COUNSELING
METHODS

Edited by
JOHN D. KRUMBOLTZ
CARL E. THORESEN
Stanford University

HOLT, RINEHART AND WINSTON   New York   Chicago   San Francisco
Atlanta   Dallas   Montreal
Toronto   London   Sydney

Library of Congress Cataloging in Publication Data

Main entry under title:

Counseling methods.

   Bibliographies.
   Includes index.
   1. Personnel service in education. I. Krumboltz,
John D. II. Thoresen, Carl E. [DNLM: 1. Counseling
—Methods. BF637.C6 C857]
LB1027.5.C67   371.4   75-43743
ISBN 0-03-089471-9

PREFACE

We want this book to be as useful as possible to counselors who ask, "What can I do to help clients with their problems?" About seven years ago we prepared another book[1] in which we expressed a desire for a counseling cookbook. A few reviewers mistakenly assumed that we intended that book to be a cookbook. For counselors a cookbook is obviously impossible because no one knows enough about what ingredients and what processes produce certain results. We still think a cookbook of well-tested recipes would be nice to have, however. In the meantime, the present volume will provide counselors, therapists, and other helping professionals (social workers, nurses, psychiatrists, teachers) with up-to-date descriptions of procedures that seem to have been successful—at least with the particular clients and under the particular circumstances described. We thus offer some tentative recipes that seem favorable enough to be tried by others.

The present book is different from the previous one in a number of important respects. All of the case materials are new and original. In order to be included in the previous book a manuscript had to meet two crucial criteria: (1) the techniques described had to offer great promise for helping clients, and (2) the techniques had to be described in sufficient detail that another counselor could duplicate the essential actions after reading the report. The present book has added another criterion: (3) each article must describe a procedure for collecting evidence about the effectiveness of the techniques tried and must present some sample of that evidence. We are no longer content with operating on the basis of faith and hope. We believe that it is essential for counselors to be able to document the effectiveness, or lack of effectiveness, of their actions.

Why do we place this stress on presenting evidence of effectiveness? In

---

[1] John D. Krumboltz and Carl E. Thoresen, eds., *Behavioral Counseling: Cases and Techniques.* New York: Holt, Rinehart and Winston, 1969.

recent years social programs and institutions such as public education have been called upon to become "accountable." Accountability, of course, means different things to different people. But the critical element for counselors is that some means must be available to demonstrate how the accomplishments of counselors are related to counselors' efforts. ("Doing these things leads to those results.") We hope that this book will help counselors design methods for demonstrating the effectiveness of their actions. Even if there were no social movement toward accountability nation-wide, obtaining evidence about the effectiveness of techniques has direct benefits for both the client and the counselor. The client benefits when he can decide what techniques seem to be valuable for him and can see how he is making progress toward certain goals. The counselor benefits by finding out which kinds of techniques seem to work better with which kinds of clients, at least in her own personal use of them. The entire profession benefits when large numbers of practitioners systematically evaluate and report to others about the value of alternative practices. No longer will administrators or members of the public be able to say that counselors are not having any impact. Counselors will be able to present evidence, perhaps much of it like the examples in this book, documenting the kind of impact that they have. Such evidence will have more than simple public relations value. It will serve to move counseling still further from a service activity to a profession. True professionals evaluate as objectively as possible the quality of their services and modify the nature of those services in light of the evidence produced.

In no sense are we claiming that each technique described here has incontrovertible evidence that it caused the changes described. Although some studies come very close to presenting convincing evidence of cause-and-effect relationships, most are content to show that certain effects occurred after certain interventions. Cause-and-effect relationships are not always clearly determined. Nevertheless, simply being able to measure or count an outcome is a step in the right direction, even if we cannot always be sure what caused it.

The previous book was organized by techniques. Each chapter described a different counseling method. The present book is organized by problems under each of the three major types of counseling goals. We had to move to a problem organization for several reasons. Most client problems are so complicated that no one single technique proves sufficient. What appears to be a simple straightforward problem is enmeshed in complicated family and cultural background factors and is usually related to a host of other problems which may only slowly come into view. In order to present the complexity and realism of client problems, we were not able to describe one technique per case. Furthermore, there is no one-to-one correspondence between problems and techniques. Knowing the nature of the problem is not enough to prescribe a given technique with an assurance that it will work. Perhaps we have enough information to suggest which techniques ought to be tried first, but from there on the process is "trial until success."

We elected to delete the adjective "behavioral" from the title of this book, though the astute reader will undoubtedly pick up a behavioral emphasis. In the seven years since our last book appeared, behavioral techniques have moved from being the practice of a few scattered counseling heretics to becoming generally acceptable by most practitioners. Furthermore, those who call themselves behavioral counselors and therapists have broadened the scope of their activities to include practices and procedures that originated in other orientations. In short, the boundary lines between what is a behavioral technique and what is not a behavioral technique have become so blurred that it is no longer useful to emphasize the differences. Counselors want techniques that can be demonstrated to work. Practical effectiveness is the emphasis in this book, and it becomes less and less important what adjective we apply to those techniques.

We hope that this book will find a use in the training and practice of school counselors, school psychologists, clinical psychologists, counseling psychologists, psychiatrists, social workers, employment counselors, and mental health workers. Case materials include examples from a wide age range and from settings ranging from schools and colleges to community mental health agencies and prisons.

Our previous book included a Diagnostic Table of Contents that was well received by many readers. The Diagnostic Table of Contents is designed to help a reader locate techniques that might be useful for a particular type of problem. We have modified the present Diagnostic Table of Contents so that you can find the articles that describe all the techniques used with any particular type of problem and age group or all the problems for which a given technique has been described.

The articles for this book were selected through a long, careful screening process. We began by writing to hundreds of professional colleagues asking about any innovations in their professional practices and also asking for names of other colleagues who were doing interesting work. We then issued invitations to selected colleagues whose work seemed to fit the requirements of our book. We specified the three criteria for inclusion as described above: practicality, replicability, and testability. Unlike our previous experience, where it was quite difficult to find enough professional colleagues whose work met our criteria, we found this time that there were many more excellent articles submitted to us than we could actually use. We selected only those that seemed most valuable to counselors, that minimized redundant descriptions of techniques, and that clearly described and evaluated procedures likely to be of use to a wide range of clients. Unfortunately, a number of excellent articles had to be declined.

We have prepared an initial section on strategy in counseling, including some notions about problem identification drawn from our prior book. Introductory comments for each major section were designed to put in perspective the developments in that problem area. We have also prepared editors' notes to comment on the procedures and results in most of the articles. These notes are entirely our responsibility, although the authors were given an opportunity to see them in advance of publication. The authors do not necessarily agree with the view we have expressed.

The problem of avoiding grammatical sex bias has been resolved through diversity. Sometimes you will find the redundancies "himself or herself," sometimes traditional male generic pronouns, sometimes female pronouns used generically, and sometimes nonsexist plural pronouns. Our intent is to represent equally both females and males as clients with problems and as counselors with skills.

The field of counseling is continuing to grow and develop. We hope this book contributes to that growth. Our purpose is to encourage counselors to experiment with new ideas that are likely to be of value to their clients. The techniques described in this book are in no way to be considered perfected or authoritative. In Part 1 we point out some of the ways in which "behavioral" counseling techniques have changed and evolved over the past seven years. We expect more change in the future.

Possibly at some future time we might prepare yet another book. We would like a dialogue among readers, editors, and authors. If you find any of these ideas particularly stimulating and useful, or dangerous and useless, we would like to hear about it. If you have developed some new techniques or ideas of your own, let us know. Possibly you will want to prepare an article for a future book.

The work of producing a book like this requires the efforts of many who do not see their names in print. At Stanford University we were aided by Sharon Washington, George Edwards, Jay Thorp, Ann Gladstone, and Ruth Bergman. Support of various kinds from the Stanford Center for Research and Development in Teaching is also gratefully acknowledged.

The Center for Advanced Study in the Behavioral Sciences deserves special recognition for creating a climate conducive to scholarly productivity in pleasant surroundings. Staff members whose efforts contributed directly to this book include Jane Kielsmeier, Heather Maclean, and Irene Bickenbach.

Finally, we are indebted to Helen Brandhorst Krumboltz and Kay Armstrong Thoresen for encouragement and help, substantive and substantial.

Stanford, California　　　　　　　　　　　　　　　　　　　　J. D. K.
February 1976　　　　　　　　　　　　　　　　　　　　　　C. E. T.

DIAGNOSTIC TABLE OF CONTENTS

The Diagnostic Table of Contents on pages viii and ix will help you quickly locate articles that describe techniques likely to be useful for accomplishing defined types of counseling goals. You may use it to identify the range of problems to which any particular technique has been applied and to locate articles in which particular methods have been used with certain age groups.

Only treatment or intervention methods are included. No diagnostic, monitoring, or evaluation methods are tabulated here unless they are being used to induce change.

Only methods described in at least some detail are tabulated. Methods that are merely named or mentioned incidentally are omitted. Check the index to locate other mentions of a method.

Standard terminology for methods has been used. If the author created a new name for a standard method, or if the author used a method without identifying it by name, it is still tabulated here under its commonly used name.

When the age of the client is indeterminate, no letter is appended to the article number. However, most methods, with appropriate modifications, can be used with almost any age group. The appended letters identify examples used in this book, but they should not be interpreted as a recommendation to restrict the use of any method to the indicated age group.

DIRECTIONS

1. Locate the type of client problem with which you are concerned in the top row.
2. Find numbers in each column to identify the article dealing with that problem. Letters after article numbers indicate the approximate grade (or age) level of the client:

    e=elementary   age 1–12
    s=secondary   age 13–17
    c=college   age 18–22
    a=adult   age 23+

3. Identify associated techniques (listed in the left-hand column) by determining which article numbers appear in the intersecting spaces.

DIAGNOSTIC TABLE OF CONTENTS

GOALS OF COUNSELING

GOALS OF COUNSELING

METHODS	ALTERING MALADAPTIVE BEHAVIOR					DECISION-MAKING	PREVENTION
	Behavioral Deficits	*Behavioral Excesses*	*Inappropriate Behavior*	*Fears and Anxieties*	*Physical Problems*		
Programmed (reading) materials	5a, 6a		23a			42e, 45c	48, 53c, 54a, 59a
Reinforcement of incompatible alternatives			23e			43s	50e, 58s
Relaxation	2c, 7a	14a	24e, 27a	30c, 36a	37, 38a, 40ca	43s, 46	56a
Role-playing	1a, 4s, 7s	12a, 14a	24e, 25e, 26a				48, 54a, 56a, 61s
Satiation		9a					
Self-instruction							
Self-monitoring	2c, 3s, 5a, 7s	9a, 10a, 11a, 12a, 18s	20a, 21e, 26a		38a, 39a		52a, 53c, 56a, 60c
Self-punishment		12a			39a		60c
Self-reinforcement	3s, 7s	9a, 10a, 11a, 18s		32a	40a		
Shaping	1a, 7a, 8e			31e, 32a		45c	48e
Simulation						46	57a
Stimulus control		10a, 12a			37, 39a		47e, 52a
Systematic desensitization	2c		24e	29a, 30c, 31e, 34a, 32a			56a
Thought stopping							
Time out		17e					50e
Token systems		17e, 18s	23e			42e	47e, 49e, 50e

CONTENTS

PART 4
METHODS FOR PREVENTING PROBLEMS AND DEVELOPING RESOURCEFULNESS   416

SOCIAL INTERACTION   495

DRUG ABUSE   510

PERSONAL APPEARANCE   517

PHYSICAL CONDITIONING   527

PEER COUNSELING   541

COUNSELOR ACCOUNTABILITY SYSTEMS   556

INDEX   567

PART 1

THE STRATEGY OF COUNSELING

Counseling is a process of helping people with their troubles. Although counseling is known by many names, like "therapy" or "helping," it is an attempt to encourage change. A troubled person comes to a counselor because he or she is unable to figure out a solution alone. Sometimes the person cannot define exactly what is wrong. He or she knows that something is wrong—that things are not going well. The counselor is often considered to be an expert at helping people to clarify problems and to find solutions to their troubles. The counselor is presumed to be an expert because he has mastered some generally accurate theories, laws, or conceptual models, which he can then apply to the specific problems presented by the client.

So the professional counselor must engage in some thought processes in order to apply these general theories, laws, or models to the specific problems of the client. But which theories, laws, or models? And what kind of thought processes? The counselor will try quite different approaches, depending upon which thought process is used with which theory.

When a client comes in with a problem, solutions do not (and should not) automatically present themselves. Unfortunately a few counselors seem to have ready-made solutions, believing that every client needs this or that solution, despite his or her particular concerns: "Here's the answer; now what's the question?" Clients' troubles have complex origins, and it is not easy for counselors to decide just what to do next or where to go ultimately. Sometimes it is not even clear what the client wants.

Some means for simplifying the terrible complexity of these problems are necessary. That is where theories come in. Theories are deliberate oversimplifications of reality. But they can be useful simplifications if they lead a counselor to take actions that are ultimately helpful to the client. A theory can be totally wrong in the sense that its constructs bear no relation to reality, yet it may still lead the counselor to take some appropriate actions. By the same token, a theory may be quite accurate but be misinterpreted or misused by a counselor in such a way that inappropriate actions are taken. Most theories are not "true," at least for very long; at best, good theories are useful for the time being.

THE NATURE OF BEHAVIORAL COUNSELING

The behavioral framework is one that offers a number of advantages. At the same time, we have to guard against the risk of closing our eyes to still better frameworks. Ideologies of any kind are comforting but inevitably interfere with the perception of alternative views.

The troubles that clients bring to us are so complex that it is difficult to see any system of help as "an elegant solution." However, behavioral counseling has demonstrated its effectiveness and requires few untestable assumptions. What is behavioral counseling?

Behavioral counseling is a process of helping people to learn how to solve certain interpersonal, emotional, and decision problems.

A Learning Process

The key word in the definition is "learn." Counselors are people who help their clients to learn. They are in the education business as much as are teachers, psychiatrists, school administrators, psychologists, mental-health workers, and social workers. All these occupations have in common the goal of producing changes in the behavior of clients. The only evidence that these professional workers are successful is that their clients do certain things or say certain things differently after receiving professional services. School children can multiply two-digit numbers that previously they could not multiply. The housewife tells the psychiatrist that her depression is gone. The unemployed person tells the social worker that he has sought and found a job. In each instance the professional is gratified to discover that the client has done something or said something to indicate that a real change has taken place.

The word "behavioral" in "behavioral counseling" serves simply to remind us that the criterion for success in any educational endeavor is changes in behavior on the part of our clientele. It serves to remind us of our purpose. Once that idea has become firmly entrenched, we need not continually remind ourselves with the redundancy "behavioral counseling." All counseling is behavioral. Soon we can drop the adjective, as we already have dropped it from the title of this book.

Client Self-Sufficiency

Another key term in the definition is "how to solve." Counselors are concerned that their clients become independent problem solvers. Continued dependence on the counselor's services is not desirable for the client, though some self-centered therapists may find it profitable. By helping people learn how to solve their problems independently counselors enhance their freedom. Clients can then assume control of their own lives and become more self-sufficient in solving their own future problems (Thoresen & Mahoney, 1974).

Problem Specification

A third key part of the definition is "certain . . . problems." Counselors cannot help people learn how to solve every problem. Some problems are beyond their interests or competence. Counselors may not be concerned with helping people learn how to change flat tires, how to solve quadratic equations, or how to bake cakes. But they are likely to be concerned with helping people learn how to choose college majors, how to become appropriately assertive, or how to communicate more harmoniously with spouses.

Counselors can help people with their interpersonal problems, with emotional problems, and with the development of learning and decision-making skills. They are concerned with habit changes that increase people's satisfaction with themselves. Counselors work to help people learn how to overcome excessive smoking or eating; to take better care of their bodies; to overcome shyness, stress, and depression. They help people learn how to overcome sexual dysfunctions, alcoholism, drug addiction, compulsive gambling, and fears and anxieties. They help people learn how to make decisions about educational plans and career choices, as well as personal decisions on marriage, divorce, and child management.

Counselors may specialize in certain problems. Each problem area requires special knowledge and skill. Counselors need not feel that they must be equally proficient in all problem areas. Eye surgeons do not perform hair transplants, even though the two problem areas seem closely related anatomically.

Prevention

The definition does not state *when* learning is to take place. Typically, counselors have waited until clients have presented themselves for help, usually after troubles have reached an advanced state. But why wait? People are going to have difficulty in solving a variety of problems in life. Would it be possible to intervene at a far earlier point and to help people to learn skills for coping with future difficulties without having first to undergo the emotional trauma of failure? Preventive approaches to helping people learn to solve their problems are needed as much as remedial approaches are. Counselors can reach out and find people who are in need of help before their problems become serious (Drum & Figler, 1973).

Preventive approaches can include anything from helping males to overcome their fear of dating females (Martinson & Zerface, 1970) to an elaborate procedure involving the use of students to orient potential clients to available counseling services (Lamb & Clack, 1974). Indeed, counseling as prevention may even help people to reduce their chances of suffering coronary heart disease (Thoresen & Coates, 1976).

Studies like those mentioned show that counselors can actually achieve better results in some types of endeavor by using paraprofessionals or other people in the environment to encourage and to reward more desirable behavior. For certain kinds of activities it is not only more expensive but also even *less* effective to use professionally trained personnel. Whereas professionally trained personnel may supervise and evaluate the operation, the people making face-to-face contact with the clientele may often be people closer to their age and status.

ORIGIN AND TREATMENT OF PROBLEMS

If counseling can be said to have a single goal, it is to help each individual take charge of his or her own life. In order to assume control of one's own life one needs two major types of skill: the ability to make decisions wisely and skills for altering one's own behavior to produce desirable consequences. Both these kinds of skills may be thought of as competence in personal management. A counselor's job then becomes one of arranging appropriate learning experiences so that people develop these skills.

Why is it that everyone does not develop these decision-making and self-control skills? The reason is that certain individuals' environments preclude their learning certain skills necessary for happy and productive lives. The environment is insufficient or inappropriate for the necessary learning to occur.

It may seem paradoxical that we can blame the environment for inadequate development of skills and at the same time maintain that each individual must learn to assume control of his or her own life. On one hand, we appear to be saying that the environment is responsible, yet, on the other, we appear to be saying that each individual is responsible. The paradox is more apparent than real, however. Certainly the environment shapes an individual's behavior, but an individual's behavior also affects the environment. Each person is subject to the environment in which he finds himself, but each person can also influence the nature of that environment to produce more desirable consequences (Thoresen & Mahoney, 1974). Counselors can teach individuals how to alter their environments to produce these desirable consequences, which in turn encourage the individuals to continue their new activities.

Let us examine the type of environmental circumstances that create the kinds of problems that are brought to counselors—and also some actions that counselors can take to help people to prevent or remedy these problems.

Insufficient Reinforcement

Some people simply receive too few of the "goodies" of life. They do not have friends with whom to share their feelings and experiences. They may work hard but see no results or receive no recognition from their employers, fellow workers, or classmates. Each day may be a boring repetition of the previous day, without such pleasant events as parties, dinners, and travel to anticipate. As a consequence of such environmental conditions, people come to counselors complaining of depression, apathy, alienation, powerlessness, and helplessness. Some of these people are so depressed that they complain that their lives have no purpose. They see no goal—life seems useless. They may even hint at suicide.

Counselors may be trapped into long philosophical discussions on the purpose of life. Some people are unhappy because they aspire to the unattainable. Discovering *the* purpose of life is an unattainable goal; however, developing or adopting a purpose or purposes for one's own life is a useful activity.

How, then, would a counselor go about helping a depressed person generate some possible purposes or activities that would produce good things for that person? The counselor, in effect, may say something like

Of course, you are feeling depressed and unhappy. It is only natural that you should be. There are not too many good things happening to you. Let's talk about some of the things you want for yourself. You want friends? Let's talk about what you can start doing right away that might help you develop some new friends. Take a bouquet of flowers to your next-door neighbor. Say hello to three strangers. Call up an old friend long distance on the phone. Volunteer to work part time for the Red Cross. Join a square-dancing class at the Y.M.C.A. You want your teacher to like you? Tell your teacher how interesting and valuable her lesson was. You want recognition for your work? Ask your boss how he likes your work. Say "thank you" to your boss for some good job that he did. Talk to other employees about what they enjoy in their jobs. See if you can devise a way to do part of your job more efficiently than you now do it. Investigate alternative job opportunities. You say that every day is the same, that there are no new thrills or excitements? Rent a motorcycle. Learn to play tennis. Join a bridge club. Try some backpacking. Ride a raft through the Grand Canyon. Make a survey of the next five people you meet, and ask them what turns them on and what they do for "kicks."

Obviously, the counselor should not give a speech like this one, but ideas for action can be developed with the active cooperation of the client. The typical depressed client, however, is likely to react to new ideas with feelings of helplessness. The client will raise objections, explaining why these activities cannot be performed: "Me? Gee, I can't. . . ." The counselor's job is to identify some immediate, small first steps toward taking action—a feasible activity that has a high probability of success. The client believes it is hopeless—in large part that is why he or she is depressed and has come to the counselor. The counselor does not try to talk the client into feeling that the situation is not hopeless. Instead, he encourages the client to begin taking action. The successful consequences of that action then serve to encourage the client to continue. And doing something (other than talking about how terrible things are) tends to reduce the experience of depression. Some people who have developed treatments for depression emphasize not only that clients should be taught to engage in some activities but also that they should be taught to anticipate the pleasure of these activities (Anton, 1974).

How can these feelings and experiences of depression and alienation be prevented? Arranging school environments, for example, that encourage active participation in learning, that challenge students with a variety of learning experiences, and that reduce the amount of sheer passive absorption of other people's conclusions would help greatly. Passive learning tends to convince people that there is nothing that they really can do to affect their own happiness. We learn that our own actions can have an impact on the environment (and, in turn, on us) only when in fact they do.

Reinforcement for Maladaptive Actions

Some people grow up in environments that provide rewards for behaviors that ultimately prove disastrous. Let us recall that Oliver Twist fell into the hands of Fagin, who was actively schooling boys in the art of thievery. But the learning of inappropriate responses is seldom that deliberate. More often it is a consequence of unplanned or "mindless" contingencies. We are learning, for example, that an ecological view is crucial to reduce the unanticipated negative effects of changing certain features of our physical environment. The same may be said of our social environment; we must cope with the effects of televised violence and poor eating habits. Sometimes problem behaviors result from well-meant but damaging responses by the adults in a child's environment.

Suppose that we want a child to learn to speak the truth. We must then be sure that speaking the truth is rewarded and that telling lies is not rewarded. Unfortunately, the experience of many people is just the opposite. The child who admits a transgression is punished immediately, whereas the child who denies the transgression avoids punishment. (Recall that any action that avoids punishment is thus strengthened.) A society that operates on punishment as a means of social control is bound to produce a high percentage of liars when admission of responsibility produces punishment. We could say to a child: "Thanks for admitting that you broke that vase. I know that it is hard for you to say so. You've shown a lot of courage. Later on when you are feeling a little better let's talk about some ways that we can arrange for you to replace the vase." A response like this one provides immediate reinforcement for telling the truth and delays the more aversive consequence of repairing the damage. The child is still held responsible for his actions but receives praise and recognition for assuming responsibility. Teaching parents and teachers to greet more desirable responses with praise and recognition is a good way to prevent or at least to reduce maladaptive responses (Krumboltz & Krumboltz, 1972).

Counselors are seldom faced with people who come voluntarily with problems of lying or stealing. However, they are frequently faced with people who are unhappy about their social relationships for reasons that they cannot identify. And often the causes consist of offensive behaviors of which the client is unaware. Some people use sarcasm, monopolize conversations, minimize other people's contributions, fail to listen, brag excessively, deprecate themselves, or feign emotions that they obviously do not feel. Such behavior has been learned. In the past it has been reinforced. It is now inappropriate, but the client does not know it.

Remediation of such problems is often best accomplished through group counseling. In the group interaction, group members can identify the strengths and weaknesses in one another's social interaction. Under the direction of a sensitive group leader new actions can be practiced and encouraged while the group members provide support. Groups can be harmful if the entire emphasis is upon the identification of weaknesses. Unfortunately, many "encounter groups" stress the confrontation of each member's weaknesses without focusing enough on positive actions. With constructive purposes in mind, however, group counselors can enlist the aid of group members in identifying maladaptive social behaviors, teaching alternative behaviors, providing a secure atmosphere in which to practice such new behaviors, and encouraging members to evaluate the results of their behaviors in the outside world (see Thoresen & Potter, 1975).

Reliance on a Single Self-Defeating Reinforcer

Some people have become so dependent on a single type of reinforcing activity that their health or welfare is seriously endangered. Overeaters, smokers, gamblers, alcoholics, and drug addicts illustrate this problem. People with these dependencies are among the most difficult to help. A variety of techniques have been tried with varying degrees of success.

One method is to provide knowledge of the consequences of changing the habit. For example, the client who overeats weighs himself frequently and plots his weight on a graph, along with a line representing the desired weight loss. By requiring that this graph be posted in a "public" place, the counselor ensures that the client's friends and relatives can see how much progress he is making and can therefore give him frequent feedback.

Another technique is to rearrange the environment so that access to addictive material is restricted. A smoker was required to carry his cigarettes taped to his thigh, so that every time he needed a smoke he had to take down his pants. Overeaters are instructed to put all food in the kitchen in a locked cupboard, the key to which is placed in some remote spot. And one desperate and discouraged overweight woman requested that her jaws be wired shut so that she could absorb only liquids.

One of the most successful methods for treating problems of this type has been group support, support from people who have suffered from the same problems. Alcoholics Anonymous has long been known for its success, and similar self-help organizations have been devised for gambling addicts, drug addicts, overeaters, and compulsive smokers. Support and encouragement from a group of people who have gone through the same trials and tribulations and know the temptations to backslide can provide far more effective therapy in many instances than can any single counselor alone. Perhaps a combination of professional counseling with membership in a self-help peer group would be an effective one for many people.

Preventive attempts usually focus on ways of helping people to find other satisfactions in life than those on which they are "hooked." For many of these people the addictive stimulus provides an escape from the problems of life. They have not yet learned how to cope actively and directly with the stresses and problems that they face. Thus they seek solace in drugs, drink, food, tobacco, or slot machines. Like people who are depressed, they need to discover for themselves the joys and satisfactions that can be obtained from many other types of social and physical activity that do not have the same self-defeating consequences. Unfortunately, these people live in an environment in which the mass media, for example, encourage eating rich food, overeating, drinking alcohol, smoking cigarettes, and enjoying other features of the so-called "good life."

Excessive Punishment

The use of punishment as a means of social control has had disastrous consequences for many people. People come to counselors with many types of problems derived either from deliberate or accidental punishing situations. People with dysfunctional sexual inhibitions and people who are afraid of high places, elevators, closed places, dentists, or other people illustrate the anxieties generated by various punishing situations.

The treatment for such people depends, of course, upon the specific kinds of anxiety that they experience. Systematic desensitization has been remarkably effective in helping many people. However, more recent evidence tends to indicate that it is better treatment to have such people experience the feared situations and learn how to cope with them or even to change them. The counselor can provide models to demonstrate how to handle the feared situation, can guide a client gradually to experience greater and greater exposure to it, and can require him to remain in the situation until his fear and anxiety begin to diminish. The counselor can also help the person to identify and change stress-producing features of certain situations. In essence, the client learns that the thing he fears is not nearly as bad as what he has anticipated. Masters and Johnson have had considerable success in helping people to overcome sexual inhibitions by teaching them in a very explicit fashion how to relax and to enjoy the touch and physical intimacy of their sexual partners.

Many fears and anxieties could be prevented if parents and teachers did not rely so extensively upon punishment as a means of social control. In the long run, positive reinforcement of desired responses is more effective and produces fewer negative side effects than does punishment of undesired responses. Punishment is used, of course, because it sometimes produces an immediate change in behavior, and that is understandably very reinforcing to the punisher. Thus its "quick and fast" effects perpetuate its use, despite its dismal long-term results. Parents and teachers need examples of ways in which they can achieve positive results from young people without the use of punishment (Krumboltz & Krumboltz, 1972). Especially needed is more patience from adults with the "slower but better" effects of positive methods.

Insufficient Cues To Predict Consequences

Another set of problems arises when people have not learned to notice or to discriminate the cues that signal when or where certain behavior is appropriate. The fact that a person has not learned to make such discriminations is not necessarily his fault but may arise from an environment that has provided either insufficient or contradictory cues. Let us take a concrete example: A child appears for breakfast wearing her brand-new blue dress. Her mother says: "You're not going to wear that dress to school. I don't want you to wear that unless you get my permission first." The next day the child comes to breakfast in pajamas and asks her mother, "May I wear my yellow dress today?" Her mother replies: "Why do I have to make all your decisions for you? You should learn to make your own decisions."

Each event is quite justified in the mother's own mind. She does not want her daughter to wear a brand-new dress without her permission, and she also wants her daughter to make her own decisions. But the effect on the daughter is one of confusion. Unable to articulate the nature of the contradictory cues, she feels vaguely inadequate about her own behavior and knows only that she is unable to do anything right. A more sensitive mother might have given clearer cues: "You may choose what to wear, except for your blue dress, which requires my ironing."

Counselors see many people who find it difficult to identify the right thing to do. They are confused and uncertain. They hesitate to take any action and sometimes blunder blindly into the first thing that comes their way. They procrastinate endlessly over the smallest decisions. They are late for appointments because they cannot decide which clothes to wear or whether to travel by bus or car. Confused and indecisive, they cannot identify what causes their difficulties.

The counselor faced with this kind of problem has to try two possible courses of action. The most important is to teach the client that the consequences of making a "wrong" decision are usually not as serious as he fears. Furthermore, the client must learn to talk to himself in more positive and constructive ways. Albert Ellis has long favored a method for teaching clients to think more rationally by identifying the irrational thoughts that terrify them. He encourages clients to say to themselves, "Yes, it might be mildly disagreeable if my girl friend didn't like the color of my shirt, but it would not be a disaster." By consciously verbalizing the consequences of making a wrong decision the client can sometimes be led to attach less importance to perfection.

A second strategy is to analyze the situation in which the client's indecisiveness occurs, to enable him to discriminate the type of response that might be best in particular circumstances. This approach involves detailed consideration of the results and the identifiable interpersonal or situational cues that will enable him to decide on the best course of action.

A rich field for research on preventive counseling can be found in the contradictory cues that are given to people in our society. When should one lie, and when should one tell the truth? When should one persist in the face of refusals, and when should one accept the first refusal as final? Does a woman's smile mean that she likes a man and would like him to approach her, or does it mean that she considers him ridiculous and wants him to stay away? Does a man's aggressiveness toward a woman mean that he is seriously interested in her as a human being or that he merely wishes to use her as a sex object? These are just a few of the discrimination problems that face people in their day-to-day decisions. The cues that are offered are ambiguous, and it becomes quite difficult for people to distinguish the best courses of action.

It is doubtful that we shall ever be able to remove all ambiguity in the cues that guide behavior, but perhaps some explicit acknowledgment that cues can be contradictory and confusing would help. People tend to internalize their confusion by assuming that the fault is entirely their own. Group counseling can be useful as a setting for "discrimination training" focused on the difficulties of distinguishing cues for appropriate action. Group members can share their confusion and discover that they are not alone with the problem.

Steps Omitted in Skill Development

Children who have skipped a year in school and missed out on some crucial arithmetic skill sometimes find their mathematical development hindered for years. There are also other skills for which omitted steps hamper development and cause unhappiness. Skills in interpersonal relations, in decision making, in job seeking, and in employer-employee relations tend to be learned step by step. When a crucial step is not learned, the entire process can become inordinately difficult.

One of the most crucial skills that counselors deal with is decision making. People come to counselors for help with their vocational decisions, their educational decisions, and their personal decisions about such things as marriage and divorce. They recognize that these decisions are crucial to their future happiness and want to make them wisely. Many feel inadequate because they are not able to make such decisions independently and are vaguely embarrassed that they do not know what to do. Many people have simply not learned how to make these decisions wisely. They seem to believe that the solutions should spring full-blown into their minds as soon as they ask the questions. It is frequently helpful for the counselor to lead the client through a step-by-step decision-making process, carefully identifying each step so that each client can learn how to make such decisions independently in the future. An eight-step decision model (Krumboltz & Baker, 1973) may be used for many purposes.

1. *Formulate the problem by specifying the client's goals and values.* The first step is often the hardest. Clients will say that they are not sure what their goals are or are not clear about their values. Considerable time may be devoted to exploring alternative goals and values, a decision-making process in its own right. A formulated problem might sound something like "I should like to decide on three colleges to which I should apply, in order to meet my requirements of desired major, cost, and location; they should differ in their probability of admitting me."

2. *Commit time and effort.* Making a decision requires time and effort. People forget that. The work involved in making a wise decision is going to take some time. Because the client must agree to work on the problem, it is sometimes useful for him and the counselor to sign a contract specifying the amount of time that each will devote.

3. *Generate alternative solutions.* Clients can often generate a list of their own alternative solutions. It is useful to ask the client to write down possible alternatives. The counselor can suggest additional alternatives, provided that he does not become an advocate of his own ideas. Many available reference books suggest alternatives. There are references on colleges, occupational guides, and lists of possible college majors. Most of these published listings, however, are so extensive that the problem facing the counselor and the client is how to narrow the alternatives to some feasible ones on which to expend investigative energy.

4. *Collect information about the alternatives.* Information about colleges and occupations is plentiful. The problem is not usually availability of information; it is sifting through that information and motivating the client to use it constructively. Somehow the information must be personalized.

We have done research on ways of encouraging vocational exploration. One outcome of this research has been the *Job Experience Kits*, which give young people simulated experience in solving problems like those solved by people working in various jobs. There are other ways of personalizing such information: visiting a college or factory, talking to people who have attended various colleges or worked in different jobs, arranging part-time work experience. Such active exploration is a crucial part of decision making, but it does require commitment. Few people have learned to take the time and effort to explore important alternatives thoroughly.

5. *Examine the consequences of the alternatives.* The information collected should enable the client to make some estimates about the probability of his success. Some of the information that is available about colleges enables counselors to estimate the probability of a client's being admitted on the basis of test scores and grade-point averages. Sometimes such information is available for occupations, though the range of ability within each occupation is so great that aptitude tests have relatively small differential predictive power. Interest inventories seem to be far more successful in helping people to identify occupations in which they might want to work.

Some people forget that the most important decision that they make is how to spend each hour of every day. A useful way of learning the importance of hour-to-hour decisions is the *Life Career Game* (Varenhorst, 1967). By deciding how much time to spend on various activities each day, students achieve different kinds of life satisfactions. They learn that a decision on how to spend an hour affects the way in which they spend their lives. Concern with time management is, of course, not restricted to students. Indeed, the decision on "What's the best use of my time right now?" is very much part of many adult problems. Much of the stress and tension that people experience is related to faulty decisions about how to use time and how to relate time to goals (Thoresen & Coates, 1975).

6. *Reevaluate goals, alternatives, and consequences.* As a result of these explorations, clients sometimes revise their values and goals. New ideas occur; values change. At this point in the decision-making process, a deliberate step must be taken: The client must be asked to reconsider whether or not his original goals and values still hold.

7. *Successively eliminate the least desirable alternatives until a tentative choice has been made.* By deliberately eliminating the least desirable alternative first, the client can then concentrate investigative energy on the more feasible alternatives remaining. When it becomes impossible to eliminate any more alternatives, then more information about the remaining alternatives is necessary. Eventually a choice can be made, but that choice must be regarded as

tentative. New opportunities may open up. Some of the information gathered may become obsolete or inaccurate. Clients should expect their decisions not to be final but to be always open-ended. Thus, if unexpected events necessitate changes in their plans, they will not be discouraged but will simply take the events as signals that the entire decision-making process must begin again.

8. *Generalize the decision-making process to new problems.* The effort to make an important decision wisely is so great that no counselor can be expected to lead every client through the steps every time. Decision-making is a personal skill. It should be learned by clients. It should be learned by people before they become clients. Once a counselor has helped a client to go through the process once, he should make sure that the client can at least verbalize the steps and can use them in solving other decision-making problems.

Perhaps the long-run solution to decision-making skills is prevention. Decision making can be taught as a skill in schools, just as multiplication skills, map-reading skills, and athletic skills are taught. Materials for developing decision-making skills are becoming available now (for example Gelatt, Varenhorst & Carey, 1973), but systematic attempts to teach them in schools have scarcely begun.

RECENT DEVELOPMENTS IN COUNSELING METHODS

The last few years have witnessed a number of changes in emphasis and in the methods associated with behavioral counseling. Counselors are using newly developed techniques and are talking in terms that would have been foreign to the counselor of seven years ago. Here are some of the major changes that will be concretely illustrated in the articles that follow.

Treating Fears through Experience as Well as Imagination

The most dramatic results in the treatment of fears have occurred when the client has been exposed gradually to increasing intensities of the feared experience itself. The client is shown models of others coping successfully with the feared situation and is then asked to experience the same situation himself. The counselor carefully guides the client through this experience and expects him to remain in the situation until the sensations of fear diminish.

The well-established technique of systematic desensitization, which is based upon the client's imagining specific situations, is less powerful than the direct experience itself. However, it would not be accurate to say that systematic desensitization is therefore ineffective. Some types of fears do not lend themselves to direct treatment, and the use of imagery may still be the best way of reaching certain types of problems. Sometimes a combination of practice with imagery and direct experience may be most effective.

Managing Fears Rather Than Avoiding Them

We cannot always avoid situations that cause extreme anxieties to develop. It seems more important now to teach clients how to handle anxieties when they arise than to teach them methods for avoiding anxieties in the first place. The technique of systematic desensitization has tended to help people reach the point at which they will not experience anxiety in a specific situation that has aroused their fear in the past. But avoidance does not always work, and the sensations of fear do arise. What then? Techniques for reducing those sensations of anxiety when they begin to develop seem to be important for the counselor to impart to his client.

Coping Models Rather Than Mastery Models

What kind of person should model a new behavior—one who is thoroughly proficient in it or one who is just beginning to learn the process himself? Recent evidence has tended to suggest that the "coping model" may be more effective in at least some problem situations. In the coping model, one who starts at the same level as the client gradually demonstrates increasing ability to master the situation. Possibly the client can see similarities between his own current behavior and the initial behavior of the model and thus can conclude: "If the model can do it, I can do it." Possibly the mastery model sets too high a standard, leading the client to discouragement: "Sure, he can do it, but that's more than I can ever accomplish."

Self-Control Rather Than External Control

Although the emphasis in behavioral counseling has been on ways in which the environment controls behavior, recent work has emphasized the ways in which an individual can control the environment. Thus, to help people to gain control over their own lives, we can teach techniques for managing or rearranging their own environments in order to influence their own behavior in ways that they consider desirable.

Covert and Cognitive Behavior as Well as Overt, Observable Behavior

Originally, behavioral counseling emphasized overt, observable behavior only. But obviously people think and engage in other, internal processes, which are not readily observable externally. These covert behaviors seem to possess many of the same characteristics as overt behaviors, and thus some of the same behavior-change principles can be used. Furthermore, people can be taught ways of thinking about their behavior that lead to quite different overt behaviors. Teaching people to observe their own emotions and to record them and teaching them to use certain thought processes for analyzing and reacting to problems are all examples of recent emphases in behavioral counseling.

Research on Individuals as Well as on Groups

Reliable knowledge can be gained from the intensive study of single individuals, as well as from controlled experimental studies on groups of individuals. For many counseling purposes the intensive single-case method has many advantages over controlled group research. In a real sense every counseling client represents a new research case, in which alternative methods must be tried out empirically to see which is most effective for that particular case. Some have even defined behavioral counseling as the intensive experimental study of the single case (Yates, 1969; Thoresen & Hosford, 1974). Of course, for the purposes of science counselors are concerned with generalizations that go beyond single cases, but even so the study of a series of single cases in an intensive manner can yield important generalizations through replication and at far less cost (Thoresen, in press).

Prevention as Well as Remediation

Counselors have shown a great deal of ingenuity in recent years in designing interventions to prevent problems, to treat groups of individuals with common problems, to help people to develop coping skills for dealing more adequately with their environments, and to create environments that reduce the incidence of problem behaviors. Although counselors still continue to treat individual clients who request help, the emphasis upon prevention is most encouraging. A major section of this book deals with preventive techniques.

Alterations in the Ground Rules for Counseling

Counseling is part of a social system in which certain customs, rules, and regulations operate unless they are deliberately altered. Some of these rules have to do with the nature of counselors' responsibilities and the permissible methods for dealing with those responsibilities. Some rules have existed for so long that it has been difficult to become aware that they even exist, so that they can be challenged. There are rules regulating what responsibilities counselors can undertake and rules preventing counselors from undertaking responsibilities designated for other professionals. There are rules stating what patterns of prior experience are necessary to fulfill the counseling function. The effort to make counselors accountable for accomplishing results, rather than merely accountable for spending time with clients, will lead to marked changes in societal expectations for counselors and in counselors' expectations of themselves. The training of paraprofessionals and peer counselors will alter notions about who can be useful to clients. Battles for licensing and certification will clarify and, it is to be hoped, not limit unduly who can perform which kinds of functions successfully. So far, however, discussions about certification and licensing more nearly represent fighting over a slice of the pie than making a flakier crust.

PROBLEM IDENTIFICATION IN COUNSELING

Very seldom do clients begin by requesting help in accomplishing specific behavior changes. A client rarely will enter a counselor's office and say, "I want to learn to speak up in class," "I wish to reduce anxiety associated with females," or "I wish to engage in information-seeking relevant to my career choice." When goals are so clearly and specifically expressed, it is relatively easy for the counselor to devise procedures that may help. Most clients do not describe their difficulties in such simple, straightforward language. Most cannot specify what behavior they desire. They are usually confused and uncertain. Can a behavioral counselor help a client who does not know what he wants, who is confused and unhappy? Certainly. One of the most exciting characteristics of behavioral counseling is its capability for successfully resolving the highly complex problems of clients (Thoresen, 1968a).

The counselor begins by listening carefully to the client's concerns. The counselor tries to understand and assess the client's thoughts and feelings. He first tries to see things from the client's point of view. He communicates his understandings to the client and attempts to determine whether or not he is accurately perceiving the client's thoughts and feelings.

But the behavioral counselor often does more initially than listen empathically and clarify perceptions of what the client is experiencing. He also seeks answers to questions. What precisely is going on in the client's everyday life? In what ways do others respond to the client's words, thoughts, and feelings? Much attention is directed to the client and the particulars of his living environment (Thoresen, 1968b).

For some clients the counselor's empathic understanding is enough. Listening without condemning may relieve guilt feelings. The sympathetic audience may enable the client to verbalize his plans and proceed without any further action by the counselor. All counselors must learn to be empathic listeners. But they must learn more. A good listener may suffice for some clients but not for most. Most clients need further assistance once the counselor understands their thoughts and feelings about their problems.

The counselor must help the client describe how he would like to act instead of the way in which he currently acts. The counselor must help the client translate his confusions and fears into a goal that the client would like to accomplish and that would begin to resolve his problems. This can be accomplished by focusing on specific behaviors in his present situation.

DIFFICULTIES IN FORMULATING GOALS

The process of translating amorphous feelings into specific goals is, of course, not easy. In the following sections we shall examine seven stumbling blocks that counselors face in making the translation and some ways that they can step over them.

The Problem Is Someone Else's Behavior

Frequently the problem as presented by the client has nothing to do with his own behavior but is attributed entirely to deficiencies in someone else's behavior. School counselors are often confronted by teachers who say: "Johnny is always causing trouble in my class. He won't pay attention. He won't do what I tell him. You are a counselor. You talk to him, and straighten him out." It is easy for a beginning counselor to make a serious mistake in accepting a referral from a teacher on this basis.

The first question a counselor must ask is "Who is my client?" In almost all instances the answer should be "My client is the person who brought me the problem." In this instance, the client is actually the teacher, not Johnny. The teacher has far more resources for controlling the contingencies of reinforcement (the antecedents and consequences of behavior) in Johnny's life than does the counselor. If the counselor were to accept the referral on the teacher's terms (taking Johnny out of class and talking with him in the counselor's office), it is unlikely that he would accomplish very much toward enabling Johnny and the teacher to develop harmonious working relations. A more fruitful approach would be for the counselor to reply to the teacher: "Yes, that does sound like a difficult problem. Maybe we can work on it together. Could you suggest a time when I might be able to visit your class to observe Johnny exhibiting this kind of behavior?" With this reply the counselor establishes himself as an ally of the teacher, his client, so that together they can work on the problem. The goal of the counseling then becomes one of discovering the types of action that the teacher (the client) can take in order to modify Johnny's inattentive and destructive behavior.

A similar situation exists with parents who bring their children to a counselor or child psychologist. The parent, like the teacher, hopes to shift responsibility to someone else, whom he or she can then blame if no progress is made. The parent, however, like the teacher, controls many more reinforcing contingencies than does any counselor or child psychologist. The client is the parent, not the child. The role of the counselor is then to work with the parent in creating an environment in which the child is able to learn and to experience reinforcing consequences of more appropriate types of behavior. The goal of the counseling is to help the parent change his behavior so that the child's behavior improves.

Not only do people in authority (teachers, parents, and employers) complain about the behavior of those for whom they are responsible, but also peers often complain about one another. Children complain about the behavior of their classmates, teachers about their colleagues, husbands and wives about their spouses. The picture presented to the counselor is one in which the presenter is virtuous—if only "they" would change *their* behavior, everything would be all right. The counselor is frequently asked for help in persuading the "offending party" to come in for some counseling.

The counselor should continue to consider the person bringing the complaint as the client. Here is the person who is bothered sufficiently by the problem to bring it to the attention of a counselor. The counselor remains sympathetic toward the person bringing the complaint but, in effect, insists, "Let us see what *you* can do that might possibly help this person change his behavior."

Does this mean that the "offending parties" in all these instances are never to see the counselor? Not necessarily. There are many instances in which it is highly desirable for all individuals involved to talk with the counselor. It is usually best, however for the counselor to avoid inviting the "offending party" to come in for counseling. The teacher may ask Johnny if he would be willing to discuss their problem with the counselor. Johnny may agree, wishing for a happier classroom atmosphere. The counselor then considers Johnny a client too. He can help Johnny to engage in behavior that will enable him to learn without antagonizing the teacher.

In all counseling situations the counselor must make a value judgment on whether or not he wishes to help a client achieve any given goal. The counselor's own interests, competences, and ethical standards are involved (Krumboltz, 1965).

In summary, when a client presents as a problem someone else's behavior, the counselor must structure the situation so that the client himself accepts responsibility for engaging in some kind of behavior that may help to remedy the difficulty. The client may elect to change the other person's behavior, to tolerate it, or to withdraw from it, but the decision and resulting action must be seen as his responsibility.

The Problem Is Expressed as a Feeling

Problems are usually presented to counselors in the form of descriptions of feelings. The client may say, "I feel inadequate," "I feel unwanted and unloved," "I feel alienated and lonely." Just as a physician encourages his patient to "tell me where it hurts," so the counselor encourages his client to describe in detail his emotional sensations. The counselor has to listen to the client tell of his feelings in such a way that he himself will be able to describe the problem and the feelings involved to the client with considerable accuracy.

This reflecting and clarifying of the client's problems and his feelings, this careful attending, serve two important purposes: First, they guarantee that the counselor has accurately perceived the problem and the feelings of the client so that he can better assess what needs to be done, and second, they establish the counselor as an important person in the client's life, one who is likely to be viewed as a social model and whose verbal responses may be effective reinforcers. A few clients even find that clear and accurate reflection of their own problems is sufficient for them to resolve their own difficulties without further attention. Perhaps these few instances have reinforced many counselors on an intermittent schedule to believe that all clients can be treated by means of mere understanding of their feelings. And sometimes clients get better independently of the counselor's efforts, thereby creating the belief—the superstition—that the counselor's listening caused the changes.

There are two basic ways of dealing with problems expressed as feelings.

Taking Action Incompatible with Undesired Feeling   A person who feels unwanted and unloved may be perceiving his environment quite accurately. And, if he talks about being unwanted and unloved in front of others, he probably drives them away. The general approach that a counselor can take is to ask, "What could you do that would make at least some people want to have you around and be their friend?" Perhaps most people want to be loved and desired for themselves without the necessity of doing anything to deserve it. The truth of the matter, however, is that we want and love those people who do things we consider desirable. We do not usually love those who make us feel guilty, who punish us, who burden us, or who do nothing for us. There are countless ways to be useful and constructive in our society. Some ways pay money, and some do not. Social-service and political organizations are always looking for volunteer workers for worthy causes. The goal of counseling for such people is that they engage in different activities until they find some pattern of behavior that gives them the satisfaction they want. Merely talking about their loneliness with a counselor will not be sufficient. Some adults, for example, regularly try to "purchase friendship" this way, but it seldom suffices.

Lonely people need to learn to take the initiative in meeting people. What does a lonely person *do* when he goes to a meeting of some organization or to a church service, for example? Does he merely stand there hoping that someone will come up and make him feel welcome? And would he know what to say if someone did greet him? He might learn to take the initiative and introduce himself to people near him, saying: "Hello, my name is _____. I'm new here."

People who feel inadequate need to develop skills. No one is inadequate in everything. One professor was once asked how he happened to have become the world's foremost authority on the ancient Greek poet Theocritus. He replied, "I'm the only one who has ever heard of him." There is an unlimited number of skills, hobbies, and interests at which one can become proficient. A counselor can help a person suffering from feelings of inadequacy to build some competence, so that he can be outstanding in at least one small area.

Establishing More Realistic Standards for Comparing Feelings   Feelings of inadequacy are often found, however, among extremely competent people. Those who are loved may feel unloved, and those with many friends may feel lonely. Building behavior incompatible with these feelings is one approach, but for some people it is not sufficient. They frequently have levels of aspiration that are unrealistically high and consider their feelings to be quite unique and unshared by others. The truth of the matter is that we all have these feelings of inadequacy and loneliness, but seldom do we express such feelings to one another. Our society does not generally reward the expression of such feelings. In subtle ways it actually punishes such expression. Yet each person knows how he alone feels. As he hears none of his fellows describing feelings similar to his own, he assumes that his fellows do not share these feelings. Each of us thinks he is alone with his own particular set of unhappy feelings because he has no opportunity to learn that others share these feelings with him.

Perhaps one of the greatest values of counseling in groups is the opportunity it provides for the sharing of feelings (Krumboltz, 1968). The discovery that feelings of guilt, hostility, hatred, lust, fear, greed, and selfishness, mixed with desires for love, tenderness, and warmth, are shared by his fellows is often a revealing experience for one who previously thought he was alone in these feelings. The goal of counseling is to enable the client and other clients to share their feelings openly with one another so that they can accurately perceive the extent to which their feelings are shared by others.

The problem of unrealistically high aspirations is a difficult one. High aspirations are undoubtedly instilled at an early age by perfectionist mothers, fathers, and teachers, as well as by the mass media. To some extent the desire for perfection should not be discouraged, but some people who by objective standards appear to be successful actually lead unhappy lives because no amount of success can ever measure up to the standards of perfection they have adopted. They are not as politically astute as the President of the United States, not as good at baseball as Hank Aaron, not as happily married as Sleeping Beauty and Prince Charming. The difficulty is that they compare their own successes with those of the most successful people in each field of endeavor. The counselor may sometimes help by bringing such people into closer contact with the real world. Clients with such unrealistically high expectations can adopt as their goals behaviors that will enable them to learn about the true range of ability that exists in each of the areas of competence to which they aspire. Discovering the number of people who are less competent, less happy, and less privileged is one possible approach to this problem: "I cried because I had no shoes until I met a man who had no feet." The counselor must discover ways to help his client take constructive steps to accomplish his highest goals, develop alternative plans if necessary, and learn that frustrations and setbacks have aways accompanied great accomplishments.

The Problem Is the Absence of a Goal

Many people do not know what they want. If they knew what they wanted they would be able to achieve it, but they are unable to make up their minds about goals. A rich vocabulary has grown up around people in this category. They are said to be "purposeless," "alienated," "other-directed." Among young people occupational goals must be decided. Older people may have already settled on occupational goals and achieved some measure of success in their occupations, but they may feel that their lives lack real purpose.

Sophisticated philosophers may dispute "the purpose of life" and "ultimate values." Our view is that purposes are made, not born. "Man's chief purpose," wrote Lewis Mumford, "is the creation and preservation of values . . . this is what gives significance, ultimately, to the individual human life." A life does not have a purpose built into it, a purpose that must somehow be discovered. Instead, people can adopt or construct purposes for their own lives. They can adopt purposes put forth by different political, religious, or social organizations. The purposes we may adopt or construct can include making a million dollars, teaching the blind, eradicating poverty, discovering beauty, stopping war, creating world unity, or finding truth. Most mature individuals have committed themselves to the attainment of some type of goal, in many instances a long-term goal that is in fact impossible to achieve during their own lives. These goals give purpose and meaning to their lives.

How do people come to adopt or to construct goals for their own lives? What kinds of experience lead them to adopt one goal, rather than another? People troubled by the absence of a goal may be encouraged to explore how other people have solved this particular problem. They may well be encouraged to experiment with different organizations and causes. They can attend meetings with people and test the goals and procedures of many organizations against their own desires. Reading biographies of key individuals to see how they have formulated goals for their own lives may often be instructive. The process of exploration must be an active one. The goal of the client is to engage in the type of exploration that will lead him to try on for size an alternative series of goals, with the expectation that eventually he will adopt or construct some goal or combination of goals that will give meaning to his life.

The Problem Is That the Desired Behavior Is Undesirable

In certain rare instances a client may desire to achieve goals that the counselor is unwilling to help him achieve. For example, the client may be a brilliant high-school student admitted to some of the best colleges in the country. He is about to decide that he will attend the local junior college because his current girl friend is going to be enrolled there. Although the counselor recognizes the boy's right to make his own decisions and to lead his own life, he feels that the boy is throwing away the chance for a brilliant career for reasons that he will very shortly regret. Should the counselor let the boy know his opinion?

In general, we consider it unwise for counselors to try to sell one choice or another to clients facing a given decision. The counselor's job is to help the client consider the alternatives and to make sure that the client is aware of all the consequences of each alternative. The final decision must be made by the client, based on his own goals and values.

But what if the client asks for the opinion of the counselor? Suppose he says: "What would you do if you were in my shoes?" Should the counselor give a frank recommendation? In our opinion, yes. The request for an opinion is to be interpreted as a request for information. The client asking for a recommendation is in essence asking for one more bit of information: what the counselor would do in his place. Our point of view is represented in the following testimony: "In the counseling I have received, I have always welcomed the opinion of my counselor; not that I have always followed his recommendation, but his opinion has always been an important factor that I have wanted to take into account in reaching my own decision."

No one can be forced to make a decision contrary to his own best judgment. The counselor's job is to help the client investigate and evaluate those factors that will influence his happiness and success in the years ahead. A thorough exploratory process means not only the evaluation of impartial information but also a thorough examination of the opinions of important people in the person's life.

Who is to say what really will make the client happiest in the long run? The client must take responsibility for the success of his own decisions. The counselor's responsibility ends when he has done all in his power to help his client to learn to anticipate the probable consequences and to weigh the values to be gained and sacrificed by each of the alternatives being considered.

The Problem Is That the Client Does Not Know His Behavior Is Inappropriate

One of the dangers in counseling is that the counselor has but one side of the story—his client's version of what is happening. People tend to distort events in order to place themselves in a more favorable light and to justify their own actions. A counselor may be totally unable to determine from the client's account exactly what the client should do in order to overcome the particular difficulty being faced.

Consider the case of an attractive young lady who wants to be married but finds that, although she attracts many invitations, no man continues to date her more than three times. She blames the fickle nature of males, wants to know what to do about it, but is totally unable to diagnose the difficulty. The first goal of counseling in this situation would be for the client to engage in behavior that would enable her to find out exactly what she has been doing that has caused men to lose interest in her. The counselor may be unable to diagnose the difficulty himself because of his own personal commitments. Yet he must help the client to structure a course of action that will enable her to find out what is wrong. Confrontation techniques may be useful. One value of marathon group counseling is that, in a relatively short period of time, through enforced contact, members of a group are encouraged to tell one another exactly what they think of one another and to share ideas about ways to improve.

Another technique available to school counselors consists of the use of sociometric devices. For example, in the "guess who" technique, pupils are asked to nominate classmates who fit various descriptions. Most people in our society are reluctant to criticize another individual to his face. We seldom communicate our negative opinions directly to the person concerned. We may reject him in various subtle or not so subtle ways, but almost never do we tell him why we are rejecting him. It is believed (probably quite accurately) that frank, critical evaluations will result in counteraggression against the one voicing such criticisms. The result of this understandable reluctance is that most people who engage in inappropriate behavior are not aware of exactly what it is that they do that causes people to shun them. Diagnosing problems of this type is extremely difficult, but clearly, if the client is to make any improvement, he must know what the difficulty is.

Our three-dates-only client, if she had sufficient "ego strength," could ask one of her girlfriends to interview boyfriends who had deserted her in an endeavor to discover their reasons for doing so. The client could ask that these interview reports be transmitted either to the counselor or, depending on circumstances, to the client herself. But the identification of the difficulty is only the first step. Insight into the problem is seldom sufficient to overcome it. The diagnosis might be that the client is too possessive, expresses jealousy, becomes bossy, attempts to demonstrate intellectual superiority, or exhibits any one of a number of possible behaviors that young men tend to avoid. Once the problem is identified, however, alternative ways of behaving can be learned.

The Problem Is a Choice Conflict

Another problem that is sometimes difficult to translate into behavioral objectives occurs when the client has a choice conflict between two desirable alternatives, both of which cannot be attained. It is the old problem of wanting to possess the eaten cake. A young man may wish to be promoted in his company yet not to put in the extra effort and time required to do a top-notch job because of pressure from his fellow employees. He sees a conflict between his desire for promotion and his desire to be accepted by his fellow workers. Or a wife may no longer love her husband but may wish to maintain the financial security she enjoys as his wife. She may be torn between wanting to leave her husband and wanting to stay with him.

If requested by the client, the counselor may see his task as helping the client to engage in a type of behavior that will enable him or her to resolve the conflict. Usually the client needs help in learning how to decide. The counselor may well begin by asking whether or not all possible alternatives have been considered. In almost every choice conflict there are more than two alternatives available. The ambitious but affiliative young man may well be able to devise ways to accomplish his work well without necessarily antagonizing his peers. The unhappy wife may well be able to devise ways of living somewhat more harmoniously with her husband or of becoming more financially independent. All possible alternatives must be uncovered and considered. "Brainstorming" by both counselor and client may turn up possibilities neither would have thought of alone.

Once the possible alternatives are in the open, the client can be encouraged to engage in activities that would test the feasibility of each possible alternative. The ambitious employee may experiment with taking some of his work home. The unhappy wife may try out some activities that she and her husband might enjoy together. The testing of alternative courses of action may eventually lead to a solution that these clients would find desirable.

The Problem Is a Vested Interest in Not Identifying Any Problem

Some clients may not even have a problem but may merely want someone to listen to them talk. People who will listen indefinitely are few and far between, and the discovery that counselors are trained to do just that may seem a god-send to some verbose people. A counselor must decide whether or not he wishes to be used in this manner. Some counselors may acquiesce, thinking it a worthwhile use of their time. Others may dismiss the client after a few sessions. A more constructive approach would be to help the client establish friendships of his own with friends who will listen to him—provided, of course, that he in turn will learn to listen to them!

The client may be attempting to enhance his social status, his "image," by seeing a counselor. At present such prestige accrues more to those who undergo some kind of "therapy," like psychoanalysis or psychiatric care, the cost of which identifies the client as a person of means. The client may have a personal interest in the counselor, perhaps a desire for a romantic attachment, but the client is not willing to express such desires explicitly. Sometimes the client finds a continuing relationship vicariously reinforcing. Other clients may wish to keep vital information from the counselor on the grounds that such information would prove embarrassing or detrimental to themselves. If no meaningful problems are identified after a reasonable period of time, direct confrontation by the counselor may be desirable: "You seem to find difficulty in expressing just what troubles you. Most clients with this difficulty have one of four problems. Let's see if one fits you."

references

Anton, J. L. An experimental analysis of training the anticipation and performance of reinforcing activities in the treatment of depression. Ph.D. thesis, School of Education, Stanford University, 1974.

Drum, D. M., & Figler, H. E. *Outreach in Counseling*. New York: Intext, 1973.

Gelatt, H. B., Varenhorst, B., & Carey, R., *Deciding*. New York: College Entrance Examination Board, 1972.

Job Experience Kits. Chicago: Science Research Associates.

Krumboltz, J. D. Behavioral counseling: Rationale and research. *Personnel and Guidance Journal*, 1965, **44**, 383–387.

Krumboltz, J. D. A behavioral approach to group counseling and therapy. *Journal of Research and Development in Education*, 1968, **1** (2), 3–18.

Krumboltz, J. D., & Baker, R. D. Behavioral counseling for vocational decisions. In Henry Borrow (Ed.), *Career Guidance for a New Age.* Boston: Houghton Mifflin, 1973. Pp. 235–284.

Krumboltz, J. D., & Krumboltz, H. B. *Changing Children's Behavior.* Englewood Cliffs, N.J.: Prentice-Hall, 1972.

Lamb, D. H., & Clack, R. J. Professional versus paraprofessional approaches to orientation and subsequent counseling contacts. *Journal of Counseling Psychology*, 1974, **21**, 61–65.

Martinson, W. D., & Zerface, J. P. Comparison of individual counseling and a social program with nondaters. *Journal of Counseling Psychology*, 1970, **17**, 36–40.

Thoresen, C. E. The counselor as an applied behavioral scientist. Paper read at the Annual Research in Guidance Institute, University of Wisconsin, Madison, June 1968. (a)

Thoresen, C. E. Being systematic about counselor training: Some beginning steps. Paper read at the meeting of the American Personnel and Guidance Association, Detroit, 1968. (b)

Thoresen, C. E. Behavioral means and humanistic ends. In M. J. Mahoney & C. E. Thoresen. *Self-control: Power to the Person.* Monterey, Calif.: Brooks-Cole, 1974. Pp. 300–322.

Thoresen, C. E., & Coates, T. A social learning approach to counseling and therapy. *The Counseling Psychologist*, in press, 1976.

Thoresen, C. E., & Coates, T. Behavioral self-control: Some clinical concern. In M. Hersen, R. E. Eisler, & L. Miller (Eds.), *Progress in Behavior Modification*, Vol. II. New York: Academic Press, 1975.

Thoresen, C. E., & Hosford, R. E. Behavioral approaches to counseling. In C. E. Thoresen (Ed.), *Behavior Modification in Education.* Seventy-second yearbook of the National Society for the Study of Education. Chicago: University of Chicago Press, 1973. Pp. 107–153.

Thoresen, C. E., & Mahoney, M. J. *Behavioral Self-Control.* New York: Holt, Rinehart and Winston, 1974.

Thoresen, C. E., & Potter, B. Behavioral group counseling. In G. Gazda (Ed.), *Basic Approaches to Group Psychotherapy and Group Counseling.* Springfield, Ill.: Charles C Thomas, 1975.

Varenhorst, B. Information regarding the use of the Life Career Game in the Palo Alto Unified School District guidance program. Unpublished manuscript. Palo Alto, Calif.: Palo Alto Unified High School District, 1967. (Copies of the game are available at mailing cost from the author.)

Yates, A. *Behavior Therapy.* New York: Wiley, 1970.

PART 2

METHODS FOR ALTERING MALADAPTIVE BEHAVIOR

BEHAVIORAL DEFICITS

Problems come in all sizes and shapes. Some problems are crisp and clear-cut, whereas others are complex and confusing. Certain problems are specific to particular life situations, whereas others are very general and seem to affect everything the person does. For the purposes of this book, we have classified problems into such categories as behavioral deficits, behavioral excesses, fears and anxieties, realizing that there is considerable overlap among such categories.

Some people have never learned how to do certain things or to do them well enough. Why haven't they? Having few chances to see others do those things, never having an opportunity to practice, and feeling very anxious about trying them out all rank as possible reasons. We can never know for sure just why a particular person is lacking or deficient. But that is not as important as recognizing that, if a person does not do something well, it *could be* because he or she simply does not know how to do it. This may seem obvious, but many people have been expected to act "appropriately" in certain situations and, having failed to do so, have been diagnosed and labeled as having various abnormalities or mental illnesses; furthermore, they have been treated *as if* they did know what to do but did not do it because of deep-seated inner conflicts. ("He doesn't relate well to women because he's a latent homosexual and undoubtedly emotionally disturbed"; "Well, of course, he hit her. It's a clear case of a sociopathic character disorder"; "She's always procrastinating, always avoiding decisions. Really, she's a neurotic personality.") A harmful sequence often begins when a person says, in effect, "I don't do it"; next comes "I can't do it" and then "I guess I'm the kind of person who can't do it." Such self-descriptions can contribute to a very dependent and self-defeating way of dealing with problems. It often is more helpful—for the person, as well as for the counselor—to look at problems as the results of faulty learning: Maybe this person lacks certain skills; maybe I can help provide a structured learning experience.

The cases presented in this first section share a common perspective: the clients did not know what to do in certain situations. Thus, counseling was designed to teach them how to overcome their deficits in the problem situations. This teaching also focused on very concrete actions, tailored to the problems involved. Such a focus requires careful assessment of what the person can and cannot do at the *beginning* of counseling. Labeling the person as emotionally disturbed or sociopathic, for example, is not as helpful as finding out what he does in certain situations. What is lacking or deficient is not viewed as entirely missing from within the person. Instead, his social environment (spouse, family, friends, colleagues) is also examined for shortcomings. For example, a painfully shy adolescent might learn rather quickly how to start interesting conversations with peers if he or she were in a social group in which such behavior was often demonstrated and encouraged.

A general strategy is used in almost all of these cases. It consists of three steps: demonstration, practice, and reinforcement of appropriate behavior. These steps are repeated in situations that come closer and closer to "real life" performance. Each problem situation is broken down into several parts. The parts are put into a teaching sequence. Then each behavior is modeled or demonstrated in some way, followed by the person's practicing (rehearsing) it. These small practice steps are reinforced (socially or otherwise) by the counselor and sometimes by others in the person's environment. Thus people typically practice certain behaviors outside the formal counseling setting. Sometimes mental or covert practice is crucial; the person uses his imagination to rehearse certain actions mentally. In all cases the focus is on helping the clients to increase certain actions that are both meaningful and appropriate.

SHYNESS

1. ASSERTIVE TRAINING IN THE WORK SITUATION

RICHARD M. EISLER[1]   Veterans Administration Center and University of Mississippi Medical Center, Jackson, Mississippi

The use of assertive training to facilitate the expression of socially appropriate behavior has been described in some detail by Wolpe and Lazarus (1966) and Wolpe (1969). Typically, in training, the client is expected to rehearse or to role-play new ways of expressing himself in interpersonal situations under the supervision and guidance of the therapist.

The following case history illustrates the procedures used in evaluating and treating a client whose problems in assertiveness manifested themselves primarily at work. Many of the clinical

[1] Many thanks to my colleagues Michel Hersen and Peter M. Miller for their editorial comments in preparing the manuscript.

techniques described have been developed through analog research at the Veterans Administration Center in Jackson (Eisler, Hersen & Miller, 1973; Eisler *et al.*, 1974; Eisler, Miller & Hersen, 1973; Hersen *et al.*, 1973).[2]

THE CASE OF MR. JONES

Mr. Jones was a thirty-nine-year-old black man who had worked for seventeen years as a bricklayer with the Acme Construction Corporation. He was admitted to the in-patient psychiatric service at the Veterans Administration Center with complaints of sleeplessness, tension headaches, and tachycardia. His local physician could find no physical basis for his complaints and had prescribed tranquillizers with no durable results.

An initial interview with Mr. Jones revealed that six months before his admission he had been promoted by his white boss to a supervisory position, in recognition of his long and dependable service with the company. Thus, it became his responsibility to supervise the work of a team of six black subordinates in performing work assignments according to specifications within a reasonable period of time. Mr. Jones admitted that his underlings often performed work of inferior quality and took too many breaks on the job. Rather than reprimand them for these deficiencies, he worked extra hours himself so that each job would be finished on

[2] *Editors' note:* See articles 54 and 55 for a description of other unassertive behaviors and methods for helping clients to act more assertively.

schedule. The few times that he attempted to assert his authority, their complaints that he was an Uncle Tom or a slave driver effectively silenced him. He also felt guilty that he was earning a larger salary than they and was unable to refuse requests to lend them money, which he knew would seldom be repaid. His plight was further intensified by his inability to discuss these matters with his boss.

In order to provide a rationale for treatment, we explained to Mr. Jones that we thought his recent symptoms arose from the fact that he had allowed himself to be bullied by his subordinates from fear of offending them. His failure to report the situation to his boss was foolish, in that he really needed assistance in solving the problem. Finally, his unassertiveness had begun to jeopardize his job and his health, a situation that was really unfair to himself and his family. At first, Mr. Jones was unconvinced that his fatigue and rapid heart beat were not the result of physical illness. However, he agreed to cooperate with the assertion training because we "were the doctors."

Assessment Procedures

We have found that the most accurate way of evaluating deficits in assertiveness is to role-play problem situations described by the client and to record his responses. These same situations are also used to initiate training and to provide measures of posttreatment improvement. For these purposes we employ students, nurses, aides, and other paraprofessionals to role-play various individuals that the client encounters in real life: his boss, co-workers, wife, waitress, clerk in a store, and so on. We also use relatively inexpensive Sony videotape equipment to record successive client performances and video playback as a method of providing feedback on progress.[3] However, therapists working without television equipment can probably be successful if they record data on patients' progress themselves or by means of audiotape.

In the case of Mr. Jones, six interactive scenes were reconstructed for the following problem situations: His subordinates were doing the job improperly; they were taking too much time on breaks; they were requesting loans and other unreasonable favors; his boss was asking why a particular job was being completed behind schedule; his boss was expressing anger that work was being performed poorly; and his boss was wanting to know whether or not he was having any trouble with his work team.

Following are examples of how the therapist structured two of the six scenes for role playing. In each instance the client was asked to respond as he would normally in that situation.

Example 1

THERAPIST: Mr. Jones, you are on a tight schedule to finish construction of a new store front. The boys have been on break for half an hour. When you walk over to them they are sitting around smoking and laughing.

ROLE-PLAYED SUBORDINATE: "Oh, here comes that slave driver again."

[3] *Editors' note:* Using videotape playbacks of the clients acting in more assertive ways can also be viewed as a type of self-modeling procedure in which the client sees himself performing assertive behaviors. See Article 56.

(Before training, the client would have replied, "The boss man is going to be angry at us.")

Example 2

THERAPIST: Mr. Jones, you are working late one evening trying to correct some work that was made with improperly mixed mortar. Your boss stops by to see why you are working so late.

ROLE-PLAYED BOSS: "How's it going, Jones? I thought we'd be done with this job by now." (Before training, the client would have replied, "Everything is going fine, Sir. We'll have this job finished tomorrow.")

Mr. Jones' responses to these scenes and the four others listed were enacted twice and videotaped. The tape was subsequently rated on components of assertiveness identified in previous research (Eisler, Miller & Hersen, 1973). For example, depending upon a specific client's deficits, we may be interested in modifying various combinations of variables like his response latency, loudness and tone of voice, speech fluency, gestures, and verbal content appropriate to the situation.

A behavioral analysis of Mr. Jones' responses indicated major deficits in the four following components of assertiveness: *eye contact* (he generally failed to look at his partner when delivering his response), *loudness of voice* (his speech was barely audible), *speech duration* (his verbal responses were short and conveyed little information), *behavioral requests of the interpersonal partner* (the context of Mr. Jones' replies reflected a failure to ask the other person in the situation to change his behavior and to help solve the problem).

Practical Aspects To Consider before Initiation of Assertion Training

Appropriate assertive behavior is inextricably related to the social reality or situational context in which it occurs. Thus, saying or doing certain things in one situation might be labeled by an observer as "assertive." In a different situation the same behavior might be labeled as "foolish or inappropriate." The therapist must be aware of the likely consequences to his client in the "real world"; will the new assertive responses meet with success, so that the client will be reinforced for the assertion, or will he be punished by the consequences?

In the Mr. Jones' case, we knew that several of his subordinates had shown concern for him by their visits to the hospital. In all probability their taking advantage of him resulted from his failure to set limits for them rather than from a genuine dislike of him. A telephone call to Mr. Jones' boss revealed he was a valuable employee who had demonstrated hard work, punctuality, and great skill at his trade. Nothing would please Mr. Jones' boss more than a chance to talk things over with his "fine foreman."

It is frequently assumed that anxiety prevents or inhibits a client from behaving assertively. However, it is equally plausible that the client has never learned the appropriate social skills in the first place and that anxiety results from behavioral deficits in his present repertoire, rather than inhibi-

tion of existing skills.[4] With most of our clients of lower socioeconomic status appropriate interpersonal behavior must be taught. Mr. Jones appeared to suffer both inhibition of existing responses and lack of social skill. For example, a black man growing up in rural Mississippi is likely to be punished for behaving assertively toward whites. Although this background could explain Mr. Jones' passivity toward his boss, it did not fully explain his lack of assertiveness with black subordinates. His lack of skills for a supervisory position seemed a more likely cause.

Whatever the reason, clients who are asked to behave assertively for the first time in role-played situations typically evidence increased levels of anxiety that must be dealt with by means of reassurance, encouragement, and persistence from the therapist. In the case of Mr. Jones, *in vivo* role playing brought to the fore all his symptoms, including tachycardia, profuse sweating, and tension headaches. The therapist handled them by informing Mr. Jones that an increase in his symptoms was expected and that once he became comfortable with his new behavior they would disappear. In some instances it is necessary for the therapist to construct a hierarchy of scenes based on the level of anxiety elicited and first to train the clients on those situations that elicit the least anxiety before progressing to the more difficult scenes. When anxiety over assertive behavior is very intense, systematic desensitization to assertive

---

[4] *Editors' note:* A chronic problem for counselors working with fearful, shy, unassertive clients is to determine whether the clients already know how to act appropriately or have not yet learned appropriate behavior for the situations involved. Technically it is a question of behavioral inhibition or deficit. Sometimes both are involved.

scenes in imagination (Wolpe & Lazarus, 1966; Emery, 1969) may be useful before assertive training.

Assertive-Training Procedures

We have found that the best strategy for training clients suffering from multiple assertive deficits is to shape one component response until demonstrable improvement is made on it before beginning training on another behavior. In the present example, instructions and feedback from the therapist were employed in successive rehearsals first to increase the amount of eye contact and then to increase the loudness of voice. Deficits in speech duration and content of response were improved by means of the therapist's modeling and feedback.

During training, the six real-life scenes were enacted ten times in different random orders. During the first series of role enactments Mr. Jones was instructed to maintain eye contact with his boss or subordinate while delivering his response. Following each enactment the therapist gave feedback on his progress. When an acceptable level of eye contact was established, instructions for Mr. Jones to talk in a louder, more forceful tone of voice were given. He continued to receive feedback on eye contact during the training on increased loudness. After a stable pattern of increased eye contact and vocal amplitude had been achieved, Mr. Jones was instructed to talk long enough so that his boss or subordinate would fully understand his position. At that point, instructions alone proved ineffective, for the client lacked sufficient verbal skills to put his point across. Therefore, in this phase of training, the therapist

modeled some replies appropriate to each situation.[5] For example, in the scene in which the boss asked how things were going, the therapist modeled the following response:

Well, boss, I am having some problems in getting this job done. That new man we just hired can't seem to lay the bricks in a straight line. I'm not sure whether he doesn't know how to do it or is just plain careless. I'll let him watch me for a few hours tomorrow. If he doesn't improve, we may have to think about letting him go.

During subsequent rehearsals the therapist continued modeling and giving feedback, and the client selected aspects of the modeled responses with which he felt most comfortable.[6] When duration of appropriate speech reached an acceptable level as judged by the therapist, he then modeled increased assertiveness by further modifying content so that Mr. Jones would request the subordinates to change their behavior. For example, for the scene in which the subordinates were taking an exceptionally long break, the therapist modeled the following reply: "Don't give me me that slave-driver business. You guys have had your break twice over. If you don't give me some cooperation in getting this job done, I'll have to deduct the time from your paychecks. I'd like you to get back to work right now."

[5] *Editors' note:* Direct modeling (demonstrating) by the counselor, immediately followed by client practice with constructive suggestions and praise by the counselor, is an extremely effective method.

[6] *Editors' note:* The client is still in charge of what he will say. The modeled responses suggested by the therapist are suggestions only.

Following observation of several therapist-modeled "requests," the client quickly learned the concept of how to request new behavior of the partner in the remaining interpersonal situations.

Assessment of Progress

A total of sixty rehearsals, or ten trials per scene, were performed in five separate training sessions. Progress was monitored by means of ratings of the videotape by trained observers. Duration of eye contact and duration of speech were timed by stop watch in seconds for each rehearsal. Loudness of voice was rated subjectively on a 5-point scale with 1 indicating barely

audible speech and 5 indicating very loud speech. Frequency of behavioral requests from partners was tallied for each scene.

Figure 1 shows the effects of treatment on the four target components of assertion presented in blocks of four scenes. In general, each of the four behaviors appeared stable at low levels before treatment.[7] Instructions and feedback worked very well in increasing the relatively simple behaviors of

[7] *Editors' note:* Figure 1 presents what is called a "multiple base-line design," in which two or more client behaviors are assessed and treatment applied sequentially to one behavior at a time. Note that in Blocks 5–7 only eye contact improved.

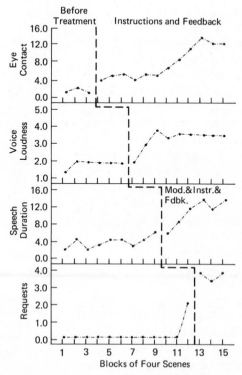

FIGURE 1   The frequency of four assertive behaviors before and during treatment.

eye contact and vocal loudness. However, supplemental modeling by the therapist, with continued feedback, was necessary to increase appropriate speech and frequency of behavioral requests. Requests for the boss or subordinates to change their behavior started to increase before specific training. This result is consistent with our previous findings that the components of assertive behavior are not necessarily independent of one another. In this instance increased speech duration led to increased opportunity for eye contact and was also probably responsible for increased frequency of "request" behaviors. However, an additional increase in request behavior also occurred after specific training.

Generalization of Training to Real Life

We have found that assertive behavior can be shaped with comparative ease in the office or hospital situation, but the crucial test is the transfer of assertive behavior to the client's natural environment. Once a hospitalized client is discharged to out-patient status or when a client is treated on an out-patient basis, it is of critical importance to monitor progress in real-life encounters. To facilitate this monitoring, we typically give the client "homework" assignments to perform with people with whom he comes into contact between training sessions. Before an assertive task is assigned, some preliminary evaluations of whether or not his skill in the office is sufficient to encourage real-life trials, are made. Another consideration is whether the client's assertions are likely to meet with success or failure during the initial attempts. The first parts of

subsequent training sessions are then devoted to discussion and additional role enactments of the client's reported real-life encounters. Evaluations of how effective his behavior seemed, how the other person responded, and how to modify his approach next time are made jointly with the client.

In the present case there was little opportunity to monitor Mr. Jones' progress in natural encounters while he was in the hospital. However, his progress as an out-patient was followed for three months. In general, the results were positive, and the client reported increased control over his subordinates and a better relationship with his boss. The initial presenting symptoms of anxiety and tension headaches had steadily diminished. During his visits Mr. Jones brought up some additional problems in assertion with his wife. Additional interactive scenes were constructed and rehearsed until he gained mastery over phrasing specific requests to his wife and reinforcing her for pleasing him. Seven months after Mr. Jones' discharge from the hospital, the therapist inadvertently made contact with the client who was working on a new shopping center. He appeared quite enthusiastic about the assertive training.[8]

[8] *Editors' note:* Such testimony is gratifying but is insufficient evidence that the assertive training has been transferred. With the client's permission, the counselor could ask the subordinates, the boss, or the wife for examples of behaviors that Mr. Jones performs more or less frequently since his hospitalization. Direct observation on the job would be the most relevant way to determine how much of the training has been transferred. However, the practical problems of collecting direct observational evidence from "real life" are sometimes insurmountable.

references

Eisler, R. M., Hersen, M. & Miller, P. M. Effects of modeling on components of assertive behavior. *Journal of Behavior Therapy and Experimental Psychiatry*, 1973, **4**, 1–6.

Eisler, R. M., Miller, P. M. & Hersen, M. Components of assertive behavior. *Journal of Clinical Psychology*, 1973, **29**, 295–299.

Eisler, R. M., Miller, P. M., Hersen, M. & Alford, H. Effects of assertive training on marital interaction. *Archives of General Psychiatry*, 1974, **30**, 643–649.

Emery, J. R. Systematic desensitization: Reducing test anxiety. In J. D. Krum-boltz and Carl E. Thoresen (Eds.), *Behavioral counseling cases and techniques*. New York: Holt, Rinehart and Winston, 1969. Pp. 267–288.

Hersen, M., Eisler, R. M., Miller, P. M., Johnson, M. B. & Pinkston, S. G. Effects of practice, instructions, and modeling on components of assertive behaviour. *Behaviour Research and Therapy*, 1973, **4**, 443–451.

Wolpe, J. *The practice of behavior therapy*. New York: Pergamon, 1969.

Wolpe, J. & Lazarus, A. A. *Behavior Therapy Techniques*. New York: Pergamon, 1966.

2. INITIATING SOCIAL CONTACT WITH THE OPPOSITE SEX

KEVIN B. McGOVERN[1] Woodland Park Mental Health Center, Portland, Oregon
JEANNIE BURKHARD Colorado State University, Fort Collins, Colorado

Most socially inhibited college students report that they are unable to initiate social interactions, feel uncomfortable while engaging in social activities, often evaluate their social behavior as inferior, and avoid attending social gatherings on campus. Some of these students can easily relate to members of their own sex but not to members of the opposite sex; others feel comfortable relating to peers but not to older individuals. There are other college students who feel comfortable interacting around the dorm but not in class. In summary, socially inhibited students represent a very heterogeneous group of individuals.

Although counselors at universities are faced with similar types of clients,

[1] Thanks to Margaret Baird, Sue Volks, and Rob Ziffer for their assistance in preparing this manuscript.

until recently the literature contained few detailed reports of behavioral programs designed to alter social inhibition. However, recent studies (Arkowitz *et al.*, 1974; Christenson & Arkowitz, 1974; Curran, 1974; Gambrill, 1973; MacDonald *et al.*, 1974; Martinson & Zerface, 1970; Melnick, 1973; Rehm & Marston, 1968; Twentyman & McFall, 1974) indicate that psychologists are now beginning systematically to assess and modify the behaviors of inhibited college students.

BEHAVIORAL CHARACTERISTICS OF THE COLLEGE-MALE NONDATER

Several years ago a social-skills training program (McGovern, 1972) was implemented for a specific group of socially inhibited college students, designated as "college-male nondaters." Briefly, the fifty college-male nondaters participating in this program read a training manual written for this project and discussed their social concern about heterosexual dating with a group of undergraduate women who had been systematically screened and trained. In some instances, the male nondaters rehearsed a set of ten social behaviors with the women trainers.

After interacting with and observing these fifty individuals, we found it increasingly clear that nondating behavior is influenced by many highly specific factors.

Distorted Self-Perception of Social Skill Level

Approximately 50 percent of the subjects were quite adequate conversationalists and demonstrated appropriate social skills at the beginning of the training program. However, these individuals possessed distorted perceptions of how they behaved in social situations. Even though many of the nondaters consistently received positive feedback from the women trainers, they persisted in believing that their social behavor was inadequate.[2]

---

[2] *Editors' note:* A major problem for clients with many kinds of difficulties. Recently Bem (1972) has demonstrated that a person's view, or perception, of himself is a function of what he observes himself doing. Thus, faulty self-perception may be best corrected by helping clients to act appropriately *and* specifically by having them observe their appropriate actions.

Low Level of Social Skill

At the beginning of this program, about 20 percent of the nondaters could not maintain a five-minute conversation without becoming extremely anxious and concerned about their performances. It was evident that these individuals were poor conversationalists and lacked self-confidence. These nondaters reported that they often intentionally avoided social interactions on campus.

High Level of Anxiety

About 20 percent of the nondaters were visibly anxious in social situations. During the training program, they chain-smoked, nervously rubbed their hands together, or continually shifted their positions in the chair. Typically, they spoke very rapidly and often lost their trains of thought. Early in treatment they usually told the women trainers that they felt extremely "uneasy" while interacting with others.

Fear of Rejection

About 40 percent of the nondaters reported at the beginning of the training program that they could initiate conversations with women and ask for dates but could not maintain relationships with the same women. Most of them reported that several times in the past they had gone on a number of dates with the same girl and then the relationships had ended abruptly. After being suddenly rejected a number of times and not knowing why, or not wanting to know why, they had stopped interacting with women and had started going to the local bar with a "few of the guys."

Whether or not a client's behavior changes in a socially competent direction depends upon the extent to which the training program allows the subject to concentrate on the specific factors that typically block his progress. Therefore, it is extremely important to emphasize that counselors should comprehensively assess an individual's level of social skills and identify the particular conditions that prevent him from dating before the beginning of treatment.[3]

THE CASE OF ART

Art was a twenty-year-old male attending the University of Oregon. An acquaintance had told him about the original training program. During open office hours, he asked the first author (a male) for assistance. At this first meeting, Art indicated that he had not had any dates during high school and college. He also mentioned that he was extremely anxious, could not interact effectively in most heterosexual social situations, and needed basic information about heterosexual dating (*social-sexual interactions*).

An analysis of the client's past social history revealed that he did not have any older brothers or sisters. In addition, his father had died when he was five years old. During his adolescent and young adult years, he had not had many opportunities to learn how to initiate or maintain satisfactory heterosexual relationships. As a sopho-

more in college, he had become extremely concerned about his inability to develop relevant social-sexual relationships.

Before the first interview, he had fantasized that many of his fears and social concerns would spontaneously change over time. However, during his third year in college, he had realized that his social behaviors would not change without professional assistance.

Assessment and Training: Phase I

Before a training program was designed to meet his specific needs, Art completed a comprehensive assessment battery. During the initial assessment phase, he responded to several self-report questionnaires, including "The Survey of Heterosexual Interactions" (Twentyman & McFall, 1974), the "Social Avoidance and Distress Scale" and the "Fear of Negative Evaluation Scale" (Watson & Friend, 1969), and the "Self-Rating Form" (Arkowitz *et al.*, 1974). In addition, he was taught how to record his social interactions in a behavioral diary (Arkowitz, 1972). More specifically, during an eleven-day period, Art recorded in the diary each male-female social interaction that lasted fifteen minutes or longer.[4] He was also asked to identify each person, to record the time of day the interaction occurred, and indicate on the back of each page how anxious he felt during these social interactions.[5]

---

[3] *Editors' note:* Sound advice! Too often counselors try to help without first determining just what the client is capable of doing.

[4] *Editors' note:* Shorter contacts could have been recorded too.

[5] *Editors' note:* A good example of behavioral self-observation. This kind of information is often more helpful to the counselor (and the client) than paper-and-pencil "personality" measures.

His scores on the self-report inventories and his comments in the behavioral diary suggested that Art felt extremely uncomfortable in most heterosexual social situations. In addition, the data from the diary revealed that he had engaged in seventy-five male and five female interactions over an eleven-day period. At the second session Art revealed that he felt "extremely tense and anxious many times a day." Because of these immobilizing feelings, he was unable to initiate conversations with undergraduate women.

During the third session, Art was taught deep-muscle relaxation exercises (Wolpe & Lazarus, 1966; Bernstein & Borkovec, 1973). In addition, a twenty-item social-situation hierarchy was constructed on 3×5-inch index cards. The first item of the hierarchy consisted of Art's saying "hello" to a middle-aged female cafeteria employee. The twentieth item included Art's visualizing himself initiating and maintaining a conversation with an attractive young female sitting alone in a booth at a college pub. Sessions 4, 5, and 6 were used to teach the client how to implement the systematic-desensitization program at home (D'Zurrila, 1969).

Over the next two weeks, the client completed six systematic-desensitization training sessions at home. At the seventh session, Art was given a social-skills training manual to read (McGovern, 1972). This manual contains six sections: "Initiating Brief Conversations," "Relevant Information About Developing Heterosexual Relationships," "Maintaining an Effective Conversation," "Personal Attractiveness," "Positive and Negative Social Behav-

iors," and "An Invalid Fear of Rejection."

After reading this manual and reducing his anxiety through systematic desensitization procedures, Art was prepared for the second phase of the assessment procedure: a practice date. By that time in the program, the client and therapist had met for eight one-hour sessions over a two-month period.[6]

Assessment Phase II: A Practice Date

The purpose of the assessment technique was to evaluate Art's social skills and related levels of anxiety in a nonclinical setting. Before the practice date, Art was told to call the second author (a female) and to arrange a time for a brief, informal interaction. Through this short meeting, they could become acquainted with each other.

The practice date took place the next evening at a pizza parlor. During the two-hour interaction, Art and the second author discussed undergraduate courses and past social experiences. After leaving the restaurant, Art accompanied her back to her apartment. At that point in the evening, they both completed the "Dating Evaluation Form" (McGovern, 1973).[7]

This six-page questionnaire was de-

---

[6] *Editors' note:* Note the combined sequence of techniques being used. First, the client's excessive stress and tension are reduced by relaxation and desensitization. Then a social-skills training program is started. Sometimes both methods can be used at the same time (see Eisler, Article 1); at other times a participant-modeling approach is quite effective (see Article 33).

[7] *Editors' note:* A practice date might also be used in the very beginning to find out how the client behaves in such situations.

signed to obtain self-report ratings on each participant's feelings of anxiety, sense of humor, conversational abilities, degree of self-confidence, and general level of responsiveness. After the participants had rated their own behavior along these dimensions, they rated their partners' dating behavior on the same dimensions. In addition, each participant was asked to list at least five positive and five negative characteristics of the partners' dating behavior. After the practice date the second author listed eleven positive and nine negative characteristics of Art's dating behavior. Some of the positive characteristics included a warm voice, appropriate laughter, optimistic attitudes, general thoughtfulness, and neatness of dress. On the negative side, Art used the expression "Oh, Gad" repeatedly, stuttered frequently, ordered the drinks awkwardly, and developed new topics of conversation at random.

Several days later, the client and authors met to discuss the details of the practice date and the responses to the "Dating Evaluation Form." Toward the end of this session, the concept of behavioral rehearsal was introduced (Lazarus, 1966; McFall & Marston, 1970; McFall & Lillesand, 1971; McFall & Twentyman, 1973). In a behavioral-rehearsal sequence, the participants practice behaviors. More specifically, the therapist first explains the details of a particular social scene. For example, the therapist says: "Over the last few days, you have been sitting next to an attractive woman in your economics class. You have talked to her briefly before and after class. On Saturday, you and your roommate are going to have a party. You would like her to attend."

The client is then given an opportunity to respond to this social situation. After the behavioral sequence is completed, the client and therapist discuss their social behaviors. The behavioral sequence is repeated until the participants are satisfied with their performances.

Behavioral Rehearsal

During the following three weeks, the second author and Art met twice weekly at the psychology clinic to discuss his concerns about heterosexual social interactions (sessions 8–13). In addition, they behaviorally rehearsed (role-played) relevant dating behaviors. The behavioral-rehearsal sequences were designed around the materials in the dating manual and the twenty hierarchical items developed by the client during an earlier stage of the program.

During the first behavioral-rehearsal sequence, the second author initiated a brief conversation with Art. He was instructed to take a passive but pleasant role. As the situations became more complex, he was instructed to take a more active role. Each behavioral-rehearsal sequence was repeated until Art was satisfied with his performance. By tape-recording these sequences, both Art and the counselor could pinpoint behavioral excesses, deficiencies, and assets (Kanfer & Saslow, 1969). At that point in the program, Art was also completing his systematic-desensitization assignments at home.

Although the initial behavioral-rehearsal sequences were practiced at the psychology clinic, the client and the second author also began to rehearse relevant dating behaviors in natural settings (sessions 14–20).[8] On several occasions, Art and she went to a nearby college pub and practiced lengthy conversations. Before each conversation, Art would leave the pub, return through the front door, walk up to her, and initiate a conversation. After the behavioral-rehearsal conversation was completed, they would discuss each other's conversational skills. Art was also instructed to initiate conversations with other female students in the pub. After these conversations were over, he would return to the table where the second author was sitting and discuss what had occurred.

While the second author and client were practicing relevant dating behaviors, the first author also met with Art once a week (sessions 21–28). Art discussed his reactions to the program and was given weekly homework assignments. During the first week of these assignments (session 21), Art was told to say "hello" to twenty college women a day.[9] During the second week, he was instructed to continue saying "hello"; in addition, he was to initiate brief conversations with two women each day. For example, he would say: "Hello, my name is Art. I just transferred here from Portland State University. Could you tell me where the clinical-services building is?" After each conversation, Art would record what had occurred in his behavioral diary. For example, after the first day, he wrote, "Thank God I got that over with." The second day he wrote: "A good day. I really timed my smiles well."[10]

Each week the assignments became more complex; that is, Art had to maintain each conversation for a longer period of time. By the fourth week of these assignments, he was initiating and maintaining at least two seven-minute conversations a day. On several days, he decided to spend several hours talking to a number of college women at different locations around the campus (in the student union, in class, at the library, and so on).

After the fourth set of weekly assignments had been completed (session 25), Art decided that these behavioral tasks were no longer necessary. Although the first author disagreed, Art wanted to try interacting with people whenever "he felt like it." After three weeks (session 28), he had interacted with only six women. He was quite disappointed with his progress and told the first author: "I needed a more structured program. . . . I really dislike these assignments because they make me anxious. However, in the long run, they will help me. I now feel more confident . . . but I still get anxious."

At the next meeting (session 29), the client and therapists met together to discuss the training program. In order

---

[8] *Editors' note:* An excellent plan. Helping clients to change in relevant natural settings greatly increases the chances that they will be able to continue changing after counseling is terminated.

[9] *Editors' note:* Homework assignments should be "doable" and highly likely to produce some success. Twenty "hellos" would guarantee some warm greetings in return, along with a few cold stares, which the client would discover to be noncatastrophic.

[10] *Editors' note:* Some socially inhibited people believe that successful social interactions involve tricks or gimmicks like memorizing clever repartee. Honest communication is the key, but the client has to learn behaviors that will put him in a position in which communication can occur.

to evaluate his progress, Art was asked to participate in a second practice date. He was told that this undergraduate woman had participated in similar practice dates.

As with the first practice date, Art called the undergraduate and set a time for a brief, informal meeting. At this meeting, the two students had an opportunity to become acquainted with each other. Art and the undergraduate woman decided to have lunch the following day. Immediately after this practice date, the participants filled out the "Dating Evaluation Form."

The ratings revealed that Art was underrating his social skills. It is important to note that, after practice dates, the two women rated his behavior higher than he rated his own behavior. A recent study (Valentine & Arkowitz, 1973) suggests that socially inhibited individuals often underrate their social skills.

In discussion of these ratings with Art (session 30), it became more apparent that he did not have an accurate perception of what occurs during most typical first dates. He believed that most college students never feel uncomfortable, are eloquent conversationalists, and use certain "lines" and "mannerisms" that "sweep women off their feet."

He also complained that the two practice dates were not realistic: "The women were too nice. They always knew what to say and what to do. What will happen when I go out on a real date with a person who doesn't work with you? I am sure that everything will be quite different. These thoughts really make me nervous."

After this meeting, the two therapists designed a procedure that would allow Art an opportunity to observe a real initial date. The therapists decided to ask undergraduate college students to participate in first dates at the clinic. By observing these interactions, Art would have a more realistic understanding of what actually occurs during initial social-sexual interactions.[11]

The Observational Date

The first author told a large class of undergraduates enrolled at the University of Oregon that he was interested in observing initial social-sexual interactions. The term "social-sexual interaction" was used because many college students detest the term "dating."[12] The students were told that their social-sexual interactions would be observed and tape-recorded.

After carefully screening sixteen volunteers, the counselors chose two individuals who did not know each other. These students indicated that they had participated in twelve or more dates over the previous six months, felt comfortable in most situations, and judged themselves adequate conversationalists.

Before the date, the man was instructed to telephone the woman. During this brief phone conversation, they were to become acquainted with each

[11] Editors' note: The counselors might have used "realistic" models of dating behavior earlier in treatment, thus helping to alter Art's faulty perceptions of what was really going on and also demonstrating typical dating behavior.

[12] Editors' note: Hmmm, we wonder how they feel about "social-sexual interaction"?

other.[13] The date took place in the group-therapy room the following evening. This room was equipped with recording equipment and a two-way mirror. The second author and Art had decorated the room earlier that afternoon. A large circular rug, floor pillows, wall hangings, and a stereo set were added to make the room look like a college student's living room. After the observational data was over, the second author, Art, and the two participants filled out the "Dating Evaluation Form." Then Art and the second author met with the participants to discuss their reactions to the evening and their responses on the evaluation form. The participants were not told that Art was a client. Instead, he was introduced as a member of the clinical observation team. Art was encouraged to ask the participants questions about the date or about past social interactions.[14]

One week later, Art and a woman undergraduate participated in a similar interaction at the psychology clinic. This woman was selected from the original sixteen individuals interviewed by the second author. During the interview, she reported feeling relaxed and comfortable in most social situations. However, she did feel that her social skills could use some improvement.

Art was instructed to engage in a brief telephone conversation with this

woman one day before the actual date. The setting and procedure for the date were similar to those used for the previous observational interaction. In this situation, however, Art was an active participant.

During the two-hour date at the psychology clinic, Art had an opportunity to use the behavioral skills that he had acquired through the behavioral-rehearsal sequences and the homework assignments. Following the date, Art, the female participant, and the second author (who had observed the interaction through the two-way mirror) filled out the "Dating Evaluation Form."

After the participants had completed the form, components of the date were discussed. Art reported feeling "fairly at ease" during the entire interaction. Both participants indicated that the artificial setting had not seemed to interfere seriously with their social behavior. The woman also revealed that their similar interests and Art's responsiveness were responsible for making the interaction a positive learning experience.[15]

In summary, by observing the first date, Art learned how other college students behave in initial social situations. He realized that his peers were not eloquent conversationalists and that they also felt anxious during various moments of dates. Also, the debriefing procedure offered Art an excellent opportunity to ask the participants questions relating to his own concerns about first dates or about other aspects of heterosexual interactions. In addition, after

[13] Editors' note: A tape recording of that telephone conversation would provide a useful model for the client too.

[14] Editors' note: As a practical matter, most counselors could not take the time and effort to structure an "observational date" for one client's benefit. But, if video- or audiotapes of such occurrences could be made readily and cheaply available, they could facilitate learning for thousands of clients.

[15] Editors' note: Art could become a "co-therapist" and help some socially inhibited women to feel more at ease. The best way to learn is to teach!

being an active participant in the second date, he realized that he had acquired a set of relevant social skills. With these new perceptions, he was enthusiastic about engaging in more complex homework assignments.[16]

During the last six weeks of the training program (sessions 31–36), Art continued to complete his behavioral homework assignments around campus. He was instructed to participate in at least two ten-minute conversations a day with two different female undergraduates. If an undergraduate responded in a friendly fashion, he was instructed to ask her to join him for another social interaction. By that point in the program, Art was extremely confident with this social repertoire and started dating several women. As these heterosexual interactions became more frequent, Art became interested in one partner.

During the last two sessions, the first author and the client designed a self-control maintenance program (Thoresen & Mahoney, 1974). At these sessions, they discussed Art's initial problems, what procedures were used to modify his concerns, and what be-

[16] Editors' note: Most counselors could not spend this much time and effort on one client. But the variety of techniques employed illustrate the alternative treatment possibilities. Maybe the same effects could be produced more quickly by judiciously selecting among techniques.

havioral techniques Art would use to modify potential troublesome behaviors. Once a comprehensive self-control schedule had been established, the formal program was terminated (sessions 37–38).

Program Evaluation

It was essential to collect and analyze data systematically while the behavioral-training program was being conducted. Through this procedure, the therapists periodically modified the program to meet Art's specific needs.

In order to evaluate the effectiveness of the entire behavioral training program, the pre- and posttraining data recorded in the behavioral diary were examined. These data, displayed in Table 1, indicate that there were several noticeable changes in the client's social behaviors after the program had been completed. For example, before treatment, the client recorded seventy-five social interactions with males and five with females over an eleven-day period. These eighty interactions occurred with thirty-two different people, twenty-eight males and four females. In addition, over these eleven days, the client did not participate in any heterosexual dates.

However, the posttreatment data collected over a similar eleven-day period revealed that the client had engaged in twenty-three interactions with

TABLE 1   A Summary of Art's Social Interactions Recorded in the Behavioral Diary Over an Eleven-Day Period

	Number of Interactions with Males	Number of Interactions with Females	Number of Dates
Pretraining	75	5	0
Posttraining	51	23	11

females and fifty-one with males. These interactions occurred with fifteen males and eight females. Eleven of the twenty-three interactions with females were defined by Art as dates. In addition, on the last page of his social-activity diary, he reported: "I felt totally at ease. This is my present attitude concerning social interactions." In summary, these data indicate that the client's nondating behavior had been modified.

The self-report questionnaire data displayed in Table 2 confirmed that the training program had been effective in changing Art's attitudes, emotions, and behaviors relevant to dating. The low scores on the first two scales and the high scores on the last two self-report measures indicate that Art felt extremely uncomfortable while interacting with others on campus. In addition,

the four pretraining scale scores reveal that Art perceived himself as extremely socially unskilled.

However, after the program had been completed, there were many noticeable changes. The higher scores on the first two scales and the lower scores on the last two self-report measures indicate that Art felt more confident and comfortable while interacting with others. He also perceived himself as more socially skilled. In addition, his posttraining scores were equivalent to those obtained by a representative group of college students. Six months after the program was completed, Art explained in a letter to the senior author that he felt very comfortable interacting in most social settings and planned to become engaged the following month.

TABLE 2   Art's Pre- and Posttraining Scores on Self-Report Assessment Scales

	Survey of Heterosexual Interactions[a]	Self-Rating Form[a]	Social Avoidance and Distress[b]	Fear of Negative Evaluation[b]
Art's pretraining scores	40	20	28	29
Art's posttraining scores	82	85	11	14
College-student sample mean	88.21	59.11	9.11	15.47
Standard deviation	18.45	23.18	8.01	8.62

[a] An increased score indicates a positive change in relevant social attitudes and behaviors.
[b] A decreased score indicates a positive change in relevant social attitudes and behaviors.

references

Arkowitz, H. Instructions for a social activity diary. Mimeo, University of Oregon, 1972.

Arkowitz, H., Lichtenstein, E., McGovern, K. & Hines, P. The behavioral assessment of social competence. *Behavior Therapy*, 1975, **6**, 3–13.

Bem, P. J. Self-perception theory. In L. Berkowitz (Ed.), *Advances in experi-* *mental social psychology.* (Vol. 6) New York: Academic Press, 1972. Pp. 1–62.

Bernstein, D. & Borkovec, T. *Progressive relaxation training: A manual for the helping professions.* Champaign: Research Press, 1973.

Christenson, A. & Arkowitz, H. Preliminary report on practice dating and feedback as treatment for college dating inhibitions. *Journal of Counseling Psychology*, 1974, **21**, 92–95.

Curran, J. An evaluation of a skills training program and a systematic desensitization program in reducing dating anxiety. *Behavior Research and Therapy*, 1975, **13**, 65–68.

D'Zurilla, T. Reducing heterosexual anxiety. In J. D. Krumboltz & C. E. Thoresen (Eds.), *Behavior counseling: Cases and techniques.* New York: Holt, Rinehart and Winston, 1969. Pp. 442–454.

Gambrill, E. A behavioral program for increasing social interaction. Paper presented at the meeting of the Association for Advancement of Behavior Therapy, Miami, December 1973.

Kanfer, F. & Saslow, G. Behavioral diagnosis. In C. M. Franks (Ed.), *Behavioral therapy: Appraisal and status.* New York: McGraw-Hill, 1969. Pp. 417–444.

Lazarus, A. Behavioral rehearsal vs. non-directive therapy vs. advice in effecting behavior change, *Behavior Research and Therapy*, 1966, **4**, 209–212.

MacDonald, M. L., Lindquist, C. U., Kramer, J. A., McGrath, R. A. & Rhyne, L. L. Social skills training: The effects of behavior rehearsal in groups on dating skills. *Journal of Counseling Psychology*, 1975, **22**, 224–230.

Martinson, W. & Zerface, J. Comparison of individual counseling and a social program with non-daters. *Journal of Counseling Psychology*, 1970, **17**, 36–40.

McFall, R. M. & Lillesand, D. B. Behavioral rehearsal with modeling and coaching in assertive training. *Journal of Abnormal Psychology*, 1971, **77**, 313–325.

McFall, R. M. & Marston, A. R. An experimental investigation of behavioral rehearsal in assertion training. *Journal of Abnormal Psychology*, 1970, **76**, 259–303.

McFall, R. M. & Twentyman, C. T. Four experiments on the relative contributions of rehearsal, modeling, and coaching to assertive training. *Journal of Abnormal Psychology*, 1973, **81**, 51–59.

McGovern, K. *The development and evaluation of a social skills training program for college male non-daters.* Unpublished doctoral dissertation, University of Oregon. Ann Arbor: University Microfilms, 1972. No. 737929.

McGovern, K. Instructions and scoring: Dating evaluation form. Mimeograph, University of Oregon, 1973.

Melnick, J. A comparison of replication techniques in the modification of minimal dating behavior. *Journal of Abnormal Psychology*, 1973, **81**, 51–59.

Rehm, L. P. & Marston, A. Reduction of social anxiety through modification of self-reinforcement: An instigation technique. *Journal of Consulting and Clinical Psychology*, 1968, **32**, 565–574.

Thoresen, C. & Mahoney, M. *Behavioral self-control.* New York: Holt, Rinehart and Winston, 1974.

Twentyman, C. T. & McFall, R. M. Behavioral training of social skills on shy males. *Journal of Consulting and Clinical Psychology*, in press.

Valentine, J. & Arkowitz, H. Social anxiety and self-evaluation of interpersonal performance. Unpublished manuscript, University of Oregon, 1972.

Watson, D. & Friend, R. Measurement of social evaluative anxiety. *Journal of Consulting and Clinical Psychology*, 1969, **33**, 448–457.

Wolpe, J. & Lazarus, A. *Behavior therapy techniques: A guide to the treatment of neurosis.* New York: Pergamon Press, 1968.

DELINQUENCY

3. ALTERING SCHOOL TRUANCY AND PETTY THEFT

DEANE SHAPIRO, JR.   Director, Webster Center, Santa Clara, California, and Stanford University Medical School

The case discussed here was treated at Webster Center, a nonprofit community mental-health center specializing in adolescent and family counseling and serving as resource consultant to the Santa Clara Unified School District and other community agencies: police, probation, social services, and county health nurses. In the majority of cases referred to the Center, the adolescent is labeled by the referral source as the "identified problem." The counselors at the Center, however, attempt to consult with many significant people (like family and school personnel) about each case and to avoid identifying any one "client." In this way, the adolescent is not merely seen at a distant clinic office to talk about his concerns and then returned to the home, school, or community environment in which the problem originally occurred. Rather, clinical strategies involve teaching the adolescent self-management, decision-making, and coping skills that can be generalized to the natural environment. And, equally important, an attempt is made to modify, as much as possible, the maladaptive aspects of the adolescent's environment. The case presented here illustrates this two-pronged approach.

This case was referred by the police department. Jack, a white male aged fifteen years, had been caught jimmying open a pinball machine to take the change inside. He was not booked and was given probation on condition that he receive counseling. The mother, Mrs. Jameson, and her son Jack attended the first session. Mrs. Jameson explained the problem briefly, saying that her son had been truant from school for the previous two weeks (since the beginning of the new quarter); that he had lied to her, saying that he had been attending school; and that, during that time, he had been arrested by the police for petty theft. Therefore, the problem, as she saw it, was her son's lying, truancy, and petty theft.

While Mrs. Jameson explained this history, Jack sat staring at the floor, saying nothing. When asked how he saw the situation, he did not respond and continued to stare at the floor.

"That's just the way he is at home when we ask him a question," Mrs. Jameson stated. "He just hangs his head and mopes and won't say anything."

METHOD OF ELICITING VERBAL BEHAVIOR FROM AN UNCOOPERATIVE CLIENT

For me, one of the most difficult times in counseling adolescents is when they refuse to respond and instead "stare at the floor," remaining silent. The tack that I took here was to try to make Jack trust me by encouraging him to feel free to speak and also by asking him very specific questions, to which there were factual, concrete answers. These "factual" questions were then followed by questions that involved Jack's feelings and might, I thought, be more difficult for him to answer.

COUNSELOR (CO): Jack, I'm not part of the school, nor am I part of the police; and I want you to know that you can feel free to say anything you want here. It will stay just between us. Were you in school today?
JACK (J): (Shakes his head no)
CO: How long has it been since you were in school?
J: About two weeks.
CO: Do you know why you decided not to go?
J: No.
CO: Do you like school? It's okay to be honest with me.
J: No.
CO: Tell me, Jack, what's the worst, the very worst class you have in school?
J: Wood shop.
CO: And, what's the best, given, of course that you don't like school?
J: Well, I like Spanish pretty well . . .
CO: What's next best?
J: Well, P.E. and math aren't bad.

As it turned out, Jack enjoyed all his classes, to some extent, except wood shop. He explained that he did not like wood shop because the teacher treated him as a child; he criticized him frequently and made him feel incompetent and stupid, "like a little kid."

CO: That must be frustrating, to be fifteen years old, almost six feet tall, and to be treated like a little child.
J: (Looking up for the first time) Yeah, it is.

CO: It seems as though you want to be treated like the adult man you almost are.
J: (Nods his head yes)
CO: I don't blame you. I'd be pretty frustrated, too, if I were fifteen, had lots of questions about what it was going to be like to be a man soon, about what I wanted to do with my life, and someone treated me like a kid. That would make me pretty angry.[1]
J: Yeah, he is always standing over my shoulder and saying, "No, you did that wrong; that's not right; boy, are you clumsy." Sometimes I want to hit him.

This dialogue represents a series of successive approximations toward the goal of increasing trust between client and counselor—and also toward increasing the client's verbal self-exploration and disclosure of his feelings. By means of certain cues, it was possible to elicit and to increase Jack's verbal behavior within a relatively short time. Furthermore, it was possible to pinpoint the problem of "not liking school" to the more specific "not liking the way he was treated by the wood-shop teacher."

USE OF IMAGERY IN THE DECISION-MAKING PROCESS

Once Jack seemed able to talk more freely with me, I asked him to close his eyes and tell me where he would like

[1] *Editors' note:* The counselor is expressing what he imagines Jack's feelings must be for Jack's unresponsiveness gives few cues. If the counselor has guessed correctly, Jack will be more likely to discuss his problem openly.

to be in five years. He immediately said, "A pilot."

CO: Do you know what is necessary to become a pilot?[2]
J: Yeah, I've checked into pilot training school and have talked with some of the pilots down at the airport.
MRS J: Yes, he loves planes. He spends most of his weekends at the airport and has model planes all over the house.
CO: Do you need to go to school to become a pilot, Jack?
J: Yeah, I guess so.
CO: You guess?
J: Yeah, I know I have to have my diploma from high school.

I then asked Jack to close his eyes again and to imagine where he would be in five years if he did not go back to school.

J: I'm on a street corner . . . leaning against some kind of post . . . looking down . . . a gutter . . . raining . . . and I'm bored . . . confused.
CO: Jack, it's your ball game. If you choose the path of not going back to school, you see what's going to happen. If you choose the path of going back to school, you see what can happen. It's your choice. I'm not going to make you go back to school. I really can't. Nor can your mother or the police. You really have to decide if you want to.
J: (Long pause) Yeah, I guess I want to.

[2] This question was asked both as a shaping device—to make Jack think about what is necessary to become a pilot—and also to determine whether he in fact wanted to be a pilot or was merely saying what he thought I would want to hear.

SELF-SABOTAGE: BEHAVIORAL REHEARSAL OF THE "TWO SELVES"

Thus, through the use of imagery, Jack seemed to see pretty clearly that, if he went back to school, in five years there would be a good chance that he could obtain his pilot's license, and that, if he didn't go back to school, there would be a good chance that he would end up on a street corner, feeling confused.

However, even though one can clearly perceive himself in the future and can clearly see the connection between present behaviors and future consequences, it is often difficult to adopt proper present behaviors, especially if they are somewhat aversive. Therefore, I asked Jack to sit back in his chair and to tell me all the reasons he wanted to go back to school:

J: So I can become a pilot; so I won't have a boring life and be . . . confused, and not know what I want to do. Yeah (thinking hard), I really do want to go back to school.

I then asked him to switch chairs and to tell me again some of the reasons that he did not want to go back to school—all the things he might say to trick himself into not going back.[3] He closed his eyes and said:

J: It's morning, and I'm tired. I don't want to get out of bed. It's pretty comfortable here . . . school's such a

[3] *Editors' note:* Switching chairs, derived from a *Gestalt* technique, is an effective way of dramatizing the conflicting reinforcers and punishments involved in major decisions.

bummer . . . and that wood-shop teacher. I don't want to see him.

CO: Switch chairs again.

J: Get out of bed, bum. —————, you're lazy.

We discussed how there seemed to be two selves within each of us, one self that tries to make us do what we really want to do and another self that seems to sabotage us, play tricks on us, and keep us from doing what we want to do.

As the counseling session took place two days before vacation and as Jack had not been to school since the start of the semester, I asked him whether or not he thought it would be a good idea to spend the next two days going back to his new classes and trying to become reoriented.

J: But I don't know where to get my class list.

CO: (Confrontive) Jack, you said that one of the things you didn't like about school was that other people treated you like a child. As an adult, tell me where you think you might get your class list.[4]

J: At the office.

CO: Um huh.

J: But there are two offices.

CO: Which seat are you talking from now?

J: (Smiling) I guess from that one there! (pointing to the sabotage seat)

CO: Tell me, how will you be able to find out which office?

J: I could ask.

CO: Thatta boy. Listen, it's a very mature thing you're doing, taking your

———

[4] *Editors' note:* Some language from transactional analysis can also dramatize the approach-avoidance conflicts.

life into your own hands. That's not an easy thing to do, and it's kind of scary. It's okay to feel nervous about it . . . and also to feel proud.

We then rehearsed, by means of covert images, what it might feel like to go back to school the next day: Some kids would tease him for being out, some teachers might give him a hard time for being behind in his work, he might feel like an outsider walking into strange classrooms.

SELF-MONITORING AND SELF-REINFORCEMENT

I then made a self-monitoring sheet for Jack, suggesting that he monitor all the times during the next five days when he had the urge not to go to school:

Whenever you hear yourself talking from that sabotage chair, mark it down on the sheet here. Then, if you are able to overcome the sabotage urge, write down a note of praise in the second column, like "Way to go man" or "This is helping me be the person I want to become" or "This takes a lot of courage; be proud of yourself."

Jack smiled and said that praising himself like that seemed a little childish. I responded:

Look, it's going to be a hard day for you tomorrow and for the next few days after that. You're going to need all the support you can give yourself. It's not at all childish to give yourself support and encouragement. I admire what you've chosen to do. I think you should admire it, too, and tell yourself so.

FAMILY CONTRACTING; ALTERING REINFORCEMENT STRATEGY IN FAMILY

At that point, I turned to the mother and, for the first time in the counseling session, brought up the issue of jimmying open the pinball machine. I asked Mrs. Jameson whether or not Jack received some sort of allowance.

MRS. J: No, but he knows that all he has to do is ask us for money and we would give it to him.

CO: Jack, did you jimmy open the machine for kicks, boredom, or because you felt like you needed the money inside?

J: I needed some money. But I don't like to ask my folks all the time for money.

CO: Are there other ways of getting money besides jimmying open a pinball machine or asking your parents?

J: I've tried to get a job, but I'm too young and the neighbors say they don't have any yard or garden work for me to do.

MRS. J: I have to say that Jack really has tried to get a job. I've seen him go around and ask the neighbors, but he's had no luck.

My initial tack in this line of questioning was to show Jack that, if the goal is money, then there are several ways of obtaining it: the pinball machine, looking for a job, and so on. I was going to point out that both ways take him to the same goal but that the first way has some aversive consequences—the police—, whereas the second method could also bring him money but without the aversive consequences. However, when I learned that he had in fact tried to find a job, without success, I changed tacks:

CO: Mrs. Jameson, does Jack do any chores around the house?

MRS. J: Yes, in fact he really does help a lot around the house, probably better than any of the other children.

CO: How would you feel about giving him an allowance for the chores he's already doing around the house? I feel that would show him that there are certain privileges that go along with acting responsible and adult-like.[5]

MRS. J: I guess we could do that. Except that since he's been cutting school, and leaving campus, we told him no more money. We also told him that, if he did go to school, he wasn't to leave campus during lunch hour.

CO: Perhaps we could look at the allowance as a preventive strategy. By giving Jack an allowance, he is learning that for doing certain adult-like behaviors—chores around the house—he gets certain privileges, like money, and the right to leave the campus during lunch. It would also be a source of money for him and probably prevent his needing to jimmy open the pinball machine again. After all, he did try hard to get a job, as you yourself pointed out.

MRS. J: I'd go along with that.

CO: Jack, your mother is willing to treat you like an adult, giving you an allowance and allowing you to leave campus during lunch. What can you do, on your part, to show her that you are in fact an adult?

[5] *Editors' note:* There may be some advantage in labeling this money "pay" or "wages" for work performed. An "allowance" is a noncontingent grant to a dependent, and the term may prolong Jack's view of himself as a child.

J: Well, I can do the chores around the house like I always do.

CO: Umm, anything else?

J: Go to school, like I said.

CO: Good. Now, what do you think should happen if you don't go to school? (Allowing Jack to choose his own consequences)

J: Well, then I shouldn't get my allowance and should be grounded from leaving campus the next day.

CO: Does that seem fair to you, Mrs. Jameson?

MRS. J: Very fair.

CO: Does that seem fair to you, Jack?

J: (Nods in agreement)[6]

It is important to note that Jack was actively involved in the formation of the contract. He chose the behaviors he was to exhibit in order to obtain the contingent allowance; he also chose what his punishment would be if he did not keep his side of the contract. These choices reinforced his role as active agent and decision maker in his own life.

The session terminated with the understanding that Jack was going to come by the next day after school to tell me how things had gone.

He did not show up the next day at my office (Thursday), and I felt pretty helpless and ineffectual. I called his mother the following morning (Friday), and she said that Jack had in fact gone to school but had forgotten to come by my office. She said that Mr. Franklin, the high-school counselor,

[6] *Editors' note:* It may seem fair to Jack now, but will it later when he actually has to forfeit his money and privilege? The money is a reward for working. Perhaps other contingencies could be arranged for attending or not attending school.

had told her that Jack had only attended five out of six classes on Thursday, cutting his wood-shop class.

MRS. J: The counselor told me that Jack had made some excuse about not being able to find the class. But Mr. Franklin said he didn't believe Jack because last quarter Jack had had metal shop, and that's right next door to wood shop.

I told Mrs. Jameson how pleased I was to hear that Jack had attended five classes and suggested that she try to give him all the encouragement she could.

MRS. J: But Mr. Franklin called because Jack cut class and sounded pretty angry. I guess I feel responsible. It's hard to encourage Jack when the counselor complains to me.

I let Mrs. Jameson know that I appreciated her feelings of responsibility and concern toward Jack and that I understood the feelings of helplessness that she must have had when the school counselor called to complain about Jack. I then asked her to listen to a story:

Imagine, Mrs. Jameson, that there is a task that you don't want to do, that you are afraid you won't do well, and that the task will make you look incompetent and ineffectual. Let's say the task consists of six parts. Finally, one day, you gather together all your courage, and tackle the task. And, lo, you find that you accomplished five of the six parts perfectly but hadn't performed the sixth. Now, imagine two different people. *Person number one* comes to you and says, "Heh, you didn't do all six. That's not good enough; I'm going to report you as inefficient, and you deserve to be punished."

CO: How would you feel after talking to this person?

MRS. J: Pretty discouraged, like what's the use . . . you can't win.

CO: Umm. Now, here's the second person:

Hey, I'm really impressed with you. That takes a lot of guts to try what you did; and, look, five parts done just right. That's not perfect; there's still room for improvement, but I'm proud of what you did; it shows a lot of courage and responsibility. Good for you.[7]

CO: And now, how would you feel?

MRS. J: I'd feel really good. Yes, I see your point. I'd feel much more like trying the sixth part.

CO: Good. So, tonight, when Jack comes home, give him all the encouragement you can. I'll call the counselor now and have a talk with him.

MRS. J: That Mr. Franklin, he doesn't seem to like Jack very much; he seems to always be trying to get him in trouble.

CO: (Ignoring the provocative remark about the high-school counselor) I'm glad to see that you are going to encourage Jack tonight.

SCHOOL CONSULTATION: ALTERING REINFORCEMENT STRATEGY IN THE SCHOOL

I then called Mr. Franklin and asked if I could engage his cooperation in an intervention strategy I was trying with one of his counselees, Jack Jameson.

MR. F: Oh, that kid; what a confused mixed-up kid he is. You know, he needs to be led around by the hand to get to class.

CO: I understand he came to school yesterday and attended five out of six classes. Isn't that the first time he's been to school in two weeks?

MR. F: Can you imagine that he couldn't find his wood-shop class? I can't believe that. It is right next door to metal shop, and he had that class last quarter. Can you believe that he couldn't find it?

CO: You're probably right, Mr. Franklin; he probably did know where that class was. Why do you imagine he didn't go?

MR. F: I don't know, but that just shows that he needs to be led around to class by the hand. Can't trust him.

CO: I wonder if he were as aware of his feelings as people like you and I are, if he wouldn't say to us, "Gee, I missed that class because I was scared to walk in there; I was feeling really insecure and didn't have much confidence in myself."

MR. F: Yes, that makes sense to me. He sure is a confused kid.

CO: You're in a tough position as middle man, aren't you, having . . .[8]

MR. F: (Cutting in) Yes sir . . . I'm right there in the middle. People blame me when the kids aren't in school, and yet sometimes those teachers aren't the most cooperative or experienced.

CO: That sure puts a lot of pressure on you, doesn't it?

MR. F: Umm. (In agreement)

CO: I'd like to see if I couldn't be of some help to you in this case. Do

---

[7] Note the use of the sandwiching technique: a positive reinforcer, a criticism, then a positive reinforcer (after L. Homme, personal communication, July 1972).

[8] *Editors' note:* The counselor now communicates that he sees how it must feel to handle the problems faced by the high-school counselor.

you think it would be a good idea for us to work cooperatively on a strategy.

MR. F: Sure, I'd like all the help I can get.

CO: Terrific.

I then outlined briefly the strategy that I was trying to use with Jack, noting particularly the fear that Jack must be feeling in returning to school after a two-week absence. I suggested that it was going to be very scary for Jack and that we should try to give him all the encouragement we could. I went through the same two-person story I had told Mrs. Jameson, in order to show the importance of reinforcing successive approximations, and I concluded by trying to involve the counselor actively in the role of helper:

CO: ˙ Maybe you could even go to the wood-shop teacher, and try to encourage him to be more positive with Jack. You could explain to the teacher how scared Jack must be and how we're all trying to give him as much encouragement as possible.

MR. F: That sounds like a good idea. Those teachers could sure learn a thing or two about being more positive with kids.

CO: That would be extremely helpful to Jack. And, by the way, since Jack is interested in airplanes, you might even see if the wood-shop teacher could suggest that Jack make a model plane in class.

The following week Jack came to my office voluntarily. He said that some of his friends had been talking about cutting school again and that he had felt himself tempted to cut with them. He pointed to the sabotage chair and said, "It sounds much more fun to cut with them than to be in school."

I asked him which he wanted to do. "Well," he said, "I want to stay in school, but I need something to give me more will power to do it."

CO: Do you have any ideas?

J: Well, I was thinking I could have all the teachers sign me in when I go to class each day.

CO: That sounds like a great idea. Then maybe you could give that sheet to your mother in the evening, and she could give you the next day's allowance.

Jack and I then drew up a form on which teachers could certify that Jack had attended class. We decided that the form looked a bit stark, so we added a note at the bottom, suggesting that the teachers smile at Jack every time they signed him in!

FOLLOW-UP

A one-month follow-up check revealed that Jack's attendance had been perfect. He had been leaving campus for lunch, receiving his allowance regularly, and doing chores around the house. I talked with the high-school counselor about Jack:

MR. F: We sure worked out a good strategy with him. He finally looks like he's going to shape up. I have to admit, there was a time there for a while when I thought it might have been hopeless.[9]

[9] Editors' note: It is a wise counselor who lets others take credit for their actions (even though that secret inner self is yelling, "Yes, but if it hadn't been for me, you never would have done it").

I also passed Jack on the school grounds, and we talked for a while. He said that there was one thing that he could not understand:

J: That counselor. He's been really nice to me. I just can't figure it out. And even the wood-shop teacher seems to have changed. He said it was okay for me to make a model plane in his class. It's going to take a long time, but, when I get done, I'll bring it by and show it to you.

COMMENTS

The intervention was short. The total time, including phone calls to the mother and the high-school counselor, was three hours.

No one client was ever identified, neither the mother, the son, nor the high-school counselor. The intervention consisted of trying to shape all three individuals' behavior. Jack was encouraged to make decisions about his own life, his mother to give him freedom to leave the school campus and money contingent upon his assuming certain responsibilities, and both his mother and the high-school counselor to be more positive toward Jack and to reinforce his successive approximations.

Past behavior was almost completely ignored, and the focus of the counseling session was on "Where can we go from here?" It seemed to me that, even though the problem that originally brought Jack to the Center from the police was jimmying open a pinball machine, to dwell on the whys of this action or to spend time figuring out how to punish it would be to dwell on the past—neither useful nor appropriate for counseling activities. Thus, the pinball-machine theft was used only as a means of understanding the present, of pointing out to the mother that Jack did not have any money of his own to spend and of pointing out to Jack that there are alternative ways to achieve the same end and that some ways have more aversive consequences than others.

The emphasis was always on Jack's making choices about his own life. Jack was "shaped" to feel that he was existentially in charge of his life. He saw, through covert rehearsal, the consequences of alternative courses of action and that he himself was the one who had to make each choice.

Data collecting was a means to an end. Jack was to record his urges not to attend school and self-reinforcement for attending. He reported that he kept the sheet for the first two days but then found it unnecessary and threw it away. It is problematical whether or not in fact he kept it at all. However, the data sheet was merely a technique by which to help Jack attend classes. Therefore, if the sheet did nothing more than make Jack more aware of how he was sabotaging himself and point out to him the importance of reinforcing himself for working toward his goals, then whether or not he actually made written notes on it was less relevant. As a Chinese saying has it: "The finger points the way to the moon. Once the moon is seen, the finger is no longer necessary."

Jack's "will power" was increased by specific environmental programming. Having Jack sign in with his teachers and persuading the high-school counselor and Mrs. Jameson to reinforce successive approximations in his behavior are both examples of altering and shaping environmental contingencies.

Finally, *relationship variables were important*. At each stage, behavioral techniques were used within the context of a relationship. The high-school counselor was willing to go along with me because he felt that I was not threatening his competence; rather I understood his middle-man position. Jack felt that he could talk openly to me about school without being punished. His mother felt that I cared about her son and was trying to make him more adult; she was therefore willing to "trust my strategy," to ignore her son's past truancy and petty theft, and to begin to give him an allowance and more rights for present appropriate behavior. It is problematical whether or not these behavioral techniques, applied in a vacuum, would have been effective. It is equally problematical whether or not relationship variables alone, without the other techniques, would have been effective. It seems that this case clearly illustrates the complementary nature of behavioral techniques and relationship variables in the counseling process.

Outline Summary of Salient Points

Self-Management and Decision-Making Strategies	Altering and Shaping Environmental Consequences	Relationship Variables

Use of imagery in foreseeing long-range goals and consequences
Connecting future goals with present behaviors
Techniques for increasing probability of present behavior
   covert rehearsal
   self-sabotage verbal
      rehearsal
   self-monitoring of urges to
      sabotage
   self-reinforcement for not
      giving into urges
	Contingency contracting with home environment
	Altering reinforcement strategy in home and school environment to increase probability that self-management strategy will occur and will be praised for successive approximations
		Eliciting verbal behavior from an initially hostile, uncooperative client
		Getting the mother (home environment) to trust the counselor enough to ignore past behavior of petty theft and to concentrate on present behavior
		Consulting, shaping the personnel of the school environment without appearing as a threat to them

---

4.   *USING MODELING TO STRENGTHEN THE BEHAVIORAL REPERTORY OF THE JUVENILE DELINQUENT*

IRWIN G. SARASON[1]   University of Washington

[1] The research reported here was supported in part by grants from the Social and Rehabilitation Service (H.E.W.), the National Institute of Mental Health, and the National Science Foundation. I am indebted to Victor J. Ganzer for his collaboration in developing the methods described here.

Juvenile delinquency is an enormous social problem. The social and vocational behavior of delinquents is a major part of that problem. The basic question is how to change certain behaviors of delinquents. Delinquency need not be viewed in terms of a "mental illness" conception. Rather, it may be viewed as a consequence of inadequate learning experiences. The delinquent is someone who has fallen out of the mainstream of his culture. He is someone who is deficient in socially acceptable and adaptive behaviors. His deviant behavior seems to be part of a rebellion against ways of responding. Much of this failure may arise from inadequate opportunities to observe and display socially useful behavior. This interpretation is consistent with empirical evidence, sociological theories, and clinical observations (Marlatt & Perry, 1975; Sarason, 1968).

The acquisition of a variety of undesirable response patterns comes about, at least in part, because of modeling effects. However, undesirable response patterns are not the only ones acquired through observation. Necessary and desirable social, vocational, and educational skills and behavior also can be learned through modeling, a process that begins with the opportunity to observe a model perform an adaptive or necessary response. There is a growing body of evidence suggesting that modeling (observational learning) may provide an effective and practical approach to the problems of delinquents and other youngsters, including many poor performers in and dropouts from school.

ESTABLISHING A MODELING PROGRAM FOR DELINQUENTS

In this article we describe a modeling program that was set up to foster better social functioning among institutional-ized juvenile delinquents. The setting was the Cascadia Reception-Diagnostic Center in Tacoma, Washington. It is part of the state juvenile-rehabilitation system. Although Cascadia receives boys and girls between the ages of eight and eighteen years, the program described here involved boys between the ages of fifteen and eighteen years. Evidence suggests that similar programs may be as effective with youngsters of varying ages in schools and other community agencies (Sarason & Sarason, 1974).

Two ingredients were needed at Cascadia in order to arrange effective modeling opportunities: an objectively describable modeling situation and good rapport between models and subjects—the models had to be liked by the subjects and had to be persons with whom boys would want to identify. Early preliminary studies led to the conclusion that, whereas the models should interact informally with the boys of Cascadia's cottages, modeling sessions should involve clearly labeled and easily identified situations. Much time was spent working on these situations and training assistants to be effective models and empathic, reinforcing individuals. A major preliminary task was preparing scripts that would capture the attention of the boys.

MAINTAINING ATTENTION

It was initially estimated that the boys' general level of attention could be maintained for twenty to thirty minutes. We then instituted several procedures to maintain better control of this short and fluctuating attention span. One "gimmick" that evolved was provision of a soft drink for each boy about midway through a one-hour session. Although initially perceived as "bribes" by many of the boys, the soft drinks were soon readily accepted as something that the group leaders wanted to share with them.

We found that an important method of maintaining attention is the actual amount of physical activity that the modeling situations require. Rather than sitting passively in chairs, the models and boys were on their feet and actually moving about the room a great deal during each session. This physical activity, combined with the heavy emphasis on affect and nonverbal expressive gestures, has done a great deal to facilitate motivation and attention to the content and purpose of the dialogues used in the groups. Because many delinquent boys are primarily action- and movement-oriented and rely considerably less on verbal skills, the nonverbal focus has proved to be very important. The third procedure for maintaining interest has been replay of the audio tapes in the groups after the boys have played the various roles. This "feedback" has proved to be of considerable interest to the boys, for it affords them the opportunity actually to hear and correct elements of their own behavior. A fourth procedure for maintaining attention has been to ask one of the boys in the group to summarize what has gone on in the scene or situation that has just been enacted. As the boys did not know beforehand who was going to be asked, it was necessary for them to be very attentive during the sessions, in order to answer the questions satisfactorily. Sim-

ilarly, the fact that each boy knew that he was expected to imitate the model's behavior promoted increased attentiveness. The procedures that were developed held the boys' attention and interest for an hour or more at a time.

TRAINING MODELS

New models occasionally had to be added to the modeling staff. In the Cascadia project new models are oriented to the purposes and procedures followed in the groups. Then they have the opportunity to read over and begin to memorize the existing scripts. Concurrently, they are engaged in writing new scenes and practicing the various roles themselves. They are also able to observe several group sessions conducted by the experienced models from behind a one-way mirror in the group room. Finally, a new model will begin working with an experienced model in the groups themselves. In general, the experienced model's behavior itself serves as an effective model on which the new model's behavior can be based.

The introduction of closed-circuit television equipment as a technical aid can have considerable impact, both in increasing the sensitivity and self-awareness of the models and on the subjects. In training, models videotape all their role-playing sessions. The tapes are then watched and evaluated by the models and staff, especially with regard to affective and expressive behavior. From observations of the tapes it is possible to point out to the models some of their habitual behaviors, which are then either eliminated or emphasized in order to maximize their effectiveness in the groups. This immediate audio-visual feedback provides a clear and objective picture of the model's behavior as it was seen by the boys.

THE ORIENTATION SESSION

In orienting delinquent boys to a modeling program, it is important to foster a practical, problem-solving atmosphere. The following is an excerpt taken from the first day's orientation at Cascadia.

First, let's all introduce ourselves, starting with me. I'm Mr. ————— and this is Mr. ————— [boys introduce themselves]. We are working with small groups of boys here at Cascadia. We are doing something new to show you some different ways of handling common situations and problems that will happen in your lives. The situations we'll work with and emphasize are often particularily important for fellows like yourselves. . . .

We want to work together with you to teach you new ways to handle problem situations. These are situations which we feel will be of importance to you in the future. They are things that probably all of you will run into from time to time, and we think that you can benefit from learning and practicing different ways to act in these situations.

The way we want to do this isn't by lecturing or advising you. Having people watch others doing things and then discussing what has been done is a very important way and a useful way to learn. It is easy to learn how to do something just by observing someone else doing it first. Often times, just explaining something to someone isn't nearly as effective as actually doing it first while the other person watches. For example, it is easier to learn to swim or repair a car if you have a

chance to watch someone else doing it first. . . .

We want to emphasize better ways of doing these things and coping with similar problems which will be important in the future for most of you. Everyone in the group will play the roles for themselves and watch others playing the same roles. This is like acting; only it is realistic because it involves situations in which you might really find yourselves. We feel that the situations are realistic because they are based on the real experiences of a lot of fellows who have gone through Cascadia. . . .

We will be playing different roles in different situations on each day. We want you to watch us and then take turns in pairs, playing the same roles yourselves. We will also discuss how everyone does, what is important about the particular roles or situations, and how they may be related to your lives. We will want you to stick closely to the roles as we play them but also add your own personal touch to your role. As you will see, it is important that we all get involved in this as much as we can. The more you put yourself into the role you play, the more realistic it will be to you and to the rest of the group. We see these scenes as examples of real situations that you will all find yourselves in sometime, and it is important to play them as realistically as possible. We will outline each scene as we go along.

Also, each meeting will be (tape-recorded or videotaped). We use these tape recordings for our own records of how each group proceeds. These tapes are identified by code numbers, and no one's name actually appears in the tape. The tapes are confidential, too, and will be used only by us. As we said, none of this information is used by the regular staff.

Before going any further, we want to give you an example of what we're talking about. Mr. ————— and I will play two roles which involve a scene that has really gone on right here in your cottage. This scene is based on information we got from a cottage counselor and other boys who have been in this cottage. This situation involves a common cottage problem, and we will show you some things that can be done about it.

A MODELING SESSION: THE JOB INTERVIEW

Each session has a particular theme, for example, applying for a job, resisting temptations by peers to engage in antisocial acts, taking a problem to a teacher or parole counselor, or forgoing immediate gratifications in order to lay the groundwork for more significant gratifications in the future. In each situation emphasis is placed on the generality of the appropriate behaviors being modeled, in order to emphasize their potential usefulness.

An example of one session is the job interview, in which roles are played by an interviewer and a job applicant. The dialogue emphasizes the kinds of questions an interviewer might ask and the various positive, coping responses an interviewee is expected to make. Also such factors as proper appearance, mannerisms, honesty, and interests are stressed. One of the models verbally introduces each scene at the beginning of a meeting. The job-interview scene introduction is a general example.

Introduction

Having a job can be very important. It is a way that we can get money for things we want to buy. It is a way we can feel important because we are able to earn something for ourselves through our own efforts. For this same reason, a job can make us feel more independent. Getting a job may not always be easy. This is especially true of jobs that pay more money and of full-time jobs. A job may be important to guys like you who have been in an institution because it gives you a chance to show other people that you can be trusted, that you can do things on your own, that you are more than just a punk kid. However, because you've been in trouble, you may have more trouble than most people getting a job. In the scene today you'll have a chance to practice applying for a job and being interviewed by the man you want to work for. Being interviewed makes most people tense and anxious because interviewers often ask questions which are hard to answer. After each of you has been interviewed, we'll talk about the way it felt and about what to do about the special problems that parolees may face getting jobs.

Scene I

A boy who is on parole from Cascadia is applying for a job at a small factory in his home town. He is eighteen and has not finished high school but hopes to do so by going to school at night. Obviously the boy has a record. This will come up during the interview. Pay careful attention to how he handles this problem. This is a two-part scene; first, we'll act out the job interview, then a part about another way of convincing an employer that you want a job.

(Mr. Howell is seated at his desk when George knocks on the door.)

HOWELL: Hello. I'm Mr. Howell, and your name?

(Mr. Howell rises, shakes hands)

GEORGE: George Smith.

HOWELL: Have a seat, George.

(Both sit down)

Oh yes. I have your application right here. There are a few questions I'd like to ask you. I see that you have had some jobs before; tell me about them.

GEORGE: They were just for the summer because I've been going to school. I've worked on some small construction jobs and in a food-processing plant.

HOWELL: Did you ever have any trouble at work or ever get fired?

GEORGE: No trouble, except getting used to the work the first couple of weeks. I did quit one job—I didn't like it.

HOWELL: I see that you have only finished half your senior year in high school. You don't intend to graduate?

GEORGE: (Showing some anxiety) Yes, I do. I intend to go to night school while I'm working. It may take me a year or so, but I intend to get my diploma.

HOWELL: How did you get a year behind?

GEORGE: I've been out of school for a while because I've been in trouble. Nothing really serious.

HOWELL: I'd like to know just what kind of trouble you've had, serious or not.

GEORGE: Well, I was sent to Cascadia for six weeks, but I'm out on parole now. I just got out a couple of weeks ago. One of the reasons I want a job is to help keep me out of trouble.

HOWELL: What kind of trouble were you involved in?

GEORGE: A friend and I stole some car parts off an engine. I guess we were pretty wild. I'm not running around like that any more, though.

HOWELL: You sound like you think you can stay out of trouble now. Why do you think so?

GEORGE: In those six weeks at Cascadia I thought about myself and my future a whole lot, and realized it was time to get serious about life and stop goofing off. I know I haven't

been out long yet, but my parole counselor is helping me with the problems that come up. I'm trying to stay away from the guys I got into trouble with. I really think that, if I could get a job and be more on my own, it would help a lot.

HOWELL: Yes, I think you're probably right—but I'm afraid we don't have any openings right now. I'll put your application on file though and let you know if anything turns up. I have several other applications too, so don't be too optimistic.

GEORGE: All right. Thank you.

(George stands and starts to leave as he says this line.)

Scene II

It is now two weeks later. George has called back several times to see if an opening has occurred. He now stops by to check again.

(George knocks on Mr. Howell's door.)

HOWELL: Come in.

GEORGE: (Enters room while speaking) I stopped by to see whether you had an opening yet.

HOWELL: You certainly don't want me to forget you, do you?

GEORGE: No sir; I don't. I really want a job; I think it's the best thing for me to do now.

HOWELL: You know, I believe you. I wasn't so sure at first. It's pretty easy for a guy who has been in trouble to say that he's going to change and then do nothing about it. But the way you've been coming here and checking with me so often, I think you're really serious about it.

GEORGE: Yes sir; I am. I started night school this week. I think I'll be able to get my diploma in a year. So, if I had a job now I'd be all set.

HOWELL: Well, I've got some good news for you, George. I have an opening for a man in the warehouse, and I think you can handle the job if you want it.

GEORGE: Yes, very much. When do you want me to start?

HOWELL: Tomorrow morning at 7:30.

HOWELL: I'll take you out there now and introduce you to Mr. Jones, who will be your supervisor.

Scene III

This is the same setting as Scene II.

(George knocks on Mr. Howell's door.)

HOWELL: Come in.

GEORGE: I stopped by to see whether you had an opening yet.

(Enters room while speaking)

HOWELL: You sure are persistent. Have you tried other places?

GEORGE: Sure, I'm checking back on them too. Getting a good job isn't easy.

HOWELL: (uncomfortably) Ah, well, look. We're not going to have a place for you here. I wouldn't want you to waste your time coming back again. We can't use you.

GEORGE: (Rises to go) Well (pause) okay. Thanks for your trouble. Look, what's up? I know that your company is hiring other fellows like me right now.

HOWELL: Er . . . that's true. Uh, I'm afraid that we have a company policy not to hire anyone with a record.

GEORGE: How come? That doesn't seem fair to me.

HOWELL: Well, er, ahem . . . that's just the company's policy. I'm sorry, but my hands are tied. There's nothing I can do about it.

GEORGE: Well, I would have appreciated knowing that right away.

HOWELL: I'm really sorry. I can see you're trying. . . . I hope you get a job.

GEORGE: Well, do you know of a place that could use me? Since you're in personnel, maybe you've heard of something.

After these scenes were played by the two models, each boy played George's role. At the end of the session, these discussion points were emphasized.

1. *The importance of presenting oneself well.* Getting a job is "selling yourself" too. In both scenes the boy takes the initiative, instead of waiting around passively for things to happen.
2. *How to deal with the fact that one has a record.* Here the boy had to admit to having a record because of the gap in his schooling. If he had lied, the interviewer would have caught him and formed an impression of dishonesty.
3. *It is understandable to feel anxious when being interviewed* because getting a job is important.
4. *Persistence is a trait that employers like.* In the first instance it was an important reason why George got the job.

Jimmy Larsen's Job Interview

About a year after he had participated in the Cascadia research, Jimmy Larsen visited the institution to describe an experience he had recently had. After returning to the community, Jimmy had sought work. He had received a number of rebuffs because of the state of the labor market and the fact that he had a "record." He was able to obtain an appointment with the personnel manager of one large company. Upon arriving for a 3:00 interview Jimmy was told that the personnel manager would be a half-hour late, and he was invited to sit in the waiting room. Jimmy's tension while waiting increased until the job-interview scene popped into his head. More as a means of distraction than anything else, he devoted his thinking to that scene and spent several minutes rehearsing it. Jimmy paid his return visit to Cascadia to tell interested people there that he had landed the job. He attributed his success to Cascadia's modeling program and his rehearsal in the waiting room. Follow-up studies have turned up other indicators of the efficacy of modeling in the vocational area.

TOPICS FOR OTHER MODELING SESSIONS[2]

The other scenes that we developed at Cascadia and used in modeling groups follow a format similar to the job-interview scene and may be categorized generally into several content areas and described as follows.

1. Scenes dealing with the problem of self-control: planning ahead, delay of impulsive actions like aggressive behavior, and so forth.
   a. One scene in this category involves a dialogue between an institutionalized boy and his caseworker on the importance of using time in the institution wisely to plan and prepare for the future.
   b. A home-problem scene involving a fight between a father and his son over compliance with rules, with the boy controlling his anger enough not to run away, which usually leads to more trouble.
   c. A scene contrasting two ways to deal with peer criticism, one based

on appropriate responses and the other leading to a fight.
   d. Two scenes based on the importance of controlling anger: recognizing it, labeling it, and emphasizing the often undesirable consequences of impulsive aggressive behavior, especially when directed toward authority figures.
2. Common situations involving negative peer influence: several scenes based on resisting pressures to conform to delinquent standards and behaviors.
   a. Two situations illustrating ways and reasons for not showing off in typical situations, one involving street drag racing, the other disruptive classroom behavior.
   b. A script illustrating the importance of regular school attendance, the "vicious circle" aspect of truancy, and the related problems it generates.
   c. A group scene with four roles, in which a parolee must resist his peers' spontaneous plan to steal a car, touching also on the fallacy "If you don't go along with the crowd, you'll lose friends."
   d. A scene related to 2a, dealing with adolescent drinking parties and some of the things an adolescent must consider before becoming involved.
3. Appropriate social-interpersonal behavior and the impressions one makes on others.
   a. The job-interview scene is an example of this concept.
   b. Examples of dialogues involving a boy's being "tested" for acceptance in a group or clique of his peers, including both appropriate and inappropriate ways to behave.
4. Aspects of taking responsibility and the consequences of not doing so.
   a. A scene concerning a boy's prompt solicitation of help with school prob-

[2] A limited supply of scripts is available from Irwin G. Sarason, Department of Psychology, University of Washington, Seattle, Washington 98195.

lems in order not to fall behind and perhaps drop out.

b. The difficult but frequently necessary task of apologizing to another and accepting responsibility for correcting a misdemeanor.

THE SEQUENCE FOR EACH SESSION

A number of procedures for presenting and working with this material within the group sessions were developed. Each session was attended by six people, two models and four boys. One complete scene was used for each meeting. Each meeting followed a sequence. First, one model introduced and described the scene for the day. Second, models role-played the scripts while the boys observed. Third, one boy was called upon to summarize and explain the content and outcome of the situation. Fourth, models commented on and discussed the scene, then replayed the recording. Fifth, pairs of boys imitated and rehearsed the roles and behaviors. Sixth, a short "break" was taken, while soft drinks were served and one of the two role-playing imitations was replayed. Seventh, the remaining boys acted out the scene. Eighth, one of the two performances was replayed. Ninth, final summaries and comments on the scene, aspects of its importance, and general applicability were emphasized.

ADAPTATIONS OF MODELING METHODS TO MEET SPECIFIC NEEDS

Variations of the methods described here can be used to meet the specific needs of various types of institutions, schools, hospitals, and community agencies. Although the principles of observational learning remain the same, it is important to identify explicitly the needs to be satisfied and the goals to be attained in a particular setting. The script that follows was written as part of a program to deal with cutting classes and dropping out among a group of boys attending an inner-city high school.

CUTTING-CLASS SCENE

Introduction

Most guys seem to agree that finishing school is a good idea. Almost everyone figures he'll get a high-school diploma someday. However, some guys think that graduating is too far in the future to worry about now. They don't study, cut school a lot, and end up out of school and in trouble. The scene today is about how to avoid cutting classes. After the scene we will talk about the problem presented and other problems that you guys might have with school.

Scene

At school during lunch. Joe and George are sitting next to each other at a table.

JOE: Hey, George, it's a really great day. Let's take off this afternoon and go to the beach. It'll sure beat getting trapped in that crummy hot classroom all afternoon.

GEORGE: Swimming would be great. I'd like to go, but, look man, the water will still be there after school. Let's go then.

JOE: After school: After the sun sets? What's the matter, have you got the hots for Miss Carlson? You used to cut school all the time.

GEORGE: No more. . . . I've got to graduate and get a decent job.

JOE: What's skipping one afternoon gonna hurt? Nobody will ever know the difference.

GEORGE: Yeah, but if I cut with you today, I'll bet I'll be the guy you'll look up the next time you want to cut out for the beach. If I get on that, pretty soon I'd hardly be going to school at all anymore.

JOE: So what? I skip a lot, and it doesn't bother me.

GEORGE: I know; I used to do it with you. I used to fool around a lot. You go ahead. I don't want to. I want to graduate, and the time to worry about doing it is right now.

JOE: Yeah, look, why don't you come on along this once?

GEORGE: Yeah, and I want to go along, but later, not now. How about getting together at three?

JOE: That's a lot of wasted sun. I'll see if Pete will go with me. If he does, we'll head out now, and we'll look for you at the beach at three. If he won't either, let's meet at the car at three. Okay?

GEORGE: Okay.

Discussion Points
1. Ability to resist temptation.
2. Importance of finishing school.
3. Reasons for skipping school and their invalidity.
4. "Vicious circle" aspects—skipping carries with it the chance of being caught, which leads to further avoidance of school (truancy) to avoid punishment.

RESEARCH ON MODELING

Research evidence indicates the value of a modeling and role-playing approach with delinquents. Sarason and Ganzer (1969; 1973) found that this approach cut recidivism rates in half. Harris (1973), in a dropout-prevention study, used material similar to that which comprises the cutting-class scene. She found the modeling of adaptive school behavior to be positively associated with students' attitudes toward themselves, school, and work. Furthermore, teachers' ratings confirmed these changes, and there were indications of improvement in grade-point averages. Why is it that modeling experiences lead to noticeable and sometimes dramatic changes in behavior? Perhaps the main reason is that these experiences provide the individual with information (Sarason, 1973).

SOME HINTS ABOUT ESTABLISHING A MODELING PROGRAM

Several important points growing out of research on observational learning bear particularly on the establishment of practical modeling programs.

1. Define the type of behavior to be modeled as explicitly as possible (for instance, persisting after an initial attempt at solving a problem fails, being patient, expressing anger and annoyance tactfully).
2. Before instituting a modeling program, plan where, when, and how often you should make the type of response you hope the observers will emulate.
3. Check the frequency of responses to be modeled *before* instituting the modeling program.
4. Check the frequency of responses to be modeled *after instituting* the modeling program.
5. Check your ideas, plans, and procedures with colleagues who will not be too polite to give you frank criticisms and useful suggestions. (Often there is no absolutely "best" behavior in a given situation.)
6. Think about the problem of getting

onlookers to attend to (listen and watch) the modeled response.

7. Consider such tactical alternatives as the use of peer models and whether or not the modeling should have a well-structured format. Models should be selected on the basis of the response to be modeled. But, in some circumstances, the most effective model may not be available. Then improvisation is required.

8. Decide on the place for practice trials (behavior rehearsals) in role-playing for your modeling. In some instances observations of modeled behavior without behavioral rehearsal will be sufficient. However, rehearsal is usually a worthwhile component.

9. Consider the question of the role of reinforcement in the program. Should either the model or the observers or both receive reinforcement for emitting desired responses? Reinforcement (for example, praise) increases the observers' interest level and motivation to learn new response patterns. We tend to remember behavior that "pays off."

10. As the program progresses, rethink it periodically. Should new modeled responses be added to the observational-learning repertory? Can it be improved or strengthened? When nonproductive patterns of activity or job performance persist, look for the presence of undesirable models or rewards.

references

Harris, G. G. The use of modeling procedures to modify vocational aspirations of high school dropouts. *Journal of Community Psychology*, 1973, **1**, 298–301.

Marlatt, G. A. & Perry, M. Modeling methods. In F. H. Kanfer and A. P. Goldstein (Eds.), *Helping people change*. Elmsford, N.Y.: Pergamon, 1975. Pp. 117–158.

Meier, R. D. The effectiveness of modeling procedures and instructions for teaching verbal employment interview behaviors to high school seniors. Unpublished doctoral dissertation, Columbia University, 1972.

Sarason, I. G. Test anxiety and cognitive modeling. *Journal of Personality and Social Psychology*, 1973, **28**, 58–61.

Sarason, I. G. Verbal learning, modeling, and juvenile delinquency. *American Psychologist*, 1968, **23**, 254–266.

Sarason, I. G. & Ganzer, V. J. Modeling and group discussion in the rehabilitation of juvenile delinquents. *Journal of Counseling Psychology*, 1973, **20**, 442–449.

Sarason, I. G. & Ganzer, V. J. Social influence techniques in clinical and community psychology. In C. D. Spielberger (Ed.), *Current topics in clinical and community psychology*. New York: Academic Press, 1969. Pp. 1–69.

Sarason, I. G. & Sarason, B. R. *Constructive classroom behavior: A teacher's guide to modeling and role-playing techniques*. New York: Behavioral Publications, 1974.

DEPRESSION

5.   ANTICIPATION TRAINING IN THE TREATMENT OF DEPRESSION[1]

JANE L. ANTON   Washington University, St. Louis, Missouri
JACQUELINE DUNBAR   Stanford University
LEAH FRIEDMAN   Stanford University

Although depression is reported to be "the most common form of mental disorder" (Irwin, 1973), it is only recently that behavior therapists have attempted to investigate and treat it. As therapists at the Stanford Institute for Behavioral Counseling, we became interested in alternative treatment strategies for depressed clients.

In general, the goal of behavioral treatment of depression is to increase the amount of positive reinforcement the individual obtains from the environment. Depressed individuals as a group have been found to engage in fewer pleasant activities than nondepressed individuals (Lewinsohn & Libet, 1972; Lewinsohn & Graf, 1973). Thus, one way of increasing the quantity of reinforcement is to increase the number of pleasant events the person experiences.

Depressed individuals, however, are characterized by pervasive negative thoughts, including negative anticipation of events (Beck, 1970). Our clinical impressions further supported this notion that depressed clients can be characterized as consistently anticipating negative consequences for themselves.

If we assume that these negative anticipations function to limit the amount of positive reinforcement received both by generating a pessimistic "attitude" and by directing attention to the unpleasant elements of an experience, then the value of adding pleasant events is diminished. Consequently, we believe that an element of treatment should be the modification of these negative anticipations. The therapist, however, cannot always work directly with the client's thought processes in order to modify them. We, therefore, were interested in developing a procedure to establish greater self-control over feelings of depression.

METHOD

Nine subjects were selected from those who answered a newspaper advertisement for women suffering from frequent states of depression and wanting to learn a method of controlling them. As depression is most commonly reported among women, only female subjects were recruited. The subjects were screeened by means of scores on the MMPI Depression (D) Scale, and an initial interview was designed to evaluate the client's level and history of depression.

Subjects completed weekly activity logs throughout the study. The activity log consisted of a sheet for identifying and rating daily activities, as well as

[1] This study was partially supported by the Stanford Center for Research and Development in Teaching.

alternate forms of the "Depression Adjective Checklist" (Lubin, 1965) for each day. Each subject was randomly assigned to one of the authors and met individually with her therapist throughout the project. Although there were some individual variations in the scheduling and completion of the treatment procedures, all three therapists attempted to implement substantially the same treatment strategy.

Treatment Procedures

Session 1   In the first session the activity log (see Figure 1) was presented, and subjects were instructed to complete it during the next week. The therapist spent approximately thirty minutes talking to the subject about her feelings of depression. During this time, the therapist attempted to be warm, supportive, and nondirective.

Session 2   The focus of the second session, which occurred one week later, was to arrange an increase in pleasant events in the client's life, as well as to begin training in the self-control of negative anticipations. The subject was told that she would select and schedule six pleasant activities to be performed during the next two weeks. Three of these activities were to be performed

ACTIVITY LOG

Name_____   Date_____

DIRECTIONS: Take a few minutes and think back over what you did today. Select the eight most important activities of the day and list them below. Don't be concerned about why an activity is important. If it seemed important to *you*, for whatever reasons, put it down. What seems like an important activity on one day, may seem unimportant on another day. Don't worry about that. For each day, select the eight activities which seemed most important on *that* day, regardless of how they compare to the activities on other days. It is essential that you list eight activities each day. After you have listed the activities, rate each activity using the seven-point scale.

extremely
unpleasant ___1___   ___2___   ___3___   ___4___   ___5___   ___6___   ___7___   extremely
pleasant

Activity   Rating

_____   _____

_____   _____

_____   _____

_____   _____

_____   _____

FIGURE 1   Activity log to be filled out by client each week. Only 5 of the 8 lines are shown.

by the subject alone, and three were to involve at least one other person. The activities were to take more than ten or fifteen minutes to perform, yet were to be performed easily within one day. Each activity was to be something that the subject expected to enjoy and that was seen as potentially reinforcing. Examples of activities selected are presented in Table 1.

The subject then selected and scheduled the first two activities. The first activity was scheduled to occur before the third session, which was to follow in three or four days. The second activity was scheduled for shortly after the third session. The subject was also encouraged to select and to schedule the remaining activities. After the activities had been scheduled, the subject, with the aid of the therapist, constructed three positive anticipation statements for each of the first two activities. Each statement began with "I will enjoy . . ." and contained a specific description of some aspect of the activity (see Figure 2).

The subject was then asked to close her eyes, relax, and imagine the first ac-tivity as if it were actually happening. She was instructed to rehearse covertly each of the three statements about the activity and to create a vivid image for each statement. For example, one subject imagined herself in the park sitting on the grass and seeing the sunlight filter through the trees (see Figure 2). She was asked to continue repeating the statements and imagining the activity until she could identify a positive feeling while doing so.[2] If the subject had difficulty creating vivid imagery, the therapist assisted by describing the activity with vivid adjectives.

The subject was then instructed to repeat each statement and to review each image for each of the first two activities three times a day at home until the activity had been performed. The subject selected three specific times during the day—usually morning, afternoon, and before going to bed—in which to review the anticipations.

[2] *Editors' note:* An important point: The use of self-statements and imagery in clinical settings without having the person actually "feel" the experience physically seldom works.

TABLE 1   Examples of Activities Planned by Subjects During Treatment

Alone	*With Someone*
Have hair done	Go to a movie
Spend an afternoon in Sausalito	Phone parents
Browse in antique shops	Take a friend to lunch
Spend three hours reading	Play tennis
Prepare a Chinese dinner	Go out to dinner
Buy new towels	Have a friend to dinner
Ride bicycle	Visit an art museum
Work in the garden	Go to San Francisco
Take a drive to the beach	Take the children to the zoo
Go to a lecture	Go to a concert
Buy a new plant	Spend an evening playing with the children
Browse in a bookstore	Go to a health club
Take a long walk	

Activity planned _lunch in the park with Edna._

Date planned for _Wed._

I will enjoy _getting sandwich & salads from deli to take out._

I will enjoy _sitting on the grass in the park & seeing the sun come through the trees._

I will enjoy _talking with Edna & the peace of the park._

Activity planned _going to plant nursery._

Date planned for _Sat._

I will enjoy _looking at all the annuals._

I will enjoy _looking at things & imagining/ designing what I will do for my garden._

I will enjoy _looking at the house plant section & selecting a plant to hang in the kitchen._

FIGURE 2   Two examples of anticipation statements.

Session 3   The third session was scheduled three or four days after session 2. The therapist reviewed with the subject the completion of activity no. 1 and discussed any problems in performing the anticipation sequence. The most common problem reported was difficulty in remembering to review the anticipations three times each day. The therapist suggested that the subject provide various cues that she would happen upon throughout the day. These cues generally consisted of reminder notes placed in obvious places, for example, on the bathroom mirror, on the refrigerator, inside a purse. The therapist then assisted the subject in constructing the anticipation sequence for the third activity. The subject was asked to construct the anticipation sequence for the fourth activity by herself and to bring it to the fourth session.

Session 4   The fourth session took place three or four days after the third session. The therapist checked out the performance of activities nos. 2 and 3 and the practice of anticipation. The subject and therapist then scheduled the fifth activity, and the subject was instructed to schedule the sixth activity by herself. The anticipation sequences for the fifth and sixth activities were completed by the subject without assistance from the therapist. The therapist also suggested that the subject apply the positive-anticipation format to her daily activities. Various daily activities were discussed, and ways of positively anticipating them were developed.

Session 5   In the fifth session, one week after the previous one, the therapist reviewed with the subject her activities and anticipations for the previous week. The therapist attempted to aid the subject in developing alternative uses for the positive-anticipation sequence. For example, if the subject was having difficulty in motivating herself to accomplish a particular task, the therapist suggested that she imagine the task completed and how she would feel about its completion. The subject was asked to continue planning activities and anticipating them as she wished, and the next session was scheduled for one week later.

Session 6   In the sixth session the therapist reviewed the subject's use of the anticipation training during the previous week, as well as the subject's evaluation of the training procedure in general. During the course of observing their activities and rating their moods, several subjects expressed the need for further counseling. They were referred for further treatment.

General Observation on Treatment Procedure

Although each subject proceeded through the treatment procedures with a unique pattern, some general characteristics were observed. Very few subjects reported disappointment, even if the planned activity did not occur on schedule. On those occasions on which anticipating the activity led to feelings of disappointment, the latter were attributed to two sources. The first was requiring someone else to react in a particular way for an activity to be pleasant. As the reactions of others are difficult to predict, such activities frequently proved disappointing.

For example, a mother anticipating a positive reaction took her daughter to lunch at a special restaurant; however, the daughter did not express gratitude for her mother's treat, and the mother was disappointed. Another woman who did not rely on another's reactions for her own pleasure, took her son for a picnic in the park. Even though the son was "in a bad mood" and did not particularly enjoy the picnic, his mother enjoyed being at the park, out of doors, and eating the picnic lunch. Consequently, it is vital that subjects select activities that they expect to enjoy and that are not contingent upon the feelings of others.[3] The fact that someone else also enjoys the activity should be viewed as a bonus and not as an essential.

The second source of disappointment was activities about which the subject had insufficient information to predict whether or not she would enjoy them. Consequently, the therapist should assist the subject in selecting activities that she knows enough about to make a reasonable prediction and also that do not require the enjoyment of other people. These two factors seem

[3] *Editors' note:* Excellent point: It is difficult enough to control one's own reactions.

most critical in the early stages of training. During the latter stages subjects are better able to deal with each of these situations and not to feel disappointed with each activity as a whole. It is essential that the therapist teach the subject to maximize the probability of success and enjoyment, especially during the initial attempt to overcome feelings of depression.[4]

RESULTS

Subjects showed substantial improvement on all dependent measures used in the study. The mean of the pretest scores for the MMPI-D Scale was 81, with a standard deviation of 6.35, whereas the posttest mean score was 69, with a standard deviation of 7.54.[5] Daily activities were rated on a 7-point scale, 1 indicating an extremely unpleasant activity and 7 an extremely pleasant activity. The mean rating of activities for the first week was 3.9, whereas the mean rating for the final week of treatment was 5.1. Subjects, however, showed great variability in the number of activities reported each day. The number of activities ranged from one to sixteen. Consequently, it

is difficult to compare ratings across subjects, and these data must be interpreted with caution. In order to avoid this problem, the activity log presented in Figure 1 was developed. This form has proved to be a more reliable way of having clients observe and rate their own activities.

The "Depression Adjective Checklist" (DACL) was scored by taking the median rating for each subject each week. Higher scores indicate greater depression. The mean for the first week for all subjects was 66, whereas the mean for the final week was 49. The standard deviations were 8.6 and 7.9 respectively. Figure 3 shows the daily median DACL scores for all subjects. As a score of 55 or less can be interpreted as a "nondepressed" score, it is evident that the subjects, as a group, moved from fairly stable ratings of depression during the base-line period to fairly stable nondepressed ratings following treatment. It should be noted that, whereas the mean scores for all nine subjects changed substantially in the direction of less depression, two of the nine subjects showed little or no change. Both these subjects had very few social skills, not positive interpersonal relationships, and almost no available sources of reinforcement in their environment. This finding suggests that, for anticipation training to be effective, the client should have at least one positive interpersonal relationship or sufficient social skills with which to develop such a relationship.[6]

---

[4] *Editors' note:* Later in the process clients could be encouraged to experiment with new (and riskier) activities, anticipating the excitement of new experiences and the satisfaction of learning whether or not they are enjoyable (even if they are not).

[5] This reduction from 81 to 69 is difficult to evaluate statistically because of the small number of subjects and the tendency for extreme scores to "regress" to the mean. A nonparametric sign test on the change does suggest that it was significant.

[6] *Editors' note:* A combination treatment involving social skills and friendship training, along with anticipation training, may be the most effective for many depressed persons.

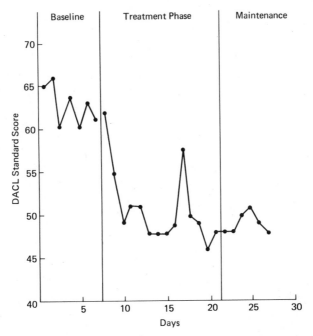

FIGURE 3   Median "Depression Adjective Checklist" (DACL) scores for all nine subjects.

DISCUSSION

The positive-anticipation training showed substantial effects in improving the subjects' reported mood level and the perceived quality of the activities. Self-reports of subjects at the end of treatment indicated that most thought they could use the procedure without further assistance from a therapist. They also indicated that they felt better able to handle feelings of depression should they occur in the future. Although the results were very encouraging, considering that the average therapeutic time with each subject was only six hours, it should be emphasized that anticipation training is not offered as a panacea for depression. Rather, it seems a very promising beginning for treatment. At the end of the project,

most subjects indicated additional problem areas on which they wanted to work. These areas included marital counseling, coping with irrational fears, assertiveness training, and improving decision making. It seems that the four weeks served not only to elevate the moods of the clients but also to aid them in defining problems more clearly. Anticipation-training procedures are therefore recommended as a first step in the treatment of depression, to be followed by specific interventions tailored to the particular needs of the client.[7]

[7] A more comprehensive study of anticipation training has recently been completed (Anton, 1974). Interested readers should write to Jane L. Anton, Graduate Institute of Education, Washington University, St. Louis, Missouri 63130.

references

Anton, J. L. An experimental analysis of training the anticipation and performance of reinforcing activities in the treatment of depression. Unpublished doctoral dissertation, Stanford University, 1974.

Beck, A. T. Cognitive therapy: Nature and relation to behavior therapy. *Behavior Therapy*, 1970, **2**, 284–200.

Irwin, T. *Depression: Causes and treatment.* New York: Public Affairs Committee, 1973.

Lewinsohn, P. M. & Graf, M. Pleasant activities and depression. *Journal of Consulting and Clinical Psychology*, 1973, **41**, 261–268.

Lewinsohn, P. M. & Libet, J. Pleasant events, activity schedules and depression. *Journal of Abnormal Psychology*, 1972, **79**, 291–295.

Lubin, B. Adjective checklist for measurement of depression. *Archives of General Psychiatry*, 1965, **12**, 57–62.

6. ACTIVITY SCHEDULES IN TREATMENT OF DEPRESSION[1]

PETER M. LEWINSOHN[2]   University of Oregon

The guiding principle for the behavioral treatment of depressed individuals is to restore an adequate schedule of positive reinforcement for the individual by altering the level, the quality, and the range of his activities and interactions. Because of the diversity and multiplicity of the symptoms shown by depressed individuals, no *single* intervention strategy that is useful for all depressives exists or is likely to be discovered. Instead, a number of treat-

ment techniques, which are derivable from the behavioral theory of depression, have evolved, allowing behavior therapists to select that combination of techniques that appears most suited to and useful for the individual case. Thus, even though the *general* goal in all instances is the same (to restore an adequate schedule of positive reinforcement for the individual), *specific* intervention techniques are expected to vary from individual to individual, depending on the circumstances responsible for the patient's low rate of positive reinforcement. The purpose of this paper is to describe the use of activity schedules for the purpose of increasing the patient's rate of behaviors that are likely to be reinforced by others or are intrinsically reinforcing for the patient —and to present data obtained from ten depressed individuals.

It is a well-established clinical and empirical fact (Lewinsohn & Libet, 1972; Lewinsohn & Graf, 1973) that depressed individuals as a group en-

[1] This research was supported in part by United States Public Health Service Grant MH-19784 from the National Institute of Mental Health. Requests for reprints should be sent to Peter M. Lewinsohn, Department of Psychology, University of Oregon, Eugene, Oregon 97403.

[2] The author wishes to thank Joe Flippo, Julian Libet, Douglas MacPhillamy, and Martin Shaffer for their many valuable suggestions and Katherin Bolstead, Bob Dittrich, Michael Graf, Pat Hines, Laurie Lerner, John Robinson, Joe Ryan, and Susan Wilson, who acted as therapists for the cases and assisted with the data collection.

gage in relatively few activities and in even fewer activities that are considered by them to be pleasant or rewarding. Some practical questions face the therapist: In what activities should the patient be encouraged to engage? How are they to be selected? Should the goal be an increase in the quantity of behavior, rather than focusing on specific behaviors because they are assumed to be especially therapeutic? What contingencies can be provided to produce an increase in pleasant activity level?

METHOD

Procedure

An activity schedule is constructed for the patient from activities and events judged by him to be pleasant. Initially, patients are asked to list activities that have been enjoyable, pleasant, meaningful, or interesting for them in the past. Many depressed individuals find it difficult to think of more than a few pleasant activities, and this step often requires considerable assistance from the therapist. Activity lists from previous patients provided useful models.[3] At present, activity schedules are generated for each patient from his responses on the "Pleasant Events Schedule" (MacPhillamy & Lewinsohn, 1971). This instrument consists of 320 events and activities generated after a very extensive search of the universe of "pleasant events." The patient is asked to rate each item in the schedule on a 3-point scale of pleasantness. An activity schedule is then constructed for the

patient; it consists of the 160 items judged by him to be most pleasant. The items are put on a ditto master, and the patient is asked to indicate at the end of each day which of the activities he has engaged in. In addition, he is asked to rate his mood at the end of each day on one of the alternate forms of the "Depression Adjective Check List" (DACL) developed by Lubin (1965). A total pleasant-activities score (the total number of activities checked) and a mood score are computed for each day. Part of such a schedule is shown in Table 1.

At the end of the base-level period (thirty days), it is possible to compute the correlation, or the relationship, between the patient's mood and his total pleasant-activity level. Also individual activities that seem especially associated with how the patient feels can be identified. The patient continues to monitor his activity level and his mood throughout the rest of treatment. He is given information about the relationship between what he does and how he feels. Specific activities that are correlated with mood are brought to his attention.

We have completed a pilot study with ten depressed individuals who were reinforced for increasing their rate of behavior for ten correlated activities by receiving therapy time, i.e., an opportunity to talk to an interested listener.

Subjects

The subjects for this study were ten depressed individuals who may be considered to have been mildly to moderately depressed with depression constituting the major presenting problem (see Lewinsohn and Libet, 1972).

---

[3] *Editors' note:* A good idea! It demonstrates practical use of modeling techniques.

TABLE 1 **First Page of an Activity Schedule Generated on the Basis of the Patient's Responses on the Pleasant Events Schedule**[a]

Name Mr. S. W.	Date	(R) Score	(W) 3 Score

Make check in the columns to correspond to the activities of this day. Only activities that were at least a little pleasant should be checked.

Activities	Frequency Check	Activities	Frequency Check
1. Wearing expensive or formal clothes (2c)		21. Getting a job advancement (being promoted, given a raise or offered a better job, accepted into a better school, etc.) (137c)	
2. Making contributions to religious, charitable, or other groups (3c)			
3. Talking about sports (4c)		22. Wrestling or boxing (148c)	
4. Meeting someone new of the same sex (5c)		23. Doing a job well (145c)	
5. Taking tests when well prepared (6c)		24. Having spare time (155c)	
6. Playing baseball or softball (8c)		25. Going to a health club, sauna bath, etc. (1d)	
7. Planning trips or vacations (9c)		26. Being with my parents (9d)	
8. Buying things for myself (10c)		27. Being at a family reunion or get-together (30d)	
9. Being at the beach (11c)		28. Being with someone I love (83d)	
10. Going to a sports event (19c)		29. Playing handball, paddleball, squash, etc. (125d)	
11. Pleasing my parents (31c)			
12. Watching TV (33c)		30. Being with my children (136d)	
13. Shaving (45c)		31. Being in the country (1c)	
14. Having lunch with friends or associates (46c)		32. Going to a rock concert (7c)	
		33. Reading the Scriptures or other sacred works (14c)	
15. Taking a shower (49c)		34. Playing golf (15c)	
16. Being with friends (74c)		35. Rearranging or redecorating my room or house (17c)	
17. Being with my grandchildren (83c)			
18. Wearing new clothes (99c)		36. Reading a "How To Do It" book or article (20c)	
19. Seeing good things happen to my family or friends (105c)		37. Going to the races (horse, car, boat, etc.) (21c)	
20. Wearing clean clothes (133c)		38. Reading stories, novels, poems, or plays (22c)	

[a] *The number at the end of each item, for example, (2c), refers to the item's number on the Pleasant Events Schedule.*

Experimental Treatment

The subjects were assigned to graduate-student therapists, who saw them between one and three times a week for ten weeks. Frequency of sessions varied with the patients but was determined early by each patient with his therapist. The patients were informed that they were participating in an experimental treatment project and that the activity schedule would play an important part in the treatment. They were told that the purpose of the thirty-day base-level period was to identify activities especially important for them and that, in order to motivate them to increase their activity levels, therapy time would be made contingent on how many activities they engaged in after the base-level period. Patients were told that they should feel free to use their time with the therapist in whatever way seemed useful to them.

The therapists were instructed to be "nondirective," and some training was provided for this purpose. They were told to adhere to the framework that is referred to in the literature by terms like "empathy," "unconditional positive regard" and "congruence." The therapists were also asked not to engage in any active interventions. The rationale for the first instruction was that a good nondirective therapist, by completely focusing on the patient, his verbalizations, and his feelings, becomes an effective reinforcer for that patient. That is, we wanted the patients to have positive attitudes toward the therapists and to be motivated to talk with them. The rationale for the second instruction was to minimize individual difference among therapists.

At the end of the base-level period, the correlations between each patient's activity scores and his mood ratings were computed. The ten most highly correlated activities were selected. A formula was then developed for each patient, according to which he would receive so many minutes of therapy time as a function of the number of activities he engaged in.[4] Sample lists and time formulas are shown in Table 2. The patients were told which activities would earn therapy time. At the beginning of each subsequent therapy hour, the patient would return his completed activity schedule and mood ratings to a research assistant, who would then score the forms, compute the amount of therapy time to which the patient was entitled, and inform the therapist about how long the patient was to be seen on this session. With very few exceptions, the therapists adhered closely to the time limits.

RESULTS

A number of questions were of special interest. First, does the total procedure lead to more patient engagement in pinpointed activities? In order to have a basis for comparison, ten "control" activities were selected for each patient. They were comparable in frequency of occurrence to the pinpointed activities, but they had not been found to be correlated with mood. The results are shown in Figure 1.

[4] *Editors' note:* An interesting procedure: Perhaps more counselors should make their time contingent upon clients' engaging in certain activities between sessions.

TABLE 2   Sample of Critical Activities and Reinforcement Schedule for Two Patients

Case 70: Female, Age 58		Case 86: Male, Age 20	
Ten Most Highly Correlated Activities		Ten Most Highly Correlated Activities	
Laughing		Doing favors for people	
Solving problems, puzzles, and so on		Talking about sports	
Being with friends		Breathing clean air	
Hiking		Driving skillfully	
Learning to do something new		Driving fast	
Being praised by people you admire		Looking at sky or clouds	
Doing physical fitness exercises		Making snacks	
Planning something		Visiting friends	
Just sitting and thinking		Seeing old friends	
Having a drink		Going to a restaurant	
Reinforcement Schedule		Reinforcement Schedule	
Number of Activities per Day	Minutes of R_x Time	Number of Activities per Day	Minutes of R_x Time
0–1	10	0–1	10
2	20	2–3	20
3	30	4	30
4	40	5	40
5 or more	50	6 or more	50

As can be seen, there was a significant increase in frequency for the correlated activities ($F = 3.4$; $df = 1$, 71; $p < .01$), which was not accompanied by a corresponding increase in either the control activities or in the total-activities score. Thus, it may be concluded that the procedure as a whole was successful in producing a significant increase in the pinpointed activities

Second, how stable are the correlations between mood and the individual's pleasant-activity scores (pinpointed and total)?

As the whole procedure capitalizes heavily on chance, a certain amount of "shrinkage" in the correlations was to be expected. Base-level and treatment data on fourteen patients (including four additional patients, who had not

been included in the time-contingency study) were available. Results are shown in Table 3.

Although there is a drop from base level to treatment in the magnitude of the correlations between mood and pinpointed activities, the correlations continue to be above chance for ten out of fourteen patients. On the other hand, the magnitude of the correlations between mood and the total pleasant-activity level remains stable. We interpret these results as justifying the use of *either* a small number of selected activities *or* of the patient's total pleasant-activities level as legitimate goals for the purpose of modifying mood level.[5]

[5] *Editors' note:* Part of what makes an activity pleasant is variety. The correlation of pinpointed activities with mood drops from

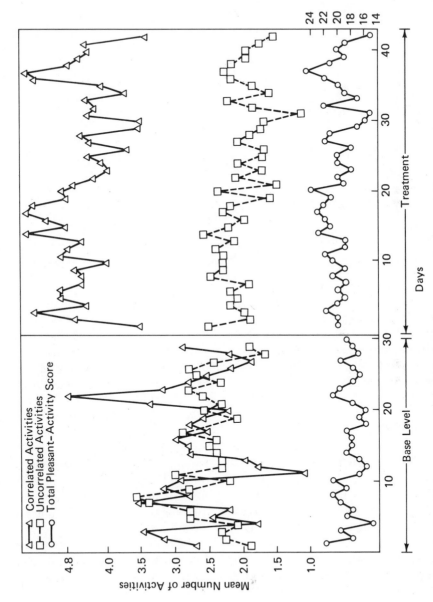

FIGURE 1 Mean correlated, uncorrelated, and total pleasant-activity scores for group of 10 patients.

TABLE 3   Correlation among the "Depression Adjective Checklist" Scores, the 10 Pinpointed
Activities, and Total Pleasant-Activity Scores for 14 Subjects Computed Separately
for Base Level (30 Days) and Treatment (42 Days)

Subject Code No.	Pinpointed Activities				Total Pleasant Activities			
	Base Level	P	Treatment	P	Base Level	P	Treatment	P
62	−.57	.001	−.31	.05	−.36	.05	−.43	.01
63	−.62	.001	−.45	.01	−.26	.10	−.51	.001
70	−.62	.001	−.75	.001	−.25	.10	−.71	.001
72	−.64	.001	−.13	NS	−.53	.01	−.10	NS
74	−.43	.001	−.28	.05	−.08	NS	−.44	.01
78	−.59	.001	.00	NS	−.46	.01	−.08	NS
86	−.67	.001	−.60	.001	−.80	.001	−.82	.001
108	−.68	.001	−.19	NS	−.52	.001	−.32	.02
113	−.63	.001	−.09	NS	−.20	NS	−.36	.01
248	−.84	.001	−.29	.05	−.26	.10	−.36	.02
840	−.66	.001	−.31	.05	−.44	.01	−.25	.10
069	−.63	.001	−.44	.01	−.35	.02	−.36	.02
082	−.72	.001	−.43	.02	−.35	.02	−.33	.05
114	−.79	.001	−.73	.001	−.66	.001	−.81	.001
Mean	−.65		−.36		−.39		−.42	

Pre- and post-MMPI scores were available for eight of the ten patients. The mean depression-scale score changed from 84 to 70, with six of the eight patients showing change in the direction of less depression and two showing no change.

DISCUSSION

One of the striking facts about depressed individuals is that, compared with normal and nondepressed psychiatric patients, they engage in fewer pleasant activities (Lewinsohn & Graf,

base level to treatment, whereas the total pleasant-activities correlation with mood increases slightly. Perhaps some patients became tired of the pinpointed activities that had initially helped to overcome their depression and found other activities more satisfying and helpful later.

1973; MacPhillamy & Lewinsohn, 1972). In these studies depressed individuals were found to engage in a smaller number of different activities (reduced range of activities), and the ones that they did engage in occurred at lower rates (fewer replications). The use of activity schedules, as described here, allows the therapist to assess what activities, or events, are potentially reinforcing for the patient; to inform the patient that his rate of engaging in pleasant activities is low; to define an increase in such activities as an explicit goal for treatment; and to measure behavior change objectively.

There are several procedural changes that we intend to make in the future. For one, the use of the ten most highly correlated activities seems, in retrospect, to have been too rigid. A considerably larger but variable number of correlated activities selected in cooperation with the patient might have been better. Also, the use of treatment time as reinforcement is but one of a number of different contingencies available to the therapist.[6]

A question can be raised about the honesty with which people fill out the activity schedules. Like other self-report measures, they are completely under the subjects' control. In our experience with about thirty patients, we have questioned the truthfulness of three. Two of them were poorly motivated, missed many sessions, and were generally critical of the approach. The third patient immediately increased her activity level substantially when the contingency program was instituted, to the point at which she was earning fifty minutes of therapy time every session. However, the majority of depressed individuals seemed to be quite conscientious about filling out these schedules. In another series of studies (MacPhillamy & Lewinsohn, 1972) we found that subjects' reports of the frequency with which they engaged in various pleasant activities were valid when compared with ratings made by both peers and independent observers.

The use of nondirective counseling in this study was dictated by experimental considerations. We have found activity schedules useful with depressed individuals when the treatment has included more directive approaches like role playing, assertiveness training, and training in social skills. Similarly, the decision to use 160 items for each subjects' activity schedules was made in

order to have the same number of items for each subject. When this parity is not important, the inclusion of all items rated pleasant by the patient would seem preferable.[7]

Therapists who do not have easy access to a computer may consider two alternatives: Using the total pleasant-activities score (the total number of activities that the patient has rated as pleasant) as the target behavior or constructing an activity schedule based on items that have been shown to be associated with improved mood for a substantial proportion of people (Lewinsohn & Graf, 1973). Such items are hypothesized to be more efficacious in counteracting depression than are other activities.

Inspection of the content of the items in Table 4 suggests that they fall into three categories. Many (21) involve *social interactional behaviors* (S) (for example, being with happy people and having people show interest in what one has said). Another group (15), *incompatible affects* (IA), involves affects and states that are assumed to be incompatible with feeling depressed (for example, laughing and being relaxed). Another group of items (8), *ego supportive* (E), involves activities presumed to lead to feelings of adequacy, competence, and independence (conducting a project in one's own way; reading stories, novels, poems or plays; planning or organizing something; doing a job well; learning to do something new).

[6] *Editors' note:* These are good points. Using a variety of pleasant activities, as well as reinforcing consequences by counselors, seems highly desirable.

[7] *Editors' note:* Yes. Unfortunately, group-oriented research designs sometimes impose severe limitations on the clinical value of research findings.

TABLE 4   Activities Associated with Mood for 10 Percent of the Sample

1. Being with happy people (S)
2. Having people show interest in what you have said (S)
3. Being with friends (S)
4. Being noticed as sexually attractive (S)
5. Kissing (S)
6. Watching people (S)
7. Having a frank and open conversation (S)
8. Being told I am loved (S)
9. Expressing my love to someone (S)
10. Petting, necking (S)
11. Being with someone I love (S)
12. Complimenting or praising someone (S)
13. Having coffee, tea, a coke, and so on with friends (S)
14. Being popular at a gathering (S)
15. Having a lively talk (S)
16. Listening to the radio (S)
17. Seeing old friends (S)
18. Being asked for my help or advice (S)
19. Amusing people (S)
20. Having sexual relations with a partner of the opposite sex (S)
21. Meeting someone new of the same sex (S)
22. Laughing (I.A.)
23. Being relaxed (I.A.)
24. Thinking about something good in the future (I.A.)
25. Thinking about people I like (I.A.)
26. Seeing beautiful scenery (I.A.)
27. Breathing clean air (I.A.)
28. Having peace and quiet (I.A.)
29. Sitting in the sun (I.A.)
30. Wearing clean clothes (I.A.)
31. Having spare time (I.A.)
32. Sleeping soundly at night (I.A.)
33. Listening to music (I.A.)
34. Smiling at people (I.A., S)
35. Seeing good things happen to my family or friends (I.A.)
36. Feeling the presence of the Lord in my life (I.A.)
37. Watching wild animals (I.A.)
38. Doing a project in my own way (E)
39. Reading stories, novels, poems or plays (E)
40. Planning or organizing something (E)
41. Driving skillfully (E)
42. Saying something clearly (E)
43. Planning trips or vacations (E)
44. Learning to do something new (E)
45. Being complimented or told I have done well (E, S)
46. Doing a job well (E)
47. Eating good meals
48. Going to a restaurant
49. Being with animals

Finally, it should be emphasized that activity schedules are not offered as a panacea for depression. The treatment of depressed individuals requires attention to the patient's instrumental skills, and his interpersonal relationships, as well as to the availability of reinforcement in his environment. It usually involves a combination of different procedures and intervention techniques (Lewinsohn, 1974).[8]

[8] *Editors' note:* Counselors should also focus on depressed clients' covert or internal activities, for example, how they anticipate events and how they imagine themselves feeling in certain situations. See Article 5.

references

Lewinsohn, P. M. Clinical and theoretical aspects of depression. In Calhoun, K. S., Adams, H. E. & Mitchell, K. M. (Eds.), *Innovative treatment methods in psychopathology.* New York: Wiley, 1974. Pp. 63–120.

Lewinsohn, P. M. & Graf, M. Pleasant activities and depression. *Journal of Consulting and Clinical Psychology,* 1973, **41,** 261–268.

Lewinsohn, P. M. & Libet, J. Pleasant events, activity schedules, and depression. *Journal of Abnormal Psychology,* 1972, **79,** 291–295.

Lewinsohn, P. M., Weinstein, M. S. & Shaw, D. Depression: A clinical-research approach. In Rubin, R. D. & Frank, C. M. (Eds.), *Advances in behavior therapy.* New York: Academic Press, 1969. Pp. 231–240.

Lubin, B. Adjective checklists for the measurement of depression. *Archives of General Psychology,* 1965, **12,** 57–62.

Lubin, B. *Manual for the depression adjective check lists.* San Diego: Education and Industrial Testing Service, 1967.

MacPhillamy, D. J. & Lewinsohn, P. M. *Pleasant events schedule.* Mimeograph, University of Oregon, 1971.

MacPhillamy, D. J. & Lewinsohn, P. M. Studies on the measurement of human reinforcement. Paper presented at the 80th annual meeting of the American Psychological Association, September 1972.

MacPhillamy, D. J. & Lewinsohn, P. M. Depression as a function of levels of desired and obtained pleasure. *Journal of Abnormal Psychology,* 1974, **83,** 651–657.

SEXUAL DYSFUNCTION

7. ELIMINATING FEMALE ORGASMIC DYSFUNCTION THROUGH SEXUAL REEDUCATION

ANDREW W. MEYERS, JO-ANN H. FARR, AND W. EDWARD CRAIGHEAD
The Pennsylvania State University

The popularity of the "how to do it" books on sexual behavior clearly indicates an increasing concern with problems of sexual inadequacy. Amidst this proliferation of lay advice on sexual functioning, Masters and Johnson (1970) have presented strong clinical evidence of the successful treatment of many common sexual dysfunctions, like premature ejaculation, ejaculatory incompetence, impotence, female orgasmic dysfunction, and vaginismus. Masters and Johnson's treatment approach is essentially a combination of *in vivo* desensitization and shaping procedures in which the client couple learns or relearns appropriate sexual behavior and sexual communication within a hierarchical framework. With male and female cotherapists serving as educators and mediators, the client couple moves from initial touching exercises to gradually extended genital intercourse. The following case history illustrates the application of these techniques to an out-patient couple with the problem of female orgasmic dysfunction.

CASE REPORT

The clients were a twenty-seven-year-old female beautician (Ms. H) and a twenty-nine-year-old male graduate student (Mr. O). The clients were not married but had been seeing each other almost daily for six months. Ms. H was seen on an emergency basis at a university psychology clinic, which served primarily the university's students and staff. Her presenting problem was severe depression arising from her "sexual hangups." She felt her sexual inadequacies were jeopardizing any possible marriage with Mr. O.

Ms. H was seen individually for two hours and Mr. O individually for one hour of history taking and problem assessment. These interviews essentially followed the outline presented in Masters and Johnson (1970). Ms. H reported the adoption of an extremely conservative attitude on sexuality from her parents and a traumatic rape experience at age fifteen years. She stated that during intercourse she experienced no pleasure and only temporary moments of excitement. The couple reported that at the time of the interview they were engaging in sexual intercourse once a week, down from an initial average of four such sexual contacts a week. Ms. H said that she had never experienced orgasm; Mr. O reported no erective ejaculatory difficulties.

Before treatment began the clients were instructed to read Masters and Johnson's *Human Sexual Response* (1966) in order to obtain an adequate conceptual and informational base for the therapy process. Additionally, Ms. H underwent a comprehensive gynecological examination in order to eliminate the possibility of any physical cause for the orgasmic problem. Treatment then proceeded one hour a week for seven weeks, followed by four one-hour sessions spread over twelve weeks.

First Session

The first treatment session was conducted in a manner similar to Masters and Johnson's round-table format (1970). The client couple and the two therapists discussed *Human Sexual Response*, and the therapists attempted to answer any questions and to clarify any misconceptions. Sexual inadequacy and particularly female orgasmic dysfunction were explained in terms of Ms. H's history. The therapists asserted that sexual pleasure and sexual skills are learned behaviors. Furthermore, they stated that anxiety over sexuality or sexual performance inhibits sexual arousal and produces a detachment from the sexual experience. As an initial step in overcoming this performance anxiety and detachment the clients were assigned a series of daily touching exercises from Gunther's *Sense Relaxation Below Your Mind* (1968). They were asked to refrain from sexual intercourse or any other attempt to achieve orgasm or ejaculation. Two objectives are accomplished by means of these exercises. First, with the ban on an orgasmic goal orientation, the clients can experience sexual stimuli in a setting free of any anxiety about performance. Second, when inhibiting anxiety has been removed, the clients, by using their new skills, can learn both to give and to receive sexual pleasure and to communicate those sensations to their partners. This emphasis on *both* giving and receiving sexual pleasure is a change from Masters and Johnson's emphasis on just receiving sexual pleasure.[1]

Sessions 2 and 3

The touching exercises continued for two weeks. The second and third treatment sessions were used for discussion and feedback regarding the pleasurable and unpleasurable aspects of the exercises and reinforcement of any productive behaviors or statements. The clients were encouraged to increase both the verbal and nonverbal (manual direc-

tion) communication that occurred during the exercises, thus refining and increasing their pleasure-giving skills and becoming more sensitive to their own sexual responsiveness.

At the conclusion of session 2, Ms. H brought up her reluctance to appear nude before her partner in the lighted bathroom and to a lesser extent in the darker bedroom. A shaping procedure was instituted, beginning with the placing of a candle at the entrance to each of these rooms and gradually moving it closer to the bed and bathtub. As the treatment proceeded the candle was eventually replaced by progressively more powerful light bulbs until Ms. H reported no further anxiety in that stimulus situation.

After two weeks of pleasurable touching exercises, the clients were instructed to include female genital manipulation in their daily exercises. Toward this end Masters and Johnson's nondemand position for female stimulation (1970) was introduced. In this position the male sits with his back supported by a wall or headboard. The female sits between the male's legs with her back against his chest and her legs spread over his. The female is in a secure position that also allows the male free access to the genital area and allows the female to direct his touching manually.[2]

---

[1] *Editors' note:* But at first the giving and the receiving take place at different times.

[2] Between sessions 3 and 4 of conjoint therapy the female therapist saw Ms. H for two sessions, for the purpose of assertion training to aid her in dealing with her mother and her mother's intrusion in her life. This therapy did not deal directly with the sexual problems or relationship of the couple.

Sessions 4–6

During the fourth session both clients reported pleasurable experiences during the exercises, but Ms. H felt anxious about being so exposed in the nondemand position. To alleviate this problem the clients were taught a physical-relaxation technique (see Paul, 1966) in the fifth session and were asked to relax themselves before the touching exercises.

The touching exercises, including manipulation of the female genitals continued for two more weeks, four weeks in all. The treatment sessions continued to function as an instructional, clarification, feedback, and reinforcement experience. During these four weeks Ms. H ended the daily exercises by manually bringing Mr. O to orgasm. This, of course, served to reinforce Mr. O's participation in the treatment process.[3]

Session 7

During the seventh treatment session Ms. H reported having experienced a great deal of sexual excitement during the daily exercises. She attributed some of this progress to the facilitating effects of the relaxation exercises. Because of this progress the next treatment step was taken. The female-superior and lateral coital positions of genital intercourse were introduced. In the female-superior position "the male is encouraged to lie flat on his back and the female to mount in a superior posi-

[3] *Editors' note:* An important consideration: Each person involved must experience periodic benefits to keep the process going.

tion, her knees placed approximately at his nipple line and parallel to his trunk. ... In this position, leaning over her mate at a 45-degree angle, she is comfortably able to insert the penis and then to move back on, rather than sit down on the penile shaft" (Masters & Johnson, 1970, p. 106). The clients were instructed that, once they felt comfortable and enjoyed the pleasure of penile containment in the female-superior position, they were to shift to the lateral coital position. This is accomplished in the following manner:

The husband with his left hand should should elevate his wife's right leg while moving his leg under hers so that his left leg (now outside her right leg) is extended from his trunk at about a 45-degree angle. The wife simultaneously should extend her right leg (the one that is being elevated) so that positionally she is now supporting her weight on her left knee with the right leg extended. . . . As she makes these adjustments, she should lean forward to parallel her trunk to that of her husband. Then the male clasps his partner with his left arm under her shoulders, his hand placed in the middle of her back, and his right hand on her buttocks, holding the two pelves together. The two partners then should roll to his left (her right) while still maintaining intravaginal containment of the penis.

Once the partners have moved into the lateral positioning, the two trunks should be separated at roughly a 30-degree angle. The male rolls back from his left side to rest on his back. . . . (Masters & Johnson, 1970, pp. 311–312)

These positions allow the female control of the coital connection and add penile containment to her growing repertoire of sexual experiences. Following the seventh appointment, the time period between each treatment session was extended to two to three weeks.

Sessions 8–11

The addition of female-controlled genital intercourse continued through session 11. In each session, Ms. H was encouraged to become more assertive in activities that pleasured her and in verbalizing about these activities to her partner. In session 8 Ms. H reported having experienced her first orgasm during the week's exercises. Sessions 9 to 11 were devoted to removing the connotation of "exercises" or "schedules" from the clients' sexual activities. They were instructed to engage in sexual contact only when they felt it appropriate, rather than each evening (though daily exercises had only been suggested and never demanded of them). Additionally, the therapists attempted to promote the generalization of mutual communication, which had proved so productive in developing satisfying sexual behavior, to other aspects of the clients' social activities.[4]

At the eleventh and final treatment session the clients labeled the preceding month "a miracle."[5] With the exception of deciding on a possible marriage, they reported no serious concern

---

[4] *Editors' note:* A good point. Sexual harmony is linked to harmony in other parts of the relationship. Good communication skills can be useful both day and night.

[5] *Editors' note:* Many "miracles" are actually the result of well-planned, systematic, and demanding effort. With the help of the therapists this couple produced their own miracle!

about their relationship. Ms. H reported feeling comfortable in all sexual situations. Frequency of sexual contacts, which had been one a week at the beginning of therapy, was now reported to be approximately five times a week. Ms. H stated that she experienced orgasm during approximately 25 percent of those contacts.

Follow-Up

At a two-year follow-up the clients had been married for just over one year. They both reported a satisfying sexual relationship, with sexual contacts approximately five times a week. Ms. H reported experiencing orgasm in approximately 75 percent of those contacts.

DISCUSSION

The present case illustrated the successful treatment of orgasmic dysfunction by means of "Masters and Johnson" and behavioral treatment. In three assessment sessions and eleven treatment sessions over twenty-two weeks, a woman who had previously had no orgasm reported a satisfying sexual adjustment both subjectively and objectively (through experiencing orgasm). At the two-year follow-up session sexual functioning was still judged satisfactory; the frequency of sexual contacts with her partner and the frequency and percentage of orgasmic experiences had increased. This finding is consistent with the results of Masters and Johnson (1970). They reported an 80.7 percent success rate with female orgasmic dysfunction, and at a five-year follow-up a success rate of 79.2 percent. With the exception of male impotence, Masters and Johnson (1970) report similar successful treatment rates for other sexual dysfunctions.

A number of questions have been raised about Masters and Johnson's findings: Will the effects be generalized from the laboratory to the "real life" setting? Can such therapy be undertaken by nonmedical professionals? Can the therapy be conducted on a weekly (or spaced), rather than a daily basis? Will the absence of certain placebo (for example, the national prominence of therapists and program) and expense ($2,500 for treatment) factors result in failure to replicate Masters and Johnson's findings? In this case study the therapy was conducted on an out-patient basis, by two advanced psychology graduate students, on a weekly (or longer intersession interval) basis at minimal ($2 a session) expense to the clients. None of these factors seemed to prevent positive treatment effects.

The shaping procedures employed here were first to instruct the clients and then to reinforce them for successive approximations to satisfying genital union. They began with simple touching exercises, progressed to genital manipulation, and then moved on to increasingly more active genital intercourse. At each step the clients learned both to give and to receive sexual pleasure. The reinforcers used in the shaping procedure were the sexual pleasure derived from the exercises and the therapists' social reinforcement. In this particular case a relaxation technique was used to further reduce anxiety associated with sexual behavior and to facilitate the experience of sexual pleasure. When anxiety is a significant component of the presenting sexual problem, the use of relaxation or systematic desensitization (Wolpe, 1958) is a recommended addition to Masters and Johnson's treatment package (1970). It is also recommended that a comprehensive gynecological examination always be included in the assessment of female sexual dysfunction.

references

Gunther, B. *Sense relaxation below your mind*. New York: Collier, 1968.

Masters, W. H. & Johnson, V. E. *Human sexual inadequacy*. Boston: Little, Brown, 1970.

Masters, W. H. & Johnson, V. E. *Human sexual response*. Boston: Little, Brown, 1966.

Paul, G. *Insight vs. desensitization in psychotherapy: An experiment in anxiety reduction*. Stanford: Stanford University Press, 1966.

Wolpe, J. *Psychotherapy by reciprocal inhibition*. Stanford: Stanford University Press, 1958.

SPEECH

8. *BEHAVIORAL INTERVENTIONS WITH A SIX-YEAR-OLD ELECTIVE MUTE*

BARBARA SEMENOFF, CATHERINE PARK, AND ELIZABETH SMITH   Santa Clara, California, Unified School District

Of all the various emotional and behavior problems present in the schools, perhaps one of the most difficult to work with and one of the most resistant to change is the problem of the child who will not talk. Speech occurs only in the presence of a select few with whom the child feels comfortable. Requests or demands to speak by anyone other than the select few result in withdrawal and physical signs of extreme fear and anxiety. The refusal to speak to others appears not to be a free choice on the part of the child but is generally a conditioned fear response that is very resistant to change. A vicious cycle develops, one that protects the conditioned fear response from extinction. The tendency to avoid the fearful situation, that is, talking to others, often precludes the possibility of a spontaneous disappearance of the maladaptive behavior. Each time the child withdraws from situations that require his speaking, the resulting reduction of anxiety tends to strengthen the withdrawal response, thus perpetuating the silence. In some instances the secondary gains of increased attention and power to manipulate and control others further reinforce the elective mutism.

The usual methods of reward and punishment, threat and demand, encouragement and understanding do not usually appear to be effective in instances of elective mutism. Further-more, the passage of time appears to make the problem even worse, and spontaneous improvement appears to be rare.

BACKGROUND OF THE PROBLEM

Roger's mother reported that he began talking at an average age. Although he was a shy child, he would talk to a wide variety of people until age three and a half years, at which time he suddenly stopped talking to most people. There was no report of any trauma or crisis that might have precipitated his silence. A move to a new neighborhood did occur around that time, but he apparently talked to others in his new neighborhood after the move. When he entered preschool he talked only to his mother, father, maternal grandmother, and one neighborhood child. The mother reported brief verbal contacts with the ice-cream man. He talked to no one else throughout his preschool year.

Conferences with the parents resulted in little information that was helpful in identifying the cause of the problem or determining a solution. His father is very pleasant and outgoing. His mother is a very reserved, quiet, shy, attractive young woman. Roger is an only child and is very close to his mother. A mutually dependant relationship was evident. When he entered preschool at age four years and ten months, his teacher reported that he screamed and cried for long periods of time when his mother left him. He had never been left with a baby sitter and was unable to do many things, like putting on his jacket, that children several years younger are able to do.

KINDERGARTEN INTERVENTION

When Roger entered kindergarten in September 1971, he still had not talked with anyone except the same four or five people. His teacher indicated that he was quiet and shy, cooperative but reserved. He would follow directions but would not speak. If he had a problem he would not ask for help but would become frustrated and begin to cry. He had only one friend with whom he would play. Most of the time he played and worked alone. He participated in the flag salute by standing and placing his hand over his heart. He enjoyed music time, sometimes mouthing the words of the song but never vocalizing. He sometimes brought items to share but stood displaying the objects without any verbalization.

When a verbal response was required he grew nervous and darted his eyes back and forth. The muscles around his mouth would tighten and his mouth would become twisted. His teacher's main goal was to make kindergarten a pleasant place to be. She created a low-pressure, relaxed, and comfortable atmosphere in the classroom.

A referral was made by this teacher to the speech therapist and the school psychologist. Conferences were held with the parents. During kindergarten and first grade, referrals were made to community mental-health agencies for professional counseling for the parents and for Roger. Communication between the agencies and the school was difficult, however, and there was no evidence of any improvement in the school setting as a result of the two brief periods of professional therapy. It was believed that, even if outside counseling was important for parental guidance, it was necessary for the school to deal with the problem where it existed. Behavioral strategies were planned by the school team and first implemented in November 1971.

SPEECH-THERAPY RECORD

November 1971: Establishing Rapport, Eliciting Nonverbal Responses

Roger was enrolled in therapy along with two other children from his class, who were delayed in language development. At first Roger was very timid, sliding along the wall all the way to the speech room and being very serious. During therapy he would respond to "yes" or "no" questions with a nod or shake of his head. Whenever a question required more of him he would put his chin down on his chest and tightly close his mouth. Most of the time during this part of therapy Roger was not pushed to communicate verbally.

January 1972: Imitation of Actions and Sounds

A program adapted from an article by Blackham and Silberman (1971, pp. 98–101) was implemented. The therapist first attempted to obtain imitation of mouth movements as suggested in the article. This effort was unsuccessful. She was unable to obtain imitation of mouth movements or any facial parts in the first session, so it was necessary to ask Roger to imitate other actions, not connected with his mouth.[1] He was able to copy three movements in sequence; tapping his foot, clapping his hands, and touching his head. Each successful imitation was rewarded with a candy in a cup. This procedure lasted for the first five minutes of therapy. Visual and auditory perceptual activities were performed: Roger wrote the sounds he heard in various positions or traced shapes, copied patterns, or completed puzzles. For these activities, Roger was reinforced with little stars, which he counted at the end of each session and copied down on paper. When the paper was full, he received a toy of his choice from the toy box. In this way, the two parts of the sessions were kept separate with different rewards. It took six sessions before Roger would imitate various sounds.

March 9, 1972: Imitation of Sounds

Roger copied movements in sequence, touching his lips, blowing out a match, and sounding out the long vowels, a,

e, and i. A continuous-reinforcement schedule was used.

March 13, 1972: Reproducing Sounds on His Own

Roger sounded out the letters in his name, as well as k and t. He wrote his name on the board, sounding out the letters. He chose M & Ms for his reward instead of valentine candies.[2]

March 15, 1972: Speaking Words Aloud

This was a red letter day! It was suggested that Roger could "read" some words, now that he could sound them so well. He was shown several pictures from the Dolch word cards, with the name written under each picture. Roger very quietly spoke the following words: "cow," "moo," "duck," "quack," "bird," "man," "kitty cat," "bus." He also counted aloud to thirty-four as he was counting his stars.

March 15, 1972: Speaking to His Teacher Alone in Class

Later on the same morning he counted aloud from one to eighteen for his kindergarten teacher. It was the first time he had spoken to her.

April–June 1972: Speaking Aloud in a Wider Variety of Situations

During the next three months various games and activities were used to increase Roger's expressive language. He

[1] *Editors' note:* Perhaps a model of another or several other children demonstrating mouth movements and other facial actions on film or videotape would have been effective.

[2] *Editors' note:* It is often effective to let the person choose his reward from among several alternatives (many of us cannot stand M & Ms!).

learned to sound out words by analysis and synthesis, to repeat sentences, to fill in missing words, to complete jingles with rhyming words, to describe and classify objects, and to work simple math problems on the flannel board as he described what he was doing. He had made great strides, but he was still talking very little outside the speech room, and his mother was fearful that he might regress over the summer. It was suggested that he attend a summer speech therapy program.

During the summer, Roger did attend summer speech therapy in a strange school. His adjustment to a different school and an unfamiliar speech therapist was very poor. He showed an extreme withdrawal reaction, no speech was evident, and his increased tension and anxiety were revealed in his behavior. The summer-session therapist's recommendation was, "Seek professional psychiatric assistance *immediately.*"[3]

FIRST-GRADE INTERVENTION

When Roger entered first grade in the fall it was apparent that there had been significant regression during the summer. There was no carryover into his first-grade classroom. There was no speech at all, and his anxiety when requested to speak was evident in his shaking and perspiring. He was back where he had started!

The consulting psychologist who

[3] *Editors' note:* Hindsight, of course, is always sharper than foresight. Given Roger's problem, the wisdom of having sent him to a strange school with unfamiliar teachers and therapists seems very questionable.

had been working with Roger had been reassigned, but one of the coauthors, who has a similar behavioral orientation, was assigned to the school and continued to provide consultation to the parents and the school team.

A similar behavioral strategy was implemented with the following differences. First, the strategy was to be applied directly in the classroom, where the likelihood of generalization would be greater.[4] Second, successive approximations to normal speech would be systematically reinforced with teacher approval administered in a nondemonstrative, matter-of-fact way, along with an occasional tangible reward like candy. In addition to positive reinforcement, some of the principles of negative reinforcement (terminating a mildly aversive situation by performing the desired behavior) would be used.

FIRST-GRADE TEACHER'S REPORT

September 1972: Creating a Climate of Trust; Building Rapport

When Roger's mother had brought him to school on his first day her face had shown her concern and apprehension. I acknowledged my awareness of Roger's problem but reassured her that progress was expected. Roger received a warm welcome, but during the first few days he was treated as one of the other children, receiving frequent smiles and affection. He was not sin-

[4] *Editors' note:* An excellent move! Whenever possible, help should be provided on the spot where the problem occurs.

gled out for special attention. One day during the second week I asked him to bring his lunch to school the next day instead of going home as he usually did. I asked him to stay in for a few minutes at lunch the next day. This suggestion seemed to fluster him a bit, as I expected it would. This day, like all those of the following week, were spent in short, ten-minute sessions getting acquainted in an informal atmosphere. We sat on a rug on the floor. I shared personal information about myself and told some funny things I had done as a child. Roger seemed to enjoy our sessions and appeared amused and relaxed, often giggling with me. As I talked with Roger, I stressed that we were "secret buddies" and that I was telling him secrets that I had not told many children. I also emphasized that some day he would be sharing his thoughts with me. I made it clear that I accepted him just the way he was, but that in the future we would be expecting some growth.

Step 2: Eliciting Nonverbal Responses

Roger nodded "yes" and "no" to questions. In class he would raise his hand for roll call. I would acknowledge responses with a wink.

In our daily sessions at noon I began to talk to Roger about the importance of learning and what my role was. I think one of the most significant comments I ever made to him was: "I am not here to get you to talk; you learned how to do that when you were little. I am here to be a good friend and to help you learn how to read and write, do math and have fun."

I continued to emphasize that we were "secret pals" and that some day he would share some of his secrets with me. He committed himself with a nod that some day he would. As time went on I reminded him that the time to keep his promise that he would share things with me was coming near. I always prepared Roger for his next step by eliciting a nonverbal commitment to agree to do something in the future.[5] This proved very effective.

Step 3: Verbal "Mumbles"

After about a week I warmed up by flashing the alphabet cards very fast. Roger nodded if he knew the letters. He began to giggle and nod his head as fast as he could. I indicated that this was the day we had prepared for, that he would tell me the names of the letters he knew, and that he could leave for lunch as soon as he told me the letters. The session took thirty minutes for one mumble. I told him I accepted what he said and trusted he was telling me the right letter (although I could not distinguish what he said). I indicated that tomorrow I would have to hear more. He left for lunch.

Step 4: Speaking in Whispers

I continued to use humor and to joke with him. The next day he began to mumble the answers. I indicated that

[5] *Editors' note:* A crucial point. By informing Roger of what behavior was expected well in advance, he was not surprised and thus made fearful. He also may have tried some cognitive rehearsal of what he was going to say.

it was unacceptable. He then responded in a low whisper. I accepted the whisper response, stressing that someday he would have to talk in a clear, loud voice. I also indicated that from now on, when he needed something, he was to come up and ask me for it. I did not make a fuss over his success as that tended to embarrass him.[6] I gave him his lunch bucket with a smile and a pat and said, "Have a good lunch."

Late October: Natural Voice and Volume

Roger talked in whispers for about three to four weeks. One Monday I told him it was too much of a strain to listen to whispers. I set Friday as a deadline and said that he and I would meet at lunch and after school every day until he responded in a natural voice.

Tuesday Roger missed his appointment after school. I called his home, and his mother brought him back to school. He had been riding his bike. When he returned, I said that I would like to see him ride and that if he would ask me in a "regular" voice I would go to his house. He indicated nonverbally that he wanted me to come. Roger was very nervous, rubbing his hands and sweating as he prepared himself to speak. After about fifteen minutes he whispered, "Come see me ride my bike." I said to say it louder, and he finally did. Although I

<hr/>

[6] *Editors' note:* A sensitive teacher. Verbal praise is not always positively reinforcing. Sometimes it is punishing—particularly for people who avoid the limelight and who feel humiliated by their inability to do what everyone else does easily.

was thrilled to hear him speak, I didn't show it outwardly because the attention embarrassed him. I just said, "Good, yes, I'd love to go." As we walked to my car, I said he would have to tell me how to find his house. He did this very comfortably, directing me all the way. After Roger responded so beautifully in the car, I knew I really had to keep going with him.

The next morning I said we had reached this point and there was "no turning back." I indicated that someday he would share what he knew with the other children. Roger knew now that, whenever he needed to respond to me, it had to be in an audible voice, not in whispers. He did not respond in class, however, if anyone else was around.

Step 6: Speaking Before Other Adults

By early November Roger appeared more comfortable around adults than around other children, so we began to add other adults to talk with, before adding children. I first called the school nurse, whom Roger knew and liked. I used the phone in the classroom, so that Roger could hear me inviting her to the room. I said I wanted Roger to show her how well he knew his alphabet. I never tried to surprise him with anything but involved him in the planning of each next step. When she arrived in the classroom he read off his alphabet cards in a low but natural voice. Gradually other adults were added: the speech therapist, the principal, other teachers, the psychologist, and mothers who helped in the classroom.

Step 7: Speaking Before Other Children

In mid-November Roger was still not talking in front of other children in the classroom. We decided he should pick a child to read his word cards to, one whom he liked and felt reasonably comfortable with. He selected a sweet, patient girl whom everyone liked. Lucy agreed to meet at noon.[7] It took a week for Roger to respond in front of Lucy. Sessions were extended from ten minutes at lunch to thirty minutes. By the sixth day I was very firm in indicating that he must read the word cards to Lucy before he could go to lunch. He became fidgety, and tension was evident in his face and hands. After thirty minutes he still had not responded, but I decided to dismiss him. He knew that I was upset, and I indicated that both Lucy and I had taken our lunch hour to work with him. He knew that he had not pleased me. My approval had become very important to him, and he seemed shocked that I had become somewhat angry for the first time.

The next day he read the word cards to Lucy within two minutes.[8] We had made a breakthrough with the children! Roger selected another child and read to him during our lunch session the first day. We added three more children all at once, and he spoke the first day that they were present. We were really making progress now!

Step 8: Speaking Before a Small Group in Regular Class Time

The next step was to speak in a small group during the regular class time. All our previous sessions had been held in the classroom but during the early part of the lunch hour, when no one was present except the selected people. In late November Roger and I talked about it and decided that the early reading group, when only half of the class was present, would be best. I told him no one else really knew how much he knew in reading. We practiced on the flash-card drills until he knew all the words well. We decided that he should volunteer to respond in class when we played a drill game. We talked of the possible reaction of the other children, acted out their reactions to his talking in class, and practiced how we would handle it.[9] This preparation seemed very important.

I planned a special word game that was fun and one that all the children enjoy. During the game Roger took his turn and responded aloud in front of the other chilrden. When he responded, the other children reacted just as we had rehearsed: "Roger talked! Roger can talk!" Receiving that much attention really embarrassed him, although I knew that he had to accept it at first. I just handled it in a matter-of-fact way and went on with another activity. As we had talked together and rehearsed the possible reactions of the other children, Roger handled them very well.

[7] *Editors' note:* Lucky for Roger she was not the Lucy of *Peanuts* fame!

[8] *Editors' note:* The expression of honest anger can have therapeutic effects when it clearly does not indicate rejection.

[9] *Editors' note:* Great anticipation!

Step 9: Responding Before the Whole Class

After performing before the small group, Roger began to answer "Here" during roll call before the whole class. He would say the flag salute with the class and would ask for things from other children when he needed them. His biggest success was participating in front of others and volunteering to speak.

Step 10: Speaking Spontaneously Before the Whole Class

Although he was still a quiet, shy child, in mid-December he began to blossom. The signs of frustration in his face began to disappear. He still would not carry on conversations with other children, but he had learned to respond and to volunteer to answer questions in a natural voice.

I never dreamed we would come so far! By January I was seeing Roger only once a week during lunchtime, but I would converse with him whenever possible during the day. He continued to be more comfortable and to respond during the rest of the school year.

I worked with Roger through the summer once a week for an hour to keep in touch. He seemed to be doing fine. I did not think that he would regress again.

There had been little regression during the summer. He was somewhat quiet but did speak in a soft voice to others in the class.

Occasional conferences with the speech therapist, school nurse, and psychologist were held to evaluate his progress. No problems were occurring. Bimonthly observations were made by the psychologist to monitor his progress.

Observations from January to April 1974 showed that Roger was responding to 100 percent of the questions directed to him. The frequency of his spontaneous, initiating remarks was at the same level as the average for the classroom. Figure 1 shows the frequency of his spontaneous remarks, compared with those of a "child taken at random." During a fifteen-minute observation period all of the spontaneous comments made by Roger were counted. During each observation a different classmate was selected at random to be observed, and his spontaneous remarks were counted.[10] The broken line on the chart shows the composite observations made for the "child at random" in the classroom. The observations were made during informal, seated activity when the students were working but quiet talking was allowed.

Roger was functioning as a member of the class. He was somewhat quieter than some students but more talkative than others. He responded to strangers in brief sentences but was initiating

SECOND-GRADE INTERVENTION

Roger was placed in a second-grade class that included some of his former classmates and some new students.

[10] *Editors' note:* Although informally selecting a "child at random" for comparison purposes does not constitute rigorous scientific control, it does provide a "quick 'n' dirty" way of assessing the extent to which appropriate speech activity is occurring.

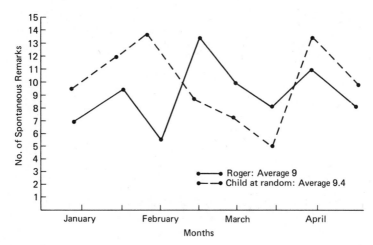

FIGURE 1   Spontaneous speech observed during fifteen-minute observations in the classroom.

more conversations outside the classroom with other students.

Observations on the playground and in other classrooms showed that his talking had been generalized to other settings. His parents indicated that he was much more comfortable with others at home and was speaking to a wide variety of people.

references

Blackham, G. J. & Silberman, A. *Modification of child behavior.* Belmont, Calif.: Wadsworth, 1971.

BEHAVIORAL EXCESSES

The ancient Greek maxim "Nothing in excess, everything in moderation" is still good advice. But as with other sage advice, the saying of it seldom suffices. More help is necessary for people who are into doing too much. The problems of "overdoing it" are certainly familiar to all of us at times—too much eating, smoking, talking, spending, drinking, drug taking, lying, gambling, arguing, physical fighting, and hurrying. The list is long. Fortunately, most of us have learned to control our tendency toward excessive actions.

Some people are caught in a vicious cycle of excess. Why? The original causes are unknown, but there is some evidence that social and cultural factors play a role. One glance at the freeway billboards, television, or magazines reveals a great deal about how excessive drinking, smoking, overeating, and spending are socially and culturally encouraged. A person often gets caught in a pattern of rewards that maintains the excessive behavior. For example, the person with an "addictive" problem (broadly speaking, all excessive behavior is addictive) finds that the immediate effects of drinking something alcoholic, smoking, overeating, using various drugs (prescription and otherwise) are very reinforcing. He or she may feel better, less tense or bored, more important and physically relaxed. Thus the person's excessive behavior is quickly reinforced, for it immediately preceded feeling better in some way. There is also the compulsive gambler who wins occasionally—just enough to keep him or her at it—even though the losses consistently outweigh the infrequent big wins over time. Even the distraught parent or frantic classroom teacher gets hooked on acting excessively. Continually shouting and threatening the children or even physically beating them at times is rewarded, in that the children's "bad" actions are immediately reduced (but often not for long). Unfortunately, the negative long-term side effects of such excessive behavior go unnoticed or, when realized, are not strong enough for the person to change.

One key to understanding excessive behavior is its expedient nature. It works in the short run. It is often a quick and easy means of dealing with various problems. But acting excessively backfires because the consequences of such behavior create other problems. This effect is perhaps best seen in this nation's number-one cause of death: coronary heart disease. The suspected sources of this pervasive disease are directly related to patterns of excessive behaviors: heavy cigarette smoking; overeating, especially of rich, fatty foods; chronic stress and tension (including hypertension); physical inactivity. Some cardiologists have even characterized people with these patterns of excessive behavior as "Type A" people. One of the problems is that Type As are rewarded and encouraged by our culture for their excessive behaviors.

In this section, a variety of interesting techniques are presented as possible ways of helping people to reduce their execssive actions, like cigarette smoking, overeating, gambling, drinking, and acting physically aggressive. Understandably these are offered in a tentative fashion. We still know very little about the sources and solutions of most behavioral excesses. Four things stand out about these promising efforts. First, several specific techniques are needed (there is no one best technique); second, because the most effective combination of methods is still unknown, the counselor must be an experimentalist, trying out things on a tentative "try and see" basis; third, what people say to themselves, along with what they expect and anticipate (personal beliefs) are important actions that often must be directly assessed and altered; and, fourth, often the antecedents (what the person experiences before the excessive action) must be the primary focus if change is to take place.

OVEREATING

9. COGNITIVE FACTORS IN WEIGHT REDUCTION

KATHRYN MAHONEY AND MICHAEL J. MAHONEY   The Pennsylvania State University

There is an interesting phenomenon that is often encountered in formalized therapy systems. Once a clinical procedure or technique has become "accepted," it is often transformed into a *routine* therapeutic strategy and administered almost *pro forma*. Behavior therapy has unfortunately not escaped this "assembly line" tendency. Relaxation training and desensitization, for example, are often preselected elements in counseling, simply because they are conventional and "established" procedures. This technical prejudice may often stand in the way of an accurate, individualized assessment in which each client is viewed as representing a new and unique clinical commitment.[1]

The behavioral treatment of obesity

[1] *Editors' note:* A serious problem. Counseling should in many ways be viewed as the experimental study of the individual case (see Thoresen & Hosford, 1973).

offers a further illustration of the tendency to formalize and routinize therapeutic strategies. This energetic marketing may be most prevalent in the therapist or counselor who views himself as a consumer of clinical research, rather than as a contributing clinical scientist. It may be easier to implement some standardized treatment regimen than to devote time and energy to individualized assessment and treatment.

The present case study illustrates the importance of viewing counseling as a personalized science, in which each client's problems are given due recognition for their uniqueness and potential complexity. It also highlights the significance of intrapersonal cognitive elements in weight reduction. Both these emphases point toward the critical importance of exploratory and experimental attitudes on the part of the counselor.

CASE STUDY

Mrs. H was a thirty-six-year-old housewife who had volunteered for participation in a long-term weight-reduction program at The Pennsylvania State University. Before treatment she weighed 173.5 pounds at a height of 62.5 inches. Mrs. H was one of twelve participants in a program, the components of which are summarized in Table 1. During the two-week pretreatment base-line period, the client gained eleven pounds. She later commented that she viewed the base-line period as a "last fling" before reduction.

TABLE 1   Weight-Program Components[a]

Self-monitoring	Using a special eating-habits diary, subjects recorded daily food patterns in three categories—food quality (high- versus low-calorie), food quantity, and situational eating. Therapeutic emphasis was placed on improved eating habits, rather than on simple weight loss.
Nutrition	Subjects were instructed in the basics of food metabolism, caloric values, and the importance of a sound balanced diet in permanent weight control. Short-lived restrictive diets lead to short-lived successes. No food categories were prohibited, and intermittent food intake records allowed evaluation of individual participants' nutritional adequacy.
Exercise	Moderate physical exercise increases the initial rate of weight loss, improves cardiovascular functioning, and actually reduces hunger. An adequate activity level also helps to maintain previous losses. Subjects were encouraged to develop individualized programs for increasing energy expenditure. Care was taken to ensure that physical activity was not confused with physical exhaustion. Participants were instructed to pursue nonstrenuous and entertaining means of energy expenditure (hiking, cycling, avoidance of elevators, and so on).
Stimulus control	Subjects were apprised of the potential influence of food-related cues in their maladaptive eating patterns. Five specific strategies were suggested: separating eating from all other activities, making high-calorie foods unavailable or inconspicuous, altering the size and appearance of food portions, eating slowly, and disposing of foods that would previously have been eaten "to avoid waste."

TABLE 1   Continued

Relaxation training	Many individuals use foods as an anxiety reducer, an antidepressant, or a reliever of boredom. Relaxation training was provided to equip participants with alternative nonfattening responses to such situations.
Family support	Establishment of a supportive social environment that would both facilitate initial progress and enhance the likelihood of maintenance after termination of the formal treatment program was recommended. Family members were encouraged to attend meetings and to share the participants' interest in the program. Two specific requests were made of spouses: "If you can't say anything *positive* to your spouse about his or her weight-loss efforts, then don't say anything at all" (no criticism or teasing), and "Never offer your spouse food, either at or between meals." In addition, program participants were trained to prime and praise their spouses, so that a reciprocal reinforcement system was established.
Self-reward	Participants were trained in the development and execution of self-reward contracts, which specified behavioral goals, explicit time intervals, and chosen reward items or privileges. Self-reward contracts were witnessed, signed, and monitored by friends or relatives to insure consistent follow-through.
Cognitive ecology	Perfectionist performance standards and maladaptive self-statements often play a major role in weight-loss failures. Extensive efforts were directed toward teaching participants to "clean up what they said to themselves" by monitoring, evaluating, and altering weight-relevant self-verbalizations.

---

[a] *Participants in the program were adult volunteers who had been screened for contraindicative variables. Dependent variables in the program were body weight, subcutaneous adiposity (measured by skin-fold calipers), mean daily adequacy ratio (a measure of adequate nutritional intake), self-records of exercise and eating habits, and questionnaire measures of relevant technical knowledge (for example, food caloric values and exercise physiology). After a two-week base line had been established, participants attended six weekly group meetings, followed by four weekly individual sessions. Follow-up contacts were begun and continued at progressively longer intervals (two weeks, three weeks, four weeks, and so on).*

During the formal ten-week treatment phase, eight different therapeutic strategies were presented.

Her progress in weight loss during the program was relatively constant and monotonic. She lost fifteen pounds in the first seven weeks. A two-week plateau ensued, followed by further reductions. After ten treatment weeks, she had shed a total of 18.5 pounds. Her progress was maintained and improved during successive follow-up contacts. A one-year follow-up found her 18.5 pounds below her postbase-line weight, and at sixteen months her cumulative loss was 20.5 pounds. After twenty months she had lost forty-two pounds. These data suggest a clean and cumulative therapeutic success—the clinician's dream and the client's delight. The "inside story," however, conveys a very different picture. Mrs. H's progress was neither smooth nor painless. It was marked by recurrent subjective distress and phases of extreme triumph and failure. Personal assessment and counseling were instituted during these phases in an effort to ameliorate their severity and to prevent their recurrence.

From interview records and client self-reports it soon became apparent that maladaptive cognitive behaviors were at least partially responsible for Mrs. H's difficulties. Her cognitive dysfunctions are briefly presented here by way of illustration.

Standard Setting

Mrs. H impressively illustrates how the cognitive behaviors that help to create the therapist's dream and the client's delight frequently become the therapist's dilemma and the client's downfall. Mrs. H quickly assumed the role of a "perfect client."[2] For several weeks her virtually perfect eating habits led to extensive positive feedback from the therapist. Even though program guidelines allowed flexible goals and occasional transgressions, Mrs. H sought to achieve errorless eating habits. Her enthusiasm and persistence were acknowledged by the group, and her perfection seeking was inadvertently praised by the therapist. The therapeutic tide turned rapidly, however, upon the first occurrence of an inappropriate eating episode. The client became extremely depressed, labeled herself a "complete failure," and wept extensively. Analysis of her distress quickly traced it to a relatively minor eating problem (mid-afternoon snacking). Interestingly, although her food habits were exemplary during 95 percent of her day, Mrs. H viewed her difficulty in avoiding small afternoon snacks as catastrophic.

[2] *Editors' note:* It is understandably easy for a counselor to reinforce such perfectionism, but it would be better to prepare the client to cope with inevitable relapses.

A problem-solving approach was employed in the resolution of this difficulty. Procedurally, this approach involves specification of the problem, analysis of its controlling influences, generation of possible solutions, selection and testing of one solution, and eventual refinement or maintenance of any observed improvement (Mahoney, 1974). In Mrs. H's case, her stringent standards, the behaviors they influenced, and the consequences of those behaviors were made explicit. Because the therapist had unwittingly reinforced her "perfect" performances, Mrs. H had set progressively higher standards and had assumed that praise from the counselor was contingent on perfection. A vicious cycle had been established and maintained.[3] To interrupt that cycle, we guided Mrs. H in re-evaluating her standards in terms of their reasonableness and efficiency in her weight-reduction efforts. One of the most provocative criteria suggested was formulated as the question: Would Mrs. H want to impose those standards on other people? Following specification of more reasonable standards (including "allowable" transgressions), Mrs. H was given training in reinforcing herself for meeting more moderate goals.

Cognitive Claustrophobia

A frequent corollary of excessively high standards is the clinical phe-

[3] *Editors' note:* The authors point out the danger of simply reinforcing improvement in the client's external observable behavior without considering how internal or cognitive behavior is changing.

nomenon called "cognitive claustrophobia" (Mahoney, 1974), in which the client feels "restricted" or "controlled" by his own extreme criteria for positive self-evaluation. Rigid standards are frequently dichotomous guides for behavior—they often involve "always" or "never" statements and allow little room for variance. For example, Mrs. H later revealed that she had begun the program with the goal of never again going on an eating binge— "no more doughnuts, no more ice cream, etc." As noted, her rigid adherence to this goal resulted in her initial progress in weight loss. Unfortunately, her dichotomous standards also restricted her degrees of freedom and comfort in reducing. Even though the program had not prohibited any foods or suggested a proscriptive diet, Mrs. H had privately compiled a long list of "forbidden fruits" that she had secretly sworn never to enjoy again. Prohibition, however, is a good way to increase the value of an item; unattainable rewards are frequently the most satisfying. Mrs. H reported feeling "suffocated" by her personal prohibitions. She was frequently obsessed about the forbidden fruits and, when she transgressed her eating habits, swung from near perfection to an all-out marathon binge of prohibited treats. There were no "minor" violations—she perceived herself as either a saint or a sinner.

It is noteworthy that Mrs. H reported an initial sense of relief when she first began a binge. Once she had transgressed, she was released from her excessive standards for that day; her self-imposed deprivation was temporarily ended. At the end of the binge, however, she became extremely self-critical, depressed, and guilt-ridden.

Emphasizing active client participation in the counseling process, the therapist and Mrs. H analyzed the cognitive, behavioral, and emotional components of the sequence described. It was challenged therapeutically in several ways. First, a modified form of "cognitive restructuring" (Mahoney, 1974) was employed to alter further her dichotomous standards. The concept of all-or-none performance was examined and evaluated as a maladaptive, inhumane, and impracticable guideline. Furthermore, Mrs. H was trained to generate and practice more reasonable goal-relevant self-statements like "Eating one doughnut doesn't mean I've blown the whole day" and "A person doesn't get fat because of one 'bad' meal or a 'bad' day—or even a 'bad' week; I'm working on a long-range pattern and a few occasional difficulties are not going to throw me." Finally, Mrs. H was given behavioral assignments intermittently to eat small quantities of her formerly forbidden foods, in order to avoid feelings of deprivation and restriction.[4]

Private Monologues

Implicit in the preceding descriptions are references to the clinical importance of private monologues—what a

[4] *Editors' note:* An excellent idea! The client can prove to herself that she can eat small quantities of the "forbidden fruits" and still be a good person in control of her own behavior. It is like deliberately practicing an error in order to bring it under control.

client says to himself. For Mrs. H, these monologues were often self-critical and discouraging. She was instructed to monitor them by means of a pocket diary and a phone-answering device, which allowed her to call and report her private monologues at any hour of the day or night. Her records dramatically illustrate the role of "internal environments" in clinical distress and behavioral dysfunction. Typical self-statements were "I am a failure" "I can't do anything right" "This will never work." It is noteworthy that many of her private monologues invoked global statements about personality traits, like "I *am* a fat slob" and "I *am* a failure." The connotation, of course, is a general and deep-seated inadequacy, rather than a specific deficiency. Furthermore, a large percentage of Mrs. H's self-statements had apparently contributed to the development and maintenance of the standard setting and claustrophobia problems described: for example, "I've got to eat perfectly" "C'mon, girl, don't blow it with a doughnut" "I can't have any of my own birthday cake." Binge eating, after the initial relief, was followed by a deluge of negative self-evaluations: "I'm a pig— I'll always be fat and ugly" or "They (the therapists) are wasting their time on me; I'm not worthy to be in the program."

In addition to a high frequency of negative self-statements, Mrs. H revealed a very low frequency of positive self-evaluations. Ironically, when her unreasonable standards were met, she felt relieved but never satisfied. Each week had to be better than the preceding one.[5] She never congratulated herself or praised her own prog-

ress. Her perseverance appeared to be dominated by anxiety over failure, rather than by anticipation of success. With her previously rigid standards, of course, failure increased as her standards rose, and a self-perpetuating vicious cycle was maintained.

Therapeutic responsibility was again shared by having Mrs. H actively monitor, evaluate, and modify maladaptive self-statements. She was trained to detect distress (depression, anxiety), to perform quick "instant replay" of her preceding self-statements, to evaluate their adaptiveness, and to generate alternative statements. She was additionally taught to cue positive self-thoughts and to practice positive self-evaluation by calling a phone-answering device and verbalizing self-praise for what she had accomplished. Tape recordings of these self-praise assignments were reviewed by both the therapist and the client, in order to stabilize, strengthen, and expand positive self-evaluation skills.

At the sixteen-month follow-up, Mrs. H reported eating habits and cognitive behaviors that were "imperfect" —a finding that was considered prognostically positive. Her standards were reasonable, her self-statements were much more adaptive, and her weight reduction continued at a slow and comfortable pace. She had shared her newly acquired skills with her teen-age son, who had also lost fifteen pounds at last contact.

[5] *Editors' note:* Progressively raising standards has inevitable limits. The counselor may best help a client by refusing to reinforce perfectionist goal statements.

DISCUSSION

The case described was probably as educational for the therapists as it was for the client. Several significant implications were deduced. The importance of individualized assessment and counseling can hardly be overemphasized. Routine strategies are often defended on the basis of statistical averages and group performance. Indiscriminately applied, however, they may impede or retard clinical improvement by permitting the therapist to overlook the complexity and uniqueness of each individual's learning history.

A second lesson lay in the deceptive dangers of the "perfect" client. Excessive performance standards and errorless progress are enticing candidates for inadvertent praise from the therapist. The ultimate consequences of perfection seeking—by client or therapist —merit thoughtful consideration. Errors, minor relapses, and occasional failures are invaluable lessons in the development of skills for coping with life. This is as true for the counselor trainee as it is for the client. These events should be viewed as valuable learning experiences, rather than threatening signs of inadequacy. The client who has learned to cope with occasional setbacks may be far better equipped for real problems than one who has been ushered through an errorless series of protected learning tasks.

One final highlight in the case of Mrs. H was the impressive role of the client's private environment in behavioral dysfunction and subjective distress. As clinical scientists, our research has only recently begun to examine the functional role of cognitive processes in maladjustment and therapeutic behavior change. Our understanding of the "inside story" of human adjustment needs rigorous cultivation. Somewhat belatedly, the behavior therapist has come to recognize that the human organism thinks a lot. A rapidly expanding literature suggests that this predilection may claim some of the most powerful influences in human behavior change (Mahoney, 1974). Our future inquiries will, we hope, offer further clarification of those influences.

references

Mahoney, M. J. *Cognition and behavior modification.* Cambridge, Mass.: Ballinger, 1974.

10.   A SELF-CONTROL PROGRAM FOR THE TREATMENT OF OBESITY[1]

SUSAN POLLY, RUSSELL D. TURNER, AND A. ROBERT SHERMAN   University of California, Santa Barbara

The problem of overeating reportedly affects from 40 to 80 million Americans (Stuart & Davis, 1972). When discussing possible treatment objectives, clients in counseling frequently mention weight loss along with other goals. Nevertheless, counselors often reveal a reluctance to deal with weight control because it is perceived as time-consuming and because results from traditional treatments for obesity have typically been poor (Stunkard & McLaren-Hume, 1959). Recent findings on the effects of behavior-modification strategies have been more encouraging (for example, Hagen, 1974; Romanczyk et al., 1973; Stuart, 1967; 1971). The behavioral treatments have generally included weekly weigh-ins and have employed such behavioral techniques as stimulus control, relaxation, social reinforcement, covert sensitization, and behavioral-programming strategies. Studies that have emphasized the self-application of such behavioral techniques (for example, Harris, 1969; Mahoney, Moura & Wade, 1973; Wollersheim, 1970) have also had good results. It has been suggested (Abramson, 1973) that self-control techniques may hold the most promise for the treatment of obesity because they can

be taught with a minimum of therapeutic time and may later be applied by the client to management of other habits as well. In the present report we first outline the basic steps of a self-control program for obesity and then illustrate the procedures by means of a case study.

The emphasis of the program is on developing self-control skills in the client. A basic familiarity with the principles of learning and behavioral counseling should enable the counselor to administer the program effectively and to support the client's efforts at self-change. As the counselor has to spend only about five minutes a week discussing the weight-control program with the client, concurrent treatment of other problems is possible.

THE SELF-CONTROL PROGRAM

During the six weeks of the program the client receives weekly instructional materials and assignments. At the outset he is given a sheet on which to record his daily food intake and daily body weight for seven days, in order to determine the base-line level of his eating problem before any attempt at behavior change. Although self-recording alone sometimes affects the "target" eating behaviors, it rarely is sufficient to promote enduring weight loss. Self-control instructional materials are introduced in a planned sequence during the second and subsequent weekly sessions. The client's experience of the

[1] Portions of the training materials described in this study were developed by the authors in the early stages of an experimental research project on behavioral self-management for college students, conducted by Dr. A. Robert Sherman at the University of California, Santa Barbara, with the support of the Exxon Education Foundation.

previous week is discussed, and he is praised for completion of program materials, habit change, and weight loss; any questions are answered, and the new materials are reviewed. At the end of each session the client is given a cover sheet that summarizes his assignment for the next week. He is encouraged to follow the instructions and to perform the corresponding self-control activities, though he is always free to skip or discontinue any activity that he finds unnecessary or unhelpful. The client is asked to bring all materials with him each week and to continue self-recording his food intake and body weight daily throughout the six-week period.[2] A self-control program with a sensible diet and an emphasis upon change in eating habits will typically allow for a weekly weight loss of one to three pounds.

The First Week

Behavior Analysis   The client is given a mimeographed introduction to the use of self-control methods and a brief description of elementary principles of behavior, which reviews the concepts

[2] Although weight is unlikely to change substantially within a twenty-four-hour period, we think it is desirable to record weight on a daily basis because, first, it will establish a meaningful base line, indicating initial weight within a range defined by the daily fluctuations; second, it will permit prompt identification of weight-change trends, particularly toward the beginning of the program, when weight losses may amount to several pounds a week (as in the case of Barbara presented here); and, third, it will probably be easier for the person to integrate the self-weighing procedure into his regular routine if it takes place on a daily basis.

of antecedent stimuli, consequences, reinforcement, punishment, extinction, shaping, behavior chains, and contingencies.[3] He is instructed to prepare a written analysis of his eating behavior, specifying what stimuli seem to prompt him to eat and what are the short- and long-term consequences of excessive eating.

Self-Recording   The self-recording instructions stress the importance of keeping accurate daily records of eating behavior, so that progress can be readily assessed. All record-keeping forms are provided. The food-intake form is divided into seven columns, one for each day of the week, with horizontal rows representing meals (breakfast, midmorning snack, lunch, snack, dinner, snack). The daily-weight form is a piece of graph paper with weight listed on the side of the chart and days of the month listed on the bottom. The form for recording antecedents of excessive eating is headed with date, situation preceding overeating, food eaten, and mood.

Planning the Eating Program   The client is given an explanation of the necessity for decreasing the number of calories consumed or increasing the calories expended, in order to lose weight. He is urged to plan a balanced diet of three meals a day by consulting a reputable nutrition guide, and he is advised to avoid fad diets, which usually have only temporary effects. Fi-

[3] *Editors' note:* Copies may be obtained by writing to Dr. A. Robert Sherman, Department of Psychology, University of California, Santa Barbara, California 93106.

nally, he is asked to write a description of his planned diet, describing proposed food intake for a typical day.

Setting Goals   In space provided in the instructions, the client is asked to indicate his ultimate long-term weight goal, as well as the amounts of weight he intends to lose during each week of the program. Clients are encouraged to set weekly goals that are realistic and attainable, usually one to three pounds.[4]

The Second Week

A major treatment focus is to help the client to rearrange and plan his environment in advance, before excessive eating takes place. This kind of environmental planning is sometimes called "stimulus control," for certain stimulus cues are arranged to facilitate more appropriate eating behaviors.

Public Self-Recording   The client is advised to post one or more of his self-recording charts prominently in his home or office so that his progress can be monitored by himself, as well as by others who can give him feedback. Encountering the charts will also serve as a reminder or cue to perform the required self-control activities.[5]

Changing Eating Behavior   The client is instructed in methods of changing his

---

[4] *Editors' note:* Counselors should insist on a client's setting a modest, attainable goal, rather than an ambitious goal that requires extraordinary efforts.

[5] *Editors' note:* Knowing that one must post tomorrow's weight for all to see provides a powerful incentive to decline a second helping tonight.

eating process, with the objective of slowing the pace of his eating. He is asked to follow two rules: first, always put the fork down while chewing and pick it up only after his mouth is empty and, second, take breaks while eating, beginning with short pauses at the beginning of the meal and working up to longer pauses near the end. The rules are intended to give the client some feeling of control over his compulsive eating. Increasing eating time also enhances the possibility that the client will become satiated before the meal has been completed, for it generally takes at least fifteen minutes to develop a state of satiety. Before actually trying to lengthen the time spent eating meals, the client is instructed to time himself while eating, in order to obtain a base line. Then, after practicing the suggested techniques, he again times himself to assess any improvement.

Breaking Eating Chains   The client is given a brief description of how a complex behavior like overeating is composed of behavioral links forming a chain (see Ferster, Nurnberger & Levitt, 1962, for further details). An example of an eating chain is presented; for example, skipping meals leads to excessive hunger, which leads to a desire to shop for fattening foods, which leads to stocking up on such foods, which subsequently leads to eating the foods, which leads to weight gain. It is emphasized that behavior chains can be broken at almost any point. The client is given examples of ways to break links in behavior chains, such as keeping food in inaccessible places, eating before shopping to make fattening foods less tempting to purchase, and eating slowly. He is asked to add to this list any additional techniques he can think of and to keep a daily frequency record for each technique that he employs during the following week or two.

Changing the Cues for Eating The importance of eliminating cues that prompt undesired eating behaviors and establishing new cues to prompt appropriate behaviors is emphasized. It is explained that the frequency of a behavior can be decreased by eliminating the antecedent stimuli that cue it. One can learn to designate new cues—new situations and conditions—to which the occurrence of certain behaviors can be restricted. For example, it may be declared that all eating is to take place in the dining room at specified times, with the added conditions that the television be turned off and that no reading take place. The client is instructed to list those situations and conditions that have prompted inappropriate eating in the past and that will now be avoided, as well as the new antecedent stimuli that will now be used to cue appropriate eating behavior.

Making It Difficult The client is given examples of how he might make it physically difficult for himself to perform inappropriate eating behaviors. If his overeating occurs in his home, he may deliberately not keep fattening foods in the house. Or, if his family insists on having fattening snacks, he should buy kinds that he does not care for so that when he is tempted to snack he will not find anything appealing. Another restraint technique is to purchase foods that require extensive preparation, thus making impulsive snacking difficult. The instructions ask the client to record for at least one week the times when he shops for food and any foods he purchases that are not consistent with his weight-control program.

The Third Week

Contingency Contracting A contingency contract states the client's behavioral goals and establishes specific positive and negative consequences of attaining or not attaining those goals. Such a contract is intended to sustain the client's motivation to continue carrying out self-control activities by providing planned consequences. The contract ordinarily specifies the behavioral goal, the date by which the goal is to be reached, the consequences of meeting or not meeting the goal, and the name of the person who will administer the consequences. Negative consequences are typically established by giving another person a personal valuable that is later forfeited if the goal is not achieved.

In formulating a contingency contract, it is suggested to the client that the goals be realistic; that any possessions subject to forfeit be given to a friend or relative at the beginning, when the contract is being written; and that the consequences be of value to the client. The following is an example of a contingency contract:

Behavioral Goal and Date
I will purchase no more than one item not on my diet plan during the week from January 10 to January 16.

Consequences of Achieving Goal
I will play eighteen holes of golf on Sunday, January 17.

Consequences of Not Achieving Goal
I will donate $5 to Citizens for a Nuclear War and $5 to People for Pollution.

Administrator
My neighbor Bill will hold the two $5 checks during the time I am attempting to achieve my goal.[6]

Contingency contracts can be formulated for long-term goals (for example, losing fifteen pounds during the six-week program), short-term goals, or both.

Using Competing Activities   An effective way to change eating behavior is to set up responses incompatible with antecedent cues to snacking. For example, if the behavioral analysis reveals that the client typically snacks around 9:00 P.M. when he is watching television, he could rearrange his schedule to go directly to bed, take a shower, or phone a fellow dieter instead. For some people, exercise or special classes can serve as competing activities for times when the inclination to overeat is strong. The client is asked to list his troublesome "eating antecedents" and to identify a possible competing activity for each. He is instructed to record for one week instances of his consciously substituting a competing activity for an overeating antecedent.

[6] *Editors' note:* Self-contracts should above all be fair to all persons involved, in terms of positive and negative consequences, and should be specific as possible. Notice the specific behavior, as well as the time limit, involved in this contract.

Altering Social Cues   Instructional materials explain that changes in behavior can be influenced by carefully choosing the people with whom time is spent. For example, if the client always lunches with overeaters, he will be likely to overeat in their presence. The client's behavior analysis will probably have revealed that some, but not all, social situations cue excessive eating. He is instructed to record for one week the persons or social situations that cue overeating and possible alternatives to being in those situations—lunching instead with slim friends or diet-club members or suggesting to the family that they dine at a seafood restaurant instead of a pizzeria.

Controlling Emotions That Cue Eating   The client is asked to identify emotions that tend to make him eat and to list possible activities that might produce different, incompatible emotions—for example, sleeping, practicing relaxation exercises, jogging, or phoning a friend. Any instances of deliberately engaging in activities to control emotions that prompt eating are recorded for a week.

The Fourth Week

Self-Reward System   General information on the nature of self-reward is provided, with the explanation that specific eating behavior can be changed by controlling its consequences. Overeating often tends to be a persistent behavior partly because the positive feelings associated with food intake are more immediate than the negative consequences of obesity and social disapproval.

A self-reward system is designed to help the client to strengthen appropriate eating behavior through immediate token reinforcement of such behavior. Instructional materials and forms are provided to assist the client with the basic steps involved in formulating and applying a self-reward system. He first identifies the many behaviors relevant to losing weight and formulates a point system indicating the relative importance of engaging in specific desirable behaviors (for example, eating proper foods at dinner, 5 points; eating slowly, 2 points) and not engaging in undesirable behaviors (for example, not purchasing fattening foods, 8 points). The client then completes the "Reinforcement Survey Schedule" (Cautela & Kastenbaum, 1967) by rating the extent to which a large number of activities and commodities have reinforcing value for him. Those rated as having "a fair amount," "much," or "very much" appeal are then incorporated into a personal-reward list with their relative desirability expressed in terms of the number of points required to earn each reward (5, 10, or 15 points, depending upon the original rating). Finally, the client employs a daily self-recording system to award himself points for performing the designated appropriate behaviors and cashes these points in for desired rewards from the list. He is generally encouraged to reward himself frequently, though points may be accumulated for several days with a view toward earning more desirable (and costly) rewards.

The Fifth Week

Self-Punishment It is explained that self-punishment techniques are sometimes helpful in controlling undesired behaviors, especially when used in combination with self-reward techniques. "Response cost" involves the loss of a specific number of self-reward points for performing such designated inappropriate behaviors as going on an eating binge (for example, loss of 10 points) or shopping while hungry (loss of 5 points). The client is instructed to list the inappropriate behaviors with point penalties for each and then to employ the response-cost system in conjunction with the self-reward system.

Another self-punishment technique consists of listing on an index card the long-term negative consequences of overeating ("People will find me repulsive," "I won't be able to fit into my clothes," and so on) and then reading the card whenever thoughts of excessive eating occur. When the card is not accessible, the same negative consequences can be recited from memory, a technique known as "negative self-verbalization."[7]

Arranging for Social Consequences Instructional materials explain that approval or disapproval by significant people in the client's life (family, friends, boss, and so on) can serve as strong incentives in facilitating his self-management efforts. By discussing his self-control activities with people who are supportive of his weight-loss goal, he may ensure that their presence cues

[7] *Editors' note:* Some prefer to avoid teaching negative self-verbalizations to clients. It is just as easy to teach positive self-verbalizations like "People will find me more attractive" and "I will be able to fit into slimmer clothes." Sometimes a combination of positive and negative self-statements works very well.

appropriate behaviors and that they will dispense or withhold social rewards contingent on his progress. For example, if the client's family knows that he is dieting, its members can apply social pressure to encourage his compliance with the diet at mealtimes and praise him for his success. The technique of posting progress charts in prominent places, introduced in the second week, also represents a way of arranging social consequences to support efforts at weight loss.

The Final Week

Food-intake forms and a daily weight graph are given in this session. The client is advised to continue monitoring his eating behaviors at least until his weight goal is achieved. Some clients will express confidence in their mastery of self-control skills with the intent of proceeding entirely on their own and reporting only periodically on their progress; others will express a desire to continue meeting with the counselor on a regular basis until their terminal weight goals are reached. On the last formal visit, whenever that occurs, the client is given a list of suggestions for maintaining his improvements. He is advised to save the self-control instructional materials for future reference, to continue to employ the stimulus-control techniques and to perform incompatible behaviors at times when the inclination to overeat is strong, to weigh himself daily for the rest of his life, to begin recording daily food intake again if inappropriate eating habits reappear, and to decide on a maxi-

mum acceptable limit for his weight and promptly to reinstate the entire program if this limit is ever exceeded.[8]

THE CASE OF BARBARA

Barbara was a twenty-three-year-old college senior who had sought treatment for depression at the university counseling center. During the course of therapy she decided that various changes had to be made in her life; one such change was weight loss. She reported that her weight problem had begun when she entered college, her weight increasing by about twenty-five pounds, and that she had felt unattractive, socially hampered, and ill at ease for the preceding several years. For weight-control counseling, the therapist referred her to an ongoing program in behavioral self-management. The week before she was to begin the self-management program the therapist gave her a base-line sheet on which to plot her weight and record her daily food intake.

Session 1.

When Barbara came for her initial appointment with the first author, she brought with her the base-line sheet,

---

[8] *Editors' note:* The one thing that is missing in this comprehensive weight-control program is direct attention to the "inside story" —those unreasonable and illogical premises and standards coupled with those excessively self-critical thoughts and images of clients that can sabotage self-control programs. See Article 9.

which indicated a weight loss of two pounds for the preceding week. As do many clients, she expressed some concern over the sort of program that she was beginning. The counselor explained the self-directed nature of the program, as well as the system of weekly instructional materials on self-control. Barbara was weighed by the counselor to establish a pretreatment measure against which progress could later be assessed; her weight at the time was 150 pounds, and her height was 5 feet 5 inches. She was told to continue monitoring her weight on a daily basis and that the counselor would weigh her again at the end of the program. She was given the materials for the first week, as described in the previous section, and told to follow all instructions and bring the materials back each week.

Session 2

Barbara brought the set of training materials, which she had completed during the first week. Her records revealed that her weight had dropped 6 pounds, to 144, which represented a rather large loss. This success heightened her enthusiasm for the program. Results from her behavior analysis revealed that a major problem in controlling her food intake was her tendency to dine out in restaurants, which she purportedly did to combat loneliness (hoping to meet people) and to save time in food preparation. She recognized, however, that her overweight condition made her less attractive and therefore reduced the likelihood of social contact.[9]

The environmental stimuli prompting her to overeat were not having adequate food in the house, so that she would have to dine out; skipping meals, which later resulted in eating large quantities of food rapidly; being alone; not planning meals; and anxiety over too much work. During the first week she had planned a very sensible eating program, concentrating on the elimination of snacks and fried foods and decreasing the quantities of her other usual foods. She had also set realistic weight loss goals of one to three pounds a week for the six weeks, with a goal weight of 138 pounds for that period. Her long-term goal weight was listed as 124 pounds, although she hoped some day to be able to reach 118 pounds. After reviewing the materials with her, the counselor praised her efforts to date and gave her the materials for the second week, briefly describing the steps.

Session 3

Barbara's weight had dropped three pounds during the second week, to 141 pounds. She had posted one weight graph on the refrigerator door and one in the bedroom.[10] She had also in-

[9] *Editors' note:* A good example of a self-defeating vicious cycle: Barbara eats out to combat loneliness, but she overeats when eating out, thus keeping herself physically unattractive and perpetuating her loneliness.

[10] *Editors' note:* Being steady and consistent is hard work. Here is a good example of how data from self-observation can serve to reward Barbara daily for her progress, however modest, as well as cue her every day about controlling her own eating behaviors.

creased the average time spent at a meal from 5–10 minutes to 15–20 minutes. In addition, she had practiced the techniques of not carrying spare change with her, eating before shopping, keeping food out of sight in her home, and buying foods that require preparation. She identified the antecedents of excessive eating as being alone, studying, and watching television. She designated new antecedents to cue appropriate eating behavior—at home eating only at the kitchen table and away from home eating only with other people (so that she could talk during the meal and therefore eat less). After discussing her progress with the counselor she received the materials for the third week.

Session 4

Weight loss during the third week was again quite large—4 pounds—bringing Barbara's weight down to 137 pounds. These losses were probably due in part to the various exercise programs that she had initiated. In a phone call during the preceding week she reported that she had not written a contingency contract because the thought of being motivated by a self-imposed negative consequence had upset her and prompted her to eat a fattening pastry.[11] The counselor reaffirmed that the contingency contract was optional and could be omitted, especially as good progress was being made without it. A discussion ensued, in which the

[11] *Editors' note:* Various forms of direct punishment sometimes backfire because of their aversive side effects. Note how unfortunately Barbara dealt with the stress—by eating rich foods!

counselor briefly outlined the steps of a self-reward system, which Barbara proceeded to initiate on her own before receiving the formal instructional materials in session 4. In keeping with the previous week's instructions, she had analyzed the emotions triggering her eating; these emotions included guilt, frustration, nervousness, loneliness, and disappointment. Activities that she had practiced to counteract such emotions included studying in the library, exercising, talking to a friend, cleaning house, and practicing the piano. The counselor encouraged Barbara's efforts at habit change and then provided a brief explanation of the materials for the fourth week.

Session 5

For the first time Barbara's weight remained unchanged from the previous week. This plateau did not seem to upset her much, perhaps because she had already lost more in four weeks than she had expected to lose in six. A quick review of completed materials revealed that she had completely filled out the "Reinforcement Survey Schedule," not only checking values for each of the listed reinforcers but also preparing a list of twenty-eight additional reinforcers. They included such things as making furniture, skin diving, taking special classes, and going to the beach at night. The self-reward system that Barbara had designed was slightly different from the one described in the materials because, as already indicated, she had proceeded with it before receiving formal instructions. She had set her goals very high, and, instead of selecting 5-, 10-, and 15-point rewards, she had set up a system whereby she would earn certain rewards if she accumulated 14–16 points daily and other, more desirable rewards if she accumulated 17 or more points (see Table 1). Her daily points were also used for weekly rewards. Barbara indicated that this self-reward technique had been the most useful of the self-control activities she had attempted. The counselor gave her materials for the fifth week.

Session 6

Barbara had achieved another 4-pound weight loss, bringing her weight to 133 pounds. She reported that the self-reward system was still working well for her and that she had added the response-cost technique—the loss of self-reward points for the performance of designated inappropriate behaviors (see Table 1). The counselor gave Barbara the option of receiving the final maintenance handout at this session or later on, and she chose to wait a few weeks. At this time Barbara expressed an interest in stopping smoking. She was told that she could try to follow the same basic techniques and was given a chart on which to graph her smoking behavior. No formal ses-

---

TABLE 1   Sample Items Adapted from Barbara's Self-Reward System

Behaviors and Corresponding Point Values			
Rewarded Behaviors	*Points*	*Response-Cost Behaviors*[a]	*Points*
Eating foods specified on menu plan for		Eating pastry or dessert	−4
breakfast	2	Drinking nondiet soda	−2
lunch	3	Eating excess amounts of food . . .	−1
dinner	5		
Exercise (swimming, running, tennis)	3		
Riding bike to school . . .	1		

Rewards for Point Accumulation[b]	
Daily Rewards	*Weekly Rewards*
17 or more points	114 or more points
buying something personal like a trinket for no more than $1.50	all-day excursion, on weekend (for example, a picnic)
going to a movie	buying something to wear, like a blouse
14–16 points	98–113 points
watching television for 1–2 hours	2–3 hour excursion . . .
visiting friend for 1–2 hours . . .	

[a] *It should be noted that response cost can also be applied to inappropriate behaviors like buying fattening foods, not eating in a designated area, watching television while eating, and so on.*

[b] *Barbara's system differs from the one described in the instructional materials in that, instead of having 5-, 10-, and 15-point reward categories, she selected more stringent daily and weekly criteria. Her system also features a dual use of daily point totals, which are summed for application to weekly rewards, in addition to their use for daily rewards.*

sions were scheduled for the next month because of school vacations and holidays.

Session 7

Barbara's final visit took place four weeks after session 6. A weigh-in confirmed her report that she had reached her "satisfactory" goal weight of 124 pounds—representing a loss of 26 pounds. She reported that she would still like to get down to 118 pounds but was extremely happy with her current weight and had received many compliments. She also reported that her daily cigarette consumption had decreased from four packs to slightly less than one pack, perhaps reflecting another favorable application of her self-control skills. Her therapist at the counseling center reported that Barbara looked slim and attractive now, having altered not only her weight but also the styles of her clothing and hair.

SUMMARY AND CONCLUSIONS

In the present report we have outlined the basic steps in a self-control program for obesity and have illustrated the procedures by means of a case study of a woman who lost twenty-six pounds within nine weeks of initiating the program. This case was selected because of the client's adherence to most procedures and her complete success in achieving her desired weight loss. It must be noted, however, that, as with other therapeutic interventions, this self-control approach cannot be expected to work effectively with all clients. Nevertheless, it is frequently worth attempting both because many people appear to benefit from it and because it requires minimal time to administer. By teaching certain general skills of self-control, the program also has the potential advantage of preparing the individual to deal with future habit problems without requiring further professional assistance.

references

Abramson, E. E. A review of behavioral approaches to weight control. *Behaviour Research and Therapy*, 1973, 11, 547–556.

Cautela, J. R. & Kastenbaum, R. A reinforcement survey schedule for use in therapy, training, and research. *Psychological Reports*, 1967, 20, 1115–1130.

Ferster, C. B., Nurnberger, J. I. & Levitt, E. B. The control of eating. *Journal of Mathetics*, 1962, 1, 87–109.

Hagen, R. L. Group therapy versus bibliotherapy in weight reduction. *Behavior Therapy*, 1974, 5, 222–234.

Harris, M. B. Self-directed program for weight control: A pilot study. *Journal of Abnormal Psychology*, 1969, 74, 263–270.

Mahoney, M. J., Moura, N. G. M. & Wade, T. C. The relative efficacy of self-reward, self-punishment, and self-monitoring techniques for weight loss. *Journal of Consulting and Clinical Psychology*, 1973, 40, 404–407.

Romanczyk, R. G., Tracey, D. A., Wilson, G. T. & Thorpe, G. L. Behavioral techniques in the treatment of obesity: A comparative analysis. *Behaviour Research and Therapy*, 1973, 11, 629–640.

Stuart, R. B. Behavioral control of overeating. *Behaviour Research and Therapy*, 1967, **5**, 357–365.

Stuart, R. B. A three-dimensional program for the treatment of obesity. *Behaviour Research and Therapy*, 1971, **9**, 177–186.

Stuart, R. B. & Davis, B. *Slim chance in a fat world: Behavioral control of obesity*. Champaign: Research Press, 1972.

Stunkard, A. J. & McLaren-Hume, M. The results of treatment for obesity. *Archives of Internal Medicine*, 1959, **103**, 79–85.

Wollersheim, J. P. The effectiveness of group therapy based on learning principles in the treatment of overweight women. *Journal of Abnormal Psychology*, 1970, **76**, 462–474.

EXCESSIVE SMOKING

11. COVERANT CONTROL OF CIGARETTE SMOKING[1]

BRIAN G. DANAHER   University of Oregon

Interest in behavioral self-control strategies has grown tremendously in the past several years. Recognition of the client's potential as an active participant in changing his own behavior has opened an exciting new perspective on behavior modification. A literature on self-control has rapidly developed; it includes a number of excellent texts (for example, Goldfried & Merbaum, 1973; Thoresen & Mahoney, 1974; Watson & Tharp, 1972) and comprehensive review articles (for example, Kanfer & Karoly, 1972; Kopel, 1973; Mahoney, 1972).

A significant contributor to the self-control literature, Lloyd Homme (1965) coined the contraction "coverants" to refer to "covert operants" or that class

of behavior that only the individual can experience and observe. Common examples of coverants include thoughts, images, and urges. Homme argued that coverants are influenced by the same contingencies of reinforcement as are the more overt forms of behavior and that they can therefore be brought into the realm of behavior-change strategies. Evidence supporting this "continuity" assumption has recently been suggested (Mahoney, Thoresen & Danaher, 1972), and the conceptual adequacy and empirical validity of the covert conditioning model have been carefully reviewed (Mahoney, 1974).

Homme contended that a strategic implementation of particular coverants might function as an effective therapeutic tool in changing maladaptive behavior. This process of covert behavior modification has become known as "coverant control therapy" (CCT). In the general procedure of CCT, the client thinks about two

[1] The assistance of Kathy Johnson and Byron Page in the present project is gratefully acknowledged. Thanks are also extended to my wife, Kathy, for her careful reading of the preliminary drafts of this paper.

covert self-instructions called "coverant statements" (GS). The first focuses upon the aversive aspects of the excessive target behavior (TB) and is called the "anti-TB statement." The second CS focuses upon the positive changes that would accrue from TB reduction and is called the "pronon-TB statement." These CSs are initiated upon prearranged cues and concluded by self-rewards. Schematically, the general CCT treatment program is:

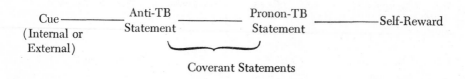

In short, the purpose of the CCT strategy is to counteract the client's prevailing disposition toward engaging in a behavioral excess by introducing self-statements that are incompatible with the target behavior.

A number of empirical investigations have been aimed at examining the efficacy of CCT in reducing excessive cigarette smoking (for example, Keutzer, 1968; Lawson & May, 1970), but the results of these studies have been complicated by conceptual and methodological issues (see Danaher, 1974). In the present case report both the procedures and the results of the CCT treatment program for cigarette smoking are described. The particular client's case history was selected from a large controlled investigation of the parameters of CCT reported by Danaher and Lichtenstein (1974).[2]

THE CASE OF JOHN

John was a twenty-eight-year-old, unmarried graduate student in physics at the University of Oregon. At the time of treatment, John had been smoking for approximately twelve years and had failed in at least ten previous attempts to quit on his own. None of these earlier efforts had involved formal smoking-reduction programs. John called the university smoking-research clinic after reading about a continuing experimental program for reduction of cigarette smoking. After a preliminary discussion with intake personnel about the details of the program (for example, individualized treatment for a limited time), John decided to participate and was assigned randomly to a consultant.

Method

During the first formal session with his consultant, John completed several informational questionnaires and briefly discussed his expectations for treatment. A contract was then agreed upon by which treatment would be limited to four weeks during which John was

---

[2] This case was chosen for detailed description because it represented a successful application of CCT to smoking. It should be noted that such success was not typical of the experience of other subjects.

required to observe his smoking behavior closely in terms of time and date of cigarettes and cigarette urges. Cigarette urges were to be evaluated further by means of a 5-point rating scale for completion of the statement "I want a cigarette now ...": 1 point, little ("not really at all"); 2 points, somewhat ("perhaps"); 3 points, moderate amount ("vague desire"); 4 points, much ("need"); and 5 points, very much ("craving"). As an incentive to help motivate John to complete the entire program, $10 was collected; $8 constituted a deposit that would be returned contingent upon the completion of all the self-observation tasks, and $2 was used to partially defray the costs of the program materials.[3]

Self-Observation John was asked to keep records of his smoking and his cigarette urges. These data were compiled on a small 3 x 5-inch observation booklet, which he carried with him at all times. The data were indicated by numbers and circles. Numbers from 1 to 5 indicated the intensity of a particular cigarette urge, the numbers corresponding to the aforementioned urge-rating scale. Circles around these urge ratings designated cigarette urges that

had resulted in smoking. *All* cigarettes had to be smoked in response to urges (no "automatic" cigarettes were allowed), but it was not necessary, of course, for all urges to be followed by cigarettes. At the end of every day, John was to indicate whether or not he had accurately recorded that day's cigarettes and cigarette urges by writing a "yes" or "no" on the back of the data page.

The exact instructions for this and subsequent phases of treatment were presented in a written "procedures manual," which was to provide the client with a ready reference source both during and after the treatment program.[4]

During this base-line week, John was cautioned to smoke as normally as possible while keeping the detailed records of his smoking.

Treatment

After the base-line week, John met again with his consultant, in order to discuss further details of the treatment strategy. At that time, the rationale behind CCT was briefly noted, and the CCT strategy was described by means of the following outline:

[3] *Editors' note:* Use of a monetary deposit at the beginning, with part of it to be returned, *contingent* on specific actions, can be very effective. See Article 12.

[4] *Editors' note:* Copies may be obtained by writing to Brian G. Danaher, Department of Psychology, University of Oregon, Eugene, Oregon 97403.

Three main points were considered: definition of the two coverant statements (CS), definition of the self-reward system, and the recording of CS events. Each of these topics will be discussed in order.

Coverant Statements Coverant statements were defined as antismoking thoughts and prononsmoking thoughts. *Antismoking thoughts* reflect those aversive aspects of smoking that had prompted John's interest in quitting smoking. The procedures manual defined them as "the various emotions, events, situations, and/or people that have in large part helped you to decide that you want to break your smoking habit." John composed the following list of antismoking thoughts: "You make George and Mary sick by your smoking," "Smoking means only twenty more years . . . ," and "Some day you may inadvertently start a fire." *Prononsmoking thoughts* were defined as the opposite of antismoking thoughts, thoughts reflecting the improvements that would occur once he had stopped smoking. John composed a list of four: "You will be able to climb mountains and ski without panting," "You will save $120 a year," "You will be strong and healthy," and "You will be more attractive."

During intervention, one of each of these CSs was to be considered in proper order every time John experienced an urge to smoke. The lists of statements were placed in the observation booklet for quick reference. The exact manner in which these thoughts were to be examined was clearly specified in the procedures manual:

You must try to concentrate and imagine vividly the events noted in a particular thought and then try to actually *FEEL* some sort of emotional reaction to it as a result. It won't be nearly enough to merely recite any reason to yourself as if it were your phone number and just let it go at that!! You should stop what you are doing, take a minute or two, and really use some effort in thinking about what you've written down. The written reasons should act as cues or prompts that will trigger other —possibly deeper—feelings and emotions which will in turn help you to strengthen your resolve and increase your resistance. This idea can be summarized in the short credo: "IT IS BETTER TO FEEL THAN TO REPEAT."[5]

Self-Reward The final link in the CCT strategy involves the client's self-administration of the reward contingent upon his remembering to emit the CS *on cue.* The procedures manual explained the definition of rewards in the following manner:

Our definition of "reward" is simply something you enjoy doing, getting, or otherwise experiencing. For the most powerful results, you should use what are known as *potential* rewards. By "potential" rewards we mean an activity or thing you'd presently enjoy experiencing but have (until now) not regularly done so. . . . The reward should [also] be something you could actually do during the day or night (a trip to Europe would be nice but it obviously wouldn't fit into a regular day for most people).

[5] *Editors' note:* An important point: The combined use of focused attention on what the person is saying to himself and vivid imagery can be very powerful and believable.

John chose the reading of science fiction and other stories as his reward.

Rewards occurred at two different times. There was an immediate self-reward after CS, as well as some delayed rewards at the end of the day. Immediate reinforcement presented some difficulties, for it was often impractical to experience it in a continuing situation. John was given the option of thinking about the delayed reward that he had partially earned by his performance as his immediate reward. For example, he was asked to think about the plot of an enjoyable science-fiction novel and then to imagine himself reading the novel that evening as his reward. The delayed reward was administered after the daily record-evaluation period if the ratio of the number of CSs to the number of urges equaled or exceeded the 90 percent criterion level. To ease the burden of these calculations, a chart was contained in the procedures manual, which indicated the levels of urges and their associated 90 percent levels of CS required for self-reward.

John in effect planned his own motivation. He assigned himself immediate rewards following the use of coverant statements (CS), as well as delayed rewards when his CS performance reached the 90 percent level.

CS Records During treatment, John was also asked to keep records of the times and days when he examined his coverant statements. These CS events were indicated in the observation booklet by a slash line, /. Typically these slashes would appear through an urge rating (for example, 3) to indicate the fact that an urge had been rated and subsequently followed by an antismoking, as well as a prononsmoking, thought. Thus John used circles, numbers, and slashes to depict his smoking cigarettes, evaluation of urge intensity, and examination of his CS, respectively.

Finally, it should be noted that treatment signaled the time when John was told that he should make every effort to try to stop his smoking. He was told to focus all his "will power," in addition to using the CCT procedures just described, in order to reduce his smoking. In other words, the CCT procedure did not exist in a vacuum but, rather, was applied in conjunction with John's strong resolve to quit smoking.[6]

Results

John was called and asked for his average daily smoking rate one month, eight months, and eighteen months after the end of treatment. These assessment probes were unannounced, in the sense that John had not been forewarned that they would occur.

The data for the baseline, intervention, and follow-up periods are presented in Figure 1. Inspection of the baseline phase reveals that John smoked an average of 24.29 cigarettes a day while experiencing a mean of 29.29 cigarette urges a day.

During the three weeks of treatment intervention, John's smoking de-

[6] *Editors' note:* A counselor should use everything and anything that may help, within ethical limits. Encouraging the client to use resolve, will, inner strength, or what have you, can sometimes help.

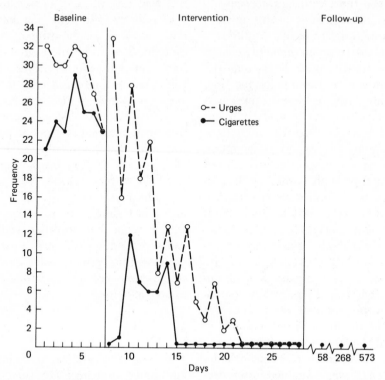

FIGURE 1 Daily frequency of cigarette urges and cigarettes smoked during the baseline (one week), intervention (3 weeks), and follow-up (one month, eight months, and eighteen months after termination) periods.

creased dramatically. The mean frequency of cigarettes smoked each day dropped from 7.71 the first week to 0 for the second and third weeks. This change was still being maintained one, eight, and eighteen months later (indicated in Figure 1 by 58 days, 268 days, and 573 days).

The frequency of cigarette urges decreased at a less pronounced rate until, in the third week of intervention, both cigarettes and urges had reached zero. The mean daily frequency of urges during weeks 1, 2, and 3 was 19.7, 5.7, and 0 respectively. Urges were also evaluated in terms of their average rating on a 5-point scale of intensity. For baseline and intervention weeks 1 and 2, intensity ratings were 2.09, 2.56, and 2.12 respectively. (As John failed to experience any cigarette urges during the third week of intervention, no analyses of urges during that period were computed.)

The frequency of urges decreased immediately after the initiation of treatment, although at a less dramatic rate than the number of cigarettes smoked. The intensity of urges, however, remained fairly constant across time.

The treatment measure of appropriate CS performance was also investigated. "Appropriate CS performance" was defined as a cigarette urge being followed by the examination of the CS. Operationally, this analysis was computed by means of the ratio between the frequency of reported CS and the frequency of urges. (Recall that John was provided with this formula to help him to determine his delayed self-reward contingency.) The results for weeks 1 and 2 of intervention were 91.3 and 100 percent. We could conclude that John was reliable and thorough in self-administering his CCT treatment and that his standard of self-evaluation (90 percent level) allowed him consistently to obtain access to the delayed self-reward for his performance.

Finally, John reported considerable satisfaction at being a nonsmoker at the end of intervention. At the eight-month follow-up probe he indicated that he had recommended the CCT program to his friends and relatives for smoking and other problem behaviors. At the eighteen-month follow-up probe John was confident of his ability to remain abstinent—he experienced occasional weak smoking urges (one every three weeks), and they were easily resisted.

DISCUSSION

Although controlled empirical research must establish the generality of these findings, the results from this case report provide suggestive evidence that CCT may be a powerful therapeutic tool in producing both immediate and long-term reduction in smoking behavior.[7] Two critical points should be underscored: The definition of relevant coverant statements requires considerable attention because their impact upon the client may well determine success or failure in any particular instance; the collection of data on cigarette urges, as well as the use of coverant statements, provided information that helped us to understand the observed changes in John's smoking.[8] The particular power of CCT in John's case may have been its efficacy in reducing the urges that led to smoking. Although difficult to achieve in many instances, the elimination of both smoking and its related urges may provide a useful predictor of subsequent prolonged abstinence.

[7] *Editors' note:* John's success is impressive but atypical, given the great difficulty many chronic smokers suffer in trying to quit. The fact that John was a moderate smoker (about one and a half packs a day) and also part of a university experimental research project may have contributed to his success. More confirming evidence is needed.

[8] *Editors' note:* It is not clear that such data were essential. Perhaps John's attention to urges helped to disrupt the almost automatic and "unconscious" chain of behaviors that characterize many smokers.

references

Danaher, B. G. Theoretical foundations and clinical applications of the Premack principle: Review and critique. *Behavior Therapy*, 1974, **5**, 307–324.

Danaher, B. G. & Lichtenstein, E. An experimental analysis of coverant control: Cuing and consequation. Paper presented at the annual meeting of the Western Psychological Association, San Francisco, April 27, 1974.

Goldfried, M. R. & Merbaum, M. (Eds.), *Behavior change through self-control.* New York: Holt, Rinehart and Winston, 1973.

Homme, L. E. Perspectives in psychology, XXIV: Control of coverants, the operants of the mind. *Psychological Record*, 1965, **15**, 501–511.

Kanfer, F. H. & Karoly, P. Self-control: A behavioristic excursion into the lion's den. *Behavior Therapy*, 1972, **3**, 398–416.

Keutzer, C. S. Behavior modification of smoking: The experimental investigation of diverse techniques. *Behaviour Research and Therapy*, 1968, **6**, 137–157.

Kopel, S. Behavioral self-control: A reconceptualization and new perspectives. Unpublished manuscript, University of Oregon, 1973.

Lawson, D. M. & May, R. B. Three procedures for the extinction of smoking behavior. *Psychological Record*, 1970, **20**, 151–157.

Mahoney, M. J. *Cognition and behavior modification.* Cambridge, Mass.: Ballinger, 1974.

Mahoney, M. J. Research issues in self-management. *Behavior Therapy*, 1972, **3**, 45–63.

Mahoney, M. J., Thoresen, C. E. & Danaher, B. G. Covert behavior modification: An experimental analogue. *Journal of Behavior Therapy and Experimental Psychiatry*, 1972, **3**, 7–14.

Thoresen, C. E. & Mahoney, M. J. *Behavioral self-control.* New York: Holt, Rinehart and Winston, 1974.

Watson, D. & Tharp, R. *Self-directed behavior: Self-modification for personal adjustment.* Monterey, Calif.: Brooks/Cole, 1972.

12.   *A BROAD-RANGE PROGRAM TO ELIMINATE CIGARETTE SMOKING*

DAVID L. GEISINGER[1]   Private Practice, San Francisco

Cigarette smoking, commonly a habit of long duration and high frequency by the time treatment for it is sought, is an enormously complex behavior. People smoke for different reasons, influenced by different cues, using varying schedules, in dissimilar living situations (life contexts), and they are subject to a wide range of reinforcers that perpetuate the habit.

[1] Claude M. Steiner, had a full share in the development and administration of the program described in this paper. The author wishes to thank the San Francisco branch of the American Cancer Society for their generous assistance.

Given this complexity, it seemed apparent that approaches to breaking this habit based upon a single technique would yield poor results. The program to be described, therefore, included a large variety of techniques, commensurate with the complexity of the habit. No attempt was made to investigate the efficacy of any particular technique, nor were appropriate controls incorporated. The plan was to develop an effective program, rather than a research study. A good deal of data from pretreatment and follow-up questionnaires were gathered, however, for possible analysis at some future date.

A perusal of the literature dealing with smoking-reduction programs reveals that adequate follow-up data are often not supplied. Furthermore, when follow-up data are available, the results have been disappointing (for example, McFall & Hammen, 1971). As it is a well-recognized fact that habits may be temporarily eliminated by a particular treatment only to return again shortly after the treatment is terminated, our intent was to provide follow-up data on each participant.

It is virtually impossible, except perhaps by using the most radical and inhumane conditioning tactics, to make a person incapable of rehabituating himself to a particular behavioral pattern. Barring such inhumane treatment, therefore, the element of will or choice can never be fully eliminated from the picture: It is always possible to choose to reengage in the behavior in question at some subsequent time and to strengthen the habit underlying it.

The participants in any program designed to "break a maladaptive habit" must be made to understand this crucial fact, for many, if not most, of them are prone to a kind of magical or wishful thinking that consists of the belief that the treatment will provide them with lifelong immunity. Any treatment at its best can only markedly reduce, and in some instances effectively eliminate, the desire or urge to engage in the "habit" (behavior). It is very likely that people who once have had a habit can more easily relearn it, no matter how long they have been away from it.

The approach described here is one that has been derived from three areas:

1. Medical information, particularly a good deal of factual material on the consequences of smoking upon physical health, has been provided. Literature from the American Cancer Society, an illustrated lecture by a physician, and a film have been used.
2. Information and techniques relating to human learning were employed. Discussions and illustrations of classical and operant conditioning and modeling were presented.
3. "Game" analysis was used. An exploration of some of the cognitive distortions commonly engaged in by people who have given up maladaptive behaviors, based on an approach drawn from transactional analysis.[2]

In addition, participants were given the set to anticipate a favorable outcome of the work they were to do in the program. Positive expectations were also structured by the fact that both group leaders had themselves successfully eliminated cigarette-smoking habits and were enthusiastic, optimistic, and supportive throughout the meetings.[3]

Participants were first made aware of the program through an ad in the newspaper or through referral from the local branch of the American Cancer Society (ACS). Each interested person was sent a "Smoking Research

[2] *Editors' note:* Careful attention to cognitive factors—what the client says to himself and what is imagined—is important. See Article 9.

[3] *Editors' note:* Generating an expectation of success is a necessary but not sufficient component of treatment. Some skeptics claim that it is all that is needed.

Questionnaire."[4] There were no criteria for selection other than a willingness to complete this questionnaire and subsequent follow-up questionnaires and to abide by the terms of the "treatment agreement" (see Appendix A). Each participant was required to deposit a certain amount of money with us in advance. This deposit was to be refunded according to the schedule outlined in the agreement, the purpose being to increase the likelihood that attendance at the meetings would be regular and that relevant data would be gathered and returned. It was made clear that the refund of money had no connection at all with success or failure in any facet of the program.

Meetings were conducted in a group setting. The group was heterogeneous, by and large, in age (ranging from the twenties to the sixties), with men and women about equally represented; most people were from the middle socioeconomic range.

Each session lasted about two hours on one evening a week for five consecutive weeks.

FIRST MEETING

At the first meeting the group leaders introduced themselves, gave their credentials, and stated that they were both ex-smokers. Participants were asked to introduce themselves and to give some statement about how long they had been smoking, how much they smoked, and how many times they had tried to quit previously. Money was returned according to the terms of the treatment agreement. Each person was given a manila envelope containing literature on smoking from the ACS and graph paper for data gathering.

The leaders then indicated that the approach of this program was a unique one in its comprehensiveness. The participants were told that they stood an excellent chance of successfully achieving their goals if they followed very carefully all the instructions given during the meetings. Emphasis was given to the fact that they would be required to expend a considerable amount of effort in overcoming their smoking "habit"—a difficult but not impossible thing to break. The decision to become a nonsmoker was one that had to be reaffirmed day after day, particularly during the next month or so. The leaders emphasized the need for honesty in reporting the data that were to be collected during the coming weeks, especially when those data might not be favorable. Remarks were made about the maladaptive role of irrational guilt in influencing people to be less than fully honest. We tried to assure the participants that the habit of smoking was neither evil nor shameful but merely unhealthy physically and therefore destructive and useless—it was to be considered morally neutral.[5]

Several commonly held myths about smoking and the cessation of smoking were discussed and explored.

[4] *Editors' note:* Copies of the questionnaire are available on request from David L. Geisinger, 341 Spruce Street, San Francisco, California 94118.

[5] *Editors note:* A good way to promote honest reporting.

Among the most important of these assumptions were, first, that, if one stopped smoking one would necessarily find a new habit like compulsive eating arising to take its place. Although in some instances such "replacements" do occur, they are not inevitable. In fact, quite often other maladaptive habits that existed concurrently with smoking may be eliminated, either as a result of the boost in morale resulting from kicking the smoking habit or because of conditioned links between cigarettes and other troublesome behaviors. In general, it appears that a slight weight gain is usual for people who stop smoking—on the order of about five pounds—and this gain is often temporary. One study suggested that the amount of extra work that the heart must engage in during the smoking of one package of cigarettes a day is roughly equivalent to the extra work required of the heart of someone who is about ninety pounds overweight. Second was the myth that, if one stopped smoking, as many people associated the habit with relaxation, one would become increasingly tense and irritable. We indicated that physiologically nicotine is itself a stimulant and an irritant, the very antithesis of a relaxant; the association of smoking with relaxation is likely a by-product of Madison Avenue advertising schemes, in which cigarettes and relaxation have been very powerfully associated.

In this connection, examples of magazine ads for cigarettes were analyzed—we had made a collection of them in advance—for their covert and irrational messages: Cigarettes were linked with relaxation, togetherness, ro-

mance, creativity, ruggedness, the spiritual enjoyment of nature, and other desirable circumstances.

A particularly invidious kind of advertisement was one that had to do with the "cigarette for the both of you," in which the scheme seemed to be to hook two people in the family into smoking. When that occurred, the probability that one of them would stop was likely to be substantially reduced by virtue of the enhancing effects of suggestion and modeling of the smoker upon the prospective nonsmoker.

The group members were asked to unmask any advertisement for cigarettes they saw in the coming weeks, in order to reveal its irrational assumptions.

There followed a brief discussion and lecture on the conditioning components of cigarette smoking. This was introduced by describing Pavlov's work with dogs and relating the principles of his work to cigarette smoking. The participants were encouraged to look at their daily lives for links between smoking and many common situations: having a cup of coffee, driving a car, talking on the phone, finishing a meal, writing, reading the paper, and so on. The parallels were drawn between the dog's salivating at the bell and people's desire for cigarettes on these occasions.[6]

In addition to this kind of conditioning that exists in terms of external events, it was pointed out that the desire for a cigarette is often governed by events of an internal, usually unob-

[6] *Editors' note:* Would it help to ask each individual in the group to analyze his or her own links?

servable, nature—events most frequently below the threshold of awareness. Smokers become conditioned to a particular artificial physiological rate of metabolism and heartbeat. It is evident that the desire to smoke a cigarette is, when it occurs, to be considered not a random event but one that arises in response to specifiable "triggers."

Following is an example of the actual presentation given on this topic:

This is called autonomic conditioning. It's a well-known phenomenon with respect to the operation of your bodily processes. It is possible to condition heartbeat, gastric secretions, muscular tension, blood flow to various areas, peristalsis of your gut and even brain waves. You can condition practically any physiological process in your body. Your heart is conditioned to beat at an increased rate by taking in the chemical nicotine, and when it begins to taper down to its normal physiological rate of about 73 and you feel like having a cigarette, you're not cognizant that your need for the cigarette at that time is anything but an accident. There are no accidents. Autonomic conditioning can be below the threshold of your consciousness or awareness, but it's there. The interesting thing is that people who smoke behave like conditioned dogs on one level, yet they have all kinds of elaborate rationalizations for why they do so.

Toward the end of the session the homework assignment for the following week was given. First, each person was to keep a daily record, on the graph paper given to him, of the number of cigarettes smoked, as well as some sense of the circumstances in which the smoking occurred. The group members were asked to make no attempt to curtail their smoking (though it is true that record keeping *per se* often alters the frequency of the behavior in question). They were to bring the graphs with them to each meeting.[7]

Second, they were to change brands the next day to the brand they *least* preferred, as indicated on the "Smoking Research Questionnaire." All cigarettes of the brand they usually smoked were to be removed from their homes and offices and specifically thrown out. They were urged not to give them away, for cigarettes are poisonous and therefore not very appropriate gifts. Our rationale here was a belief that it might be easier ultimately to break from brands they disliked than from brands they enjoyed. Incidentally, it was our experience that many people rather quickly adapted to the brands they had formerly deemed repugnant.

Third, cigarette packages were to be thoroughly wrapped in sheets of newspaper held on by rubber bands. In this way the decision to smoke would require greater effort than usual (wrapping and unwrapping the pack each time) and would make it unlikely that they would reach for cigarettes in an automatic, semiconscious fashion. They were to smoke no cigarettes other than their own.

Fourth, "delay periods" were to be implemented in two ways: They were to allow five minutes to elapse between their desire for a cigarette and the actual lighting of it, and they were to

---

[7] *Editors' note:* Wrist golf counters or leather bracelet counters would facilitate the daily counting.

wait approximately five seconds between the desire to take a drag on the cigarette and actually doing so.

Again in this instance we were increasing the effort attached to a formerly rather effortless habit, and we were demonstrating to the participants that they could begin to exercise some self-control over the habit. After waiting the five-minute delay period, some people would forget about or no longer want a cigarette. Also, the delay periods prolonged the time interval between the antecedent stimulus and the response of smoking. In this way, conditioned associations were being weakened (extinction).

Fifth, everyone was asked to begin to read at leisure the literature provided in the envelopes (see "References"). It was stressed that group members were to have read all the material by the end of the program, even though most of them were familiar with many of the well-publicized facts on smoking and health.

Paper and pencils were provided, and group members were encouraged to take notes during the meeting, particularly on their assignments. Throughout the program questions were encouraged, personal experiences were elicited by the leaders, and spontaneous discussions were frequent. An air of camaraderie, good humor, and support pervaded the sessions.

All participants were weighed on a medical scale before leaving this and all other meetings, and their weights were recorded. They were told that after the next meeting they would be required to reduce their daily consumption of cigarettes by 50 percent of their base-line average.

SECOND MEETING

As the participants entered the room they were refunded a sum of money in accordance with the stipulation in the treatment agreement. The graphs representing the numbers of cigarettes smoked during the previous week were collected, and the mean number of cigarettes smoked per day during the previous week was computed for each person. The graphs were then returned.

Following some general discussion in which experiences of the previous week were shared, a film put out by the ACS was shown. This film showed research on animals linking chronic exposure to certain components of cigarette smoke with disease. The effects of smoking on human beings were illustrated on both the microanatomical and functional levels. Lung diseases like cancer and emphysema were explored in some detail and their destructive nature made evident. The tone of the film was scientific, not sensational— it did not propagandize but just presented some factual material and some modest speculations based upon the findings.

The film was followed with a lecture by a physician, an internist, who spoke more extensively about his own personal experiences with long-term smokers whom he had seen in his practice.

The physician mentioned the fact that, whereas emphysema and cancer are not reversible, upon the cessation of smoking, other diseases, like chronic bronchitis, do reverse themselves. Some statistics supporting the relationship between stopping smoking and returning to health were quoted.

The ACS had provided actual specimens of human lungs that were extremely damaged by cancer and emphysema; these were passed around among the participants for a closer look while the physician gave his talk. Questions about the medical aspects of smoking were answered at length.

When the internist had completed his presentation, the group leaders discussed the effects of modeling on others in the smokers' environment. Relevant research, like that of Bandura (1969), was cited to demonstrate how social-learning processes may bear on the matter of smoking cigarettes.

It was noted that children of non-smoking parents are less frequently smokers themselves upon reaching adulthood than are children of families in which one parent is a smoker, and they in turn smoke less than do children who have been raised in families in which both parents smoke.

Smoking as a "pure" stimulus activity was then described. Essentially this technique consisted of having the participants smoke in a manner in which the cigarette was detached from its usual environmental contexts. The cigarette was to be smoked while facing a blank wall and relating only to the cigarette, so as to encourage the breaking of the bond between smoking and other common daily events associated with it.

A "smoking machine"—a small plastic device distributed by the ACS in which cigarette smoke is drawn through a filter, demonstrating the trapped tar, nicotine, and other coagu-

lants—was demonstrated next.[8] It was pointed out that these poisons normally are filtered by the lungs and remain lodged there to some extent. Again it was emphasized that the lungs systematically "clean themselves" and that, if smoking is terminated, the lungs in time tend to return to their normal state.

A variation on "thought stopping," a technique described by Wolpe and Lazarus (1966), was presented in detail. Each person was provided with a one-eighth-inch-thick rubber band and was instructed to wear it on one wrist during all waking hours until further notice. The band was to be stretched four to five inches and snapped vigorously against the wrist whenever the desire to smoke occurred and the person did not want to smoke. The band was to be used repeatedly until the desire left. It was made clear that the thought of having a cigarette and the snap of the rubber band had to occur almost simultaneously for maximum effect to be obtained.

As each person was required to reduce his smoking frequency by 50 percent during the coming week, thought stopping was viewed as a timely and practical technique at this juncture of the program.

The basis for this procedure was explained as follows: Any behavior that is closely associated in time with a noxious stimulus will decrease in frequency and intensity. Thus the participants

[8] Editors' note: The wealth of demonstrations, lectures, and equipment is impressive. The necessity for these procedures, however, remains unknown, for no attempt was made to evaluate each treatment component. Possibly a far simpler program could produce equal or even superior results.

were told to expect that the frequency and intensity of their desires to smoke were likely to be diminished during the course of the week. The rubber band was to be used on a continuous schedule: All impulses to smoke that were not to be honored should be followed immediately by snaps or series of snaps.[9]

Before the group left, as usual each member was weighed. The homework was as follows.

First, group members were to continue to read the literature provided, including notes personally taken during the meetings.

Second, at the start of each day they were to put exactly 50 percent of the original base-line number of cigarettes in the package.[10] These cigarettes are to continue to be of the brand "least preferred" and are to be wrapped in newspaper with a rubber band around it.

Third, whenever a desire to smoke occurred that was not to be honored, the rubber band was to be used until the desire abated for at least thirty seconds.

[9] *Editors' note:* The rationale for this technique is puzzling. Although the purpose is to punish the urge, one would also be punishing the act of refusing a cigarette. It would seem more consistent to snap the rubber band *during the act of smoking* or when lighting up—or to follow the rubber-band snap (and the successful resistance to smoking) immediately with a positive event. In that way the urge would be reduced and the nonsmoking rewarded.

[10] *Editors' note:* A sudden 50 percent reduction could be excessive. Others have recommended a more gradual tapering off, with the client specifying in advance the maximum number of cigarettes allowable each day.

Fourth, group members were to continue keeping charts of urges to smoke and the actual number of cigarettes smoked.

Fifth, each was to smoke two cigarettes as a "pure" activity each day.

The group was told that its members would stop smoking completely at the next session.

THIRD MEETING

As the group entered, a spontaneous discussion in which people shared the experience of reducing their cigarette consumption by 50 percent began. Participants by and large had been successful in attaining this subgoal; most people were surprised at how easy it was. The few who had not quite achieved a 50 percent reduction were asked individually to describe how they had exceeded the limit set for them. In nearly all instances they had rationalized their behavior in one way or another or had failed to use the techniques described during the second meeting in any consistent fashion. We indicated in as neutral and nonjudgmental a fashion as possible that we considered this to be a serious warning signal, suggesting that these people had to be even more dedicated and precise in following the instructions if they were to achieve their goals of becoming nonsmokers.

The money for attendance and record keeping was returned as usual.

As this was "Q day," quitting day, everyone was requested to throw his cigarettes in a garbage can placed in the center of the room. They were instructed to throw out all cigarettes remaining in their homes, cars, and offices immediately upon arriving at these places.

Being nonsmokers from this time on meant that they were not to have even a puff of a cigarette, cigar, or pipe. We cautioned them that becoming reconditioned to smoking could readily happen and that they were to refrain, therefore, from using any tobacco at all. We asked that they also refrain from smoking marijuana for several weeks at least—those who used it—for it tends to weaken self-control. Furthermore, it might cause them to have powerful urges to smoke cigarettes because of the generalization of the smoking response.

"Quitting games" were explored next. Essentially, these are common rationalizations that people engage in, attempting to justify their return to smoking. We requested that notes be taken on the four major "games" as we explored them.

First was "What the hell." In this rationalization—a process of making rational something that is fundamentally irrational—the person told herself that pollution of the air, atomic testing, the fact that people in her family died early anyway, the fact that one could die tomorrow in a highway accident, and so on made stopping smoking insignificant. The counter to this argument is that, despite the fact that death is inevitable for all of us, we should do nothing to hurry our deaths or to increase the likelihood that we shall fall ill.

Second was "This is killing me." In this instance, the individual, noting a temporary increase in such symptoms as irritability, sleeplessness, weight gain, and distractibility told herself that the *absence* of a poison (cigarette smoke) is harmful. The counter is that refraining from a destructive habit can only be a healthy move in the long run, even if some unpleasant consequences do develop temporarily.[11]

The third game was "I've got it licked," a game in which the individual, convinced that she has conquered the habit for all time, tries to show herself or others how invulnerable she is to its former hold over her. She tries one drag or even a whole cigarette in a smug demonstration of her power over the pernicious habit, and most often before very long she has returned fully to her former smoking level. The counter is the nearly certain knowledge that returning to the habit is always going to be the easiest of possibilities with a behavior that has had such a powerful reinforcement history. Everyone knows of people who have stopped smoking for varying lengths of time only to have returned again after this kind of experimentation: "Stopping smoking is easy; I've done it many times." There can be no rational justification whatever for experimenting with smoking once one has stopped.

Fourth is "I didn't want to quit anyway" a rather crude denial of one's original motivation and commitment to terminate the habit. Often this is accompanied by a message in which the individual tells herself that she only wanted to prove to herself that she

[11] *Editors' note:* This "consequence" is probably the biggest problem in the self-control of habits with immediate positive consequences but long-term negative results (smoking, overeating, drugs, drinking, physical inactivity and so on).

could stop smoking any time she wanted to; now that she has done so for days, weeks, or months she will return to smoking and will stop permanently when she "really" decides to do so. Counter to this fabrication are the reminders that every additional puff on a cigarette is a step closer to ill health and that it will never be easier to stop than it is now, for the habit becomes stronger the longer a person engages in it.

The group members were asked to reread their notes on these common bits of illogic once a day for the next few weeks in order to acquire a heightened awareness of them. They were instructed to be vigilant in the future for any evidence that they might be telling themselves such nonsense and to counter each instance with its rational antithesis.[12]

The next stage of this session was devoted to emotional role playing. An experienced psychodramatist arranged a scene in which a group member volunteered to play the part of a patient being told by a physician, played by one of the group leaders, that the results of laboratory tests had confirmed the presence of lung cancer. The "physician" gently and with great seriousness told the patient that she could make no promises as to the success of the surgery that would now be necessary nor could she make any predictions about the future. No knowledge was yet available as to whether the cancer had metastacized, but the pa-

tient was advised that this could not really be ruled out. The physician suggested that the patient might want to make certain preparations in case the worst proved to be true. She offered to help break the news to the patient's family.

During the enactment of this scene the psychodramatist stood behind the patient and played the role of "double." This consisted of speaking aloud in a dramatic way the thoughts and feelings that a person first hearing such shocking news might be having. For example, the patient might be thinking, "This can't be happening to me—it's a dream, a nightmare!"; "She's made a mistake; I'm too young to have cancer"; "I'm going to die! I'm going to die!"; "What about the vacation we had been planning, the house we had been saving for"; or "Just when things seemed to be going so well, this! Oh God! Oh God!"

Usually the room was deadly silent during this drama. Occasionally someone would laugh defensively or look about distractedly as if to deny the possibility that such a scene could become a reality.

Immediately after the presentation the group leaders walked over to each participant one at a time, being careful to make eye contact, and said in a quiet tone, "This could happen to you." At times we repeated this sentence with a particular person until we were convinced he or she had given it serious personal consideration.

The participants were congratulated on having stopped smoking. They were urged not to take even one drag of a cigarette again—they had taken their very last puff on a cigarette for their entire lives. Again they were re-

---

[12] *Editors' note:* Anticipating these mental games is excellent. We owe thanks to transactional analysis for showing the clever ways that people can reward their inappropriate behaviors.

minded to throw out all remaining cigarettes and butts where they lived and worked. They were reminded to use the thought-stopping technique diligently on a continual basis for the first five days of the week. For the remaining two days before the next meeting the rubber band was to be used on an intermittent-ratio schedule: Every fourth or fifth thought of smoking was to be permitted to go unpunished by the rubber band. Of course, this meant that on these occasions the person would use only "will power" to overcome the desire to smoke.[13] We explained the rationale for this alteration in the way the rubber band was to be used by indicating, with examples, how intermittent schedules of reinforcement tend to increase the strength of the responses related to them. In this instance we were interested in strengthening the ability to suppress or eliminate thoughts of smoking.

Group members were instructed to continue their records on the number of thoughts or desires to smoke during the week. If cigarettes were offered them they were told to refuse, saying, "No thanks, I'm going to remain a nonsmoker," or something equivalent. We specifically asked that they not brag about having stopped, though they

[13] *Editors' note:* Unfortunately, the popular reference to "will power" is often self-defeating, leading to another game: "I guess I don't have any (will power)." It may be better to avoid this notion altogether.

might tell some of their friends or relatives about it in a modest fashion. In no way were they to consider their smoking habits eliminated.

FOURTH AND FIFTH MEETINGS

The primary intent of the next two meetings was to support and consolidate the gains made thus far and to give the participants an opportunity to share their personal experiences. We devoted a good deal of the time to a review and clarification of the material of the previous sessions.

No new techniques were introduced; however, at the fourth meeting we told the members to use the rubber bands only about two thirds of the time and to use them only half the time during the week after the fifth meeting. They were to wear the rubber bands daily, whether they used them or not, for at least one month after the termination of the program and were to snap them, when necessary, more or less at random.

As usual, records were collected, refunds of money were made, and weights recorded.

Those people who had failed to quit smoking after the third meeting were asked to give their analyses of why they had not achieved their goals. In most instances they apparently had used one of the four rationalizations we had warned them against. We asked these people to make another attempt

Percentages Not Smoking at Different Follow-Up Times (N=21)			
1 Month	*4 Months*	*12 Months*	*20 Months*
57	48	43	48

to stop and to return for the fifth meeting only if they were successful.

RESULTS AND DISCUSSION

A total of twenty-one people, in two groups of eleven and ten, began the program. Of this number nineteen completed at least the first four sessions. Follow-up questionnaires were sent to all the participants after the program's last meeting, on a one, four, twelve, and twenty months' basis (see "Appendix B"). Money was refunded by mail upon receipt of these completed questionnaires. Each questionnaire was accompanied by a note asking for complete honesty in reporting and stating that the money would be refunded, regardless of whether or not smoking had been resumed. No other verification of the accuracy of these self-reports was made.

Among those who failed to stop smoking completely several people indicated that they had cut down their daily intake of cigarettes substantially or were motivated to try to stop at a future date. The mean weight gain during the course of the program was approximately four pounds, with a range of zero to ten pounds.

Although a good deal of additional data were gathered, they have not yet been analyzed.

CONCLUSIONS

Considering the breadth and intensity of this program, it does not seem likely that incorporating still more techniques (like monetary rewards) would have substantially increased its success rate. After a certain point, extending such techniques becomes impractical and may lead to diminishing returns.[14]

It is an inescapable fact that a fairly large number of people are able to stop smoking, no matter how strong or long their habits, merely after physicians' suggestions that they do so or even on their own—at times with relatively little effort.

Perhaps, therefore, the most significant predictors of success in "habit"-breaking programs will turn out to be what might be called "personality-trait variables" that relate to "strength of decisions" or what is called "will power." Tests should be devised to measure these variables, and their results should be correlated with outcome criteria.[15]

More stringent selection procedures, based upon measurements of pretreatment motivation, would probably also enhance the success of such programs. It may be possible to increase motivation by manipulating expectations more carefully and by requiring greater effort from applicants in order to be selected.[16]

---

[14] *Editors' note:* We simply do not know what the best combinations of various treatment components are at this point. Perhaps some chronic smokers need fewer different techniques but more continuing group support, whereas others need more emphasis on training in self-control skill.

[15] *Editors' note:* Perhaps some smokers successfully quit with "relatively little effort" because they use a variety of cognitive and environmental techniques that are not readily apparent to others. Thus it seems as if they have succeeded because of "will power."

[16] *Editors' note:* The monetary refund for meeting attendance and data completion was an excellent idea. What would happen if a sizable part of the refund were contingent on stopping smoking?

APPENDIX A: STOP SMOKING AGREEMENT

Treatment Agreement

Each participant in the "Stop Smoking" program will be required to deposit a $70.00 (seventy dollar) money order or check prior to the beginning of this program, payable to the Interagency Counsel on Smoking & Health. Fifty-seven ($57.00) dollars of this will be returned to you according to the following schedule.

		Amount Returned
There will be five meetings in the program:		

A) For attendance at each meeting @ $3.00 per meeting. $15.00
THERE WILL BE FOUR FOLLOW-UP QUESTIONNAIRES AFTER THE TERMINATION OF THE PROGRAM.

B) For return of each completed questionnaire @ $5.00 per questionnaire. $20.00
YOU WILL BE REQUIRED TO KEEP CERTAIN RECORDS AND CHARTS:

C) *Smoking Incidence:* During the second and third meetings you will be required to hand in a detailed record of the number of cigarettes smoked each day. For the return of these records @ $3.00 each. $6.00

D) *Desire To Smoke:* During the course of the program you will be required to hand in after the first meeting a record of the number of the separate thoughts or desires to smoke you had each day. For the return of those records @ $4.00 each. $16.00

Thirteen dollars ($13.00) of the fee will be *non-returnable* and will be used to cover the expenses of the program. $13.00

                                           TOTAL $70.00

I, _____ _____
      (PRINT NAME)   (ADDRESS)

agree to abide by the above terms and understand that if I fail to carry out any of the above requirements, I will forfeit that proportion of the deposit stipulated in this agreement.

                                  _____
                                        (SIGNATURE)

APPENDIX B: STOP SMOKING PROGRAM FOLLOW-UP QUESTIONNAIRE

Name: _____ Date: _____
      (LAST)   (PLEASE PRINT)   (FIRST)

1) Do you presently smoke at all (excluding marijuana)? YES NO (circle one)
2) Have you smoked at all since the end of the program? YES NO (circle one)
   If answer to question #2 is *YES*, answer questions 3–7 only.
   If answer to question #1 is *NO*, accept our warm congratulations and return the
   questionnaire with comments on reverse side of this page.
3) How many days were you abstinent after "Q" day? _____
4) State *in detail* how you came to resume smoking: _____
   _____
   _____
   _____

5) Are you *presently* motivated to quit smoking? YES NO (circle one)
6) Have you made any attempts to quit smoking *since you left the program?*
   YES NO (circle one)   Describe these attempts you have made, including their
   results _____
   _____
   _____

7) Did your participation in the program affect your smoking behavior in *any* way?
   YES NO (circle one)   If *YES* please describe the effects it had _____
   _____
   _____
   _____

references

Bandura, A. *Principles of behavior modification.* New York: Holt, Rinehart and Winston, 1969.

Blakeslee, A. *It's not too late to stop smoking cigarettes!* New York: Public Affairs Pamphlets, 1966.

Brecher, R. & Brecher E. *Smoking—The great dilemma.* New York: Public Affairs Pamphlets, 1964.

Brecher, R. *et al. The Consumers Union report on smoking and the public interest.* New York: Consumers Union, 1963.

Hammond, E. C. The effects of smoking. *Scientific American,* 1962, **207**, 39–51.

Hammond, E. C. Evidence on the effects of giving up cigarette smoking. *American Journal of Public Health,* 1965, **55**, 682–691.

McFall, R. M. & Hammen, C. L. Motivation, structure, and self-monitoring: Role of nonspecific factors in smoking reduction. *Journal of Consulting and Clinical Psychology,* 1971, **37**, 80–86.

McGrady, P. *Cigarettes and health.* New York: Public Affairs Pamphlets, 1960.

Wolpe, J. & Lazarus, A. A. *Behavior therapy techniques.* New York: Pergamon, 1966.

World conference on smoking and health: A summary of the proceedings. New York: American Cancer Society, 1967.

COMPULSIVE GAMBLING

13. *TREATMENT FOR HABITUAL GAMBLING*

SUSAN M. FITCHETT AND DONALD A. SANDFORD   Psychological Services,
Justice Department, New Zealand

INTRODUCTION

Habitual gambling has traditionally been regarded as a psychological, rather than a medical, problem. There has never been any doubt that it can have serious social consequences, as is demonstrated by the number of people imprisoned for "borrowing" money solely to place bets or to pay gambling debts. As both authors work in a prison setting, we became interested in devising a treatment program for compulsive gamblers.

Conceptualized in terms of operant-learning theory gambling is an excellent example of behavior supported on a variable-ratio reinforcement schedule. "Winning depends on placing a bet and in the long run on the number of bets placed, but no particular pay-off can be predicted. The ratio is varied by any one of several systems. The pathological gambler exemplifies the result. The long-term net gain or loss is almost irrelevant in accounting for the effectiveness of the schedule" (Skinner, 1953). Such a view also accepts that any change in the behavior is possible only through manipulation of the environmental consequences of the behavior. A review of the publications of other behavior therapists who had attempted to alter gambling behavior led us to conclude that efforts in this area have been spasmodic and ill defined. Rather than duplicate such efforts, we decided that it would be more useful to develop a treatment that would use existing knowledge in a programmatic fashion.

BASIC RATIONALE FOR TREATMENT

The program is divided into three stages, each involving different contingencies.

Stage 1: Unavoidable Punishment

Rachman and Teasdale (1969), referring to homosexual behavior-modification programs, reported that the most successful were those in which punishment was unavoidable (this procedure has often been called "respondent conditioning"). However, other experimental data suggest that behavior produced by such contingencies is prone to rapid extinction following contingency withdrawal (Kimble, 1962). For this reason, two further stages of treatment were also instituted.

Stage 2: Development of a Competing Response

Azrin and Holtz (1966), in a review of operant-punishment literature, reported that training the organism to perform an alternative response leads to more lasting response suppression than occurs in the absence of such an alternative. Rachman and Teasdale (1969) also concluded that an aversive stimulus has a more lasting effect as a punisher when the person is given an alternative positively reinforced response to perform. Stage 2, therefore, involves the client's being able to escape from the aversive situation by performing a competing response, which is then reinforced.

Stage 3: Partial Reinforcement of the Competing Response

The only difference between the second and third stages is that in the latter not all competing responses are positively reinforced. The rationale is twofold: First, behavior maintained on a variable-ratio schedule is highly resistant to extinction, and, second, the situation more closely approximates the real-life situations that such clients will encounter outside prison.

THE CASE OF MR. JONES

Mr. Jones was a thirty-one-year-old married man who had been convicted of "theft as a servant" ($27,200) and who had no previous convictions. He had embezzled his firm's money to pay debts acquired through betting on horses. At the time the treatment program was begun he had spent nine months in prison, and during that period he had received verbal psychotherapy, which had not weakened his interest in gambling. Although there was less opportunity to listen to races

and to place bets in prison, he had taken part in illegal sweepstakes, listened to racing broadcasts when he was able, and placed two illegal bets. He approached one of the authors, who was a member of the prison classification board, because he was concerned about the possibility of his gambling's again becoming a problem when he was released.[1]

An analysis of Mr. Jones' gambling behavior showed that he did not attend race meetings but listened to the races on the radio. It was decided to focus treatment on this behavior. Base-line data collection included finding out how many times each week he listened to the races on the radio. This figure was expressed as a percentage of the total number of times that he could have listened in a week, because race broadcasts are not constant from week to week. The percentage of illegal prison sweepstakes in which he took part each week was also recorded.

To simulate "listening to a race broadcast" several such broadcasts were taped on twin-track tape. An old radio case with the knobs still attached was used to simulate a "working" radio. When the client switched the "radio" knob one way he heard the tape of the race broadcast; switching the knob the other way allowed him to hear the other tape track.

The client had told us that his relationship with his wife was very important to him and that, being in prison many miles from his home town, he

---

[1] *Editors' note:* Note that the treatment was begun when a client voluntarily requested help, even though his environment was confining.

missed her very much. We thus considered that a treatment program might be more effective if we could arrange for his wife to participate in it. One of the authors was able to interview her and gained her agreement to assist us in the treatment program. We recorded her telling her husband that she loved him and also being upset and saying, "Please don't bet on the races." Mr. Jones had also told us that he found the sound of a woman screaming very aversive, and this sound was simulated by a colleague and recorded.[2]

Session 1

Preparation for the first session involved inserting the wife's aversive comments and the woman's scream into the tapes of the race broadcasts. Placement of these aversive stimuli was random, so that the client could not learn to predict when the aversive stimuli were going to occur. There was one session of five practice trials, during which the client listened to a race broadcast and the aversive stimuli. He was not allowed to turn the radio off or to leave the room.

Sessions 2–6

During the second part of treatment Mr. Jones could escape the aversive stimuli by turning off the racing broadcast, which automatically turned on the other tape track, from which he heard light music and at random intervals his wife's voice telling him that she loved him. Thus he was positively reinforced for turning off the race broadcast.[3] There were five sessions during this stage, and each session consisted of five practice trials.

Session 7

Session 7 was similar to the preceding ones, except that not all the escape responses were reinforced. This stage consisted of one session of five trials.

Prison-staff members were asked to observe whether or not Mr. Jones listened to any race broadcasts outside treatment sessions. He was also asked to make report on his own "listening to races" behavior. To compare progress with base-line data, we translated the information received from staff and Mr. Jones into a percentage of "racing broadcasts listened to" (see Figure 1).

Progress and Problems

The client came to the first treatment session displaying considerable skepticism about the proposed program. However, following the first session his attitude had changed. He said that the tape had made a tremendous impact on him, and he was visibly upset. During the broadcast he wrung his hands, shook, wanted the radio turned off, screwed up his cigarette, and made hostile comments to the therapist. He reported later that he thought the ini-

---

[2] *Editors' note:* Notice how the authors carefully selected personal experiences that were both realistic and influential with Mr. Jones.

[3] *Editors' note:* A good example of combining negative reinforcement (turning off the "radio" was strengthened by the resulting avoidance of the aversive comments) and positive reinforcement.

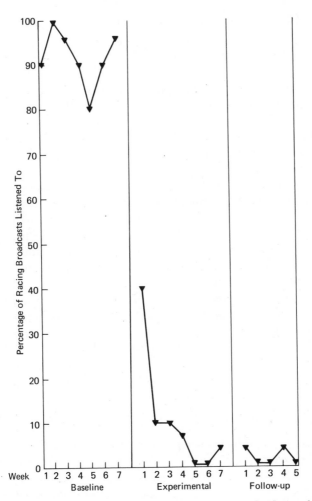

FIGURE 1 Percentage of racing broadcasts listened to by Mr. Jones during baseline, experimental, and follow-up periods.

tial punishment trials had been suffi- cient to stop his listening to, or betting on, horse races.

In a book written by another in- mate about his prison experience the treatment given to our client was dis- cussed (Justin, 1973, pp. 86–88). From this source we received objective vali- dation of the impact of the initial trials on Mr. Jones. Mr. Jones himself re- ported that, following session 1, he had turned off the radio in his cell whenever a race broadcast was about to com- mence, without "consciously knowing why." Later in the treatment program he reported that he had lost all interest in betting and sweepstakes. He found that he could be in a room while a rac- ing commentary was being broadcast without becoming so upset that he wanted to turn it off but that such commentary had become so much a part of the background noise that he did not pay attention to it. The client continued to report loss of interest in all gambling activities, despite the fact that other gamblers often urged him to continue to bet and that as a work parolee he had access to betting-shop facilities.

Mr. Jones encouraged other gamblers in the prison to approach the authors and inquire about treatment. At the end of treatment he said that his liking for the music used on the reinforcement tape had increased to such a degree that he wanted to know its source so that he could purchase the record after his release. Again, objective validation of a change in his behavior was received from statements made in Justin's (1973) book. The major problem encountered during treatment was occasional technical difficulties with the tape recorder. We had also begun treatment not really knowing how effective the use of auditory aversive stimuli would be in changing the client's behavior.

The Outcome of the Treatment Program

Following release from prison Mr. Jones returned to his family. To carry out the follow-up investigation it was necessary to enlist the assistance of his probation (parole) officer, as he lived in a city several hundred miles away from the prison in which he had been treated. The officer was initially asked to send us information on Mr. Jones' progress every six months. In the officer's first report he said, "Mr. Jones stated that he no longer had any inclination to gamble . . . claims that it [the treatment] has been entirely successful." Suggestions were made to the probation officer about important variables in the maintenance of new behavior and the suppression of gambling. It was hoped that he might explore them with Mr. Jones and encourage certain behaviors that would be incompatible with gambling.

One possible danger in the client's home environment was the tendency for his relatives to gamble heavily. The officer's second report indicated that the client "was highly thought of" in his job and that his wife had "noted a change for the better." Mr. Jones stated "that he dislikes gambling and is tired of his relatives talking about gambling. . . . He said that the sport, now, holds no interest for him whatsover. . . ."

In the third six-month report the officer stated that he had spoken to both Mr. Jones and his wife: "Both he and his wife stated that he has no interest in gambling." A year later the officer reported verbally that he had again spoken to Mr. Jones, who still claimed that he was free of the problem. Six months later, that is, about two years after conclusion of treatment, the authors visited the client's city and were able to speak both to him and to his wife. They both said that he was free of the problem and that gambling did not interest him.[4]

---

[4] *Editors' note:* Success seems to have been so sudden and complete that we cannot help but wonder whether or not other variables, unknown to the authors, might have played a part.

PROCEDURAL VARIATIONS

The major differences between the case presented and others is in the selection of the appropriate stimulus, response, and reinforcers. It is theoretically possible that any one of the three contingencies used may be just as effective when used alone as when combined with the other two, for example, the unavoidable-punishment procedure may be the primary cause of behavior change. Recently we have been looking into such possibilities. A client has been taken through a simple respondent-conditioning program in which a noxious unconditioned stimulus was presented on a variable-interval schedule while he was watching a videotape of himself looking through racing periodicals. The treatment has apparently been a complete success, according to one six-month followup.

Another change has been the introduction of a contingency-management program for "significant others" like wife, friends, and other relatives of each client. For one particular client, several sessions were conducted with his wife, to whom the learning basis of her husband's gambling was explained and with whom several areas were explored. The first area was discriminative stimuli that had in the past controlled her husband's gambling responses. The wife was informed about the responses that her husband had been asked to make in relation to these stimuli and about the importance of perceiving subtle cues that could be interpreted as danger signs of her husband's recurring interest in gambling. The importance of perceiving correct responses was also emphasized.

The second area explored was the strengthening of "correct" behavior and the suppression of "incorrect" behavior. The wife was taught how she could contingently strengthen certain responses made by her husband, for example, responses incompatible with gambling responses, and how she could contingently weaken "dangerous" responses, like his bringing home a racing periodical.[5]

[5] *Editors' note:* These techniques sound like excellent additions to the procedures used with Mr. Jones.

references

Azrin, N. H. & Holtz, W. C. Punishment. In W. K. Honig (Ed.), *Operant behavior: Areas of research and application.* New York: Appleton, 1966. Pp. 380–447.

Justin, J. *Prisoner.* Christchurch: Whitcombe & Tombs, 1973.

Kimble, G. A. (Ed.). *Conditioning and learning.* 2nd Ed. New York: Appleton, 1962.

Rachman, S. & Teasdale, J. *Aversion therapy and the behaviour disorders.* London: Routledge & Kegan Paul, 1969.

Skinner, B. F. *Science and human behavior.* New York: Macmillan, 1953.

ALCOHOLISM

14. TRAINING CONTROLLED DRINKING IN AN ALCOHOLIC THROUGH A MULTIFACETED BEHAVIORAL TREATMENT PROGRAM: A CASE STUDY[1]

G. TERENCE WILSON   Rutgers University
RAYMOND C. ROSEN   College of Medicine and Dentistry of New Jersey,
Rutgers University Medical School

Mr. V was a thirty-year-old, white electrician, who was married with two sons aged seven and eleven years. He was also an alcoholic. His case came to our attention in the course of the second author's treatment of Mr. V's mother-in-law through the Rutgers Mental Health Center. Mr. V had a history of drinking since he was thirteen years old, and reported that he had been an alcoholic for the previous twelve years. His drinking had seriously interfered with his health and his social and economic functioning. He had experienced periodic blackouts and withdrawal symptoms on occasion; these symptoms led him to be verbally and physically abusive toward his wife and sons. He was distrustful of Alcoholics Anonymous (A.A.) programs and had derived no benefit from an extended and expensive course of therapy with a psychodynamically oriented therapist. The experience left him and his wife somewhat antagonistic toward psychiatrists. Mr. V was currently living with his father-in-law and on the brink of being divorced by his embittered wife, when the second author,

whom both partners had come to trust, suggested that he make one final attempt at rehabilitation. Mr. V was eager and highly motivated; somewhat grudgingly, his wife agreed to one "last ditch" effort. As the first author was codirector of a behavioral treatment program for alcoholics at the Rutgers Alcohol Behavior Research Laboratory, it was decided by both authors to develop an out-patient treatment program for Mr. V.

There is evidence (for example in Pattison et al., 1968; Sobell & Sobell, 1973a) indicating that alcoholics can become controlled social drinkers. In some instances this goal is perhaps more viable than abstinence. "Loss of control" drinking, customarily attributed to an involuntary, physiological addictive process, can be conceptualized as learned behavior, differing from normal social drinking only in terms of rate, amount, and the circumstances under which alcohol is consumed. Several factors recommended controlled drinking as the appropriate therapeutic objective for Mr. V. He was reluctant to give up drinking completely, the abstinence doctrine of A.A. had already proved ineffective, he had been able to control his drinking for some period in the past, and he appeared to have suffi-

[1] This program was supported by a grant from the National Institute of Alcohol Abuse and Alcoholism, AA-259-04.

cient potential familial and social support to support controlled drinking.[2] The only drawback was his wife's skepticism. We persuaded her to cooperate with us for an initial limited treatment period of approximately one month. If we failed to produce some significant improvement by then, we would change strategies, or she would be free to file for divorce.

Our immediate goal was to win some breathing space by at least temporarily decreasing Mr. V's alcohol consumption, using a modified form of aversion therapy. A more detailed behavioral assessment was deferred to a later date. Lovibond and Caddy (1970) have described a promising treatment method by which alcoholics are first taught to discriminate their own blood-alcohol level. In the second phase they learn to modify their drinking. Any consumption of alcohol that exceeds a predetermined upper limit of 0.065 percent alcohol concentration in the blood is followed by contingent shock; drinking below the target level is allowed with impunity. Mr. V and his wife freely consented to his participation in this program, which they understood to be completely voluntary.[3] The self-control nature of the procedure was emphasized, and the more general principles of self-regulation of behavior were carefully explained to the cou-

ple. For example, Mr. V was cautioned against going into a bar to buy cigarettes or soda, which he could purchase elsewhere without exposing himself to the cues associated with drinking.

FIRST SESSION

The first treatment session took place in the simulated bar setting of the Alcohol Behavior Research Laboratory (see Nathan *et al.*, 1972) on December 22, 1972. Mr. V was given two ounces of 86-proof blended whiskey to drink. Following the necessary twenty-minute interval, he was given a Breathalyzer test.[4] He was asked to estimate his blood-alcohol level and then was provided with feedback on the accuracy of his estimation. This procedure was repeated every twenty minutes after he had consumed approximately a half-ounce of alcohol (which he mixed with soda) until a level of 0.07 was reached. All drinking was done while Mr. V and the two authors sat around a table and engaged in a typical male "bull" session.

As his blood-alcohol level increased, Mr. V became noticeably talkative and assertive, almost to the point of being aggressive. In fact, it was possible to identify two distinct phases during the course of his drinking. During the first phase, Mr. V became red in the face, felt his "ears light up," began tapping his foot in time to the

---

[2] *Editors' note:* Training in controlled drinking is recommended not for every instance of alcoholism but for those in which certain conditions seem to indicate it is the least undesirable alternative.

[3] *Editors' note:* Aversive techniques are risky and should be used only when the client freely consents after being fully informed of the procedures and their purposes.

[4] Estimating blood-alcohol level directly from exhaled ethanol in the breath has become the accepted method for rapid determination of blood-alcohol levels. The instrument used was a model 900 from the Stevenson Corporation, Red Bank, New Jersey 07701.

background music, and was congenial. During the second phase, however, his speech became slurred; he became quiet and introspective and began downgrading himself. At a level of about 0.06 he himself reported that, if left to his own devices, he would have continued to drink until completely inebriated. On the basis of these observations the target blood-alcohol level was set at 0.045 to maximize his chances of maintaining control over further alcohol intake.[5] In keeping with Lovibond and Caddy's findings, Mr. V proved to be adept at learning to identify his blood-alcohol level accurately during the two-hour session.[6]

SECOND SESSION

After six days Mr. V reported only one drinking episode. He had bought half a pint of whiskey, but in what he called an "act of self-control" he had poured half of it down the sink before consuming the remainder. In the past he had typically drunk whiskey or would start drinking beer and then switch to whiskey and continue drinking until he became very intoxicated or passed out. He had been sober on Christmas Day for the first time in eleven years. This initial improvement may have been

due to the demand characteristics of entering treatment.

The therapy session began with our determining an appropriate level of shock, administered via Beckman electrodes to the wrist of his nondrinking arm. A level of 7 milliamps, which was subjectively painful and caused an arm flexion, was chosen. Thereafter Mr. V's blood-alcohol level was raised to about the target level around 0.045 as in the previous session. At this point the electrodes were reattached, and he was informed that he could expect a shock each time that he finished approximately one ounce of whiskey. He was at liberty to pour it for himself from a bottle on the table.

As in session 1, there was an attempt to make the setting as "naturalistic" as possible. The two authors engaged Mr. V in friendly conversation; his wife was asked to sit in on the session, in order to allay her apprehensions about the shock and to involve her closely in the program. Mr. V began by drinking rapidly. After the first two shocks (administered by one of the authors) Mr. V's pattern changed to one of sipping, or "nursing," his drink, as he started to avoid the shock. The session ended after an hour, with Mr. V pouring out the remaining contents of his glass. He became acutely conscious of the punishment contingency and none too fondly nicknamed the shock apparatus Betsy.[7] He was instructed to conjure up images of Betsy, should he experience the desire to drink between sessions.

---

[5] Editors' note: Notice that the authors commendably used the actual problem situation (drinking) to find out how Mr. V. handled alcohol before setting a goal.

[6] Silverstein et al. (1974), however, have recently reported more difficulty in training for accurate discrimination of blood-alcohol level in chronic alcoholics.

[7] Model #102K, Scientific Prototype, 615 West 131st Street, New York, New York 10027.

THIRD SESSION

At the next session Mr. V reported that he had consumed a total of four beers and two shots of whiskey. He had sipped them, however, as opposed to his former practice of gulping, and he claimed that thoughts of Betsy had deterred any further drinking.[8] He had been sober on New Year's Day and on his birthday the preceding day. His wife was pleasantly surprised with this progress, despite her distaste for the punishment procedure.

The session started with Mr. V. drinking until his blood alcohol reached the target level. He was then given a glass containing one ounce of alcohol mixed with three ounces of soda in a glass with ounce measures clearly marked on it. It was explained that, if he consumed about one ounce over a period of one hour, his blood alcohol would probably not increase and that this pace would result in controlled drinking. During the session he was shocked if he consumed more than one ounce of the contents of the glass (that is, a quarter-ounce of alcohol) in less than fifteen minutes. He incurred one shock within the first fifteen minutes but successfully avoided further shocks. Once again he concluded the session by pouring out the alcohol that remained. In lieu of drinking Mr. V had begun studying to obtain a superior job. This studying was verbally reinforced by the therapists.

His wife's attitude had also changed considerably. The couple had decided to move to Florida, provided that Mr. V maintained his sobriety, the authors sanctioned the move, and he could find a suitable job.

FOURTH SESSION

The fourth session was a repeat of the previous one, except that Mr. V was able to avoid all punishment by controlling his drinking. However, he had been drinking beer every night during the intervening week. Although his wife agreed that he had probably not exceeded the 0.045 level, she objected to the frequency of his alcohol intake. In effect, we had somewhat shortsightedly modified the rate and quantity of alcohol consumption. However, we still had the problem of establishing the circumstances under which drinking could appropriately occur.[9] Accordingly, we initiated the next phase of therapy by conducting a searching behavioral analysis of Mr. V's drinking problem. This analysis revealed that his drinking was reliably precipitated by feelings of anger, frustration, and depression. In particular, conflicts with his boss, his wife, or family members almost invariably led to his drinking with the avowed intention of anaesthetizing himself against disagreeable thoughts and feelings. He would drink by himself at home. Interestingly, Mr. V had no difficulty controlling his

[8] *Editors' note:* With some clients the skillful use of imagined aversive consequences (just when they have an urge to smoke or drink) can be as effective (or more so) as experiencing the "real" consequences.

[9] *Editors' note:* A good example of why focusing only on consequences without considering the cues (the antecedents of behavior) often fails.

drinking when he was in a good mood and in a social situation. But he lacked appropriate assertive skills for handling troublesome interpersonal situations. Once emotionally aroused, he would become bent on intoxication, literally telling himself, "To hell with it; I'm going to get drunk."

SUBSEQUENT SESSIONS

The technique of behavior rehearsal was employed in an attempt to reproduce some of the stressful situations that had served to instigate excessive drinking in the natural environment (Sobell & Sobell, 1973b). During succeeding sessions, one of the authors would role-play an adversary and deliberately expose Mr. V to increasingly more stressful social situations. All conversation was centered around emotionally charged themes that appeared to function as antecedent stimulus events for intoxication.[10]

Alcohol was available to Mr. V throughout each session but with the punishment contingency as introduced in session 3 (shock if he exceeded a quarter-ounce in a fifteen-minute drinking period). After two sessions, in which Mr. V successfully avoided shock, despite becoming quite emotional during the behavior rehearsal scenes, the shock contingency was discontinued. On no subsequent session did he exceed the target behavior of

drinking more than a quarter-ounce within fifteen minutes.

During this period Mr. V was disabled by reinjuring his back on the job. Despite considerable physical pain and psychological stress engendered by being out of work, he refrained from getting drunk, although he stated that he often had to fight the urge. He also moved back with his wife, who proved to be very supportive and sympathetic at this time.[11]

During these sessions the authors also modeled and differentially reinforced alternative, more appropriate assertive responses to stressful situations.[12] In addition to these therapeutic strategies, "thought stopping" was used to help Mr. V eliminate the rumination that often acted as a precursor to his drinking.[13] Two sessions were also devoted to relaxation training, in order to equip the client with a means of reducing tension other than alcohol.[14]

At that point (ten weeks after the beginning of therapy) Mr. and Mrs. V both felt sufficiently confident to contemplate seriously the move to Florida. It was decided that Mr. V would go down for about ten days to look for a job and a place for the family to live. Although he unfortunately met with little success (he was unable to gain acceptance in the Florida electricians'

---

[10] *Editors' note:* It was a good idea for him to practice some newly learned skills in the same emotionally charged setting that had previously been associated with excessive drinking.

[11] *Editors' note:* A fortuitous factor—but not entirely so. Remember that the authors had invited the wife to participate in the treatment, despite her initial skepticism.

[12] *Editors' note:* See articles 54 and 55 on assertiveness training.

[13] *Editors' note:* Thought stopping is described in Article 32.

[14] *Editors' note:* Examples of relaxation have been provided in articles 2, 7, 24, 27, 30, 36, 37, 38, 40, and 56.

union), he remained completely sober for the duration of the trip. On his return he became very depressed, drank about half a pint of whiskey over the course of the first day after his return, but still did not exceed the rate of intake established during the training sessions.

Mr. V was seen for only three sessions over the next three months. The recurrence of his back problems continued to frustrate his vocational plans and necessitated his wife's taking a job. It is striking, however, that, even under such stressful conditions, he was able to control his rate of drinking within the prescribed limits. Not once did his wife report that he had become drunk, despite the fact that the authors had impressed upon both Mr. V and his wife the importance of providing accurate information, so that the program could be changed if necessary.

Shortly after Mr. V's return from Florida, contingency contracting was introduced, in order to facilitate the maintenance of his newly acquired self-control of alcohol consumption (see Miller, 1972).[15] The couple agreed to sign a contract with the authors, stipulating the appropriate stimulus conditions under which drinking could take place. Drinking was permitted only if Mr. V was in a good mood and in a social situation. All other instances, particularly when he was upset, angry, or depressed, were strictly prohibited. In addition, the acceptable rate and amount of alcohol consumed were specified: a maximum of four ounces of

alcohol over a period of two consecutive days. A breach of the contract resulted in forfeit of $10 (a sizable sum for the financially hard-pressed couple), which had been deposited with the authors, to the organization that Mr. V most disliked—the Salvation Army—together with a letter commending it on its efforts!

Mr. V violated this agreement within two weeks of its inception, thus losing the money to the Salvation Army. He protested and tried to dissolve the contract, but he quickly settled down and reluctantly accepted the arrangement. Interestingly, Mr. V himself phoned the authors to report his "infraction" without his wife's intervention. We regarded this as a sort of confirmation of our impression that he was very candid in monitoring his drinking and that the admittedly subjective data that we had been receiving were valid. (Not all clients will be this cooperative, and contingency contracting in more difficult cases will undoubtedly raise problems of how breaches are to be ascertained and by whom.)

No other excesses occurred during the approximately two-month period that the contract remained in effect. Mr. V was last seen toward the end of July 1973. Although he continued to have serious difficulties with his back, which severely impaired his ability to function as an electrician, he had not relapsed into his former alcoholic pattern. His drinking was largely confined to social situations. On occasion he did consume some alcohol in response to the physical discomfort that he was experiencing. However, he reported that he was now able to monitor his drinking appropriately and to

15 *Editors' note:* Other examples of contingency, contracting are provided in articles 3, 7, 11, 17, 19, 31, 32, 39, 52, and 60.

maintain his level of intoxication within socially acceptable limits at all times. He appeared to have learned alternative strategies for coping with emotional stress and was relating well to his wife and family, who in turn were substantially happier and more supportive of Mr. V. No further contact was had with Mr. V. A social worker on the case of Mr. V's mother-in-law, who also had some contact with Mr. V and his wife, had not reported any subsequent drinking problems by the beginning of 1974.

references

Lovibond, S. H. & Caddy, G. Discriminated aversive control in the moderation of alcoholics' drinking behavior. *Behavior Therapy*, 1970, 1, 437–444.

Miller, P. M. The use of behavioral contracting in the treatment of alcoholism: A case report. *Behavior Therapy*, 1972, 3, 593–596.

Nathan, P. E., Goldman, M. S., Lisman, S. A. & Taylor, H. A. Alcohol and alcoholics: A behavioral approach. *Transactions of the New York Academy of Sciences*, 1972, 34, 602–627.

Pattison, E. M., Headley, E. B., Gleser, G. C. & Gottschalk, L. A. Abstinence and normal drinking: An assessment of changes in drinking patterns in alcoholics after treatment. *Quarterly Journal of Studies on Alcohol*, 1968, 29, 610–633.

Silverstein, S. J., Nathan, P. E., & Taylor, H. A. Blood alcohol estimation and controlled drinking by alcoholics. *Behavior Therapy*, 1974, 5, 1–15.

Sobell, M. B. & Sobell, L. C. Evidence of controlled drinking by former alcoholics: A second year evaluation of individualized behavior therapy. Paper read at the 81st annual convention of the American Psychological Association, Montreal, August 31, 1973a.

Sobell, M. B. & Sobell, L. C. Individualized behavior therapy for alcoholics. *Behavior Therapy*, 1973b, 4, 49–72.

DRUG ADDICTION

15. TREATING DRUG ABUSE BY TREATING ITS CAUSES[1]

RICHARD BALE   Veterans Administration Hospital, Palo Alto, California
BEVERLY POTTER   Lewis and Allen Associates, Palo Alto, California

One of the most difficult problems facing the counselor of students is the

[1] This work was supported by grant DA-00384 from the National Institute of Mental Health. The authors also wish to thank Mr. Robin Gilbert, Director of the 101A1 Family at the Veterans Administration Hospital, Palo Alto, California, for his support and input to our thinking about these issues.

abuse of drugs. Concerned teachers and distressed parents often refer the student, who is likely to have no desire to enter counseling or to discontinue his use of drugs. The therapeutic relationship becomes one of coercion by the counselor (to help the student "break the habit") and intimidation by the client (through the use of street language and talk about previous drug experiences). In trying to establish rapport with the student, the counselor may react positively to extensive talk about drug experiences (sometimes called "drugalogs") and may even share verbally some of his own experiences with drugs. The failure of this approach results from the fact that the conditions or antecedents of drug use are not attended to by the counselor. In fact, the counselor is himself behaving in a way perfectly analogous to that of the client himself: *He is addressing real-life problems of coping and competence by dealing with drugs!* Whereas the client takes drugs to avoid confronting stresses and other difficulties, the counselor now talks about drugs instead of those difficulties in living.

The central question is as follows: Are drugs really the problem to be addressed by the counselor? Certainly the use of illegal drugs, particularly the amphetamines and barbiturates, can cause physical impairment and loss of health and can subject the client to risk of arrest for their use. In the case of narcotics, the high expense of the drug normally creates a need for substantial illegal activity and further risk of arrest and confinement.

However, what is often ignored is the fact that these same drugs provide highly effective, if only short-term, solutions to many of the stresses and agonies so acute in adolescence: anxiety, alienation, interpersonal inadequacies, feelings of worthlessness, and boredom. Through the use of various drugs the individual is able to regulate his mood states, lower his anxiety, feel more powerful, and stimulate himself. The tragedy of the pattern is that he

has used an external agent to alleviate problems and has failed to develop skills necessary to deal with the inevitable future pressures and problems in his life. This cycle becomes vicious and destructive until the person is finally overwhelmed by problems and comes to the attention of therapeutic or legal systems.

THE FAMILY: DRUG-ABUSE TREATMENT IN THE HOSPITAL

An alternative approach to dealing with the use of drugs is virtually to ignore drugs while teaching the client the interpersonal and other skills necessary to solve problems productively and to deal with emotional stress. This is the approach taken by many therapeutic communities, including the one described here, the 101 Program at the Palo Alto Veterans Administration Hospital, known as The Family. Talk about drugs is forbidden, and many members have difficulty in remembering which drugs are abused by their fellow patients, although they are aware of an enormous amount of other personal information. Members of the community work on a variety of core problems, which are best illustrated by presenting the results of a rating scale used in The Family. It asks the question, "Which three of the following behaviors and attitudes are most important for (a particular program member) to be working on in the next week?" Each patient was ranked by each other patient and staff member as to his three most important problem areas. The frequency with which the items were rated in the top three for all patients in the program appears in Table 1.

TABLE 1   Patient-Staff Ratings of Problems at The Family

Problem	Percentage
Understand his problems better	65.0
Learn to express his honest feelings	50.0
Learn to like himself	45.0
Learn to get close to people	37.5
Resolve his guilt feelings	32.5
Become less passive	22.5
Develop new interests	17.5
Learn to make and carry out plans	10.0
Learn to ask for help	10.0
Become more independent	5.0
Learn to assume responsibility	5.0

$N = 40$.

Different patients are ranked quite differently on their three most important core areas, and the treatment system of The Family, though thoroughly structured, is individually designed for members' specific skill deficits and areas of relative incompetence. One individual may be able to fulfill various responsibilities quite reliably but may be unable to discuss his feelings openly with others. Another person may find it difficult to complete any task without constant supervision yet may display a variety of interpersonal skills.

The twenty-five or so members work with the assistance of a small group of paid staff to help one another with these core problems in a twenty-four-hour residential setting. (All members live in the program during their six months' tenure before "graduation.") Time and space limitations preclude a thorough description of the treatment process.[2] However, the process essen-

[2] Editors' note: A more thorough description is available from Robin Gilbert, Ward 101A1, Veterans Administration Hospital, Palo Alto, California 94304.

tially involves the use of a wide variety of social sanctions (like approval, physical affection, increased responsibility, and acknowledgment of increased status) and increased privileges (like greater personal freedom, weekend passes, overnight passes, release from household duties) to reinforce appropriate behavior.

Individual patterns of inappropriate and self-destructive behavior are invariably recreated in the treatment program, and feedback on present behavior is given constantly during many hours of intensive group sessions. Members are required to be extremely assertive in every behavior, which begins by yelling for the attention of the group leader in order to be recognized at any group meeting. Newer members are easily able to identify with the older patients and staff, who have gone through the same treatment process and serve as models for appropriate behavior. Inappropriate behavior is publicly pointed out to the extent that members are required to wear signs describing this behavior: "I am a motor mouth," "I deny everything," "I am a private person," and so forth. At all times, behavior and not the person himself is criticized.

The therapeutic process and its relation to an individual's problem areas and drug use may better be understood from a summary of the case of Paul, a former patient in The Family.

THE CASE OF PAUL

Paul, a twenty-four-year-old single white man of working class parents, had been periodically addicted to heroin; he had used amphetamines, barbiturates, and alcohol extensively and had completed several jail sentences for possession of drugs, breaking and entering, and driving while under the influence of alcohol.

When Paul entered high school, he had felt unattractive and extremely self-conscious in social situations. His feelings of inadequacy in heterosexual relationships were unshared with peers, as he progressively withdrew. He did poorly in his academic work (although tests revealed him to be of above average ability) and never participated in sports. He felt lonely, cut off, and unique.

Paul was introduced to alcohol by some acquaintances. He found that it helped him to feel relaxed and confident in social situations. In his sophomore year he began smoking marijuana and found that the act, not the effect of the drug itself, gave him entrance to an elitist group. He began to feel acceptance, status, and a sense of belonging. Later he began to use barbiturates in combination with alcohol to alleviate feelings of boredom and emotional distress.

Paul continued his pattern of heavy drinking and using marijuana and barbiturates during his two-year term in the marines. Returning to his home town, he discovered that his former friends now rejected him because of his military service. Once again he began to feel depressed, lonely, and separate. He escalated his drug use first to include amphetamines and then heroin, taking both intravenously. He found that these drugs made him feel more powerful and alleviated his loneliness, both by raising him from his depression and providing a new group of accepting peers, the junkie community.

Paul had tried repeatedly to stop using amphetamines and heroin. Each time that he would stop, his feelings of loneliness and inadequacy would return. His relationships with coworkers and women remained superficial and exploitative. Paul's periodic but heavy use of drugs led to overt rejection by nonusing friends and coworkers, further confirming his own view of himself as worthless and undeserving. In fact he "set up" these rejections in a passive way; others would always terminate the relationships.

Finally, after several brief but insincere attempts at therapy, and with a lengthy jail sentence hanging over his head, Paul was accepted by The Family. "For the first time in my life people didn't put up with my games. I had to be responsible for what I did. The emphasis was on trust and honesty, and I felt good. I felt important."

What Paul wanted was available in The Family: warmth, love, acceptance, a sense of belonging, a feeling of importance and competence. These had *always* been reinforcing to him, and his use of drugs had, for temporary periods in his life, been useful in gaining them. But in The Family, the *contingencies*, or requisite behavior, for these personal and social reinforcements were changed. These reinforcements were now consequences of honest and responsible behavior and of assertive actions. His former patterns of manipulation and self-destructive behavior were now dysfunctional and resulted in the loss of reinforcing events and privileges.

During his six months in the program, Paul worked on major problem areas. He learned to assume *responsibility* for his actions by being held publicly accountable for a multitude of duties (household work, scheduling, watch duty, leading therapy groups) and by accepting the consequences when he failed to fulfill a duty adequately. He learned to be *assertive*. "Before, I stuffed my feelings and hid. In the program, I learned to direct my anger verbally at what I was angry with and assert myself on what I wanted."[3] As with the other program members, Paul gained his privileges (like being able to make phone calls, to leave the program on a pass, to stay out overnight) by strongly asserting his wants directly. To each request, the patients and staff in positions of power in the program would maintain a consistently skeptical and negative view, so that only the most assertive behavior would sway them.

Paul's "stuffed" and displaced anger was not tolerated by other Family members, who required him to wear a large sign around his neck; it read, "I'm a private person and don't express my real feelings." Once again, he was able to gain the "privilege" of removing the sign after a week had elapsed by vigorously asserting why he no longer deserved to wear the sign and by presenting concrete behavioral evidence of the change before the group.[4]

Through mandatory personal "one to one" conversations with more than fifty other program members (in which he was required to gain a great deal of personal information, which was checked at various times) Paul learned how to share his personal feelings and came to understand various similarities in feelings and experiences with many others. By taking risks and sharing his privately held fears and doubts about himself, he learned to trust other Family members, who did not use his exposure of himself against him and who did not retreat from his revelations. (Paul's fear—like that of many others —was best expressed in the sentence "But who could love me *as I really am*?" The experience of trust in others and the training in many intimate and sharing exchanges laid a basis for the development of reciprocal friendships outside The Family. "I had to learn to let people know where I'm at and what I'm thinking and feeling, rather than be pleasing. I had to be sensitive to the

---

[3] *Editors' note:* Direct verbal expression of anger, though probably therapeutic within The Family, is not consistently reinforced in the larger community. Thus learning to discriminate when such expression will be helpful might be necessary.

[4] *Editors' note:* A good example of negative reinforcement. Paul worked hard to remove the aversive event (the sign). Thus his assertive behavior was strengthened by getting rid of the sign.

fact that others had needs. I could give part of myself and fulfill others' needs, and I had a *right* to ask for these things back."

Finally, Paul developed a feeling of self-worth and competence by being responsible, by helping others, and by being a role model for others.[5] He worked his way through a succession of roles involving increasing responsibility and became a "section leader," in charge of seven group sessions for one half the program's members each week. His good work was often praised by both the senior staff and program members, and his development was continually commented upon in community meetings involving the entire Family.

After graduation from The Family, Paul became a counselor in one of the rehabilitation programs in which he had previously failed. This program had experienced a leadership change and was in a transition period. At first there was some antagonism toward Paul because he favored and sought to use some of the techniques (including a heavy confrontation approach) that he had learned in The Family. This approach frightened and alienated many of the other staff.[6] However, in the eight months he has been on the staff, Paul has resolved these conflicts and made radical changes in his new program. He has been able to express his anger and other emotions during this

[5] *Editors' note:* Clearly these improved feelings seem to be the consequences of Paul's improved behavior.

[6] *Editors' note:* These reactions may have helped him to learn more precisely how and when anger can best be expressed.

painful transition process directly to other staff members and has been able to elicit and hear their hostility and fears. He has established a respected reputation for honesty and straightforwardness. He expresses confidence in his self-worth as an integral part of the program leadership.

When Paul was in The Family, he began an intimate relationship with a woman he hoped to marry. After he left the program, they lived together for seven months before Paul terminated the relationship. He thought that his girlfriend was "not willing to continue growing" with him and that they had begun to "play games" with each other. In the past, Paul would have behaved irresponsibly enough to push the other person into terminating the relationship and thus would have assumed no responsibility for the decision. While making this decision, Paul returned to an evening therapy group of The Family to share his fears, guilt, and hurt in leaving one he had loved. He asked for support and received it. He moved out of his apartment and began rooming with a staff member, with whom he is developing a deep friendship. When asked about his loneliness, he said: "I get lonely, and when I do I seek out a close friend and talk about it. I don't sit around and feel sorry for myself. I go out and try to meet new people."

In addition to working full time, Paul attends a local junior college in the evenings. He is doing well and is able to use others for help and resources. When he was having difficulty with a recent paper, he sought out one of the authors for assistance.

Paul still has problems. The difference after his experience in The Family is the process with which he solves those problems directly and assertively, without the short-term facilitation of drugs. He says: "In many ways, I'm socially retarded. I feel uncomfortable around new people, especially women. I don't know exactly what to say or how to act. But I push myself and confront these fears. I'm making a constant effort to meet new people." Paul reports that he has begun to "get himself together" but that he has many conflicts and unresolved problems. He is planning to seek individual counseling to help him in dealing with these continuing problems.

Paul is not very different from most of the people with drug problems who come to The Family. Problems achieving intimacy with others, as well as feelings of loneliness, alienation, and despair have been alleviated with drugs, and the skills necessary to deal with these problems have never been learned. Paul's particular self-destructive pattern—using drugs—was rarely discussed during his six months as a program member, and many of the newer members were relatively ignorant of his *addiction* history. What they did attend to, as did Paul, was his failure to learn the skills necessary to lead a meaningful life, which resulted for a period of time in his use of drugs.

CONCLUDING COMMENTS

The case of Paul presents several important dimensions of personal change —assertiveness, responsibility, and the ability to relate to others—and the contingencies that facilitate these changes, in an informal and anecdotal report. Currently, we are assessing

these and other important variables more systematically in several of the drug programs at the Veterans Administration Hospital in Palo Alto. We are administering the "Rathus Assertiveness Scale" and Wolpe and Lang's "Fear Survey Schedule." The "Rotter Internal-External Locus of Control Scale" gives us information on the individual's sense of personal control and responsibility. The "Schutz FIRO-B" and Cautela's "Reinforcement Survey Schedule" shed some light on the value and valence of interpersonal relationships. Finally, we have assessed, and are continuing to assess, patient functioning on a wide variety of social, economic, legal, and interpersonal variables at several points after they leave the drug programs.[7]

The residential setting has many advantages not available to the counselor in the school setting or to the therapist in private practice. Counselors and therapists are probably not faced with clients who are as severely disabled as are those in an institution. However, we can see from the case of Paul that self-destructive patterns were evident early in adolescence and might have been treated then.

The counselor usually encounters people when they are just beginning to use drugs. Although he does not have the same degree of control, the time, and the opportunity to observe each client in a wide range of behaviors, he can incorporate elements of the approach used in the residential program.

[7] *Editors' note:* Information and research results are available from Dr. Richard Bale, Veterans Administration Hospital, Palo Alto, California 94304.

In particular, he may focus the sessions away from talk about drugs by directly communicating that intention, as well as by ignoring drug behavior when it does occur. In treating the drug user, the counselor must focus on giving the client something—new skills—rather than merely taking something (drugs) away from him.[8] This is important in eliciting a commitment from the client, for his involvement in the drug culture has given him an identity as "addict," "junkie," "dealer," or "user" that is often his only source of competence and status. To have this sole identity stripped away is terrifying, and the counselor should expect clients to cling to it tenaciously. Through a skill-oriented approach, in which various personal competencies are developed *outside the context of drug use*, the counselor can increase his chances of gaining the confidence of his drug-using client. He can also help to develop the personal strengths that will alleviate the need for resorting to drug use to solve problems.

[8] *Editors' note:* An important point! Interpersonal skill in coping effectively with life's problems have to be learned. Drugs provide only a temporary and progressively destructive escape.

TEMPER OUTBURSTS

16. *THE TURTLE TECHNIQUE: A METHOD FOR THE SELF-CONTROL OF IMPULSIVE BEHAVIOR*

MARLENE SCHNEIDER AND ARTHUR ROBIN   State University of New York, Stony Brook

Mrs. S could see the blood rush to Dennis' face; the muscles of his back were becoming tense, and his shoulders began climbing up around his ears. Before she could do anything, it happened. He had ripped his writing paper into pieces and was throwing his desk over. The contents of the desk spilled out on the floor, and Dennis began to cry. Mrs. S felt helpless. She could see that Dennis felt helpless too. He looked around the room and saw all the children glaring at him.

Brian was working intently on his math paper. He wrote each answer carefully, putting the numbers down in perfect form. Tommy, having just finished, left his desk and went charging to the back of the room to turn in his work. In his enthusiasm, he bumped Brian's desk, causing a jagged line on a previously neat paper. Brian looked at his paper and then looked at Tommy; his eyes flashed, and he charged after him. Grabbing Tommy by the back of the neck, he threw him down and started banging his head on the floor.

Susan was curled up under the table in the back of the classroom. Mrs. B saw her there and went over to talk to her. She gently put her arm on Susan's rounded shoulders in order to coax her back into the group. Susan's eyes widened at the unexpected intrusion; her breathing quickened, and, without warning, she bit Mrs. B's arm and ran wildly to the front of the room.

What can we do for these children who lack the ability to cope with failure, who, out of frustration, throw temper tantrums, hit others, call them names, and suffer unnecessarily from the inability to control their impulses?

Behavior modifiers have traditionally responded to such problems with a series of contingency-management techniques, including systematic praise-ignore procedures, token economies, and punishment (O'Leary & O'Leary, 1972). All these techniques have in common an external locus of control in the person of the contingency manager. Although clearly successful, such external contingencies may not result in sufficient maintenance of improvement after termination of the treatment. Furthermore, such procedures are sufficiently time consuming so that, for many teachers, long-term treatment programs are not feasible.

Recently, self-control procedures for dealing with a wide variety of behavior problems in children and adults have been developed (Goldfried & Merbaum, 1973; Thoresen & Mahoney, 1974). These techniques hold out the promise of increased maintenance of behavior and decreased participation of contingency managers.

THE TURTLE TECHNIQUE

At the Point of Woods Laboratory School in Stony Brook, a self-control procedure was developed to help young emotionally disturbed children to control impulsive and aggressive responses to provocations in the classroom. The procedure is called the "turtle technique" because of the analogy to a turtle's going into its shell when threatened. The technique consists of four stages.

Learning To Respond to the "Turtle" Cue

The turtle technique can be applied flexibly to a variety of impulse-control problems in many situations. We shall present the procedure for implementing the technique in a group to reduce aggression and tantrums. More details can be found in Schneider (1974) and in the *The Turtle Manual* by Schneider and Robin (1973).[1]

Teaching the child to respond to the cue word "turtle," by closing his eyes and pulling his arms to his body, is initiated with the following story:

Once upon a time there was a handsome, young turtle. He was six years old, and he had just started first grade. His name was Little Turtle. Little Turtle was very upset about going to school. He preferred to be at home with his baby brother and his mother. He didn't want to learn school things; he wanted to run outside and play with his friends, or color in his coloring book. It was too hard to try to write letters or copy from the board. He wanted to play and giggle with friends— he even loved to fight with them. He didn't

[1] Those interested in more detailed instructions for instituting the turtle technique can send $1.00 for *The Turtle Manual* to Point of Woods Laboratory School, Department of Psychology, State University of New York, Stony Brook, New York 11794.

like sharing. He didn't like listening to his teacher or having to stop making those wonderful loud fire engine noises he used to make with his mouth. It was too hard to remember not to fight or make noise. And it was just too hard not getting mad at all the things that made him mad.

Every day on his way to school he would say to himself that he would try his best not to get in trouble that day. But, despite that, every day he would get mad at somebody and fight, or he would get mad because he made a mistake and would rip up his papers. So he always would get into trouble, and after a few weeks he just hated school. He began to feel like a "bad" turtle. He went around for a long time feeling very, very bad.

One day when he was feeling his worst, he met the biggest, oldest tortoise in his town. He was a wise old turtle, who was 200 years old and as big as a house. Little Turtle spoke to him in a very timid voice because he was very afraid of him. But the old tortoise was as kind as he was big and was very eager to help him. "Hey there," he said in his big bellowing voice, "I'll tell you a secret. Don't you realize you are carrying the answer to your problem around with you?" Little Turtle didn't know what he was talking about. "Your shell—your shell!" he shouted. "That's why you have a shell. You can hide in your shell whenever you get that feeling inside you that tells you you are angry. When you are in your shell, you can have a moment to rest and figure out what to do about it. So next time you get angry, just go into your shell." Little Turtle liked the idea, and he was very eager to try his new secret in school. The next day came, and he again made a mistake on his nice clean paper. He started to feel that angry feeling again and was about to lose his temper, when suddenly he remembered what the old tortoise had said. He pulled in his arms, legs, and head, quick as a wink, and rested until he knew what to

do. He was delighted to find it so nice and comfortable in his shell where no one could bother him. When he came out, he was surprised to find his teacher smiling at him. He told her he was angry about the mistake. She said she was very proud of him! He continued using his secret for the rest of the year. When he got his report card, it was the best in the whole class. Everybody admired him and wondered what his magic secret was.

After the story is told, there is a practice session in which the whole class is instructed to imitate the turtle response as demonstrated by the teacher. The response consists of pulling the arms in close to the body and putting the head down so that the chin rests on the chest. Then the teacher asks individual children to model the technique in response to various imaginary frustrating situations. These exercises are held daily, and the children are rewarded for good performances.

Learning Self-control
Relaxation Techniques

The rationale for relaxation is presented to the children by means of a continuation of the story, in which Little Turtle goes back to Big Turtle because he is still left with some "angry feeling in his stomach," despite his appropriate use of the turtle response. The children are instructed first to tense the muscles of the part of the body being trained and then suddenly to relax, with suggestions, delivered in a calm and gentle voice, that they be aware of how nice that part of the body feels when relaxed. This procedure is repeated with the arms, legs, hands, face, chest, stomach, and so on until the whole body is relaxed. After the relaxation has been practiced separately and mastered, it is incorporated into the turtle response. When the child is in the turtle position, the whole body is tensed for a slow count from 1 to 10, after which the body is suddenly relaxed. This relaxation is maintained for as long as necessary, usually a few moments.

Up until this time the cue word, "turtle," has been under the control of the teacher. The children are subsequently encouraged to initiate the turtle response and relaxation in frustrating situations themselves. Whenever a child is seen using this response, he is rewarded.

Learning Alternative Problem-Solving Strategies

Even though most children's initial reactions to the turtle technique are good, it is clear that some children lack the ability to find an appropriate behavior after finishing the turtle response. To help children to deal with this difficulty, social problem-solving techniques (D'Zurilla & Goldfried, 1971) are taught. Examples of various responses to a frustrating situation are given, and the alternative solutions are discussed with special reference to their ultimate consequences. Here are two examples.

If I hit Johnny, the teacher will get angry. She will punish me, and it will ruin my day. On the other hand, if I choose to control myself and ask the teacher to help me get my toy back, the day will continue to be good, and I can show myself how big I am.

If I rip my paper up because I made

a mistake on it, I will only have to start again. Another choice is to cross out my mistake neatly and continue so I do not waste time. That way I will have more time to play.[2]

Daily ten-to-fifteen-minute instruction sessions are held in the class, during which problem situations that have recently occurred are presented as material for the problem-solving activities. The teacher supports the problem-solving technique by cueing the children with the question "What are your choices?" She then supports appropriate choices with praise and by encouraging peer support. Later, the problem-solving technique is incorporated into the turtle response by having the children use the time in the relaxation phase (previously described) for imagining behavioral alternatives and their consequences. This step is very important. The child now has an opportunity to choose from among several alternative responses, whereas previously he was locked into only one impulsive response. This choice gives him a power over his environment that he did not have before learning to control these impulses.

Developing Peer Support

Long-term maintenance of the turtle technique in the classroom requires that the social environment support

[2] *Editors' note:* These problem-solving techniques involve "self-instructions," in which the child directs himself to engage in a certain action, as well as a type of personal decision-making based on selection of what to do from among alternatives.

and reward children for use of the procedure. This is accomplished by means of a peer-support program. From the first introduction of the turtle program and all through the instruction sessions, peers are rewarded for supporting the child who is "doing turtle." They are taught to praise and applaud the child using the technique. They also learn to help fellow students by cueing them when they seem to be in situations that might precipitate fights or tantrums. The peer supporter is rewarded in the same way as the child who is "doing turtle." For example, if Johnny sees Bill and James about to fight and cues them to use the turtle technique, then he will be praised along with Bill and James. In addition, the teacher can call attention to the fact that it is more difficult and takes more strength to "do turtle" than to give in to the first impulse to fight. In this way, the peer-support stage of the program provides the child with the needed environmental support to maintain use of the procedure.

Teaching the technique takes fifteen minutes a day for approximately three weeks, after which instruction sessions are gradually reduced to a frequency of twice a week. Group activities are supplemented by individual practices sessions, in which the teacher involves children in role playing in problem-solving situations.

OUTCOMES

In a recent evaluation of the effectiveness of the turtle technique (Robin & Schneider, 1974), the procedure was taught to fifteen emotionally disturbed children in three special-education classrooms. Trained observers were sent into the classrooms three times a week to record aggressive behavior. Dennis, Brian, Tommy, and Susan are four typical children who participated in the research. As a result of the teachers' cooperation and the children's efforts, aggression and tantrum behavior was reduced 61 percent by Dennis, 70 percent by Brian, 57 percent by Tommy, and 36 percent by Susan. Overall, two of the participating classes manifested respectively decreases of 46 percent (significant at .001 level) and 54 percent (significant at .005 level) after eight weeks of treatment. In a third class in the study the technique was introduced too late in the semester to provide meaningful results.

After implementation of the turtle technique, the climate of the classes showed a marked improvement. Dennis could be seen smiling proudly as he displayed his work on the rear bulletin board. Susan spent much of her time helping others with their work. Brian continued to spend much time by himself, but he was the first one to give peer support if there was a hint of a disturbance in the classroom. Perhaps most important, the teacher could spend much more of her time assisting the children with their academic work, rather than functioning as a referee or disciplinarian.

In our experience, a child often starts "doing turtle in my head" without prompting a few weeks after the introduction of the technique. He no longer has to depend on physical withdrawal reactions for self-control. It appears that for some children a reduction in aggression is maintained, regardless of the continued presence of an overt response.[3]

This technique has produced some interesting and unexpected side effects. Only one week after introducing the technique, a teacher was absent for two consecutive weeks. In her absence several of the children took on her role of cueing "turtle" whenever a disturbance was brewing and reinforced their peers for appropriate use of the turtle procedure.

In another class two withdrawn children in the room responded so well to the peer-support program that they started joining their classmates in giving other positive support. Robert, aged ten years, formed a close friendship with a girl in his class. It was the first time he had made friends with any of his peers at school.

Jim had learned the technique at Point of Woods Laboratory School. His parents were involved in a bitter divorce proceeding. One night his father came into the house, beat his mother, pulled the telephone out of the wall, and kidnapped his little brother. When the father left, Jim's mother found him in his bed relaxing in the turtle position. She believed that Jim's knowledge of the technique had helped him to cope with this difficult experience.

Other clinical indications suggest that there is a carryover outside the classroom situation. Several parents have asked that we clarify to the children that one of their choices is to hit back when appropriate. It seems that some children had been "doing turtle" when confronted or attacked during street play, with the consequences of a few bloody noses, of course. We would like to emphasize here that the purpose of this technique is not to stop children from being aggressive altogether—only to give them control over their aggressive impulses. Clearly, it is important to teach the child that self-defense may be an appropriate alternative.[4]

We are now in the process of revising the technique for use with adults and older children. In one instance of marital abuse, the husband was successfully taught the technique, using the cue word "stop," and a modified version of the turtle position. He was instructed in relaxation techniques and problem-solving paradigms that were appropriate to his situation. In a clinical case involving a ten-year-old, the technique was successfully taught by the therapist with only a minimum of support from the classroom teacher.

In addition to the teachers' manual, a clinical manual is now being developed for use by counselors. It will outline the procedures to be used by the counselors to help a child outside the classroom. Counselor instruction would cut down considerably on the class and teacher time that is now necessary to institute the technique.

---

[3] *Editors' note:* Not surprisingly, for self-control is primarily a covert, or "in the head," process. But note that the training is not designed to inhibit the honest expression of emotion, a problem Paul exhibited in Article 15. Instead, it is to train a constructive response to that emotion.

[4] *Editors' note:* A turtle has to stick its neck out to get ahead.

references

D'Zurilla, T. J. & Goldfried, M. R. Problem solving and behavior modification. *Journal of Abnormal Psychology*, 1971, 78, 107–126.

Goldfried, M. R. & Merbaum, M. (Eds.). *Behavior change through self-control.* New York: Holt, Rinehart and Winston, 1973.

O'Leary, W. D. & O'Leary, S. G. *Classroom management.* New York: Pergamon, 1972.

Robin, A. L. & Schneider, M. The turtle technique: An approach to self-control in the classroom. Unpublished manuscript, State University of New York, Stony Brook, 1974.

Schneider, M. Turtle technique in the classroom. *Teaching Exceptional Children*, 1974, 7, 22–24.

Schneider, M. & Robin, A. L. *The turtle manual.* Technical publication, Point of Woods Laboratory School, State University of New York, Stony Brook, 1973.

Thoresen, C. E. & Mahoney, M. J. *Behavioral self-control.* New York: Holt, Rinehart and Winston, 1974.

17.   HELPING BILL REDUCE AGGRESSIVE BEHAVIORS: A NINE-YEAR-OLD MAKES GOOD

THOMAS S. TOBEY AND CARL E. THORESEN[1]   Learning House, Palo Alto, California

In the last five years, family-style residential treatment facilities, in which behavioral methods are used, have helped many children and adolescents to change (Bailey, Wolf & Phillips, 1970; Phillips *et al.*, 1971; Wolf, Phillips & Fixsen, 1972). These small treatment "homes" have been developed as alternatives to the large, costly, and often problem-producing institutions typically used for delinquent and emotionally disturbed youth. Learning House, a family-style residential treatment facility in Palo Alto, California, is one such facility. In this article a variety of methods are described to illustrate this approach to helping problem children and their parents.[2]

In the Learning House program the traditional diagnostic categories that are so often used to classify deviant children are disregarded. Instead, specific target behaviors of the child are identified that require change in home, school, and community settings. A refined point system, contingency contracting, behavioral observation,

[1] Thomas S. Tobey is a former Learning House teaching parent and program coordinator. Currently he is a doctoral candidate in counseling psychology at Stanford University and chairperson of the Learning House Committee of Community Resources. Carl E. Thoresen is founder and Executive Director of Learning House. The suggestions and comments of Janis Wilbur, Curtis Wilbur, and Karen Tobey are gratefully acknowledged.

[2] General information on behaviorally oriented residential-treatment homes for children can be obtained by writing to Learning House, 534 Channing, Palo Alto, California 94301, as well as to Achievement Place, Lawrence, Kansas 66044.

teacher consultation, and parent counseling are used at Learning House to provide a consistent treatment system for each child. These methods allow decisions about each child to be made primarily on the basis of observed frequencies of specific behaviors.

Learning House emphasizes its family-style setting for four boys and two girls who reside there. The children and their families are referred from various social agencies like the Department of Juvenile Probation and Social Services. Two professionally trained married couples serve as "teaching parents" on an alternating weekly basis. The two sets of teaching parents are assisted by a part-time program coordinator (a former teaching parent) and an executive director in such areas as revising the program, developing specific treatment procedures, working with community agencies, and consulting with school personnel. In addition, a board of directors composed of local community members provides help on a variety of problems such as home repair and community relations.

OVERVIEW OF THE LEARNING HOUSE PROGRAM

A point system is used to provide an immediate, explicit, and recordable measure of behavior for each child. The behaviors of each child earn consequences, according to a specific list. Table 1 presents a small sample of such behaviors. A typical day offers the opportunity for each child to earn points in such areas as personal hygiene (like brushing teeth), household chores (like vacuuming), social skills (like proper greeting of a visitor), peer interaction (like cooperative play), academic skills (like class participation), and recreation (like sportsmanship). Designated behaviors are observed and earn positive or negative

TABLE 1   Sample of Observed Behaviors and Their Point Consequences

Behavior	Points Earned or Lost
Social	
cooperative play	+ 1,000/30 minutes
temper (slamming objects, voice out of control)	− 500
interrupting another	− 500
volunteering to help	+ 500
lying	− 1,000
good hygiene (washing face, hands, brushing teeth)	+ 1,000
Maintenance	
setting table	+ 500
putting groceries away	+ 300/sack
vacuuming	+ 1,000–2,500
washing dishes	+ 3,000–4,000
Academic	
late leaving for school	− 100/minute
homework (at home)	+ 5,000/hour
trouble call from school	−10,000

points.[3] The subtotal of points, recorded on a point card each day, is exchanged for privileges (see Table 2). Each child carries the point card with

[3] *Editors' note:* A controversial feature of this point system is that points are subtracted for undesired behavior, thus introducing a mild form of punishment of the child. An interesting experiment would compare the effects of this system with other variations, for example a system in which points were not permanently subtracted but were put in a "trust fund," so that they could be restored to the child when some subsequent desired behavior had occurred.

him or her so that points can be awarded (or lost) as soon as possible after the behavior has occurred. Privileges are activities that children typically enjoy, like bicycle riding, watching television, receiving allowance, and swimming. Table 3 presents a partial list of privileges. Each child becomes eligible for a greater variety of privileges as he proceeds through the promotional system.

Each child progresses through a series of steps based on a combination of demonstrated competencies and

TABLE 2   The Daily Point Card

Points Made	Code	Description of Behavior	Points Giver	Points Lost	Code	Description of Behavior	Points Taker
1250	A	Reading	KT	400	S	Late to bed	KJ
1000	S	Quiet bedtime	KT	300	S	Neg comment	BJ
500	M	Good manners	KT	300	A	Being mean	BJ
500	S	Neat appearance	KT	300	S	Name calling	KJ
1000	S	Early to school	KT	500	S	Back talk	KJ
4000	A	Good school report	KT	1000	S	Swearing	KJ
2500	A	Reading	KT	1000	S	Lying	KJ
500	A	Homework	KT	500	S	Back talk	KJ
5000	A	Reading	KT				
500	M	Making rice	BJ				
200	S	Answering phone	BJ				

TABLE 3   Partial List of Privileges on Weekly System

Privilege	Weekly Point Exchange
"Basics" (care privileges)	1,500
going outdoors on Learning House property	
using telephone to call friends in the local area	
(all calls to parents must be approved by teaching parent)	
using house games in study room and sports equipment	
on Learning House grounds	
using radio and record player	
Bedtime stories	1,500
Television time	5,000
Use of bicycles	4,000
Allowance $ .50/week	5,000
$1.00/week	10,000

point accumulations. At first, a child's program is limited to a simple exchange of one isolated behavior for a single privilege (the item-exchange system). For example, "Bill, when you have finished putting your clothes in the dresser I will show you around the house." Typically a child spends about one day on the item system. The child then progresses through a sequence of daily, weekly, merit, and homeward-bound systems in an effort to attain the final objective of returning home or "graduating" to a foster home. The daily and weekly systems are based upon the point system, as well as on success in accomplishing individual behavioral goals.[4] For example, one child's goal was to go for ten consecutive school days without getting into any physical fights at school. To help him accomplish this goal, new ways of developing self-control in typical fighting situations were taught through modeling, rehearsal, and instructions to achieve this goal.

The merit system is the first step toward a more natural contingency program, one without points and with the privileges usually enjoyed by children. The final phase is called "homeward bound." In this phase the child is given more responsibility for his own behavior. He also begins to make a systematic reentry into his own family's style of living. A carefully monitored system of behavior observation continues during this period, in order to

pinpoint areas of potential trouble and reversion to old behavior patterns. Observation also provides the opportunity to reinforce the child and his family for adaptive behaviors. The behavioral-observation data on the child and parent are also used during the weekly parent counseling sessions.[5]

THE CASE OF BILL

Bill was a nine-year-old ward of the juvenile court and was referred to Learning House after spending three months in the local juvenile detention facility. He had been in trouble with the juvenile authorities since he was six years old. He had been cited for running away from his natural mother's home in an attempt to locate his natural father. Later both parents were cited for child abuse and inability to control the child. Bill was then placed in the custody of the juvenile probation department for placement. At least five attempts had been made to place him in a suitable foster family, without success. He would frequently become aggressive with younger peers, would seldom attend school, and, when he did, was difficult to control. He spoke in almost inaudible tones and displayed noticeable fear when dealing with most adult figures, especially males.

Bill was one of four brothers. His older brother had been successfully placed in a foster home. He had two infant half-brothers, who lived at the

---

[4] At first, a child's progress through the various systems was based solely on the acquisition of points. Recently, however, points have been combined with accomplishing specific behavioral goals ("goal target behaviors").

[5] Editors' note: As the child's behavior is largely a function of the parents' behavior, it is vital that the parents learn ways of responding more positively to the child's improvements.

home of his mother. In Bill's last placement before Learning House, he had been removed because of an attempted suicide and because of physically abusive behavior with a foster sibling. Despite flagrant abuse by his own mother, Bill still expressed a strong desire to return to her home.

Bill's first few weeks at Learning House were comfortable and secure for him. He arrived two weeks before Christmas as the first child in a new facility. He adapted to the contingency-point system with little difficulty. He responded very positively to the teaching parents' expressions of warmth and affection, and he especially enjoyed the frequent reading of stories at bedtime. He expressed great surprise when informed that he could exchange his points for such privileges as leaving the Learning House grounds, watching television, and eating special afternoon treats. He seemed noticeably impressed that he was being trusted to care for his own behavior.[6]

The opportunity to visit his real home for Christmas became the first objective that Bill worked to achieve. A special contract was drawn up with him; it stated explicitly, "When this contract is completed, you will have earned the privilege of going home to see your family on Christmas." Bill completed the contract by earning a predetermined number of points (a total of 50,000). A further stipulation

[6] It may seem paradoxical that a child would perceive a tightly structured point system as offering more freedom and privileges. The key seems to be consistency, predictability, and a sense of control; that is, the child knows in advance what will happen if he behaves in certain ways.

was that he must earn a minimum of 5,000 points each day. He carefully charted his progress by coloring in a blank outline of a Christmas tree with each day's total. Bill completed this contract with little difficulty. He was very pleased that he had done it himself.

Dealing with Problem Behaviors

Shortly after Christmas, with the start of school, some of Bill's problem behaviors appeared. He disliked being "forced into doing things," to use his words. On the second day of school he announced that he was not going to school and that he did not like it at Learning House. As this kind of verbal behavior had been a problem in the past, special attention was paid by the teaching parents to the events that followed. They explained that attending school was something that he must do as part of the program at Learning House. Reluctantly, Bill finally agreed to leave for school, but he did not report to his classroom. Instead he "ran away." Thanks to close coordination with the local school authorities, the teaching parents were immediately informed of his absence. Within one hour Bill returned to Learning House to announce that he had been "sent home by the principal." He was told that this was not true. He was also told how many points he had lost for lying and for disobedience in not reporting to school on time. Bill seemed confused at this point because he had not been able to manipulate his new parents.

Bill turned and ran out of the house, despite a reminder that such behavior would result in a further loss of points. Shortly afterward he returned, this time brandishing a tire iron in his hand. He informed the teaching parents that he had found the iron in the bushes next door. He added, "If I am bad enough, I can go back to Juvenile Hall." This contingency had worked in the past with numerous foster parents, so Bill had every reason to believe that it would work again. The teaching parents told Bill: "You have just two choices—either you decide to return to school, or you will sit in this chair and do nothing else for the remainder of the day. Those are your choices. What are you going to do?"[7]

Bill became belligerent, swinging the tire iron, swearing, and flailing at the teaching parents. This kind of behavior was deemed dangerous and beyond the reasonable limits of what could be ignored. Thus the teaching parents physically subdued Bill, took the tire iron, and placed him in the "time out" room. He was told, "When you can be quiet, that means no noise at all, for at least three minutes, then you can come out."[8] Bill was quiet after five minutes. However, he became belligerent immediately after the door to the time-out room was opened. He was again placed in the room. He was even more aggressive this time, banging on

the walls and swearing profusely. He settled down, however, a few minutes after the same terms as before were stated to him.

Bill returned to school that same day. He seemed to realize that the teaching parents intended to, follow through on what had been said. They were not going to be manipulated by his physical outbursts and verbal threats. Bill received a similar message from his classroom teacher at school. After the first ten days of school Bill did not miss a day, nor did he ever again indicate that he disliked school. This was a real beginning for Bill. Although outbursts occurred at least six times under similar circumstances over the next few weeks, Bill did begin to change.[9]

His running away and threats to run away usually occurred when he did not get his way in some activity. He would frequently become angry in these situations. Being asked to go to bed was an example. When pressed on this request, Bill would run out of the house, dressed only in his pajamas. Rather than disappearing, he would try a series of antics that included tapping on the windows of the house, yelling expletives from the street, and screaming in a loud voice. These behaviors were purposely ignored by the teaching parents and other residents. In addition, the other children at Learning House could lose points for inappropriate behavior by responding to Bill's antics in any way. Within thirty minutes, after no response to his behavior,

---

[7] *Editors' note:* A nice way of putting it! Bill still had a choice.

[8] Rather than use direct physical punishment to suppress extreme negative behaviors that cannot be ignored, for example, uncontrollable temper outbursts and threats of physical violence, the teaching parents used "time out from positive consequences." The child was placed briefly in a small room away from others, with nothing to do. The terms for leaving the time-out room were always clearly specified to the child in advance.

[9] *Editors' note:* The teaching parents' consistent follow-through in word and deed was probably unique in Bill's experience.

Bill would typically return to the house, quietly walk up the stairs, and climb into bed. When he was finally in his bed, Bill was informed by the teaching parents: "Bill, we are glad you decided to come to bed by yourself. You will lose points, but it will be less because you did so voluntarily. If you go to bed the next time you are asked without any hassle then you can receive points for being cooperative." The following morning he would record his point loss on his card. Bill's pattern of behavior was not easily extinguished because it had always worked for him in the past. Progress was slow, nerve-wracking, yet sure. To balance Bill's loss of others' attention for negative behavior and to strengthen actions that were incompatible with running away, swearing, and verbal abuse, he was given significant amounts of attention for *any sign* of cooperative behavior and following directions. Bill seemed initially puzzled by this response because he had received attention in the past only for negative behaviors. He was learning, however, that being cooperative, following directions, and doing his share of work around the house would provide a great deal of attention and approval.

At school, a few target behaviors were being observed, for example, paying attention to the teacher's instructions, positive interactions with peers, and daily attendance. The teacher reported the results daily to the Learning House staff by means of a daily school card (see Figure 1). Bill could earn or lose points for his behavior at school, as well as at home. He was able to correct his inappropriate behavior at school within a few weeks. He seemed to enjoy his teacher, especially her attention, and he met new friends and earned many points for his school behavior. Bill knew that by earning more

---

DAILY SCHOOL CARD

Name: BILL HARPER

Class/School: Madison

Date: January 19

YES	NO	
☐	☐	Paid attention and studied during class time.
☐	☐	Obeyed the classroom rules.
☐	☐	Completed assigned work on time.
☐	☐	Arrived to class on time.

SIGNATURE

FIGURE 1   Daily school card.

points he would soon become eligible to go home to visit on a weekend.

Bill's behavior began changing, although not with the same ease and speed as in the beginning. His actions were still inconsistent. He continually "tested" the Learning House system for consistency and consequences: threatening to return to Juvenile Hall, engaging in excessive teasing of peers, hiding from adults when asked to do something, and returning home late from activities at school. It took a series of individualized behavior contracts (see Figure 2), points, and a great deal of patience before Bill began moving up in the promotional system. A coordinated effort between Learning House and Bill's parents was essential to his eventual success.

When Bill came to Learning House, his natural mother and stepfather agreed to work one hour each week with the staff in a regular series of parent counseling sessions. However, a number of problems immediately arose. First, the teaching parents did not have a well-established standard procedure to follow with the parents.[10] Too much time was spent in trying to cover child-management skills that the parents seemed to know (but seldom to use). Second, Bill's step-

[10] Since then a formal written contract has been developed in which commitments of time and responsibility are detailed. The contract is signed by the parents, the teaching parents, and the referral agency staff worker. Although it has no legal force, the contract has proved effective psychologically.

BEHAVIOR CONTRACT

Name: BILL HARPER   Date: 5/12/73

Agreement

Me   During the next week (Mon.-Sun.) at Learning House I will volunteer for household tasks at least 2 times each day w/o reminder.

Them   During the next week (Mon.-Sun.) at Learning House, the teaching parents will post lists of household chores that need to be done.

Reward

Me   Get to stay up on Monday to watch a special television program of my choosing that ends before 10 P.M.

Them   Enjoying Bill's positive attitude when he volunteers to do a task. Make the TV available to him.

Give Up

Me   Television privileges for Mon. & Tues.

Them   Desserts at dinner for Mon. & Tues.

PARTICIPANT

WITNESS

FIGURE 2   Bill's behavior contract.

father refused to come to the weekly counseling sessions, viewing the efforts of Learning House as part of the "police establishment." As an ex-convict on parole, he was Learning House as another agency of authority. He also viewed Bill as a "problem kid," one that the mother should handle completely.

Bill's mother was very interested in regaining custody of her son. She attended sessions regularly. She was reminded how important her cooperation was in following through on Bill's behavior contracts, target behaviors, and other Learning House contingencies when Bill visited her at home. It was stressed that Bill should not successfully "manipulate" her as he had done in the past. Fortunately, Bill's mother was able to follow through with this commitment. Bill gradually learned that the pattern of consistent "cues and consequences" that he experienced at Learning House and at school was going to continue when he returned home.

Some of Bill's Changes

It is difficult to delineate all of the changes that Bill made while at Learning House during his seven-month stay. The specific causes or functional relationships between certain procedures and particular behavior changes remain unknown. However, Bill did demonstrate change, and he did succeed in completing the program.

Some changes do deserve mention. Bill's school attendance problem was eliminated, thanks to consistent follow-through by teaching parents, teachers, and other school authorities. Undoubt-

edly the daily monitoring (school card), point consequation, and consistent contact between teaching parents and Bill's teacher made a difference. The behavior contracts for such behavior as going to bed when told the first time helped Bill to become responsible for his own behavior. Bedtime was no longer a problem situation.

Bill learned to control antagonistic behaviors when dealing with peers because he knew that inappropriate behavior could result in point losses and slow his progress in the Learning House program. Many times contracts were set to enable Bill to work on very specific target behaviors, like teasing. He was able to reduce his teasing remarks from an average of more than ten a day to fewer than two. It is important that his reduction in teasing was reinforced by peers, as well as by adults. He seemed to have learned that more cooperative actions yield far more pleasant consequences from everyone.

Bill also demonstrated changes in his school behavior. One of his target behaviors was following the teacher's directions. Before leaving Learning House Bill would almost always accept requests by his teacher to put his materials away without fuss or anger. When he had first come to Learning House he had been unable to play any kind of board game (like checkers) that required concentration and cooperation. The same was true for organized sports. Invariably he would lose his temper when he lost or was losing. Yet Bill really enjoyed games and sports more than any other activity. When he left the program he was able to play a variety of board games (checkers, Monopoly, and so on), as well as to participate in such sports as touch football and basketball. He demonstrated a great deal of control and good spirit even when he lost. The fact that other children at Learning House were also working on these behaviors was undoubtedly helpful.

Bill was very much like most nine-year-old boys. He did not like such household chores as picking up his clothes, making his bed, cleaning the floor, and putting games away. A "no breakfast" rule worked well in establishing better behaviors. These house jobs had to be done before he could have breakfast. Learning how to do household jobs consistently was a very practical skill. Like other children at Learning House, Bill came from a large family in which everyone was expected to do his share of the work.

After several months, Bill was serving as a student manager at Learning House. He was appointed by the teaching parents to see that all household tasks were completed each day by the other children. He enjoyed this role of responsibility and performed well. He knew that he would lose points if jobs were not done properly after he had given his approval. He, of course, earned points and a lot of attention for doing a good job as manager.

A special problem of Bill's was his inappropriate verbal behavior. He generally spoke very softly, barely audibly, to adults (except, of course, when he had emotional outbursts). He seemed to have a generalized fear of verbally interacting with adults, and he rarely spoke above a whisper when in their presence. The teaching parents used practice sessions with a tape recorder and rehearsed telephone calls and answering to encourage Bill to increase his voice volume and the frequency of his interacting with adults. When he left the program, Bill was still speaking quietly. Some improvement had been made, especially in number of conversations initiated by Bill, eye contact, and voice loudness. Bill still has a speaking problem, especially when dealing with his stepfather. However, it is no longer considered a problem at school by teachers and peers.

Some Follow-Up

Bill had changed his behavior in a number of positive ways at home and at school. The boy who left Learning House after seven months was a different child in many ways. How well has Bill maintained these changes in the year since his departure? Unfortunately, only verbal reports from Bill's mother on his behavior at home are available. The uncooperativeness of his stepfather has prevented systematic behavorial observation by others in the home. Bill's classroom teacher has provided monthly information on a checklist of specific behaviors (see Figure 3). In addition, a staff observer, using a specific behavior checklist, provided data on Bill's home behavior for the first eight weeks of his stay at home. Results indicated that Bill had maintained his progress very well.

Since Bill left Learning House he has not been in trouble with the juvenile authorities. His mother reports that he is a "pleasure to have around." He has household chores, which he performs regularly without being reminded. There have been no incidents of run-

Name _____

School _____

LEARNING HOUSE BEHAVIOR SHEET

Please rate the above child in your classroom on a scale of 1-5 in the following behavior categories: 1–excellent performance, 2–very good performance—occasional encouragement needed, 3–average performance—could stand some improvement, generally acceptable behavior, 4–below average, frequently out of order, 5–below average, extremely poor performance, beyond my control most of the time.

Behavior

Following instructions of teacher	1	2	3	4	5	NA
Completion of assigned work on time	1	2	3	4	5	NA
Follows school rules	1	2	3	4	5	NA
Relations with peers (makes friends, talks to, is friendly with)	1	2	3	4	5	NA
Running away from authority (hiding from teacher and other adults)	1	2	3	4	5	NA
Putting tools away (books, paper, and other class items)	1	2	3	4	5	NA
Participation in group activities on voluntary basis	1	2	3	4	5	NA
Talking in an audible voice	1	2	3	4	5	NA
Academic performance (measured against self)	1	2	3	4	5	NA
Academic performance (measured against others)	1	2	3	4	5	NA

Please add any comments you may feel are pertinent to an objective description of the above child. Also, we would be interested in your own feelings regarding the child's adjustment to school community, home influence and citizenship.

FIGURE 3 Behavior assessment sheet.

ning away. The behavior checklist filed by Bill's teacher indicates a similar pattern of consistently acceptable behavior at school. The teacher rated Bill either excellent or very good 98 percent of the time in all ten categories on the checklist. She has always rated him as excellent in "respect for authority," a significant problem area before he came to Learning House. Bill's teacher also made the following comment about Bill's relations with his peers: "He serves as an excellent role model for many of my problem children." It seems apparent that Bill has maintained the progress made at Learning House and has established a new reputation in his own right.

references

Bailey, J. S., Wolf, M. M. and Phillips, E. L. Home-based reinforcement and the modification of pre-delinquents' classroom behavior. *Journal of Ap-*

plied Behavior Analysis, 1970, **3**, 223–233.

Phillips, E. L., Phillips, E. A., Fixsen, D. L. & Wolf, M. M. Achievement Place: Modification of the behaviors of pre-delinquent boys within a token economy. *Journal of Applied Behavior Analysis*, 1971, **4**, 45–59.

Phillips, E. L., Phillips, E. A., Fixsen, D. L. & Wolf, M. M. *The teaching-family handbook*. Lawrence: University of Kansas Printing Service, 1972.

Wolf, M. M., Phillips, E. L. & Fixsen, D. L. The teaching-family: A new model for the treatment of deviant child behavior in the community. In S. W. Bijou and E. L. Ribies (Eds.), *First symposium on behavior modification in Mexico*. New York: Academic Press, 1972.

PHYSICAL AGGRESSION

18. A GROUP APPROACH WITH ACTING-OUT BOYS

NANCY BROWN MILLER   Neuropsychiatric Institute, U.C.L.A. Center for the Health Sciences
RICHARD A. BROWN   Behavioral Medicine Associates, Santa Ana, California

Deviant classroom behavior has been effectively modified through the efforts of teachers, parents, and peers working as primary change agents within the school setting. In this paper we describe a program in which a school social worker, teachers, and a group of seventh-grade boys worked together to improve the social behavior and academic performance of the boys.

Disruptive classroom behavior is one of the most frequent reasons that children are referred for counseling in schools. Referrals are usually not made until after the teacher has been unable to modify the behavior through traditional methods of reasoning, threats, punishment, sending children to "the office," and calling parents. Most of the children referred are boys, and in junior-high-school settings, as peer influences gain more importance, more than one boy is often referred at a time. Typically, however, each boy is referred individually for counseling, and teachers frequently lay the "causes" of the disruptive behavior on emotional problems within the child or in his home environment. Disruptive behavior is frequently accompanied by poor academic performance.

The four junior-high-school boys described in this paper were all referred for individual counseling after "everything" had been tried and had failed. A group approach was used because the boys were exhibiting similar problems, shared the same classes, and had social contacts with one another. All the boys were of average intelligence, with long histories of low academic achievement and "failure to comply with rules." By the time that they had reached junior high school, they were all one to two years behind in reading and math skills and had been placed in the lowest of three "tracks" with other students who were also underachievers. Their reputations for disruptive behavior had preceded them into the junior-high-school setting, so the teachers were expecting them to present problems.

The program was carried out in a public school in a middle-class suburb of Chicago. The school included grades kindergarten through eight; the sixth, seventh, and eighth grades operated on a departmentalized program.

PROBLEM

Four seventh-grade boys were referred for counseling because of frequent talking out, hitting others, throwing objects, making noise, getting out of seats, chewing gum, and eating candy. They had all been suspended several times and at the time of referral had been told by the principal that they were on the verge of suspension again. (Both the principal and the boys recognized that suspension had no lasting effect on their behavior.) The social worker asked the teachers to rate the frequency of inappropriate social behaviors and appropriate academic behaviors, using the form shown in Figure 1. The results of their baseline ratings are shown in Figure 2.

METHOD

The social worker met with the teachers and proposed a plan for focusing on appropriate classroom behavior through the use of a daily behavior chart, on which each boy would receive a "grade" of "one," "two," or "three" for his behavior at the end of each class. The teachers were skeptical but willing to try "anything." They were instructed to praise observable appropriate behaviors and to ignore the disruptive behaviors for one week, at the end of which the program would be discussed and evaluated.

The social worker then met with the four boys, described the behaviors reported in the referrals, and proposed the new program. They were told that good "grades" could be traded in for a reward at the end of the week and asked what they would like to work for. The unanimous, enthusiastic response was money. In order to maximize the initial success of the program for both the boys and the teachers, the social worker agreed. Nickels would be paid for "ones" (for no inappropriate behaviors during one-hour classes) for one week. The boys would be able to earn a maximum of $1.10 each for "perfect" behavior. By the end of the week three of the boys had earned all "ones," and one boy, Tom, had received two "twos" (one or two inappropriate behaviors in a class) out of a total of twenty-two class periods.[1]

The teachers expressed both delight and pessimism ("This can't possibly last") and agreed to continue with the program. The social worker asked the boys to select a new reinforcer that would not cost money, and they decided that they would like to earn points to eat lunch at school (a practice forbidden by the district at that time). Permission was granted by the administration, and the boys decided that the goal should be 150

[1] *Editors' note:* These results clearly demonstrate that the boys had a great deal of control over their own behavior.

Student _____

Teacher _____

	Frequency of Occurrence				
Behavior	Very Fre-quently	Fre-quently	Occa-sionally	Rarely	Never
Initiated Talking Out					
Talked out but did not initiate					
Threw objects					
Made noise with objects					
Hit other student (initiated it)					
Hit back other student					
Chewed gum or candy					
Got out of seat					
Other inappropriate behavior:					
1.					
2.					
3.					
Academic					
Turned in homework					
Had proper materials for class					
Participated in class discussions					
Answered questions when called on					
Answered questions voluntarily					
Other:					
Scale Weighting	(3)	(2)	(1)	(0)	(0)

Comments: _____

_____

_____

FIGURE 1   Rating scale of acting-out and academic behaviors.

"ones"—which would take a minimum of six weeks to earn. The goal was reached within the minimum time by all four boys.

About four weeks into the program the teachers became tired of giving daily grades for behavior and began to expect the boys to behave appropriately without their efforts—in spite of the fact that they were no longer spending most of their class time reprimanding inappropriate behaviors. During this time, the social worker was meeting weekly with the teachers in a group; as they became less enthusiastic about the program, weekly individual sessions with each teacher were added to reinforce their efforts.[2]

During the fifth week of the program the teachers were again asked to rate the behaviors of the four boys. A decrease in acting-out behavior was noted along with an increase in academic work (see Figure 2). The same week the boys, in their weekly meeting with the social worker, began to talk about academic work and commented that, since they had begun to behave in classes, there was nothing to do except listen to the teacher or do classwork. They asked if they could modify their chart so they could earn points for academic work.[3] At this point the responsibility for developing a program was given entirely to them. They

devised a weekly report card on which each teacher was to record whether or not each boy brought books and so on to class, turned in homework, took a test, earned good grades on homework or test papers, and behaved in class. The boys presented the revised chart to the teachers for their approval. Points were assigned for both social and academic behaviors, with bonus points for any grade above a C and demerits for grades of D or F. They decided to work in teams of two, and whichever team reached 150 points first would be the winner.[4] A large chart, with two "thermometers" for recording progress, was hung in the social worker's office. The boys asked for and received additional time in the office to help one another with academic work. The social worker asked the boys what goal they would like to work for, but they could not decide and, in fact, never did decide.

This program began in the seventh week, at which time one of the boys, Tom, dropped out because he did not think he could do as well as the others.[5] The boys held a meeting with him and offered to modify the rules to make it easier for him, but he declined. Another boy from their class with similar problems entered the group at this time, and Tom was seen in individual counseling.

[2] *Editors' note:* A common problem. Unfortunately, improvement by others is often not enough of a reinforcer for the parent, counselor, or teacher, especially after some time has passed.

[3] *Editors' note:* A smart move! Why not directly encourage behavior that is incompatible with "acting out" in the classroom right from the beginning?!

[4] *Editors' note:* The rule could just as easily have been "As soon as your team reaches 150 points, you are a winner." Then there would not have to be any losers.

[5] *Editors' note:* Competition is great motivation for those likely to win. Those likely to lose would rather drop out: thus, the necessity of devising motivational systems so that everybody can be a winner.

In the eighth week the teachers again rated the behavior of the original four boys. Inappropriate social behaviors remained at an acceptable level, and academic behaviors showed a marked increase except for Tom's behaviors, which had begun to deteriorate in both areas (see Figure 2).

In the twelfth week, the social worker "forgot" to leave copies of the charts for the boys and was not in the school until Wednesday. A reversal occurred, as the boys decided to "get even." There was a significant drop in academic performance and an increase in acting-out behaviors. The teachers responded by increasing their yelling and reprimanding and once again filled out rating sheets (see Figure 2).

The charts were reintroduced, and the boys and the teachers began to behave appropriately again. The chart system continued for twenty-four weeks until the end of school. The social worker attempted to fade out the charts, but the boys stated emphatically that the charts helped them. The social worker told them it was important to test out their appropriate behaviors and erroneously insisted on a week without charts. The boys made their own charts out of paper towels and convinced the teachers to sign them. The charts were officially reinstated the following week. The rating scale demonstrated that academic work continued to be maintained and disruptive behavior continued to decrease. The exception was Tom, who was eventually transferred to a private school because he had failed the seventh grade and his classroom behavior had become unmanageable.

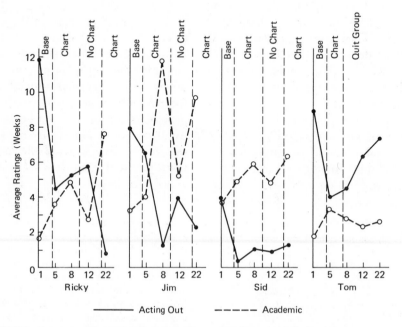

FIGURE 2   Average of teacher ratings for acting-out and academic behaviors.

DISCUSSION

The program described in this paper was designed to restructure the teacher-student interaction by focusing on appropriate behavior. All the boys had entered the junior-high-school setting with "negative halos"—everyone in their environment, including themselves, expected them to be disruptive and to show poor academic performance. It may also be argued that the disruptive behavior served as a negative reinforcer, providing them with a means for avoiding academic tasks that were aversive and usually resulted in failure. The inappropriate behaviors appeared to be maintained by both teachers and peers, for the reported behaviors were seldom produced by one boy in isolation. The success of the program indicates that teacher approval was still highly reinforcing to the boys. Although it was not tested, it appears probable that an individualized approach would have been far less successful because of the concomitant importance of peer attention. A group of boys can maintain peer support and earn teacher approval at the same time.

The use of charts served as a means for both giving the boys immediate feedback and providing a structure that would give consistent cues to the teachers to praise appropriate behavior.

One important aspect of the program was the development of a serious community problem that the social worker had inadvertently stimulated by using money as a reinforcer in the initial week of the program. As knowledge of the program spread in the community, parents began calling the principal to complain about children being "bribed" to be good. Of all the parental complaints, none ever came from the parents of the boys in the group. One of the parents in the district was on the school board and asked for a review of the program before the board. The social worker received complete administrative backing, the program was described in detail and the issue was resolved.[6]

In any behavioral program it is important to monitor the client's level of progress continually and to modify the program to maximize his functioning. In this program, the boys "got ahead" of the social worker when they asked to be graded on academic as well as social behavior. Timing is often critical, however, and it is possible that part of the success of the program was related to the boys' initiating the request and indicating their readiness to work on their academic behaviors. When the social worker tried to fade out the charts, the boys indicated that they were not ready; they wanted the structure and did not want to test their abilities to function without it. It is possible that the fading procedure was too rapid. A more gradual plan, with greater involvement by the boys, might have been more successful in testing the improved behavior of both the boys and the teachers.

[6] *Editors' note:* Sometimes it is more effective to use activities or special events as reinforcers in the beginning instead of money, in order to avoid problems with community and colleagues.

references

Backer, W., Madsen, C., Arnold, C. & Thomas, D. The contingent use of teacher attention and praise in reducing classroom behavior problems. *Journal of Special Education*, 1967, **1**, 287–307.

Bushell, D., Jr., Wrobel, P. & Michaelis, M. Applying "group" contingencies to the classroom study behavior of preschool children. *Journal of Applied Behavior Analysis*, 1968, **1**, 55–61.

Hall, R., Lund, D. & Jackson, D. Effects of teacher attention on study behavior. *Journal of Applied Behavior Analysis*, 1968, **1**, 1–12.

Patterson, G. *Teaching parents to be behavior modifiers in the classroom.* Eugene: Oregon Research Institute, 1970.

Patterson, G., Shaw, P. & Ebner, M. Teachers, peers, and parents as agents of change in the classroom. In Benson, F. (Ed.), *Modifying deviant social behaviors in various classroom settings.* Eugene: University of Oregon, 1969.

Thomas, D., Becker, W. & Armstrong, M. Production and elimination of disruptive classroom behavior by systematically varying teacher's behavior. *Journal of Applied Behavior Analysis*, 1968, **1**, 35–45.

19.   CONTROL OF PHYSICAL AGGRESSION THROUGH SCHOOL- AND HOME-BASED REINFORCEMENT

MARIE M. BRISTOL   Southeast Mental Health and Retardation Center, Fargo, North Dakota

"See me as soon as possible about a crisis in Mrs. Harris' class," the principal's note to me read. Attached to the note was the official referral form requesting my help. I was the visiting counselor who served three elementary schools and an experimental preschool program.

The "crisis" was an eight-year-old second-grader named Andrew. Three different views of his problem emerged from interviews with his teacher, his mother, and Andrew himself. According to the teacher, Andrew clearly had a poor self-concept. He did not like himself or others and showed his feelings of inadequacy by continually fighting on the school bus, in the classroom, and on the playground. His mother, who hadn't taken psychology courses, as the classroom teacher had, knew only that Andrew was unhappy

and did not have any friends. Andrew's statement of the problem was quite simple: "Nobody likes me, not even my teacher."

Before a counseling plan could be devised, it was important to decide which of the stated or implied behaviors should be the focus. If Andrew had a poor self-concept, should he be encouraged to make more positive statements about himself or to record the number of positive strokes he received from his teacher or classmates? Should he be taught more approach behaviors or skills in making friends, or should the first order of business be training Andrew to decrease or eliminate his verbal and physical assaults on his peers? The last problem seemed the most pressing and was much too serious simply to "ignore" while we worked on other problems.

Observation of Andrew in his classroom quickly convinced me that his feeling that others did not like him was a reasonably accurate judgment. In class children would walk two aisles away rather than go by his desk, for fear he would trip or poke them. On the bus no one wanted to sit with Andrew because he "got them into trouble." At my request, the teacher drew up a sociogram, asking the class to choose partners for both indoor and outdoor activities. Andrew was not selected for either type of activity by anyone in class. Any effort to change Andrew's self-concept without first changing his behavior toward his peers seemed clearly doomed to failure.[1]

The teacher, a dedicated and competent woman, had tried to reason with Andrew and to point out how his aggressive behavior caused the loss of friends, but to no avail. Andrew steadfastly maintained that no one liked him and acted in such a way that he continually confirmed his worst fears. Even if Andrew's fighting were to stop immediately, the other children had learned to avoid him. Somehow, Andrew had to stop fighting and to convince his classmates that he could "be a friend" at the same time.

To formulate a realistic counseling goal, I asked the teacher what seemed to be the worst times of day for Andrew. She said that he fought almost every single day immediately before

[1] *Editors' note:* An excellent observation. Our "self-concept" is based on observations of our own behavior and the reactions of others to us. Andrew's self-concept of being disliked was accurate. To change his self-concept, he would first have to act in more likable ways.

school in the morning, again at noon, and at the end of the day. I asked her to keep track of the number of times Andrew fought during these three problem periods for the next school week. At the end of the week, she reported that Andrew had had "a very good week." He had fought "only" nine out of fifteen possible times, or 60 percent of the time!

At that point, I met with Andrew to draw up a plan of action and to help him select reinforcers from a list of activities that his mother and teacher had previously agreed to supply. Both home and school reinforcers were included, so that Andrew would be receiving support from at least two significant adults in his life. This arrangement also guaranteed that Andrew's good behavior would not go unrewarded if one of the adults failed to follow through.

I was in the building only periodically at that time of the year because of preschool commitments. To accommodate my schedule, the technique chosen to change Andrew's behavior was contingency contracting. In most counseling situations the counselor and the client have an implicit "contract" or agreement. Each asks something of the other, and both are working toward a common goal. Sometimes the contingencies for mutual reinforcement can be made quite explicit in the form of a behavior contract or a contingency contract. A contingency contract is a written agreement between two or more people stating that prearranged contingencies will be attached to specified behaviors for a stated period of time. A contingency contract requires the subject to help formulate and to commit himself publicly to clear and precisely defined goals in anticipation of consequences that are agreeable to him. In addition, others involved in giving the client support make the same public commitment to the treatment program.[2]

With Andrew's consent, we drew up and signed a contract at a formal meeting attended by Andrew, his mother, his teacher, and myself. The contract (see Figure 1) outlines the treatment procedure.

Each morning Andrew was to receive a "smiley card" (see Figure 2) as soon as he entered the classroom. If he had fought or argued, the teacher was simply to hand him the card, without comment, as a reminder of the agreement. If he managed to make it to his seat without fighting, the teacher was to welcome him to class, give him his card, and sign it. The same procedure was to be used at lunch and at the end of the day. It would provide immediate social reinforcement to Andrew for his appropriate behavior, a tangible reminder of his success, and a cue for good behavior later in the day.

When Andrew brought his card home with signatures, his mother was asked to post it in a conspicuous place and to congratulate him on his successes. She was asked not to punish him for the absence of signatures or even to comment on it in any way. His mother agreed to allow Andrew to delay his bedtime by fifteen minutes for each three signatures he received. This served the double purpose of reward-

ing Andrew for his good behavior and training his mother to respond actively to that behavior. When Andrew earned fifteen signatures, he could choose one of ten reinforcers selected from the list that he and I had prepared. Some of the choices were simply things that Andrew really wanted to do at school, like being first in line for lunch and playing with the classroom pet. Others were deliberately included in the list because they gave Andrew opportunities to interact appropriately with his classmates and gave them a stake in helping him to succeed. They included choosing a friend for a math game, bringing a treat from home for the whole class, and earning an extra story time for the class with a book of his choice.

Ordinarily, the list of reinforcers would have been assigned different exchange values to ensure Andrew's success in earning a reward in school without undue delay. For example, holding the class pet might have been contingent upon receiving three signatures, bringing a treat from home contingent on five signatures, and going to the library contingent on eight signatures. In this instance, however, the teacher, who was reluctant to give "special privileges" to individual students, insisted that the minimum criterion be fifteen signatures, or five good days.[3] The success of the program

[2] For a more detailed account of contingency contracting see J. D. Krumboltz and C. E. Thoresen (Eds.), *Behavioral counseling: Cases and techniques.* New York: Holt, Reinhart and Winston, 1969. Pp. 87–129.

[3] *Editors' note:* The problem of fairness to all class members is a tough one. However, treating everyone exactly alike can be most unfair: We do not make everyone wear clothes of the same size, and we give appendectomies only to those who need them. Ideally, each school child should be reinforced for improving his or her current level of performance, whatever it is.

DATE

CONTRACT NO.

Mrs. Harris will initial a smiley card for Andrew each time he does one of the following:

1. Comes into school, hangs up his wraps, and takes his seat without arguing or fighting with another child.
2. Eats his lunch and has his noon recess without arguing or fighting with another child.
3. Clears his desk, gets his wraps, and goes to the bus without arguing or fighting with another child.

When Andrew has received 15 signatures from Mrs. Harris and has had his cards signed by one of his parents, he may choose one of the following rewards:

> Read a story to someone.
> Be first in line for lunch.
> Pass out supplies.
> Get notes from the office.
> Bring a treat from home for the class.
> Go to the library for free reading.
> Choose a book for Mrs. Harris to read to the class.
> Choose a friend for a math game.
> Bring a carrot for Chopper and get a chance to hold him.
> Be a student helper in math for 30 minutes.

I, Andrew, agree to the terms of the above agreement.

_____

I, the classroom teacher, agree to provide Andrew with the reinforcers specified above if Andrew keeps his part of the agreement. I also agree *not* to provide Andrew with any of the above reinforcers during the term of the contract if he does not earn the necessary signatures.

_____

I, Andrew's parent, agree to sign each card that Andrew brings home, to post the cards where Andrew can see them, and to help Andrew keep track of the number of signatures he has earned. Andrew can earn 15 minutes of extra "stay up" time by bringing home 3 signatures.

_____

WE UNDERSTAND THAT THIS IS NOT A LEGALLY BINDING CONTRACT, BUT RATHER A FIRM COMMITMENT OF GOOD WILL AMONG PARTIES WHO CARE ABOUT EACH OTHER.

FIGURE 1   Andrew's contingency contract.

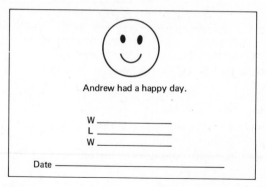

FIGURE 2   A "smiley" card.

depended, then, on the teacher's immediate social reinforcement, on the parents' delayed social and later bedtime reinforcement, and on the social reinforcement that it was expected Andrew would receive from his peers when his behavior changed.

The teacher continued to keep track of the number of times Andrew fought during the problem periods each day. I checked this daily record when I was in the building and periodically called the teacher and parents to check on Andrew's progress.

As the graph (see Figure 3) shows, Andrew went from fighting 9 out of 15 possible times during the baseline period to fighting only 2 out of 150 possible times during contracting. At this time, another sociogram was

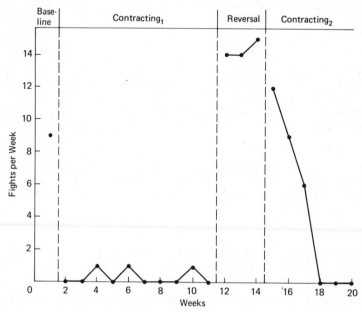

FIGURE 3   Weekly summary of the total number of fights occurring out of a possible maximum of fifteen.

drawn up, showing that Andrew now had a friend. The teacher reported that Andrew had stopped fighting throughout the day, even during the times when no contract was in force. During the period of the contract, I had observed Andrew playing games and interacting appropriately with his classmates both before school and at the noon hour.

At the end of this time, Andrew's mother and teacher asserted that Andrew was "cured" and that there was no reason to continue the cards. However, during a three-week interval after the program had been discontinued, Andrew fought forty-three out of forty-five possible times. The teacher stated that this was typical of his precontracting behavior. At that time, I set up a consultation with Andrew's teacher and mother. Both requested that a new contract be drawn up. The new contract was identical to the first, except that some different reinforcers were added to avoid satiation.[4]

When I saw that Andrew had a high rate of fighting during the first week after the contract had been reinstated, I met with him to discuss the situation. Andrew said that his teacher was not giving him the cards anymore. When asked, the teacher said simply that she made a "slight adjustment in the program" and was keeping a tally of Andrew's good behavior on a pad on her desk instead of giving him the cards.

The teacher's "slight adjustment" eliminated the immediate social reinforcement for Andrew's good behavior and also deprived him of his discriminative stimulus, or cue, for good behavior. With no cards to show for his labors, his mother, living up to her part of the agreement, assumed that he was not doing well and discontinued his later bedtime and extra attention.

During the second week the teacher was still not consistently giving Andrew the cards. Finally, by the end of the third week, the program was being carried out as planned. Andrew fought six times the third week and no times for the remainder of the school year (three weeks). The teacher reported that Andrew's new friend sometimes went home with him after school. His mother commented that Andrew "smiles a lot now."

Because Andrew had never been formally shifted from a continuous to an intermittent reinforcement schedule, I feared that the rather dramatic behavior change would not be maintained over time.

In the meantime, I changed jobs and was not able to observe Andrew in class the following year. However, seven months after the end of the program, Andrew's mother reported that he was still doing well without any special assistance. At parent-teacher conferences his teacher reported to his mother that Andrew was "a typical third-grade boy" and not considered a behavior problem.[5] Andrew's mother

[4] *Editors' note:* Stopping the program temporarily to see what will happen represents a reversal design (ABAB) to test the effect of reinstating the original conditions (absence of a contract). Clearly, the contract was helping Andrew to control his fighting.

[5] *Editors' note:* Andrew wanted to be liked. When he stopped fighting, he had to do something else with his time. Undoubtedly, he found some behaviors that worked better for him.

also commented that, although no specific counseling plan had been set up for the year, she and her husband were careful to "look at the doughnut and not at the hole." They focused on and reinforced Andrew's positive behaviors, as they had been instructed to do the year before. Because it was impossible to do so every time that Andrew behaved appropriately, his parents, without knowing it, had put Andrew on a variable-interval, variable-ratio schedule of reinforcement, a powerful means of maintaining behavior change.

The treatment required approximately ten hours of counselor time. Some secretarial time was involved in typing the contracts. The classroom teacher spent approximately six minutes a day when the program was in effect. The mother estimated her time at three to five minutes a day. Both the teacher and the mother thought that they spent less time in carrying out the program than they had previously spent in reprimanding Andrew. The treatment program, then, cost very little. In addition

to making a significant difference in Andrew's life, it also removed a serious problem from the classroom.

For similar problems encountered since my experience with Andrew, I have found it helpful to write formal reinforcement-fading programs. For Andrew that would have meant gradually reducing the number of signatures received (from three a day to one a day to one a week, and so on) until eventually reports home would be only on the standard report card at the end of each marking period.

All of my contracts written since that time have also included a sliding scale of values for reinforcer exchange.

I believe that some of the difficulties encountered in implementing the program for Andrew could have been avoided if the teacher had had some preliminary in-service training in behavior principles.[6]

---

[6] *Editors' note:* See articles 50 and 51 for descriptions of some teacher-training programs.

INAPPROPRIATE BEHAVIOR

In the cases so far considered the primary emphasis has been on either increasing or decreasing the frequency of a specific behavior. But there are some problems that are not solved by simply increasing or decreasing frequencies. Some behavior occurs at the wrong time, in the wrong place, or under inappropriate circumstances. In such situations the clients need to identify cues that signal when or where the responses are appropriate.

There is nothing wrong with striking matches *per se*. Lighting a cigarette or starting a fire in a fireplace is not generally considered a serious problem. But setting fire to combustible materials in the basement of an apartment building is indeed a serious offense. Similarly, removing one's clothes in front of other people is not in itself an undesirable behavior. Appropriate settings include a doctor's office, a locker room, or a bedroom with one's spouse. However, removing one's clothes on a public street is still frowned upon in polite society and may result in a jail sentence.

In this section we shall examine methods for helping clients to learn the appropriate times, places, and circumstances for engaging in specific types of behavior. The following general methods for dealing with inappropriate behavior are described and illustrated in the articles in this section.

1. *Instruction.* Clients can be given verbal directions or "coaching" to enable them to formulate appropriate cognitive strategies for dealing with their problems.

2. *Overt Practice.* A behavior can be practiced deliberately at preset times or places, so that the client can deliberately control its occurrence. Instead of allowing the behavior to occur impulsively in response to internal whims or urges, the individual learns to control his own behavior by initiating it at designated times or places.

3. *Covert Rehearsal.* The steps leading up to the actual execution of the

behavior can be practiced in imagination. The client can mentally rehearse the manner in which he will respond.

4. *Covert Sensitization.* The client can be taught to imagine aversive consequences accompanying his inappropriate behavior. He can also be taught to avoid the unpleasant consequences of inappropriate behavior by imagining some pleasant consequences that occur after his "escape."

5. *Reinforcement of Incompatible Behavior.* Instead of focusing on the inappropriate behavior itself, the counselor can teach the client to engage in some behavior incompatible with it and can arrange for rewards to be given upon the occurrence of the incompatible behavior.

6. *Reinforcing Successive Approximations.* Improvement usually takes place gradually, and the counselor must be sensitive to small degrees of improvement in order to reinforce them. It is a mistake to wait until the behavior is perfect before arranging rewards.

7. *Reinforcing on an Intermittent Schedule.* Maintenance of the more appropriate behavior is often a difficult problem. Gradually changing the schedule of rewards so that they occur less frequently but at intermittent intervals is a method for maintaining gains.

MARITAL-COMMUNICATION DIFFICULTIES

20.   INCREASING POSITIVE BEHAVIORS IN MARRIED COUPLES[1]

MARK KANE GOLDSTEIN   Veterans Administration Hospital, Gainesville, Florida, and University of Florida

For many couples, getting married is a far more satisfying experience than being married. Hicks and Platt (1970) reviewed the preceding decade research on marital happiness and stability. From the findings of six major studies, they surmised that marital satisfaction and happiness decrease with the length of time married. Even spouses in so-called "happy marriages" see their relationships as growing worse, find each

[1] This report is based on a paper delivered to the Annual Meeting, Association for the Advancement of Behavior Therapy, New York, October 1972.

other less admirable, and, at best, learn to live with the irritants. For those who rate their marriages as unhappy, the decline over time is far more profound and dismal.

Pineo (1961) cited the following as areas of severe decline and disenchantment: companionship, demonstrations of affection, common interests, and consensus. Blood and Wolfe stated, "Corrosion is not too harsh a term for what happens to the average marriage over the course of time" (1960, p. 264). Feldman (1966) and later Rollins and Feldman (1970) demonstrated that marital satisfaction declines severely during the child-rearing stages of marriage.

Mindful of findings on dissatisfaction and the difficulty of reestablishing rewarding marital interaction, we developed a set of accelerative behavior techniques at the Schuyler County Mental Health Center, Watkins Glen, New York, and later at the Family Behavior Analysis and Training Laboratory of the University of Florida and the Gainesville Veterans Administration Hospital Medical Outpatient Clinic. These techniques are part of a larger group of family health-care intervention strategies (including medical care) based on the principles of applied behavior analysis.

THE DAILY INTERACTION-RATE RECORD

This daily interaction-rate recording format permits continual systematic feedback between spouses about their interpersonal responses, judged pleasant or unpleasant by the recipients (see Figure 1). Ordinarily, specific instruc-

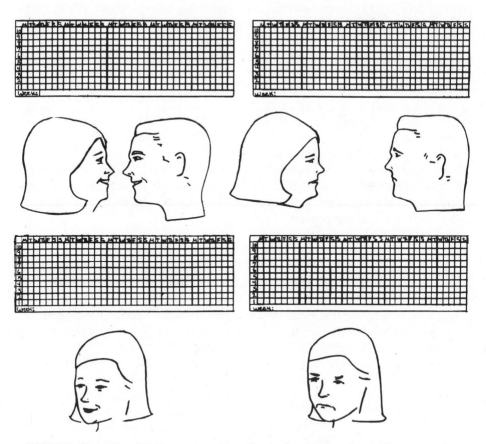

FIGURE 1   The wife's daily interaction chart. The husband's chart has male faces at the bottom.

tions are given to the couple on precisely which interaction events to record in accordance with their specific desires for change. However, we do not focus directly on "deceleration desires," those behaviors that one person wants the other to decrease or cease. For example, couples may complain of a high rate of arguments that they wish to reduce. In this instance we would not attempt direct reduction of arguments, for this approach could have a generalized dampening effect on constructive marital interaction. Instead, we would assess the probability of positive and negative *outcomes* of arguments, and within a short period of time (as soon as possible) following a disagreement the couple would record its *appraisal of the outcome* of the event by marking one side of the record or the other[2] with an X (as many as 10 separate Xs are possible for each day of recording).

The specific outcome recorded may be a simple personal assessment of whether each partner feels that the couple is "closer together" or "farther apart" after each disagreement. Alternatively, the couple may define particular instances of positive or negative argument outcomes (the difference in physical distance between the couple on the left side of the chart in Figure 1 and the couple on the right, along with the expressions depicted, facilitates appropriate recording).

The data are brought or telephoned to the laboratory, usually after several days; there they are reviewed with behavior managers (counselors), who assist the couple in evaluating their progress. If data on the right-hand side of the record (negative behaviors) exceed those on the left side by a wide margin (three or four to one), the right side of the record is *cut off* by the manager, who points out the incompatible effects of punishment with prosocial behavior. Surprisingly, this effort is rarely necessary, for most spouses seem to prefer to reward, not to punish, each other when they are recording interpersonal events. Gratifying results found with this general technique have been recently reported in a large-scale experimental investigation (Welch & Goldstein, 1974).

MR. AND MRS. A: SHIFTING OUTCOMES

The following case, suggesting a learned shift in argument outcomes, illustrates the use of this procedure.

Behavior Antecedents

Mr. and Mrs. A were twenty-six and twenty-three years old respectively, had respectively completed seventh and eleventh grades, and had been married and living together for four years before their request for marital assistance. Mrs. A wished to come alone to the clinic, stating that her husband was adamantly not interested in attending. She was instructed to send her husband a get-well card by registered mail to his place of work, to include the time and date of the clinic

[2] *Editors' note:* An excellent strategy. "Accentuating the positive" is the way to travel. Clients often know what they should not do. The task is to help them to act more positively.

appointment, and to sign it with "love."[3] She was asked to avoid all further discussion of his refusal and was instructed to arrive on time, whether he joined her or not.

Behavior Pinpointed

Mr. and Mrs. A appeared together and complained mutually of frequent intense and physically abusive arguments, which had led Mrs. A to consider separation or divorce. They denied that any one topic generated worse fights than did others and indicated that arguments ordinarily terminated after six to eight hours but occasionally lasted several days.

The couple was first asked to list those outcomes or endings to arguments that both members agreed were good or wholesome and had occurred at least once. The list included kissing, mutual touching, the husband's laughing, continued talking at lower volume, admitting any value to the partner's point. The negative list included hitting spouse, throwing objects at spouse, Mr. A's drinking liquor, Mr. A's leaving the house for more than half an hour, Mrs. A's crying without talking, calling the police, and sleeping in separate rooms.

Recording Arrangement

Mr. and Mrs. A were instructed to record on the left side of their respective marital records any good or whole-

[3] *Editors' note:* A clever idea. Sometimes the right medium (for example, a written card, instead of verbal conversation) can help to say something loud and clear.

some outcomes of arguments that had occurred before and had not been followed by negative outcomes. A negative outcome was to be recorded upon occurrence.

The records were to be kept at all times on the refrigerator door and patched with tape if they were torn. The couple was instructed neither to discuss the recorded data nor to threaten or promise each other about their responses before or after charting.

Reporting Arrangement

Mr. and Mrs. A were instructed to phone their data to a secretary each night for the first four days and were told that they would receive an appointment on the fifth day, contingent upon the calls having been made. Each spouse was instructed to initiate half of the calls.

Behavior Outcome

Telephone data for the four days before the clinic appointment revealed six positive outcomes and one negative outcome.[4] Mr. and Mrs. A reported that the negative outcome was an extension of an earlier positive one that had later deteriorated. The couple's individual outcome ratings were consistent for each incident (they recorded the events in identical fashion). They

[4] *Editors' note:* These data were probably influenced positively by the systematic recording and charting system (every occurrence posted on the refrigerator door), as well as by the daily "accountability program" of calling in the data each day. Self-observation methods like these can really help.

stated that neither had applied pressure to the other in arriving at agreement. They were pleased with the outcomes and continued charting for six weeks, during which time they were seen at five-day intervals.

The final data totaled fifty-three argument outcomes, forty-six of which had been "wholesome." Reevaluation of the couple after a three-month interval suggested maintenance of the shift, which they mutually concluded was highly significant and had had a powerful influence on their relationship.

MR. AND MRS. B: PLANNING SYSTEMATIC OBSERVATIONS

In this use of the marital recording system, spouses carry on continuing evaluation of each other's performances for some preset time interval. It is sometimes difficult to elicit the cooperation of couples (even though they may claim profound interest) in tracking and recording the events that they agree are important to increase in their interactions. Without a clear, novel, prearranged stimulus situation, some couples fail to provide regular records of behavior and thus miss much of the feedback available for corrective responding. The programmed performance interval was developed to overcome this problem.

The same marital record (see Figure 1) is used, but a behavior, or outcome, is not recorded *per se*. Instead, the partners' evaluation of each other's performances over some unit of time is registered. Whenever the husband and wife are together in their home, a kitchen timer is set for intervals, initially ten minutes long, which are usually enlarged by ten-minute increments weekly after discussion with the manager. The couple is instructed to set the timer for the agreed-upon interval. When the interval has terminated the partners immediately reset the timer and place a mark on the upper left-hand, or positive, side of the chart *if* their spouses' performances during that interval have warranted positive ratings in their opinion. The upper right-hand side is used when the opposite is true. The white area in the middle is marked if the recorder cannot select between the positive or negative alternatives. (Feldman, 1970, suggested that the use of a computer card, with each column containing the numbers 0 to 9 be used as a "Likert Scale" of spouse-behavior performance, and this approach has been attempted successfully with some couples.) The lower section of the marital record is used for an end-of-day evaluation, in which the spouses assess each other's total daily performance on a 20-point (10 positive and 10 negative) scale before retiring for the night. Only one mark is to be made. A mark of 10 on the lower left side suggests exemplary performance, which could not have been improved on; a 1 on the left side suggests that the performance was not unpleasant but could have been a good deal better; a 10 on the right side suggests that behavior during that day could not possibly have been more contemptible or unrewarding. Surprisingly, most couples using this format admit that they tend to err toward more favorable evaluations than their spouses really deserve. They seem to reward each other for successive approximations.[5]

Behavior Antecedents

Mr. and Mrs. B were both thirty-two, years old, had completed high school, and had been married for nine years. They had three sons and had been legally separated for three months early in the previous year of their marriage. They had participated in couples' group therapy for four months before requesting assistance. They stated that both the therapist and the couples in the group had "given up on them" and had advised them to consider divorce, for they had "showed no progress" and were extremely hostile to each other. They agreed that the marriage was painful, but each accused the other of causing the distress. Mrs. B said that she was prepared to engage a lawyer for a divorce and was "humoring" her husband, who desired a final attempt to save the marriage.

Behavior Pinpointed

The Bs used abusive and demanding language in describing each other's behavior to the manager. When asked, they could not compile a list of assets or positive attributes. Mr. B did state that his wife was "good in bed," to which she responded that he was in-

experienced.[6] In an effort to extract and document the existence of any positive behavior, the manager asked Mr. and Mrs. B to mark the marriage record in the event that their spouses made any desirable response during the ensuing week and to describe on the back of their records the particular behavior noted. Only the left half of the record was given to the Bs. The records were unmarked on the following week; the partners claimed that they might have overlooked some slight positive change but that there had been nothing good enough to mark. An alternative program was then considered, and the partners agreed that they could distinguish between pleasant and unpleasant spouse performance and were willing to record it in time intervals.

Recording Arrangement

The manager instructed the Bs to set a kitchen timer for ten minutes as soon as Mr. B came home from work and to reset it after it rang. Furthermore, they were to mark the appropriate box on the left grid of their respective marital records if the interval was pleasant and on the right side if it was unpleasant. As the grid had only 10 spaces for each day and covered 100 minutes of behavior, additional data sheets were supplied to extend each day's recording to 40 intervals, or 400 minutes (a little less than seven hours). Weekends were extended to 100 intervals.

[5] Editors' note: We all really prefer being rewarded to being punished. As each person evaluates the other, they quickly learn that the receipt of positive evaluations is facilitated by the giving of positive evaluations.

[6] Editors' note: Wow! She really knows how to punish a guy. But the remark is a clue that their sexual adjustment needed some attention too.

A slash mark in the middle of the chart indicated inability to differentiate. This procedure was to continue until bedtime; when the Bs moved around the house or when they left together, the timer and records were to accompany them. The process was to continue in the presence of visitors, should any arrive. Just before retiring, the Bs were to place their records on the refrigerator with magnets, and each was to evaluate the spouse's performance for their total time together that day. A mark of 10 on the lower left grid indicated maximum pleasant total performance by the spouse—"It couldn't have been better"; a mark of 10 on the lower right grid suggested maximum unpleasant performance.

Reporting Arrangement

The Bs were given an appointment to return to the clinic in one week. However, they were instructed to report by telephone on any day during the week when half or more of the marks were on the upper left grid (pleasant), when a day's performance evaluation was on the pleasant side, or when husband's and wife's data showed general agreement.

Behavior Outcome

On the fifth morning Mrs. B called the clinic and reported that the fourth day's data satisfied these instructions. When the Bs arrived for their appointment at the end of the first week, their data had been entered for each ten-minute interval that they had been together.

Data analysis (with the couple assisting) revealed an accelerative movement from 20 percent combined pleasant evaluation on the first day's recording to 67 percent on the fourth day. However, the data turned negative on the ensuing days and culminated in an 8 percent pleasant rating on the day before the appointment. The end-of-day ratings followed the same general daily trends—slightly positive when the performance intervals were pleasant more than half of the time and strongly negative when the intervals were mostly unpleasant.[7]

Mr. B's interval marks agreed with Mrs. B's marks 82 percent of the time, but when they differed (18 percent of the time) he tended toward the positive, whereas she marked the intervals as negative. Their end-of-day evaluations were quite similar, but Mr. B's evaluations were slightly more favorable. The couple expressed surprise with the results on "good" days and wished to continue but asked to extend the intervals to one hour, for they thought ten minutes too demanding. The compromise arrived at was half-hour intervals.

The following week showed some improvement, with four "good" days' combined data revealing 52–74 percent pleasant intervals. The sessions continued for five weeks, and the intervals had been extended to two hours by the final week of consultation. The data on the intervening weeks averaged four to five days a week when pleasant intervals accounted for more than half the time spent together. The average "pleasant"

[7] *Editors' note:* Using a *daily* recording system is often invaluable. In this way the clients and counselor are alerted to specific events that cause the fluctuations.

day for weeks 3 through 7 yielded 76 percent positive evaluations. After the third week the couple performed its own data analysis before coming to the clinic, and this effort shortened the consultation time considerably.

At a three-month checkup the Bs expressed mutual interest in continuing their marriage. No interest in divorce was expressed by either party. They had continued using the charts on an attenuated basis (morning and evening daily evaluations were made).

Mr. and Mrs. C: Overcoming Inertia

The only aversive procedure that we employ is in overcoming inertia, and it is used when a couple's expression of verbal interest in securing a more rewarding marriage is not followed by positive changes in behavior in the natural environment. Problems include failure to keep records; strong resistance to data-based procedures, including "I forgot my record" (repeatedly); and reluctance to record data ("Making marks on paper is much too time-consuming"). Furthermore, *marital inertia* sometimes appears insurmountable with other techniques that require greater effort. Marital inertia (a spouse-rewarding operant at rest tends to stay at rest) is the psychological equivalent to Newton's Law of Motion, suggesting that a body at rest tends to stay at rest. We have found that spouses have to overcome the forces of "psychological" inertia to deliver rewards (positive reinforcers).

The procedure is a simple direct attempt to overcome marital inertia and can be used to establish some stable (if somewhat contrived) responding, especially when verbal interaction and reinforcement are low or nil. Both husband and wife are asked to put ten sticky file labels on their clothing where the labels will be clearly visible. The only way in which the labels can be removed is by the partner. The partner removes one label *if* the spouse demonstrates some behavior deemed pleasing. The labels remaining on the clothing at bedtime are placed on a blank 5×8-inch, off-white card that is later brought to the manager. The same technique may be used with parents and children or with whole families.[8]

Behavior Antecedents

Mr. and Mrs. C were thirty-five and thirty-one years old respectively, had been married five years, and had two children by Mrs. C's previous marriage, which had lasted six years. Mr. C had not been married before and had completed three years of college; Mrs. C had completed high school. The Cs complained of sexual difficulties, which had become more pronounced during the previous two years. They had spoken about the problem to their minister, who had referred them to the clinic.

Specifically, Mr. C stated his wife was not interested in having sexual relations and resisted his advances. Mrs. C indicated that her husband was

[8] *Editors' note:* As the labels are aversive, the wearer is rewarded for taking some positive action to remove them. This procedure nicely illustrates the process of negative reinforcement.

only interested in her as a "sex object" and showed no interest in her other than sexual interest. They agreed that frequency of sex relations had declined from about twice a week in early marriage to about once every one or two months in the previous year. Mrs. C admitted to a recent extramarital sexual relationship which had lasted two weeks and had been terminated several months before the clinic visit. The partners had not discussed divorce, but Mr. C said that he believed he had made a mistake in marrying Mrs. C and would "wind up like her first husband" (who was a former pal). Mrs. C denied that her husband's sexual technique was inadequate and attributed the difficulty to her receiving inadequate attention and little nonsexual affection.

Behavior Pinpointed

The Cs were initially asked to record the occurrence of nonsexual affectionate gestures (including physical contact and verbal behavior) received each day on the upper left half of the posted marital records and to rate their enjoyment of any occurrence of sexual behavior on a 20-point dimension, using the lower left half of the record, as described earlier.

In discussion with the couple, the counselor withdrew the sexual-rating system when he realized that it was potentially aversive for the couple (there might have been a wide divergence in their evaluations). A simple report of the occurrence of sexual intercourse was substituted.

Mr. C did not join Mrs. C at the second meeting five days later. She reported that he had refused to participate further. No data were offered, and Mrs. C stated that none had been gathered and that no sexual behavior had occurred. The manager telephoned Mr. C, who agreed to join his wife the following week in order to try a different approach. At the second meeting the Cs were given fifty file labels each and instructed to place ten of them on a sleeve, dress, or pair of pants each day when they were together. Only the spouse could remove the sticky labels, one at a time, immediately after behavior that he or she found rewarding. However, consecutive repetitions of the same response that had resulted in a label removal could not result in a second "rip-off"; a new and different response deemed enjoyable or rewarding by the partner had to occur. The manager made no other requirement for recording, except that at bedtime the remaining labels were to be removed and placed on a 5×8-inch off-white card.[9]

Recording and Reporting Arrangement

The card containing unused labels was the only recording device used. The Cs were given an appointment to return in five days.

Behavior Outcomes

The Cs arrived together on schedule for the second appointment. They presented their cards with twenty-seven of Mr. C's and twelve of Mrs. C's labels

[9] *Editors' note:* The counselor was appropriately and commendably flexible about data gathering.

affixed. Mrs. C had removed twenty-three of her husband's fifty labels from his clothing, and Mr. C had removed thirty-eight from her clothing during the preceding five days. Mr. C stated that it "seemed like a game and was kind of silly." But he noted that his wife had been more affectionate during the week and that they had had sexual intercourse on the night before the clinic visit. Mr. C requested fifty more file labels and agreed to continue the program until the next visit.[10] The manager suggested adding a timed-interval observation program, which, he explained, might further strengthen the relationship. Mr. C rejected the suggestion, explaining that it would be too time-consuming. The couple agreed to add a "spouse-absent self-control program,"[11] although Mrs. C expressed

some resistance to praising her husband to others, especially as she had done the opposite in the past.

In the ensuing two clinic visits Mrs. C returned 21 of 100 labels, and Mr. C returned 29. Thus, Mrs. C had removed seventy-one of her husband's labels for responses that she considered rewarding or enjoyable, and Mr. C had ripped off seventy-nine for behaviors that she had emitted. Both claimed that affectionate behavior had increased, and Mrs. C said that her husband was still primarily interested in sex but that she did not mind. The partners had experienced sex relations on three occasions in ten days. She also indicated that her friends did not believe her reports of Mr. C's improvement. The couple was telephoned after a two-month interval, during which no labels were used, and both indicated that the gains in affectionate and sexual behavior had been maintained.

---

[10] *Editors' note:* A little well-timed reinforcement always helps.

[11] The program is introduced by asking partners to compile a written list of a number (ordinarily five to ten) of virtues that their mates possess. After sharing the lists with each other they are instructed to praise (in the course of everyday conversation) at least one of the attributes each day to a different friend, coworker, secretary, boss, graduate student, and so on, and to record which virtue was extolled to whom. The couple is further instructed to post the daily results on the refrigerator and to bring them to meetings with their manager.

references

Blood, R. O. & Wolfe, D. M. *Husbands and wives.* New York: Free Press, 1960.

Feldman, H. *Development of the husband-wife relationship.* Research report, Cornell studies of Marital Development, New York State College of Human Ecology, Cornell University, Ithaca, New York, 1966.

Feldman, H. Personal communication, 1970.

Hicks, M. W. & Platt, M. Marital happiness and stability. In C. Broderick (Ed.), *A review of the research of the sixties.* Minneapolis: National Council on Family Relations, 1970. Pp. 59–78.

Pineo, C. Disenchantment in the later years of marriage. *Marriage and Family Living,* 1961, **23**, 3–11.

Rollins, B. C. & Feldman, H. Marital satisfaction over the family life cycle. *Journal of Marriage and the Family,* 1970, **32**, 20–27.

Welch, J. & Goldstein, M. K. *28,000 minutes of marital intervention: An experiment in non-delivery.* Unpublished manuscript, University of Florida, 1974.

CHILD MISBEHAVIOR

21. *CHANGING A PRESCHOOLER'S MISBEHAVIOR BY DECREASING PARENTAL PUNISHMENT*

MARILYN GILBERT KOMECHAK[1]   The Center for Behavioral Studies, North Texas State University

A "BAD LITTLE GIRL"

Joanie was brought to the guidance center[2] because her parents believed that she was totally unmanageable. The family had been referred to me by a staff social worker, who requested my involvement as a consultant to furnish a system for working out a possible solution to this family's problem. The worker's impression was that the mother was a very angry and hostile woman, who would not acknowledge her need for parenting skills and always referred to her young daughter as a "very bad little girl." The social worker, as well as others who had seen the mother, recommended that she undergo psychiatric care. The stepfather impressed the worker as inexperienced as a parent. He appeared to be simply following his wife's lead in dealing with Joanie.

Conversations with the parents revealed that they had, within the previous two months, spanked Joanie daily and with so much force that they were frightened about how they were to continue to control her without inflicting real damage. They reported that belt whippings simply did not change her behavior for the better for any length of time. They indicated that no other form of discipline worked and that at least the whippings brought Joanie's behavior momentarily under control.[3]

On the occasion of the initial visit, I observed Joanie in the play room. She appeared ill at ease and answered ques-

---

[1] The author completed this study as a staff member of the Child Study Center, Fort Worth, Texas, and is currently Associate Director of The Center for Behavioral Studies, North Texas State University, Denton, Texas.

[2] The guidance center is located within the complex of the Child Study Center, Fort Worth, Texas.

[3] *Editors' note:* The devastating thing about physical punishment is that it often succeeds "momentarily," only to have the problem grow worse. A vicious, escalating cycle of more severe punishment is thus set in motion and often ends in physical harm, psychological alienation, and guilt.

tions in rapid bursts of words. When asked how she was disciplined ("Do you ever get spankings?"), she denied that she was ever spanked. As she bent over to retrieve a toy, several buckle marks could be seen on her back.

During this family's second visit to the center, the members were observed from a one-way mirror while they interacted in a play room. During an observation time of thirty minutes, the father continually tried to attract Joanie's attention and involved himself in her play, even when she asked to play alone. The mother did not talk to Joanie, except to mumble an answer to a question or to tell her, "No, do not do that." The mother said that she continually had to talk to the child in a harsh and prodding fashion at home.

MODELING POSITIVE PARENTAL BEHAVIOR

The parents had difficulty understanding how a child can be controlled without physical punishment. (It should be noted that "the belt" had been used liberally on both parents when they were children.) The next three sessions involved the use of modeling procedures. The social worker and the mother (the father explained that he could lose no more time from work) observed the counselor and the child from behind a one-way mirror as they interacted in the play room. Affection and consistency were modeled by the counselor, with an emphasis on words that would elicit cooperation from Joanie. The result was that she complied with cheerfulness to any requests that the counselor made.

During these observation sessions the social worker pointed out to the mother how cooperative behaviors resulted from what the counselor said and did, how the counselor consistently reinforced the behavior that she wanted. The mother's reaction could be summed up in these words after the third observation session: "I do not think it is what she [the counselor] says or does; it is just that my child likes the pretty toys." It was apparent that the mother could resist indefinitely recognizing the reasons for Joanie's good behavior. The impasse suggested the need for another approach to persuade the mother to gain control of her daughter without physical punitiveness.

GAINING A HOSTILE MOTHER'S COOPERATION

The full "game plan" was not revealed to Joanie's mother at the time, for it was feared that she would employ enough countercontrol to sabotage the effectiveness of her training. I solicited her cooperation by reacting in a very empathic way to her plight: "She certainly does not mind you well"; "Just how many times a day do you have to scold her?"; "That must be very tiring." The mother brightened considerably when she realized that she was not going to be accused of being an ineffective parent.[4]

[4] *Editors' note:* Empathic understanding serves several important functions, one of which is to convince the client that both counselor and client are working on the same side. The initial use of modeling contains the implicit message "I can do a better job than you" and may antagonize the client.

She agreed to a self-monitoring mechanism, using a golf wrist counter to count her "scolds" and "praises" of her daughter. She was also to count Joanie's misbehaviors. (The counter had three digital windows, which revealed the "score," or frequency, of the three behaviors being counted.) A misbehavior was defined as refusal to comply with a reiterated parental request. Scolding was defined as a harsh comment directed to the child when she was engaged in behavior that the mother did not want; it would cause the child to frown or pout. Praising was also modeled for the mother. It consisted of gentle or enthusiastic comments that would cause Joanie to

smile, laugh, or look at her mother without pouting or frowning.

DISCRIMINATING THE EFFECTS OF WORDS

Figure 1 presents the data. The baseline rate of Joanie's misbehaviors was forty-five for one week. The mean was 6.42 a day. Scolds also occurred at a higher rate than praises. At this point, I did not reprimand the mother but simply asked her to try very hard in the following week to bring the circular symbols (praises) on the graph "higher than" the dots (scolds). When she returned with the second week's

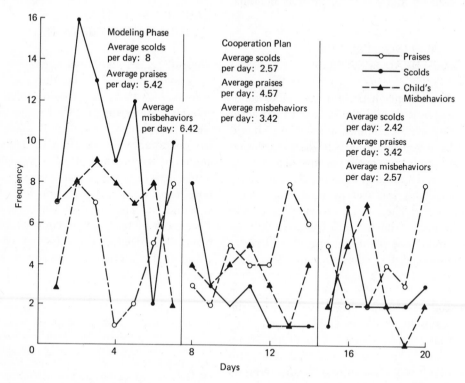

FIGURE 1   Number of mother's "praises" and "scolds" and child's "misbehaviors" per day.

data and it was evident that she had indeed raised the "circles over the dots," I enthusiastically reinforced her for her achievement. The effects on the decrease in misbehaviors were also pointed out to her. She was beaming with pride, as were the counselor and the social worker.

A "GOOD LITTLE GIRL"

By the end of the first experimental week, the number of misbehaviors had been reduced by 47 percent of the baseline rate. The mean was 3.42 a day. The final period shows a reduction of 60 percent of the base-line rate, with a mean of 2.57 a day. The reduction in Joanie's misbehaviors was fairly consistently related to the decrease in her mother's scolding comments. The mother said that the data indicated that scolding did seem to "make her worse" and "me too." She began to praise appropriate behaviors and to use time outs (that is, time out from her attention), rather than scolding or whipping as a response to misbehavior.

It should be noted that the reliability of the mother's data was confirmed by the stepfather's spot checks two or three times a week. He stated that he was in agreement with her rate taking at those times. For him, this too acted as a training period. He voiced his enthusiasm for the results of decreased whippings and scoldings and increased kind words.

SOME IMMEDIATE EFFECTS

It seems that this little girl's cooperative behavior was encouraged by her mother's increased use of positive comments and the decrease in scolding comments. Fortunately, the social environment helped as well. Her mother began to report that people were saying things to her about her skills as a parent. She reported that someone had said to her: "Joanie certainly has been behaving herself. How do you do it?"; "You always seem to know what to do"; and "I wish my child behaved as well as yours; she is such a *good girl!*" A client's progress is certainly aided when other people in the environment reinforce the same behaviors that the counselor is trying to elicit.[5]

---

[5] *Editors' note:* A counselor does not have merely to hope for such environmental support but can plan for it. See Article 9.

references

Bandura, Albert. *Principles of behavior modification.* New York: Holt, Rinehart and Winston, 1969.

Goldiamond, Israel. Self-control procedures in personal behavior problems. *Psychological Reports*, 1965, 17, 851–868.

Komechak, Marilyn. The client as change agent: Tactics in behavior modification for counselors and clinicians. Paper presented at the annual meeting of the Texas Personnel and Guidance Association, Houston, October 14–15, 1973.

Skinner, B. F. *Science and human Behavior.* New York: Macmillan, 1953.

22. REDUCING OUT-OF-SEAT BEHAVIOR WITH A VARIABLE-INTERVAL GROUP REWARD

ROBERT R. PHILLIPS   Teachers College, Columbia University

The purpose of this study was to reduce a student's excessive disruptive behavior (being out of his seat at inappropriate times) by helping the teacher to adopt a behavioral view of the problem. The value of this case is its illustration of how extraclassroom personnel (like the guidance worker, assistant principal, teacher trainer, psychologist, and social worker) can work with a teacher in developing a repertoire of behavioral strategies appropriate to an immediate problem and a conceptual operational model that may be incorporated in future teaching plans and practices.

Mark was an eight-year-old second-grade boy who had repeated the first grade. His teacher, Miss Lee, nevertheless considered him one of the better students academically. She said, however, that Mark frequently left his seat and interfered with other pupils engaged in work. This behavior was reported to be worse on the days when he came to school upset over problems at home. His parents were divorced, and he was the middle one of three children living with his mother.

The author had conducted counseling sessions with the boy in a traditional one-to-one fashion, attempting to identify possible emotional causes for his disruptive behavior and through this approach to develop a psychotherapeutic strategy to eliminate the mental disturbances assumed to be responsible for his inappropriate behavior. Subsequent consultation with Miss

Lee showed that this strategy had been ineffective. At this juncture it was decided that a new strategy based on the behavioral model would be developed and tried.

Finding a powerful reinforcer that would increase the response rate of in-seat and appropriate out-of-seat behavior in the natural classroom environment presented special problems. It is difficult for all members of a class continuously to ignore a specific behavior, the behavior might be disruptive only in regard to the teacher's perception of effective classroom management, and the behavior might be self-reinforcing for the student (as when he left his seat for a drink of water). A final problem was to devise a method of reinforcing the teacher's new behavior pattern if, indeed, the behavior she engaged in during the experimental phase of the study did significantly reduce the boy's rate of disruptive behavior.

The author made two independent thirty-minute visits to the classroom for the purpose of determining the conditions that were maintaining Mark's out-of-seat behavior[1] and to obtain in-

---

[1] Inappropriate out-of-seat behavior was defined as any occasion when Mark stood upright behind his desk or moved from behind his desk without Miss Lee's permission. If he was sitting with his knees in his seat or standing with his elbows resting on his desk, while directly behind it, he was not considered out of his seat. However, if he rested his elbows while standing beside his desk he was counted as

formation necessary for the design of an intervention strategy. The results of an analysis of these two observation periods follow.

The boy's seat was isolated from the rest of the class—located to one side far from the teacher and his peers (the teacher said this seating was a strategy that she used in an effort to reduce his interference with other pupils). This location made communication with his peers impossible unless he left his seat or talked loudly. He was observed out of his seat nine times during the first observation period (a rate of 1.5 times every five minutes) and five times during the second—the fifth time for fifteen consecutive minutes (a rate of 1.2 was derived by counting him out-of-seat three times during the fifteen-minute segment, once for every five-minute interval).[2]

Observations indicated that out-of-

seat behavior was preceded by two kinds of events: apparent disinterest in the classroom activity (for example, a music lesson) and completion of an assignment. When he left his seat he talked to classmates, helped them with class work, sat in an empty chair among other students, drank water, stared out the window, and moved about in the play area. Miss Lee attended to his out-of-seat behavior by scolding, physically taking him to his seat, and removing his chair so that he had to sit on the floor (this punishment resulted in disruptive laughter from the rest of the class). He always smiled when his inappropriate behavior was attended to, suggesting that even the negative consequences he received were perceived as rewards.[3]

These observations were invaluable in that they established that Mark was frequently away from his desk and provided valuable information so that a plan of intervention could be devised to take into account many variables that had previously been unidentified.

TRAINING OF OBSERVERS

Four observers (two teaching aides, the principal, and the author) were trained to record out-of-seat behavior on a student in a different classroom until they attained 90 percent consistency among their observations. During the formal experiment at least two observers were present during each observation period to ensure reliable data.

---

out of his seat. Essentially, when his body presented a visual or physical obstruction at his desk or when he was completely removed from the desk, he was viewed as out of his seat.

[2] It was subsequent to this second observation that the author decided to report the out-of-seat frequencies in five-minute intervals because it was possible that Mark would be out of his seat for extended periods of time during the course of the formal study. This decision is viewed as liberal, in that the 1.5 rate gleaned from the first observation was greater than the 1.2 rate derived during the second period, in spite of having counted him out of seat once every five minutes during the fifteen-minute segment. Therefore, an out-of-seat tally was recorded for each occasion when Mark was out of his seat for less than five minutes but only once if he was out for five minutes or longer or twice for ten consecutive minutes and so on.

[3] Editors' note: It seems in many ways that this student had good cause to leave his desk.

DESIGN AND INTERVENTION

Period 1: Before Phase

In the first period of five days the frequency of Mark's out-of-seat behavior was recorded. Miss Lee was instructed to interact with him as she normally did.

Period 2: Intervention

During the next eight days Miss Lee was asked to move Mark to an empty seat among his classmates. She was given an oven timer and a variable-interval schedule based on a five-minute average. Her instructions were to tell the class, in Mark's presence, that the timer would be set to ring at different times during the day; if he was either in his seat or out with her permission when the timer rang, everyone would receive an extra minute of physical education, but if he was out of his seat without permission one of the extra minutes would be taken away.[4] She was asked to select at random, at the start of each day, a different interval on the variable-interval schedule, in order to prevent Mark from learning to adjust his behavior to the natural sequence of a schedule. The minutes he earned were to be tallied on the chalk board for everyone to see, and the timer was kept on the teacher's desk with its face turned away from the students.[5] She

[4] Prior contacts with the subject had revealed that his favorite school activity was physical education; therefore, extra physical-education time was selected as the consequence best suited to reinforce his appropriate behaviors.

[5] *Editors' note:* It is a brilliant idea to use an inexpensive oven timer as a way of structuring variable intervals!

was encouraged to provide seat projects for him to manipulate when he had free time.

Period 3: After Phase

The seven days following the use of the physical-education consequence were used to check on any changes that were maintained after the group reward had been terminated.

The intervention treatment was not reintroduced because the school term ended on the last day of period 3.

DATA COLLECTION

Data were recorded during two fifteen-minute observation periods each day. Observers were seated in an area void of student activity, where their presence was minimally distracting. A chart was devised so that each inappropriate out-of-seat behavior could be represented by a tally. The recorded data were reported in five-minute intervals in the event that occasions would occur when Mark would be out of his seat for more than five consecutive minutes, as he had been during the preexperimental observations. An average rate of out-of-seat behavior for each day's observations was obtained by dividing the total frequencies by six (the number of five-minute intervals in thirty minutes).

Interobserver reliability was obtained by calculating the percentage of agreement among observers' tallies. The reliability indexes calculated revealed a mean of 86 percent, with a range of 76–100 percent. Three observers achieved 89 percent agreement, and two observers attained 95 percent agreement.

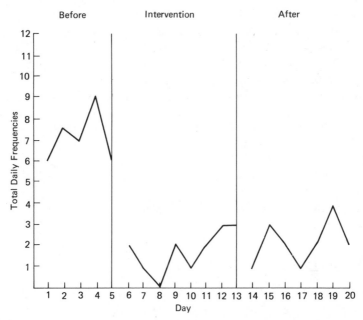

FIGURE 1   Total daily observations of inappropriate out-of-seat behavior.

Figure 1 illustrates the total number of times that Mark was inappropriately out of his seat on each day through the three phases. Average frequencies for each period were 7.1 in period 1, 1.8 in period 2, and 2.1 in period 3.

During period 1 Mark was out of his seat a rate of 1.2 times per interval. In period 2 he was out of his seat a rate of .28 times per interval, which represents a decline in frequency of 77 percent from period 1. During this period the only occasion when he moved from his seat was immediately after the timer rang but only for a few brief seconds while Miss Lee reset the oven timer.

In period 3 Mark remained at a level comparable with that of period 2, although the intervention contingency had been removed. His rate of out-of-seat behavior was .36 times per inter-

val. This figure represents an increase over that of period 2 but still remained 70 percent less than in period 1.

The teacher moved Mark to a desk among the other pupils, but there was no evidence of her supplying him with materials for seat work during free time.

Out-of-seat behavior clearly exhibited a decline during treatment. However, three variables (change of seat location, patterns of peer reinforcement, and the power of extra physical-education time administered as a reinforcer on a variable-interval schedule) were not assessed independently.

The power to earn or lose extra physical-education time served as a stimulus that prompted the emission of a consistent pattern of reinforcement from Mark's classmates. Observations indicated that they positively reinforced his in-seat behavior with verbal praise and punished his out-of-seat behavior with verbal reprimands.

There was no major reversal in the response rate recorded in period 1 during period 3. This result could lead to the conclusion that Mark's behavior had generalized. However, it seems there was no reversal because the teacher's behavior, learned during the intervention condition (period 2), continued during period 3, that is, she continued reinforcing the desired be-

havior and ignoring the undesired behavior.[6] As period 3 took place during the last seven days of school, which are usually marked by improvised activities after the redemption of textbooks and are a time when classroom management is most difficult, the results are particularly significant.

[6] *Editors' note:* Good for her! It is encouraging to learn that good things beget better ones: The boy improved, and the teacher got better.

COMPULSIVE FIRE SETTING

23. *ELIMINATING A FIRE-SETTING COMPULSION THROUGH CONTINGENCY MANAGEMENT*

LOUIS GERSHMAN   Villanova University

Myriad speculations, heavily laden with symbolism and unconscious motivation, have been suggested by psychoanalytic therapists to explain the psychological meaning of fire: a state of sexual excitation, substitute masturbatory impulses, urethral sadistic fantasies, blocked homosexual drives, acting out parents' forbidden wishes, and others. Despite these "explanations," no specific treatments have succeeded in dealing with this problem. If a counselor, confronted with a compulsive fire-setting patient, searches the behavioral literature, he will find that this problem has seldom been written about. In the present report we describe an effective treatment that involved teaching a mother to control the fire-setting obsession of her eight-year-old boy by means of contingency management.

THE CASE OF JOHN

John was described by his mother as insecure, lacking confidence, unaggressive, and unassertive with his friends and others. In school John's teacher complained of his lack of attention, loud talking in class, and short attention and memory span. As a result, John was frequently criticized by his teacher and mother for his inadequacies. The mother and father differed in their perceptions of John's problems. The mother, burdened with the care of invalid parents (a progressively deteriorating senile mother and a paraplegic father), was often tense and nervous. Her depressed feelings were associated with frequent criticizing and shouting at John. The father was rarely home, his business necessitating a great deal of travel. When he was at home, he was permissive with John, often rationalizing, "I did worse when I was a little boy." The mother, on the other hand, bore down hard on John and set high requirements for him at home and school. Among the more serious of John's fire-setting incidents had been setting fire to a wood pile in the apartment building, frequently taking matches from cigarette machines and lighting them, throwing lighted matches into bundles of trash in the apartment-house basement, and playing with matches in his room.

Teaching the Mother

Reinforcement Procedures I rejected the idea of requesting John to come to my office in a one-to-one relationship with me.[1] The reasons for doing so were simple: To change John's behavior would have taken a much longer time; it would have become very expensive; and, most important, my contact with John, no matter how skillful I claimed to be, would not be the crucial factor in modifying his maladaptive behavior. In interviews with his mother, it was obvious that she continually contributed to John's deviance. As a matter of fact, she realized this, but she did not know what to do about it. It was strategic, then, to change her behavior, so that she could exercise

---

[1] *Editors' note:* That's great! It is tough for a counselor to break the habit of accepting a "client" who does not state a problem. It is better that the counselor establish a partnership with the referrer (in this instance, John's mother); "Why don't you and I work on this problem together?"

proper behavioral controls over herself, as well as over John. Unless she could understand how she contributed to John's deviant behavior and what steps should be taken daily to alter his behavior, the probability of permanent success was slim. Because she seemed the most appropriate change agent, I constructed a special program of training for her.

Five sessions were spent in teaching her reinforcement principles. She was given a copy of *Parents Are Teachers* (Becker, 1971) and was assigned additional programmed exercises to complete daily during the week. These exercises were taken from the first three chapters of Homme's book (1969), which highlights the principles of contingency management and emphasizes the basic rules for using rewards effectively. John's mother became fascinated with the behavioral approach and, being an intelligent woman, caught on quickly to the aims, theory, and application of contingency management.

Contingency Contracting It was obvious that most of the mother's interactions with John were characterized by directing, criticizing, and punishing. In devising the training procedures, a careful analysis was made of differential reinforcement procedures that could be used by her to increase John's constructive and adaptive behavior. For example, John was negligent in doing his homework. This had caused several rifts with his teacher and detentions after school. John was unhappy about school and his teachers, and he was remiss in doing his homework. His mother attempted to control him by taking away privileges, like playing with friends, television, and sweets, as well as by stiff physical punishments.

A contingency-contracting program centered around homework activities, based on the procedure set forth by Homme (1969), was constructed by John's mother and me. I taught her specifically how to take the following steps:

1. Make task cards (small tasks, shaping procedure). Every day John's mother prepared one task card for each of the main areas of school work: arithmetic, spelling, and reading (see Figure 1). Often the task cards dealt specifically with the daily homework. When homework was not assigned by the teacher, John's mother constructed task cards for review of previous work or introduced additional appropriate exercises. I showed her how to arrange tasks aimed to provide John with many successes each evening. Even when the assignments became more difficult and longer, her job was always to combine the tasks, questions, and points so that successes followed. Being an intelligent, well-educated woman, she caught on very quickly to these procedures. The total amount of John's time required for an evening's work was forty-five to sixty minutes. After a week all assignments were being completed before

dinner, so that he would be able to enjoy his daily reinforcement, watching television. To be sure, John showed high enthusiasm for the point program from the very beginning. As for his mother, the system of reinforcements proved to be a godsend, for it helped to eliminate the constant bickering and punishment by which she had previously tried to control John.

2. Reward each completed task with points. John and his mother mutually agreed upon a system of daily, as well as weekly, rewards for completed tasks. The purpose of the daily reinforcer was to motivate John to earn immediate rewards. For example, as he had a special liking for several television programs, watching them became an appropriate daily reinforcer. A weekly reinforcer was valuable because it generated continuity in performance, in order to achieve a desired reward. Furthermore, it was teaching John the value of delayed gratification. To implement these goals, a chart was constructed for the purpose of recording John's earned points. Below the chart an explicit agreement between John and his mother, involving earned points, privileges and responsibilities, was stated.

3. Accompany point reinforcement

JOHN'S TASK CARD IN ARITHMETIC

Task: Problems 3 to 12 on page 52.

Check: When you finish, bring your paper to Mother for checking.

Reward: 1 point for each correct answer.

FIGURE 1   One of the task cards (5×8 inches), constructed by John's mother each day for arithmetic, spelling, and reading. Each card specifically stated the task, the requirement for checking results, and the specific reinforcement to be administered.

TABLE 1   John's Daily and Weekly Earned Points

	Mon	Tues	Wed	Thurs	Fri	Week
Arithmetic	7	6	10	13	9	45
Spelling	8	10	10	15	12	55
Reading	6	10	15	18	20	69
Total	21	26	35	46	41	169

Agreement

Arithmetic	John earns one point for each problem solved correctly. If he makes a mistake, he is required to redo the problem correctly before he records his points on the chart.
Spelling	John earns one point for each word spelled correctly. He must correct any misspelled word before he records his points on the chart.
Reading	After reading a certain number of assigned pages, John will be asked questions by his mother. The number of points earned will depend upon the length of the reading matter, type of question, and number of questions.
Daily rewards	John gets ½ hour of television for at least 20 points.
	John gets 1 hour of television for at least 30 points.
	John gets 1½ hours of television for at least 40 points.
	John gets 2 hours of television for at least 50 points.
Weekly rewards	John will go bowling this weekend if he earns at least 125 points this week from Monday to Friday. It is agreed that points cannot be carried over from week to week.
Changes	Changes in this agreement will take place through discussion and mutual agreement.

_____
(JOHN)

_____
(MOTHER)

_____
(DATE)

with positive social reinforcement. John's mother reinforced him frequently during and after his work, in addition to the points that he earned. For example, when he spelled a hard word correctly, completed a sticky arithmetic problem, or thoughtfully answered a reading question, she made a favorable comment. She was given a list of appropriate social-reinforcing statements like "That's good work," "Well done," "That showed good thinking," "You're doing better," "That's fine," "You sure are improving," and "You're really working now."

4. Determine appropriate reinforcers. Back-up reinforcers, that is, pleasant activities that John could purchase with his points, like ice skating, bowling, movies, friends at the house overnight, piano lessons, story telling, and reading, were effective in stimulating him to collect points. John himself was the best source of information on what the back-up reinforcers should be. Often his mother would start the ball rolling by asking, "What would you like to earn for 125 points this week?" John would respond, "Bowling." If he suggested an activity that was not

appropriate (like a day trip to New York City, a weekend at the seashore, an expensive pair of ice skates), both mother and son would engage in an exchange of positive communication, which always culminated in a mutually agreeable activity. At the end of each week, John and his mother would discuss and agree upon a new backup reinforcer, which would become the new target for the next week.

Two daily charts were prepared. One was privately recorded by the mother to keep her aware of the need to reinforce appropriate behavior, and to reduce her tendencies to criticize and punish (see Figure 2). To help her in the latter task, I gave her a list of "taboo" words and phrases to illustrate the kinds of expressions that she should avoid in interacting with John. These expressions connoted scolding, criticism, disapproval, and punishment; they included the follow-

ing: "That's childish," "Don't you have better sense?" "Stupid," "You're hopeless," "Stop wasting time," "Dummy," "You're so undependable," "Where's your brain?" "I'm getting tired of your behavior," "Stop that nonsense," "You'll never change," "Can't you think?" and "How many times do I have to tell you?" She was able to supply many other such expressions that were idiosyncratic to her and that she had frequently used.

The second chart (see Figure 2) showed John's progress in completing his homework activities (see Table 1). This chart was hung on his bedroom door.

TREATMENT GOALS

Two major goals (as suggested by Holland, 1969) were agreed upon by the therapist and mother. First was to

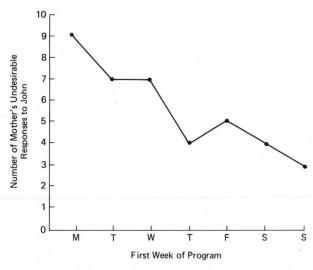

FIGURE 2 The initial week's record of John's mother's scolding, criticizing, disapproving, and punishing behavior. In the following weeks, the curve flattened out in the 0–2 range.

strengthen John's behavior of bringing matches to her when she was available (to prevent fire setting). Second was to strengthen the behavior of not striking matches when they were available but his mother was not present (to control John's fire-setting behavior in and outside the house after he was no longer being reinforced).

The traditional "why" of John's behavior was ignored: The suggested psychoanalytic interpretations were discarded as irrelevant, untestable, and unmeasurable. In connection with the first goal, John's mother was trained to engage in a step-by-step method as follows:

Bringing Matches to Mother: Goal 1

1. She was to tell John that, if he found matches or match covers around the house, he should bring them to her immediately.[2] She was to provide John with continual reinforcement; that is, to give him 5 cents each time that he brought matches.

2. She was to place an empty match book conspicuously around the house (as this book would have little value to John he would bring it to her).[3]

3. When John brought matches, he was to be reinforced immediately with 5 cents. His mother was also to provide

social praise when giving him the money; for example, "Thank you," "That's nice of you, Johnny," "Gee, I'm glad you picked this up for me; I've been trying to clean up papers and all this kind of stuff." A smile, kiss, hug, pat on the cheek, or pat on the back[4] varied the reinforcements. John's mother was also instructed to use a pleasant tone of voice, not to overact, to be naturally pleased, and to act natural. After reinforcing him, she was to tell him that he could go to a nearby candy store immediately and could buy whatever he wanted (candy, gum, and so on).

4. During the next nine days, she placed other match books around the house, using the following schedule of the number of matches in each packet:

day 1	empty
day 2	empty
day 3	1 match
day 4	2 matches
day 5	2 matches
day 6	5 matches
day 7	8 matches
day 8	15 matches
day 9	3 matches

She was instructed not to say anything to John if any of the matches were missing when he brought the books to her. If he brought her match books that he had picked up elsewhere, she was also to reinforce him.

5. Starting on day 10, she was to vary the magnitudes of reinforcement from 2 cents to 10 cents. The money reinforcement was always to be paired

[2] *Editors' note:* The best way to stop an undesirable behavior is to reward some other, incompatible behavior. In practical situations it is not always easy to find a feasible incompatible behavior. Bringing matches to his mother was a good one for John.

[3] *Editors' note:* An excellent idea. The boy was rewarded at first for an easy step toward the goal under conditions that did not present any temptation.

[4] *Editors' note:* It is important to remember that positive physical contact can be a very powerful reinforcer. Too often we rely only on words.

with a social reinforcement. John's mother was to appear natural when she gave him more or less money, to treat him with humor, not to argue or to discuss but to be nice. She used the following schedule:

day 10   5 cents
day 11   5 cents
day 12   4 cents
day 13   2 cents
day 14   8 cents
day 15   3 cents
day 16   1 cent
day 17   4 cents
day 18   10 cents
day 19   3 cents

6. Starting on the twentieth day, the mother was to tell John that he was not to expect money every time. She was to say this naturally and pleasantly, and she was to adopt the following schedule:

day 20   0
day 21   4 cents
day 22   0
day 23   7 cents
day 24   3 cents
day 25   5 cents
day 26   0
day 27   6 cents
day 28   0
day 29   0
day 30   0

Not Striking Matches: Goal 2

John's mother was to start work on the second goal after match-bringing behavior had been strongly established.

1. At dinner, she was to introduce a book of matches and to tell John that he could strike matches if he liked. She was to place twenty pennies beside the book of matches and to tell John that,

for every match not struck, he was to take one penny.
2. She was to give social reinforcement for unlit matches, no matter how few remain unlit.
3. She was to continue with this program until John showed no desire to light matches.[5]
4. On days when John showed no desire to light matches, he was to be encouraged in a casual manner to light a match once. If he did not, his mother was to avoid making an issue of it.

What happened:

dinner 1   0 matches lit
dinner 2   0 matches lit
dinner 3   2 matches lit
dinner 4   3 matches lit
             (John said: "I love to light matches.")
dinner 5   3 matches lit
dinner 6   0 matches lit
dinner 7   3 matches lit
dinner 8   5 matches lit
dinner 9   2 matches lit
dinner 10   1 match lit
dinner 11   1 match lit
dinner 12   0 matches lit
dinner 13   0 matches lit
dinner 14   1 match lit
dinner 15   0 matches lit
dinner 16   0 matches lit
dinner 17   0 matches lit
dinner 18   0 matches lit

At the end of this time, the family went on spring vacation, the first time that the parents had taken John with them on vacation. He said: "You know, Mom, I really don't care about the matches. You'll see, I won't light any more."

[5] *Editors' note:* Extinction could have been an alternative procedure. The boy could have been *required* to light matches for hours until he tired of the sensation.

RESULTS

A rapid reduction in fire setting followed the use of the behavioral approach described here. The procedures not only eliminated the fire-setting compulsion but also led to the development of many adaptive behaviors at home and in school. For example, John's behavior in school had improved, he did his homework enthusiastically, he participated in class, he was invited more frequently to friends' houses, he frequently helped his mother with chores, and he was an enjoyable child to have around.

His mother called three weeks after the end of treatment to report that John had not lit any matches, that he was doing well in school, and that the relationships at home were better than they had ever been. Contact with the mother four months, one year, and two years after treatment revealed the same results: John's interest in matches had disappeared.[6] He was having a great deal of success and enjoyment playing the piano. He was more assertive with his friends in play activities. Both at home and at school he had turned into a very likable boy.

John's mother continued to use reinforcement procedures when problems arose. She herself seemed to have found a new zest for life, feeling confident that she had the tools to face new situations with John. Though she still had to care for her invalid parents, she found herself applying the behavioral principles with them also, helping to make life much more bearable for her.

[6] *Editors' note:* Ideally we would like to see the exact frequency of fire-setting attempts before, during, and after treatment. With behavior as dangerous as fire setting, however, a counselor might understandably forgo collecting precise base-line data. The evidence is clear that a dangerous practice was reduced to zero frequency.

references

Holland, C. J. Elimination by the parents of fire-setting behavior in a 7-year-old boy. *Behavior Research Therapy,* 1969, **7,** 135–138.

Homme, L. *How to use contingency contracting in the classroom.* Champaign, Ill.: Research Press, 1969.

Becker, W. C. *Parents are teachers.* Champaign, Ill.: Research Press, 1971.

ENURESIS

24.   A DIVERSIFIED APPROACH TO CURING ENURESIS

LOUIS GERSHMAN   Villanova University

Barbara was a shy, docile twelve-year-old girl. Her enuretic problem dated back to infancy and had never been resolved. During the previous two years, her parents had tried unsuccessfully to use the bell-and-blanket apparatus, which they had purchased through a newspaper ad.[1] After an up-down experience of bed wetting, accompanied by extreme frustration and exasperation, the parents brought Barbara to me for behavioral treatment. At that time and for several months previously, she had been wetting her bed every night. The parents made one request: "Please do not use the bell and blanket." The apparatus had become anathema to Barbara, who agreed to come for treatment only when she was assured that the apparatus would not be used.

I agreed to the condition. I was especially motivated at this particular time to try other techniques for eliminating enuresis, as a result of having come across a paper by Ditman and Blinn (1954) that presented physiological evidence that enuretics, with the exception of the very young, are awake or nearly awake before wetting their beds.

In addition, they experience somatic signs of distress previous to and during the bed wetting. If this is so, I hypothesized, I should be able to make use of behavioral techniques other than the bell and blanket, which I had used with frequent success in the past, to change the maladaptive enuretic response.

As a rule, the normal child experiences the following sequence: Bladder pressure increases, sleep becomes shallower, and the child awakens, gets up, and urinates. In this paradigm, bladder tension becomes the conditioned stimulus that leads to the appropriate response. The enuretic child, on the other hand, apparently feels the stimulus of the full bladder but fails to respond to this cue in the appropriate manner by awakening and urinating. Thus, Barbara had experienced eleven years of bed wetting and had strengthened the undesirable enuretic habit. As a matter of fact, this instrumental act had been repeated so frequently over the years that any cause that might have been identified years ago had become insignificant at the present time.[2] On the basis of such reasoning, I was primarily concerned with direct treatment aimed at eliminating the maladaptive behavior by helping Barbara learn

---

[1] It consists of two foil pads with a separating sheet between. When the first drops of moisture strike the foil pads, the moisture passes from the top pad to the bottom, and a buzzer alarm goes off and alerts the sleeper. This system helps to condition him to stop bed wetting. The supplier is Sears, Roebuck (No. 8KH 1164).

[2] *Editors' note:* A good point. The original causes are of historical interest but offer little help now.

some new habits. Only by preventing a wet bed could the vicious cycle be broken and the child's problem and accompanying anxiety be eliminated. To achieve this goal I made use of the following procedures.

MULTIPLE TECHNIQUES

Relaxation

For Barbara to wet her bed or to think of wetting her bed was anxiety-evoking. The purpose of relaxation training was twofold: to reduce Barbara's tension in thinking about and anticipating enuresis and to use relaxation as a counter-conditioner in a desensitization approach. Barbara was taught progressive muscular relaxation (Wolpe, 1958). She was an excellent learner and became deeply relaxed in the first training session.

Balloon Blowing

As bladder tension is the immediate forerunner of the undesirable enuretic response, my purpose was to train Barbara to reproduce bladder tension and then to introduce an adaptive response to this tension, which would be followed immediately by reinforcing consequences. Then the goal was to build up, through repetition, a new contingency relationship between the new response and the desirable consequences.

I handed Barbara a balloon and asked her to inflate it. "As you blow," I told her, "notice how you feel the tensing of your stomach, just like when the stomach gets tense when the blad-

der is filling up with urine." After a few tries, Barbara agreed that blowing up the balloon made her feel those peculiar feelings in the stomach that resembled the filling of the bladder before wetting the bed.

"Now, let's practice this exercise," I said. "Start inflating the balloon.... Feel the tension in your bladder.... Now stop inflating and say to yourself, 'I should go to the bathroom.' Visualize yourself going to the bathroom.... After you finish, feel good about it. Feel real good about it, knowing that you did what you ought to do."[3]

Barbara was told to practice this exercise every night, sitting on her bed dressed in pajamas, right before she turned the light out to go to sleep. It occurred to me afterward that pursing the lips and blowing would have produced the same stomach tension feelings as trying to inflate a balloon. However, even if I had thought of this at that time, I would have continued with the balloon technique because the novelty of the balloon approach was enticing to Barbara.

Desensitization

A modified imaginal-desensitization procedure was used. Its purpose was to help Barbara to learn to make a new specific response. Customarily, in standard desensitization, a patient is exposed to an aversive stimulus under relaxation, with the intent of counterconditioning the stimulus through pro-

[3] *Editors' note:* An example of covert self-modeling, in which the person practices imagining himself acting appropriately in problem situations. See Article 55, as well as 37.

gressive confrontation. With Barbara, however, I changed the procedure somewhat by having her relax, gradually exposing her through a hierarchy to the fearful enuretic-stimulus situation, helping her learn to respond appropriately, and reinforcing this response.

My first interview with Barbara indicated clearly that the items in the desensitization hierarchy should center on the following dimensions:

1. Sleeping location
   a. home
   b. Nana's house
   c. friend's house
   d. hotel room
   e. at home a few days before summer camp
2. Number of people present
   a. client only
   b. one other person in room
   • c. two other people in room
   d. several people in room
   e. ten girls in room (camp)
3. Depth of sleep
   a. "You've almost fallen asleep"
   b. "You've just fallen asleep"
   c. "You are in heavy sleep"
4. Bladder distention
   a. "Your bladder is slightly full"
   b. "Your bladder is half full"
   c. "Your bladder is really full"
   d. "You feel a slight wetness"

Here is a sample item:

You are lying in your bed at home (1a, 2a), lights turned off, you are almost asleep (3a). You begin to have feelings in your bladder (4a). It is annoying. You know that you should go to the bathroom. You get out of bed, go to the bathroom, urinate, walk back to your room, get back in bed and cover yourself. You feel good.

You know that you did what you should have done. When you have this good feeling, raise your left index finger.

The combination of dimensions that were used at any particular moment was related to the time of presentation. Naturally, in the early sessions, the a dimensions were most important, for they involved the lowest amounts of anxiety. However, with each succeeding session, as Barbara showed greater ability to face higher-anxiety items, such items were gradually incorporated into the hierarchy. The following combinations of dimensions were used in each session:

Enuresis Hierarchy

Session

(1)	1a	2a	3a	4a
	1a	2a	3a	4b
(2)	1a	2a	3a	4b
	1b	2b	3a	4b
(3)	1b	2b	3a	4b
	1a	2a	3b	4a
	1b	2b	3b	4b
(4)	1b	2b	3b	4b
	1c	2b	3b	4a
	1a	2a	3c	4a
(5)	1a	2a	3c	4a
	1b	2b	3c	4b
	1c	2c	3c	4b
	1d	2d	3c	4b
(6)	1d	2d	3c	4b
	1e	2a	3b	4b
	1e	2a	3c	4c
	1e	2a	3c	4d
(7)	1e	2a	3c	4d
	1e	2d	3a	4b
	1f	2e	3b	4c
	1f	2e	3c	4c
	1f	2e	3c	4d

I did not ask Barbara to indicate the existence of anxiety by lifting her finger, which is the usual procedure in standard desensitization. I felt that in the case of this twelve-year-old, I did not want to take the chance of motivating her to feel anxiety. I preferred to give her the impression that, when she did what she was supposed to do, she would feel good and happy.

I frequently asked Barbara how she felt. When she would say "I feel good," or the equivalent, I would verbally reinforce her. As desensitization proceeded from session to session, I frequently shortened the ideas used in presenting an item. I deliberately made use of a variable presentation, sometimes presenting the full item, other times shortening the phrases or eliminating words and phrases. Sometimes I would merely say to her, "Now visualize that whole scene once again, and this time really feel good about what you are doing."

In the first two sessions only two items were presented, each three or four times. The tempo of presentation was slow because it was important for Barbara to become accustomed to the desensitization procedure. The total presentation time was approximately fifteen minutes. In subsequent sessions all items were presented two or three times, covering twenty to twenty-five minutes. In sessions 3 and 4, three items were presented, and in the next four sessions the number of items was increased. In session 7, the final desensitization session, five items were presented. By that time, Barbara was feeling very confident: She was more assertive, and she exhibited greater self-esteem. She completed the five hierarchical items in the last session with minimal or no anxiety in approximately twenty-five minutes.

Assertive Training

I introduced assertive training during the fourth session. Barbara was a shy girl. The inability to make the appropriate response in bed in order to avoid enuresis may very well have been tied in with her general unassertive tendencies.[4] If I could strengthen Barbara's assertive ability, I hypothesized, it would give Barbara greater confidence and self-esteem, which should help to generalize these assertive feelings to the enuretic situation.

During this session I engaged in role-playing and behavior-rehearsal practice. At first, Barbara was uncomfortable. After initial failures, she wanted to stop. However, with a lot of modeling on my part and friendly, often humorous pressure to continue trying, she eventually began to get over her embarrassment and reluctance.[5] During this session we made use of the following items:

1. A girl (boy) pushes you out of lunch line.
2. A girl (boy) steps on your toes.
3. Your teacher asks for a volunteer to do some work.
4. A student unjustly criticizes a teacher whom you like.

The topics for assertive training in the next four sessions were as follows:

[4] *Editors' note:* An interesting speculation. Perhaps the ability to act appropriately is related generally to self-control skills and a sense of one's own competence.

[5] *Editors' note:* Good work. The client's resistance to trying a new treatment procedure should not prevent its being used. Of course, the client must consent, but gentle and persistent persuasion may be needed to obtain the consent.

Session 5
1. Your teacher blames you unjustly for writing in your textbook.
2. Your friend wants to see a movie, but you prefer to see a different movie.
3. Begin to converse with a new girl who just moved into your neighborhood.
4. You tell the waitress in the restaurant that the bread in your sandwich is stale.

Session 6
1. You are visiting your girl friend. She wants to read. You want to play.
2. Your teacher misspells a word on the board.
3. Your friend asks to borrow your brand new bike.
4. After paying for lunch, you realize that you were short-changed.

Session 7
1. The meat doesn't taste fresh in the restaurant.
2. You tell your mother you would prefer to stay home rather than to go with her.
3. After buying a blouse in the department store, you decide you don't like the way it fits.

At this time, to consolidate changes that had taken place as a result of the assertive training, I introduced a direct cognitive approach for the purpose of further implementing these gains. I took several of Barbara's common daily experiences and converted them into affirmative, assertive statements, with the purpose of helping her to strengthen a new way of regarding herself and her behavior.

Giving her a typewritten page, I said: "Now, I would like you to read each of these statements three times. Read them meaningfully. Don't just read them with your lips. Sort of read them with your whole body even though you only move your lips."

1. When I am right, I am not afraid to say that I am right.
2. When my teacher is wrong, I should politely tell him he is wrong.
3. Everybody makes mistakes. I make mistakes, too. So what?
4. When something should be done, it's best to do it at the time.
5. Sometimes I'm tired, like in bed. But if I know that I should do it, I will do it.
6. Sleepy or not sleepy, if I know something should be done, I aim to do it, not be sorry afterwards.
7. Sometimes my mother makes a mistake. She's human too.
8. Sometimes my father makes a mistake. He's human too. So what's the big deal?
9. If I can help it, I don't want to make mistakes.
10. If something has to be done, it's best to do it now.
11. When I make up my mind to do something, I'm going to do it—now.[6]

In session 8 we went over all of the previous assertive items and several others suggested by Barbara. It was obvious not only that she had dissipated a great deal of her shyness but also that she had become quite a different girl. Whereas before therapy she had been withdrawn, it was amazing to see the positive personality changes that had taken place. By this last session, approximately six weeks later, she was a changed girl. The best way that I can describe Barbara is by comparing her to a flower that had burst into bloom. Not only was this change obvious to

[6] *Editors' note:* Actually Barbara is practicing, through self-instruction training, how to talk to herself more appropriately. Notice the "cognitive restructuring" flavor to those new "beliefs." See Article 9.

me in the therapy sessions, but it was also confirmed enthusiastically by her mother.

RESULTS

Figure 1 represents Barbara's progress during the six weeks of counseling. There was a total of eight counseling sessions. During the first two weeks there were two sessions each week but only one for each of the remaining four weeks.[7]

At that time, Barbara thought that she could comfortably handle the situation. She did not want to come to therapy anymore. A few weeks later she left for two months of summer camp, which she enjoyed very much.

---

[7] *Editors' note:* As complete success was achieved in the fourth week of treatment (during the middle of the assertion-training exercises), it is not at all clear just which procedures accounted for the results. The case does suggest some promising possibilities that future research studies might test.

Follow-Up

Follow-up contact was made after six months, one year, two years, and three years. During this entire three-year period, Barbara wet her bed only two times. Both of these occasions occurred during the first year and were preceded by events causing great excitement, like going on a plane trip with her father to Jamaica and looking forward to her first boy-girl date.

PERSONAL EFFECTS OF THE THERAPIST

I experienced a peculiar change in my own personal behavior as this case was coming to an end. During the wee hours of the morning, I noticed that I was awakening as a result of bladder tension. Half-awake, I would go to the bathroom and urinate. Several weeks later, after almost daily trips to the bathroom in the early morning hours, the thought struck me that I might have developed diabetes, for never before in

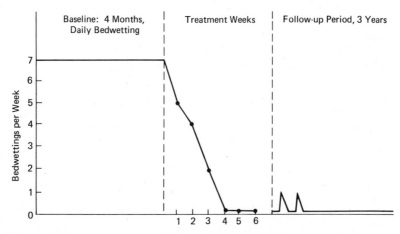

FIGURE 1 Number of nights of bed wetting per week during the four-month base-line period, in 6 weeks of treatment, and during the three-year follow-up.

my life had I felt the urge to urinate in the early morning hours. A physical checkup turned out to be negative. My doctor, however, suggested that I take a glucose-tolerance test and consequently made arrangements at the hospital.

About two days before my appointment, I was discussing with a friend this particular case, pointing out that I was going to use the same methodology with a sixteen-year-old enuretic girl, when suddenly I stopped and muttered, "My God." I repeated this phrase several times like a record player whose needle is stuck in a groove. "My God," I said, "I conditioned myself while I was reconditioning my patient. It has to be that. . . . It's unbelievable!"

The next morning I called up my doctor to cancel the appointment and to inform him of my opinion. He still thought that I should go through with the examination. However, I assured him that if my hypothesis was correct, I should be able to decondition myself as easily as I had conditioned myself to getting out of bed and urinating

whenever I had these "feelings" in my bladder. I immediately set up a procedure of counterconditioning.

First, I reproduced the feelings in my stomach by blowing with my lips, then followed with the words "When I am asleep, I will urinate only after I get up in the morning."

Second, before going to sleep, I again reproduced the bladder feeling and said numerous times, "I will fall asleep in a few minutes and will sleep deeply until I hear the radio music in the morning."

Third, during the day, also, I disregarded any slight buildup in bladder tension by becoming involved in activity.

In approximately one week, I was back to normal. There were no more night trips to the bathroom.[8]

[8] *Editors' note:* Maybe the old standard notion of "helping oneself by helping others" has real merit. Why not train enuretics (or shy, withdrawn people, hyperactives, and so on) to help other enuretics, using very specific techniques.

references

Cautela, J. R. Covert reinforcement. *Behavior Therapy*, 1971, 1, 33–50.

Ditman, K. S. & Blinn, M. D. Sleep levels in enuresis. Paper presented at the 110th annual meeting of the American Psychiatric Association, St. Louis, May 1974.

Wolpe, J. *Psychotherapy by reciprocal inhibition*. Stanford: Stanford University Press, 1958.

ENCOPRESIS

25. ENCOPRESIS: THE CASE OF JASON AND THE GOLDEN FECES

SUSAN R. PERKINS   Southeast Mental Health and Retardation Center, Fargo, North Dakota

When Jason's mother called the Center, her call was routed to me, the "new person" on the staff.[1] She explained that none of the other three counselors she had seen had been able to help Jason. She also stated that she and her husband were not coming in for more counseling because it was their son who had "the problem." When I asked her to be a little more specific, she said that Jason was refusing to do his chores around the house. Mrs. Montgomery also said there was "something else" about her son that she would tell me when she saw me. To a behavioral consultant, this problem seemed ideal for a behavior-change program, so I invited her in for an interview the following week.

When Mrs. Montgomery entered my office, she sat down and immediately began to tell me about the problem that she and her husband were having in obtaining even minimal cooperation from their son regarding his share of the household tasks. She said that she had followed a program outlined to her previously and that, although it had helped for a while, Jason had become very careless about his responsibilities. Then she paused.

Actually, the real problem is that Jason is still messing his pants, and after four years of this, I'm getting a little tired of cleaning up after him. And don't tell me to come in with my husband, because he won't, and besides, Jason's the one messing his pants, not us!

I could hardly argue with the last statement,[2] so I scheduled Jason for an appointment for three days later and went to look up his old records.

Jason and his family had been seen fourteen months before my first conversation with Mrs. Montgomery, when Jason had been just seven years old. The problems then had been identical with those presented to me, that is, a three-year history of encopresis (socially unacceptable bowel control) with a minimum of two accidents a week and a maximum of two accidents a day. There was also a reported lack of cooperation on Jason's part with regard to his share of the household duties (making his bed, picking up his toys, and so on). In addition, Jason was not doing well in school, and was collecting more than his share of "yellow cards" for misbehavior (like talking out of turn, out-of-seat behavior, and fighting). And Jason had no friends. There was also a report that he had been hit by a car, which resulted in multiple

---

[1] This case was handled in the Children's Services Division of the Southeast Mental Health and Retardation Center, Fargo, North Dakota.

[2] *Editors' note:* Although Jason was the one guilty of messing around, his parents may have been contributing to his odoriferous delinquency.

injuries, including a concussion. To make matters worse, this accident had occurred slightly before the onset of encopresis. Intelligence testing at that time had produced several significant indicators of brain damage, although a subsequent neurological report was negative.

Another part of Jason's folder contained a six-page (single-spaced) behavior-modification program including one procedure for toilet training and another for household responsibilities. The program looked flawless, and reinforcers seemed ideal.[3] By that time I was not looking forward to seeing Jason.

FINDING APPROPRIATE REINFORCERS

Jason appeared at 3:30 the next afternoon. Actually, his mother appeared to be hauling him into the reception area. His attitude toward seeing another counselor was not positive. One of his most outstanding aspects was his appearance. With crooked teeth, yellowish complexion, shaggy dirty-blond hair, and tattered clothes, he was not the kind of child that others were likely to pat on the head. Once in the office, I found that Jason was very verbal and maintained a constant stream of chatter about his school, his teacher, his brother, and whatever else came to mind. He also responded with a big smile to anything positive that I said to him. Here was a boy who obviously re-

sponded well to praise. Conversation then centered on his past experiences at the Center and his household chores. Jason reported that, although he was supposed to finish a certain number of jobs before he was allowed to go swimming, he had found a way around that. If he made a "real big fuss," his mother would let him go without doing any of the tasks. This "real big fuss" included yelling, stamping his feet, and pounding on the floor or wall with his fists. This behavior was fail-safe—he was always permitted to leave the house![4]

When I asked what his mother did when he did something good, he said she did nothing.

"Does she say she's happy you did your jobs?"

"No."

"Does she smile at you when you've done your jobs?"

"No."

"Does she give you a hug or a squeeze when you've done your jobs?"

"No! She don't do nothin'."

Things were becoming a little clearer. Jason received little or no reinforcement for completing his household chores, but he did receive a reward, in addition to attention, when he did not complete them.

Then our conversation turned to the encopresis. Jason announced loudly that he had decided not to mess his pants any more. He had not had one accident that entire day, so he thought that should prove it to me. I praised him, which produced the expected grin, and asked him whether or not he

[3] Editors' note: Flawless yet abstract. What counts, of course, are realistic programs that elicit the cooperation of the key people, not idealistic plans on paper.

[4] Editors' note: Despite his appearance, there was nothing shaggy about Jason's understanding of human behavior!

thought he could use a little help. He admitted that help would be okay with him. We then discussed all the advantages of having clean pants, and Jason indicated that maybe the kids would like him better if he did not have any accidents. He also indicated that it would probably make things a lot happier at home.

Because of the immediacy of the encopresis problem (school was starting in a few weeks), we decided to focus on this behavior. First, obviously, Jason's mother would be unable or unwilling to embark upon another program for Jason at home. Furthermore, she had not learned how to praise or reinforce her son when he did perform the tasks outlined. Jason did respond well to praise from me, and he truly seemed to want to stop the encopresis.

"Jason, do you like to talk to people on the telephone?"

"Yeah!"

There was my answer. I told Jason that, if he had a "perfect" day all day, he could call me tomorrow morning on the telephone. He really seemed to be excited about this prospect. Then I wrote down my telephone number for him, and we did some role-playing, including how to ask for me when the receptionist answered the phone. When he said, "Wow, this is neat!" I knew this approach might be appropriate, at least for a while.[5]

The next morning Jason called bright and early. He said that every-

thing was fine and that he had had clean pants all the day before.

"Hey, Jason, that's really great! I'm so proud of you. I knew you could do it."

"Yeah, and I'll call you tomorrow if I have a good day."

"Great. I'll be waiting for your call."

The next morning produced another call, and at the end of a perfect week I invited Jason in to have his picture taken with a Polaroid camera. This, I explained, was a special treat because he had done so well.

Jason's visit resulted in a discussion with him about continuing the telephone calls. He said that he enjoyed the telephoning. I then saw Mrs. Montgomery without Jason. She indicated that she was honestly pleased with her son and hopeful that this time things would work out. I told her about the procedure that was being used with Jason and questioned her about her reactions to Jason at the end of the day. Although she said she was happy, she was still saying nothing to her son to reinforce him for his good performance.[6] I gave her several suggestions about what she might say to Jason, and she agreed to give some of them a try.

At the beginning of the second week, Jason called as usual to report his progress to me, but this time he added, "My mom said she was proud of me!"

---

[5] *Editors' note:* It is an excellent idea to use daily telephoning as an immediate consequence for having clean pants. Role-playing how to call was also good anticipation.

[6] *Editors' note:* Unfortunately, this consequence is a very common one. We "expect" others to do what they should do but typically fail to communicate directly to them our happiness about their good work.

A REVERSAL

At the end of the second week of daily calls, Jason had maintained good performance, but I was scheduled to be out of town for the next three days, and I told him he would be unable to call me on the phone on each of those days. When I returned, there was no call from Jason. The next day, however, he called with the news that, although he had had a perfect day the day before, he had had three accidents previously, one on each of the days that he had been unable to call me! The daily phone-call system was reinstated immediately, and Jason finished off that week and the next two with a perfect record.[7]

SELF-PACED REDUCTION OF DEPENDENCE ON COUNSELOR REINFORCEMENT

By the end of the seventh week, the calls were coming irregularly, sometimes before school, sometimes afterward. It was apparent that Jason had come to realize some other benefits from giving up encopresis. His mother told me about his new friends (two of them) and also mentioned that he had not received one yellow card at school. She also said that she had started using the program prescribed for Jason's household tasks the year before and that he was "doing beautifully."

[7] Editors' note: Jason's three "accidents" suggest that the daily telephone contact was helping to control his messy behavior. The interrupted treatment served much as does an experimental reversal phase, in which treatment is withdrawn in order to assess its effect.

When I asked her if she had been praising Jason she said that she had and that, if she "forgot," Jason would ask her whether or not she was proud of him. "Yesterday, I had to tell him seven times that I was proud of him, but I didn't mind it, and even my husband said he was glad."

So Jason's mother and father had taken on some of the responsibility for reinforcing Jason when he did a good job, and Jason was reminding them to do so if they forgot.

Jason's phone calls to me were also changing in content. They were still less than two minutes in length, but less and less time was spent reinforcing Jason's good behavior, and more time was spent "just talking." For example:

"Well, Jason, any accidents yesterday?"

"Of course not. Hey, did you know that my teacher's in the hospital?"

I invited Jason to come in to see me, so that we could discuss the frequency of the calls. He said that he did not need to call me every day any longer, but he thought that three times a week would be good. I agreed to this schedule and asked him what days he would like to call. Jason picked Monday, Tuesday, and Friday.

Monday came, and there was no call until 3:30. Jason said that he had just called to report that he had broken his collar bone and was in the hospital but that I should not "worry" because he was doing fine. He asked whether or not he could call on Thursday instead of Tuesday and also whether or not it hurt when they removed stitches. The next week (week 9) Jason said that three times a week might be too much but that he would finish off this week and then just call me on Mondays and Thursdays. I agreed, but Jason was not able to reach me by phone until Wednesday, and he scolded me for being out of the office. Friday brought a call just before 5:00, and Jason said that he had been busy but hoped it was all right to call that late. He then stated that once a week would now be enough, and I spoke with him the following Tuesday. At that time, I told Jason that he had done so well that I wondered whether or not he needed to call me at all. He said that he did not think so, but his tone sounded somewhat doubtful, so I invited him to call "when he really needed to."

Jason called approximately one month later to report that all had been well and that he might visit me one of these days. I told him to stop in any time.

"Well, what I really called about is that I think maybe my brother should come down and see you, 'cause he does what I used to do."

"Really? How old is he?"

"Oh, eighteen months, I think."

OTHER APPLICATIONS OF FREQUENT TELEPHONE CHECKS

Very often individuals who appear to be the logical figures to deliver reinforcement for improved behavior to children are unable or unwilling to do so. Even with considerations of case load, it may be possible for the counselor to deliver the reinforcement himself. In the case of Jason, the initial conversation with the boy took approximately twenty minutes. Daily phone calls took less than two minutes each,

and the three visits to my office were kept to less than one-half hour each. With very little prompting from me, Jason was able to reduce the frequency of his calls very systematically, and at that point there had been no recurrence of the encopresis behavior, although another month has passed since Jason has called to talk with me. Figure 1 summarizes the results.

This technique has been used successfully with other children. Some of them live so far from the Center that weekly or even bimonthly personal contacts with them are impossible, but the telephone enables them to "check in" with me on a regular basis. (One ten-year-old boy reports his attendance from school each morning on the principal's office phone, and another girl calls weekly to report the number of stars that she has accumulated on a wall chart for completing household tasks.) Periodic checks with parents or teachers ensure reliable information, and often these calls are used to reinforce the adults for reinforcing the children. The calling schedule varies from child to child, but the majority consider use of the telephone to be a very special privilege and enjoy contact with adults, especially when this contact comes as an "earned" activity. In each of these cases, the initial program has been developed at the Center with the cooperation of the child.[8]

---

[8] *Editors' note:* This case clearly demonstrates how positive consequences can be rearranged to help a person do what he is clearly capable of doing.

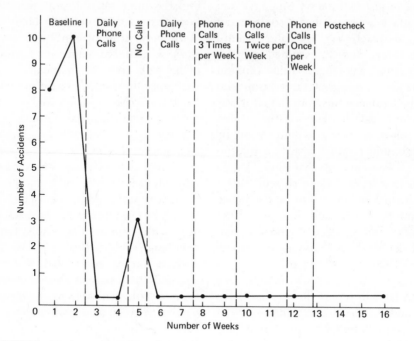

FIGURE 1   Number of Jason's bowel-movement accidents before, during, and after treatment.

EXHIBITIONISM

26.   TREATMENT FOR EXHIBITIONISM

HALMUTH H. SCHAEFER   University of Auckland

Exhibitionism, the compulsive display of the genitals in public, is probably the most common of all sexual offenses. Hirschfeld (n.d.), the pioneer sex researcher and neurologist, declared that in Germany around the turn of the century it accounted for about one third of all sex crimes. Wallace (1967) regards it as the most common sex offense in Australia and New Zealand. Arieff and Rotman (1942) and Coleman (1972) make the same statement for the United States. Statistics from New Jersey State Police files of known sex offenders reported by Ellis (1967) show the incidence of exhibitionism second (18 percent) only to rape (45 percent) for that state.

The behavior seems to be a problem for males only (Dengrove, 1967), although inappropriate nudity of female patients in mental hospitals is well known, and there are several reports in the psychiatric literature on defiant or provocative exposure of the genitals or buttocks by females during court hearings for hospital commitment. Witzig (1968) reports only a single female among the many males he treated for the problem. Kinsey and his associates (1948) report that more than 99 percent of all males who admitted to sex play as boys began this activity by exhibiting themselves.

There is a remarkable and uncharacteristic agreement among clinicians, quite regardless of their respective orientations or the periods during which they have written, on the behavior patterns of the exhibitionist: He has no idea why he exhibits himself or, indeed, how he is capable of such an act, given his normal outlook on life; he has usually been reared by over strict or puritanical parents in an environment in which there has been little personal warmth and love (Rickles, 1950); he has a stereotype *modus operandi*, in that he exhibits at a fixed place or kind of place (park, automobile, beach, and so on) and sometimes even at a fixed time of day; his sexual fantasies are limited to scenes of exhibiting; he is not sexually adequate with others (Hirning, 1947); before and during exhibition he feels sexual urges, but only of the vaguest general nature and never of the type that would eventuate in normal sexual intercourse with the subjects (nearly always women and children) to whom he exhibits; he is never a member of a nudist club (Witzig, 1968).

Nearly all psychodynamic clinicians and some behaviorally oriented therapists consider exhibitionism relatively easy to treat and unlikely to recur once treated. But this belief seems at odds with the large number of practicing exhibitionists, many of whom most certainly would seek help if they believed it were available. It also does not square with the clinical observation that many of the patients referred for treatment of the problem have had previous treatment. It may be that the situation is misleading in that the exhibitionist who happens not to be exhibiting is not only appalled at such times at what he has been doing but is quite sincerely convinced that he will never succumb to the compulsion again now that he has received what he believes to be successful therapy. There is not much follow-up reported in the older studies, perhaps because the offenders have moved because of the usual publicity that surrounds the offense.

Behavioral therapists are more likely to be aware of the control that the environment outside the hospital, jail, or office is likely to exert. An excellent example of the complexity of the behavior, in particular its dependence on a great variety of stimuli, is given by Bond and Hutchison (1960), who describe a case in which systematic desensitization was used. Over a period of about two years the authors time and again were able to extinguish the behavior *in a given situation*—much to the relief of the patient and his wife—only to find that there was yet one more stimulus complex that had not been touched.

Not all exhibitionists are likely to have a wide range of stimuli that requires individual extinction. Abel and his colleagues (1970), Dengrove (1967), Evans (1967), and Kushner and Sadler (1966) employed behavioral techniques in various ways. The results seem to favor a combination of aversion and subsequent avoidance procedures.

From a behavior-analytic point of view exhibitionism is easy enough to understand. The behavior is compulsive in the sense that like gambling, it must have been acquired under some variable-ratio schedule of reinforcement. It also occurs under socially inappropriate conditions, and in that sense it is an abnormal behavior. Ullmann and Krasner best describe the most commonly held behavioral view: "Over a period of time, the pairing of sexual release with exhibiting may lead to the various situations in which exhibiting behavior comes by itself to have strong stimulus control not unlike that of the fetish object" (1969, p. 481).

This logical description does not take into account, however, that some, and perhaps many, exhibitionists do not achieve orgasm during their offensive actions or immediately following them. Indeed, if there were continuous pairing, the behavior would lose its compulsive appearance, because it would now be operating under a schedule of continuous reinforcement. Nevertheless, it is possible to regard the behavior itself, the opening of garments and the display of the genitals, simply as an activity that may or may not lead to reinforcement, depending, perhaps, on the reactions of onlookers.

If that approach to analysis is used, the sexual feelings, whatever they are, become merely one facet of the stimulus complex that prevails at the time. This way of thinking suggests at once a novel and highly attractive therapeutic approach: If it were possible to elicit the behavior in the presence of stimuli other than the highly specific ones in the presence of which it is normally emitted, then these new stimuli should weaken the exclusive control of the old. Among these new stimuli would be strong conscious feelings of inappropriateness, shame, awareness of the situation, self-ridicule, and common sense, none of which is normally present during exhibitions, according to accounts by nearly all exhibitionists.

These feelings, it should be pointed out, are well known to the exhibitionist, but they are invariably experienced after, never during, an exhibition. It is the presence of these stimuli, along with "vague" sexual urges, that probably prevents normal adults from exhibiting themselves in public. To explore this notion, the following study was undertaken.

SUBJECTS AND PROCEDURE

The first subject, J, a thirty-eight-year-old, married construction worker, had been referred for treatment as part of a suspended sentence for exhibiting himself on a construction site repeatedly to two small school girls on their way to and from school.[1] He had six previous arrests, resulting in either convictions or suspended sentences. He had started exhibiting himself at age fifteen years and, since then, he believed he had averaged two exhibitions a week. He maintained a diary of such activities, which he preserved for four

[1] Special thanks are owing to the officers of the Probation Department in Auckland, especially Mr. Fred Masters and Mr. M. J. Hazel for encouragement to the author in the conduct of this study and for their special efforts in conducting follow-up procedures.

to five years to protect himself against unjust accusations, which he believed are commonly leveled against known sex offenders. This record showed that during the six months preceding his arrest he had exhibited himself an average of 4.2 times a month.

On three previous occasions he had been given therapy by one psychologist (using rational counseling) and by two psychiatrists (using transactional analysis in one instance and supportive counseling combined with an antidepressant-drug regimen in the other). He reported that all of these approaches had helped for a while but that he had relapsed soon after treatment had been terminated.

He was highly motivated to receive professional help, but at the same time he had little hope that anything could be done to help him permanently. He was accepted for treatment and seen a total of seven times for approximately one hour each in a private office. The progression of sessions was structured as follows.

First Week

During the first week an intake interview was held to assess the stimuli present when the exhibiting behavior occurred. A baseline record of the occurrence of sexual thoughts (and the content of such thoughts in general terms, for example, heterosexual activity with one or several partners of a certain age, a seduction scene, an exhibiting scene, and so on), erections, urges to exhibit, actual exhibitions (and prevailing conditions at the time, including fantasies), and sexual outlets and types of outlet (masturbation, inter-

course, and so on) was established. J was instructed to keep an hourly record and was given seven of the sheets shown in Figure 1.

Second Week

In the second session we discussed the baseline data obtained during the previous week. The behavioral approach was explained in general terms, and J was assigned to continue baseline data collection and to "practice exhibitions" once every hour, starting immediately after awakening in the morning and ending before going to bed at night. He was asked to use discretion and to arrange for the exhibitions not to take place in crowded streets.[2] Each exhibition was to consist of opening the trouser flap, extracting the penis and scrotum, counting to five, and then restoring the proper appearance again. It was explained to J that this exercise had to be undertaken if treatment was to continue and that at this stage he should trust the therapist's judgment.

Third Week

At the third session we discussed the baseline data obtained during the previous week. Both J and his wife discussed the problem and the general approach, and general advice on normal sexual practices was given to the couple. Continued data collection and practice exhibitions were assigned.

[2] *Editors' note:* Exhibitions, it is hoped, without exhibitees! Using an "exhibiting on cue" (to the clock—once every hour—instead of to urges and fantasies) method is an excellent way to help people gain more control over their compulsive behavior.

Day:_____ Date:_____

Hour	Sexual Thoughts and Contents of Thoughts	Erections	Urges to Exhibit	Exhibitions and Situation	Sexual Outlets and Type
01					
02					
03					
04					
05					
06					
07					
08					
09					
10					
11					
12					
13					
14					
15					
16					
17					
18					
19					
20					
21					
22					
23					
24					

FIGURE 1   Convenient daily base-line record form given to subjects to record absence or presence of behaviors and coincidental stimuli for each hour of the day.

Fourth Week and After

At the fourth session we discussed progress, and continued practice exhibitions were assigned. After the fifth week, beside discussion of progress, arrangements were made for J and his wife to visit a public sauna. Practice exhibitions were discontinued, the performance record was continued.[3] Seven weeks went by, and a session was held in the twelfth week to discuss progress. Almost a year later (the fifty-second week) there was discussion of progress, and therapy was terminated.

Six other exhibitionists, ranging in age from twenty-four to fifty-five years, were subjected to the same regimen, which differed only in the involvement of wives: Three of the subjects were not living with their wives.

Follow-up throughout eighteen months for the most recent and two years for the first case was undertaken by means of personal contacts with the subjects, their families, friends, and employers and through the services of the probation officers of the New Zealand Department of Justice, through which all these subjects had been referred.

RESULTS

During and following the practicing of exhibitionism none of the seven offenders either felt urges to exhibit of the type he had previously found irresistible or actually exhibited himself inappro-

priately. The record of the first subject, J, has been presented in detail. From the very beginning, J kept excellent baseline records. This is not surprising, for he had recorded his behavior for many years previously, though not in such detail and with such frequency. Other subjects had to be coached, and in three instances an additional baseline week had to be used before practice exhibitions could commence. Figure 2 shows J's performance during the first week of baseline data taking. He actually exhibited three times during this period (on days 4 and 5) and had fifteen separate urges to do so. He distinguished those urges clearly from what he called "dirty thoughts," which might involve fantasies about exhibitions but were often vaguely connected with females. These thoughts averaged about eight a day.

At the end of the second week J reported that he felt silly and stupid when having to engage in the practice assignments. He stated that he had faithfully executed the exhibitions but asked that his practice be discontinued. Amazingly, only when it was pointed out to him with the graphic representation that his urges to exhibit had remained at zero every day between days 8 and 14 did he realize the effects of the practice exhibitions on his immediate problem.[4]

By the end of the third week the patient stated that any thoughts he had about exhibiting were now like other thoughts of lurid content: They did not

[3] *Editors' note:* Notice the progression of practice from exhibiting under voluntary control by the hour (not in response to uncontrolled urges) to "exhibiting" (being nude) in a public bath with his wife and others.

[4] *Editors' note:* The client often does not think a treatment is working when in fact it is. Data collection has advantages for the client too.

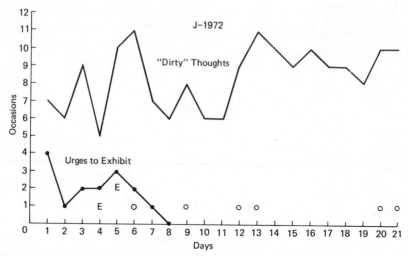

FIGURE 2 Frequency of daily involuntary exhibitions (E), sexual orgasms (O), urges to exhibit, and sex fantasies regarded initially as "dirty thoughts" by subject J.

and need not lead to immediate action or any action. He reported that his marital sex life had somewhat improved but that he was not happy with the results yet.

Sometime during the third month the patient, though not his wife, attended a public mixed sauna bath. The patient dated his personal confidence in not offending again to this event.[5]

[5] *Editors' note:* Perhaps prolonged exposure to the gaze of others under socially

Figure 3 permits a comparison of the patient's behavior and after therapy. The three exhibitions during March were those shown for days 4 and 5 in Figure 2. After the first day of practice exhibitions (day 8 in Figure 2), which took place in March, there were no

permissible conditions serves to extinguish the behavior—a variation of the flooding technique. If so, possibly a useful inexpensive treatment would be to require the exhibitionist to attend a mixed public sauna or a nudist camp.

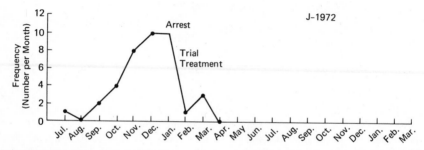

FIGURE 3 Frequency of self-exhibition for eight months before, during, and for twelve months after treatment.

further exhibitions or uncontrollable urges to exhibit. The incidence of sexual orgasms (small circles in Figure 2) was not affected by the treatment. Figure 3 also shows the seasonal effects on exhibiting: July, August, and September are the winter months in New Zealand. Like their counterparts in the northern hemisphere, they show the lowest incidence of exhibitionism.

After eighteen months J's probation officer wrote:

. . . there is an obvious change in "J," which manifests itself in many ways. It stems, I believe, from his vastly improved confidence about ever offending again. As an example, you know that he is a keen church chorister, and he is now singing solos for the first time in his life. Mrs. "J" seems by now to have adjusted to her new masterful spouse. Indeed, she seems pleased that she has relinquished her role as the dominant partner.

At the time of this writing J has also for the first time in his life, applied for and received promotion at his job.

With the exceptions already mentioned (additional coaching in baseline taking and insertion of an additional week of baseline taking before practice exhibiting), the course of therapy and subsequent performance were essentially the same for the other subjects. One of the divorced older men has now married again, another has become a modest "swinger," and the third has entered a steady homosexual reltionship.

The patterns of sexual activity for all of the subjects changed toward greater frequency and variety of sexual intercourse and toward greater assertiveness. It is very likely that the attendance at a mixed sauna greatly contributed to this particular change by providing the most explicit socially acceptable practice of "exhibition" behavior.

references

Abel, G. G., Levis, D. J. & Clancy, J. Aversion therapy applied to taped sequences of deviant behaviour in exhibitionism and other sexual deviations: A preliminary report. *Journal of Behavior Research and Experimental Psychiatry*, 1970, **1**, 59–66.

Arieff, A. J. & Rotman, D. B. Psychiatric inventory of 100 cases of indecent exposure. *Archives of Neurology and Psychiatry*, 1942, **47**, 495–498.

Bond, I. K. & Hutchison, H. C. Application of reciprocal inhibition therapy to exhibitionism. *Canadian Medical Association Journal*, 1960, **83**, 23–25.

Coleman, J. C. *Abnormal psychology and modern life.* (4th ed.) Glenview, Ill.: Scott, Foresman, 1972.

Dengrove, E. Behavior therapy of the sexual disorders. *Journal of Sex Research*, 1967, **3**, 49–61.

Dengrove, E. Sex differences. In A. Ellis and A. Abarbanel (Eds.), *The encyclopaedia of sexual behavior.* Hawthorn, N.Y.: 1967. Pp. 931 ff.

Ellis, A. The psychology of sex offenders. In A. Ellis and A. Abarbanel (Eds.), *The encyclopaedia of sexual behavior.* Hawthorn, N.Y.: 1967.

Evans, D. R. An exploratory study into the treatment of exhibitionism by means of emotive imagery and aversive conditioning. *Canadian Psychologist*, 1967, **8**, 162.

Hirning, L. C. Genital exhibitionism, an interpretive study. *Journal of Clinical Psychopathology*, 1947, 8, 557–564.

Hirschfeld, M. *Sexual anomalies and per-*

versions, London: Aldor, n.d. (approx. 1935).

Kinsey, A. C., Pomeroy, W. B. & Martin, C. E. *Sexual behavior in the human male*. Philadelphia: Saunders, 1948.

Kushner, M. & Sadler, J. Aversion therapy and the concept of punishment. *Behavior Research and Therapy*, 1966, **4**, 179–186.

Rickles, N. K. *Exhibitionism*. Philadelphia: Lippincott, 1950.

Ullmann, L. P. & Krasner, L. *A psycho-logical approach to abnormal behavior*. Englewood Cliffs, N.J.: Prentice-Hall, 1969.

Wallace, V. H. Sex life in Australia and New Zealand. In A. Ellis and A. Abarbanel (Eds.), *The encyclopaedia of sexual behavior*. Hawthorn, N.Y.: 1967. Pp. 193 ff.

Witzlig, J. S. The group treatment of male exhibitionists. *American Journal of Psychiatry*, 1968, **125**, 75–81.

HOMOSEXUALITY

27. COVERT SENSITIZATION FOR HOMOSEXUALITY[1]

EDWARD J. CALLAHAN   Camarillo-Neuropsychiatric Institute Research Program, University of California, Los Angeles

Covert sensitization is a verbal aversion-therapy technique used to suppress feelings or behaviors that are unwanted by the client. The term "covert sensitization" was coined by Cautela (1966), who has stimulated much interest in the technique. Previously, a very similar technique was used by Miller (1959; 1963) with hypnosis for the suppression of alcoholic desires and overeating.

[1] The author wishes to thank Robert Moore, William Frey, and Charles McArthur for their work in helping to treat this client. The opinions stated are those of the author and do not necessarily reflect the views of the California Department of Health or the University of California Board of Regents. The writing of this paper was supported in part by Grant No. MH-R20-C from the National Institute of Mental Health.

Covert sensitization has proved to be a fairly flexible technique and has been found useful in the treatment of alcoholism (see, for example, Anant, 1967), obesity (for example, Janda & Rimm, 1972), drug abuse (for example, Wisocki, 1973), and sexual deviation (Barlow, Leitenberg & Agras, 1969; Callahan & Leitenberg, 1973).

The purpose of the present article is to spell out how to reach the decision to use covert sensitization when dealing with homosexuality, how to take an intensive sexual-learning history, what salient measures of continuing sexual arousal might be taken, and how covert sensitization was applied in one case of homosexuality.

There is increasing sentiment that homosexuality should not be labeled a sexual deviation. At a recent American Psychiatric Association symposium (Stoller, 1973) this issue was debated, and later the same association removed homosexuality from its list of psychiatric disorders. Davison and Wilson (1973; 1974) have made a point that improved homosexual functioning can be a legitimate goal for behavior therapy with homosexual clients. Kohlenberg (1974), in fact, has used Masters and Johnson's sex-therapy techniques with a homosexual pedophilic to improve his sexual functioning with adult males.[2] These developments are indeed important, for changing sexual orientation in therapy is quite difficult and cannot be the therapist's sole option for the homosexual client. This implies the presentation in part of value-free therapy. That is, the therapist can encourage the client's choice of a life style different from that of the therapist and much of society yet within the fairly extensive moral bounds of the therapy. As Strupp (1974) has pointed out, however, even therapists claiming to be "value free" would not help a pedophilic reduce the guilt that he feels when molesting children. Thus, a therapist ought to be open to whatever goals a homosexual client selects. However, as Marmor (1973) points out, homosexuality can be a painful state for some individuals; for such individuals, treatment to change sexual arousal is the legitimate choice. With such people covert sensitization provides a usable and potentially successful treatment for reaching goals. The option of

covert sensitization or other treatment is first laid out in the presenting interview.[3]

REDUCING HOMOSEXUAL AROUSAL

Presenting Interview: Session 1

As in any treatment, the first interview is a crucial start in establishing rapport and in outlining therapeutic options for reaching the client's goals. The initial complaints of the client ought to be elicited while it is emphasized that he will have the support and expertise of the therapist in undertaking whatever reasonable therapeutic goals he chooses. For the "sexually deviant" client, the therapist can point out that sexual arousal is learned and can be changed or can be accepted as a natural and normal human experience.

In setting the goals for treatment, a critical question is what has motivated the client to seek treatment at the present time. As far as I know, court referral is no longer used for homosexuality in the United States. This is fortunate because it allows homosexuals optimal freedom and it increases the possibility of successful treatment. In addition, court-referred pedophilics (child molesters) or exhibitionists must be worked with more slowly and more carefully than self-referred homosexuals.

---

[2] *Editors' note:* See Article 7 for a description of a variation of Masters and Johnson's technique for heterosexuals.

[3] *Editors' note:* Indeed, it is important for the counselor to act in such a way that the choice of goals is up to the client. Of course, counselors may differ in their willingness to accomplish certain goals. Treatment should proceed only when client and counselor are agreed on the goals.

Court referral is not a reason to deny a client treatment, but it may indicate that the client is less well motivated for change than is a client who comes on his own initiative. The pressures that the homosexual feels when seeking treatment are critical and may be used to support treatment. However, if the client chooses, he can be taught to overcome pressures to live as a homosexual.

What are the therapeutic goals open to the client? Obviously, the first alternative is the acceptance of homosexuality. This option may well require less therapy time than trying to bring about a complete change in his sexual arousal. Some options for achieving this goal are systematic desensitization to anxiety about discovery, assertion training for interactional deficiencies, and referral to gay-liberation groups. A second therapeutic goal is to work on increasing heterosexual arousal (see Barlow, 1973, for a review of these techniques). The increase of heterosexual arousal can be undertaken in lieu of covert sensitization with the goal of creating bisexuality or in conjunction with covert sensitization. If the client is married or can find a female partner, a training program of the type identified with Masters and Johnson may well be in order for increasing heterosexual satisfaction.

Following the description of options for the client, he should be asked to record all instances of his own sexual arousal and activity during treatment. This will be important in evaluating treatment progress for both therapist and client. Arousal can be recorded using the following categories for both males and females:

1. *Sexual urges:* quick-striking sexual arousal in response to the sight or thought or another person
2. *Sexual fantasies:* any sustained thoughts of sexual interaction with another person
3. *Masturbation:* self-stimulation to orgasm (recording the content of the accompanying fantasies)
4. *Contact:* any sexual encounter with another person.

These categories can be tallied in a small notebook, and can be fantasies explained in the therapy hour or written out. These data can be tallied in a pocket-sized notebook under code so that others will not know what is being recorded. While the client records these pretreatment measures, other aspects of the clinical interaction can be continued.[4]

Sessions 2–5

Several things must be accomplished in the second section of therapy. First, the client must be trained in relaxation. Second, measures of homosexual arousal and activity must be monitored. Third, a detailed sexual-learning history must be taken.

Relaxation training is conducted in the manner described by Wolpe (1958). Generally, it consists of having the client lean back in a recliner chair, close his eyes, and then proceed through the various parts of the body, first tensing the muscle groups and then

---

[4] *Editors' note:* There are, of course, a variety of self-observation techniques. Some persons may find wrist counters (leather or golf type) helpful in recording their actions.

relaxing them. This procedure takes twenty to thirty minutes. Homework assignments to practice the relaxation each night before falling asleep are given. A tape recording of relaxation instructions can be made by the therapist if the client has his own recorder to use. It is important to monitor the progress of the relaxation homework, both to ensure that it is being practiced and to help the client with any particular difficulties that he may encounter in relaxing. The relaxation will probably have to be practiced in these sessions as well. Gradually, the amount of instruction can be faded back to the point at which the patient relaxes by thinking about particular parts of the body. The other area that must be monitored closely in early treatment is the recording of sexual arousal and activity.

Pages from the recording notebook should be examined, and fantasies and contacts should be reviewed to determine their contents. This detailed information will be important in shaping the therapy sessions to cover the current arousal patterns of the client. The other source of information on arousal is a well-detailed sexual-learning history.

In gathering the sexual-learning history, a good starting point is to obtain a report of the first remembered instances of both homosexual and heterosexual activity. Detailed information for both these histories is quite important. It often leads to a view of the patient as reaching his sexual puberty just at the time of treatment; that is, he may be viewed as ready to discover sexual arousal toward women for the first time. The next step in the learning history is to determine what other forms of sexual arousal have been important to the person in the past and what other forms of sexual arousal occur currently. These experiences may provide fantasy "crutches" to increase heterosexual arousal; that is, the client during treatment may briefly imagine these scenes, in order to maintain an erection while masturbating to a heterosexual fantasy or while having intercourse with a woman. These crutches can be decreased in duration and frequency over time (see Marquis, 1970). Thus, it is critical to know the content of fantasies during masturbation.

At an overt level, it is important to know what sort of homosexual seeking behavior, or "cruising," goes on; what antecedents trigger the cruising episodes, where the cruising occurs; and who is involved. It is further necessary to learn what forms of homosexual activity occur, who the most likely partners are, and where the activity is likely to happen. Finally, it is important to know whether or not there is any heterosexual dysfunction. Some reporting on this matter from both the client and any heterosexual partner is important.

Next, it is very important to discover the content of the client's current sexual-arousal hierarchies. First, determine what the most attractive woman is, what her age is, what her body build is like, what her hair is like, what her face is like. Second, find out what the least attractive woman is like. Third, find out the most arousing heterosexual situation. Fourth, find the least arousing heterosexual situation. This same process should be repeated with homosexual partners.

THE CASE OF LOWELL

The client, Lowell, was a twenty-five-year-old single male living with his parents. He had been referred by his family doctor because he considered himself abnormal owing to homosexual arousal and continuing tension and anxiety. He dated the onset of his sexual difficulties to the age of six years, when a twenty-year-old uncle taught him to masturbate and later to masturbate him (the uncle). He had continued this activity sporadically with his uncle for several years. In the second grade, he and a young male friend had practiced mutual masturbation and had experimented with each other's erections. Lowell reported that he and his friend would undress in a barn and smell all the areas of their bodies. He had then continued to masturbate but had had no further involvement with others until junior high school, when he and another boy had engaged in mutual masturbation and fellatio for approximately one year. After this boy had moved away, Lowell had continued to masturbate quite frequently but had had no further male sexual contact.

Lowell's own masturbation then took on aspects of fetishism. Initially, he had defecated in his bed, rubbed his groin with feces, and then masturbated. Eventually, he had ceased using feces but instead had urinated in the sheets, had held the sheets next to his groin, and had masturbated. In the more recent past, he had used vaseline rubbed into the groin and anus, instead of urine. In addition, he had begun to seek anal stimulation by inserting candles into his anus during masturbation.

By the tenth grade he had sought help from his mother on the issue of the normality of masturbation. He had refused to talk to his father, telling his mother that his father would never understand. At that time he had confessed these activities to his priest, who had given him advice on how to control himself. He had attempted to control himself and had become devoutly religious but had continued much of the sexual behavior.

In high school he had dated three different girls. Each relationship had lasted about six months, although he had never become aroused by the girls. During these dating periods he had not masturbated. He had had little desire to kiss the first two girls and cannot remember ever having had erections while with them. He had begun to date the third girl as a high-school senior and had done some minor petting with her, which included some fondling of her breasts. He had had erections on occasion while with this girl. Because of this he had become obsessed with the idea of marrying her, and he had begun to look through ring catalogues. Later he recalled feeling very guilty because he had frequently missed church to be with her. He had broken up with her on grounds of religious differences.

After having been graduated from high school he had begun working at a local company. He had continued to live at home and had later joined the national guard. During his service in the national guard he had become very tense and nervous. (It was the first and only time that he had been away from home.) He had felt the urge to masturbate more frequently but had been too embarrassed to masturbate in the barracks, where he might be seen. He had had no homosexual contacts while in the national guard.

After leaving the national guard and before treatment he had dated two girls, each relationship lasting four to five months. He reported that he had broken up with each of these girls because of his feelings of inadequacy and confusion. With the second girl he had actually discussed marriage, but as he felt that he was sexually incapable of making love to her he had broken up with her. Since then Lowell had felt anxious, depressed, and in need of psychiatric help. At that point he began to consult his own physician. Talking about his sexual problems made him feel less tense; however, during the same period he had also noticed an increase in his attraction to males. He had found himself looking at "men's rears and where their penises are." He would become sexually aroused but would feel very guilty and then would become even more anxious. His physician referred him to the University of Vermont's Clinical Research Unit.

First Few Interviews

At intake to the twelve-bed clinical research unit, Lowell stated that he had always floated through life, had never felt committed to anything, and had always felt dependent upon his family to make his decisions. He felt that he had never had any manly traits, having had many fears, having felt very cowardly, and lacking aggressive instinct. He felt as if he were the butt of jokes whenever he was in a large group, and he felt anxious having to speak to girls. Lowell had only recently been able to talk to his father generally about the

issue of masturbation. His father had responded to the "problem" by saying that it is completely normal, and that had ended the conversation.

Aside from the sexual-learning history, Lowell was interviewed to determine other life problems. They included asking girls for dates, being afraid to feel foolish (someone might be watching, the girl might say no), feeling hurt when people said things even if they did not mean them, being forced to fight back. (As a child he had always feared and felt weaker than the other guy; instead of fighting, he would go home and tell his folks about it. His mother would encourage him to be passive, while his father and brother would encourage his fighting. He usually remained passive.)

He also never felt that he could communicate with a girl very well. Other anxiety came at work, where he felt that people were out to "screw" him and were keeping information from him. Still another source of anxiety was the fact that there were two known homosexuals working in the same area of the plant. He was very much afraid that he was behaving as they did.

Session 5: Review of Alternatives

After gathering baseline measures of sexual arousal, training the patient in relaxation, and taking an extensive learning history, it was time to review the learning history and the various options available to Lowell for treatment. It is often helpful for the client to understand his sexual arousal as learned through a combination of his life circumstances and the fantasies that he had available for masturbation. At this point he can be given a behavioral explanation of how masturbation reinforces the fantasies that it occurs with and how orgasm's being paired with a stimulus makes that stimulus more erotic (Maguire, Carlisle & Young, 1965; Abel & Blanchard, 1974). With this understanding of how the sexual-arousal pattern has been established and maintained, the client then can feel free to accept or alter that pattern.

In the case of Lowell, this decision point led to a firmer conviction that he wanted to try to do away with his homosexual arousal and to learn heterosexual arousal. In fact, he viewed the learning-history explanation of his sexual-arousal patterns with relief and a feeling of lessened guilt. He chose at that point to begin covert sensitization.

From his history and the description of his current sexual arousal we drew up the following list of sexually arousing scenes from his experience:

1. Sitting with a group of men at the national guard camp around the fire and seeing one man stand up in his underwear, go to the fire, and bend down, exposing his penis.
2. Walking into the men's room at work and looking at a man sitting on the john defecating.
3. Sleeping on a crowded truck at the national-guard camp, rolling over, and hitting his hand on the penis of the man next to him.
4. Walking into the locker room at work and seeing a man lying on the bench with his legs spread wide apart.
5. After drinking with another man, pulling off the road to masturbate.
6. Being at the national guard camp, walking up to the latrine, and finding another man defecating.

These items were roughly equal in their arousal value; their content was varied by using different scenes with descriptions of the most and least attractive persons (see Table 1).

Covert Sensitization

With this information, covert sensitization was started in the sixth session. Sessions were held twice each day while Lowell was hospitalized. Each

TABLE 1   Physical Characteristics Related to Sexual Arousal.

	Men	Women
Most attractive		
physique	muscular	well proportioned
age	18–50 years	20–25 years
hair	blond, wavy	blonde
looks	handsome, strong face	pretty, delicate features
clothes	stylish, not mod	stylish, not mod
Least attractive		
physique	obese	obese
age	very young or old	under sixteen or over 30 years
height	very short	very short or tall
looks	pock-marked from acne	pock-marked from acne
clothing	loud or wild	loud or wild

session consisted of four punishment scenes and two escape scenes. Each scene lasted three to four minutes, with about one minute between scenes, so that each covert-sensitization session lasted between thirty and forty minutes. Assertion training was conducted concurrently by another therapist, who focused on work-related scenes. The following are examples of one punishment scene and one escape scene used with Lowell early in treatment.

Punishment: "I want you to imagine that you are on the truck at night with the national guard. It's been a long and tiring day, and it's been quite hot. You are lying on the truck quite tired but somewhat edgy and you start to remember times during the day when you looked at the crotches of men working around you. You start to feel hot and uncomfortable as you're lying there, and you can feel a slight cramping sensation in your stomach. Your head starts to feel a little light, and you feel the sweat forming on your neck and your forehead. You start to turn over on the truck, and you realize that the fellow lying next to you has rolled closer. You start to think more about him lying there and about his penis just a foot away from you. You look toward him and see he's pulled his blanket off to be more comfortable, and you know you can look down to see his penis. You start to turn more towards him and you feel yourself getting aroused, but your gut is getting hotter and more queasy. You can feel your stomach floating heavily inside. You try to turn away from the guy, but you're too close to the side of the truck. You're getting hotter and more sweaty as you turn back towards him, and your hand slips off your side and rubs up against his exposed penis. You pull your hand back as he grunts, and you look down and see his penis. Your stomach is really hot now as you feel the puke rolling slowly from one side of your stomach to the other—and the hot chunks start to press up into the back of your throat. You tentatively put your hand back near his penis, but as you do, you begin to gag on the bitterly acidic chunks of puke—they are gagging and choking you. You're really feeling hot now, and you roll closer to him just wanting to stroke his penis with your hand. Your hand touches his penis, and you puke down on him and see the chunks of puke splatter on his face and down on your hand and on his penis. He wakes up gagging and glares at you as your hot, stinking puke rolls slowly between your fingers and down on his underwear and his penis.

Escape: You're at work, and its almost quitting time. It's been a hard day, and you are feeling tense because one of the homosexuals at work seemed to be staring at you a lot. You're walking to the locker room to get some cigarettes from your coat. You start to get aroused thinking there might be someone drying off from his shower whom you could look at. The thought of it makes you nervous but turned on. As you walk in, that idea gets stronger and stronger for you. You start to feel a cramping in your stomach as though you're going to have diarrhea. You walk toward your locker and see in the next row that there is a guy lying on the bench with wet legs—and you want to get closer. You start to walk closer and you see more of his leg and up to his thigh. You want to get closer to see his penis and his anus if you can. You see his legs are spread, and you really feel turned on, but then that cramping in your stomach starts to get worse. All you can feel is that cramping with an acidic feeling in your throat and sweat starting to break out on your forehead. You think you're going to be sick as you walk along, and you turn quickly and run out of the locker room. As you get out, the cramping stops in your stomach—an overhead fan cools your forehead—you walk to the fountain and take a slow, cool sip of water and feel immensely better. Then you walk to the outside door of the plant and feel a breeze from outside. You see an attractive blonde secretary coming in from outside —you look at her and smile. She smiles back, and you say hello while watching her breasts sway gently and her hips move from side to side as she walks. She stops, and you talk briefly about what a beautiful day it is and how the smell of the flowers is really filling the air. She speaks warmly and makes you feel a warm glow as the two of you talk.

During treatment, these scenes were varied with other attractive scenes from the homosexual hierarchy. Different noxious stimuli were used, including being stopped by the police while masturbating with another man, being stung by bees, and having the homosexual partner develop diarrhea. The point at which the noxious event was introduced was slowly and systematically placed earlier in the sequence of arousing events. For example, instead of vomiting as he stroked the penis of the man sleeping next to him on the national-guard truck, he would vomit as soon as he thought of stroking the other man's penis. In like manner, escape scenes become less and less homosexually oriented, with escape occurring to the thought of heterosexual contact or arousal. The escape to females became gradually more complex, with dating, petting, and intercourse ultimately introduced into the fantasies.

Lowell was given fourteen sessions of covert sensitization during the final ten days of hospitalization. During that time · his reported homosexual urges dropped from fourteen to six a day (with a mean of 10.2 a day during the

baseline period) to a frequency of zero. Data averaged in three-day blocks are presented in Figure 1. Lowell was then discharged and seen once a week for the following three months. During that time he reported spontaneous sexual arousal to the sight of women for the first time.

FOLLOW-UP

Booster sessions are probably quite important to the success of covert sensitization. Although no empirical studies exist to support the need for booster sessions, most clients from a large-scale study (Callahan, 1972) reported some new sexual urges or recurrence of old sexual urges after treatment. It is recommended that the frequency of treatment be faded gradually after the client reports that he has control of the problem and that additional trials of covert sensitization be run in these follow-up sessions. This format was used with Lowell.

At the initial follow-up, he reported a continued lessening of arousal to males and further reported that any arousal that did occur was now quickly and easily suppressed. Although he had started to feel sexual arousal for a woman for the first time, it brought up a new anxiety source: Could he perform intercourse?

This anxiety was handled by reassuring him that it would indeed be quite possible to have intercourse and describing the processes of foreplay and intercourse. At a five-month follow-up he reported that he was continuing to date one girl regularly. By that point, he thought that his main

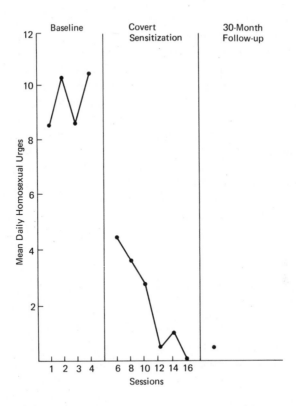

FIGURE 1.

problem involved whether or not to marry her. He was very concerned about being sure of his love for this woman. He reported regular sexual arousal and foreplay with his girlfriend, but they avoided sexual intercourse for religious reasons. He reported that, at that point the male fantasies of arousal had not recurred. He thought that the desire to have intercourse was there; however, he would not test it because of his religion, which taught that intercourse was appropriate only to marriage.[5] He continued to avoid masturbation completely, although he reported that he no longer felt guilty about his autoerotic behavior in the past. At that point he seemed more self-confident and reported

marked improvement in interpersonal relations. He was given a booster session of covert sensitization.

At one year's follow-up his major reported problem continued to be whether or not he was in love and whether or not he should marry. At a two-and-a-half-year follow-up he had maintained his improvement. He did report about one homosexual urge every three days for the two weeks be-

[5] *Editors' note:* There is a complex ethical dilemma here! It is usually assumed that a client's religious beliefs and practices should never be confronted. At times, however, such beliefs, if allowed to go unchallenged, may preclude attainment of the counseling goal desired by the client.

fore this session (see Figure 1). He had married the girl he was dating fourteen months after treatment had ended and reported no problems with intercourse. At the latest follow-up, Lowell reports that his progress has been maintained throughout the four and a half years since treatment ended, that there is now no problem with homosexual arousal, and that he has a good sexual relationship with his wife. Over that period of time, he and his wife have had two children. His wife was aware of all of his prior problems but accepted everything in his past and seemed to be very happy in the marriage, according to Lowell. However, at this final interview, he reported a problem with sleeping at night and a recurrence of anxiety problems related to work. These anxiety issues were treated with assertion training. The result was that the sleep disturbance disappeared and that reported anxiety decreased significantly.

references

Abel, G. & Blanchard, E. B. The role of fantasy in the treatment of sexual deviation. *Archives of General Psychiatry*, 1974, **30**, 467–475.

Anant, S. S. A note on the treatment of alcoholics by a verbal aversion technique. *Canadian Psychologist*, 1967, **8**, 19–22.

Barlow, D. H. Increasing heterosexual responsiveness in the treatment of sexual deviation: A review of the clinical and experimental evidence. *Behavior Therapy*, 1973, **4**, 655–671.

Barlow, D. H., Leitenberg, H. & Agras, W. S. The experimental control of sexual deviation through manipulation of the noxious scene in covert sensitization. *Journal of Abnormal Psychology*, 1969, **74**, 596–601.

Callahan, E. J. Aversion therapy for sexual deviation: A series of within-Ss examinations. Unpublished doctoral dissertation, University of Vermont, 1972.

Callahan, E. J. & Leitenberg, H. *Aversion therapy for sexual deviation: Contingent shock and covert sensitization. Journal of Abnormal Psychology*, 1973, **81**, 60–73.

Cautela, J. R. Treatment of compulsive behavior by covert sensitization. *The Psychological Record*, 1966, **16**, 33–42.

Davison, G. C. & Wilson, G. T. Goals and strategies in behavioral treatment of pedophilia: Comments on a case study. *Journal of Abnormal Psychology*, 1974, **83**, 196–198.

Davison, G. C. & Wilson, G. T. A survey of the attitudes of behavior therapists towards homosexuality. *Behavior Therapy*, 1973, **4**, 686–696.

Gray, J. J. Methods of training psychiatric residents in individual behavior therapy. *Journal of Behavior Therapy and Experimental Psychiatry*, 1974, **5**, 17–25.

Janda, L. H. & Rimm, D. C. Covert sensitization in the treatment of obesity. *Journal of Abnormal Psychology*, 1972, **80**, 37–42.

Kohlenberg, R. J. Treatment of a homosexual pedophilic using in vivo desensitization: A case study. *Journal of Abnormal Psychology*, 1974, **83**, 192–195.

Marmor, J. Homosexuality and cultural value systems. In Stoller, R. J. (Chm.), Should homosexuality be in the APA nomenclature? Symposium presented at the meeting of the American Psychiatric Association, Honolulu, 1973.

Marquis, J. N. Orgasmic reconditioning: Changing sexual object choice through controlling masturbation fantasies. *Journal of Behavior Therapy and Experimental Psychiatry*, 1970, **1**, 263–271.

McGuire, R. J., Carlisle, J. M. & Young, B. G. Sexual deviations as conditioned behavior. *Behavior Research and Therapy*, 1965, **2**, 185–190.

Miller, M. M. Hypnotic aversion of homosexuality. *Journal of the National Medical Association*, 1963, **55**, 411–414.

Miller, M. M. Treatment of chronic alcoholism by hypnotic aversion. *Journal of the American Medical Association*, 1959, **171**, 1492–1495.

Stoller, R. J. (Chm.) Should homosexuality be in the APA nomenclature? Symposium presented at the meeting of the American Psychiatric Association, Honolulu, 1973.

Strupp, H. H. Some observations on the fallacy of value-free psychotherapy and the empty organism: Comments on a case study. *Journal of Abnormal Psychology*, 1974, **83**, 199–201.

Wisocki, P. The successful treatment of a heroin addict by covert conditioning techniques. *Journal of Behavior Therapy and Experimental Psychiatry*, 1973, **4**, 55–61.

Wolpe, J. *Psychotherapy by reciprocal inhibition.* Stanford: Stanford University Press, 1958.

FEARS AND ANXIETIES

"We have nothing to fear but fear itself." Franklin Roosevelt's famous comment made during the darkest days of the Great Depression had much truth to it. There was for many at that time a great deal to be aroused about—no money, little food, few jobs. But Roosevelt was addressing the fear and anxiety that are caused by fear and anxiety themselves—the vicious cycle in which a person's fearful thoughts and physical arousal stimulate even more stress and tension. Like a forest fire spreading rapidly, fears and anxieties are fanned by the physical and mental arousal the person experiences. At the extreme, some people become physically immobilized, almost frozen in place as it were; others suffer from wildly racing thoughts and frightening images. Often, a devastating combination of physical and mental upset is experienced.

Many fears are irrational, in that the situation feared will not in fact take place or cause physical harm. But the person acts *as if* serious physical or social danger were at hand. He may, of course, be extremely aroused because he cannot, or believes he cannot, do a thing well enough—because he suffers a behavioral deficit (for example, inability to give a speech to a large audience). A person may know how to do something but cannot because of the tremendous tension involved ("I could do it, but I'm so upset just thinking about it"). Behavioral excess is a factor here—too much tension and arousal. Understandably the person moves quickly to reduce this extreme tension, often by avoiding or escaping the situation. Thus an endless assortment of feared people and situations are scrupulously avoided: the dentist, an attractive girl (boy), exams, walks in the country, parties, elevators, tall buildings, speaking up in groups. There is hardly anything that is not feared by someone. But avoiding the feared situation does not reduce the fear. On the contrary, avoidance increases the fear by constantly proving the phobic's belief: "I won't experience panic as long as I stay away from X."

Much time and effort have been spent focusing on fine discriminations among fears, phobias, and anxieties. Perhaps it would be more helpful to view them as various *tension responses* that a person experiences physiologically, motorically, or cognitively *in reaction to some actual or anticipated stressful event or object*. In this way attention would be focused more on those features of the environment that bring about excessive arousal.

As tensions are often experienced across the board—as dry throat, butter-flies in the stomach, jerky movements, disrupted speech, confused thinking, and so on—a combination of treatments may be most helpful. In the following articles a variety of tensions are dealt with by means of a variety of techniques. Some of the procedures have already been introduced in the sections on behavioral deficits, excesses, and inappropriate behaviors. One theme is apparent throughout these papers: On a gradual, step-by-step basis the person learns how to take action in the stressful situation. The best overall solution for tensions, regardless of their origins and specific contents, seems to be variations of "show, do, and shine." First, show the person in some way, step by step, how to act in the stressful situation; then have the person do what has been demonstrated; and, finally, make sure that the person receives some type of encouragement and support for efforts to enact these steps.

Sometimes the tension is so extreme that it must first be reduced by means of physical relaxation or other means before the person can attend to and benefit from the sequence of modeling, practice, and reinforcement described. At other times the structured opportunity to observe how to act and to practice with ample physical and social support suffices. One rule of thumb for reducing ex-treme tension tends to emerge: Any action that is antagonistic or incompatible with tension *for that person* can be used. Thus physical relaxation or breathing-focused meditation may be more effective in reducing tension for one person, whereas jumping right in and doing what has been modeled is better for another. The general thrust is (and should be) to teach the person the skills of self-control so that future stress can be managed in order to keep tension within tolerable limits. After all, not all tension is bad. Too much of it is what causes problems.

TREATMENT OF PHOBIAS

28. EFFECTING CHANGE THROUGH PARTICIPANT MODELING[1]

ALBERT BANDURA Stanford University

Social learning principles can be implemented in many different ways, some of which are more effective than others. The optimal procedures for achieving enduring changes in behavior include induction through modeling, refinement through enactment, and reinforcement through successful use. The treatment approach that combines modeling with guided reinforced performance has therefore yielded the most impressive results under diverse psychological conditions. In the present article we analyze the method of participant modeling as applied to the treatment of behavioral deficits and defensive behavior. Let us first consider the principal components.

MODELING

Desired activities are repeatedly modeled, preferably by different models, who demonstrate progressively more difficult performances. In competence training, complex patterns of behavior

[1] Research discussed by the author in this paper was supported by Public Health Research Grant M-5162 from the National Institute of Mental Health. Some of the material that is incorporated in this paper was originally presented at a conference on The Behavioral Basis on Mental Health, Galway, Ireland.

are broken down into the requisite subskills and organized hierarchically to ensure optimal progress. To eliminate inappropriate fears and inhibitions, anxious individuals observe models engaging in threatening activities without experiencing any adverse consequences.

GUIDED PERFORMANCE

After the demonstration, individuals are provided with necessary guidance and ample opportunities to enact the modeled behaviors under favorable conditions at each step until they perform them skillfully and spontaneously. Various response-induction aids are used whenever needed to assist participants through difficult performances.

REINFORCING EXPERIENCES

Modeling and guided performance are ideally suited for inducing psychological changes, but the resulting behaviors are unlikely to endure unless they prove effective when put into practice in every-day life. People must therefore experience sufficient success in using what they have learned. This is best achieved by a transfer program in which newly acquired skills are first tried in natural situations likely to produce favorable results and then extended to more unpredictable and riskier circumstances.

In the weakest treatment approaches, those relying upon conversational influences, all three components are typically lacking. Therapists favoring such techniques tend to model a restricted range of conduct, and what they do exemplify most prominently may have limited functional value for those seeking help.[2] In addition, clients are, for the most part, left to their own devices to develop and to try new styles of behavior in their daily lives. Modeling is now increasingly employed, but in many instances its potential is not fully realized because the treatment either fails to provide sufficient practice in the modeled activities or it lacks an adequate transfer program that helps clients become adept in their new conduct under advantageous conditions.

Given appropriate demonstration, guided practice, and success experiences, the multiform method achieves excellent results. Because, in participant modeling, people learn and perfect effective ways of behaving under life-like conditions, problems of transfer of learning are largely obviated. An additional advantage of this approach is that a broad range of resource people can be enlisted to serve as therapeutic models.

ERADICATING DYSFUNCTIONAL FEARS AND DEFENSIVE BEHAVIOR

In modifying fearful and defensive behavior, therapists tend to focus their efforts primarily on eliminating emotional arousal. The desensitization approach devised by Wolpe (1969) is conducted on the principle of minimization of anxiety arousal. Treatment strategies are therefore keyed to this factor. Aversive stimuli are presented in small doses and promptly withdrawn whenever the clients experience anxiety. Should disturbing emotional reactions be evoked, there are essentially two things the therapist can do: relax the client and reduce the threat value of the aversive scenes. As emotional responses to weaker threats are eliminated, more stressful situations are progressively introduced.[3]

More recently, avoidance behavior has been treated by means of flooding procedures, which rely upon maximization of anxiety arousal (Gath, 1973; Watson & Marks, 1971). In this approach, intense anxiety is elicited through prolonged exposure to the most threatening situations. The therapist's main efforts are aimed at inducing and sustaining anxiety at high levels without relief until the reactions are extinguished.

Coupled with the focus on anxiety is heavy reliance upon symbolic renditions of aversive events. In both desensitization and flooding treatments emotional responses are typically extin-

[2] *Editors' note:* An excellent point. Clients rarely have a goal of learning to give fifty-minute monologues, yet this may be the only type of learning experience they have in some forms of counseling.

[3] *Editors' note:* See Article 30, on the use of systematic desensitization to reduce emotional arousal. One use of flooding is illustrated in Article 26.

guished in relation to visualized representations of feared situations. Results of numerous laboratory studies reveal that elimination of anxiety related to imagined threats improves behavioral functioning. However, there is a notable loss of therapeutic effects in transfer from symbolic to real-life threats (Agras, 1967; Barlow et al., 1969). It is not at all uncommon for clients to respond fearfully when confronted with intimidating situations after the imaginal counterparts have been thoroughly neutralized. Such transfer decrements are understandable, considering that complete generalization rarely occurs when treatment events differ significantly from the natural ones.

The arousal-oriented treatments are based on the assumption that anxiety activates defensive reactions. To eliminate defensive responding it is therefore considered necessary to eradicate its underlying anxiety. This theory, though still widely accepted, has been found wanting (Bandura, 1971b). Autonomic arousal, which serves as the principal index of anxiety, may facilitate, but is not required for, defensive learning. Maintenance of avoidance responses is even less dependent upon autonomic feedback. The overall evidence indicates that anxiety and defensive behavior are coeffects, rather than causally related. Aversive experiences, either of a personal or a vicarious sort, create expectations of injury that can activate both fear and defensive conduct. Because they are coeffects, there is no fixed relationship between arousal and action. Until effective coping ,skills are developed, threats produce high emotional arousal. But after people become adept at self-protective

behaviors they perform them in potentially threatening situations without having to be frightened. Should their habitual modes fail, they reexperience heightened arousal until new defensive learning reduces their vulnerability.[4]

The participant-modeling approach favors successful performance as the primary vehicle of psychological change. Avoidance of subjectively real but objectively unwarranted threats keeps behavior out of touch with existing conditions of reinforcement. Participant modeling provides a dependable and effective means of reality testing. There is nothing more persuasive than the experience of successful action in feared situations.

Persons suffering from intractable inhibitions, of course, are not about to do what they dread. The therapist must therefore arrange the environment in such a way that incapacitated clients can perform successfully despite themselves. This is achieved by enlisting a variety of supportive aids and protective controls. To begin with, the *threatening activities are repeatedly modeled* to show the client how they can be best performed and that the feared consequences do not in fact occur. By weakening inhibitions, modeling influences facilitate the use of other performance inducements should they be needed. *Joint performance* with the therapist, who offers physical assistance when required, further enables apprehensive clients to engage in threatening activities in which they

---

[4] *Editors' note:* Counselors, therefore, should be helping clients to learn better ways of coping with threatening situations, not merely to reduce anxious thoughts about them.

would not consider engaging on their own. Highly demanding or intimidating performances are reduced to *graduated subtasks* of increasing difficulty, so that at any given step participants are asked to do only what is clearly within their immediate capabilities. Treatment is conducted in this step-by-step fashion until eventually the most difficult activities are performed skillfully and fearlessly. If clients can perform with assistance the most threatening activities from the outset, the graduated procedures can be dispensed with.

Another method for overcoming response inhibition is to have the client practice the avoided behavior over *graduated temporal intervals*. As will be shown later, obsessive-compulsives who wash repeatedly to avoid contamination can be led to handle dirty objects without ritualistic washing for manageable short periods, but they will refuse if required from the outset to endure distress over a long time. By gradually extending the time interval, clients learn to perform with equanimity activities that earlier would have produced intolerable distress.

Arrangement of *protective conditions* that reduce the likelihood of feared consequences is a further means of weakening dysfunctional restraints that retard change. Thus, for example, snake phobics are willing to touch a snake, which ordinarily they refuse to do, provided that the model holds a snake securely by the head and tail (Bandura, Blanchard & Ritter, 1969), and acrophobics will climb scary heights given the security of the therapist's physical support (Ritter, 1969). Most of the preceding methods at-

tenuate the fear-arousing potential of the threat while keeping it at a high level. Animal phobics, for example, are exposed to scary animals, but performance supports and safeguards are temporarily introduced so that participants can do what they previously were too frightened even to contemplate. If such environmental arrangements prove insufficient to induce the desired behavior, incapacitating restraints can be overcome by *reducing the severity of the threat itself*. Weaker threats are presented.

During the early phases of treatment, therapists use whatever induction aids are necessary to initiate behavioral changes. As treatment progresses, however, the supportive aids and protective controls are gradually removed until clients function effectively without assistance. The provisional supports undoubtedly attentuate emotional arousal, but performance is not deferred until anxiety reactions have been extinguished. Successful action is considered the best eradicator of anxiety.[5]

Accelerating Change Through Response-Induction Aids

The manner in which provisional induction aids influence the rate of therapeutic progress is revealed in a study by Bandura, Jeffery, and Wright (1974).[6] Adult phobics received participant modeling with either low, moderate, or high numbers of per-

[5] *Editors' note:* Perhaps developing successful action through "doing it" is the best strategy for all client problems!

[6] *Editors' note:* See Article 33 for a description of participant modeling and response-induction aids.

formance aids. Clients given the same amounts of treatment progressed rapidly when therapists had recourse to an array of performance aids, whereas progress was slow and arduous when therapists had only a few induction aids at their disposal. In subsequent assessments, clients who had had the benefit of high and moderate induction procedures surpassed their minimally aided counterparts in behavioral improvement, in attitudinal changes, and in reductions in anticipatory fears.

When induction procedures are used to ensure continuous progress, the severity of clients' debilities determines the number of response facilitators that will be required—but not the level of attainment. Given sufficient aid, even the severely incapacitated can eventually gain full benefit. These findings indicate that, in developing powerful treatments, attention might be more profitably directed at the scope of therapists' serviceable skills than at the clients' limiting characteristics.[7]

[7] *Editors' note:* Counselors and teachers habitually place the blame for lack of success on clients or students, seldom on themselves. If Bandura is right, our failures must be partly attributed to our not using the best possible techniques. A disquieting thought but one that can serve as an impetus for improving our effectiveness. Desensitization anyone? Or would it be better to master some new coping skills?

Generalizing Change Through Self-Directed Performance

Social learning theory distinguishes among three basic change processes: *induction, generalization,* and *maintenance* of behavior (Bandura, 1969). Analysis of treatment in terms of these processes provides a more informative basis for evaluating and improving therapeutic methods than do undifferentiated assessments of outcome.

Table 1 depicts different patterns of effects that might obtain for any given treatment. Plus and minus signs signify successes and failures respectively. From this perspective, the general issue of therapeutic efficacy is divided into the more analytic questions of whether or not a method induces psychological changes, whether or not the changes are generalized across situations and response systems (behavioral, affective, attitudinal), and whether or not the changes are maintained over time.

Applying this multiprocess analysis, the first treatment shown in the table fails on all counts. The second induces changes, but they are circumscribed and transitory, which does not necessarily mean that the method is inadequate. Quite the contrary. It may be effective for creating changes, but it requires a supplemental transfer program and proper maintaining condi-

TABLE 1   Possible Patterns of Success and Failure.

Processes	Treatment Accomplishments				
	1	2	3	4	5
Induction	−	+	+	+	+
Generalization	−	−	+	−	+
Maintenance	−	−	−	+	+

tions. The third treatment produces generalized changes that are short-lived. Here the deficiencies lie in the maintenance component of the approach. The fourth treatment achieves enduring but circumscribed changes, thus requiring supplementary procedures to enhance transfer effects. The fifth, and most powerful, treatment succeeds on all indexes—induction, generality, and durability. Just as therapists do not rely upon unplanned influences to initiate psychological changes, they should not leave generalization and maintenance to fortuitous circumstances.

Aided participant modeling is a demonstrably powerful way of creating psychological changes. Although the positive effects are generalized across both stimuli and responses, there is room for improvement in the amount of transfer achieved (Bandura, Blanchard & Ritter, 1969; Bandura, Jeffery & Wright, 1974; Blanchard, 1970a). When disinhibition is facilitated by extensive supports, clients may attribute their performances to external aids, rather than to restored capacity. Generalization may also be reduced by judgments that the probable consequences of feared activities differ under circumstances with varying safeguards. As a result, clients may behave boldly under secure conditions but remain somewhat fearful in less protected situations.

In applications of participant modeling, erroneous attributions and protective discriminations can be minimized by fading the response aids and having clients repeatedly engage in the activities unassisted. Any lingering doubts they may have either about their capabilities or about probable response consequences can be easily dispelled in this manner.[8]

Self-directed performance can enhance the efficacy of participant modeling in several ways. It serves to extinguish residual fears. Observable success disconfirms erroneous attributions of the source of attainments. And it reinforces a sense of personal efficacy in coping with threatening situations. People who feel less vulnerable and expect to succeed in what they do will behave more boldly and persistently than if they harbor self-doubts. Evidence bearing on these issues is provided in a study of the generality and durability of therapeutic changes achieved through participant modeling as a function of the amount and variety of self-directed performance (Bandura, Jeffery & Gajdos, 1975).

Adults whose functioning was adversely affected by snake phobias were matched in triads on strength of phobic behavior and received aided participant modeling until they completed all the therapeutic tasks. This method achieves terminal performances within a relatively short period, requiring on the average only one hour of treatment time. Clients who received *participant modeling* alone were tested after they had successfully performed all the therapeutic tasks. Those assigned to the *self-directed performance* condition

[8] *Editors' note:* Helping clients to credit themselves for successful outcomes is vital, especially if self-control and competence are to be enhanced. Counselors will have to get their "ego satisfaction" from knowing that they have contributed to clients' self-sufficiency, not from clients' dependence or gratitude.

spent an additional hour interacting freely by themselves with the same snake (a boa constrictor) used in treatment. A third group, which had the benefit of *varied self-directed perform-ance*, spent the additional hour handling not only the familiar boa but also an unfamiliar king snake markedly different in color and activity level.

Results of this study attest to the therapeutic benefits of a brief period of self-directed performance. It thoroughly extinguished clients' fears and substantially boosted their self-confidence in dealing with snakes under diverse circumstances. It produced similar gains in behavioral functioning. Figure 1 depicts the percentage of clients in each of the three treatment conditions who were able to achieve terminal performances with the snake used in treatment and with an unfamil-

iar corn snake. Those who received participant modeling supplemented with self-directed performance behaved fearlessly toward the treatment snake and showed virtually complete transfer of boldness toward the generalization threat. Most clients who received participant modeling alone also behaved fearlessly toward the treatment snake, but they displayed transfer losses in coping with the generalization threat.[9]

Varied self-directed treatment did not surpass the gains from successful coping with a familiar threat. The latter treatment in fact extinguished fears most thoroughly and induced the strongest sense of competence. A

[9] *Editors' note:* See Article 33 for additional details and discussion of how self-directed performance aids facilitate transfer.

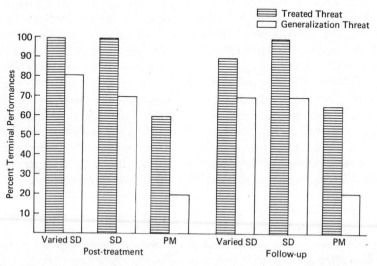

FIGURE 1 Percentage of clients who achieved terminal performances with the treatment and generalization snakes, depending upon whether they received participant modeling alone (P.M.) or supplemented with self-directed performance, either with the same (S.D.) or with varied (varied S.D.) threats.

number of the clients in the varied condition were taken aback by sudden confrontation with an unfamiliar snake. Premature performance demands in the face of severe threat can undermine self-confidence and partially reinstate fears that have been extinguished. These findings indicate that tasks that are more forbidding are best introduced after an ample foundation of success has been established.

Treatments aimed at improving behavioral functioning produce diverse collateral changes in affect, attitudes, and self-evaluation. Just as traumatic experiences simultaneously create avoidance, fear, negative attitudes, and self-perceptions of vulnerability, conversely, powerful success experiences concurrently attenuate fearfulness and instill positive attitudes and a sense of competence. The majority of clients in the previous study were repeatedly plagued by distressing ruminations and nightmares over which they could exercise little control. The treatments virtually eliminated the nightmares, even though they were never selected for change.

Generalized reduction of fearful behavior in areas not specifically treated may result from several processes (Bandura, Jeffery & Gajdos, 1975). The first includes generalization of fear extinction on the basis of stimulus similarity. The greater the likeness between treated and subsequently encountered events, the greater the transfer. The second process relies upon reinforcement of personal capability through success. By instilling expectations of success, action-oriented treatments can enhance transfer of boldness toward dissimilar threats. The third

process entails acquisition of a generalizable skill for coping with stress. In the course of treatment, clients learn a serviceable method for overcoming their fears, which they can apply on their own. Some of the generalized improvements are thus products of self-administered treatment under natural circumstances.

Comparative Effectiveness of Participant Modeling

The comparative effectiveness of participant modeling in producing behavioral, affective, and attitudinal changes was initially evaluated in an elaborate design by Bandura, Blanchard, and Ritter (1969). The participants in this project were adolescents and adults who suffered from snake phobias that, in most cases, adversely affected their lives or restricted their occupational functioning in troublesome ways.

One group received the standard form of desensitization, in which relaxation was paired with snake scenes of increasing aversiveness. A second group participated in a self-administered symbolic-modeling treatment in which they observed a film depicting children and adults engaging in progressively more intimidating interactions with a snake. They reviewed threatenng scenes repeatedly under self-induced relaxation until the depicted events were thoroughly neutralized.

The third group of phobics received the treatment combining live modeling with guided performance. This earlier version of the method, however, did not include the full array of induction aids or the self-directed component. After observing the therapist interacting closely with the snake, clients were aided through other induction procedures to perform progressively more frightening responses themselves. At each step the therapist himself performed the activities fearlessly and gradually led clients to touch, stroke, and hold the midsection of the snake's body with gloved and then bare hands for increasing periods. After clients could touch the snake under these secure conditions, anxieties about contact with the snake's head area and entwining tail were similarly extinguished. The therapist again performed the responses fearlessly, and then both therapist and clients performed them

jointly. As clients became more courageous, the therapist gradually reduced his level of participation and control over the snake until eventually clients were able to tolerate the squirming snake in their laps without assistance, to let the snake loose in the room and retrieve it, and to let it crawl freely over their bodies.

As depicted graphically in Figure 2, untreated controls remained unalterably fearful. Symbolic modeling and desensitization produced substantial reductions in phobic behavior, whereas participant modeling proved to be unusually powerful, eliminating phobic behavior with substantial transfer after

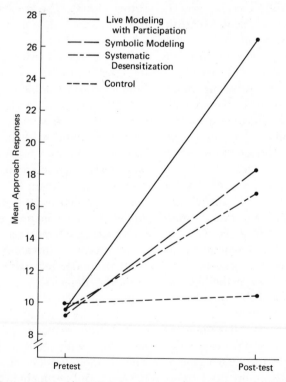

FIGURE 2   Mean number of approach responses performed by individuals before and after receiving different forms of treatment and by untreated controls (Bandura, Blanchard & Ritter, 1969).

approximately two hours of treatment. These procedures not only eliminated defensive behavior of long standing but also altered attitudes and reduced fears in other areas of functioning. The extent of the collateral changes was roughly proportional to the potency of the treatments.

In order to demonstrate that, in cases in which only partial improvement was achieved, the major deficits reside in the method, rather than in the client, those who failed to attain maximum performances, including the controls, were subsequently administered the participant-modeling treatment. Phobic behavior was thoroughly extinguished in all these individuals within a brief period, regardless of their age, sex, proneness to anxiety, and severity of avoidance behavior (see Figure 3).

Other Clinical Applications

Hardy (1969) has evolved a highly promising method for treating agoraphobia (fear of open spaces), a condition that has been highly refractory to change. The treatment essentially involves joint performance of activities during graduated massive exposure to feared situations until the clients' anxieties and phobic behaviors are eliminated. Clients accompany the therapist

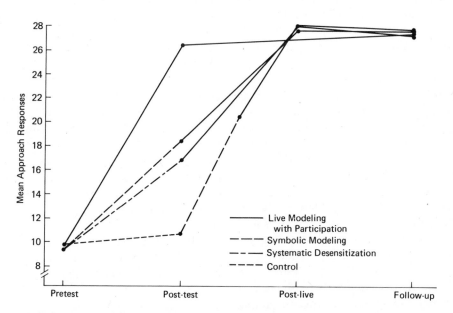

FIGURE 3   Mean number of approach responses performed by individuals before and after (posttest) receiving different treatments. Controls were subsequently given symbolic modeling without relaxation. All individuals in the desensitization, symbolic-modeling, and treated-control conditions who failed to perform the terminal tasks then received the treatment combining live modeling with guided participation (post-live). Approach behavior was measured again in a follow-up study conducted one month later (Bandura, Blanchard & Ritter, 1969).

into the avoided situations over a period of several days. The longer they are exposed to the aversive events, the more dramatic is the experience that what they dread does not happen. As a variety of things may produce fear, the specific performance tasks differ from client to client. Transportation phobics ride trains and buses, those who dread automobile travel drive freeways and mountain roads, those with flying phobias board planes during servicing and then make regular flights with the therapist to neighboring places, clients who fear bridges repeatedly cross bridges, those who shun supermarkets or department stores accompany the therapist on shopping trips, acrophobics ride elevators and climb scary heights, claustrophobics visit enclosed places, those who become apprehensive in crowds walk through busy city streets, clients who dread public speaking deliver talks, and obsequious individuals who invite maltreatment through their passivity are given self-assertive training.

As the clients' fears diminish, therapists reduce their support and guided participation. They send the clients on gradually longer missions alone while they stand by and wait for them. Later, excursions are arranged for clients to carry out on their own. They are asked to perform previously threatening activities that bring them to specific locations from which they call after completing their missons. To reinforce and extend therapeutic changes, alumni functions are scheduled. Ex-phobics regularly engage in groups in activities they formerly dreaded. They convene social gatherings, automobile jaunts,

mountain excursions, shopping trips, and theater outings.

Hardy reports that of 100 severe phobics treated by this method, 80 percent achieved extinction of their phobic behavior after several days of intensive treatment. Of these cases, approximately half required some supplementary treatment in the form of additional performance assignments or modification of family interactions to ensure continued improvement.[10]

Participant modeling with ritual prevention has been recently applied to chronic obsessive-compulsives who have remained incapacitated for many years because of their incessant rituals (Rachman, Hodgson & Marks, 1971; Rachman, Hodgson & Marzillier, 1970). Most dreaded contamination and spent countless hours each day scrubbing themselves and their households. Their lives were further constricted by avoidance of situations in which the feared contamination might occur. Others suffered from ruminations about safety that prompted repetitious checking rituals. Not only did they make life miserable for themselves; they also imposed intolerable restrictions on others. Neither insight therapies, drug treatments, nor relaxation training had brought them any relief.

Rachman, Marks, and Hodgson (1973) compared the relative efficacy of modeling, in which clients perform

---

[10] *Editors' note:* Counselors may have to modify their work schedules and arrangements to provide the concentrated doses of feared situations, the telephone follow-ups, and alumni-maintenance activities.

increasingly disturbing behavior demonstrated by the therapist, and flooding, in which they are encouraged to perform the most disturbing activities from the outset without prior modeling. Both methods proved equally successful. In some comparisons, however, the treatment that has produced the best results combines modeling with performance of the most uncomfortable activities and prevention of rituals. Therapists first demonstrate the repugnant behavior. Clients are then asked to engage in the same activities and to refrain from performing their compulsive rituals for increasing periods of time. They are also asked to resist rituals between sessions. Assessments based on a variety of measures reveal enduring reductions in compulsive behavior. Success rates of different versions of the multiform approach indicate that ritual prevention, a method originally reported by Meyer (1966), plays a vital role in the extinction process.

The following report provides a detailed description of how the procedures and the transfer program were implemented in treating a thirty-eight-year-old woman, whose fear of contamination ruled her household.

She had a 20-year history of compulsive handwashing and other rituals centering round a fear of tuberculosis infection. Her rituals had worsened since the birth of her son 2 years previously. She was unable to feed him for fear of contaminating him and the husband had to spend hours daily boiling bottles and feeding utensils to feed the child. The child was not allowed to play outside his playpen and was confined to it most of the day. The patient's mother, who lived nearby, had never been allowed to play with the child for fear of infecting him and indeed had never held him. The home was not swept because dust was thought to contain TB germs so that a thick layer of dust accumulated in most of the house. On returning home from work, if dirty, the husband sometimes had to strip naked outside the home before he was allowed to enter and don clean clothes inside.

The patient was admitted to a hospital and did not improve during 3 weeks of control relaxation treatment. She was then given exposure in vivo with modeling (e.g., she watched her therapist rub a biscuit on the floor and then eat it and was asked to follow suit). She was asked to rub her hands in dirt and to hold stained slides of bacteria without subsequent washing. The patient was most co-operative and rapidly lost all her rituals. However, it was feared that improvement would not transfer from hospital to her home 200 miles away, so the husband and son were brought to London to lodge near the hospital. The son was brought into the ward, and the patient was required to feed him after touching the food on the floor first. The husband was asked to participate. In the ward the patient soon lost her rituals concerning her son. At discharge the precaution was taken of sending a nursing sister with her and the family on the train home. As soon as the patient went on the train further rituals appeared such as avoidance of touching handles on doors and windows. The nurse prevented this avoidance on the train. On arrival at home the nurse ensured that the patient swept the house so that it was "contaminated." The husband had to be taught to desist from cleaning rituals his wife had engrained in him over the years. After 36 hours the nurse left the family, but regular contact was maintained by telephone and by further home visits. The patient remained free of most of her rituals over 2 years' follow-up. . . . (Marks, 1973, p. 424)

Rachman and Marks suggest that supervised home treatment, in which clients perform disturbing activities but refrain from compulsive rituals, can augment the therapeutic benefits. As compulsives tend to impose burdensome restrictions on those around them, family members can expedite changes by withdrawing reinforcement of compulsive behavior and substituting rewarding activities as clients become free of their time-consuming rituals.

Durability of Therapeutic Changes

If defensive behavior can be removed by corrective experiences, is it likely to be easily reinstated by a few adverse incidents? Not necessarily. There are several factors that favor persistence of changes long after treatment has been discontinued. Removal of unwarranted anxieties alleviates distress and enables people to participate in rewarding activities that they have formerly avoided. A compulsive who spent inordinate amounts of time scrubbing and avoiding contact with "dirty" objects, for example, was able to hold a job, to go swimming, and to walk on grass for the first time in many years after his compulsive rituals had been eliminated (Rachman, Hodgson & Marzillier, 1970). Reinstated behaviors are thus supported by favorable conditions of reinforcement without requiring a special maintenance program. Furthermore, reinforcement of personal competence often improves functioning in nontreated areas (Bandura,

Blanchard & Ritter, 1969; Bandura, Jeffery & Gajdos, 1975).[11] The benefits of restored competence can counteract the effects of occasional distress.

The capacity of adverse events to reinstate fears and defensive behavior depends upon the total pattern of experience in which they occur. Occasional mishaps among many positive or neutral experiences have little negative effect (Rescorla, 1969). Favorable experiences curtail inappropriate generalization of fear, as well as neutralizing aversive events (Hoffman, 1969). Therefore, an effective way to reduce people's vulnerability to mishaps is to have them perform extensively the formerly threatening activities under advantageous conditions after treatment has been terminated. A dog phobic who, following treatment, has had many benign interactions with different dogs will not be much affected by a few unpleasant encounters. At most, such experiences will establish discriminative avoidance of realistic threats, which has adaptive value. By contrast, for people who have had limited contact with previously feared objects after treatment, a few unfavorable experiences are likely to reestablish defensive behavior that is generalized inappropriately.

The oft-repeated dictum that maintenance of change depends upon environmental contingencies conveys the impression that behavior is at the

----

[11] *Editors' note:* Here is evidence to refute the symptom-substitution argument. Removing a "symptom" does not necessarily cause a new "symptom" to replace it. On the contrary, it may encourage the development of other coping skills.

mercy of fortuitous circumstances. This belief has retarded research on how supplemental experiences can be arranged in the immediate posttreatment phase to reduce vulnerability to defensive relearning. Findings based on studies of self-directed performance and rate of reconditioning under varying circumstances indicate that sustained therapeutic benefits can be achieved at the point at which treatments are usually terminated. Among procedures that eliminate avoidance behavior, some leave subjects more susceptible to aversive relearning than others (Polin, 1959). The therapeutic value of a given treatment should therefore be judged in terms of vulnerability to defensive relearning, as well as of success in the initial eliminaton of defensiveness.[12]

If disinhibited behavior frequently results in punishing consequences, then therapeutic changes will be short-lived unless the adverse social conditions are also modified. No psychological methods that can render an organism insensitive to the consequences of its actions exist. Nor would imperviousness be desirable, were it possible, for individuals who remained unaffected by response feedback would function in a grossly maladaptive way.

It might also be noted in passing that those whose unwarranted fears have been extinguished do not behave recklessly. Elimination of an automobile phobia does not dispose clients to saunter heedlessly into onrushing traffic on busy thoroughfares. Rather, stereotyped avoidance is replaced by flexibly adaptive behavior that is cognitively controlled by judgments of probable consequences resulting from prospective actions.

PARTICIPANT MODELING AND BEHAVIOR DEFICITS

Participant modeling figures even more prominently in the modification of problems arising from behavioral deficits. Fears can be overcome without the aid of models, but competence learning would be exceedingly laborious, not to mention perilous, if it proceeded solely on the basis of trial and error without the guidance of models to exemplify the patterns. For this reason, most competence, whether it involves social or vocational skills, is acquired and perfected by the combined influence of instructive example and reinforced practice. In the treatment program devised by Lovaas (1967), behavioral repertoires are established in autistic children, who display little functional behavior, through reinforced modeling. Complex skills are gradually elaborated by means of modeling activities in small steps of increasing difficulty and of rewarding matching performances. Manual prompting and other induction aids are used when children fail to respond. The provisional supports are then gradually withdrawn to promote natural responsiveness.

Although all children improve during the course of treatment, their subsequent levels of functioning, as assessed one to four years later, vary,

[12] *Editors' note:* An intriguing question to ask about all counseling methods for various client problems.

depending upon environmental circumstances (Lovaas, *et al.*, 1973). Those whose parents are trained to conduct treatment at home maintain their gains or improve further. By contrast, those who are discharged to state hospitals, for lack of better alternatives, abandon most of what they have learned and revert to their former autistic conduct. The skills they have acquired are not lost, however. Brief reinstatement of the therapeutic conditions restores the original gains in the institutionalized children.

Development of assertiveness provides another illustration of the clinical application of participant modeling (Bandura, 1973). People who are unable to behave assertively, a common problem, are likely to suffer considerable mistreatment. In teaching people how to behave affirmatively, assertive styles of conduct must be modeled for them. Depending upon individual needs, these might include such things as complaining about inadequate service, returning purchases, refusing arbitrary or unreasonable demands, responding to unfair criticism, making rightful claims to goods and facilities, defending a position in the face of opposition, and in other ways standing up for one's rights.[13]

Clients then practice by behaving assertively and receiving feedback that rewards their successes and corrects their errors. Fear of revealing one's inadequacies creates initial reluctance to engage in behavior rehearsals, even

[13] *Editors' note:* See Articles 54 and 55 for examples of techniques with unassertive clients.

under simulated conditions. There are several ways in which such resistances can be reduced. First, participant modeling is structured in a nonthreatening manner aimed at fostering new competences and confidence, rather than at exposing deficiencies. Concern about poor performance is further decreased by noting that in all successful skill learning initial efforts are awkward; it is thus progressive improvement with practice, rather than instant proficiency, that is expected. In an optimistic, forward-looking program clients more readily accept and profit from their mistakes. Prior modeling provides a helpful guide for new styles of behavior. Participants therefore do not have to grope around for appropriate responses, which reduces needless failure experiences. In addition, assertion tasks are graduated, beginning with relatively easy performances. As apprehensions are diminished through repeated practice, progressively more difficult encounters, demanding more assertive actions, are introduced.

In a comprehensive treatment, clients must also learn when and where assertiveness is appropriate. And they need positive reinforcement for asserting themselves in their daily interactions. Transfer of assertiveness from the training situation to the natural environment should be an integral part of the treatment, rather than being left to chance. A transfer program might proceed as follows: After clients have perfected their social skills and overcome their timidity, they accompany the therapist on excursions into the field where they witness further demonstrations of how to handle situations calling for assertive action.[14] The therapist then reduces the level of participation to background support and guidance as clients try their skills in situations likely to produce favorable results. By means of careful selection of encounters of increasing difficulty, the assertion requirements can be adjusted to the clients' momentary capabilities to bolster their sense of confidence. As a final step in the program the clients are assigned a series of assertive performance tasks to carry out on their own.

COMPONENT ANALYSIS OF PARTICIPANT MODELING

The influence of some of the factors contained in participant modeling has been examined singly, especially in modifying defensive behavior. Observation of bold models can, by itself, produce substantial reductions in phobic behavior, both in children and in adults (Bandura, 1971b). Similarly, repeated performance of frightening activities without untoward effects can eventually eliminate fears and inhibitions (Bandura, 1969).

Some efforts have been made to assess the relative contributions of the

[14] *Editors' note:* Counselors may fear that they cannot model the desired responses well enough. Counselors have fears too! However, it may be more helpful to the client to observe a stumbling approximation than a polished performance. The counselor can say, "Look, I'm not perfect either, but I'm willing to try." Of course, the counselor need not be the model. He can draw on resource people who can provide good models for assertiveness.

constituent influences in the multiform procedure. The proportional weights furnished by a given study must be accepted with reservation, however, because only a single value of each component is assessed, whereas other versions of the same factor may have different efficacy. In a study comparing the outcomes associated with various component combinations, Blanchard (1970b) found that modeling accounted for approximately 60 percent of behavior change and 80 percent of changes in attitude and fear arousal; guided participation contributed the remaining increments. Factual information about what is feared, on the other hand, had no significant effect on any of the measures.

The guided-participation component of the treatment under discussion can be further analyzed into separable elements. When clients are assisted in performing the desired behavior the protection afforded by the model may facilitate changes by reducing behavioral restraints. As participants engage in the feared activities, some of the changes are undoubtedly attributable to feedback. In evaluating the contribution of protective guidance and response performance, Ritter (1969) reports that modeling accompanied by physically guided performance decreased acrophobic behavior more effectively than modeling with verbally guided enactment, which, in turn, was superior to a brief demonstration alone.

Numerous studies have also been conducted on the relative contributions of modeling, performance, and reinforcement influences to development of new modes of behavior or to facilitation of responsiveness unencumbered by restraints (Bandura, 1971a). The evidence generally shows that modeling plays a paramount role in the acquisition of novel and complex behavior, whereas learning is difficult to achieve through response consequences alone. In enhancing conduct that is already learned, modeling serves a secondary function, whereas response inducements and reinforcing consequences emerge as prominent determinants. Regardless of whether deficits or defensiveness is the problem of concern, modeling, supplemented with guided performance and reinforcing consequences, is the most powerful means of effecting psychological change.

references

Agras, W. S. Transfer during systematic desensitization therapy. *Behaviour Research and Therapy*, 1967, **5**, 193–199.

Bandura, A. *Aggression: A social learning analysis.* Englewood Cliffs, N.J.: Prentice-Hall, 1973.

Bandura, A. *Principles of behavior modification.* New York: Holt, Rinehart and Winston, 1969.

Bandura, A. (Ed.) *Psychological modeling: Conflicting theories.* Chicago: Aldine-Atherton, 1971a.

Bandura, A. Psychotherapy based upon modeling principles. In A. E. Bergin and S. L. Garfield (Eds.), *Handbook of psychotherapy and behavior change.* New York: Wiley, 1971b. Pp. 653–708.

Bandura, A., Blanchard, E. B. & Ritter, B. The relative efficacy of desensitization and modeling approaches for inducing behavioral, affective, and attitudinal changes. *Journal of Personality and Social Psychology*, 1969, **13**, 173–199.

Bandura, A., Jeffery, R. W. & Gajdos, E. Generalizing change through self-directed performance. *Behaviour Research and Therapy*, 1975, **13**, 141–152.

Bandura, A., Jeffery, R. W. & Wright, C. L. Efficacy of participant modeling as a function of response induction aids. *Journal of Abnormal Psychology*, 1974, **83**, 56–64.

Barlow, D. H., Leitenberg, H., Agras, W. S. & Wincze, J. P. The transfer gap in systematic desensitization: An analogue study. *Behaviour Research and Therapy*, 1969, **7**, 191–196.

Blanchard, E. B. The generalization of vicarious extinction effects. *Behavior Research and Therapy*, 1970a, **8**, 323–330.

Blanchard, E. B. The relative contributions of modeling, information influences, and physical contact in the extinction of phobic behavior. *Journal of Abnormal Psychology*, 1970b, **76**, 55–61.

Gath, D. H. Implosion therapy (flooding) for phobic patients: Results of a controlled trial. Unpublished manuscript, Oxford University, 1973.

Hardy, A. B. Exposure therapy as a treatment for agoraphobia and anxiety. Unpublished manuscript, 1969.

Hodgson, R., Rachman, S. & Marks, I. M. The treatment of chronic obsessive-compulsive neurosis: Follow-up and further findings. *Behaviour Research and Therapy*, 1972, **10**, 181–189.

Hoffman, H. S. Stimulus factors in conditioned suppression. In B. A. Campbell and R. M. Church (Eds.), *Punishment and aversive behavior.* New York: Appleton, 1969. Pp. 185–234.

Lovaas, O. I. A behavior therapy approach to the treatment of childhood schizophrenia. In J. P. Hill (Ed.), *Minnesota symposia on child psychology.* Vol. 1. Minneapolis: University of

Minnesota Press, 1967. Pp. 108–159.

Lovaas, O. I., Koegel, R., Simmons, J. Q. & Stevens, J. Some generalization and follow-up measures on autistic children in behavior therapy. *Journal of Applied Behavior Analysis*, 1973, **6**, 131–166.

Marks, I. M. New approaches to the treatment of obsessive-compulsive disorders. *The Journal of Nervous and Mental Disease*, 1973, **156**, 420–426.

Meyer, V. Modification of expectations in cases with obsessional rituals. *Behaviour Research and Therapy*, 1966, **4**, 273–280.

Polin, A. T. The effects of flooding and physical suppression as extinction techniques on an anxiety motivated avoidance locomotor response. *Journal of Psychology*, 1969, **47**, 235–245.

Rachman, S., Hodgson, R. & Marks, I. M. The treatment of chronic obsessive-compulsive neurosis. *Behaviour Research and Therapy*, 1971, **9**, 237–247.

Rachman, S., Hodgson, R. & Marzillier, J. Treatment of an obsessional compulsive disorder by modeling. *Behaviour Research and Therapy*, 1970, **8**, 385–392.

Rachman, S., Marks, I. M. & Hodgson, R. The treatment of obsessive-compulsive neurotics by modeling and flooding *in vivo*. *Behaviour Research and Therapy*, 1973, **11**, 463–471.

Rescorla, R. A. Pavlovian conditioned inhibition. *Psychological Bulletin*, 1969, **72**, 77–94.

Ritter, B. The use of contact desesitization, demonstration-plus-participation, and demonstration alone in the treatment of acrophobia. *Behavior Research and Therapy*, 1969, **7**, 157–164.

Watson, J. P. & Marks, I. M. Relevant and irrelevant fear in flooding: A cross-over study of phobic patients. *Behavior Therapy*, 1971, **2**, 275–293.

Wolpe, J. *The practice of behavior therapy*. New York: Pergamon, 1969.

TEST ANXIETY

29. TEACHING A STUDENT TO ASK QUESTIONS IN CLASS: A CASE REPORT

DAVID M. WARK   University of Minnesota

The basic technique of systematic desensitization has been explained previously by Wolpe (1969) and Yates (1970). The application to academic problems by Emery (1969) covers both theoretical and applied considerations. In the present paper we shall discuss the use of a modified desensitization program for a previously unreported problem: an adult student's fear of asking and answering questions in a college classroom.

The client, Juanita, was a mature, married student in an adult extension course. The title of the course, "How to Study," attracted a wide range of students. They all wished to learn, or to relearn, techniques for effective study in college. Part of the class content covered behavior modification of study problems. Students were given a brief lecture on basic behavioral mechanisms and on the effects of muscular tension upon study, memory, and test taking. The notion of the problem hierarchy was presented as part of the lecture. The students were required to develop and to present a desensitization hierarchy as an exercise. For those who wished, succeeding class sessions were devoted to practice in relaxation and desensitization.

As a demonstration for the students, one section of the course ($n = 19$) went through a group desensitization exercise.[1] Each member picked a target item on his individual hierarchy. The group members were relaxed and then told to imagine their items while experiencing relaxation. The instructions were repeated three times. Students were instructed to hold the images for ten, twenty, and finally thirty seconds. At the end of the session, they were asked to rescale the level of subjective units of discomfort (SUD) for the target items.

The scale represents an attempt to quantify the tension or unpleasantness that a client feels in a given situation. Typically, these scale values go from 0 SUD (completely relaxed and calm) to 100 SUD (extremely tense and anxious). Changes in the personally perceived SUD scale are one measure of improvement by systematic desensitization. For these nineteen students the mean of prerelaxation scores was

39 SUDs. The mean postrelaxation score was 19 SUDs, an average drop of 20 points. The data showed that it was possible to reach relaxation and to achieve some reduction of anxiety through the course (Wark, 1971).

Juanita stood out as needing desensitization from the very first class meeting. At that time she could not respond with more than a barely audible whisper and a deep blush when her name was called in the roll call. She appeared to suffer a constant level of discomfort in the successive class sessions. She rarely talked to other students and never asked questions or volunteered answers in class. At the time when students were required to turn in hierarchies, she submitted seven more or less unrelated but painful experiences having to do with school. These are presented in Table 1. Later, in an individual session, she was guided in redefining them into the four items listed as the derived hierarchy in Table 1.[2]

The initial plan was to present four scenes from the derived hierarchy to Juanita in individual desensitization sessions following class. The four sessions were to occur between April 7 and 28. Her behavior in class meetings following the desensitization was to be used as a criterion for evaluating therapeutic effectiveness. However, at the end of the third session, on April 21,

---

[1] Editors' note: For a comprehensive discussion of group systematic desensitization see Article 30.

[2] Editors' note: It is not at all unusual for clients to require help in constructing hierarchies. In the derived hierarchy we might have tried to have items 1 and 2 specify client behaviors, as do items 3 and 4, for example, "Answering 'I don't know' to a question asked me by the professor with other students present."

TABLE 1   Original and Derived Hierarchies Related to Talking in Class.

Original Hierarchy Scenes Presented by Juanita	SUD
1. Failed test	100
2. Blank test day	90
3. Study for test—not meaningful	70
4. Not taking part in class discussion	40
5. Embarrassed, not knowing answer in class	20
6. Did not study for assignment	10
7. Not understanding	5
Derived Hierarchy Scenes	
1. Students present when you can not answer a question	80
2. Only professor present when you can not answer a question	50
3. Students present when you raise a question	40
4. Only professor present when you raise a question	20

Juanita said that she felt confident enough to postpone the fourth scene, at least temporarily. In conjunction with her training, Juanita was told two things: At no time would she be called upon to answer a question in a class discussion and, if she raised her hand to answer a question presented to a class, she would be immediately acknowledged and allowed to answer. Table 2 outlines the training sessions after class and Juanita's behavior in the class session conducted the following week.

Notice that the first night that her classroom behavior was recorded, April

TABLE 2   Events in Class and Therapy Session Related to Improvement in Talking in Class.

Date	Class Behavior Related to Talking	Relaxation Sessions after Class
4/ 7	None	See self answering question. (scene 4)
4/14	Answered general questions in class; raised hand	See self raising hand, asking question; know answer. (scene 4)
4/21	Asked question with known answer; raised hand	1. See other students in room—PANIC. (scene 3) 2. See self raising hand and asking; know answer. (scene 3) 3. See self raising hand and asking; answer unknown. (scene 3)
4/28	None	none
5/ 5	Asked questions with known answer; raised hand	none
5/12	Volunteered comments twice; asked questions twice; answers not known; raised hand	none
5/19	Asked questions; answers not known; raised hand; no blush	none
5/28	Volunteered comments twice; evaluation of instructor; did not raise hand; did not blush	none

7, she demonstrated no relevant asking or answering behavior. However, on May 28, not only did she answer questions, but she also twice volunteered comments. These included a rather pointed evaluation of the instruction. She made these evaluations unblushingly.

Juanita's case illustrates a very direct and practical application of desensitization. The problem is not uncommon—fear of asking and answering questions in a classroom. But as a counseling strategy it may be necessary to contrive questions. Students may in fact be encouraged to ask questions, even when they know the answers, so that they have the positive experience of actually asking.[3] In addition, Juanita received concrete assurances that her attempts to develop new behavior would be encouraged. It is reasonable for a behaviorally oriented counselor

[3] *Editors' note:* Some students might fear even more the asking of questions to which they know the answers, thinking, "If dumb me already knows it, the professor will think I'm totally ignorant if I ask it." An alternative would be for the student to ask for the professor's opinion, for example, "Do you think the government could have done anything to prevent inflation?"

to arrange with a faculty person to provide similar treatment.[4]

There is one final aspect of Juanita's behavior that is worth noting. She was helped to ask and answer questions. Notice that she eventually demonstrated that behavior on May 5. At the very next class she added something new. On May 12 she was volunteering comments, not questions or answers. The new behavior continued on May 28. Eventually she was demonstrating a whole new skill: assertive, even confrontational, evaluation. This mode of behavior was a radical departure from her original shy, uncommunicative responding in class. Apparently the question asking had been generalized.

[4] *Editors' note:* If so, should the client know that such an arrangement was made? In situations in which the counselors are part of education teams employed by schools, it may not always be necessary or desirable, although in most cases it seems highly desirable. The client's consent could be obtained in a way something like this: "With your permission I would like to explain to Professor X what you are trying to accomplish and recommend that he make it a point to call on you whenever you raise your hand during the next week."

references

Emery, J. Systematic desensitization: Reducing test anxiety. In J. D. Krumboltz & C. Thoresen (Eds.), *Behavioral counseling: Cases and techniques.* New York: Holt, Rinehart and Winston, 1969. Pp. 267-288.

Wark, D. M. Case studies in behavior modification. In G. B. Schick & M. M. May (Eds.), *The Psychology of reading behavior: 18th yearbook of the National Reading Conference,* Milwaukee: 1969.

Wark, D. M. Test panic, daydreaming and procrastination. In D. M. Wark (Ed.), *College and adult reading VI: The 6th yearbook of the North Central Reading Association.* Minneapolis: North Central Reading Association, 1971. Pp. 131–151.

Wolpe, J. *Practice of behavior therapy.* New York: Pergamon, 1969.

Yates, A. *Behavior therapy.* New York: Wiley, 1970.

30. *GROUP SYSTEMATIC DESENSITIZATION OF TEST ANXIETY*

ROBERT A. OSTERHOUSE   University of Maryland

Systematic desensitization has gained increasing acceptance among counselors as a treatment method for clients with phobic and specific anxiety reactions. Because there currently exist a number of excellent reviews of this treatment (for example, Paul, 1969), no attempt will be made here to specify the theoretical rationale underlying systematic desensitization.[1]

As initially conceived by Wolpe (1954; 1958) desensitization was an individual treatment method. However, when it became clear that this technique was useful for reducing a wide variety of fears and anxieties, other investigators began to explore the possibility of treating more clients by using desensitization with groups, rather than with individuals. A number of investigations (for example, Ihli & Garlington, 1969; Mann & Rosenthal, 1969; Paul & Shannon, 1966) have found that group desensitization is equally as effective as individual desensitization.[2]

The standardized procedures for individual systematic desensitization have already been described in detail elsewhere (for example, Emery, 1969; Paul, 1966). Less information is available, however, on the procedures used for group desensitization. The purpose of this article therefore is to describe the procedures that the author and several of his students have developed for the group systematic desensitization of clients with high levels of test anxiety. Although the procedures described here are designed for six sessions of approximately sixty minutes each, the number of sessions can easily be increased by increasing the frequency with which the anxiety hierarchy items are paired with relaxation.

THE TECHNIQUE OF GROUP DESENSITIZATION

Instructions to Clients

It is important that clients understand the treatment process. Following the introduction of the therapist, group members are given an opportunity to share their previous reactions to testing situations. The therapist then explains that our treatment procedures will be based on the assumption that anxiety is a learned reaction to specific events and that it can be unlearned through appropriate techniques. The therapist then distributes the following explanation (adapted from Garlington & Cotler, 1968) to each subject, with instructions to read it carefully:

[1] *Editors' note:* The rapid and effective "modeling and guided participation" method described in Articles 28 and 33 seems even better for certain anxieties. Variations of systematic desensitization might be the treatment of choice when the potential threat to the client is real or when it is impossible to arrange conditions so that coping with feared stimuli can be repeatedly demonstrated (modeled) to the client during treatment.

[2] *Editors' note:* Note that using an individually based treatment with several people at the same time (group-administered treatment) does not necessarily qualify it as group counseling or group therapy. The latter procedures require interaction (primarily verbal) among group members as an essential factor in treatment.

Introduction to Desensitization Principles
The procedure we will use to help you overcome any unusually strong fears of examinations is called desensitization. It was developed a few years ago by a psychiatrist named Joseph Wolpe. He and a number of other psychiatrists and psychologists have used this method with many kinds of fears and anxieties, and they have reported a high level of success.

This approach is based upon the fact that it is impossible to be afraid and relaxed at the same time. For example, a student might want to ask a professor a question, or perhaps criticize something the professor has said. He may find, however, when he starts to speak that he experiences shortness of breath, his heart pounds, or his hands perspire. He is unable to make his point. These are anxiety reactions and don't occur when the student is relaxed. Therefore, an important part of the method involves teaching you to relax as completely as possible. You may think that you don't have to be taught how to relax, but the fact is that most people are frequently unaware of their tensions.

Once you have learned how to relax, then this group will develop a list of situations in which the anxiety occurs. This list will be made up so that it contains items representing many different degrees of anxiety. For example, when an instructor announces an examination will be given in two weeks, you may experience a slight degree of anxiety. That anxiety, however, is ordinarily nothing compared to the anxiety you experience as he actually passes out the examination in class. In between these two extremes there are probably a number of situations that call out varying degrees of anxiety. This group, working together, will put the items on a list in order from the one that produces the least amount of anxiety up to the one that produces the most. This list is called a hierarchy.

One of the most interesting aspects of this procedure is that it tends to generalize to real life situations. Even though the procedure only requires you to imagine yourself in situations related to fear of examinations, there is a strong tendency for fear to decrease in the actual situation.

We will go through the various steps in this procedure over a period of six weeks. In the first week you will learn relaxation techniques. The second week will be devoted to developing the hierarchy, learning to visualize clearly, and practicing relaxation techniques again. The final four weeks will be spent in going through the hierarchy and actually reducing your fear of examinations.

Now, are there any questions about the program?

After all of the clients have indicated that they have read the information, the opportunity is given to raise and discuss questions that they might have about desensitization.

Training in Muscle Relaxation

The remainder of the first session is devoted to explaining the use of relaxation procedures in the treatment process, to initial training in deep muscle relaxation, and to distributing forms that are to be used by the client for additional practice in muscle relaxation at home.

The explanation of the importance of relaxation in desensitization is given verbally by the therapist; the content is almost identical to that already described by Emery (1969). Following an opportunity to raise questions about the relaxation process, group members are instructed to settle themselves as comfortably as possible in their chairs.

The room is darkened, outside noise reduced to the extent possible, and clients are instructed to remove glasses, watches, and anything else that might interfere with relaxation.[3]

In order to train clients in muscle relaxation, we have prepared our own version of a thirty-minute tape recording originally developed by Gerald Davison. This tape employs "progressive relaxation," in which the clients alternately tense and relax twenty-one different muscle groups. Throughout the recording, clients are urged to become aware of the difference between feelings of muscular tension and feelings of muscle relaxation.

It should be noted that some clients have difficulty in the early stage of the initial session in muscle relaxation. In our experience, this has occurred much more frequently in groups than in individual treatment. Many clients look occasionally at the other group members during the first portion of the tape, perhaps for assurance that the other group members are also participating and that this is not some type of "put on." In any event, this difficulty ordinarily disappears very rapidly.

Following the conclusion of the relaxation tape, clients are given the opportunity to share their reactions to the relaxation training with one another and with the therapist. They are also given a copy of the following "Guide for Training in Muscle Relaxation," in order to help them practice relaxation exercises at home or in the dormitory.

[3] Editors' note: Although physical relaxation is the most common "incompatible" action used to reduce anxiety, a variety of other behaviors can be used, as Gershman and Stedman point out in Article 34.

Guide for Training in Muscle Relaxation
Instructions: The following exercises will help you learn to relax more completely, so that you can achieve the maximum benefits from the procedures which are to follow. After you feel the tension associated with each movement, hold that position for five seconds. Become aware of the feelings of tension. Then completely relax, allowing the affected muscles to become absolutely limp. Note the feelings of pleasantness associated with the relaxation. Do each of the following exercises twice.

1. Clench left fist—note tension in hand and forearm—relax.
2. Clench right fist—note tension in hand and forearm—relax.
3. Bend left arm upward at the wrist, point fingers at the ceiling—note tension in back of hand and forearm—relax.
4. Bend right arm upward at the wrist, point fingers at the ceiling—note tension in back of hand and forearm—relax.
5. Touch shoulders with fingers, raise arms—note tension in biceps and upper arms—relax.
6. Shrug shoulders, raise as high as possible—note tension in shoulders—relax.
7. Wrinkle forehead—note tension—relax with eyes lightly closed.
8. Close eyes tightly—study tension—relax with eyes lightly closed.
9. Press tongue into roof of mouth—note tension in mouth—relax.
10. Press lips together tightly—note tension in mouth and chin—relax.
11. Press head backward—note tension in back, shoulders, and neck—relax.
12. Push head forward, bury chin in chest—note tension in neck and shoulders—relax.
13. Arch your back, move away from the back of the chair, push arms back-

ward—note tension in back and shoulders—relax.

14. Take a deep breath and hold it—note tension in chest and back—exhale—relax.
15. Take two deep breaths of air, hold and then exhale—note your breathing become more slow and relaxed—relax.
16. Suck in stomach, try to make it reach your spine—note feelings of tension in the stomach—relax, noting your breathing becoming more regular.
17. Tense stomach muscles—note tension in stomach—relax.
18. Tense buttocks by pushing them into the chair—note tension in buttocks area—relax.
19. Tense thigh muscles, straighten legs—note tension in thighs—return legs to original position—relax.
20. Point toes upward toward face—note tension in foot and calves of legs—relax.
21. Curl toes downward, as if burying them in sand—note tension in arches of feet—relax.

Each client is also given a copy of "A Report of Practice in Muscle Relaxation" (Figure 1), on which to record the frequency of practice sessions. We have found a nonsignificant but positive correlation between the number of practice sessions in muscle relaxation and improvement following treatment. We have also found that our clients practice relaxation significantly more frequently when they are asked to record their practice sessions and to return this report to the therapist than when they are not asked to do so.

Constructing Anxiety Hierarchies

The construction of anxiety hierarchies differs substantially in individual and group desensitization. In individual desensitization, the therapist is free to explore and to list those specific situations in which the client feels anxiety. It is

Name: _____

Directions: Please note below the amount of time spent in practicing muscle relaxation. Use the entries below as examples.

	Day	Date	Numbers of Exercises Engaged in		Time Spent
(e.g.)	Weds.	Oct. 12	exercises 1–18	(18)	25 mins.
(e.g.)	Thurs.	Oct. 13	all of them	(21)	32 mins.
1.					
2.					
3.					
4.					
5.					
6.					
7.					
8.					
9.					
10.					

FIGURE 1   A report of practice in muscle relaxation.

then relatively simple for the client to rank these situations from the least to the most anxiety provoking. In group desensitization, however, the therapist is confronted with five to ten clients, each of whom has somewhat different situations in which anxiety is aroused, as well as a different ordering of anxiety-provoking situations. The most common solution to this problem has been to have all clients rank the final list of hierarchy items from least to most anxiety provoking and then to average the rankings. The first hierarchy item presented to group members would thus be the one that is ranked *on the average* as least anxiety provoking by the group. There is considerable evidence (for example, Emery & Krumboltz, 1967; McGlynn, 1971; Osterhouse & O'Connell, 1973) that shows that hierarchies constructed by averaging the responses of the group members are equally as effective in reducing anxiety as are individualized hierarchies.

There is also some difficulty in the development of a hierarchy that will meet the needs of all of the group members. Some therapists have solved this problem by using one full therapy session for clients to generate a list of situations in which they all feel anxious. The group then selects the most representative items and ranks them from least to most anxiety provoking. As is true with many other therapists, we have developed our own list of situations that are specific to test anxiety. Clients are asked to rank these situations from least to most anxiety provoking at the beginning of the second session.[4]

Although we have previously used other test-anxiety hierarchies, we are currently using one developed by McMillan (1973). This hierarchy includes fifteen situations that elicit varying degrees of anxiety and range in time from the first announcement of an examination to the actual examination period.

Test-Anxiety Hierarchy

Instructions: Below are fifteen items which tend to elicit varying degrees of anxiety. You are to rank these items, from *least* to *most* anxiety-provoking *for you*! In the space before each item, place a number corresponding to the degree of anxiety you normally feel when you encounter it. Number 15 would be the item which elicits the most anxiety. Work carefully and slowly.

_____You are sitting in your class and the instructor announces that you will have an examination during the next class session. You wonder if you can prepare in time. There is so much material to be covered.

_____It is the day before an important examination. You talk to some of your classmates who tell you how much preparation they have done for this examination. You have spent far less time on the readings.

_____You are studying for an important examination to be given the next day. Your grade in this course will probably depend upon your performance on this examination. You are wondering how you will remember the information on the test.

_____It is late evening before an important examination. You are tired and having trouble concentrating, but you do not feel really prepared.

_____You are in bed the night before an important examination which will

[4] *Editors' note:* An alternative to ranking would be to use the SUD rating technique explained in Articles 29 and 34.

determine your final grade. Your mind flashes to the examination.

_____You wake up and realize that you have an examination today which will determine your final grade. The test is scheduled for later that same day.

_____You have an hour of study time left before you will take a very important examination. As you look over your notes, you realize that you have become confused. You wonder whether you should continue reviewing your notes or just put them aside.

_____You are walking to an important examination which will probably determine your final grade.

_____As you enter your classroom on the day of an examination, you hear several students discussing possible questions. You realize that you probably could not answer these questions if they were asked on the test.

_____You are sitting in class, waiting for your examination to be passed out.

_____You receive your examination. You look at the first question and cannot recall the answer.

_____As you read over your examination, you realize that many of the items are very difficult. You look up from your test, wondering where to start, and notice the students around you writing furiously.

_____Many questions on this examination request information that is hazy to you. You realize that you must have skipped over some important facts in your study.

_____On this extremely important examination, you find that you have spent too much time on the first portion of the test and must hurry up a bit in order to finish on time.

_____With five minutes left on this examination which will probably determine your final grade, you see that you have left a number of items blank.

Following the ranking of hierarchy items, the clients are encouraged to share their reactions to their practice in muscle relaxation the previous week. An attempt is made to resolve any difficulties that a client may have had in the practice sessions and to answer questions about muscle relaxation. The relaxation tape referred to earlier is then used again, in order to train group members even more thoroughly in relaxation. At the completion of the relaxation tape, the clients are given training in visualizing neutral scenes. The therapist informs the group members that they will now hear another tape, which will describe two neutral scenes. The clients are urged to continue their relaxed state and to attempt to project themselves into the situations they will hear described to them.

The visualization tape, prepared by the author, represents an attempt to depict vividly two common experiences ordinarily shared by most people. The first scene involves the experience of lying on a beach. The second scene involves the experience of lying on a lawn chair in the back yard of a friend. In both, there is an extensive use of adjectives (for example, "hot sun," "bright-red bathing suit," "purple-and-white-striped beach towel," "sputtering lawn mower," "pale-yellow flowers"), so that group members can gain practice in imagining themselves in real-life situations.[5]

Working Through the Hierarchy Items

The last four sessions of our treatment program are devoted to working through the individual items of the test-anxiety hierarchy. The first fifteen minutes of each session are used to induce a deep state of relaxation among the clients. The remaining forty-five minutes are used to work through four or five items on the hierarchy.

As the group members have had two previous experiences with the recorded relaxation instructions and have practiced relaxation procedures at home for two weeks, we have found that most can be relaxed in approximately fifteen minutes during the third session. The instructions for relaxation are given verbally by the therapist, with only one tensing and relaxing of each of the muscle groups. After the relaxation instructions, the therapist announces that in a few minutes the clients will have read to them a description of the scene that they had ranked at the previous session as the least anxiety provoking. The group members are told that, if they experience any anxiety or muscle tension whatever during the visualization of themselves in that situation, they should alert the therapist by simply raising the index finger of either hand. They are also urged to try to project themselves as completely as possible into the description of the hierarchy item. For example, if the bedroom is mentioned, they are asked to picture their own rooms. If an instructor is mentioned, they are asked to think of a specific instructor with whom they are familiar.

After a few more minutes of relaxation instructions, the therapist reads an expanded version of that hierarchy item that was rated as least anxiety provoking by the group. Expanded versions of two of the hierarchy items are presented here.[6]

Expanded Hierarchy-Item Descriptions

You are in your bed, trying to get to sleep. As you roll over on to your side, your mind flashes to the examination you will have tomorrow. You feel that you are uncertain as to how well you will do, even though you have studied for the examination. Somehow, you can't seem to get very comfortable. As you shift your position, your mind flashes once again to the examination.

You are sitting in class in your normal seat. Your instructor has just walked into the room with the examinations under his right arm. A few students are talking together a short distance away, and one of them laughs loudly. There seem to be more students in the room than is usual. You look over a few notes and they seem familiar as you read them. When you put them away, however, it is hard to recall what you had just read.

One difficulty with group desensitization is the number of presentations of the individual hierarchy items that is of maximum benefit to each client. In individual desensitization, hierarchy items are repeated until the client can

---

[5] *Editors' note:* Such practice may not always be necessary, but if it is, individuals from different ethnic, cultural, and geographic backgrounds may require different scenes.

[6] A complete set of items may be obtained from Robert A. Osterhouse, Department of Psychology, University of Maryland, College Park, Maryland 20742.

visualize himself in each situation without any feelings of anxiety or muscle tension. It is frequent in group desensitization, however, for one client to signal anxiety for many presentations, long after other group members have stopped signaling their anxiety.[7]

Two major methods of presenting hierarchy items have emerged as a response to this problem. One group of therapists tends to favor an approach in which the hierarchy item is presented until the last client no longer signals anxiety. At that point, the therapist introduces the next least anxiety-provoking item from the hierarchy. Along with other therapists, we favor a different approach. We have a maximum number of presentations for any one hierarchy item, and we then move on to the next hierarchy item even if one or more of the clients is still signaling anxiety following the last presentation. Our rationale for this decision is that many clients have reported to us that they find it difficult to continue to relax when they are confronted with many additional presentations of an item that no longer arouses anxiety or muscle tension for them. The minimum number of presentations we make is three, the maximum number five. If none of the group members signals anxiety following the third or fourth presentation of an item, the therapist moves on to introduce the next hierarchy item.

One potential problem with our procedures is that clients may feel some pressure not to signal anxiety following the fifth presentation, even if they still feel anxious. We have tried to solve this problem by assuring clients that we will work with them individually on any hierarchy item about which they still feel anxiety following the final presentation. Individual work is done with clients either following the group session or at some other convenient time. Our experience has been that approximately 20 percent of the clients need individual attention at some point during the treatment program.

After each presentation of a hierarchy item, clients are given fifteen to twenty seconds of relaxation instructions (for example, "Let your arms relax even more fully"; "Feel the relaxation proceed down your chest and stomach"; "Take a deep breath and hold it—now feel the enjoyment as you relax completely"). When all of the presentations of a hierarchy item have been completed, clients are given approximately one minute of relaxation instructions before the initial presentation of the next hierarchy item is made.

During the fourth, fifth, and sixth sessions, we begin desensitization with one or two presentations of the hierarchy items that have been worked through in previous sessions. One presentation is made if no client signals anxiety during the item description; two are made if any client signals anxiety. A typical outline for the final four sessions, then, looks something like this:

7 *Editors' note:* This may not be a problem if a variation of desensitization is used. Instead of immediately stopping the scene, the person continues to imagine it, using relaxation to reduce anxiety.

Session 3
1. Collection of relaxation practice forms from client.
2. Fifteen minutes of relaxation instructions by therapist.
3. Explanation of signaling of anxiety and projecting self into situations; assurance of individual help if anxiety is still signaled following final presentation.
4. Two minutes of relaxation instructions.
5. Presentation of item 1 from the hierarchy (three to five presentations, interspersed with fifteen to twenty seconds of relaxation instructions).
6. One minute of relaxation instructions.
7. Continuation with hierarchy items 2–5, as shown in 5 and 6 above.

Session 4
1. Fifteen minutes of relaxation instructions.
2. One or two presentations of hierarchy items 1–5.
3. Presentation of hierarchy items 6–9.

Session 5
1. Fifteen minutes of relaxation instructions.
2. One or two presentations of hierarchy items 1–9.
3. Presentation of hierarchy items 10–12.

Session 6
1. Fifteen minutes of relaxation instructions.
2. One or two presentations of hierarchy items 1–12.
3. Presentation of hierarchy items 13–15.

EVALUATION OF OUR PROCEDURES

The basic procedures for group desensitization of test anxiety described earlier have been evaluated in a number of research investigations conducted by the author and several of his students. The two outcome measures used consistently in this series of investigations have been changes in self-reported test anxiety following treatment and changes in academic performance following treatment. A copy of the self-report measure, the "Inventory of Test Anxiety" (Osterhouse, 1972), is shown here.

Inventory of Test Anxiety
Directions: Read each of the following statements carefully. In the space before each item, indicate how you *actually* felt during your psychology examination. Use the following scale:
1. The statement did *not* describe my feeling or condition.
2. The feeling or condition was barely noticeable.
3. The feeling or condition was moderately intense.
4. The feeling or condition was strong.
5. The feeling or condition was very strong.

_____ 1. I felt panicky while taking this examination.
_____ 2. I felt during this examination that I wouldn't be able to finish the examination on time.
_____ 3. My mouth got dry during this examination.
_____ 4. Prior to taking this examination, I felt that other students were better prepared for this examination than I was.
_____ 5. My mind went blank at the beginning of this examination. It took me a few minutes to function.
_____ 6. I feel that I let myself and other persons down by my performance on this examination.
_____ 7. I felt my heart beating fast during this examination.

_____ 8. I found myself worrying about a low grade before this examination.

_____ 9. During this examination, I found myself thinking about the consequences of failure.

_____10. I got so tense during this examination that my stomach became upset.

_____11. After finishing this examination, I feel that I could have done better than I actually did.

_____12. I got a headache during this examination.

_____13. While taking this examination, I found myself thinking of how much brighter other students are than I am.

_____14. My hands perspired during this examination.

_____15. I did not feel very confident of my performance before I took this examination.

_____16. I got so nervous during this examination that I forgot facts which I really knew.

There has been a consistent tendency for clients who have undergone these treatment procedures to report greater reductions in test anxiety related to examinations following treatment than do untreated control subjects, selected on the same basis as treatment subjects (McMillan, 1973; O'Connell, 1971; Osterhouse, 1972; Osterhouse & O'Connell, 1973).

There is less consistency, however, in improvement in academic performance. Some investigations have discovered a significantly greater increase in academic performance following treatment, compared to that of control subjects (McMillan & Osterhouse, 1972; Osterhouse & O'Connell, 1973). Other investigations report no significant differences between control and treatment subjects in academic performance following treatment (McMillan, 1973; O'Connell, 1971; Osterhouse 1972). Currently it is unclear what factors in the treatment process or selection of clients account for these differences in outcome with respect to academic performance.[8] Nevertheless, there does appear to be substantial evidence for the usefulness of the treatment procedures reported here.

[8] *Editors' note:* Many factors other than excessive stress and tension influence how well a person does on an examination. Thus it is not surprising that a student could experience much less stress yet not significantly improve her grades.

references

Emery, J. R. Systematic desensitization: Reducing test anxiety. In J. D. Krumboltz & C. E. Thoresen (Eds.), *Behavioral counseling: Cases and techniques.* New York: Holt, Rinehart and Winston, 1969. Pp. 267–288.

Emery, J. R. & Krumboltz, J. D. Standard versus individualized hierarchies in desensitization to reduce test anxiety. *Journal of Counseling Psychology,* 1967, **14**, 204–209.

Garlington, W. K. & Cotler, S. D. Systematic desensitization of test anxiety. *Behaviour Research and Therapy,* 1968, **6**, 247–256.

Ihli, K. L. & Garlington, W. K. A comparison of group vs. individual desensitization of test anxiety. *Behaviour Research and Therapy,* 1969, **7**, 207–209.

Mann, J. & Rosenthal, T. L. Vicarious and direct counterconditioning of test anxiety through individual and group desensitization. *Behaviour Research and Therapy*, 1969, **7**, 359–367.

McGlynn, F. D. Individual versus standardized hierarchies in the systematic desensitization of snake avoidance. *Behaviour Research and Therapy*, 1971, **9**, 1–5.

McMillan, J. R. The effects of desensitization treatment, rational emotive therapy, and a combination treatment program for test-anxious students with high and low levels of generalized anxiety. Unpublished doctoral dissertation, University of Maryland, 1973.

McMillan, J. R. & Osterhouse, R. A. Specific and generalized anxiety as determinants of outcome with desensitization of test anxiety. *Journal of Counseling Psychology*, 1972, **19**, 518–521.

O'Connell, T. J. The effects of motivational factors on desensitization treatment for high test-anxious students. Unpublished master's thesis, University of Maryland, 1971.

Osterhouse, R. A. Desensitization and study-skills training as treatment for two types of test-anxious students. *Journal of Counseling Psychology*, 1972, **19**, 301–307.

Osterhouse, R. A. & O'Connell, T. J. The effect of individual vs. group treatment, "live" vs. recorded relaxation training, and individual vs. standard hierarchies on the desensitization of test anxiety. Mimeograph. College Park: Department of Psychology, University of Maryland, 1973.

Paul, G. L. *Insight vs. desensitization in psychotherapy*. Palo Alto: Stanford University Press, 1966.

Paul, G. L. Outcome of systematic desensitization, II: Controlled investigations of individual treatment, technique variations, and current status. In Cyril M. Franks (Ed.), *Behavior therapy: Appraisal and status*. New York: McGraw-Hill, 1969. Pp. 105–159.

Paul, G. L. & Shannon, D. T. Treatment of anxiety through systematic desensitization in therapy groups. *Journal of Abnormal Psychology*, 1966, **71**, 124–135.

Wolpe, J. *Psychotherapy by reciprocal inhibition*. Palo Alto: Stanford University Press, 1958.

Wolpe, J. Reciprocal inhibition as the main basis of psychotherapeutic effects. *American Medical Association Archives of Neurological Psychiatry*, 1954, **72**, 205–226.

SCHOOL PHOBIA

31. *FAMILY COUNSELING WITH A SCHOOL-PHOBIC CHILD*

JAMES M. STEDMAN   University of Texas Health Science Center, San Antonio, and Community Guidance Center, Bexar County

Mr. and Mrs. Sanchez brought their nine-year-old daughter Alice to the Community Guidance Center[1] in November 1971, complaining that she was refusing to attend school. In fact, she had been out of school for two weeks. Mr. and Mrs. Sanchez also spoke of Alice's having various "nervous symptoms" and stated that she had few friends.

The Sanchez couple also had two teen-age daughters and an older son, who was away at college. The initial session, conducted with all family members except the older brother, suggested that the family was rather tightly knit and closed, with the parents being bound up in child rearing and having few activities outside the family circle. The major unresolved issues appeared to involve Alice's lack of independence from the family, particularly from the influence of her mother; Mrs. Sanchez' tendency to communicate, both verbally and nonverbally, in an infantilizing manner that encouraged Alice's dependence; and a lack of marital satisfaction on the part of the parents. The resistance to school seemed to have resulted from the broader issue of Alice's lack of appropriate separation from parental figures and from anxiety

more directly associated with school performance.

This global analysis of the family interaction was gradually translated into the following behavioral goals:

1. To return Alice to school on a daily basis and to enable her to complete academic work successfully.
2. To increase the number of Alice's observable, developmentally appropriate independent behaviors.
3. To decrease the number of Alice's responses that were directly controlled by her mother.
4. To increase the frequency of "releaser statements" made to Alice by Mrs. Sanchez.[2]
5. To decrease Alice's anxiety over school performance, particularly related to reading and music.
6. To increase reciprocally reinforcing responses between Mr. and Mrs. Sanchez, particularly those related to their marriage.

As these family issues emerged and the various behavioral goals were established, it seemed clear that a variety

---

[1] An out-patient guidance agency affiliated with the University of Texas Health Science Center at San Antonio.

[2] "Releaser statements" are loosely defined as any verbal or nonverbal communications from Mrs. Sanchez to Alice indicating approval of appropriate independent behaviors on Alice's part. For example, in session 4, Mrs. Sanchez sat physically apart from Alice for the first time, and, about midway through the session, she commented with approval on Alice's remaining in school three days that week.

of behavioral counseling strategies would be required. Total treatment consisted of sixteen face-to-face meetings with the family and two contacts with the school.

As Eisenberg (1958) has pointed out, getting the school-resistant child back into school is a primary therapeutic task. However, prior to accomplishing this goal, it was crucial to understand Alice's actual school-resistant behavior and the parental responses to it. Further detailed investigation revealed that Alice was not totally resistant to school and, in fact, would go to school after much urging. However, each day she would leave school immediately before reading class, and Mrs. Sanchez would walk halfway to school to meet Alice at that time each morning. Further exploration of Alice's pattern revealed that each day she became anxious before reading class and avoided that anxiety by leaving school. Once home, Mrs. Sanchez was mildly reinforcing, in that Alice was allowed to do as she wished for the rest of the day.[3]

On the other hand, Mr. Sanchez was becoming increasingly angry and was pressing both Alice and his wife about Alice's babyish ways and her refusal to go to school. Thus, his return home each evening constituted a punishing contingency, directed mostly toward Alice.

In summary, Alice's school-resistant patterns seemed to incorporate an anxiety component connected with her performance, which involved a specific "dreaded" activity at school. The approaching reading activity and thoughts about her mother both acted as specific discriminative stimuli for leaving school. Additionally, it became clear that Mrs. Sanchez reinforced "school leaving" behavior, as well as reinforcing dependent behavior in general. Mr. Sanchez was rapidly becoming a nightly punisher, a factor that was leading him to take on aversive properties for Alice.[4]

INITIAL BEHAVIORAL STRATEGIES WITH ALICE AND HER FAMILY

In the course of three evaluative contacts with the family, I decided on two behavioral strategies, a desensitization program to counteract Alice's specific fear of reading and an operant contingency-contracting program to counteract her resistance to school. Actually, the contingency contract was designed to accomplish several target behavioral goals, all of which were coordinated with the previously stated goals. Thus, the contingency contract was designed to enable Alice to remain in school, to increase mutually compatible responses between Mr. and Mrs. Sanchez in their roles as "parent managers" of the contract, to establish Mrs. Sanchez as a reinforcer of more mature and independent behavior, and to decrease the

---

[3] *Editors' note:* Actually Alice was handling a very anxious situation (reading class) quite understandably. Avoiding class was highly reinforcing, for it reduced her stress and tension (the process of negative reinforcement at work!). And Mrs. Sanchez added some positive reinforcement for leaving school.

[4] *Editors' note:* Unfortunately, too many fathers behave in this fashion as "after-work aversives."

frequency with which Mr. Sanchez acted as a nightly "punishing stimulus."

In my experience, I have found that some families do not readily accept a contingency-contract approach, considering it a form of "bribery" and perhaps sensing that other changes in the family homeostasis are likely to occur should they engage in contingency-contract programs.[5] Thus it is sometimes difficult to elicit parental cooperation. The following is an excerpt demonstrating how this family was "sold" on a contingency-contracting program.

THERAPIST: I think it's very important for you to know that your mother is wanting you to get over your fear in school. Now let's get back to my explaining about how Alice may have learned these things. In my view, Mr. and Mrs. Sanchez, most of the problems we see with kids are not some mysterious illness that we don't have any control over. From my point of view, most of what we see in kids is really learned by them during their growing-up period. I think Alice has learned to fear some things in school and has also learned to fear growing up in general. It's like she feels safer being little than big. She's definitely not crazy, but she's learned to fear many things—we need to help her learn new ways of dealing with her scared feelings. Does this make sense?

MOTHER: Yes, I guess it does.

FATHER: Yes, it does.

[5] Editors' note: "Bribery" is a common misnomer for using positive consequences systematically in any context. To bribe is to reward a person for engaging in an illegal or immoral act.

THERAPIST: Well, you know maybe we should try something to help Alice unlearn some of her fears about going to school. There should be some payoff for Alice's being able to go to school and stay there all day. It's kind of like her job. What would happen to you, Mr. Sanchez, if you left your job in the middle of every day?

FATHER: I'd get fired pretty quick, I guess.

THERAPIST: Yeah, I suppose so. I guess one of the reasons you go to your job every day is that once a month, or maybe once a week, you get some payoff from going to your job—you get a paycheck.

FATHER: Yes, I guess that's right. If I didn't go to work I wouldn't get paid.

THERAPIST: Well, Alice's job at her age is going to school and getting herself ready to grow up, right?

FATHER: Yes.

THERAPIST: Alice, is that right?

ALICE: Yeah, I guess so.

THERAPIST: What do you think, Mrs. Sanchez? Is that Alice's job—getting ready to grow up?

MOTHER: Yeah, I guess so.

THERAPIST: Well, let's design a program so that we can help Alice get some payoff or some rewards for staying in school. [Therapist proceeds to sketch out a data sheet, similar to that in Table 1, for the parents.]

The contingency contract itself was simple, with only a single target behavior: school attendance. The system was arranged so that Alice had to spend about 5 points a day (about 75 percent of the Tuesday, Thursday, and Friday totals) to gain the privileges she usually wanted on a daily basis. It should be noted that points gained on one day were used to purchase priv-

TABLE 1   Point System for School Attendance

Time	M	T	W	T	F
Morning	3		3		
	Music 3	3	Music 3	3	3
Noon	2	2	2	2	2
Afternoon	1	1	1	1	1
Total	9	6	9	6	6

ileges on the following day. Surplus points, when earned, were spent for "special" privileges. Privileges and their costs are listed here:

1. *Television:* 1 point for thirty minutes (Alice usually spent 3–4 points daily for this).
2. *Allowance:* 1 point for 10 cents, to be earned on a daily basis up to 50 cents a week (Alice usually spent 1 point for this).
3. *Movies:* 5 points on a weekly basis (Alice spent available surplus points for this).
4. *Trips to the store with her father:* 1 point about three times a week (Alice spent available surplus points for this).

Contingency-Contracting Results with Alice and Her Family

Observable changes in Alice came rather quickly. The system was initiated in the third therapy session, and she managed to complete three of five days by session 4. However, she had left school on Monday and Wednesday just before music class and was now complaining about anticipatory anxiety with regard to music. Reading was no longer cited as a source of anxiety, a matter that will be discussed later. It was interesting to note the qualitative changes in Mr. and Mrs. Sanchez. Mrs.

Sanchez sat physically separated from Alice for the first time and also produced more nonverbal cues suggesting relaxation: smiling, less muscular tension, sitting back in the chair (rather than on the edge). Mr. Sanchez also seemed less physically tense and made a comment on Alice's "getting more guts" with regard to handling the school situation.

Results in later sessions continued to be much the same for both Alice and her parents. Alice continued to attend school (except on music days) and received access to her privileges. Mrs. Sanchez continued as manager of the system and seemed to be releasing control over more of Alice's behavior. The following is an excerpt from my notes on session 8:

I asked Mr. Sanchez about his perception of his wife's management of Alice, and he reinforced several aspects of his wife's increased feelings of being ready to release his daughter. He commented on the separation and growth of Alice, stating that she is no longer as interested in sleeping with her mother as in the past and that she spontaneously gave up the habit she had of taking baby bottles and dolls with her on trips away from home. I reinforced these behaviors as indications of Alice's "growing up" and being stronger inside.

In session 9, Mrs. Sanchez spontaneously commented that she had decided to learn to drive because it would give her more autonomy in her various pursuits, an indication of her own growth. Later results with Mr. Sanchez seemed to indicate a sharp decrease in his role as nightly punisher and an increase in his support of Mrs. Sanchez, as manifested by an increase in positive statements about both Alice and his wife. Additionally, Mr. Sanchez acted as the dispenser of "special reinforcers," which Alice could gain as part of her point program. This role increased his importance as a mediator of positive reinforcement in Alice's life. Unfortunately, I have only my notes to document these changes in Mr. and Mrs. Sanchez.

The problem of Alice's anxiety over music took on special proportions when it became obvious that she had "switched" her anxiety from reading to music. I must admit a few shaky hours pondering the possibility of symptom substitution, which, of course, is not supposed to occur. However, once again careful behaviorally oriented inquiry brought forth an explanation. Most important, I ascertained that reading *per se* had not been the specific cue for anxiety. Rather, Alice reacted with anxiety to any situation requiring her to perform a new or poorly mastered academic task in front of the class.

Of special interest is the fact that Alice's decrease in anxiety over reading was apparently facilitated by a "home remedy" program devised by her parents. This procedure required Alice to spent several thirty-minute periods reading into a tape recorder while in a room by herself. Later these tapes were played before the rest of the family, with Alice present in the room. Then Alice herself read briefly in front of the family and gradually lengthened the time during two additional sessions. Apparently, this parent-generated "*in vivo* desensitization program" was sufficient to decrease Alice's anxiety specific to reading and complemented the operant program.[6]

The Systematic Desensitization Program

Concurrent with the operant program, I began desensitization designed to counteract Alice's specific anxieties experienced in the school situation. Deep muscle relaxation proved successful. Establishment of a hierarchy at first took the form of items involving reading, but it was soon noted that Alice became anxious when called upon to perform any unfamiliar, complex academic task in front of the teacher and the class. Also, because of her absence from school, she had missed a number of music lessons and now suffered acute anticipatory anxiety with regard to performing on the recorder in music class. Thus, a later hierarchy, focusing on music but designed also to counteract anxiety over performance of un-

[6] *Editors' note:* An excellent program. It seems likely that the Sanchez family got the general idea from the counselor. The tape-recording procedure can also serve as an induction aid, as described in articles 28 and 33.

familiar school work, was established;
a sample of items is presented here.

*Excerpts from Music Class and
Academic Hierarchy*

1. I am at home at night thinking about sitting in music class watching the others play their recorders. . . .
5. I am in music class with the teacher by herself. I am playing an easy, familiar tune on my recorder, and the teacher looks pleased. . . .
9. I am in music class with the teacher by herself. I am playing a hard tune on which I make many mistakes, and the teacher looks slightly displeased. . . .
14. I am in music class with the teacher and all the students. I am playing an easy tune in front of the class, with the teacher watching me. . . .
18. I am in front of the music class, playing a fairly hard tune on which I make many mistakes, and several students smile and laugh. . . .
22. I have played poorly in front of the music class, and the teacher corrects me after class for a poor performance. . . .
26. I am in reading class, and the teacher calls on me to stand up and read. I stumble over words, while several students laugh at me and the teacher looks impatient. . . .
29. I am in reading class, and the teacher calls on me to stand up and read. I stumble over words, and the teacher asks me to sit down and comments that I should know the work. The whole class laughs.

Desensitization began in session 3 and continued through session 14. Alice's progress followed conventional desensitization lines, in that she reported progressive anxiety reduction as the various hierarchy items were completed. By session 14, Alice was attending all classes without anxiety. Formal desensitization sessions were discontinued at that point.

LATER BEHAVIORAL STRATEGIES WITH ALICE

Meanwhile Alice continued to report anxiety over music and continued to leave school on Monday and Wednesday before music class, although she was able to remain in school on other days. By session 8, it seemed to me that additional measures, specific to music class, were in order, so I decided to incorporate Alice's teachers into the therapy program and to attempt an *in vivo* desensitization strategy, which would run concurrently with the imagery-desensitization program. This procedure was discussed in a separate meeting with Alice's music teacher and then presented to Alice and her parents during the following therapy session. The procedural steps were the following:

1. Alice's music teacher would tutor her outside the school setting until she reached a level equal to that of the class.
2. Alice would reenter music class for twenty-minute periods but would not be required to play her recorder.
3. Alice would remain in music class for the full time and would play the recorder.

Alice responded positively to this proposal and immediately began special tutoring sessions. By session 11, she had learned to play the recorder up to the level of her class. However, through a mistake by a substitute music teacher who was unaware of the program, Alice not only reentered music class but was invited to play. She responded by playing the recorder and staying through the entire music class.[7] After a hasty consultation with Alice's regular music teacher, I decided to continue this procedure if Alice showed no significant increase in anxiety. This decision proved successful, thus ending the *in vivo* desensitization program.

An additional behavior strategy became necessary when it was discovered in session 9 that Mrs. Sanchez had continued to accompany Alice to school and to walk her to the door each morning. As Mrs. Sanchez apparently was serving as a necessary stimulus support for the girl's attendance, I decided to employ a stimulus-fading strategy, which contained the following steps:

1. The mother was to ride to school with Alice but not to accompany her to the door for four days.
2. She was to accompany Alice to the car but not to ride to school with her for four days.
3. She was to remain in the house and to allow Alice alone to complete all steps required to go to school.

This program was monitored through three additional sessions and resulted

---

[7] *Editors' note:* Success in mastering the anxiety-producing situation reduces the anxiety. All other desensitization programs become superfluous.

in Alice's attending school without further support from Mrs. Sanchez.

GETTING THE PARENTS TOGETHER

As noted earlier, lack of reciprocal reinforcement in the Sanchezes' marriage relationship seemed to have been causal in the development of the intensive overinvolvement between Alice and her mother and remained a source of concern after the resolution of some of Alice's problems. After some additional probing of Mr. and Mrs. Sanchez's social learning history, I decided to use an operant approach to their marriage difficulties. Starting at session 10, I began to identify more precisely areas of social bankruptcy, a concept developed by Stuart (1973) to describe communication deficits in marital interaction. Then I proceeded to outline the general notion of marital relationship, based on mutually reinforcing behavioral exchanges. I suggested that the Sanchezes complete the Stuart marriage forms as a preliminary step in establishing a marital contingency contract.

This procedure resulted in cancellation of the following session and a "no show" for the next session. I realized that I had made an error in attempting such a formalized system without proper consideration of possible cultural background factors. I had not reordered my contract with the family to one calling for specialized work with them, as opposed to work with Alice, and I had not assessed their readiness to work on these problems. I contacted Mr. Sanchez and discussed the fact that I had probably "stuck my nose in where I had no business."[8] He quickly confirmed my impression and stated that he and his wife felt no need to probe or to change a "happy marriage." I accepted this level of readiness and urged them to return for one final visit, which I said would focus primarily on Alice.

They did return, reporting that all school issues were going well and that Alice was playing well with children in the family and around the neighborhood. Later in the session Mr. Sanchez casually mentioned that he had made some changes, like staying up longer at night to be with his wife, sharing some of the recent decision making with her, and planning more family activities. Although these were precisely the areas his wife had mentioned in her complaints, Mr. Sanchez went on to state that his shifts were minor and of little importance in their overall relationship. My response was cautious, as I felt that aggressive pursuit of these issues would result in "flight from therapy," as before. However, I did inquire whether or not Mrs. Sanchez had let her husband know of her appreciation for these changes and pointed out the similarity between Alice's and Mr. Sanchez' need to be reinforced for successful completion of pleasing behavior. Except for one follow-up visit, this was our final face-to-face session.

[8] *Editors' note:* Good for you. It takes courage to acknowledge mistakes to clients (or to anyone), but mistakes can be corrected. Counseling is an intelligent trial-and-error process as long as the counselor remains open to the feedback from the trials and errors.

SOME RESULTS

Results can be analyzed with reference to the target areas outlined earlier.

Alice's Return to School

Alice did, in fact, return to school and remained there, free of symptoms, for a number of sessions; she was still symptom-free at a follow-up session one month after the final family session. As part of the preparation for this paper, I made contact with the Sanchez family and discovered that, after two years, Alice continues to do well. Mrs. Sanchez reported that Alice has attended school with no problems. Additionally, she has many friends and a variety of interests, including music. In fact, she recently marched in a downtown parade with her school band. With regard to performance before groups, Mrs. Sanchez reports that Alice regularly leads her classmates in singing at the school mass. Thus, Alice seems to be completely symptom-free at present.

Increase in Alice's Observable Independent Behaviors

As noted earlier, Mr. Sanchez was reporting that Alice was acting as if she had more "guts." In session 5 he continued this theme, and by session 8 he was speaking with pleasure about his wife's management of Alice's situation and commenting that his daughter had given up sleeping with her mother and was no longer taking baby bottles and dolls on trips away from home. Such comments continued throughout the rest of therapy. At our final follow-up session, Alice reported that she had joined the school band and was playing the flute, had joined the Girl Scouts, and was making As and Bs in her schoolwork. These unmeasured but reported behaviors indicated an increase in independent behavior on Alice's part.

Fewer of Alice's Responses Controlled by Her Mother

Results here are hard to assess, but it was noted that Mrs. Sanchez did cooperate in the "fading" program and that Mr. Sanchez commented frequently on Alice's increased distance from her mother. Additionally, perhaps Alice's observed increase in more mature behavior patterns is an indicator that fewer of her response patterns were controlled by Mrs. Sanchez.

Increase in "Releaser" Statements by Mrs. Sanchez

There is no way to assess this goal accurately. However, it was interesting to note that Mrs. Sanchez' pattern of comments about Alice's improvement or regression tended to vary with her own assessment of the probability of having her needs met by Mr. Sanchez. Qualitative analysis of my notes suggests that, whenever Mrs. Sanchez perceived Alice as likely to "become independent" without noticeable improvement in her own marital relationship, she would make more comments about Alice's regression and lack of progress. Whenever there seemed to be more hope for change between her husband and herself, she tended to talk more about Alice's progress. Unfortunately, I have no quantitative analysis of this interaction pattern.[9]

Decrease in Alice's Anxiety Over Performance Before Groups

Two strategies were used to alleviate this target problem, systematic desensitization and in vivo desensitization. As noted, Alice did report anxiety decrease to zero with respect to the imagined hierarchy. However, as these data are based on imaginary practice, they are subject to doubt. The in vivo program did result in appropriate approach responses to music class and then full participation. It is impossible to tell whether the two strategies interacted to produce results or whether some third, unknown factor played a major role. Nevertheless, Alice did reintegrate into all classes and reported no anxiety by the end of treatment.

[9] Editors' note: Mrs. Sanchez probably desired certain emotional responses that she obtained from her daughter if she could not obtain them from her husband.

references

Eisenberg, L. School phobia: A study in communication of anxiety. *American Journal of Psychiatry*, 1958, **114**, 712–718.

Stuart, R. Operant-interpersonal treatment for marital discord. In Stedman, J. et al. (Eds.), *Clinical studies in behavior therapy with children adolescents, and their families*. Springfield, Ill.: Thomas, 1973. Pp. 311–323.

FEAR OF SOCIAL REJECTION

32. A TREATMENT PROGRAM FOR SOCIAL INADEQUACY: MULTIPLE METHODS FOR A COMPLEX PROBLEM

PATRICIA A. WISOCKI   University of Massachusetts, Amherst

Within the last few years more than half the people in my client population have requested therapy for "central life problems" or "personality restructuring." These people are generally deficient in social responses, have few positive attributes, and often regard themselves as inferior, many times for good objective reasons. In short, they are people whose lives are miserable because they cannot "get along" with others in daily living. Usually, they have been referred to a behavior therapist because they have not responded to other therapeutic methods.

In treating this type of case, the behavioral counselor has an opportunity to incorporate a variety of therapist and situational variables into the treatment program, along with the "standard" behavioral techniques.[1]

About two years ago I was presented with a particularly difficult case, involving a thirty-one-year-old female, Lois, who complained, "I have no hope for the future, and I don't enjoy the present." Lois was of average height and extremely thin build; her face was long, colorless, and unanimated; her hair was pulled away from her face,

emphasizing the sharpness of her features; her clothes were dark and plain. She reported having frequent headaches, bowel disturbances, and insomnia, along with a poor appetite. She felt tense and panicky, depressed, lonely, and inadequate. She occasionally contemplated suicide. Although she held a doctorate in physics, she was working at a demeaning and boring job. She could not remember a happy time in her life. At the time, she had one friend (female) and rarely spoke with anyone else. In her entire social history she had dated four men (briefly) but had never felt comfortable with any of them. Weekends, which were particularly distressing times, were generally spent sewing or "walking around," although even then she believed that people were watching her and thinking of her as a social misfit.

Lois wanted therapy to change all that. She wanted to be attractive, sociable, and busy. She wanted an interesting job that demanded creativity. She wanted to think well of herself. Most of all, she wanted friends.

She had been referred by a male behavior therapist, who had employed for eight months the standard techniques: relaxation and desensitization for her anxiety in social situations and for feelings of loneliness; thought stopping for ruminations on her inadequa-

---

[1] *Editors' note:* Unfortunately, counselors too often use "standard" techniques that are not tailored to the clients' particular problems. Then, if therapy fails, the counselors rationalize that it is because of the clients' "unreadiness for therapy"!

cies; covert reinforcement for attempting various social gambits. He had even arranged a few dates for her and had rehearsed appropriate social responses with her in a role-playing format.

To my mind his treatment program had been logical and functional, but I concluded that he had tried too much too soon. After his unsuccessful experience, it was apparent to me that the client needed more rudimentary skills of social intercourse before taking on complex interactions.

BEHAVIORAL ANALYSIS

Obviously, the information that I had to date was only topographically descriptive. It served to define boundaries for me and provided a basis for what questions to ask. The next steps were to obtain a functional description, specifically of the operational limitations of therapeutic activity in terms of establishing target behaviors; to choose procedures; and to determine a method of measuring the client's progress.

Each goal presented by Lois was operationally defined through joint consideration of each element necessary to achieve that goal. During the course of that discussion we found that some of the categories were defined similarly (for example, "being sociable," "having friends," and "being busy"; "being attractive" and "thinking well of self"), and so we integrated them.

Next, through direct questioning and an examination of several self-report assessment scales (the "Life History Questionnaire," Wolpe, 1969; the

"Fear Survey Schedule," Wolpe & Lang, 1964; the "Reinforcement Survey Schedule," Cautela & Kastenbaum, 1967; and the "Job Fear Survey Schedule," Wisocki, 1970a) I determined which of Lois' behaviors it would be necessary to increase or to strengthen and which to weaken or to decrease in order to achieve the desired goals. I also found out what assets she possessed relevant to the target behaviors. She had a sharp wit, excellent written-communication skills, her own car (allowing for ease of mobility), interests in art and music, and a history of independent living. I also explored the types of reinforcing and punishing stimuli that were available for use. Finally, I assessed other possible fears that she associated with daily life and work.[2]

In Table 1 I have diagrammed the results of this assessment operation, which occurred over a two-week period. The goals are presented in the order of priorities set by Lois herself.

The design of the treatment program followed directly from the assessment. Although in the course of treatment these specified categories overlapped, I tried as much as possible to focus on one problem area at a time. There are several reasons for this strategy: First, there is a greater likelihood of immediate gain, which usually provides the client with more confidence in achieving future success and results in a greater willingness to cooperate with the therapist's suggestions

[2] *Editors' note:* These self-report assessment scales serve as handy short-cuts in the time-consuming task of asking the client many questions.

TABLE 1 Behavioral Assessment of Lois

Goals Stated by Patient	Operational Translation by Therapist and Patient	Necessary Therapeutic Operations for Reaching Goals			
		Increase	Techniques	Decrease	Techniques
1. Be attractive (and think well of self).	Frequent positive thoughts that "people like me; I am attractive; I am a valuable person," etc. Elicitations of positive statements from others regarding personality, appearance, value, etc.	Buying brighter, more stylish clothes; change in hair style; use of make-up; smiling; walking quickly. Positive self-statements; verbal expressions of feelings.	Shaping, verbal reinforcement. Contingency contracting; covert positive reinforcement; verbal reinforcement; behavior rehearsal (modeling).	Negative self-statements.	Thought-stopping. Verbal extinction.
2. Be sociable (and have friends), which would result in "being busy."	Feeling comfortable (nonanxious) in social gatherings. Making conversation easily.	Presence in groups by accepting and extending invitations. Conversation skills in various settings and emission of positive statements to others.	Covert positive reinforcement; covert negative reinforcement; and overt and covert reinforcer sampling. Prompting-shaping; behavior rehearsal.	Feelings of anxiety among people. Thoughts that people are unfriendly or unconcerned.	Relaxation-desensitization. Thought-stopping.
3. Have a creative job.	Change present job to one which has more variety and elicits more "professional" feelings or make current position more acceptable.	Behaviors necessary to confront present employer about personal dissatisfactions. Appropriate interview behavior: ways of handling questions; expressions of enthusiasm.	Assertive training. Covert reinforcement. Behavior rehearsals.	Fears of: people in authority; failure; making mistakes; rejection; criticism. Tension over being supervised. Feelings of personal inadequacy.	Desensitization.

for the rest of therapy; second, with a specific direction in mind, the therapist is better able to maintain control over the treatment process; third, usually the client has had these problems for years, and a few weeks' delay has no effect on ultimate success.

THE ATTRACTIVENESS PROGRAM: TARGET 1

We began with the goal of "learning to be attractive" because the client believed it to be the most urgent and I felt it was central to the other problems. If Lois could feel that others were interested in her, she would be less hesitant to attempt the more active behaviors required to meet the other established goals. Operationally, this first goal consisted of arranging external contingencies to elicit positive statements from others and of increasing specific positive personal attitudes.

I began by prompting Lois about possibilities for makeup, a more pleasing hair style, a new wardrobe. She immediately informed me that she did not intend to wear makeup, had tried every hair style possible, had no money for new clothes and no patience with self-styled "Pygmalions." At this point (and many times thereafter) I realized that, with this client, I would be required not only to increase desired responses but also to overcome an unpleasant past history.[3]

My approach then became a process of shaping small changes in appear-

ance, posture, gait, and facial expression through verbally administered personal approval and deliberately arranged compliments from "outsiders" (for example, my colleagues in the office). To carry out such a program thoroughly and sincerely, it was necessary for me to take careful notes and to amass a large repertoire of compliments delivered with variations in timing and tone. For instance, sometimes I gushed over Lois' clothes as soon as I saw her; sometimes I paused in the middle of a conversation, looked "thoughtful," and mentioned some change; at other times, as she was leaving the office, I casually remarked about how happy she had appeared during the session.

Incidentally, not all people respond well to praise; some people, in fact, find it extremely aversive. The selection of a reinforcing stimulus is made on the basis of efficacy. If after six weeks or so I had not observed behavioral changes in the desired direction, I would have tried something else.

Such consistent attention occupied very little therapy time, but I believe it was a significant factor in facilitating a change in Lois' appearance and in establishing "rapport" between us.[4]

The majority of therapy time was given over to raising Lois' self-confidence by means of three separate methods: decreasing the frequency of negative self-statements by means of the thought-stopping technique (Wolpe, 1969) and verbal extinction; increasing

---

[3] *Editors' note:* Resistance to treatment is frequent. It may be a signal to slow down —but not to stop.

[4] *Editors' note:* Maybe some type of modeling experiences would have been more efficient. See Article 28 on participant modeling.

the frequency of positive self-statements with the use of covert positive reinforcement (Cautela, 1970) and contingency contracting (Homme, 1966); and practice in the overt expression of personal feelings by means of modeling and behavior rehearsals.

To deal with the things Lois believed—and needed to believe—about herself, I pointed out in great detail that constantly ruminating about her inadequacies, even if those inadequacies were objectively correct, usually prohibited constructive change and led to "depressed" feelings. On the other hand, deliberate thoughts about her value also affected behavior, but in a positive direction.

To illustrate a way to control these thoughts beneficially, I asked Lois to think of a specific self-destructive phrase that recurred frequently and to signal me when it was clearly in mind. At that point I shouted "stop," in order to produce an interruption in the pattern. We repeated the formula, but this time I stopped the thought *as it began*. Then, to demonstrate that she herself could end the same thought, I asked her to begin the thought pattern and to shout "stop" subvocally. Next, Lois constructed a list of negative statements that she commonly made about herself, and we alternated shouting "stop" for each one of them.

I also decided to extinguish verbally any self-deprecatory references Lois made in my presence by banning them from our conversations. In order to prevent "hard feelings" and to enlist Lois' cooperation, I informed her of my intention. Figure 1 details the weekly progress of this contractual arrangement.

To increase the frequency of positive self-statements with the technique of covert positive reinforcement, three steps were followed: construction of "scenes" containing stimuli sufficiently pleasurable to effect changes in Lois' behavior; a test for the speed of visualization, the degree of clarity, and the amount of familiarity associated with various images; and the presentation of the target behaviors followed immediately by the reinforcing stimulus. For example, to increase the frequency of the statement, "Once people get to know me, they would like me," Lois imagined the sentence and informed me when it was clear in her mind; I then pronounced the word "reinforcement," signaling her to think of the pleasurable stimulus that we had previously chosen. Lois was then asked to repeat the procedure without intervention from me. (For further clinical details of this technique, the reader is referred to Wisocki, 1970b; 1973.)[5]

For the other self-statements we wanted to increase we employed a similar format, varying reinforcing stimuli to avoid satiation problems.

These techniques were rehearsed for an entire session. Afterward I asked Lois to schedule two specific fifteen-minute periods each day for practice at home. These time periods were to be independent of any random occurrence of the problem behavior, but she was also told to make use of both whenever necessary.

[5] *Editors' note:* The research literature on covert reinforcement is incomplete. It appears that some clients do not need to "reinforce" their thoughts as such but are helped by various cues or reminders to think positive self-thoughts.

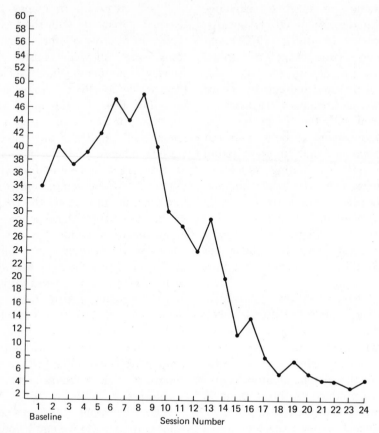

FIGURE 1 Results of the verbal-extinction program for self-deprecatory statements made during the therapy session.

In the development of new habits, practice is obviously an important element, one that a counselor or therapist cannot stress too strongly. In addition to "homework" assignments for a client, large portions of the office sessions are given over to practice, at least until adequate changes in the target behaviors are seen. Merely advising the client on a course of action without assisting him to reach the goal is generally insufficient for ensuring a behavior change, particularly during the initial stages of therapy. In fact, in order to encourage at-home rehearsal and to be able to make any necessary changes immediately, even when the office training has been discontinued, it is important each week for the therapist to inquire about the client's use of the techniques.[6]

With Lois I also found it helpful

[6] *Editors' note:* Sometimes calling the clients (or having them call in) every day or so is necessary, especially in the beginning, to ensure consistent home practice. (See articles 9 and 25 for examples of the uses of more frequent short contacts.)

to buttress the homework assignments with contingency contracts in which the performance of certain routine behaviors (like having a cup of coffee, brushing her teeth, looking at the clock) were made conditional upon the performance of certain desirable behaviors (for example, uttering ten positive self-statements).[7]

After sixteen weeks of therapy in this kind of format, Lois felt confident enough to begin behavior rehearsals of overt self-expression, a most difficult phase of treatment.

Behavior rehearsals, amalgams of desensitization components, modeling, and immediate feedback, were very important in this case. They permitted the client opportunities to learn several complex behaviors in an anxiety-free atmosphere.

The first set of rehearsals concerned the client's ability to express her personal feelings under various circumstances. Sample items indicating the range of these "personal feelings" follow. Each level demanded an increasing amount of personal involvement and risk of rejection or criticism.

Sample Items for the Behavior Rehearsal of Self-Expression
Polite Questions
  How are you?
  What's new?
  How are things going?
  Did you enjoy your trip to Europe?
Personal Feelings (level 1)
  I hope you're feeling better.
  I like your outfit.
  I was sorry to hear about the death in your family.

  I hope to take a trip myself soon.
Personal Feelings (level 2)
  I have a terrible headache.
  I went to the movies last night (possible implication that she didn't have a date.)
  Work is getting boring for me.
  I hope my article is published soon.
Personal Feelings (level 3)
  I despise my boss.
  I spent Saturday night watching TV.
  I'm thinking about changing jobs.
  I was cheated out of authorship on an article that was mostly my work.

Along with learning the correct words, it was necessary for Lois to acquire variety in phrasing, an "alive" tonal quality, and spontaneity (that is, speed of response and facility with casual phrases) in order to sound natural.

We worked for three months on this treatment area, employing the following format:

1. Lois would describe a troublesome situation to me.
2. We would discuss various possible ways of handling it.
3. I would suggest several responses connoting the target intentions.
4. She would imitate my behavior exactly.
5. We would discuss how she felt about it and what problems could have arisen in a real-life trial.
6. I would describe the same situation to her, and she would play out several responses.
7. I would make corrections, asking for more spontaneity, a change in tone, and so on.
8. We would rehearse the situation again.
9. We would discuss problems surrounding potential responses from other members in the interchange.

---

[7] *Editors' note:* A good example of using daily high-frequency activities as cues or reminders, as well as reinforcers.

10. Lois would be told to practice whatever we had rehearsed with as many people as she could find and to keep detailed accounts of her attempts.

Once Lois had mastered an item (mastery was determined by office demonstration, at least ten successful outside trials recorded by her, and a self-statement about feeling unconstrained and comfortable) we would begin work on the next one. Gradually, the time we allotted for practice on one item was decreased from sixty minutes to ten minutes, and we were able to include discussion of the preceding week's events in terms of the opportunities presented, Lois' specific behavior, possible improvements, and unanticipated problems.

Improvement occurred slowly in small increments, with plateau stages and occasional defeats. After the first twelve weeks, however, we both saw a steady gain toward the established goals. Lois expressed more strength and confidence in herself, reported a higher frequency of casual interactions (with waitresses, taxi drivers, salespeople, fellow employees, and so on) with greater ease and comfort. I, therefore, thought it was time to move on to more complex interactions and extended conversations.

SOCIAL-BEHAVIOR PROGRAM: TARGET 2

The social-behavior portion of the treatment program consisted of three phases: reducing the anxiety associated with social events, teaching the requisite skills for social exchange, and arranging for Lois to participate in different groups.

Detailed descriptions of each of these phases follow. In actual fact, however, they did not proceed in such orderly fashion but overlapped and intertwined continuously.

Phase 1

Lois reported frequent occasions of circular thinking related to the fact that people were basically unfriendly and unconcerned about her. She experienced a high degree of muscular tension induced by authority figures, questions about her professional status, lulls in speech, remarks about her personal characteristics, and mistakes she could make in conversation.

For a reduction in these circular thoughts, I encouraged her to design her own program combining the thought-stopping and covert-reinforcement techniques that she had used successfully before. For the anxiety cues, relaxation and desensitization appeared most appropriate.

Relaxation training was completed in two sessions, but, for long-term benefits, I instructed the client to set aside at least two periods each day for practice. In addition, she was encouraged to make use of the procedure whenever she anticipated joining a group, whenever she found herself among people, and whenever she left a group. Relaxation also served as the necessary prelude to systematic desensitization.[8]

---

[8] *Editors' note:* Providing clients with an audio cassette tape of relaxation instructions often helps. See articles 30 and 37 for examples of this.

Desensitization hierarchies were constructed from the data provided by Lois' ranking of the amounts of anxiety evoked by the stimulus cues described previously. The imaginal presentation of scenes from the hierarchies followed Wolpe's detailed prescriptions (1969). *In vivo* desensitization also occurred through behavior rehearsals. Lois required thirty-two sessions of desensitization, averaging one and a half hours apiece, for the elimination of anxiety associated with most aspects of the three categories of stimuli presented.[9]

Phase 2

Concurrently with desensitization, which was employed for anxiety reduction, I instituted a program to increase these specific social behaviors: making small talk, making "witty" remarks, feeling calm, issuing and accepting invitations, giving and receiving compliments. These sequences of socially effective responses were necessary for the maintenance of social contacts.

For each of these target behaviors, a covert reinforcement paradigm was useful. To strengthen Lois' embryonic conversational skills further and to provide her with another source of reinforcement, I introduced a male therapist into the sessions; he took primary responsibility for the behavior rehearsals and modeling practices (described

[9] *Editors' note:* Could the modeling and guided-practice techniques described in articles 28 and 33 have produced speedier results? Maybe, but human beings pose many more threats than snakes. Still, it would be well to develop and test more feasible and efficient procedures for overcoming social anxieties.

earlier in another context).[10] These techniques, combined with the client's memorization of a "guide to conversation" (Wisocki & Tierney, 1971), proved helpful in this area.

I also decided to try a procedure called "covert negative reinforcement" (Cautela, 1970). Derived from the escape-conditioning paradigm, it involves the presentation of an intensely aversive stimulus that may be terminated only by the performance of a correct response. Theoretically, after several such trials, the correct response increases in frequency because it has been instrumental in causing the elimination of the aversive stimulus. In this instance, for example, Lois selected a scene of personal rejection as one very repulsive to her. She was able to imagine it clearly, to feel anxious over the image, and to terminate it immediately at my request. Once these trials to meet necessary conditions were successful, I described the scene to her. When she reported it vividly in her mind, I pronounced the word "switch," and she imagined a scene in which she was feeling relaxed and carrying on a witty conversation with an attractive male. Lois had some problems making the imagery clear and sufficiently detailed, so I described a wider range of items and asked her to imagine the scenes in smaller segments. She then repeated the entire procedure by herself. Every week this scene and others like it were practiced for about ten minutes in the office and assigned for homework that week. Lois spent three

[10] The author gratefully acknowledges the invaluable assistance of John L. Tierney in the conduct of this case.

fifteen-minute periods practicing her assignments each day.

The choice of negative reinforcement as a treatment technique was made not only for its obvious clinical value but also because it provided much-needed variety for the client and for me. (Incidentally, along with learning to make a desired response through the use of this procedure, the client often learns also to tolerate the aversive stimulus more easily.)

Phase 3

While preparing the client for what to do upon entrance onto the social scene, we were confronted with the problem of arranging for her to do it in fact. To accomplish this objective we employed a variety of procedures: verbal prompting, shaping, reinforcement (described earlier), and overt- and covert-reinforcer sampling.

Reinforcer sampling was devised originally by Ayllon and Azrin (1968) as a method of increasing the use of a potential reinforcer among institutionalized patients. In essence, the patients were simply given opportunities to consume, hear, or take part in various scheduled events and activities for an allotted time span. The effect of several such trials was a significant increase in requests from the patients themselves for participation in those same activities.

By asking Lois to join us in restaurants and nightclubs, at museums, flea markets, and barbecues, we effectively introduced her to a diversity of novel social experiences. We were even able to contrive instantaneous practice conversational gambits, for example, casu-

ally questioning strangers about their reactions to particular events and gradually giving Lois the responsibility for continuing the conversations. As an apparent result of several of these trials, Lois reported lessened anxiety in her thoughts about attending various functions and she slowly increased her actual overt behavior as well.[11]

In order to extend the range of social activities Lois could sample in the absence of the therapists, I decided to adapt the reinforcer-sampling procedure to an imaginal model (Wisocki, 1971). I therefore instructed her to sample the potentialities of a target event by imagining all the sensory stimuli inherent in it. She was not required to imagine herself performing any specific behavior; neither were any reinforcing contingencies applied.

For instance, in trying to coax her into joining a hiking club, I described this scene:

Imagine you are in the Vermont mountains on a cool, sunny day. Imagine you have on heavy boots for walking, a backpack, a sweater, shorts and a hat with a wide brim. Imagine you are walking with about five other people and you are all talking about the beauty around you. You see a stream nearby. It looks cold and inviting. You feel exhilarated—glad to be alive on such a day.

Over a three-month period of my inserting five minutes of similar descriptions into the hour, Lois became an

----

[11] *Editors' note:* A commendable and highly relevant effort by the counselor. Obviously a great deal of modeling was provided by the counselor and others whom Lois met in natural settings.

active member of a hiking club, a church choir, an advanced French class, and a women's group; she attended her youngest sister's wedding and two professional conventions, and she went to Europe for two months alone.

At that point Lois and I had been working together for fifteen months. This period included approximately eighty hours of formal therapy, conducted once a week in my office, and another thirty hours of direct sampling experiences during a five-month period. Behaviorally, on both overt and covert levels, Lois had improved markedly. She had acquired a variety of hobbies, was meeting socially with friends two or three times a week, was planning activities, and was carrying them out. She reported *feeling* happy, confident, and busy.

She had not become a social butterfly by any means. For instance, she was still hesitant in conversations on occasion; she was still fearful of men, and she sometimes experienced uncertainties about her personal characteristics. No one would refer to her as anything more than a "pleasant" person, an adjective of indistinct character. "Pleasant," however, was a definite six steps above "unpleasant." Perhaps most important, she was definitely happy with herself, except for her job, which was the next item on our therapeutic agenda.

JOB-SATISFACTION PROGRAM: TARGET 3

After some discussion of alternate plans of action and the reasons for her dissatisfaction, Lois decided to remain at her present job and to try to improve the conditions. This decision reduced our goals to elimination of the anxiety-provoking elements of her job situation, as indicated by her responses to the "Job Fear Survey Schedule" (Wisocki, 1970a). We also had to prepare for a confrontation with her employer.

Lois reported very high anxiety with people in authority positions, in being supervised, and in hearing comments from others that she interpreted as rejection, criticism, and failure. Three desensitization hierarchies were devised for these fears, and Lois carried them out herself at home. Having her do this on her own simultaneously enabled me to focus on increasing her assertive responses.

Assertive training (Salter, 1961) is a highly effective technique for dealing with clients who are prevented from doing or saying what is reasonable and correct in an interpersonal context.[12] I asked Lois to write out a speech detailing her demands exactly in the manner in which she would like to express them to her employer. When it was completed, I added various assertive statements, like "I demand my rights," "I believe you have treated me unfairly," and "I deserve a better deal for all the work I've put in around here." We practiced the speech over and over until I was satisfied that her voice was firm and convincing. During these behavior rehearsals, her physical stress noticeably diminished.

As a further aid to success, I di-

[12] *Editors' note:* Assertive training is actually a rich combination of techniques like modeling, role playing, rehearsal, social reinforcement, and cognitive restructuring. See articles 54 and 55.

vided the speech into various segments, ending with an assertive statement. I then had Lois imagine speaking each segment to her employer, and I reinforced that behavior with a pleasurable image (covert reinforcement).

In two months (eight sessions) the client was able to dispel her tension over the anxiety-producing stimuli and to recognize her unrealistic fears. Also, before I had okayed it,[13] she had forced the issue with her employer to a happy end.

TERMINATION AND FOLLOW-UP

Therapy did not terminate with the successful completion of the program but continued for another two months until Lois decided that she had better things to do with her time (which completely delighted me, of course). During that two-month period, however,

[13] *Editors' note:* That is what comes from teaching her to be assertive!

we reviewed what she had accomplished over the seventeen months of therapy, we identified the skills that she had acquired for application to future problems, and we discussed what difficulties she might expect "on her own," for example, beginning a relationship with someone and finding it disappointing, possible clashes with her supervisor at work, and feeling lonely among groups of people. I tried to stress the fact that therapy could not guarantee a completely rosy, tension-free existence and that she should take care to deal with problems as they arose.

Six months later the client came to my home for a visit. She had gained weight, looked lively, could sustain a ten-minute conversation without stopping, easily shifted topics, asked pertinent questions of me, and reported feeling content, "professional," and creative at work and happy with her social life. Five months after that I saw her again over dinner and noted that the changes in her "personality" had been maintained.

references

Ayllon, T. & Azrin, N. *The token economy.* New York: Appleton, 1968.

Cautela, J. R. Covert conditioning. Paper presented at a Conference on the Study of Private Events, University of West Virginia, Morgantown, 1970.

Cautela, J. R. & Kastenbaum, R. A reinforcement survey schedule for use in therapy, training, and research. *Psychological Reports*, 1967, **20**, 1115–1130.

Homme, L. E. Coverant control therapy: A special case of contingency management. Paper presented at the annual meeting of the Rocky Mountain Psychological Association, Albuquerque, May 1966.

Salter, A. *Conditioned reflex therapy.* New York: Putnam, 1961.

Wisocki, P. A. Covert reinforcement sampling. Unpublished manuscript, University of Massachusetts, 1971.

Wisocki, P. A. The job fear survey schedule. Unpublished manuscript, University of Massachusetts, 1970a.

Wisocki, P. A. The successful treatment of

a heroin addict by covert conditioning techniques. *Journal of Behavior Therapy and Experimental Psychiatry*, 1973, **4**, 55–61.

Wisocki, P. A. Treatment of obsessive compulsive behavior by the application of covert sensitization and covert reinforcement: A case report. *Journal of Behavior Therapy and Experimental Psychiatry*, 1970, **1**, 233–239.

Wisocki, P. A. & Tierney, J. L. Conversation guide. Unpublished manuscript, University of Massachusetts, 1971.

Wolpe, J. *The practice of behavior therapy*. New York: Pergamon, 1969.

Wolpe, J. & Lang, P. A fear survey schedule for use in behavior therapy. *Behaviour Research and Therapy*, 1964, **2**, 27.

SNAKE PHOBIA

33. REDUCING FEARS THROUGH PARTICIPANT MODELING AND SELF-DIRECTED PRACTICE[1]

ROBERT W. JEFFREY   University of Missouri, St. Louis

In this report we describe an extension and refinement of participant modeling to eliminate phobias. Participant modeling has been effective in group and individual applications with a variety of fears and client populations (Bandura, 1971; Ritter, 1968; 1969a, b; Rachman, 1972). It has also proved superior to other techniques (Bandura, Blanchard & Ritter, 1969).

Participant modeling is based on the assumption that successful performance is the most effective means of inducing psychological change. As people with persistent fears resist doing things they dread, however, the counselor must arrange the environment in such a way that a frightened individual can perform successfully. This is achieved by providing the client with a variety of supportive aids that reduce the aversiveness of threatening situations.

Participant modeling includes three basic treatment components: modeling, guided participation, and success experiences. In the initial stage of the treatment the counselor demonstrates the activities that the client fears. To enhance the effectiveness of the modeling, threatening performances are subdivided into graduated series of tasks, each of which is repeated several times.

Next the client is asked to engage in the same activities by himself. The counselor remains nearby to provide support and protection in the event that the client experiences difficulty. If the client is unable to perform the activities, a variety of response-induction procedures is introduced. As the client is able to master feared behaviors with the support and guidance of the counselor, the aids are gradually withdrawn

[1] The research discussed in this paper was supported by Public Health Research Grant M-5162 to Dr. Albert Bandura.

so that he performs the feared activities unassisted.[2]

The principal role of the counselor in participant modeling is to assist the client when he is unable to perform feared activities on his own. The types of aids that facilitate approach behavior include the following:

1. Modeling feared behaviors to show the client how they may be effectively accomplished and that anticipated aversive consequences do not in fact occur.
2. Arranging performance tasks in an order of increasing difficulty so that the client is asked to do only what is within his immediate capabilities.
3. Performing activities jointly with the client, offering physical support when needed.
4. Performing threatening activities over graduated time intervals, beginning with brief periods and then extending them as the client's fears diminish.
5. Reducing the likelihood of feared consequences by physically controlling the source of the threat or by providing the client with protective equipment (like gloves).
6. Reducing the magnitude of the threat itself.

CLIENTS AND THEIR SELECTION

The studies reported next illustrate how response-induction aids can be used to accelerate change and self-directed performance to generalize change. The projects included a total of sixty-six snake phobics who had been plagued with this problem for many years.[3] They were solicited through advertisements placed in local newspapers and were screened by means of a rigorous behavior test. This test of avoidance consisted of a series of twenty-nine performance tasks involving increasingly more threatening interactions with a boa constrictor. The tasks required clients to approach the snake in a glass cage, to look down at it, to touch and hold it with gloved and then bare hands, to let it loose in the room and return it to the cage, to hold it within five inches of their faces, and finally to tolerate the snake in their laps while they held their hands passively at their sides. Those who could lift the snake inside the cage with a gloved hand were not considered fearful enough for inclusion in the study.

The selected clients varied somewhat in phobic behavior. At one end of the continuum were individuals who could approach the snake but balked at the prospect of touching it. At the other extreme were those who refused even to enter the room to view the snake.

Virtually all the participants in the study had abandoned recreational activities like hiking, swimming in lakes, camping, and gardening because of their fear of snakes. Some experienced difficulty with their vocations, as did a geologist who had extreme difficulty conducting field work. Others suffered social or residential restrictions, being unable to visit friends or to purchase homes in rustic areas.

A few individuals were incapaci-

---

[2] *Editors' note:* Essentially, it is a "show and do" strategy with emphasis on the client's mastering the situation.

[3] *Editors' note:* Although this article deals with snake phobia, its basic ideas are applicable to virtually any phobia.

tated in more unusual ways. One woman, for example, had been unable to use her bathroom for several weeks upon learning that a snake had escaped into the sewer system of a distant city.[4] Another had severely beaten her son, of whom she was very fond, when he innocently brought a dead snake into her house for inspection.

The most pervasive consequences of snake phobia were disturbing thoughts. ("During the spring and summer they are constantly on my mind when I am out of doors"; "Once I've seen one or a picture of one it is hard for me to get them out of my head"; "Now that I know they are on some land we purchased I feel tense about living there"; "My husband and I went camping at Big Sur, and I couldn't sleep at all thinking about the snakes"). Many had recurrent nightmares in which snakes chased and attacked them.

USING AIDS TO HELP CLIENTS ACT

In this project clients were matched in triads on the basis of their pretreatment avoidance behavior and were randomly assigned to three treatments that varied in terms of the number of inductive aids used. In all three conditions, a fearless behavior, taken from a standardized sequence, was first modeled by the counselor. Clients were then asked to perform it themselves.

When clients in the *high aids*

---

[4] *Editors' note:* A good example of how a specific fear can be generalized to many seemingly unrelated situations.

treatment were unable to do what had been modeled, the counselor used a variety of aids: joint performance, graduated time intervals, protective gear, and a smaller snake. In addition, contact with the snake was facilitated by the counselor's holding it securely by the head and tail.

In the *moderate aids* treatment the performance aids, in addition to the standard modeling and task gradation, included joint performance and temporal gradation. During physical-contact activities the counselor exercised partial, rather than full, control over the snake. Neither any physical protector nor the smaller, less frightening snake was used.

Clients in the *low aids* treatment had only the benefit of the counselor's modeling and gradation of tasks and time. Furthermore, the counselor maintained no control whatever over the snake to facilitate contact responses by the client.

THE FIRST SESSION

Treatment was conducted in a carpeted room with several chairs and a table. A three-foot boa constrictor was placed in a glass-enclosed cage on the table, and the chairs were evenly spaced from the door of the room to the table at the opposite end. The room was equipped with a one-way mirror, connecting it to an adjacent observation room. To illustrate the procedures, the treatment employing the largest number of aids will be described in some detail.

At the outset clients were given the following information:

To help you overcome your fear of snakes, you will first watch from a distance while I handle the snake to show you that he's a harmless creature. Gradually I'll help you to look at, to touch, and eventually hold him. At no time will I force you to do anything you don't want to do, but I will encourage you to do things that at any given point you could do with some extra effort. If you find yourself absolutely unable to do what I describe, there are things that I will do to help you overcome your difficulty.

Upon learning that they would be asked to handle snakes, many clients voiced their fears and resistance ("I can't possibly handle a snake"; "Not today"; "Aren't snakes dangerous?" "Does this treatment really work?"). Questions were answered succinctly, to avoid conversational excursions into the nature of fears or treatment approaches. The clients were told that their apprehension was natural but that action is the best way to overcome fears. They were also reassured that the treatment was tailored to help them overcome irrational fears of harmless snakes, rather than to make them insensitive to real dangers.

The First Task

The counselor then entered the treatment room and asked the first client to join him. This was the first performance task. If the client refused to enter the room, he was again encouraged to do so ("It is only natural to feel tense and upset at this stage, but the only way to get over this feeling is to do what I ask you to do"). If he continued to resist, he was told that he could re-

main outside the room and enter when he felt more comfortable.

Although most clients were able to look into the room from the hallway, the severely phobic even refused to look in. A response-induction aid was therefore introduced. The boa was replaced with a tiny king snake that could barely be seen from the entryway. The client was asked to enter the room in the presence of the small snake. If he still remained immobile, he was led to the adjoining observation room and observed the caged snake through the one-way mirror. All were able to do this much.[5]

After the client had observed the snake from a distance, the counselor modeled how to handle it. The client was urged to come as close to the counselor as possible while the latter lifted the boa from its cage, placed it in his lap, petted it, lifted it up with both hands, held his hand in front of its face, held its head within five inches of his own face, and then returned it to its cage. During the demonstration the therapist gave the client factual information about the snake, including its name, species, the function of its tongue, its cold-bloodedness, and how it could be easily controlled.[6] He also offered to demonstrate any activities that the clients found particularly upsetting. Clients who began treatment with the small snake or from

[5] *Editors' note:* Note that throughout this treatment the counselor was insistent that the clients take the next step. Refusal was interpreted as a request for an additional aid —not as a definitive determination to stop.

[6] *Editors' note:* Such cognitive information may have contributed to the success of treatment for some clients.

the observation room were given live demonstrations with the boa following their initial experiences with the smaller snake.

The Second Task

Next each client was to observe the snake in its cage from a distance of one foot. The client was asked to do so on his own first. If that proved too difficult, the counselor stood beside him and walked up to the cage with him, physically supporting him if he hesitated. If the client resisted the joint procession to the cage, approach was attempted in graduated steps, a foot or two at a time. If this procedure also failed, the client was asked to come forward, with the counselor, for a short period of time and then to move back again. The time interval was increased on successive trials and the distance from the snake shortened to ensure continual progress.

If the client was unable to progress with the combined influence of joint performance, reduced distance, and graduated time intervals, the counselor asked him to recommend an aid that he thought would help him to approach the snake. As might be expected, clients with long-standing fears were not readily able to generate solutions to their own difficulties. Few offered suggestions, and those recommended were uniformly unhelpful. One client, for example, thought that approaching the snake would be easier if a "tree" were placed in its cage to make the environment more "natural." Much to her chagrin the counselor immediately produced a piece of driftwood, a terrain enhancer normally enjoyed by the

snake in its off-duty hours. The result was even greater resistance to approaching the snake, suggesting that the recommendation was actually an attempt to avoid taking relevant action.[7]

Clients who were still unable to approach the boa with these multiple aids then performed the approach tasks with the small king snake. The combined use of performance aids with the weaker threat ensured success. After they were able to view the king snake close up, the boa was substituted, and the approach performances were repeated. By this means even the most phobic clients experienced success.

Additional Tasks

Thirteen additional performance tasks were used in the treatment procedure. In each instance the same format was followed: The client was asked to perform a fear-provoking activity after the counselor had first modeled it. In the event that the client refused, the counselor introduced whatever aids were necessary to ensure successful completion of the task.

The graduated tasks and available aids were as follows:

1. The client was asked to sit next to the counselor while he held the snake securely with both hands in his lap. Aids: beginning in a distant chair and moving to a closer chair; moving to a closer chair for a reduced period of

[7] *Editors' note:* Many clients want to be cured without, understandably, directly facing their fears. The counselor's job is to make sure that they engage in the necessary direct actions.

time; transferring to the baby snake and repeating the steps.

2. The client was asked to touch the midsection of the snake while the counselor held it securely with both hands. Aids: touching the snake for a reduced period of time; moving the hand from the top of the counselor's hand to the midsection of the snake; touching the midsection with a gloved hand (two pairs of gloves were available, a light cotton pair and a heavy leather pair that offered more protection); transferring to the baby snake and repeating all these steps.

3. The client was asked to support the midsection of the snake while the counselor held the head and tail. Aids: supporting the snake's midsection for a reduced time; support the midsection with a gloved hand; transferring to the baby snake and repeating these steps.

4. The client was asked to touch the tail section of the snake while the counselor controlled the head area. Aids: touching for a reduced period of time; moving the hand from on top of the counselor's hand to the tail section; touching the tail section with a pencil or ruler; touching the tail section with a gloved hand; transferring to the baby snake and repeating the steps.

5. The client was asked to support the tail section of the snake while the counselor controlled the head area. Aids: the counselor's holding the tail section with the client and then withdrawing his hand; the counselor's withdrawing his hand for a reduced time; supporting the tail section of the snake with a gloved hand; transferring to the baby snake and repeating the steps.

6. The client was asked to place his hand in front of the snake's face.

Aids: the counselor's holding his hand between the client's and the snake and then withdrawing it; joint performance at graduated distances from the snake's face; joint performance with graduated distance and reduced time periods; placing a gloved hand in front of the snake's face; transferring to the baby snake and repeating the steps.

7. The client was asked to touch the head area of the snake while the counselor controlled the tail section. Aids: touching the head area of the snake for a reduced time; moving the hand from the top of the counselor's hand to the head area of the snake; touching the head area with a pencil or ruler; touching the head area with a gloved hand; transferring to the baby snake and repeating these steps.

8. The client was asked to support the head area of the snake while the counselor controlled the tail section. Aids: the counselor's holding the head area jointly with the client and then removing his hand; joint performance and reduced time; supporting the head area with gloved hands; transferring to the baby snake and repeating these steps.

9. The client was asked to hold the entire snake. Aids: the counselor's holding the snake with the client and then letting go; joint performance and reduced time; holding the snake with gloved hands; transferring to the baby snake and repeating the steps.

10. The client was asked to allow the snake to move freely in his lap with his hands at his sides. Aids: wearing a protective lab coat; allowing the snake to move about for a reduced time period; the counselor's holding the snake in the client's lap and gradually letting

go; transferring to the baby snake and repeating these steps.

11. The client was asked to hold the snake's face six inches from his own. Aids: joint performance with the therapist; joint performance with graduated distance; joint performance with graduated distance and reduced time; wearing a protective visor; transferring to the baby snake and repeating these steps.

12. The counselor placed the snake on the floor of the treatment room and the client was asked to retrieve it. Aids: joint performance with the counselor; picking up the snake with gloved hands.

13. The client was asked to remove the snake from its cage, let it loose on the floor of the room, and return it to its cage. Aids: joint performance with the therapist.

For each of the fifteen performance tasks clients were urged to do as much as possible on their own, despite any tension they might feel. To ensure rapid progress, graduation from one performance task to the next was keyed to the behavioral accomplishments of clients, rather than to their reports of comfort or distress.[8] Supportive aids were withdrawn as quickly as possible once aided performance had taken place. If the client was able to hold the snake with gloved hands, for example, he was asked to attempt the same performance bare-handed. Intermediate supports were omitted unless they were needed. Thus progress through the

treatment was not hindered by unnecessary pauses or diversions.

RESULTS

Clients were treated in the study until one member of each matched triad had completed the fifteen performance tasks in treatment. All three were then administered the behavior test described earlier.

Treatment was completed by one or more members of the various triads in a relatively short period. Mean treatment time was eighty-one minutes, with 75 percent of the successful performances occurring in an average of forty-one minutes.[9] Figure 1 shows that treatment successes were directly related to

[9] *Editors' note:* Amazingly fast!

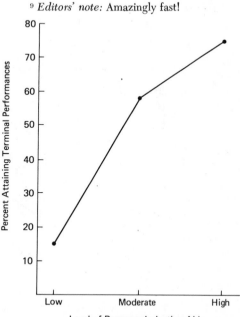

FIGURE 1   Percentage of clients who completed treatment as a function of the number of response-induction aids.

---

[8] *Editors' note:* An excellent point. It is the actual performance ("doing it") that can often influence in turn how the person feels about it.

the number of supportive aids available to the counselor. Compared to the condition in which minimal assistance was offered to clients, both high and moderate levels of performance aids produced significantly higher rates of treatment completion.

Figure 2 shows the changes in approach behavior on the behavioral test as a function of the level of supportive aids. In the posttest, clients' approach responses to both the boa constrictor used in treatment and a corn snake that they had never seen before were assessed. Clients in both the moderately and highly aided treatments behaved more boldly on the posttest than did those who had received little support. These results were also paralleled by changes in self-reported fear during the behavior test and in attitudes toward snakes.

Some interesting correlational data also emerged from the study. Neither initial attitudes toward snakes, severity of phobic behavior, performance-aroused fears, nor proneness to fear was correlated with behavior change. On the other hand, the number of tasks completed in treatment, a factor determined by the options available to the counselor, was highly correlated ($r = .71$) with later approach scores.[10]

Data on the highly aided treatment indicated, as expected, that the number of performance aids necessary to induce approach behaviors was related to the client's initial degree of fearfulness. The subjects who required

[10] *Editors' note:* The moral: To overcome the fear of doing something, do it! And do not worry about "attitudes" as revealed by paper-and-pencil tests.

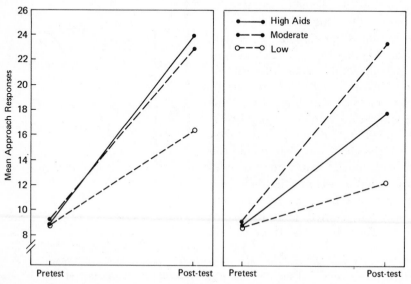

FIGURE 2   Mean number of approach responses performed by clients toward the boa constrictor (left) and the corn snake (right) in the low-, moderate-, and high-aid treatments.

the greatest number of induction aids to perform feared behaviors were those who had been most phobic behaviorally ($r = .40$), who had experienced the greatest distress during the pretest ($r = .62$), who had the most animal fears ($r = .41$), and who most detested snakes ($r = .43$).

At the conclusion of the experiment ten of the subjects who had achieved only partial improvement were available for further treatment. They were treated by means of the maximally aided procedure, which was continued in each instance until the client had completed all tasks in the treatment. Though these individuals represented the most refractory phobics in the sample, they all completed the program in an average of 101 minutes. Their improvement on a subsequent behavior test was equivalent to that of the maximally aided clients who had finished earlier.

DISCUSSION

The results of this experiment reveal that the efficacy of participant modeling depends upon the number of supporting options that the counselor has at his disposal to aid people in overcoming their fears. Given a variety of aids, people make rapid and substantial progress, whereas with more limited aids their gains are slower and often disappointing. These findings underscore the degree to which psychotherapeutic effectiveness is dependent upon the range of a counselor's serviceable skills. Progress in developing powerful treatments would be better achieved by seeking ways of expanding these skills than by focusing on limiting client characteristics.[11]

Although aided participant modeling appears to be a powerful way of inducing behavioral, attitudinal, and affective changes, there was a significant generalization decrement from the snake used in treatment to the unfamiliar snake. Further work was therefore needed to identify conditions that maximize generalization and maintenance of these changes.

The design of the experiment required the termination of treatment as soon as a client was able to perform the final tasks unassisted. There was, therefore, little opportunity for him to practice his new skills on his own. It was expected that, had these clients been allowed to engage in snake-handling behavior for longer periods of time, their gains would have been more pronounced. The overall evidence seems to indicate that widespread changes are best achieved by highly aided participant modeling supplemented with self-directed practice to extinguish residual fears and to develop a sense of personal mastery.

PROCEDURES TO IMPROVE TRANSFER TO NEW SITUATIONS

A second experiment was conducted to assess systematically the generality and durability of changes produced by participant modeling as a function of the amount and variety of self-directed

---

[11] *Editors' note:* An important issue: "Weak" treatments have too often encouraged the search for client characteristics as the important factor.

practice. In this study three groups of matched snake phobics were treated by means of highly aided participant modeling until they had completed all the treatment tasks. Then they received no additional therapeutic experiences and either engaged in self-directed performance with one snake or practiced self-directed performance with two snakes.

In the self-directed component clients were asked to perform a sequence of ten interactions with the snake taken from the treatment series. These interactions included lifting the snake from its cage, supporting the snake's midsection, supporting the snake's tail section, placing a hand in front of the snake's face, stroking its head, supporting the head area of the snake, holding the snake's head six inches from the client's own face, allowing the snake to move freely in the client's lap, placing the snake on the floor, and picking up the snake from the floor and returning it to its cage.

Clients were instructed to perform these tasks three times but were allowed considerable performance latitude. They could do the tasks in any order they wished, omit any tasks that they found too distressing, and draw on the available protective devices (lab coat, towel, gloves, ruler, and face visor).

The counselor did not assist the client in any way. During the first two times through the tasks he remained in the room for reassurance. Clients completed the final task sequence alone, while the counselor watched from an adjacent room through a one-way mirror. The self-directed performance lasted one hour.

Clients in the *varied self-directed performance* group handled two snakes. They initially performed the tasks with the familiar boa constrictor, then with an unfamiliar king snake, and finally with either or both, as they preferred. Those assigned to the *self-directed performance* group handled only the boa constrictor, and clients in the *participant modeling* condition received no self-directed practice.

At the conclusion of treatment all clients were again tested for phobic behavior. As in the previous study, behavioral assessment was conducted with an unfamiliar corn snake, as well as with the boa. In addition, a follow-up assessment was administered one month later.

All the clients who had had opportunities to engage in either form of self-directed performance were able to perform *all* the tasks in the behavioral post-test with the boa constrictor. Among those who had had no opportunity to do so, only 60 percent achieved terminal performances. The therapeutic benefits of self-directed performance were even more striking on the generalization test. Seventy-five percent of the clients who had had self-directed experiences were completely fearless with the unfamiliar corn snake, whereas only 20 percent of those who had not had such experiences achieved terminal performances. The therapeutic changes were stably maintained during the follow-up period.[12]

Six months after treatment, clients were mailed questionnaires inquiring about their experiences since partici-

[12] The results of this experiment are illustrated graphically on page 254.

pation in the treatment program. Virtually all who responded reported that they were able to engage in activities that they had formerly avoided ("I don't lock my child out of the house when he brings home a snake or lizard"; "I went to the aquarium and could really enjoy the snake exhibit"; "I go on field trips, hike, and am willing for the first time to try camping"; "My husband and I pruned the trees in my aunt's orchard, and I gathered the twigs, in tall grass, with my bare hands!"). Obsessive thoughts about snakes had also lessened ("I am not preoccupied with looking for snakes in the grass"; "My bad dreams no longer have snakes in them"; "I just figure that if there should ever be a snake in my bed, I'd just have to pick him up and put him on the floor until morning"; "Actually, until I sat down to fill out this questionnaire, I had not thought about snakes for some time").

A few clients attributed dramatic and generalized changes in their behavior to the treatment experience ("Before treatment I had a fear of worms and some bugs. I am now able to handle them with gloves"; "The feeling of accomplishment at having overcome the fear of snakes gave me the confidence to overcome my fear of public speaking"; "I feel that if I could lick this major thing, I could lick any problem and I've started!"). Some even expressed warm feelings toward snakes ("I find myself feeling sympathetic toward the harmless snakes being misunderstood"; "I would like to have a garden type snake to eat the bugs in my yard").

Although a few did indicate that their fear had been only partially eliminated ("I'm not afraid of harmless pet snakes and would even handle one, but I still get hysterical when I see one in the wild and don't know if it is poisonous or not"), all the clients reported enduring benefits and none gave any indication of being resensitized.

Powerful treatments usually include several components, each of which adds an increment of influence. Participant modeling, which combines modeling, guided participation, and success experiences is one such treatment. Evidence reported here and elsewhere demonstrates that fearless behavior can be induced rapidly through modeling with aided performance of fear-provoking activities. A relatively brief period of self-directed performance is an effective means of enhancing generalization and maintenance of performance gains.[13]

Counselors should develop a repertoire of procedures that can aid clients to achieve continuous rapid progress, however fearful they may be. Generalized changes in behavior are best induced and maintained by careful attention to conditions throughout the change process. Reliance on limited techniques or premature client initiative is likely to retard progress and to create needless stress and discouragement.

[13] *Editors' note:* The self-directed practice gives each client the opportunity to try the experience alone and enables him to say, "Yes, I know now that I can do it on my own."

references

Bandura, A. Psychotherapy based upon modeling principles. In A. E. Bergin and S. L. Garfield (Eds.), *Handbook of psychotherapy and behavior change*. New York: Wiley, 1971. Pp. 653–708.

Bandura, A., Blanchard, E. B. & Ritter, B. The relative efficacy of desensitization and modeling treatment approaches for inducing behavioral, affective, and attitudinal changes. *Journal of Personality and Social Psychology*, 1969, **13**, 173–199.

Rachman, S. Clinical applications of observational learning, imitation and modeling. *Behavior Therapy*, 1972, **3**, 379–397.

Ritter, B. Eliminating excessive fears of the environment through contact desensitization. In J. D. Krumboltz and C. E. Thoresen (Eds.), *Behavioral counseling: Cases and techniques*. New York: Holt, Rinehart and Winston, 1969a. Pp. 168–177.

Ritter, B. The group desensitization of children's snake phobia using vicarious and contact desensitization procedure. *Behaviour Research and Therapy*, 1968, **6**, 1–6.

Ritter, B. The use of contact desensitization, demonstration-plus-participation, and demonstration alone in the treatment of acrophobia. *Behaviour Research and Therapy*, 1969b, **7**, 157–164.

COMBINATIONS OF FEARS

34. *USING KUNG FU TO REDUCE ANXIETY WITH A CLAUSTROPHOBIC MALE*

LOUIS GERSHMAN   Villanova University
JAMES M. STEDMAN   University of Texas Medical School, San Antonio

Research and clinical evidence over the past ten years have substantially corroborated Wolpe's (1958) principle of reciprocal inhibition: "If a response which is inhibitory of anxiety can be made to occur in the presence of the anxiety-evoking stimuli, it will weaken the bond between these stimuli and the anxiety."[1] In clinical behavioral practice the most frequently used counterconditioner in the treatment of phobias has been muscle relaxation. In general, because of the ease with which relaxation can be learned by the patient and

[1] *Editors' note:* Although systematic desensitization and many variations of it have proved effective clinically, the adequacy of Wolpe's theoretical rationale for reciprocal inhibition, with its neurophysiological emphasis on anxiety and the autonomic nervous system, has been seriously challenged. It seems that any behavior that is incompatible with and antagonistic to fearful actions for the individual can be used to reduce fears and avoidance behaviors without necessarily "neutralizing" the fear-arousing situations step by step.

controlled by the therapist, the clinician tends not to look for other counterconditioners unless the patient is unable to relax effectively.

The first author has successfully treated several hundreds of patients, making use of different counterconditioners, including assertive responses, sexual responses, emotive imagery, induced anger, and different kinds of physical and motor responses. Theoretically, as well as practically, it is good strategy for a clinician to seek and to capitalize upon counterconditioning activities that are idiosyncratic to a particular patient, for they are likely to have special therapeutic efficacy. One case, in which the self-defense activity kung fu was used to countercondition anxiety, will be described. Kung fu is an oriental method of self-defense. Karate, a Japanese system of unarmed self-defense and counterattack, converts the hand, fist, elbow, or foot into a weapon aimed at an opponent's weak spots. As taught in this country, kung fu, of earlier Chinese origin, is similar to karate but is considered more of an art and requires much more training for proficiency. It seems likely that these exercises inhibit anxiety in much the same way that assertive behavior does, by evoking responses related to anger.[2]

[2] *Editors' note:* If a client finds that he is never anxious while practicing kung fu, then kung fu may be a suitable "counterconditioner" for him. Relaxation is usually used because it is common to almost everyone. Many activities are antagonistic to fears and anxieties. Knitting, sewing, smoking, and drinking are socially acceptable under certain circumstances. Perhaps we counselors ought to work at finding the specific response that is best for each client.

THE CASE OF MR. PATRICK

Mr. Patrick, thirty-one years old and married, reported a history of anxiety involving elevators, enclosed places, trains, buses, and locked rooms. Over the previous five years, secondary generalization of the anxiety to the wearing of tight-fitting clothing, underwear, and his wedding ring had occurred. These maladaptive behaviors interfered with Mr. Patrick's occupational adjustment and family life. In the course of the history taking Mr. Patrick indicated that he was a practitioner of kung fu, liked to engage in this activity, and felt like a "man" when he did. As he mentioned this, the small, timid man seated in the comfortable chair jumped up and propelled himself vigorously into various kung fu manipulations. After no more than sixty seconds, he said, exuding confidence, "How do you like that?" This exhibition of assertive, "manly" behavior convinced us immediately of the usefulness of these kung fu exercises as an appropriate idiosyncratic counterconditioner.

So that he would be able to measure changes in anxiety, Mr. Patrick was taught how to use the "subjective units of discomfort" (SUD) score (Wolpe, 1958). A scale from zero (complete relaxation) to 100 (panic) was sketched on paper, and he was asked to describe situations illustrating each of these extremes. Pertinent examples of other dimensions of the scale were then presented. This was followed with about fifteen minutes' practice, requiring him to estimate the SUD scores for various events, like waiting in the office (60), eating dinner with his wife (10), wearing a loose tie (30), wearing a tight-fitting shirt (90), and ascending five floors in an elevator by himself (100). It was obvious that Mr. Patrick understood and discriminated well the use of the SUD score.

A trial claustrophobic item was then presented. "Imagine sitting in a room, approximately 6 by 6 feet, for two minutes. As soon as you feel any anxiety, go right into your kung fu. Continue kung fu until you feel comfortable." Mr. Patrick's anxiety level had shot up to 60 SUDs. After one minute of kung fu, the score had plummeted to zero. Because we had a small, windowless room available, we decided to use an *in vivo* (live), rather than imaginal, approach.[3] When we pointed the room out to Mr. Patrick, his SUD level jumped to 80. He voiced the pessimistic thought that, as he had practiced kung fu exercises numerous times in the past without any alleviation of his fears, why should it be different now? To reduce doubt and reservations about the technique and to give him a motivational lift, we described in simple language several phobic cases that we had treated using the principle of reciprocal inhibition. We purposely selected these two cases because we thought they would be especially significant for him. In both we stressed the importance of linking anxiety with a behavior that is incompatible with excessive arousal (in his case, fung fu)

---

[3] *Editors' note:* There is nothing socially unacceptable about practicing kung fu exercises in a small, windowless room alone. However, it is a good thing the client did not become anxious at cocktail parties!

---

and of the gradual, progressive confrontation by the individual of his fears through a desensitization procedure.

A client was afraid to be alone in a dark room. He was placed in a dark room for increasing periods of time and instructed to sing at the top of his voice, vigorously to punch the sofa chair, or to run energetically in place. In a short time his fear disappeared.

A client who loved the movies had a fear of sitting in a movie theater. At times he could sit in the very last row. Arrangements were made with the manager of a movie theater to admit him several times each day for the price of a single admission, which was then subtracted from the therapy fee. A desensitization program was planned; it required him to sit in the back row, then the second from the back, and so on. He was never to sit in the next row until he felt comfortable sitting in the preceding one. In gradual stages, within a few weeks, the client became able to sit comfortably in the middle sections of movie theaters.

Finally, the whole idea was made clear to Mr. Patrick in this manner:

Look, Pat, the object, as you can see, is to get rid of small doses of anxiety at a time by engaging in behavior which is incompatible with anxiety. Look at this circle that I draw on the paper. Imagine that all of your fear about sitting in a small room is contained in this circle. Now suppose we take this little portion here on the right . . . see how I blacken this small bit. This represents a small bit of your anxiety. If you only had to contend with this small bit of anxiety instead of all anxiety—the big circle—that would be pretty easy for you to do. Right? Okay, that's exactly what we're going to do. Little by little, we're going to get rid of this anxiety, never going on to the next step until you feel comfortable with the last step. Just like the fellow who had the fear of darkness and the one who couldn't sit in the movie house, we're going to confront you with small doses of your particular fear, sitting in a small room without windows, and ask you to kung fu immediately, as you did before. Then we will ask you to sit for increasingly longer periods of time until you feel comfortable and nonanxious.

We proposed to lock Mr. Patrick in a room for progressively longer times, starting with ten seconds, and to have him engage immediately in kung fu exercises as soon as the door was closed.[4] After ten seconds all feelings of anxiety

[4] *Editors' note:* Mr. Patrick need not be locked in the room unless it was the being-locked-in that he feared. Otherwise asking him to stay in the room with the door closed but unlocked would seem appropriate.

were eliminated during the first trial. At twenty seconds, the kung fu exercises reduced his anxiety level to zero in two trials. Our strategy involved two dimensions: gradually increasing the time spent in the locked room and gradually reducing the time spent using kung fu exercises. For example, one step in the hierarchy required Mr. Patrick to spend the first thirty seconds going through kung fu exercises, then spending the remaining fifteen seconds without the benefit of kung fu. As the end of the hierarchy approached, Mr. Patrick was able to sit comfortably in the room reading a newspaper. If he felt the least twinge of anxiety he was to start "kung fu-ing," and quickly to dissipate it. Eventually, a forty-five-minute trial was followed by a one-hour trial. Mr. Patrick had no difficulty remaining relaxed during the latter trial (see Table 1).

TABLE 1   Claustrophobia Hierarchy

Trial	Time in Room	Duration of Kung Fu	Duration of Newspaper or Playboy Reading
1	10 seconds	10 seconds	
2	30 seconds	30 seconds	
3	60 seconds	60 seconds	
4	90 seconds	90 seconds	
5	120 seconds	120 seconds	
6	45 seconds	30 seconds	15 seconds
7	90 seconds	60 seconds	30 seconds
8	2 minutes	60 seconds	60 seconds
9	3 minutes	90 seconds	90 seconds
10	5 minutes	3 minutes	2 minutes
11	8 minutes	4 minutes	4 minutes
12	12 minutes	4 minutes	8 minutes
13	15 minutes	4 minutes	11 minutes
14	20 minutes	3 minutes	17 minutes
15	30 minutes	3 minutes	27 minutes
16	40 minutes	1 minute	39 minutes
17	45 minutes	0 minutes	45 minutes
18	60 minutes	0 minutes	60 minutes

Mr. Patrick felt incredulous about what was happening. For the first time in many years, he found himself in a live, realistic, fear-producing situation and was able to confront his fear without cracking up. Following the elimination of anxiety in the locked room, Mr. Patrick was enthusiastic about trying the method in elevators. At the end of the second session in an elevator, he was able to go up and down without experiencing anxiety.[5]

Generalization of extinction was apparent when Mr. Patrick reported that he could again don tight underwear and was no longer disturbed at wearing his wedding ring. At six-month follow-ups, he had maintained his recovery.

[5] Editors' note: It is rather interesting to contemplate Mr. Patrick's doing kung fu in a crowded elevator. Perhaps certain cognitive (nonphysical) behaviors offer some advantages as incompatible actions.

reference

Wolpe, J. Psychotherapy by reciprocal inhibition. Stanford, Calif.: Stanford   University Press, 1958.

35. COPING WITH INESCAPABLE DISCOMFORT THROUGH IN VIVO EMOTIVE IMAGERY

JOHN J. HORAN   The Pennsylvania State University

Emotive imagery is a behavior-therapy technique that resembles systematic desensitization.[1] In lieu of deep muscle relaxation, however, classes of images assumed to arouse positive feelings, like self-assertion, pride, affection, and mirth, are used to block the anxiety arising from a given hierarchy scene. This procedure has proven to be particularly effective in the treatment of children's phobias. Lazarus and Abramovitz (1962), for example, described how a child's fear of dogs was overcome by the therapist's vivid description of a sports-car racing event in which the child was depicted as a hero. Images of driving an Alfa Romeo in

the Indianapolis 500 produced strong feelings of self-confidence, which successfully inhibited the anxiety arising from dog-related scenes that were then gradually included in the narration.

The process of focusing on similar covert events during actual distressing situations has been called "in vivo emotive imagery." Unlike traditional emotive imagery, the noxious stimuli occur in real life, rather than in imagination, and simultaneously with, rather than intermittently woven into, the positive fantasy. The technique appears to have strong potential for enabling people—both clients and counselors—to cope with inescapable discomforting situations, ranging from the relatively

[1] Editors' note: See Article 30.

trivial experience of a turbulent airplane ride to the highly dramatic occurrence of childbirth (Horan, 1973).

Support for the utility of *in vivo* emotive imagery has recently been furnished by an analogue study, in which it was found that subjects who listened to tape-recorded relaxation-producing images (walking through a lush meadow, looking at a clear blue lake, and so on) were able to keep their hands immersed in ice water nearly three times as long as subjects who were given no treatment at all and more than twice as long as those who were given a placebo distraction treatment (Horan & Dellinger, 1974).

Apparently two mechanisms influence the effectiveness of *in vivo* emotive imagery. In the first place, the positive feelings stimulated by pleasant images seem to block the anxiety arising from uncomfortable situations, in a manner similar to that of systematic desensitization.[2] Second, the images themselves may serve to lessen "real" pain. This latter hypothesis is supported by the related work of Segal (1971), who has shown that the holding of certain images raises the threshold of the particular sense modality involved.

PRACTICAL APPLICATIONS

Childbirth

To date, a number of expectant parents have been successfully trained in the use of *in vivo* emotive imagery as a means of reducing childbirth anxiety

[2] *Editors' note:* This "blocking" process is also similar to participant-modeling techniques. See articles 28 and 33.

and discomfort in hospital labor rooms. No more than two counseling sessions are usually required for a couple to become proficient in the procedure. During the first session the counselor presents a rationale like the following:

Through extensive medication it is entirely possible to have your baby with almost no discomfort at all. Of course you know that any drug in any amount represents a potential hazard to the infant. *In vivo* emotive imagery may enable you to experience childbirth with less discomfort so that you will require less medication.

Some women are able to deliver without any anesthetic at all. You and your physician will have to decide the amount and kind that is most appropriate for you. A good procedure is to request beforehand that you be given as little medication as possible, with the understanding that more may be required as labor progresses.

Here is how *in vivo* emotive imagery works: In this culture women often learn to expect excruciating pain in childbirth. Even intelligent sophisticated women have a hard time shaking this belief. Consequently, the prospect of childbirth is often fraught with considerable anxiety. In the labor room, early contractions are seen as signals for unbearable pain to follow. The result is that even more anxiety occurs.

Now, since anxiety has a magnifying effect on childbirth discomfort, the more anxious you become the more actual pain you will probably experience. This "vicious circle" happens all too frequently.

The process of *in vivo* emotive imagery involves having you focus on scenes or events which please you or make you feel relaxed while the contractions are occurring. You simply cannot feel calm. happy, secure—or whatever other emotion the scenes engender—and anxious at the same time. These opposing emotions are incompatible with each other.

So, *in vivo* emotive imagery blocks the anxiety which leads to increased childbirth discomfort. There is also some evidence which suggests that the holding of certain images can raise your pain threshold. Thus, *in vivo* emotive imagery not only eliminates anxiety-related discomfort, but it also has a dulling effect on what might be called real pain!

After answering any questions that may arise from the foregoing explanation, the counselor begins to build an inventory of scenes and events that foster positive emotions. This process must be tailored to the individual. Scenes that give rise to extremely deep tranquillity or contentment in some women leave other women quite aroused. Suggestions from the husband are encouraged at this point. Use of the "Reinforcement Survey Schedule" (Cautela & Kastenbaum, 1967) or a similar device may also be of some help. And, of course, the counselor is free to offer (not to push!) his own ideas. It is usually a good idea to include imagery training as part of the program, as advocated by Phillips (1971).

As homework between the first and second counseling sessions the couple should be asked to identify any other images or events that produce positive feelings. During the interim it is also important that the husband gain practice in describing these scenes as vividly as possible.

The second counseling session, if needed, is essentially a role-playing or behavorial rehearsal of the labor-room scenario to follow. With the wife lying down and signaling the onset of contractions, the husband selects an image from the inventory and begins to describe it with appropriate feeling. For example, if the scene is supposed to induce relaxation, his voice should be calm and reassuring. If delight or pride is called for, his speech should reflect it. As the contractions become more frequent and intense, the scenes may lengthen into vignettes. It apparently does not matter whether or not the events are recounted repetitiously; it matters only that they be described as vividly as possible.

Minor Medical and Dental Problems

In vivo emotive imagery is potentially applicable to many other medical problems. Receiving injections, minor surgery (like removal of warts, moles, and so on), and chronic recurring pain are examples of situations that can probably be made much less aversive by the concurrent imagination of various positive events.

The process of having one's teeth cleaned can also be quite uncomfortable, particularly when calcium deposits between gums and teeth are extensive. A controlled study of the effects of *in vivo* imagery on this form of dental discomfort in women is now in progress (Horan, Layng & Pursell, 1975). Preliminary evidence collected in a pilot phase is indeed promising. When heart rate was used as the major stress index, four subjects exhibited a five-minute pretreatment base line averaging seventy-seven beats a minute. During teeth cleaning, while the subjects listened to five minutes of tape-recorded neutral images (numerals printed on a white poster board), their heart rates declined to an average of seventy-three beats a minute. A further drop to sixty-five beats a minute was found when the following five minutes of relaxation-producing emotive imagery were introduced:

Now close your eyes, sit back, and relax. Eyes closed, sitting back in the chair, relaxing. Now visualize yourself standing by the shore of a large lake, looking out across an expanse of blue water and beyond to the far shore. Immediately in front of you stretches a small beach, and behind you a grassy meadow. The sun is bright and warm. The air is fresh and clean. It's a gorgeous summer day. The sky is pale blue with great billowy clouds drifting by. The wind is blowing gently, just enough to make the trees sway and make gentle ripples in the grass. It's a perfect day. And you have it entirely to yourself, with nothing to do, nowhere to go. You take from your car a blanket, towel, and swim suit, and walk off through the meadow. You find a spot, spread the blanket, and lie down on it. It's so warm and quiet. It's such a treat to have the day to yourself to just relax and take it easy. Keep your eyes closed, thinking about that warm, beautiful day. You're in your suit now, walking toward the water, feeling the soft, lush grass under your feet. You reach the beach and start across it. Now you can feel the warm sand underfoot. Very warm and very nice. Now visualize yourself walking out into the water up to your ankles; out farther, up to your knees. The water's so warm it's almost like a bath. Now you're moving faster out into the lake, up to your waist, up to your chest. The water's so warm, so comfortable. You take a deep breath and glide a few feet forward down into the water. You surface and feel the water run down your back. You look around; you're still all alone. You still have this lovely spot to yourself. Far across the lake you can see a sailboat, tiny in the distance. It's so far away you can just make out the white sail jutting up from the blue water. You take another breath and kick off this time toward the shore swimming with long easy strokes. Kicking with your feet, pulling through with your arms and hands. You swim so far that when you stop and stand the water's only up to your waist, and you begin walking toward the beach, across the warm sand to the grass. Now you're feeling again the grass beneath your feet. Deep, soft, lush. You reach your blanket and pick up the towel, and begin to dry yourself. You dry your hair, your face, your neck. You stretch the towel across your shoulders; dry your back, your legs. You can feel the warm sun on your skin. It must be ninety degrees, but it's clear and dry. The heat isn't oppressive; it's just nice and warm and comfortable. You lie down on the blanket and feel the deep, soft grass under your head. You're looking up at the sky, seeing those great billowy clouds floating by, far, far, above.

Self-Management in Daily Life

In all of the practical applications discussed so far, the treatment by *in vivo* emotive imagery has been administered by external agents to people experiencing stressful situations. The expectant father, for example, describes the images while the wife endures the contractions. Similarly, the dental patient listens to a tape-recorded pleasant event while the hygienist works on her teeth. Once learned, however, *in vivo* emotive imagery can be used by clients in appropriate situations without the aid or presence of a counselor. For instance, in conjunction with stimulus-control procedures, several insomniac clients have found relaxing images to be of use in falling asleep.[3]

[3] *Editors' note:* See Article 37.

Another illustration was originally suggested by Thoresen (1972), who described how the image of skiing down a slope (while "the fine snow-mist billowed from the sides of the skis" and so on) made a cramped airplane ride much more endurable. The author of this chapter had a chance to replicate Thoresen's experience on a recent turbulent flight over the Alle-gheny mountains. Even though the storm tossed the small propeller-driven craft up and down, the ski scene was quite refreshing. In fact, the constant bobbing and weaving motion of the plane actually served to enhance the vividness of vicarious participation in a slalom race. Thus, the entire experi-ence was tinged with a modicum of delight, rather than panic.

references

Cautela, J. R. & Kastenbaum, R. A rein-forcement survey schedule for use in therapy, training, and research. *Psychological Reports*, 1967, **20**, 1115–1130.

Horan, J. J. "In vivo" emotive imagery: A technique for reducing childbirth anxiety and discomfort. *Psychological Reports*, 1973, **32**, 1328.

Horan, J. J. & Dellinger, J. K. "In vivo" emotive imagery: A preliminary test. *Perceptual and Motor Skills*, 1974, **39**, 359–362.

Horan, J. J., Layng, F. C. & Pursell, C. H., A preliminary study of the effects of in vivo emotive imagery on dental discomfort. In *Behavioral counseling: Training and treatment research*. Symposium presented at the annual meeting of the American Edu-cational Research Association, Wash-ington, D.C., April 1975.

Lazarus, A. A. & Abramovitz, A. The use of "emotive imagery" in the treat-ment of children's phobias. *Journal of Mental Science*, 1962, **108**, 191–195.

Phillips, L. W. Training of sensory and imaginal responses in behavior ther-apy. In R. D. Rubin, H. Fensterheim, A. A. Lazarus & C. M. Franks (Eds.), *Advances in behavior therapy*. New York: Academic Press, 1971, Pp. 111–122.

Segal, S. J. (Ed.) *Imagery: Current cog-nitive approaches*. New York: Aca-demic Press, 1971.

Thoresen, C. L. Behavioral humanism. Paper presented at the colloquium sponsored by the Department of Counselor Education, The Pennsyl-vania State University, University Park, July 1972.

GENERALIZED ANXIETY

36. *ANXIETY MANAGEMENT TRAINING TO CONTROL GENERAL ANXIETY*

RICHARD M. SUINN   Colorado State University

Anxiety Management Training (AMT) was developed in 1971 (Suinn & Rich-ardson, 1971) to meet the deficiencies of systematic desensitization and of implosion and flooding techniques. De-sensitization is an important procedure for controlling tensions when the cue conditions prompting these tensions are specifiable. Such specificity permits construction of the anxiety hierarchy. Desensitization has the advantage of enabling the client to remain subjectively calm during treatment while imagining specific situations.[1] On the other hand, implosion and flooding do not require cue specificity, though the client completes a treatment session feeling emotionally drained and fatigued from the anxiety arousal. AMT does not require cue specificity and permits the client to learn anxiety-reduction techniques, so that sessions end with subjective feelings of control or calmness, rather than arousal.

The original format for AMT has been changed as clinical experience has been gained. Thus, the more complicated early use of mood music and recordings to help initiate anxiety arousal has been discarded. Currently, AMT involves relaxation training, imagery to initiate anxiety arousal, attention to the physical cues of anxiety arousal, training in switching from arousal imagery to relaxation imagery, and experience in anxiety arousal followed by self-induction of anxiety control. Theoretically, AMT was conceived by me to be a conditioning process by which the stimuli of the anxiety experience are connected through training with anxiety-reduction responses. Presumably it is a learned process not dependent upon conscious, cognitive control. Rather, it was thought to occur automatically. Thus, the client would experience anxiety arousal in the future, and these cues would automatically trigger anxiety-reduction actions. I suspect that this does occur for some

---

[1] *Editors' note:* See Article 30 for a discussion of systematic desensitization.

clients who report, "I begin to notice myself becoming tense, but then relaxation seems to just take over and things are all right again." On the other hand, experience now suggests that other clients actually are learning a self-control style of coping in AMT. They are the ones who report, "I can now identify when I'm becoming anxious, and when I see that happening, I use the deep breath and take a moment to regain control."

I shall report on a case involving a client for whom AMT was a crucial part of treatment. The case involved a complaint of diffuse tensions, mixed within a framework of high emotionality.

THE CASE OF ELAINE

Elaine was a thirty-seven-year-old married woman with three children. She sought my aid because we had met professionally and she had become interested in behavior modification approaches. She had seen the value of operant procedures in working with children and was hopeful that similar short-term methods were available for herself. Her primary complaint was a diffuse emotionality, which often swept her out of control. She saw herself as an intense person who seemed to have only strong emotions, ranging from anger to the point of "bursting" to joyful excitement, with happiness "welling up inside," to immobility from depressed moods. Even her verbal self-descriptions to me seemed full of exclamation points! Her voice quality would shift from a happy lilt to a somber plea for insight and control.

Her life had been full of examples

in which her emotions were in control of her rather than she in control of her emotions. When appearing in court in connection with a minor car accident, she had become angry at losing the case and had followed the attorney down the hallway, yelling at him. She had become so involved in a school issue that she had cried and had had a stomach ache when reading a newspaper article referring to the topic. She had begun to develop an awareness of her tendency to overreact to situations, and this had led to her starting to fret over what she might do in important interactions. She had soon found herself spending an entire morning feeling anxious and on edge before a meeting on a personally crucial issue. Her general anxieties had also begun to influence her ways of relating to others. When she became anxious, she would engage in compulsive self-disclosure statements, revealing her personal feelings and anxieties. The sheer volume and intensity of these statements often became aversive to her listeners, and, as she noticed their discomfort and apparent withdrawal, she became more anxious and reacted by becoming even more involved in self-centered revelations.[2]

In many respects, Elaine was actually a successful person. She had an air of spontaneity and extroversion. She was attractive and lithe and graceful in her movements. She was a partner in a growing business, which brought a modest supplementary income and the personal gratification of contributing to

[2] *Editors' note:* A good example of "arousal-induced arousal"; realizing that she is behaving in a certain way leads to even more of the same.

the development of her students. She was gaining a regional reputation for her efforts. Her husband was an acknowledged expert in his own right, having left a well-established private consulting firm of his own to take a faculty administrative position.

I selected anxiety management training because a primary component of Elaine's behavior was the heightened basic tensions. On some occasions, these tensions seemed actually to reflect anxiety, as when she fretted before an important meeting or indulged in uncontrolled talking about herself. On other occasions, the layer of continuing tension seemed to set the stage for blowing other emotional states out of proportion. This was evident in her quick irritability, explosive anger, and steep slides into depression. In a way, she was acting as does the tense executive under work pressure who suddenly blows up angrily over a trifling matter that he would not have reacted to under calmer conditions. I was also hopeful that the self-control training would be generalized to emotional reactions other than the anxiety.

Treatment began with relaxation training, a brief version of the deep muscle-relaxation method (Jacobsen, 1938). During the first attempt Elaine reported being a little too "hyper" to become fully relaxed. However, focusing on each muscle group longer seemed to be useful. At the end of thirty minutes she said she felt physically relaxed, a little "twitchy" occasionally in the muscles, but "my mind still seems to be racing a mile a minute . . . funny, but my body feels solid and relaxed . . ." I thought it important that she could accept my instructions to talk to me during various parts of the relaxation procedure, without the talk's being a detriment.

I shifted to relaxation imagery as a means of replacing the heightened mental activity and of substituting a single, controlled relaxation scene for her varied and random thoughts. She was able to develop a clear image of "sitting in front of her easel in her studio with the morning sunlight coming through the window." This scene brought with it a deeper sense of peace, "a different level of relaxation for me." Two more sessions were conducted, with emphasis on controlled relaxation. Each session offered a briefer relaxation induction and increased emphasis on her initiating the relaxation, with less help from me. She chose some additional relaxation scenes, some of which were imagined from earlier days before she felt burdened with anxieties, increased responsibilities, and situational stresses. Each of these scenes was used with emphasis on the relaxation stimulated by the images.

By the fourth session, Elaine was able to sit in the reclining chair, to close her eyes, and to achieve a deep level of comfort within a minute and without any instructions other than "Get comfortable, close your eyes, and signal me when you're deeply relaxed."

Because she was so emotional, the first exposure to AMT was aimed at determining whether or not she could develop an image to arouse some tension. I did not want her to develop a high level of arousal for fear that it would not be controllable at this stage. The typical AMT instruction was used: "Switch on some scene which aroused some tension or anxiety for you. It might be a situation which always seems to trigger anxiety. Or it might be simply the last time you were anxious. Put yourself back in that scene again. Let yourself really be there. As soon as you begin to feel that anxiety returning again, signal me."

As might be guessed, Elaine had no difficulty in retrieving a scene and the accompanying anxiety! She did have some trouble returning to relaxation, even though the anxiety scene was immediately switched off. Generally at this stage I prefer to go from the anxiety scene to focusing on muscle groups: "Turn off that scene. Now focus on the right hand and the fingers of the right hand. Attend to deepening the relaxation. Just increase the sensation of relaxation in the right hand. Now continue to flow the relaxation up the right forearm. . . ." I believe that this verbal instructing helps to anchor the attention of the client to my voice as a cue, the content of the instruction, and the actual muscle groups. This focusing distracts or removes any residual thought from the anxiety imagery. As it turns out, the relaxation imagery also proved to be a powerful means for regaining relaxation. In the rest of this session we repeated the process of starting anxiety arousal, followed by immediate return to relaxation under my verbal instructions.

By the fifth session, Elaine was being taught to initiate anxiety arousal to a moderate level by herself and to pay attention to how she experienced anxiety: "Notice for yourself how you act; perhaps it is in your increased heart rate, or in some persons it is in their throat or stomach; maybe your neck muscles; how *you* tend to feel when you become anxious, what cues you have in your body." This stage is aimed at changing the response properties of anxiety to stimulus properties (details of the theory of AMT may be found in Suinn & Richardson, 1971).[3] This step permits AMT to develop in accordance with either the conditioning model or the self-control model.[4] After each anxiety arousal, relaxation was again induced through my verbal instructions. After a number of these arousal-relaxation sequences, Elaine was asked to complete the entire sequence by herself: "Switch on the anxiety scene, pay attention to how you feel the anxiety, then switch off the scene, and do whatever seems to be the best method for bringing back the relaxation." Verbal feedback was obtained to determine how she did. As with most clients, she accomplished this task without difficulty.

During the sixth session, verbal instructions for anxiety arousal were again introduced by me with emphasis on using the scene to experience heightened anxiety. "Just let yourself become really anxious, as anxious as you feel in those really stressful conditions. Notice your anxiety building, let it build even further, use those internal cues that tell you you're becoming anxious to become even more anxious." I then told her to

___

[3] *Editors' note:* The basic idea here is that the client learns to use the tense muscles and stomach butterflies as signals that it is now time to relax.

[4] *Editors' note:* That is, the signals may automatically trigger the learned relaxation process (conditioning model), or the client may note and verbalize the signals and deliberately initiate the relaxation steps (self-control model).

switch off the scene and to pay attention to the muscle relaxation and finally to the relaxation scene. This technique was followed for the rest of the session. The next session followed the pattern of the fifth session, in which Elaine was trained in initiating anxiety herself, with gradually more and more responsibility being placed on her for completing the entire arousal-relaxation sequence by herself. Ordinarily, this process is achieved in four or five sessions; however, I progressed more cautiously with Elaine because of her volatile emotionality.

SOME RESULTS

A variety of gains were already being reported by Elaine after the fifth session. She began to realize her anxiety during some conversations with others and could then focus on controlling it instead of automatically talking more. She would find herself suddenly becoming aware ("I'm anxious; I'm talking too much") and would discover that the desire to talk was being replaced by "disinterest." Before events that she knew might cause her to become overemotional, she practiced relaxation. By the twelfth meeting she had experienced a number of changes. She found herself less out of control emotionally during a very ego-involved experience: "I was involved emotionally, and I hated to see the outcome turn out as it did, but I was no more aroused than other people participating . . . and I didn't feel like I had to scream and shout." She also took a family trip that had been planned for weeks and was suddenly faced with a dangerous drive through a predicted snow storm over a threatening mountain pass. She recognized the difficulty and even the danger of the drive ahead of her, but "I wasn't at all disturbed."

The number of situations in which tension was aroused seemed reduced; the level of emotion when she was faced with stress settings seemed better controlled; and her day-by-day perceptions of herself as an anxious and emotional woman seemed to have been replaced by a firmer sense of control over her environment and herself. In a way, she saw herself less as a person possessing the traits of emotionality and anxiety and more as a person who might face situational stresses.[5]

Follow-up contact was made two years later. Elaine's general emotionality was still in control, although there were occasions on which anxiety was sometimes triggered. There was still evidence that talkativeness was sometimes a symptomatic response to aroused tension, but the frequency was well in hand. Elaine used the AMT approach as preventive action whenever

she anticipated facing difficult interactions or experiences.[6] For example, she used the sequence of anxiety arousal and anxiety reduction just before telling a difficult student that she was breaking off further lessons.

In one sense, this case was a partial success, inasmuch as other clients, with lower emotionality but suffering from diffuse or general anxiety, seem no longer to experience the anxiety attacks at all. On the other hand, the AMT approach may actually have two possible objectives: reduction or elimination of frequent anxiety (what might be called "trait anxiety") and training in control of anxiety that is situationally prompted (so-called "state anxiety"; Cattell & Scheier, 1961; Spielberger, 1966). We have some evidence of the reduction of both types of anxiety in experimental research (Edie, 1972; Nally, 1975; Nicoletti, 1972). The case of Elaine may have involved some success in the handling of trait anxiety, without complete elimination of the occurrence of state anxiety.

[5] *Editors' note:* It is an excellent idea to teach clients to anticipate stressful situations, so that they can mentally rehearse how they wish to react.

[6] *Editors' note:* Good for her! The "enduring trait" approach to personality has caused more harm than good. Elaine was fortunately discovering that what she experienced was primarily due to specific situations—ones that she could actually change.

references

Cattell, R. & Scheier, I. *The meaning and measurement of neuroticism and anxiety.* New York: Ronald Press, 1961.

Edie, C. Uses of AMT in treating trait anxiety. Unpublished doctoral dissertation, Colorado State University, 1972.

Jacobsen, E. *Progressive relaxation.* Chicago: University of Chicago Press, 1938.

Nally, M. AMT: A treatment for delinquents. Unpublished doctoral dissertation, Colorado State University, 1975.

Nicoletti, J. Anxiety management training.

Unpublished doctoral dissertation, Colorado State University, 1972.

Spielberger, C. *Anxiety and behavior.* New York: Academic Press, 1966.

Suinn, R. & Richardson, F. Anxiety management training: A non-specific behavior therapy program for anxiety control. *Behavior Therapy,* 1971, **4,** 498–511.

PHYSICAL PROBLEMS

An invigorating change in recent years has been the growing awareness that not all somatic and physiological processes and problems are "medical"
ones. Indeed many so-called "physical" problems seem to have quite a social and
psychological flavor to them. Is depression, for example, a physical or a social-
psychological problem? How about high blood pressure, smoking, tension headaches, physical conditioning, hypoglycemia, and malnutrition? Many still dichot-
omize problems broadly as either "physical-medical" or "social-psychological,"
as if they were all one or the other. In fact, almost all human problems have
important physical, as well as social-psychological, features. Sometimes the
physical-somatic part of the problem is very obvious, as in a physical defect. At
other times the mental component seems paramount (for example, in depression). Calling a problem "psychosomatic" has done little to reduce this artificial
division, for the term is usually translated to mean a psychological problem with
some physical symptoms (like a skin rash caused by "nerves").

In labeling this section "Physical Problems" we may be perpetuating this di-
chotomy. We do so, however, in order to direct the reader's attention to a more
familiar category. As each paper makes clear, the problems treated are experienced by the clients as both physical and psychological. Therein lies an
important point. Various professional areas like counseling, clinical psychology,
psychiatry, and internal medicine have long traditions of conceptualizing problems and basing treatments on these conceptions. Medical training, for example,
still gears the doctor to fight infectious diseases, although the major sources of
death and disability in our culture are degenerative problems associated with
habits of living (like the cardiovascular diseases). Clinical training for many
psychologists still places a premium on trait-oriented personality testing to
classify people, despite the fact that results from most of these tests seldom show
people how to change or improve. Writing out a prescription for a migraine
headache or interpreting several psychological tests to clients may help to

alleviate the problem. The pain diminishes; the confusion is reduced. But the sources of the problem often remain. In one area (insomnia), there is even substantial evidence that sleeping drugs (prescription or otherwise) actually make the "physical" problem worse. The person may lose consciousness, but the drugs cause serious disruptions in the level and quality of his sleep.

As suggested by these papers, a promising strategy for dealing with "physical" problems has started to emerge. Regardless of a problem's designation, treatment procedures are designed to alter specific problem behaviors. Furthermore, there is a strong emphasis on self-managed change. That is, people are taught how to treat their own problems. Thus, those suffering from severe headaches are helped to explore just what is going on in their day-to-day situations that may be triggering headaches, how to alter these situations, and what they can do physically and psychologically at the first signs of a headache. It is to be hoped that over the next decade more professional helpers from various disciplines will spend less energy on labeling problems as "physical" or "psychological" and more on offering the kind of help that really does help.

INSOMNIA

37. TREATMENT OF INSOMNIA WITH STIMULUS-CONTROL AND PROGRESSIVE RELAXATION PROCEDURES

THOMAS D. BORKOVEC[1]   University of Iowa
PATRICK A. BOUDEWYNS   Iowa City Veterans Administration Hospital

Insomnia represents a frequent and significant problem in this culture. The quantity of nonprescription sleeping pills purchased daily attests to the pervasiveness of periodic sleep disturbance in the general population. Surveys in 1971 and 1972 at the University of Iowa

[1] Preparation of this manuscript and the research studies cited was supported by Biomedical Sciences Support Grant FR-07035 from the General Research Support Branch, Division of Research Sciences, Bureau of Health Professions, and Education and Manpower Training and Grant MH 24603-01 from the National Institute of Mental Health awarded to the first author.

revealed that 15–18 percent of college sophomores not only reported needing an average of thirty minutes or more to fall asleep at night but also felt that this represented a difficulty for them and desired treatment for the problem. Although such anecdotal data on normal samples may be somewhat unexpected, it is not surprising to the clinician when he hears reports of sleep disturbance from his clients. Insomnia has been related to anxiety states, large numbers from both in-patient and out-patient psychiatric populations report sleep problems, and sleep disturbance is included as one of the diagnostic criteria for primary and secondary affective disorders. Understandably, problems in daily living that lead individuals to seek professional help frequently produce problems in night-time sleep.

The majority of case studies and most controlled research on insomnia treatment have focused on medical (primarily drug) intervention. Aside from indications that drug effects are unlikely to result in more than brief improvement, the attractiveness of drug treatment is reduced by a variety of undesirable side effects. Identification of effective psychological techniques that can be easily administered by the therapist and quickly learned by the client would have distinct advantages for the sleep-disturbed individual.[2]

The purpose of this article is to outline assessment and therapy procedures for the short-term treatment of sleep disturbance, with specific focus on difficulty in falling asleep initially. The procedures are derived from our experience over the past several years in both clinical practice and continuing research programs for evaluating the impact of therapeutic interventions on insomnia. Although the presence of sleep disturbance is frequently symptomatic of other adjustment problems or real life circumstances, the assumption is that direct treatment of insomnia is often a reasonable and desirable therapeutic goal. In many cases of insomnia there is little evidence of underlying problems. Even in the presence of underlying factors, poor sleep itself may

be aggravating the adjustment difficulties that led to its occurrence. Although counseling or referral for those adjustment problems is obligatory for the responsible therapist, brief and effective treatment of the complicating sleep disturbance will often facilitate both client motivation and ability to respond to other treatment.

For several reasons, the psychiatric disorder of depression deserves specific attention by the counselor. Insomnia is probably more common in depression than in any other psychiatric disorder. As depressive patients offer a higher than usual suicide risk, inappropriate or ineffective treatment may increase the risk. Furthermore, many depressed patients believe that their other symptoms are caused by their insomnia and will request treatment of the sleeping disorder only. Thus we strongly recommend that before a counselor treats a client for sleep disturbance he should routinely check for the following signs of depression (Feighner et al., 1972):

1. Dysphoric mood (sad, blue, despondent, hopeless, "down in the dumps," irritable, fearful, worried or discouraged)
2. Poor appetite or recent weight loss (without dieting)
3. Loss of energy (fatigability, tiredness)
4. Agitation or retardation (motor)
5. Loss of interest in usual activities
6. Decrease in sexual drive
7. Increase in feelings of self-reproach or guilt
8. Complaint of diminished ability to think or concentrate
9. Recurrent thoughts of death or suicide, including thoughts of wishing to be dead
10. Hypersomnia (sleeping too much)

[2] Editors' note: Actually almost all prescribed sleeping drugs cause more sleeping problems; that is, the "cure becomes a cause."

Patients who display a few or even many of these symptoms may not be suffering from clinical depression, but these signs should warn the counselor of its possible presence.[3]

ASSESSMENT

Once the factors described have been considered, the counselor can proceed with symptomatic treatment for the sleep disturbance, either alone or concurrently with counseling for other problems. The first step is to determine specific contributors to the problem by interview and collection of data on the client. The "General Sleep Questionnaire" (Figure 1) and discussion of its contents with the client will help to identify the components of his sleeping problem and contributing factors in his environment. The counselor can use the questionnaire as an outline for interviewing, or the questionnaire may be filled out by the client and used as a basis for further interviewing. In addition, a daily sleep questionnaire modeled after the outline and including those items relevant to the client's daily behavior and environment should be constructed during the initial session and sent home with the client. (Frequently used daily-questionnaire items are indicated by asterisks.) He is asked to fill out the brief questionnaire each morning upon awakening for the next two weeks and to return it at each interview. The resulting daily data will help to clarify observations obtained from the initial interview and will give

the counselor a clearer impression of the pattern of his client's sleep behavior and sleeping environment. The use of the daily questionnaire must be emphasized. The general and sometimes vague reports to open-ended questions in an interview often lack sufficient detail to allow for a useful functional analysis of the problem. Furthermore, we have regularly found the accuracy of interview reports to be poor. As with any problem behavior, the client should learn to observe his own behavior and the conditions under which it occurs. The daily questionnaire promotes this learning and provides more complete and eventually more accurate information.

Questions on the history of the sleeping problem should focus on duration of the disorder, circumstances of its origin, and past attempts to eliminate it. Ordinarily, if the disturbance has been present for several years, the therapist can expect that the client may require a good deal of practice to develop new skills. Historical circumstances may suggest current causal factors to be addressed by means of other counseling methods (for example, onset of disturbance associated with separation from a loved one, suggesting current fears of separation), but at the very least such information can be used to reassure the client. Many people experiencing particular life situations may have sleeping difficulties as a consequence of those situations; once the sleep situation becomes associated with behaviors incompatible with sleep, maintenance of the disturbance in the absence of the original causal factors is possible and understandable.

It is advisable to determine the

[3] *Editors' note:* See articles 5 and 6 on the treatment of depression.

methods and outcomes of previous treatments devised either by the client or suggested by other counselors. Experience with unsuccessful strategies should not discourage the client's future attempts, for the methods may have been inappropriate, employed for too brief a duration, or inadequately supervised. Briefly successful strategies may suggest methods that will be helpful, in addition to the program recommended here.

Finally, information on current drug use is important to the probable ultimate success of treatment. Quite frequently, the sleep-disturbed individual will be using prescribed or unprescribed medication to facilitate sleep. Our goal is always to replace such drugs with the client's own skills for controlling his arousal and sleep. For two reasons it is not always appropriate to ask the client to terminate drug use immediately: First, abrupt termination may result in withdrawal effects that can complicate both treatment effects and the counselor-client relationship and, second, termination of a drug that has been helpful because of its active or placebo effects leaves the client with no aids while he is attempting to implement the counselor's suggestions. On the other hand, ultimate elimination of drugs is highly desirable. The procedures employed in this program involve learning. Whether or not generalization of learned behaviors from drug to non-drug states will occur for every client is questionable. It is often best then gradually to reduce frequency and dosage commensurately with the client's progressively increasing skills in applying the psychological techniques. Specifically, a recommendation to reduce

the amount of drug use during the next week can occur each week that the client reports successful application of procedures and some improvement in sleep. Keep in mind that such recommendations should be made in consultation with the client's physician.[4]

Questionnaire items regarding the target behavior itself will serve two purposes. First, because the targets represent the most common complaints presented by sleep-disturbed individuals, the questionnaire will reveal the specific components involved in a particular individual's problem and the severity of each component. The vast majority of sleep-disturbed clients report that their principal, or only, sleep problem involves the initial onset of sleep. This difficulty will therefore be the usual focus of treatment intervention. For some individuals, however, additional components may be present. Although elimination of the onset problem frequently results in reports of improvement in other sleep areas, direct treatment of these secondary components may sometimes be required. Second, data on the target behaviors obtained both from the general questionnaire and later from the daily questionnaires will serve as the dependent measures of treatment effects. Such weekly information gathered throughout the duration of treatment supplies continuous feedback to the client on his success in applying therapeutic suggestions and to the therapist on their appropriateness.

The remaining questions address

[4] *Editors' note:* Since drugs may have been prescribed for more than one purpose, no counselor should recommend changes without consulting the client's physician.

History of the Disturbance and Past Treatment

1. When did you first notice that you had a sleeping problem? Date:_____

2. Was anything significant occurring in your life at that time? _____
   Specify those events.

3. Have you received counseling for the sleeping difficulty before? _____
   Indicate approximate dates, what was attempted, and how much benefit was derived.

* 4. Indicate anything that happens to you or anything that you do *during the day* that
   a. makes it easier for you to sleep at night.
   b. makes it more difficult for you to sleep at night.

5. Indicate anything that you have tried in the past *when you retire* that makes it easier to sleep at night.

6. Indicate anything else that makes it easier or more difficult to sleep at night.

7. Have you taken any prescribed or nonprescribed drugs to relieve the difficulty?
   _____ Please specify drug, duration of use, and how much benefit was derived.

8. Are you currently taking any drugs for the difficulty? _____
   Specify type of drug and dosage.

9. Do you currently take other types of prescription or nonprescription drugs for any other purpose? _____ Specify.

10. What do you think is causing your current sleeping problem?

Please answer the remaining questions in terms of your *average* or *typical* experience with your sleep situation during the *past month*.

Target Sleep Disturbance Components

11. How many nights per week do you experience sleeping difficulties? _____ nights per week

* 12. How long does it take you to fall asleep after retiring? _____ minutes

13. How many nights per week do you awaken during the night? _____ nights per week

* 14. How many times per night do you wake up? _____ times per night

15. When you do awaken during the night, what percent of the time do you have difficulty falling back to sleep? _____% of the time

16. How often during the week do you awaken and are unable to fall back to sleep at all? _____ times per week

* 17. How much difficulty do you have falling to sleep?

0	1	2	3	4	5	6	7	8
no difficulty		some difficulty		moderate difficulty		a good deal of difficulty		extreme difficulty

FIGURE 1   The "General Sleep Questionnaire." (Asterisked items may be modified for use in daily questionnaires.)

(Figure 1, cont.)

*18. How rested do you feel in the morning?

0	1	2	3	4	5	6	7	8
very rested		somewhat rested		moderately rested		not very rested		no feeling of being rested

*19. How much enjoyment do you get from sleeping?

0	1	2	3	4	5	6	7	8
very much enjoyment		much enjoyment		moderate enjoyment		a little enjoyment		no enjoyment whatsoever

20. How often do you feel tired during the day bceause of poor sleep from the preceding night? _____ days per week.

21. Does your sleeping difficulty cause other disruptions in your daily living? _____ Specify.

Bed-related Environmental Factors

*22. At what time do you retire?
    Weekdays: _____ o'clock
    Weekends: _____ o'clock

*23. At what time do you awaken in the morning?
    Weekdays: _____ o'clock; By yourself _____ or by alarm clock _____?
    Weekends: _____ o'clock; By yourself _____ or by alarm clock _____?

24. Check appropriate spaces to describe your bedroom situation?
    a. Own room _____ or shared room _____?
    b. Own bed _____ or shared bed _____?
    c. Typical noise level at night in your dwelling:
       high _____   moderate _____   low _____
       outside your dwelling:
       high _____   moderate _____   low _____
    d. Describe the physical characteristics of your bed (e.g., size, firmness, comfortableness).
    *e. Do you use your bed for any purpose other than sleeping (e.g., studying, reading, listening to music, watching TV, resting, eating)? _____ Specify and indicate how often per week you use your bed for each stated purpose.

*25. How often per week do you take naps? _____ times per week
    At what time do you nap? _____ Where do you nap? _____
    Usual duration of nap: _____ minutes

Cognitive and Physiological Activity after Retiring:

*26. After you retire, do you notice that you are thinking a lot about things? _____ If yes, specify what kinds of things you think about.

(Figure 1, cont.)

27. Do you ever have disturbing or re-occurring dreams that awaken you or make your sleep seem less restful? _____ If yes, how often *per month* does this occur? _____ times per month

*28. After you retire, do you notice any bodily sensations like heartbeat, muscle tension, feelings of arousal? _____ If yes, specify what you notice.

*29. How would you describe the way you usually feel when you retire?
_____ Physically tired, but alert
_____ Not physically tired, and alert
_____ Physically tired, and not alert
_____ Not physically tired, but not alert

Relaxation Homework Information (on daily questionnaire upon initiation of relaxation training)

How often did you practice relaxation today? _____ At what times? _____ _____ _____
How long did you practice each time? _____ _____ _____
Where did you practice? _____

what are usually the current and most immediate factors maintaining the client's sleep disturbance: stimulus conditions of his sleep behavior and cognitive or physiological events in the sleep situation. In many cases, one or more of the following factors will be clearly involved in the client's sleeping difficulty. First, bed-related stimuli (both temporal and physical) are frequently associated with behaviors that are incompatible with sleep. Individuals who use their beds or bedrooms to read, watch television, listen to music, eat, socialize, and so on inadvertently create conditioning that increases the probable elicitation of sleep-interfering responses in the presence of bed stimuli. Individuals who vary their hours of retiring and awakening similarly prevent temporal conditioning of sleep behavior. Second, Monroe (1967) has demonstrated that poor sleepers display higher levels of physiological arousal before and during sleep than do good sleepers.

In our own experience, most clients do report awareness of such arousal at bedtime, although specific reports will vary from general or localized muscle tension and irregular breathing to nervousness and physical discomfort. In addition, however, questioning routinely elicits reports of the third factor, intrusive cognitive activity subsequent to retiring. Specific thought patterns and content vary, but common statements include thoughts about past events, worry over coming events, attempts to solve current problems, concern about the inability to fall asleep, and a "racing mind" cluttered with a variety of unrelated thoughts and images. Each instance precludes rapid onset of sleep and may set the occasion for further interfering activity, should the client awaken during the night.

Dealing with these three areas represents the model treatment program for many cases of sleep disturbance. The recommended two-part program can be stated simply and in terms of its goals. First, our client should engage in sleep-related behaviors only under specific and regular environmental conditions and should avoid engaging in behaviors not related to sleep under those same conditions. Second, within this regular environment, our client should learn, and use at bedtime, behaviors that are incompatible with high physiological arousal and intrusive thinking and that are compatible with the onset of sleep. The first goal will be accomplished by structuring the temporal and physical aspects of the client's sleeping environment and behavior. The second goal is attainable by training the client in relaxation techniques.

TREATMENT

Rationale Given to Client

Base-line data collected for two weeks by means of the daily questionnaire can be integrated with information from the assessment interview to yield a meaningful and functional description of the client's sleeping problem. The counselor begins treatment with the following (or a similar) rationale based on that analysis. Emphasis on specific points and use of specific examples from the client's own reports will vary.

Over the past two weeks, you have supplied me with a good deal of information about yourself and your sleeping problem. The questionnaires that you have been filling out each morning have been especially important, for they give us an exact idea of your current situation. You've probably become quite good now at observing the details of your problem and the circum-stances at home that are related to that problem. Based on all of this information, we can now begin to do something to make it easier for you to fall asleep. Let me first describe for you what kinds of things are often associated with sleep disturbances and then what you and I will do to change those things in your own situation.

Most sleep disturbances are caused by three things. First, problem sleepers have had a long history of wakefulness and fitful sleep associated with bedtime and the bedroom itself. Given such a history, nonsleep behaviors have been conditioned to those situations. Such conditioning occurs frequently in our lives whenever certain situations are regularly present when we are engaging in certain behaviors. An obvious example is the association of time and eating. If we have a long history of always eating our meals at 8:00 A.M., 12:00 P.M., and 6:00 P.M., we tend to get hungry as those times approach. If we always ate in the same place, entering that place would result in our becoming more hungry than entering any other place. Sleep (or nonsleep) can be similarly conditioned to certain times and places. In your case, a lot of nonsleep behavior has been conditioned to your bedroom, making it more difficult for a strong association between bedroom and sleep to occur. To change that, we'll simply make sure that the bedroom is always associated with sleep-related behaviors and only at regular times. I'll explain this and other steps we'll take to guarantee this association in more detail later on.

Secondly, problem sleepers often have a lot on their mind when they go to bed, and since they continue to think about those things after they're in bed, it's difficult to fall asleep. The thoughts keep them alert and awake. I'm sure that you've noticed this to be true and also that simply telling you to stop thinking when you go to bed isn't going to help. I need to give you something else to focus your attention on, so that those thoughts can't intrude and keep you awake.

Thirdly, problem sleepers are often overaroused, physiologically speaking, when they go to bed. This activity is, of course, essential for daily behavior, but it is likely to interfere with sleep unless we learn to "shut down" that activity at bedtime. Again, just telling you to relax in bed isn't going to help. So I'll be teaching you how to reduce the arousal by instructing you in a technique called "progressive-relaxation training" that will allow you to do this.

This particular type of relaxation training will help you in two ways. Instead of thinking about the day's events, or whatever you have to do tomorrow, you'll learn, through practice, to concentrate your attention on pleasant internal sensations. Since this requires little thinking on your part, falling asleep isn't prevented by a lot of troublesome thoughts. Second, relaxation itself reduces physiological activity. Your body can't be physiologically active and completely relaxed at the same time. So, by learning to relax, activity in your body decreases, thus facilitating the occurrence of sleep.

Be sure to ask whether or not the client has any questions about the rationale. Once he understands your analysis of his situation and its relation to the general therapy strategies, then proceed with training in stimulus-control and relaxation techniques.

Stimulus Control

In order to establish stimulus control of sleep behavior, the following instructions are presented. It would be helpful to give a verbatim copy of these instructions to the client so that he can refer to them at home, if necessary.

1. *Rearrange Your Bedroom.* Because your current physical environment has been associated with poor sleep, start with a new environment. At least put your bed in a different part of the room, facing a different direction. Change other furniture and decorations, if possible.

2. *Decide on a Reasonable Bedtime and Awakening Time.* Those times should be the same every day. You may have to arrange your day so that you can keep to that schedule. But stick to that schedule! It is important that specific times become associated with retiring and awakening. Your body will become accustomed to a routine only if you follow that routine.

3. *Do Not Use Your Bed or (If Possible) Your Bedroom for Anything Other Than Sleep-Related Behaviors.* Ideally, you should be in your bedroom only when you're going to bed at night to sleep. If you must be in the bedroom for an extended period of time, avoid visual or physical contact with your bed. Keep in mind that the bed is to be associated only with sleeping and with no other activity. The more often this is true in the future, the more likely you are to respond with sleep-compatible behavior instead of sleep-incompatible behavior.

4. *Do Not Take Naps During the Day.* Taking naps harms your program in two ways. First, day naps reduce your need for sleep, making night sleep less likely. Second, by napping, you are associating sleep with the wrong temporal and physical stimuli. You may feel that you need naps because you get tired in the afternoon. But it may be the case that you get tired in the afternoon because you're accustomed to sleeping at that time. If you need a break during the day, do something

relaxing (for example, reading or listen-to music), but avoid lying down or falling asleep.

5. *Take Whatever Steps Possible To Reduce Distracting Stimuli Around Bedtime.* There may be several sources of noise or lights that interfere with sleep and can be eliminated. For example, heavy drapes over windows can eliminate random lights from outside; electric clocks are quieter than wind-up clocks. You may need to talk to roommates or neighbors if they are a source of distractions. Be diplomatic but firm in such discussions. You have a right to your sleep.

The counselor should discuss each of these points in terms of the specific situation revealed by the assessment information. It is advisable to work out the details of their application during the therapy hour, rather than simply to allow the client to make those decisions later. Notice that point (5) will vary widely in detail from client to client; the counselor must be prepared to offer a variety of suggestions, depending on the particular bedroom situation. A helpful general principle to keep in mind is that we want to establish a relatively monotonous sensory environment. Total dark and quiet represent only one example of such an environment and may be practically unachievable. The alternative is reduction of distractions as much as possible and the temporary use of monotonous masking stimuli (for example, a quietly humming fan).

Progressive Relaxation Training

Subsequent to discussion of stimulus-control procedures with the client,

training in relaxation can begin. As mentioned earlier, intrusive cognitive and physiological activities are common causal factors in sleep disturbance. It is unknown whether heightened arousal is a function of increased cognitive activity or the reverse. For the therapist's pragmatic purpose, it is best to consider the cognitive and physiological components as interactive (increases in either factor contributing to increases in the other). The most efficient treatment program therefore involves training the client in techniques that reduce both sources of difficulty. Although there may be a variety of strategies for accomplishing one or the other of these two goals (for example, folkloric suggestions to count sheep, drink warm milk, exercise before retiring) we recommended use of progressive relaxation training on three bases. First, research (Paul, 1969a; 1969b) suggests that progressive relaxation is effective in reducing physiological arousal and responsiveness to stressful imagery. Second, use of the technique gives the client a specific internal stimulus on which to focus his attention and, in this way, supplies a behavior incompatible with other cognitive activity. Finally, several recent studies have demonstrated that brief progressive relaxation produces immediate, as well as long-term, beneficial results in the treatment of sleep disturbance (Borkovec & Fowles, 1973; Borkovec, Kaloupek & Slama, 1975; Borkovec, Steinmarak & Nau, 1973; Gershman & Clouser, 1974; Nicassio & Bootzin, 1974; Steinmark & Borkovec, 1974).

Progressive relaxation involves the systematic tensing and releasing of various muscle systems throughout the body and direction of attention to the sensations that result.[5] Initial training sessions lasting some forty-five minutes each involve the sequential tensing and releasing of sixteen different muscle groups interspersed with indirect suggestions by the therapist of feelings of warmth, heaviness, calmness, and relaxation. The client is asked to practice the procedure daily between therapy sessions. As he practices and becomes successful in producing feelings of deep relaxation and attending to those feelings, muscle groups are gradually combined over subsequent sessions. Ultimately, tension and release of muscle systems are eliminated altogether, and the client learns to relax himself first by recalling the sensations resulting from previous tensing and releasing and eventually by a simple counting procedure. Progress through these steps is ordinarily completed within ten weeks with a motivated client who is practicing well; it results in the development of a highly efficient means of producing deep muscular relaxation and arousal reduction in a matter of moments.

Training in basic progressive relaxation techniques can be acquired by the counselor from a recent book specifically designed to teach individuals in the helping professions the details of these techniques and how to apply them to appropriate clinical problems (Bernstein & Borkovec, 1973). There are several additional suggestions that can be made, however, and that are particularly helpful in using progressive relaxation for the specific treatment of insomnia.

[5] *Editors' note:* See Article 30 for a summary description of the progressive relaxation treatment.

First, the client frequently *falls asleep* during a relaxation training session! In usual circumstances, this event is a "problem," in that the client is obviously not learning the procedure if he is asleep. The therapist will ordinarily raise the volume of his voice or call the client's name in order to arouse him as soon as sleep is apparent. In cases of insomnia, however, we recommend that the therapist allow the client to sleep for several minutes before gently awakening him and terminating the session. What is lost in training time is more than offset by the client's discovery that the procedure can indeed produce rapid onset of sleep. Additionally, the stimulus of training procedures has now been associated with the occurrence of sleep, increasing the probability that relaxation will elicit sleep behavior upon its future occurrence.

Second, although the therapist's verbalization of calmness and relaxation during training should be relatively monotonous with any client, softer volume and greater monotony are recommended during training of sleep-disturbed individuals.

Third, any client learning progressive relaxation procedures is requested to practice at home twice a day. With the sleep-disturbed client, the second practice session must be at bedtime. Instruct the client to begin his practice immediately after retiring, when he is not required to leave the bed again.

Fourth, during the practice session at night, the client should tense and release muscle groups and focus on the resulting sensations, just as he did during the therapy hour. In addition, however, he should periodically (once every twenty to thirty seconds) think of the words "relax . . . calm" in the same soft, monotonous manner used by the therapist.

Finally, as the client will be filling out daily sleep questionnaires, a question on the frequency, location, and times of home practice should be included (see the end of the "General Sleep Questionnaire," Figure 1). This item will allow monitoring of practice and will encourage the client to be regular in his practice.

Monitoring Client Progress

Evaluation of both process and outcome is important throughout treatment. To monitor process, the counselor should begin each therapy session with a review of the frequency and quality of relaxation practice and the steps taken to guarantee that sleep has been associated only with regular temporal and physical stimuli. General and daily sleep questionnaires, which serve as assessment devices, also supply baseline data on the occurrence of the target behaviors.[6] For monitoring outcome once treatment has begun, a briefer daily questionnaire (including items 12, 14, 17, 18, and 19 from the "General Sleep Questionnaire" in Figure 1) can be used. In our clinical experience, clear evidence of improvement frequently begins within the first three weeks of treatment, and gains continue as the

[6] *Editors' note:* One problem in relying solely on sleep questionnaires involves the validity of the data. People are typically not very accurate in estimating how many minutes it takes for them to fall asleep or how many times they awake during the night and how long it takes to go back to sleep. With practice, however, they do improve.

client progresses to the recall and counting stages of relaxation training (ninth or tenth session). At that point, if the client has successfully followed treatment suggestions and if clinically significant reduction in target problem measures has occurred, termination should be considered (assuming absence of other difficulties). The client is encouraged to continue the use of stimulus-control and relaxation procedures and to begin the program from its start (tension and release of muscle groups) if difficulties are encountered in the future.

TREATMENT VARIATIONS AND ALTERNATIVES

Although the program described here is the therapy of choice when other factors are not involved, occasionally the method may not be possible, or its application may fail. Perhaps the client does not have the ability to relax well, or the use of such extensive procedures is inconvenient (for example, the client lives too far from your office to meet with you on a regular basis). Financial considerations may interfere with therapy, and a less expensive procedure may be in order. Finally, other aspects of the assessment information may indicate the desirability of variations in technique. Alternatives for several such situations are described here.

Paradoxical Intention

One client, treated by the second author, was certain that his insomnia was incurable and asked for treatment almost as a challenge, certain that the therapist would fail. The case exemplifies the use of Frankl's technique of paradoxical intention (1960).[7]

Mr. M was a forty-three-year-old merchant who complained of severe initial sleep disturbance. Although he had entered the hospital after a very superficial suicide gesture, prompted by some recently incurred financial difficulties, his insomnia had troubled him for more than ten years. His recent problems had only served to aggravate the sleep disorder. Thus, after his family had agreed to help him out of his financial straits, treatment for the insomnia was requested. The patient was referred by his psychiatrist, who believed that continued "overuse" of sleeping medications was neither effective nor advisable at that time. Mr. M was annoyed with his physician for reducing his sleep medication and very skeptical about the effectiveness of psychological treatment. According to Mr. M he had not slept at all for the previous few nights. To make matters worse, he was obsessed with the idea that he had to have some sleep. It seemed obvious that the potential positive effects of progressive relaxation training would be too slow in coming for this impatient client. Instead, he was told that he could not sleep because he was trying too hard and that his belief that he must go to sleep kept him awake. He accepted this interpretation but predictably pointed out that it was understandable that he should be concerned, for his insomnia was severely interfering with his life. At that point, it was suggested

that one way he might overcome his concern was to do just the opposite of what he wanted: to try to stay awake all night. At first he chided the therapist for making light of his problem, but he was assured of the seriousness of the recommendation.

The next morning a red-eyed patient appeared at the office door still in his hostile mood. He stated, with an "I told you so" attitude, that he had followed the instructions and that he had in fact not slept one second all night. He was congratulated for sticking so tenaciously to the instructions and was encouraged to try again that night. This is one of the significant factors of paradoxical intention: The therapist never loses credibility. If the patient stays awake, he can be reinforced for cooperating, and if he goes to sleep you have won your case.[8] The next morning he arrived at the office to communicate the fact that he had again tried to stay awake but had fallen asleep for a couple of hours. According to the hospital sleep chart, however, a "couple" of hours was in fact seven! Mr. M continued using the technique for the next five days. His sleep chart credited him with from six and a half to eight and a half hours a night.

On the day of his discharge Mr. M asked what was the longest continuous period of time anyone had stayed awake by trying to as he had. He was given the stock answer to this question: The world's record is held by a disk jockey who kept himself awake for seven days and nights on a marathon radio show. Of course, Mr. M wanted

[7] *Editors' note:* See Haley (1973) for several examples of how paradoxical intention and "negative practice" can be used.

[8] *Editors' note:* Rare it is when the counselor wins, no matter what the result!

to know what happened to the fellow afterward, and he received the stock reply: He fell asleep.

Unfortunately, there is no systematic research on paradoxical intention that would suggest its active mechanism. But it seems logical to hypothesize that the procedure lowers arousal level and intrusive cognitions by reducing the anxiety caused by the client's fear that he may never go to sleep.[9]

Autogenic Relaxation

Autogenic-relaxation training (Schultz & Luthe, 1959; Luthe, 1963) represents a possible alternative to progressive relaxation therapy. This procedure allows the client to use a kind of hypnotic suggestion or "self-suggestion" for the purpose of lowering his arousal level. The technique itself is quite simple. The client is asked to lie back in a comfortable position and to listen to (and silently to repeat to himself) statements that suggest that he relax various parts of his body ("My feet feel heavy and relaxed.... My ankles feel heavy and relaxed.... My knees feel heavy and relaxed...." and so on).

Although research evidence sug-

gests that progressive relaxation may be more effective in reducing autonomic arousal than other relaxation techniques, the counselor might employ autogenic relaxation with rare clients for whom progressive relaxation techniques are inappropriate (see Bernstein & Borkovec, 1973).[10] One obsessive-compulsive patient of the second author, for example, found that she had difficulty with the tension-release cycles. She kept questioning (doubting) whether or not she was performing the procedure correctly. This concern, in turn, increased her anxiety level and thus intruded on her relaxation experience. But the autogenic procedure (tape-recorded in this case) did not seem to stimulate this self-doubt and significantly increased sleep time according to her reports.

Additional Stimulus-Control Procedures

On the theory that for many insomniacs bedtime has become a cue for behaviors that are incompatible with sleep, Bootzin (1973) developed a treatment designed to "separate the cues for falling asleep from the cues for other activities." Bootzin instructs his subjects to follow typical stimulus-control procedures, but in addition he tells them to leave their beds and go to other rooms

---

[9] *Editors' note:* Sleep may be thought of as a respondent behavior—one that automatically occurs under certain stimulus conditions (like salivation in the presence of delicious food). But *trying* to make a respondent behavior occur, especially if anxiety is associated with its failure to occur, reduces still further the chances of success. Hence, the value of the instruction to try the opposite. Sexual arousal, another respondent behavior, is also facilitated by instructions that it is not to occur (see Article 7). A new motto is needed: If at first your (respondent) behavior does not succeed, don't try, don't try again.

[10] *Editors' note:* Formal autogenic training involves a prescribed sequence of statements to oneself starting with "I am completely relaxed" and "My arm is very heavy" and ranging to "Forehead pleasantly cool." These statements are repeated several times along with self-instructions, like "Eyes are tired and heavy" and "'I fall asleep quickly." The procedure is very similar to what might be called "self-hypnosis."

if they do not fall asleep within ten minutes. This procedure is to be repeated as often as necessary and aims at associating the bedroom environment with *rapid* onset of sleep. Bootzin (1973) has investigated the effects of this procedure in an experimentally controlled study and has found it to be potentially more effective in reducing time to go to sleep than progressive-relaxation training; both of these procedures were more effective than placebo and no treatment.

Nightmares

In rare instances, sleep disturbances may be functions of periodic nightmares. In such instances, it is not surprising that sleep is unenjoyable or otherwise disturbed. A positive response to the dream item on the general questionnaire should alert the counselor to this possibility. If the content of the dreams is recurrent, the use of systematic desensitization may be appropriate. Hierarchy items simply involve components of the dream (see Geer & Silverman, 1967, for an example of such treatment). More often, the negative dreams that are potentially disturbing sleep vary in content. If a common fear theme (for example, separation, negative evaluation by others, aggression) appears to run through many of them, systematic desensitization of that theme (Wolpe, 1973), assertion training (Alberti & Emmons, 1970), or other adjunctive procedures will be necessary. In any case, daily sleep-questionnaire items should be expanded to include a more detailed measure of dream behavior, both for assessment and outcome-evaluation purposes.

Stimulus Control for Intrusive Thoughts

Because of severe cognitive intrusions, a rare client may have great difficulty learning to focus his attention on relaxation at night, despite frequent practice. Although separate counseling will ordinarily be required in such instances, some attempt to achieve stimulus control of "worrying" behavior may be attempted concurrently. The client is instructed to establish one location and a set of specific times for worry. He can worry (plan his next day, attempt problem solving, and so on) as long as he does so only in that location and at scheduled times. He cannot engage in those behaviors outside of those conditions. Thus, he should not retire, ideally, until he has planned his next day or completed his worry work and has determined when he can allow himself to worry again the next day (see Goldiamond, 1965, for a case example of similar stimulus-control procedures for sulking behavior).

Additionally, in such instances, single-item desensitization (Geer & Katkin, 1966) may be employed. Once the client is deeply relaxed in the therapy office, one item is repeatedly presented: The client visualizes lying in bed, his mind begins racing, and he visualizes himself turning off the thoughts and focusing on the feelings of relaxation.

Multiple Interventions

Assessment may clearly indicate that the cause of the intrusive thoughts or physiological arousal is related to specific life problems. If the client reports that bedtime thoughts frequently involve current crisis situations or difficulties in financial, marital, sexual, or social areas, these problems must be addressed directly in therapy. Keep in mind, however, that concurrent symptomatic treatment of the sleep disturbance may have therapeutic value and that elimination of the problems in living are no guarantee that sleep will return to normal. The sleep disturbance may now be simply a function of poor stimulus control and elicitation of sleep-incompatible behaviors in the bedroom, regardless of the presence or absence of the other difficulties.

Ms. A represents an example of this situation. She came to the first author, who was serving as a part-time counselor at a private college. Her presenting complaint of insomnia involved the presence of high degrees of physiological arousal and cognitive intrusion at bedtime. Assessment revealed that the onset of the difficulty had occurred two years previously, when she had declared a major in music and had begun performing in front of large audiences. The performance anxiety had been ag-

gravated by her current music instructor, who was placing very strong demands on her. Average latency to sleep onset was two to three hours, and she had been taking tranquillizers to relax herself during the day and just before retiring. Treatment involved stimulus-control procedures and progressive relaxation training for the sleep disturbance, differential relaxation for reducing general arousal during the day (see Bernstein & Borkovec, 1973), systematic desensitization to a performance hierarchy (including the presence of her instructor), assertion training to handle the instructor's unrealistic demands, and graduated withdrawal from night-time drug taking and, later, from day-time drugs, as she increased her skills in progressive and differential relaxation. Therapy lasted for fifteen sessions and resulted in reduction of sleep-onset latency to less than twenty minutes, elimination of all medication, successful confrontations with her instructor, and a decision to continue confidently pursuing her professional career in music.

references

Alberti, R. E. & Emmons, M. L. *Your perfect right*. San Luis Obispo, Calif.: Impact, 1970.

Bernstein, D. A. & Borkovec, T. D. *Progressive relaxation training*. Champaign: Research Press, 1973.

Bootzin, R. Stimulus control of insomnia. Paper presented at the annual meeting of the American Psychological Association, Montreal, September 1973.

Borkovec, T. D. & Fowles, D. C. A controlled investigation of the effects of progressive and hypnotic relaxation

on insomnia. *Journal of Abnormal Psychology*, 1973, **82**, 153–158.

Borkovec, T. D., Kaloupek, D. G. & Slama, K. The facilitative effect of muscle tension-release in the relaxation treatment of sleep disturbance. *Behavior Therapy*, 1975, in press.

Borkovec, T. D., Steinmark, S. W. & Nau, S. D. Relaxation training and single-item desensitization in the group treatment of insomnia. *Journal of Behavior Therapy and Experimental Psychiatry*, 1973, **4**, 401–403.

Feighner, J. P., Robbins, E., Guze, G. B., Woodruff, R. A., Winokur, G. & Munoz, R. Diagnostic criteria for use in psychiatric research. *Archives of General Psychiatry*, 1972, **26**, 57–63.

Frankl, V. E. Paradoxical intention: A logotherapeutic technique. *American Journal of Psychotherapy*, 1960, **14**, 520–535.

Geer, J. H. & Katkin, E. S. Treatment of insomnia using a variant of systematic desensitization: A case report. *Journal of Abnormal Psychology*, 1966, **71**, 161–164.

Geer, J. H. & Silverman, I. Treatment of a recurrent nightmare by behavior modification procedures: A case study. *Journal of Abnormal Psychology*, 1967, **72**, 188–190.

Gershman, L. & Clouser, R. Treating insomnia with relaxation and desensitization in a group setting by an automated approach. *Journal of Behavior Therapy and Experimental Psychiatry*, 1974, **5**, 31–35.

Goldiamond, I. Self-control procedures in personal behavior problems. *Psychological Reports*, 1965, **17**, 851–868.

Haley, J. *Uncommon therapy: The psychiatric techniques of Milton H. Erickson, M.D.* New York: Norton, 1973.

Luthe, W. Autogenic training: Method, research, and application in medicine. *American Journal of Psychotherapy*, 1963, **17**, 174–195.

Monroe, L. J. Psychological and physiological differences between good and poor sleepers. *Journal of Abnormal Psychology*, 1967, **72**, 255–264.

Nicassio, F. B. & Bootzin, R. A comparison of progressive relaxation and autogenic training as treatments for insomnia. *Journal of Abnormal Psychology*, 1974, **83**, 253–260.

Paul, G. L. Inhibition of physiological response to stressful imagery by relaxation training and hypnotically suggested relaxation. *Behaviour Research and Therapy*, 1969, **7**, 249–256.

Paul, G. L. Physiological effects of relaxation training and hypnotic suggestions. *Journal of Abnormal Psychology*, 1969b, **74**, 424–437.

Schultz, J. & Luthe, W. *Autogenic training: A Psychophysiological approach in psychotherapy.* New York: Grune & Stratton, 1959.

Steinmark, S. W. & Borkovec, T. D. Active and placebo treatment effects on moderate insomnia under counterdemand and positive demand instructions. *Journal of Abnormal Psychology*, 1974, **83**, 157–163.

Wolpe, J. *The practice of behavior therapy.* New York: Pergamon, 1973.

TENSION HEADACHES

38. SELF-MANAGED RELAXATION IN THE TREATMENT OF TENSION HEADACHES

LEONARD H. EPSTEIN, JEFFREY S. WEBSTER, AND GENE G. ABEL
Veterans Administration Center and University of Mississippi Medical Center

In the present case the self-managed application of relaxation training for long-standing, debilitating tension headaches is presented. The use of self-managed relaxation has been discussed by Goldfried (1971), and Sherman and

Plummer (1973) have demonstrated its effectiveness in helping college students to cope with stressful situations. In addition, Tasto and Hinkle (1973) have reported the use of relaxation training in successful treatment of tension headaches, and Epstein, Hersen, and Hemphill (1974) have provided data on the importance of using antitension exercises at home to reduce tension headaches.

THE CASE OF MR. PAYNE

Mr. Payne was a fifty-three-year-old, married, white male. He had completed two years of college and had begun working as a sales manager for a family business. However, he reported his effectiveness at work was influenced by his brother, for whom he worked, and by his constant tension headaches. Apparently, his brother gave him few responsibilities because of both lack of confidence in his abilities and Mr. Payne's repeated sick days caused by headaches. The daily headaches had begun twelve years before treatment.

Mr. Payne was medically evaluated, in order to assess the possibility of organic causes for his headaches. In addition, numerous medications had been prescribed without success. The diagnosis of tension (muscular-contraction) headache was confirmed by evaluation of neurological findings, tension-headache symptoms, and repeated frontalis (forehead-muscle) electromyogram (EMG) recordings. Before beginning treatment, Mr. Payne was gradually withdrawn from his pain medication, Valium, to which he had been addicted.

Treatment Measures

Treatment effects were assessed by means of physiological measures and self-reports. During relaxation training sessions Mr. Payne's heart rate, respiration rate, and frontalis EMG (for muscle tension) were recorded. These measures provided an estimate of his progress in relaxation training. It is important to ensure that clients have learned to relax in the therapist's office before using this as a self-managed relaxation technique. Although most counselors do not have a physiograph at their disposal, they can obtain estimates of progress in relaxation. For example, pulse rate can be sampled throughout training, and respiration rate can be observed through changes in chest volume. Also, the counselor can obtain subjective ratings of discomfort before and after relaxation training.

Headache activity was rated by the client on a 6-point scale of headache discomfort (Budzynski et al., 1973) four times a day (before breakfast, lunch, and dinner and at bedtime). No headache was represented on the scale as 0, and an incapacitating headache was represented by 5. Specifically, the definitions for each level were as follows: 0, no headache; 1, a low-level headache that is noticeable only when you think about it; 2, a low-level headache that can be ignored at times; 3, a painful headache that still allows you to continue at your job; 4, a severe headache that makes concentration difficult but permits you to perform tasks of an undemanding nature; 5, a very severe headache that makes it almost impossible to do anything until it is over.

At each recording time, if a headache were present, Mr. Payne was asked to describe the situation that had preceded the headache and the result of the headache. All the self-report data were collected in a pocket-size spiral notebook with prestamped pages. A hypothetical day's record, providing information on headache levels, antecedent conditions, and effects of the headache is presented in Table 1.

Information on events that precede and follow the headache can be useful in determining both the stimuli that cause it and the response to it. The response can be either from the client, for example, lying down, or from the environment, as when Mr. Payne's wife gave him a neck rub or brought him soup in bed.

Treatment Procedures and Results

Before beginning treatment, base-line self-report measures were obtained. These self-reports provided a basis for comparison with treatment effects. Mr. Payne's self-reports during base-line,

treatment, and follow-up phases are presented in Figure 1. Thus the baseline measures collected for one week indicate that Mr. Payne was experiencing on the average about a level-4 headache, during which the pain was intense and only simple tasks could be performed. The headache reports did not appear to be related to any particular environmental stimuli that might be manipulated during treatment. Following this assessment, training in progressive relaxation was begun.

During training, which was conducted in a quiet, dark room, Mr. Payne sat back in a comfortable, stuffed reclining chair. The relaxation instructions involved contracting and releasing muscles in major muscle groups. Instructions were adapted from those presented in detail by Wolpe and Lazarus (1966).[1] The instructions for training were pretaped to ensure uni-

[1] Editors' note: See articles 30 and 37 for descriptions of the progressive relaxation method.

TABLE 1   A Hypothetical Day's Record

Time	Situation	Level	Result
Breakfast	Good breakfast, no problems	0	
Lunch	Brother indicated I was not selling enough goods, and I got aggravated	2	Checked my books; attempted to relax
Dinner	Books do indicate sales down; talked to several salesman and still bothered	1	Lay down after dinner; played relaxation tape
Bed	Relaxation helped; talked with wife about business; she is understanding	0	

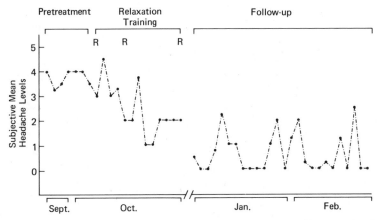

FIGURE 1 Self-report of headache levels during pretreatment, self-managed relaxation, and follow-up phases. Each datum point represents the daily mean headache level, computed from the four daily self-observations.

formity of presentation and lasted about twenty minutes. Days on which there were training sessions are indicated in Figure 1 by R. Three half-hour laboratory training sessions were used over a period of thirteen days. In addition, a tape of the progressive-relaxation instructions was provided for Mr. Payne. He was instructed to practice relaxation daily at home in an attempt to prevent headaches and to use relaxation procedures whenever he detected a headache. He was instructed to relax when he detected the slightest pain resulting from muscle contractions, that is, when he detected a level-1 headache, and to try not to wait until his headache reached level 5 before relaxing.

The therapy was designed to teach Mr. Payne a tension-reducing response that he could make when he detected a headache. He was thus in control of managing responses that could reduce his headaches. Mr. Payne reported that he practiced relaxation two to three times daily and specifically attempted

to stop what he was doing and to relax whenever a headache began.

The effect of self-managed relaxation, supplemented by three laboratory assessment sessions, on the client's tension headaches was immediate. Figure 1 shows a gradually decreasing trend, stabilizing around a level-2 headache (a headache that cannot be ignored but that does not interfere with work or accomplishing tasks). Follow-up data were collected for two months beginning four months after treatment had begun. These data indicated that continued self-managed relaxation had decreased headache reports to a mean headache level of less than 1 (very slight headache pain that could be ignored) a day, with many no-headache days.[2] Mr. Payne does not think that

[2] *Editors' note:* We wonder how Mr. Payne is getting along with his brother? It is possible that assertiveness training by itself or in addition to relaxation training might have been effective. Changing the social environment that often causes the problem is another way of using a self-control approach.

his relationship with his brother has noticeably changed. However, he reports that he can now better handle negative comments and criticism from his brother.

In summary, the use of self-managed relaxation was associated with a significant decrease in both intensity and frequency of reported headaches, an improvement lasting throughout the five-month assessment. This treatment approach can be used for many other problems related to tension. Engaging in many complex behaviors is often disrupted by tension. Thus, a client can be taught to manage tension that takes place before, as well as during, some activity. Self-managed relaxation can be extended to the treatment of problems associated with public speaking, dating skills, and study habits.[3]

[3] *Editors' note:* Self-management of stress and tension is one of the most valuable personal competences to be learned. See Article 37 for examples.

references

Budzynski, T. H., Stoyva, J. M., Adler, C. S. & Mullaney, D. J. EMG biofeedback and tension headaches: A controlled outcome study. *Psychosomatic Medicine,* 1973, **6,** 509–514.

Epstein, L. H., Hersen, M. & Hemphill, D. P. Music feedback in the treatment of tension headache: An experimental case study. *Journal of Behavior Therapy and Experimental Psychiatry,* 1974, **5,** 59–63.

Goldfried, M. P. Systematic desensitization as training in self-control. *Journal of Consulting and Clinical Psychology,* 1971, **37,** 228–234.

Sherman, A. R. & Plummer, I. L. Training in relaxation as a behavioral self-management skill: An exploratory investigation. *Behavior Therapy,* 1973, **4,** 543–550.

Tasto, D. L. & Hinkle, J. E. Muscle relaxation treatment for tension headaches. *Behaviour Research and Therapy,* 1973, **11,** 347–349.

Wolpe, J. & Lazarus, A. A. *Behavior therapy techniques.* New York: Pergamon Press, 1966.

PHYSICAL CONDITIONING

39.   A BEHAVIORAL APPROACH TO INDIVIDUALIZED EXERCISE PROGRAMMING[1]

RUSSELL D. TURNER, SUSAN POLLY, AND A. ROBERT SHERMAN

University of California, Santa Barbara

The importance of regular exercise has been emphasized by recent research in medicine and physiology demonstrating that insufficient physical activity is correlated with the occurrence of certain medical disorders. Individuals who are physically inactive exhibit a higher rate of coronary artery disease (Fox & Haskell, 1968) and greater susceptibility to coronary attack (Kannell, Castelli, & McNamara, 1967) than physically active individuals. Vigorous physical activity can help to prevent factors that contribute to heart disease; for example, it can lower the levels of certain serum lipids circulating in the blood, may help to reduce high blood pressure, and can be a factor in the prevention of obesity (Fox & Haskell, 1968; Mann et al., 1969; Mitrani, Karplus & Brunner, 1970; Skinner, 1970).

In addition to the physiological desirability of physical activity, there is evidence that exercise may also provide psychological benefits. Experimental studies have found that exercise may

decrease anxiety, submissiveness, and neuroticism (Popejoy, 1968), improve sleeping patterns (Baekland & Lasky, 1966), improve cognitive performance in geriatric patients (Powell, 1972), and reduce hallucinations and delusions in sensory-deprivation studies, suggesting the possibility of its use with psychotics (Zubek, 1963). In an extensive review of the psychiatric application of exercise, Layman (1960) reported that it can contribute substantially to psychological adjustment.

Despite the prospective physiological and psychological benefits of exercise and the promotional messages from such organizations as the American Heart Association and the President's Council on Physical Fitness and Sports, few people participate in regular exercise programs (Cunningham et al., 1968). Individuals frequently find the short-term aversive consequences of exercise, for example, fatigue and time away from other activities, to be more salient than the potential long-term gains (see Ferster, Nurnberger & Levitt, 1962). Also most people lack the knowledge necessary to devise exercise programs suitable to their personal needs.

The behavioral approach to individualized exercise programming presented here includes information about

[1] Portions of the training materials described in this study were developed by the authors in the early stages of an experimental research project on behavioral self-management for college students, conducted by Dr. A. Robert Sherman at the University of California, Santa Barbara, with the support of the Exxon Education Foundation.

elementary principles of behavior,[2] exercise, translating goals into behavioral terms, and teaching self-control skills for development and maintenance of the exercise program. The approach is illustrated by its application to Suzanne, a twenty-six-year-old married woman referred to the first author through the university counseling center because of an expressed interest in initiating an exercise program.

[2] Copies may be obtained by writing to Dr. A. Robert Sherman, Department of Psychology, University of California, Santa Barbara, California 93106.

SESSION 1: SELECTING AN EXERCISE PROGRAM FOR DESIRED BENEFITS

As the physiological effects of exercise are specific to the particular activities performed, the counselor will ordinarily have to assist in the formulation of a program appropriate to the client's goals. For example, weight lifting increases the strength of the muscles involved but does not strengthen other muscles or condition the cardiovascular system; stretching exercises increase the flexibility of connective tissues but do not increase muscular strength or cardiovascular fitness; cardiovascular exercises condition the heart and circulatory system and increase endurance

TABLE 1   Outline of Representative Exercise Activities and Some Prospective Benefits

Activities and Benefits	Type of Exercise		
	Strength	Flexibility	Cardiovascular
Exercise activities	Weight lifting Isometrics Gymnastics Some calisthenics (for example, push-ups and sit-ups)	Stretching exercises (like touching toes) Yoga Gymnastics	Running or jogging Swimming Bicycling Sports with extended activity (for example, handball, tennis, mountain climbing)
Prospective benefits	Increase muscle strength or size Improve performance in certain competitive sports Provide psychological benefits	Increase range of movement Improve performance in certain sports requiring flexibility Provide psychological benefits	Improve cardiovascular fitness Prevent hypokinetic disorders Build endurance in muscles used Improve performance in sports requiring endurance Promote loss of excess weight Provide psychological benefits

in the muscles employed. In Table 1 exercise activities that provide benefits in each of the three categories—strength, flexibility, and cardiovascular fitness—are outlined.

The initial interview with Suzanne was focused on determining the specific benefits she desired from an exercise program. Her weight of 118 pounds was within the average range for her height of 5 feet 4 inches. She expressed an interest in slimming down and firming her figure and in becoming more physically fit, both for the long-term health benefits and to assist her in keeping up with her one-and-a-half-year-old son in the coming years. As Table 1 suggests, cardiovascular exercises are the most useful for attaining these benefits. In order to provide Suzanne with information about cardiovascular exercises, she was advised to read *The New Aerobics* (Cooper, 1970) before the next meeting.[3] It was also suggested that she have a physical examination in the interim to confirm the absence of any medical problems that might contraindicate vigorous physical activity. This first meeting lasted thirty minutes, and the next session was scheduled for the following week.

---

[3] Cardiovascular exercise has the potential of providing extensive physiological and psychological benefits and will generally be useful for most clients. However, for the person with a particular strength or flexibility goal, for example, the man desiring to develop his physique, appropriate sections of *Foundations of Conditioning* (Falls, Wallis & Logan, 1970) may be assigned. This book provides technically accurate and clear descriptions of strength and flexibility exercises, in addition to a general discussion of exercise programs.

SESSION 2: TAKING BASE-LINE MEASUREMENTS, SETTING GOALS, AND SELF-MONITORING

Base-Line Measurements

At the beginning of the second meeting with Suzanne two base-line measurements were taken. As she had not been participating in any systematic exercise, her frequency base line was zero. In addition, a standardized cardiovascular test was administered.[4] In *The New Aerobics* (Cooper, 1970) several such cardiovascular tests that require administration outdoors over a measured distance are described. A more convenient procedure called the "Harvard Step Test" (Brouha, 1943), which can be administered in the office, was used with Suzanne. The step test is administered as follows:

The subject stands in front of a bench, chair, or other firm surface that is 20 inches high. At the signal "Up" he places one foot on the bench, at the count of 2 he steps up placing both feet fully on the bench with legs and back straight, and at the counts of 3 and 4 he steps down again, one foot at a time. The pace is counted by the administrator, "Up-2-3-4, up-2-3-4," as in military marching, the command "up" coming every two seconds, so that the subject is stepping up and down thirty times a minute. The subject is advised that it is easiest to begin with the same foot each time and to alternate feet

---

[4] For strength or flexibility programs the client's present maximum performance on the planned exercise activities can be assessed —how many pounds he can lift, how many push-ups he can complete in two minutes, how close he can come to touching his toes, and so on (see Falls, Wallis & Logan, 1970).

only after one leg has grown tired. The administrator employs a watch with a second hand to time the test, which is continued for five minutes or until the subject stops from exhaustion. If the subject falls behind and is unable to keep pace for about ten seconds, the test is also discontinued. When the subject has stopped he is promptly instructed to sit down and rest while the administrator records the duration (in seconds) of the subject's performance. One minute after the test was discontinued the administrator takes the subject's pulse count for thirty seconds, waits thirty seconds, takes the pulse for thirty seconds, waits thirty seconds, and takes the pulse for thirty seconds. In other words, a thirty-second pulse count is taken one, two, and three minutes after stopping the activity. The fitness score is then calculated, according to the following formula:

$$\text{Fitness score} = \frac{(\text{Duration of performance in seconds}) \times 100}{2 \times (\text{Sum of the three thirty-second pulse counts})}$$

The fitness score for college-age males may be interpreted approximately within the following guidelines: below 55, poor physical condition; 55–64, low average; 65–79, high average; 80–89, good; above 90, excellent (from Brouha, 1943).[5] The score serves the function of a base-line; that is, it provides information relevant to setting realistic goals and establishes a reference for future appraisal of improvement.

Suzanne completed eighty seconds of the step test before stopping from exhaustion. Her three thirty-second pulse counts were 54, 47, and 43, yielding a fitness score of 28, which is poor but not unusual for nonexercisers.

Setting Goals

Written materials explaining how to set short-term behavioral goals were given to Suzanne with a brief verbal explanation. Physical conditioning requires that stress be imposed on the body and then removed to allow the body to adapt. This means that a person must "push" himself slightly each time he exercises; the extent of the exercise is specified in behavioral terms. For cardiovascular exercises the duration or the intensity (or both) is *gradually* increased.[6] Defining the appropriate exercise amounts and increments (short-term goals) to be achieved over a given time period for a variety of exercises can be a complex task. However, the aerobics system (Cooper, 1970) makes it a simple matter for the counselor and client to specify how much exercise will be performed at each session for several weeks in advance, without having to specify the activities themselves. In other words, within that system it is unnecessary for the client to decide in advance whether he will run, swim, or the like; in fact,

[5] These norms were based upon a male college population, which had a mean score of 75 with a standard deviation of 15. Although it would not be appropriate to apply the same norms to women or older men directly, they can serve as reference points for assessing improvement.

[6] For strength exercises the number of exercises or the amount of weight used (or both) is gradually increased.

he is encouraged to vary his exercises to sustain interest.[7]

Self-Monitoring

Self-monitoring materials were given to Suzanne with instructions to keep an accurate record of her exercise behavior. Included was a graph with the horizontal line indicating the days and the vertical line indicating the cumulative number of exercise sessions. Each time she completed an exercise session as defined in her short-term goals Suzanne was to mark it on this graph. She was advised to post the graph, along with a list of her short-term goals, in a prominent place, where it would serve as a reminder. The desirability of posting it in a place that would be visible to friends or family, a technique called "public self-monitoring," was also explained. This introduces social contingencies by which other people can serve to support the person's exercise efforts. Suzanne chose to post the graph in the kitchen.[8]

Suzanne was also instructed to keep track of changes in the amount of time it takes her to run or swim the distances specified in her exercise program. This provided her with another index of improved fitness and a basis to reward herself for her efforts. It was agreed that the step test would be re-

administered in five weeks to provide an objective measure of her progress. The inclusion of the counselor in such fitness checks often provides additional motivation for the client to adhere to the program.[9]

This second session lasted thirty minutes.

SESSION 3: SCHEDULING EXERCISE SESSIONS, ARRANGING SOCIAL CONSEQUENCES, AND CONTINGENCY CONTRACTING

At the next meeting one week later the previous material was reviewed. Suzanne had begun her program and reported no difficulties. She had established the following short-term goals: exercise three times a week for the first two weeks, four times a week for the next two weeks, and five times a week thereafter. Over the next five weeks she also planned gradually to increase the duration of her exercise sessions from five to ten minutes, with a long-term goal of twenty minutes a session. During the previous week she had exceeded her first short-term goal by exercising five times: four sessions of jogging and one of swimming. Table 2 summarizes Suzanne's weekly exercise activities and the results of her fitness tests. To assist Suzanne in developing her program she was given written materials explaining the following self-control techniques.

[7] *Editors' note:* Here is one real advantage of having the assessment distinct from prescribed treatment activities. Success is measured by how the body performs, regardless of the specific activities that may have contributed.

[8] *Editors' note:* Also a good place to post a weight chart when the goal is to lose weight (especially by the refrigerator).

[9] *Editors' note:* Ideally, such counselor support should gradually be phased out. The client can learn to recruit a close friend or relative to serve the same function.

TABLE 2   Suzanne's Exercise Activities and Fitness Tests

Pretreatment Fitness Test: Week 2	
Duration: 1 minute, 20 seconds	Fitness Score: 28

	Weekly Exercise Activities During Exercise Program[a]			
Week	Number of Exercise Sessions	Activities	Average Duration per Session	Weekly Aerobic Points[b]
3	5	4 jogging 1 swimming 3 swimming 2 tennis	10 min.	5
4	6	1 jogging	14 min.	7
5[c]	4	4 jogging in place	7 min.	5
6	5	5 jogging in place 3 jogging	5 min.	7½
7	5	2 swimming	7½ min.	11¼

Posttreatment Fitness Test: Week 8	
Duration: 2 minutes	Fitness Score: 43

First Follow-up Fitness Test: Week 12	
Duration: 3 minutes, 40 seconds	Fitness Score: 69

Second Follow-up Fitness Test: Week 16	
Duration: 4 minutes, 25 seconds	Fitness Score: 76

Third Follow-up Fitness Test: Week 21	
Duration: 5 minutes	Fitness Score: 91

[a] Suzanne exercised regularly for the twenty weeks from the pretest to the third follow-up. However, only those sessions she reported during the formal treatment program are detailed here.

[b] These points, based upon Cooper's aerobic system (1970), best reflect the amount of weekly exercise completed. These were computed by Suzanne each week, using the intensity of exercise, in addition to the frequency and duration (for example, ten minutes of running was worth 1 point if a quarter-mile was covered but 3 points if a half-mile was covered).

[c] Suzanne reported that she had had the flu during the fifth week.

Scheduling Exercise Sessions

The client is advised to schedule times for exercise within his weekly routine *in advance* and to regard such scheduled exercise sessions as important appointments. If he prefers, he may register for physical activity classes at a Y.M.C.A. or adult-education center. This introduces motivating contingencies related to instructor and classmate attention, which may serve further to encourage regularity of participation in exercise. That may also be accomplished by arranging to exercise with a friend on a planned schedule.

Arranging Social Consequences

Approval or disapproval by important people in the client's life—like family, friends, and work associates—can serve as strong incentives supporting his exercise program. People with whom he has discussed his exercise activities, goals, and schedule may later serve as reminders to exercise, and they can also praise or deride him depending on his progress. Comments like "You really look healthy and energetic since you began exercising" can serve as very strong reinforcers.

Contingency Contracting

Contingency contracts are documents in which clients state behavioral goals and specify valuables or pleasurable activities to be lost if the goals are not reached and gained if the goals are reached. Such contracts are intended to sustain clients' motivation to continue carrying out their exercise programs by introducing contingencies beyond those that initially prompted them to attempt to improve their physical fitness. A well-formulated contract would specify realistic behavioral goals, the dates by which the goals are to be reached, and the consequences of achieving or not achieving the goals. If the contract provides for the forfeit of valuables for failure to fulfill goals, it is recommended that the valuables be given in advance to another person, who can later return them or direct

them to a designated recipient, depending upon the client's progress. Such contingency contracts can be formulated in relation to both short- and long-term goals. For example, a female college student who had not been exercising at all formulated seven increasing weekly goals, culminating in 15 aerobic-exercise points by the seventh week. She gave a friend seven $4 checks, with instructions to return a check to her each week if she met her weekly goal or to mail the check to a designated organization if she failed to meet her weekly goal. The weekly goals are given in Table 3.

It should be noted that contract goals must be individualized to reflect the person's own needs and capacities and may at times be revised by agreement between the subject and the other person, if both agree that the original goals were inappropriate. As with all other self-control activities introduced in this behavioral program, the client is advised to familiarize himself with the procedures but to continue employing only those that prove helpful.

The third session with Suzanne lasted ten minutes. The next meeting was scheduled for one week later.

TABLE 3   Sample Contingency Contract: Weekly Goals

Week	Number of Exercise Sessions	Weekly Aerobic Points
1	3 times	5 points
2	3 times	6 points
3	3 times	7 points
4	4 times	9 points
5	4 times	11 points
6	4 times	13 points
7	4 times	15 points

SESSION 4: SELF-REWARD, SELF-PUNISHMENT, AND MAINTENANCE

At the beginning of the fourth meeting the previous week's material was discussed along with Suzanne's progress. She had exercised six times during the previous week, including such activities as jogging, swimming, and tennis (see Table 2). She had been unable to register for an exercise class but had found someone to exercise with, had scheduled the exercise sessions in advance, and had informed her husband and a neighbor about her program. She had not written a contingency contract because she thought she did not require the additional motivation. She was given materials explaining how to arrange a self-reward system to support her new behaviors through contingent rewards and punishments. As her progress was such that weekly meetings no longer seemed necessary, she was also given maintenance materials at that time. These described techniques for maintaining exercise behavior once her long-term goals had been reached. The set of materials given at this session included the following procedures.

Self-Reward

The self-reward system is designed to help the client strengthen appropriate exercise behaviors through systematic reinforcement of those behaviors. The first step is to identify the behaviors relevant to exercise programming and to formulate a point system, which will indicate the relative importance of engaging in specific desirable behaviors (for example, beginning scheduled exercise session on time, 2 points; completing all the required exercises, 5 points) and not engaging in undesirable behaviors (for example, not joining friends for a social discussion when it is time to exercise, 3 points). Next the client rates the extent to which a large number of commodities and activities have reinforcing value for him by completing an adapted version of the "Reinforcement Survey Schedule" (Cautela & Kastenbaum, 1967). Those rated as having "a fair amount," "much," or "very much" appeal are then arranged in a personal-reward list, with relative desirability expressed by the number of points required to earn each reward (5, 10, or 15 points, depending upon the original rating). Finally, the client employs a daily self-recording system to award himself points for performing the designated appropriate behaviors and "cashes in" these points for desired rewards from the list. He is generally encouraged to reward himself frequently, though points may be accumulated for several days with a view toward earning more desirable (and costly) rewards.

Self-Punishment

The self-punishment technique called "response cost" can be used in combination with self-reward techniques to help some individuals control their undesired behaviors. This involves the loss of a specific number of self-reward points as a penalty for performing certain inappropriate behaviors, like having a meal immediately before exercising (for example, lose 5 points) or skipping a scheduled exercise session (for example, lose 8 points). The client first lists the inappropriate behaviors with point penalties for each and then applies the system of response costs in conjunction with the self-reward system.[10]

Maintenance

Physical fitness requires consistent activity. Once the client has reached his long-term fitness goals he will have to continue exercising regularly in order to maintain his gains. Suzanne was asked to read instructional materials that encouraged her to continue self-monitoring and recording exercise sessions indefinitely, a task that can be facilitated by having several graphs prepared in advance; preparing a description of long-term fitness goals and the exercise program required to maintain them and posting it near the exercise graph to serve as a daily reminder; saving the self-control instructional materials in a convenient place for immediate reference in the event of future difficulties in maintaining the exercise program; making certain that she is not falling below her fitness goals by testing herself periodically with the step test or some other appropriate fitness test. If the counselor is included in the periodic reassessment plans, the client may be more motivated to maintain

the exercise program.[11] The fourth meeting lasted ten minutes.

SESSION 5: FITNESS TEST

At the next session three weeks later the step test was readministered. Suzanne completed 120 seconds of the test this time. Her three thirty-second pulse counts were 53, 45, and 40, yielding a fitness score of 43 (see Table 2). This 53 percent improvement over her initial score was owed to a forty-second increase in duration of performance, as well as to a slight decrease in pulse counts. The improvement was consistent with her subjective report that her figure was slimmer and firmer (though she had lost only one pound), she could now fit into clothes that had previously been too tight, and she felt "healthier." Over the previous three weeks she had exercised four, five, and five times a week, emphasizing jogging and swimming activities. She had not attempted to formulate a self-reward system because she was having no difficulty in meeting her short-term goals. It was agreed at that time that, as Suzanne had mastered self-control techniques appropriate to her own needs

[10] *Editors' note:* Clients may differ in their abilities to administer self-punishment or self-reward. The particular self-control methods used can be tried out by each client.

[11] *Editors' note:* As any owner of a car or home knows, the "maintenance problem" is naggingly real. Things simply do not take care of themselves. Clients will not maintain their progress unless they receive help in knowing just how to do so. If a counselor is unavailable, sometimes a friend, neighbor, or colleague can help the client in his maintenance efforts.

and was experiencing no difficulties, further treatment sessions were unnecessary. However, further fitness tests were planned. This fifth meeting lasted ten minutes.

FOLLOW-UP FITNESS TESTS

Four weeks after the end of formal treatment, a fitness test was administered. Suzanne completed 220 seconds of the step test before stopping from exhaustion (see Table 2). Her three thirty-second pulse counts were 58, 54, and 48, yielding a fitness score of 69, which represents a "high average" rating by male standards. This score constituted an overall improvement of 146 percent over her initial score nine weeks earlier and of 60 percent since the test four weeks earlier. Suzanne noted that she had lost an additional two pounds and clothes that previously had been too tight were now actually loose on her. She had noticed the most dramatic change in her fitness during the preceding three weeks. Furthermore, she was enthusiastic about the future of her program.

Suzanne had previously told the counselor that she and her family were planning to visit her parents in Europe. She wanted very much to be physically fit for that trip because her father, who is deeply involved in an exercise program of his own, had chided her in the past for her poor physical condition. It was decided, therefore, to administer a fitness test just before she left. This occurred eight weeks after the end of formal treatment. She completed 265 seconds of the step test with a fitness score of 76. It represented an overall improvement of 171 percent and a 77 percent improvement since the end of the formal program.

Following her trip to Europe, Suzanne was reached and asked to return for a final fitness test. At that time, twenty-one weeks after the initial meeting and thirteen weeks after the end of the formal program, she completed the full five-minute test with an excellent score of 91—equivalent to an overall improvement of 225 percent and improvement of 112 percent since the end of the program.

SUMMARY AND CONCLUSIONS

In the present report we have employed a case-study format to illustrate a behavioral approach to individualized exercise programming. The client in this case achieved moderate improvement in her cardiovascular physical fitness within five weeks of formal training and exhibited substantial further improvement in each of three follow-up tests. She was highly motivated in her pursuit of physical fitness because of a desire to impress her father; as with other therapeutic interventions, this approach may not prove equally effective with clients who are less motivated. Nevertheless, considering the prospective benefits of exercise and the brief administration time required of the counselor, the approach is often worth initiating. Success employing self-control techniques for exercise programming may also prepare and prompt the client to attempt similar strategies in pursuing behavioral goals associated with other areas of personal improvement.

references

Baekland, F. & Lasky, R. Exercise and sleep patterns in college athletes. *Perceptual and Motor Skills*, 1966, **23**, 1203–1207.

Brouha, L. The step test: A simple method of measuring physical fitness for muscular work in young men. *Research Quarterly*, 1943, **12**, 31–35.

Cautela, J. R. & Kastenbaum, R. A reinforcement survey schedule for use in therapy, training, and research. *Psychological Reports*, 1967, **20**, 1115–1130.

Cooper, K. H. *The new aerobics*. New York: Bantam, 1970.

Cunningham, D. A., Montoye, H. J., Metzner, H. L. & Keller, J. B. Active leisure time activities as related to age among males in a total population. *Journal of Gerontology*, 1968, **23**, 551–556.

Falls, S. M., Wallis, E. L. & Logan, G. A. *Foundations of conditioning*. New York: Academic Press, 1970.

Ferster, C. B., Nurnberger, J. I. & Levitt, E. B. The control of eating. *Journal of Mathetics*, 1962, **1**, 87–109.

Fox, S. M. & Haskell, W. L. Physical activity and the prevention of coronary heart disease. *New York Academy of Medicine Bulletin*, 1968, **44**, 950–965.

Kannell, W. B., Castelli, W. P. & McNamara, P. M. The coronary profile: 12 year follow-up in the Framingham study. *Journal of Occupational Medicine*, 1967, **9**, 611–619.

Layman, E. Physical activity as a psychiatric adjunct. In W. R. Johnson (Ed.), *Science and medicine of exercise and sports*. New York: Harper, 1960.

Mann, G. V., Garrett, H. L., Farhi, H., Murray, G. H. & Billings, F. T. Exercise to prevent coronary heart disease. *American Journal of Medicine*, 1969, **46**, 12–27.

Mitrani, Y., Karplus, H. & Brunner, D. Coronary atherosclerosis in cases of traumatic death. In D. Brunner & E. Jokl (Eds.), *Medicine and Sport*. Vol. 4. *Physical activity and aging*. Baltimore: University Park Press, 1970.

Popejoy, D. I. The effects of a physical fitness program on selected psychological and physiological measures of anxiety. *Dissertation Abstracts*, 1968, **28**, 4900.

Powell, R. Psychological effects of exercise therapy upon institutionalized geriatric mental patients. *Dissertation Abstracts*, 1972, **33**, 2771.

Skinner, J. S. The cardiovascular system with aging and exercise. In D. Brunner & E. Jokl (Eds.), *Medicine and sport*. Vol. 4. *Physical activity and aging*. Baltimore: University Park Press, 1970.

Zubek, J. Counteracting effects of physical exercise performed during prolonged perceptual deprivation. *Science*, 1963, **142**, 504–506.

DEVELOPMENT OF ATHLETIC SKILL

40. *VISUO-MOTOR BEHAVIOR REHEARSAL FOR ADAPTIVE BEHAVIOR*

RICHARD M. SUINN   Colorado State University

Although operant reinforcement and assertive training techniques aim at helping the patient to learn adaptive skills, each relies heavily upon *in vivo* practice of such behaviors and is therefore limited by the availability of appropriate situations. In addition, the therapist has little control over reinforcement during such practice for non-hospitalized adult clients. With hospitalized adults and with children, the therapist may have more control over the environment, for example, through token economy wards or engineered classrooms. Another problem with such techniques is related to the principle that the strength of the adaptive behavior being learned is a function of the number of reinforced trials: The more frequently the patient can practice the new behavior, the better the learning. But again this is limited by the opportunities within the patient's everyday life. Finally, techniques based upon reinforcement for change rely upon immediate occurrence of the reward if the behavior under question is to be strengthened. With careful planning, the therapist can help a patient to select circumstances for trying out the adaptive behavior in which there is high likelihood of quick reinforcement. However, there is no way of being certain that this will happen, for life is fraught with unforeseen contingencies.

Behavior rehearsal, or active role playing, has been discussed by behavior therapists as a useful technique (Gittelman, 1965; Lazarus, 1966; Salter, 1949; Wagner, 1968; Wolpe, 1958). The procedure is basically role playing, in which the patient is often given direct instructions on what to say or what to do in his role. It has the advantage of being available for use in the therapist's office and thus is less reliant upon *in vivo* circumstances. The major drawback is that behavior rehearsal is still lacking in realism for many clients. The stimuli facing the client in the therapist's office are not identical with those facing him in his every-day encounters. Thus, although some transfer of the behavior-rehearsal effects can be expected to occur, there can well be occasions in which the role playing has little or no effect.

A few therapists have begun to experiment with a combination of imagination and rehearsal (Lazarus, 1968; Suinn, 1972b; Wells, 1970). This involves behavior rehearsal after the patient has visualized the real-life problem situation. The value of this approach is in the control afforded the therapist. Previously therapists have used the method because it has enabled them to face patients with stimuli (imaginal scenes) that are identical or nearly identical with those of the problems. I have further developed the technique as a means of controlling the occurrence of reinforcers and as a means of developing insights in clients;

I have also extended it to be applicable to talented normal people who wish to improve musical or athletic skills (Suinn, 1972a; 1972c). "Visuo-motor behavior rehearsal" (VMBR) is the label for this treatment technique.[1]

FEAR OF PUBLIC SPEAKING

Jack L is a successful executive with a large industry, responsible for making oral presentations on programs. During a previous affliction with polio, he was unable to speak because of paralysis of the facial muscles and vocal area. However, his slight residual paralysis was considered by a speech pathologist as having no further functional effects. The client's presenting problem was weakness of the vocal cords and inability to speak with any volume during public presentations. The symptomatology was absent during relaxed conversations.

In the VMBR technique, the client is first relaxed through standard deep muscle relaxation (Jacobsen, 1938) instructions. Then he is directed to visualize himself in a specific situation, followed by instructions to perform (role-play) certain adaptive behaviors. For Jack L this procedure involved visualizing himself in the conference room filled with managerial personnel, some hostile to his program, and having orally to present and defend his plans. He was instructed not simply to *observe* himself in the conference room but also actually to *be* there looking at the audience, thinking about his presentation, and feeling the emotional arousal. Once the scene had developed, the client was directed to begin his oral presentation, actually saying aloud the words. I have found that clients can communicate verbally without losing the relaxation or the visual imagery.[2] This approach enabled Mr. L to achieve a means of rehearsing the desired oral activities under controlled conditions. His treatment was terminated after six sessions and after he had successfully performed in two high-pressure situations in real life. The procedure in the first two sessions was similar to standard desensitization, in that he was relaxed, then directed to visualize being in his office just before stepping into the board room to make his presentation. The emphasis was on attending to calm emotions in the presence of the office cues: "Continue to notice your relaxation as you are in the office before going to the board room. Take another deep breath to retain those relaxed feelings." In the remaining sessions we emphasized the presentations to the audience:

You are in your office just prior to your scheduled presentation; take a deep breath to retain that relaxation as you con-

[1] *Editors' note:* The "mental practice" technique described here is also used to help people who block on introducing people to one another and who forget the last names of their best friends. The recommended procedure is mentally to rehearse the introduction several times in advance of the actual event.

[2] *Editors' note:* Note the differences among the various techniques that use imagination. VMBR involves imagining a successful performance under realistic conditions. Horan's emotive imagery (Article 35) involves imagining pleasant distractions while pain is being endured. Systematic desensitization involves imagining potentially painful situations while relaxed.

sider how you will start your talk. All right, now you see it is time to go to the board room, so you have picked up your papers and are walking to the room. As you enter, continue that relaxation; you notice the people there, some showing interest, others not. There are a few words introducing you. Now you begin, using the overall organization of presenting which you planned. So, begin your talk. . . .

The oral presentation was permitted to go on in imagery for a short time span during the first scene presentation, then gradually lengthened until the client was completing the full presentation. This gradual extending of the oral presentation with each successive phase was based on the premise that a type of successive approximation was important in chained sequences. In between scenes, the client answered questions about his level of comfort (questions about his level of discomfort were avoided, to prevent reinforcement of negative affect).

FEAR OF ORAL EXAMINATIONS

Mark U was a graduate student who had failed twice on his doctoral oral examinations. He had blocked during these examinations, unable to pull together his thoughts.

During treatment, Mark was instructed to visualize being in the examination setting, in front of the examining board. When this scene was developed, he was then asked a typical doctoral examination question by the therapist. The hope was to train him in proper ways of answering such questions. However, the scene was so realistic for Mark that he experienced an emotional block and was unable to respond. He was then taught to deal with this block by visualizing it as a substance, attending to the fact that it was really amorphous, then "thinning" it out through more careful inspection.[3] Following this, Mark was again taken through behavior rehearsal involving answering examination questions.

He was treated in ten sessions, during which he was able to work his way through three separate emotional blocks without help. At the end of treatment he was also able successfully to pass his final doctoral examination.

Visuo-motor behavior rehearsal was used without any attempts to focus on anxiety control. Hence, unlike the treatment for Jack L, this treatment contained no emphasis upon a scene involving "noticing your ability to remain relaxed in the examining room." Instead, the early sessions began with Mark's first listing a few questions that he thought his particular examiners were liable to ask. He was relaxed, then instructed to

be in the examining room. . . . You are able to identify each of the faculty on your committee. . . . These people you know quite well and can see their characteristics. As soon as you have this scene clearly, signal me with your index finger. All right, you are taking your seat, and now one of the examiners is asking you the first question. "Tell us something about how you conceptualize therapy." Take a moment to organize your reply, and as soon as you are ready start in with your answer.

[3] *Editors' note:* Possibly any one of a number of other visualizations might have been equally effective.

The first time this scene was presented, Mark began an answer, floundered after a brief beginning, then said that he was having trouble continuing. The scene was terminated. Mark, while still relaxed with eyes closed, then indicated that he had experienced mental blocking. A first attempt to eliminate this block was figuratively to "encapsulate it"; I told him to visualize being examined again and to let these cues prompt the blocking. As the first signs of the blocking returned, he was to imagine himself "moving further and further away from this block, leaving it further and further behind you. Take a deep breath to increase your relaxation . . . and as you become even more relaxed, you can move further away from this block, leaving it far behind you." When this procedure did not work, I decided to have the client move toward the block, instead of away from it:

Let's have you again facing the examiners. Now let the block begin to build. Examine it more carefully. Perhaps it seems like a mist. But let's have you move through it, increase your relaxation and thin it out, so that it gradually becomes thinner and thinner as you examine it more carefully. It's as if you can move through it. Thinning it out more. Have you become rid of it yet?

Once I had determined that this approach did seem to help, I told Mark to use this procedure anytime he encountered a block: to stop for a brief moment, to take a deep breath, to examine the block, and to thin it out until he could proceed with his reply. The treatment sessions were then refocused on the oral examination. The next time

a block appeared, Mark was readily able to rid himself of it and to deal with the examination question.

Further training in dealing with the examination process involved two behavioral objectives: emitting the correct verbal answers and controlling the examiners' behavior. For the former a typical oral-examination question was asked, and the client was required to answer it. In connection with the latter, it was discovered that the client lacked the skill to deal with two examiners who asked different questions simultaneously. Such a scene was initiated, and Mark was instructed to say: "Let me take those one at a time. First . . ." In each of the treatment sessions the standard procedure was relaxation, visualizing being in front of the examining committee and being asked a question by a committee member (although the committee person was being visualized by the client, the actual question was vocalized by me, so that the client did not know what to expect), and giving an answer out loud. Some scenes in which Mark was to visualize more than one question's being asked were introduced in order to determine progress on the second behavioral objective.

This case is interesting because it demonstrates the feasibility of recovery without treatment of anxiety components. As Mark had been unsuccessfully treated by desensitization therapy and had been (unsuccessfully) on tranquillizers, I chose to train him in adaptive behaviors and to leave the anxiety untouched. Indeed, during the final oral examination. Mark reported *feeling* anxious but indicated that his "brain was clear." Thus, he experienced sweating palms and fidgeted yet was able to think out answers clearly.[4]

FEAR OF MUSICAL PERFORMANCE

Jennifer C was given help in preparing for a musical competition. Performance in music is one example of a circumstance in which there is chaining of responses, that is, in which the person gives one response that in turn is the cue for the next in a series. Thus, practice of only one response or one set of responses is insufficient.

VMBR was used; Jennifer was asked to visualize being on the stage, seeing the judges in the audience, and awaiting a signal to begin. The therapist then gave a verbal signal ("All right, start now"), at which she began to play the piece selected for the competition. She was instructed to signal the therapist upon finishing the piece, so that the rehearsal could be repeated. As time sequences in visualization do not correspond on a one-to-one basis with the passage of real time, it is possible to have clients practice several times within a one-hour session.

Jennifer C was seen once a day for five consecutive days. Subsequently she qualified as one of the semifinalists in an open competition. As of the completion of this paper, she was a semifinalist for a regional contest.

DEPRESSION

Lorraine K was treated partially for depression on an out-patient basis. The depression involved "hating myself" and an inability even to list positive self-referent traits. During interviews, the therapist could not identify any reinforcers that occurred with sufficient frequency in Lorraine's life to be dependable. VMBR was therefore used as a means of presenting reinforcing events with greater frequency than would have occurred in real life.[5] To achieve this, Lorraine first visualized a scene involving a positive trait of herself. Immediately following this scene, she was instructed to shift to another scene involving her participation in a reinforcing activity. This procedure was aimed at reinforcing her for positive views of herself and is consistent with an operant-reinforcement approach used with depressives (Todd, 1972). Here is a typical example of a scene during these sessions: "You are looking at yourself in the mirror, seeing how you look in that attractive outfit. It is the one which your husband has always liked on you. All right, now switch to the scene of being in the swimming pool, feeling the warm, positive sensations." A relatively neutral scene was usually initiated first, so as not to challenge her self-perceptions too rapidly; thus the scene was presented as "seeing yourself . . . in the *attractive outfit*," rather than "seeing

---

[4] *Editors' note:* Helping the person to increase appropriate behavior (typically incompatible with the problem behavior) is highlighted here. Actually, VMBR represents a type of self-modeling; that is, the person sees himself in the problem situation acting in an effective manner.

[5] *Editors' note:* Compare this imagined-reinforcement technique with the technique for anticipation of positive reinforcement developed by Anton, Dunbar, and Friedman in Article 5.

yourself as attractive." In later sessions we associated the adjective "attractive" with "self," as Lorraine seemed more able to accept this as congruent. This approach avoids the typical problem of the depressed client's rejecting the positive self-evaluative scene as not realistic. Later sessions are then directed toward expanding the number of different positive traits visualized. Within six sessions after the initiation of the VMBR, Lorraine was reporting no longer hating herself for the first time in two years.

ATHLETIC PERFORMANCE

Ted C was an alpine ski competitor, who was being treated to enhance his performance at races. During a recent contest, he had fallen at the seventh gate; upon being asked what caused the fall, his "insight" was that it was the slushy ice conditions at that gate. Ted's conclusion about the origin of the particular problem (his fall) is similar to insights from other patients who consider their previous behaviors and arrive at statements about causation. Ted's statement and the insights of other patients are based upon current reflection on past events and are therefore subject to memory problems.

Through VMBR, Ted was asked to visualize being on the slalom course, standing at gate 7 and actually seeing himself skiing through the gate. In effect, he was asked to observe himself as if he were watching a movie of his race. Normally, V.M.B.R. directs the client to "be there racing and *not* to "observe yourself" or "see yourself" racing (Suinn, 1972a). But in Ted's case our objective was to identify behavioral errors in order then to use further VMBR practice to correct the errors. During his observation, Ted was to pay careful attention to the circumstances of the fall, reporting them to the therapist as he was observing them. In effect, this technique relied upon direct observation, rather than upon memory; such a procedure had been shown to be feasible with other clients, often leading to discovery of information not available through recall. During this procedure, Ted observed and reported that the fall was associated with his "stepping up" into the gate and placing his weight incorrectly on both inside edges of the skis. Once this was discovered, he was asked to develop a means of correcting the problem in the next visualization. To complete the session, he was then run through several imaginary slalom courses involving gates that required him to step up.

The VMBR in this case was useful in diagnosing the cause of the problem, in identifying means for correcting the problem, and in giving the client practice in the adaptive behavior. The fact that Ted had attributed his fall to snow conditions when he had used memory earlier but that he actually observed something else through VMBR highlights the need for caution about clients' reports based upon memory, even of recent events.

references

Gittelman, M. Behavior rehearsal as a technique in child psychiatry. *Journal of Child Psychology and Psychiatry*, 1969, **6**, 251–255.

Jacobsen, E. *Progressive relaxation*. Chicago: University of Chicago Press, 1938.

Lazarus, A. Behavior rehearsal vs. nondirective therapy vs. advice in effecting behavior change. *Behaviour Research and Therapy*, 1966, 4 209–212.

Lazarus, A. Variations in desensitization therapy. *Psychotherapy: Theory, research and practice*, 1968, **5**, 50–52.

Salter, A. *Conditioned reflex therapy*. New York: Farrar, Strauss, 1949.

Suinn, R. Behavior rehearsal training for athletes. *Behavior Therapy*, 1972a,

Suinn, R. Removing emotional obstacles to learning and performance by visuo-motor behavior rehearsal. *Behavior Therapy*, 1972b, **3**, 308.

Suinn, R. Sports psychology and Nordic competition. *Nordic Sports Medicine Journal*, 1973c, **1**.

Todd, F. Coverant control of self-evaluative responses in the treatment of depression: A new use for an old principle. *Behavior Therapy*, 1972, **3**, 91–94.

Wagner, M. Reinforcement of the expression of anger through role playing. *Behaviour Research and Therapy*, 1968, **6**, 91–95.

Wells, W. Relaxation-rehearsal: A variant of systematic desensitization. *Psychotherapy: Theory, research and practice*, 1970, **7**, 224–225.

Wolpe, J. *Psychotherapy by rceiprocal inhibition*. Stanford: Stanford University Press, 1958.

PART 3

METHODS FOR PROMOTING WISE DECISION MAKING

A major responsibility of counselors is teaching how to make decisions and to solve problems. The concern is not merely with finding a solution to today's problem but also with teaching a method that people can use to solve future problems.

Career decision making is one of the big problem areas. Many people expect that they should be able to make good decisions about their career goals without any effort. Many are unhappy because they lack goals and consider the lack a personal weakness. After all, if a five-year-old child can say that she wants to be a fire fighter, why can't a twenty-year-old make up her mind? No one should feel guilty about not having a career goal. The absence of a goal merely means that the client has not learned a method for arriving at a goal or has not yet gone through the necessary steps.

But career-planning decisions are not the only kinds of decisions people must make. There are some general steps in decision making that can be applied to a wide range of problems. The articles in this section describe and illustrate the following aids and methods for developing decision-making skills.

1. *Instructional Materials on Decision Making.* Booklets and audiotapes have been prepared to teach the general decision-making process.

2. *Group-Interaction Techniques.* A variety of games and group experiences have been devised to help people confront the realities of career development. Role playing, fantasy, confrontation, and group discussion are techniques that can be used to expand the horizons of young people.

3. *Automated Information Sources.* Techniques have been developed for making information readily available to those who simply dial a telephone number. (Computerized guidance-information systems have also been developed, although we shall not be dealing with such systems in this book.)

4. *Systematic Instruction.* Formal classes have been established to teach the decision-making process. The courses involve setting goals, examining values, keeping journals, confronting racism and sexism, assessing interests, promoting exploration, making tentative choices, and assessing outcomes.

5. *Evaluating Decision-Making Skills.* If the goal of career guidance were merely to make a career choice, it would be easy to know when the process had been successful. As soon as the student said, "I have decided to become a plumber," we would know the process had been terminated successfully. But, when the goal is to teach the skill of decision making, then we must have some way of assessing whether or not the general skill has been learned. To do so, we must find out whether or not the student can apply the skill to new problems, as well as to the problem initially brought to the counselor. Some first approximations to the evaluation of decision-making competences are described here, but a great deal of further work will be needed to improve assessment methods.

WITH FAMILIES

41. COACHING MARITAL PARTNERS IN FAMILY DECISION MAKING[1]

EDWIN J. THOMAS, KEVIN O'FLAHERTY,[2] AND JOYCE BORKIN
The University of Michigan

In this paper we describe a new coaching procedure that was developed to train marital partners in family decision making. The procedure is relevant to training marital partners who have recurring difficulties in making joint decisions when there are clear deficits in decision-making skills. If there are other problems, like drug abuse, faulty child management, and sexual or financial difficulties, that clearly interfere with or dominate the content of the decision making, then such difficulties themselves should be addressed first, by means of other techniques.

The procedure presented here is called "coaching" because it very much resembles the training methods used to develop and strengthen complex response repertoires, as in athletic, dance, and operatic coaching. Individualized training is accomplished by having the behavior in question practiced in a lifelike manner under the surveillance of the person functioning as coach and with the use of a variety of influence techniques.[3]

The coaching procedure is used during actual discussions between marital partners of real-life decision issues currently facing them. The procedure consists of three main components: first, decision making in ordered steps, with successful completion of each step required before progress to the next; second, light-signal feedback by the coach to the marital partners for on-topic and off-topic decision making; and, third, interventions by the coach as necessary to provide instruction, clarification, and guidance.

At the end of a coaching session, the couple has successfully completed the five decision-making steps: agreeing to work together on a problem, choosing one particular part of the problem to work on, listing possible solutions, selecting a solution or solutions for implementation, and deciding on action (determining what is to be done, who will do it, when it will be done, and how).[4] Although not part of

[1] The first portion of the research upon which this report is based was supported in part by SRS Grant No. 10-P 56023/5-02, Social and Rehabilitation Service, Department of Health, Education and Welfare. We would like to acknowledge the helpful contributions of Claude L. Walter, who participated actively in the formative stages of this research.

[2] Now in the Social Welfare Division, Social Security Department, Australia.

[3] *Editors' note:* Coaching has some similarities with participant modeling, in which the counselor demonstrates the appropriate behavior and then helps the client practice it. See Article 33.

[4] *Editors' note:* Note the similarities and differences between these five steps and the decision-making procedures recommended in Part 2.

the office training in coaching, the two additional steps of taking and reviewing action are also integral to the training regimen. With this emphasis on training the marital partners, the coach's task is to facilitate successful movement through the steps and not to give substantive advice. The coach, of course, can assist substantively when his expert opinion would be critical, but such occasions are very much the exception. This coaching procedure is thus restricted to decision areas in which the practitioner can and should take a neutral position concerning the outcome of the decision making.

Although some attention has been addressed to the behavioral aspects of decision making (D'Zurilla & Goldfried, 1971; Krumboltz & Thoresen, 1969; and Skinner, 1966), behavioral procedures have been relatively undeveloped in this area. The coaching procedure described here grew out of prior work by the authors and their associates on the assessment and modification of family verbal behavior. Attention was first given to marital communication; the marital partners produced response displays by discussing selected topics. In a series of single-couple experiments, it was found that difficulties in marital communication could be reliably specified and baseline data could be gathered; furthermore, change in selected areas of verbal response could be successfully achieved with corrective feedback and instructions and with light-signal feedback (Carter & Thomas, 1973a; Carter & Thomas, 1973b; Thomas, Walter & O'Flaherty, 1974a; Thomas, Walter & O'Flaherty, 1974b). Because many of the couples we saw had decision-mak-

ing difficulties in addition to poor communication, we endeavored to extend and apply our procedures to marital decision making. These efforts culminated in the development of the coaching procedure that has now been used in one or more training sessions with more than thirty couples.

CASE EXAMPLE

The case presented here was drawn from a series of single-couple experiments conducted to evaluate the effectiveness of coaching in modifying difficulties of marital decision making. Each couple was seen for four ninety-minute training sessions. Following referral to the research project from collaborating family-service agencies for assistance in marital decision making, each couple was screened to be sure that there were no overwhelming nonverbal problems and that the decision-making problem did indeed involve difficulties that had persisted over some time and involved several decision areas. All couples agreed that the decision areas addressed needed handling, that joint decision making was desirable, and that each partner would have a say in decisions.

The marital partners in this case were in their mid-forties. Among the current decision issues facing them were the following: what to do about their nine-year-old son's eating in the television room, how to cope with long and often unexpected weekend visits by their twenty-year-old boy, whether or not to give money to this boy and his fifteen-year-old brother, whether or not to let the nine-year-old make more decisions, how to work out individual and joint leisure-time activities for themselves, and how to handle their disagreements about the fifteen- and twenty-year-old boys. The decision-making difficulties of the parents involved not discussing subjects to completion, heated arguments, becoming upset with each other after discussion, and, on occasion, the wife's becoming disgusted and walking out of the room in the middle of a discussion and the husband's talking apologetically and hopelessly about his own behavior.

Setting and Apparatus

All sessions with the couple were conducted in an office setting in which the partners sat opposite each other at a table and the coach was close by in an adjoining room, where he was able to monitor the decision-making discussion and to provide verbal instructions and light-signal feedback as required. Before each partner was placed a light box in which the illuminated green light signified "on topic" and the lighted red meant "off topic." The coach did the signaling. The signal system used was the "Signal System for the Assessment and Modification of Behavior" (SAM), described elsewhere (Thomas et al., 1970; Thomas, Carter & Gambrill, 1971), which was connected to an eight-channel encoder-decoder and a four-channel tape deck that assisted in storing and retrieving the light signals along with the content of what was said (Thomas, O'Flaherty & Walter, 1972). In addition, a step-indicator sign was visible to both partners at all times during the session; it consisted of a list

of the steps in decision making and an arrow pointing to the current step.

Coaching Procedure

The following excerpt was drawn from a tape-recorded transcript and contains verbatim coaching instructions given in the italicized quotations and a summary of what transpired at each step.

Step 1: Agreeing To Work on the Problem. You have listed this topic [topic previously listed by clients] *as a possible topic to discuss during decision-making training. Do you agree to discuss this topic now and to try to reach a decision about it?*

The couple agreed to discuss the topic, which was how to help Carl, the nine-year-old, make more of his own decisions.

Because you are both agreeing to work on this topic now, we will move on to step 2, choosing one part of the problem [topic] *to work on.* (The pointer on the step-indicator sign was moved to step 2.)

Step 2: Choosing One Part of the Problem To Work On. There may be several different parts of this topic which you would like to work on. Select one now for discussion and decision making. You may deal with any other parts later. Select a part that you think is important enough to work on and small enough to actually make a decision on now. Go ahead with step 2.

The couple began with a general discussion of the need for Carl to make his own decisions and with several illustrations of how the father did not let him make them. In response to the generality of the discussion, the coach intervened to inquire what was meant specifically by "Carl's decisions." The couple then gave an example of the father's selecting a book for Carl to read, rather than letting him make the selection himself. The couple then launched into a discussion of possible solutions to this problem, at which time the coach intervened to ask what types of things the couple wanted the boy to make decisions about. From the ensuing discussion it was clear that the couple did not expect Carl to make adult decisions involving the family or the marriage; rather, they expected him to be able to make decisions within his capabilities and pertaining to his own personal situation. The coach then asked for additional details about examples of these types of decision. Following further discussion, the couple finally indicated that they wanted Carl to be able to make decisions on what to eat, what books to read, what books to obtain from the library, what to wear to school, and what television programs to watch.

Then the coach said, *Have you agreed on the part of the topic that you want to work on?* The parents indicated that they had and, in response, the coach said, *What is the part that you both agreed on?* In reply, the husband repeated the particulars just given about the areas in which they wanted Carl to be able to make decisions by himself.

Step 3: Listing Possible Solutions.   List as many possible solutions, or suggested actions, or plans as you can, which you think could solve the problem or help

with solving the part you have chosen to work on. In this step, each of you simply tries to suggest as many actions or solutions as you can without commenting on them or evaluating them. The objective of this step is to state all of the possible solutions or actions you can. Evaluating them or judging them will come later. Go ahead now to list all actions or solutions that you can think of that might help in handling the part [or parts] *of the problem you have chosen to work on.* (The pointer on the step-indicator sign was moved to step 3.)

The following were among the possible solutions suggested: to offer Carl choices like "Would you like egg or cereal this morning?" "Which book would you like to read—A, B, or C?" (suggested by W, the wife); to give Carl a choice and then have the father leave the room, in order to decrease the likelihood of his making the choice for the boy (suggested by H, the husband); to send Carl to the library by himself to obtain books (suggested by H); to take Carl to the library and let him decide which books to take (suggested by H); to have Carl take out the food he wants when food is being prepared (suggested by H); to have Carl select his own clothes (suggested by H); to let Carl decide what television programs he wants to watch (suggested by W); when Carl asks a question involving a decision that he can make himself, to turn the question back and to ask him to decide for himself (suggested by H); and when Carl asks his father a question, the father is to stop and think before answering, in order to avoid making the decision for Carl (suggested by H). Several times during the discussion the couple drifted off the topic but was promptly brought back by the red light or, if it failed, by the coach's instruction.[5]

Then the coach said, *Would you review your list of possible solutions so that you each know what has been suggested?*

Following a summary by the wife, who had written down the solutions on a pad provided for this purpose, the coach then said, *These suggestions are sufficient for you to move on to step 4, where you will consider them and select one [or more] suitable for helping with the part of the problem you have chosen to work on.* (The step indicator was now moved to step 4.)

Step 4: Selecting the Appropriate Solution. Select those actions which you think best for addressing the part or parts of the problem chosen to work on in step 2.

In regard to reading, it was agreed that Carl should be given choices and allowed to make his own decisions about which books would be read to him. He was also to make his own selection of books while visiting the library. It was concluded that Carl could watch anything he wanted on television until 9 P.M., after which time on Fridays and Saturdays, when he stayed up later, the parents would give him a choice of programs from among those not involving violence. When Carl asked questions of his father, it was agreed that the father would stop and think before answering, again, to try

[5] *Editors' note:* An impressive list of possible actions generated under a structured format with direct encouragement from the counselor.

to avoid making decisions for the child. In regard to the suggestion that the child be allowed to take out his own food, the wife objected because it would be difficult to do at breakfast; however, it was agreed that it could be done at lunch. In regard to going to the library, it was again affirmed that it was possible for the child to walk to the library, for it was really not far and involved few streets to be crossed.

Following the discussion, the coach said: *Have you agreed on your selection? Would you summarize briefly what you have selected?*

The couple then summarized.

Step 5: Deciding Action. Plan the detailed action you will need to carry out the alternatives just selected. Decide what is to be done, who will do it, when it will be done, and how. You will have discussed some of these details already, but make sure you state them all clearly now, so that each of you knows exactly what you have decided to do. The aim of this step is to clearly specify all of the actions needed to carry out the alternatives agreed to so that, if necessary, you could each carry out your decisions satisfactorily without requiring further discussion in the future. (The pointer was moved to step 5.)

Most of the details discussed in connection with step 4 were affirmed, but there were some additional specifications. For example, in regard to the selection of television programs, it was agreed that the husband and the wife would decide what is violent, preferably in advance, by discussing the matter. However, if it turned out that a program was unexpectedly found to be violent while they were watching it, they agreed that they would simply turn off the television or change channels.

There was also discussion of what would happen if Carl made a decision with which one or both of the parents disagreed. At first, the husband wished to provide some means of reversing the decision, but the wife argued that Carl must be allowed to make his own decisions even if they are occasionally incorrect by parental standards. Finally, with some reluctance, the husband agreed that Carl should be allowed to make decisions in the areas specified, without veto. He suggested that he should somehow be reminded if he began to question Carl on the wisdom of any decision. It was then agreed, at the wife's suggestion, that, if the husband began to disagree with a decision that Carl had made, she would remind him that they had "made an agreement"; this reminder was to be a signal for the husband to back off.

At the conclusion of the discussion the coach said: *Are you clear regarding the details of each action you have agreed to? Are there any other details that you need to consider? Would you briefly summarize what you have decided to do regarding helping Carl to make his own decisions?*

The parents then gave a summary.

Evaluation

The coaching session lasted approximately an hour, during which time the light feedback was preponderantly positive. Specifically, ninety-two on-topic light signals were given to the husband and eighty-six to the wife; only three off-topic signals were given to the husband and one to the wife. A total of eleven coaching interventions were given; six of them dealt with the initiation or the termination of steps, and the remaining five were questions for clarification, intended to redirect discussion. The light signals cued the partners and gave them feedback but did so without disrupting the flow of discussion. The coaching interventions briefly interrupted discussion and served to give it new direction. In regard to efficacy, this transcript indicates that the desired behaviors for the couple had been produced at each step before it moved on to the next. At the end of the session, operationally specific decisions for action were made.

Figure 1 shows the percentage of appropriate verbal units for steps 2–5 of this couple's decision making for three periods. In the first, precoaching period, there was an assessment on topic 2, which was how to let Carl make more decisions. The second period occurred during coaching on this same topic, as described. The third period was after coaching, and it involved topic 3, how to get the fifteen-year-old boy up in the morning. In the postcoaching period, no coaching was undertaken, and the couple was left to its own devices to solve the problem. The verbal units coded as appropriate for each step were the sentences or parts of sentences that were "on topic" for each step. Specifically, appropriate verbal units were parts of the topic for step 2, possible solutions for step 3, evaluation and selection of possible solutions for step 4, and specification of the decision response for step 5. Percentage agreement of coders in classi-

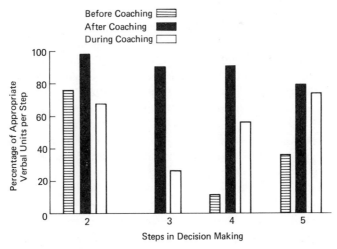

FIGURE 1 Percentage of appropriate verbal units in decision-making steps before, during, and after coaching.

fying verbal units into one of these categories ranged from 80 to 90 percent for this case, which was also the same level of reliability for all other cases in this series.

Figure 1 clearly indicates that the percentage of appropriate verbal units was very high for each step during coaching. Furthermore, only at step 2, when aspects of the problem were discussed, do we find in the precoaching assessment that there was a high percentage of appropriate verbal units. The findings after coaching indicate that the couple had learned to apply some of the decision-making skills to a new problem area. The 2×2 chi square for the sum of appropriate and inappropriate verbal units across steps 2–5 was 164 ($p < .001$) for the comparison of the precoaching assessment with coaching, 59.6 ($p < .001$) for the contrast of coaching with the carryover session, and 23.9 ($p < .001$) for the difference between the pre- and postcoaching sessions.

The couple was seen several times following these sessions, and it was learned that husband and wife had had an opportunity to implement successfully the different aspects of solutions discussed. The wife also described several instances in which the husband had noticeably refrained from making decisions for Carl, and she was approving of these changes.

The results for this couple are typical of those for the eleven couples in this series. During coaching periods for all couples, 88 percent of the verbal units in each step of the decision making were appropriate. This figure compares with 22 percent for the precoaching sessions and 36 percent for the postcoaching assessment. Thus, for all couples in the series, the coaching procedure also clearly served to produce the behaviors intended for each step in the decision making and to produce a modest but noteworthy carryover of the decision-making skills when applied to new decision areas. Additional details may be found in O'Flaherty (1974) and in forthcoming reports.

Although it is very helpful, the light-signal feedback used in these studies is not essential in practice, for feedback can be provided verbally by the coach at strategic points, along with other verbal interventions. The step-indicator sign is also a helpful visual reminder, but it too is not required.

As part of a modification program for marital decision making, the coach should ordinarily expect to provide one or more training sessions for different decision areas and to monitor concur-

rently the adequacy with which the decisions are implemented, as well as carrying out periodic reviews of the adequacy of the decisions. Furthermore, clients should set aside regular times at home to make decisions by means of the step procedure.

The coaching procedure is exacting for the coach, who must continuously track the flow of what is said for both on-topic and off-topic content. Interventions by the coach must be given carefully; they should be minimal, in order to keep the discussion moving properly; and they must be procedurally oriented, so that the coach does not impose his points of view on the discussion. With some experience and diligent application, the procedure can be mastered, however.

references

Carter, R. D. & Thomas, E. J. A case application of a signaling system (SAM) to the assessment and modification of selected problems of marital communication. *Behavior Therapy*, 1973a, **4**, 629–645.

Carter, R. D. & Thomas, E. J. Modification of problematic marital communication using corrective feedback and instruction. *Behavior Therapy*, 1973b, **4**, 100–109.

D'Zurilla, T. J. & Goldfried, M. R., Problem solving and behavior modification. *Journal of Abnormal Psychology*, 1971, **78**, 107–126.

Krumboltz, J. D. & Thoresen, C. E. (Eds.) *Behavioral counseling: Cases and techniques.* New York: Holt, Rinehart and Winston, 1969.

O'Flaherty, K. W. *Evaluation of a coaching procedure for marital decision making.* Unpublished doctoral disser-

tation, University of Michigan, 1974.

Skinner, B. F. An operant analysis of problem solving. In B. Kleinmuntz, (Ed.), *Problem solving: Research, method, and theory.* New York: Wiley, 1966. Pp. 225–257.

Thomas, E. J., Carter, R. D. & Gambrill, E. D. Some possibilities of behavioral modification with marital problems using 'SAM' (Signal System for the Assessment and Modification of Behavior). In R. D. Rubin, H. Fensterheim, A. A. Lazarus & C. M. Franks (Eds.), *Advances in behavior therapy.* New York: Academic Press, 1971. Pp. 273–287.

Thomas, E. J., Carter, R. D., Gambrill, E. D. & Butterfield, W. H. A signal system for the assessment and modification of behavior (SAM). *Behavior Therapy*, 1970, **1**, 252–259.

Thomas, E. J., O'Flaherty, K., & Walter,

C. L. Modification of problematic family verbal behavior using instructions and light signal feedback. In E. J. Thomas, C. L. Walter & K. O'Flaherty, *Socio-behavioral techniques for open welfare settings.* (Final Report on Research Supported by the Department of Health, Education and Welfare, Social and Rehabilitation Service, Grant No. 10-P-56 02315-02.) Ann Arbor: University of Michigan School of Social Work, 1972.

Thomas, E. J., Walter C. L. & O'Flaherty, K. Computer-assisted assessment and modification: Possibilities and illustrative data. *Social Service Review,* 1974a, **48**, 170–183.

Thomas, E. J., Walter, C. L. & O'Flaherty, K. A verbal problem checklist for use in assessing family verbal behavior. *Behavior Therapy,* 1974b, **5**, 235–246.

WITH CHILDREN

42.   *TEACHING DECISION-MAKING SKILLS TO CHILDREN*

MICHAEL L. RUSSELL   Pacific Medical Center, San Francisco
CARL E. THORESEN   Stanford University

Children are seldom directly taught the skills to make good decisions. Counselors, teachers, and parents expect most youngsters somehow to acquire this ability through a natural process during childhood. Although this method of learning to solve personal problems is sufficient for some children, many others never seem to achieve the basic set of skills (D'Zurilla & Goldfried, 1971).

The children at Learning House, a residential treatment home in Palo Alto, California, for neglected and acting-out preadolescents, generally lack effective decision-making skills. In talks with the youngsters about their past troubles they typically make such comments as "I knew it was wrong, but I wanted the money," "It was the first thing I thought to do, so I did it," "I didn't know what else I *could* do," "I didn't know *that* [result] would happen."

These children, when faced with difficult problem situations, have often adopted the first solutions that have occurred to them. Frequently they have neglected to consider other alternative behaviors or the probable consequences of their actions. In short, they have not learned a systematic method for attacking personal problems.

SELF-MANAGEMENT AT LEARNING HOUSE

As part of a behaviorally based treatment program, Learning House uses a token-economy system to encourage and maintain appropriate social and academic behavior.[1] The Learning

---

[1]*Editors' note:* See Article 17 for further details about the Learning House environment.

House treatment program helps each child gradually to change his behavior through the consistent and systematic application of positive and negative consequences coupled with the use of social modeling, stimulus cuing, and behavioral-rehearsal procedures. Early in the development of the Learning House treatment program, however, it was realized that the children also needed to develop greater self-control skills. In this way, when a child returned to his family, he could better "manage" many of the problems that still existed in his own home, school, and neighborhood environments.

Following the rationale of Thoresen and Mahoney (1974), a behavioral approach was used in designing a self-control training program. Self-control was considered to be a complex pattern of actions (self-controlling behaviors) that the child could learn in order to manage his behavior (behaviors to be controlled). Self-controlling behaviors were viewed as ways of altering the child's environment that would, in a reciprocal way, influence the child. Crucial to the development of the child's self-management skills is the modification of his private, or internal, environment (his thoughts, perceptions, and images).

Making good decisions was identified as one important self-management skill that each child should learn. He should be able to anticipate the probable consequences of his behavior from staff, teachers, peers, and parents. In addition, he should be able to generate and select from several alternatives those actions that will lead to the consequences he desires. In this way, after leaving Learning House and returning

to his family, the child will have expanded this "adaptive capacity" and be able to generalize appropriate behaviors learned at Learning House to his own home and school setting. More important, there will also be an increased probability that the child would be able to maintain appropriate behaviors when the immediate consequences for his actions are minimally positive, absent, or in some instances punishing. Even when the actions of others are not helpful, the child should see himself as more in control of his actions.

THE DECISION-MAKING BOOK FOR CHILDREN

The steps in good decision making have been incorporated into the *Decision-Making Book for Children* (D.M.B.C.), a self-contained set of written materials integrated with a cassette audiotape for children ages eight to twelve years (Russell, 1974).[2] The book has been designed to allow each child to progress through the training program at his own rate. He learns that the process of good decision making includes identifying the problem, generating choices, collecting information, recognizing personal values, making the best decision, and then reviewing the decision at a later time.[3]

[2] Copies of this book and tape may be obtained by writing to Michael L. Russell, Department of Psychological and Social Medicine, P.O. Box 7999, Pacific Medical Center, San Francisco, California 94120.

[3] *Editors' note:* Decision-making steps may be defined in various ways. Compare these, for example, with those in Articles 45 and 46.

The materials have been designed to teach a logical method of attacking a current problem, together with a means of improving future decisions. The child, therefore, is given skills to self-manage his current behavior and the flexibility to adapt more successfully to future situations.

One objective of the D.M.B.C. is to teach each child how to use a decision chart (see Figure 1). The decision chart includes all the components of the decision-making process and requires the youngster to complete each step in sequence. Several decision charts must be correctly filled out for real and simulated problem situations before the child completes the training program.

To allow maximum individualization with minimal staff monitoring, the D.M.B.C. uses an informal, programmed text structure. First, the child reads a simple explanation for each step of the problem-solving process with examples, pictures, and a cartoon character who "thinks out loud" for the reader.[4] The child then listens to a story on the audiotape demonstrating an application of the step by another child or posing a problem for the listener to solve. In this way the child listens to a social model using the decision process and then obtains practice in applying each of the decision steps to a problem situation himself. At the conclusion of each section the child completes a brief quiz requiring knowledge of all the steps taught in previous sections.

[4] Throughout the book the written material is presented at about a third-grade reading level since poor problem solvers frequently have poor reading ability.

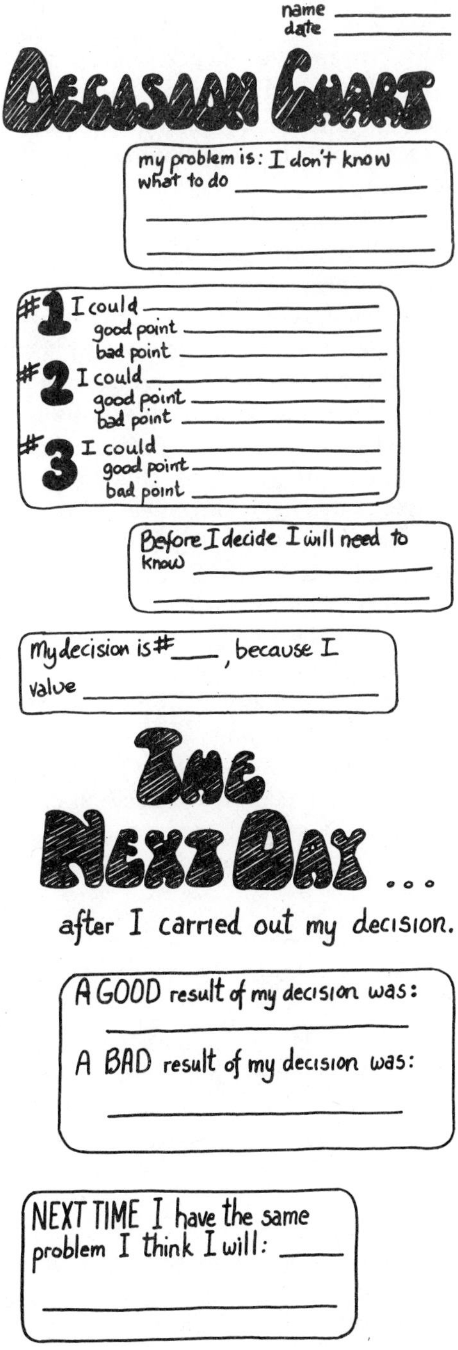

FIGURE 1   A decision chart.

Each of the six sections and exercises can be completed in thirty to forty-five minutes, depending upon the individual child's reading and writing ability. Additional small-group activities can also be incorporated into the training if several children are using the materials at the same time.

When each part of the book has been finished, the child is allowed to color the appropriate area of a success chart, which is prominently displayed in the family room at Learning House. As learning decision-making skills is a valued part of the Learning House treatment program, the child also receives points in the token-economy system for successful completion of each section of the D.M.B.C.

Just acquiring knowledge of the decision-making sequence does not, of course, ensure an improvement in the child's problem-solving ability. To help the child use his newly acquired knowledge of the decision-making process, he is required to complete a decision chart for each of several personal problems as they occur over the succeeding weeks.

TENTATIVE RESULTS

The effectiveness of the D.M.B.C. and the training program for the children at Learning House has been initially evaluated according to the following objectives:

1. After completing the D.M.B.C. the child can demonstrate knowledge of the decision-making sequence by writing all the problem-solving steps in order and drawing a decision chart.
2. After completing the D.M.B.C. the child can demonstrate an improvement in decision-making skills as measured by a significant increase in the number of possible alternative solutions and probable consequences offered in several simulated problem situations.[5]

Knowledge of Decision-Making Steps

Each child completes a written quiz of his knowledge of the problem-solving steps after finishing the D.M.B.C. This procedure requires him to recall each of the important parts in the decision-making sequence and to draw a model of the decision chart. The decision-making sequence on the decision chart includes the following steps: stating the problem, listing choices, indicating good and bad points for each choice, and choosing the best solution for the child. It was expected that if a child had acquired knowledge of the decision-making process, he would score at least 90 percent on the knowledge test. It was found that the children ($n=5$) were able to recall the decision-making sequence with a group average of 90.7 percent. The range of scores was between 80 and 100 percent. In addition, all children could reproduce a decision chart from memory, with at least 90 percent of the major sections included.

Improvement of Decision-Making Ability

In order that we might assess the effect of the knowledge of the decision-making sequence on the children's actual

[5] Anecdotal data have also been gathered on how well each child actually uses the skills in "real life" problems as they occur. However, to date this objective has not been systematically examined.

problem-solving ability, each child responded to two separate simulated problem situations before and after using the D.M.B.C. These hypothetical situations were audiotaped for uniformity and required the child to solve problems faced by a child, either involving guilt for past performance of socially unacceptable behavior or requiring actions to remove himself from a double-bind (avoidance-avoidance) conflict. These stories included ones about finding a lost wallet with money in it, stealing flowers from a neighbor's yard, keeping a friend's baseball when the friend thought it was lost, and setting off firecrackers at school. These problem situations were considered typical but not severe dilemmas for children at Learning House.

The four stories were randomly assigned to each child, with two situations employed in the pretesting and two in the posttesting situation. The group means, standard deviations and t test values are presented in Table 1.

The children demonstrated a significant improvement ($p<.10$) in the number of possible alternative solutions, as well as in the probable consequences for their actions. The mean number of alternatives stated by the children almost doubled (from 4.8 to 7.6). These results are highly tentative, however, for adequate control groups were not available. The data are suggestive at this point that the D.M.B.C. and training program are instrumental in improving decision-making skills.

Some Additional Evidence

To gather additional information on the effects of the D.M.B.C. on a child's actual problem-solving ability, a real problem situation was created for each of the children before and after he had completed the training program. The children were told that the staff "wanted to see how well you can follow directions" when instructed to purchase a specific article for $1 or less (a light bulb, sandpaper, green thread, a notebook, or the like). The children had to choose from numerous articles in the store that fit the descriptions they had received. Each article had several dimensions upon which the child could base his decision (for example, color, shape, cost, quality, "best buy," efficiency). After purchasing their items, the children were asked to list the reasons why they had chosen them, describe the other items that had been available, and state the reasons why they had not chosen any of the other items.

Illustrative of the results of this exercise is the dramatic improvement in the decision-making ability of one

---

TABLE 1   Number of Choices Considered in Simulated Problem Situation

	x	Standard Deviation	t Value
Pretest	4.8	1.48	2.215[a]
Posttest	7.6	1.34	
$n=5$			

[a] $p<.10$.

twelve-year-old boy, Dan. On the pre-test Dan was instructed to purchase "gift ribbon." On his return from the store, however, it was discovered that he had actually purchased blue yarn. When asked if he had had any difficulty in following the directions to purchase gift ribbon, he replied: "No. I had no problem selecting the correct item since blue is my favorite color. There were other colors but they weren't my favorite."

Five weeks later, after Dan had completed the D.M.B.C. and training program, he was again sent to the store, this time to purchase a "note-book." He returned with a spiral note-book and explained that he had chosen the particular notebook because he wanted to buy the type of notebook that the staff wanted, he had seen staff members using a notebook of similar size and shape at Learning House, and the notebook he had chosen had a picture on the cover of two people in love, which he thought the live-in parents would like. It appeared that, unlike Dan's pretest decision, which had resulted in the purchase of the wrong item and was based solely on his own personal preference, his posttest decision had involved consideration of several alternatives, the anticipation of consequences, and the tastes of other people.[6]

This pattern was typical for many of the children at Learning House who

---

[6] *Editors' note:* Anecdotal evidence of this type is appealing but, as the authors recognize, inconclusive. Perhaps Dan placed a higher value on notebooks than ribbons and would have given the same amount of thought to each item if the assignments had been given in reverse order.

participated in the decision-making program. Initial purchases at the store were commonly made for reasons like "It was the first thing I saw, and I was in a hurry," "This is green thread, and that's what you wanted. Green thread is green thread!" "There were no other selections." Decisions made after completing the training program were more frequently made for such reasons as "I wanted to get the best buy for the money," "I bought it [medium-grade sandpaper] because I thought it would sand more than finer grades and that's what you would want," "I bought it because it was better quality."

Anecdotal reports from the residential staff and children at Learning House also contribute information about the effects of the decision-making program:

In an evening "family" group meeting, the children were attempting to solve a family problem affecting all members of Learning House. The group was trying to decide what to do about a rcent increase in the frequency that a few children were running away from the house. One twelve-year-old boy, Don, stated that to solve the problem the group should follow the decision-making sequence. He then outlined each of the steps and asked the children with the problems to complete each step to make a better decision.

In talking with thirteen-year-old Carol about the decision-making materials, she reported that when she had a real problem with a close personal friend, she decided to use the decision chart to help her organize her thoughts and decide what she should do. She said she carried out her decision and reports that it was a successful experience for her. Carol stated that the program has made her think about solving problems and evaluating how her decision worked.

The residential staff has reported that the decision-making sequence is used as a structure to solve personal problems as they occur in the house. The teaching parents frequently refer to the decision-making steps and suggest that the children use the steps to help solve their problems. They report that the sequence gives the children a way of attacking a problem.

Data from this preliminary study are suggestive of the exciting potential offered by explicit self-management training programs for children. The D.M.B.C. and training program have given children at Learning House a decision-making sequence to use with personal problems. As such, it represents a first step in a series of training experiences designed to provide children with self-control competences. Other self-control skills will involve self-observation, self-contracting, and self-modeling.

The utility of self-control training for children that incorporates internal activities like thoughts and perceptions, along with external behaviors, is clearly not limited to Learning House children. Indeed, one of today's most pressing educational needs is to provide self-control training for all students (Glaser, 1972; Mahoney & Thoresen, 1974). Effective self-management by the child offers a method of reducing the often authoritarian institutional management of the children by others and thereby enhances his freedom to decide and to act (Thoresen, 1973).

references

D'Zurilla, T. & Goldfried, M. Problem solving and behavior modification. *Journal of Abnormal Psychology*, 1971, **78**, 107–126.

Glaser, R. Individuals and learning: The new aptitudes. *Educational Researcher*, 1972, **1**, 5–13.

Mahoney, M. F. & Thoresen, C. E. *Self-control: Power to the person.* Monterey, Calif.: Brooks-Cole, 1974.

Russell, M. L. *The decision-making book for children.* Unpublished manuscript, Stanford University, 1974.

Thoresen, C. E. Behavioral humanism. In C. E. Thoresen (Ed.), *Behavior modification in education.* Chicago: University of Chicago Press, 1973. Pp. 385–421.

Thoresen, C. E. & Mahoney, M. J. *Behavioral self-control.* New York: Holt, Rinehart and Winston, 1974.

WITH HIGH-SCHOOL WOMEN

43. EXPERIENCE-BASED CAREER EXPLORATION

JANICE M. BIRK   University of Maryland

Repeated instances of young women coming to the university's counseling center with limited notions about their career options prompted a colleague, Mary Faith Tanney, and me to deal with the question, What can we do to intervene in people's lives so that as young adults they consider the whole range of careers—from traditional to nontraditional? As notions about what is appropriate to consider for a career are fairly firm by late adolescence, we felt the urgency to intervene at an earlier age; thus began the development of a career-exploration program for high-school women.

We intended the program to act as a catalyst for exploration of career goals based on awareness of the influence of sex-role stereotypes on decision making. In a specific way the program was developed to sensitize participants to their acceptance of the *status quo* regarding women's roles, to broaden participants' awareness of *what can be* regarding women's roles, and to explore attitudes that prevent them from moving from the *status quo* to what can be, that is, the *reasons for the gap*.

To achieve these goals several activities that could be scheduled within an average class period were planned. During and following these sessions we envisioned the school counselor (or classroom teacher) as assisting the student in the career exploration vis-à-vis provision of occupational information, value clarification, and decision making.

We conducted the program for volunteer tenth-grade women at a large public high school. Counselors at the school were present for the sessions, thereby facilitating continuing exploration after the program sessions. The sessions were structured so that participants would be active, rather than passive; that is, the program was designed for experience-based, rather than didactic, learning.

THE MODEL

Session 1 (What Is)

Living Careergram (Twenty Minutes). In preparation for session 1 we posted placards around the room. On each placard was lettered the name of an occupation. Some occupational titles represented traditional roles for women (for example, secretary, nurse, teacher, waitress, homemaker), and others represented nontraditional roles (for example, barber, electrician, psychiatrist, college professor). Participants were instructed to mill around the room, to observe the placards, and then to sit below those that approximated what they envisioned themselves doing or training for in five years.

After everyone was seated under one of the posters, the participants shared with one another their reasons for choosing those particular posters. We observed the configuration of the total group in the room. For example, we noted where most people were clustered and which posters were left vacant. We then discussed some inferences based on our observations, like responding to career possibilities as we think society expects us to respond.

Myths and Realities (Thirty Minutes). On an "opinionnaire" comprised of thirteen statements related to women and work, the participants expressed their agreement or disagreement. After everyone had completed the opinionnaire we drew a simple chart on the blackboard in order to plot the number of "I agree" responses for each item. We then explained that the opinionnaire stated commonly held myths about women and work; for each myth we supplied the reality. For example, a *myth* is that women have higher turnover and absenteeism rates than men do; the *reality* is that in numerous studies it has been found that higher turnover and absenteeism rates are related to less rewarding jobs, regardless of sex. By looking at the plotted responses the group could see the extent to which misinformation affected their impressions of working women—and possibly affected attitudes about themselves as workers.

Session 2 (What Can Be)

Group Fantasy (Twenty-Five Minutes). The students, grouped in clusters of five or six, were provided with a written description of a hypothetical situation:

Anne and Alan Johnson have been married for four years and have one child, Jamie, age 2½. They had met while in high school. After he graduated Alan went into the military, and immediately after his discharge he and Anne were married. Currently Alan is a full-time college student and is working part time to supplement the income provided by the G.I. Bill. He is majoring in business, hating it, and recently decided that he wanted to transfer to engineering. With only one year remaining to complete his business degree, switching majors would necessitate another three years in college. Anne, who has not been working since Jamie was born, is quite disappointed. She and Alan had agreed that after he completed college she would enroll in college. If Alan switched to engineering it would mean another postponement of her college plans.

After reading the description, the young women were instructed to complete the story imaginatively, as if it were occurring five years in the future. Each person added something to the fantasy. We moved from group to group, noted the solutions or alternatives generated, and occasionally reminded the total group that it was to be future-oriented, that is, not to be constrained in its fantasizing by today's realities. After all had had time to finish the story, we asked each small group to share its fantasy with the total group. This sharing stimulated discussion of how stereotyped roles for women and for men can close options to both sexes, whereas putting aside stereotyped roles can expand options. By approaching a problem situation through fantasy, participants were encouraged to view career dilemmas through an expanded perspective and with a pool of alternatives that went beyond the attitude, "This is the way things are, and this is the way they'll always be."

Triads (Twenty Minutes) We divided the participants into groups of three. Each member of each resulting triad was to take a turn assuming the role of *speaker, receiver,* and *observer.* The speaker's task was to share her perceptions of the receiver in terms of an unconventional occupation (different from the traditional jobs typically filled by women). For example, "I see you as an airline pilot." Following this the speaker was to give a rationale for her choice: "Because I see you as quite precise, calm. . . ."[1] The receiver's task was to listen to the speaker's comments and then to share her reactions: for example, "I was amazed you suggested that field to me because I sometimes think I'm sloppy about details. . . ." The observer's task was to watch the process and then to share with the speaker and the receiver her perceptions of what had been transacted between them. For example, "You seemed unable to explain clearly why you saw her as an agronomist" or "You didn't seem very happy with her choice of an occupation for you. Were you?"

Approximately five minutes were devoted to each interaction among speaker, receiver, and observer before we instructed the participants to switch roles. In the final five minutes of the activity we solicited reactions to the triadic interaction from the total group. This activity forced the students to thnk of one another in terms of unconventional occupations; thus, career alternatives were broadened. From the occupation suggested to her, along with the concomitant rationale, the receiver obtained positive feedback about strengths that she may not have valued previously.

Session 3 (Reasons for the Gap)

Role Playing (Forty Minutes) After a brief explanation of what is meant by "role playing," we explained how it could sensitize the students to some stereotypes about women, men, parents, counselors, and the like that they might share. We also explained how often we behave according to our own stereotypes, rather than according to the demands of a particular situation. We posited to the group that, when people become aware of how sex-role stereotyping affects them, they have taken the first step toward freeing themselves from the limitations imposed by such stereotyping.[2]

Volunteers were solicited to role-play the following vignettes. First, a female lawyer and her male secretary are discussing his performance, and he has requested a raise (allowing eight minutes); second, a female eleventh-grader is discussing her plans to become an industrial-arts major in college with her parents, her boyfriend, and her high-school counselor (allowing five minutes for each of the three exchanges). If male students or male faculty members are available, they may be invited to assume the male roles within each vignette.

Following the role playing of each vignette, we asked the total group to react in terms of the realism of the scene, the stereotyping they had wit-

---

[1] *Editors' note:* Emphasizing strengths, not weaknesses, would be important.

[2] *Editors' note:* Additional ways to combat stereotypes are described in Article 45.

nessed in mannerisms and dialogue, and the resolution (if any) of the problem. As the role players had portrayed their roles according to how they imagined characters would react in the actual situations, feedback from them was significant. What was it like, for example, to assess a male subordinate's performance and possibly to tell him that you did not believe that he merited a salary increase—particularly when you were probably making four times his salary? Did you feel more inclined to give him an increase than you might feel about giving one to a female secretary? If so, why?

Evaluation (Ten Minutes) A brief evaluation form was distributed in order to assess informally the participants' learning and to calculate their reactions to the total program. After completion of the form, we used it as a vehicle for stimulating verbal reactions from the total group and for soliciting suggestions for program revision.

REACTIONS

The response of the tenth-grade women was generally positive. We could gauge that from the negligible absenteeism rate during the three sessions, numerous requests for occupational information, and the apparent interest and enjoyment with which the participants approached the various activities. Additionally, over half the participants felt that their awareness of the obstacles preventing women from choosing nontraditional careers, of the need to plan immediately for career satisfaction in the future, and of the extent to which others would influence their career decisions had increased. When asked to rank the activities according to what they considered the most interesting, they ranked the role-playing and the triad activities first and second consistently.[3]

My colleague and I also responded positively—although with hindsight we think that a few changes would increase the program's effectiveness. Longer sessions, for example, would facilitate fuller discussion and integration of the activities with the conceptual notions underlying them. With additional time it is more likely that the program's activities will become linked to the participants' personal experiences and that the fun of the activities will be linked with the message of the activities.

Among the informational materials we provided were pamphlets from the Women's Bureau of the U.S. Department of Labor, like "Careers for Women in Conservation," "Why Not Be an Engineer?" and "Why Not Be an Optometrist?"[4] Unlike most career-information resources, these brochures use women and not men as representatives of the careers. More materials of that kind should be accessible to participants; examples of the more com-

[3] A detailed report on the program materials and the research used to evaluate this program is available in a paper presented by J. M. Birk and M. F. Tanney at the National Education Association conference, Warrington, Virginia, in November 1972. Copies of the paper are available upon request from Janice M. Birk, University of Maryland, Counseling Center, College Park, Maryland 20742.

[4] These pamphlets are available from Women's Bureau, U.S. Department of Labor, Washington, D.C. 20020.

mon occupational information (pamphlets depicting only young men as engineers or barbers) can be displayed to highlight the subtle influence of stereotyping in resource materials. We observed that the career materials in the counseling office were almost entirely based on sex-role stereotypes, as were the films used for career exploration. Taking the time and effort to select nonstereotypical occupational information is an important adjunct to an effective program.

Finally, our volunteers were middle-class urban females, and the activities we designed were congruent with their general life experiences; however, for participants from other socioeconomic settings it would be necessary to modify the situations accordingly. The situation described in the group-fantasy activity illustrates an inappropriate stimulus for noncollege-bound participants. Most of the activities, in fact, can be adjusted so that they are appropriately geared to multiple age groups and varying sociological or ethnic groups.

FOLLOW-UP

Several months after the program's completion I asked the school counselor to arrange for me to talk with any two participants. I hoped to obtain some impressions of the program's impact. From both of the young women with whom I spoke, Laura and Ruth, I found that the program had supported career directions that they had been tentatively considering—for Laura speleology and for Ruth veterinary medicine. These women are representative of the not-so-traditional young women who are beginning to consider career options beyond the typical feminine cluster. Both Laura and Ruth had parents who encouraged them to pursue their nontraditional interests; the career-exploration program had become for them yet another support for sustaining their interests. In light of the many discouraging influences on "pioneers" like Laura and Ruth, support systems are crucial to ensure free career choices, rather than "expected" decisions.[5]

An incident recounted by Ruth typifies what she and others like her usually face when acknowledging nontraditional interests. Recently, while taking the family's pet to the veterinarian, she mentioned her plans to become a veterinarian herself. "It's nice that you're thinking about that," he responded, "but there are some things you had better seriously consider. For example, how could you ever give a shot to a cow?" The anecdote reminded me of Rossi's observation (1965) several years ago that more women scientists would be produced if we stopped using the pretext of reality when exploring clients' career options. The extent and manner in which counselors use "reality" to dissuade women from "masculine" careers were particularly evident in Pietrofesa and Schlossberg's research (1971).

[5] *Editors' note:* Care must be taken to ensure that career programs really do promote free choices and do not merely create pressures to make nontraditional choices. Some young women now feel guilty about wanting to be nurses, stewardesses, or housewives. A strong, supportive career program would encourage exploration of both traditional and nontraditional occupations and would not exert pressure to choose either kind.

Career-exploration programs like the one just described are not (and should not be, I believe) intended to steer all women into "masculine" careers. Women, and men as well, do need a climate, however, in which it is possible to consider a wide array of career options and then to have the freedom to make a choice based on their interests, abilities, and values— not on social expectations.

references

Pietrofesa, J. & Schlossberg, N. K. Counselor bias and the feminine occupational role. In N. Glazer-Malbin & H. Y. Walker (Eds.), *Women in the* *society and economy.* Chicago: Rand McNally, 1971.

Rossi, A. S. Women in science: Why so few? *Science,* 1965, **148,** 1196–1202.

WITH COLLEGE STUDENTS

44. TELE-TIP: INFORMATION AND ADVICE ON DEMAND

RAY W. ALVORD AND DAVID L. GALLACHER   Brigham Young University

Tele-Tip was conceived primarily as a result of the study of problems associated with students typically characterized as "below standard" academic performers. Analysis of this group's difficulties (Moses, 1971) suggested that a major two-dimensional problem existed: First, such students frequently lack information about significant policies and procedures in the university, and, second, they tend to be the most reluctant to seek information or assistance that might provide a basis for the prevention of academic problems. Methods of encouraging student use of counseling services through written communications (McGuire & Noble, 1973) and the "crisis line" techniques used at many universities had not satisfied the needs suggested by the nature of the problem. Some evidence suggests that the simple offering of counseling services for the discussion of personal problems is also relatively ineffective (Gelso & McKenzie, 1973).[1]

Recognizing that many of the problems of low achievers are also common to college students in general, we envisioned a new approach to the delivery of information that could potentially influence behavior. The method would have to be designed to satisfy several criteria. First, expert assistance was mandatory. Second, it must cover a broad range of administrative, personal, social and academic areas re-

[1] *Editors' note:* Probably true: Mere discussion of problems is seldom enough to help.

lated to student needs. Third, it should permit confidentiality and total anonymity. Finally, it should be accessible "on demand" to students. The result was Tele-Tip, offering the possibility of directly influencing the behavior of students through telephone advisement.

THE TELE-TIP METHOD

In its simplest sense Tele-Tip provides direct telephone access to a library of expertly prepared tapes, usually three or four minutes long, that respond to a series of direct questions typically asked by students (see Table 1). The tape library initially included sixty-six tapes developed in response to common student questions. The questions most often asked were identified, and then the experts were requested to prepare responses to them. The responses were taped (on cassettes) and then installed in the University Library Learning Resource Center. A designated direct-dial telephone line was obtained and connected to a tape-player console. Lists of the tapes were then widely distributed through the campus community. Students with any of the problems on the list were advised simply to dial the specified telephone number and to request by code numbers the tapes containing the responses to their problems or questions of the moment. Tabulations of requests for each of the tapes were maintained by the library clerk answering the call.

The actual reference file of tapes is limited only by practical considerations and the specificity of questions to be offered through the system. The first listing was deliberately limited. Subse-

quently, the tape file was increased to the 163 separate titles listed in Table 1. The general philosophy followed in preparation of the taped responses was to take a conversational mode as if the individual were in a face-to-face situation, to be brief but complete in providing answers or suggested sets of actions, and to state where (phone, office, person) additional assistance might be obtained.[2] For example, Tape 212, in answer to "How can I get rid of my self-defeating behavior?" includes the following content in a three-and-a-half-minute message:

First of all, let us understand what we mean by a self-defeating behavior. A self-defeating behavior can be any behavior which keeps you from being your best self in a moment of living or that keeps you from achieving your potential as a person. Such behavior might include inferior feelings, depression, sexual behaviors, losing your temper, bad study habits, procrastination, etc. There are many behaviors that are self-defeating, and all of us have one or more.

Let me give you seven steps to help you eliminate one of these behaviors. It is best to work only one behavior for a period of time until you feel you have conquered it. [Seven steps follow in brief detail suggesting a procedure the individual can apply on his own.]

Short three-to-five-week workshops are provided on the B.Y.U. campus at no cost for students and faculty to help you apply these seven steps. In such a workshop you need not divulge to others the

TABLE 1   List of Taped Responses Available Through the Tele-Tip Information System

TELE-TIP 377-1625

Want help on a problem? What to do, where to go, who to see? Tele-Tip assistance is as close as the tip of your finger. For information or help on the questions or problems listed, you can call *Tele-Tip*, 377-1625, from 7:00 A.M. to 10:45 P.M. daily (except Sunday) and receive an immediate answer. Dial 377-1625 and, when the operator answers, simply give the *number* listed to the left of the question or problem of interest to you. A specially prepared tape response to your question will then be played for you. Listen carefully for instructions or supplemental sources of assistance. Hang up when the tape ends. Call again whenever you can use a Tele-Tip on one of the problems listed.

Administrative Potpourri

100   How do I change my major?
101   How do I discontinue all classes after I've registered?
102   The ombudsman: the person to see when no one else will help.
106   What academic standards must I achieve in the University?
108   Do I qualify for an Associate of Arts degree?
109   How do I remove an incomplete or get a grade change on my record?
110   As a veteran, for what benefits am I eligible?
115   What if I've lost my student activity card?

Academic Assistance

100   How do I change my major?
106   What academic standards must I achieve in the University?
107   Suppose my course grade isn't what I expected?
109   How do I remove an incomplete or get a grade change on my record?
126   Repeating failed classes to improve my GPA.
127   What is a CAC? Services and benefits of the College Advisement Center.
128   I'm on academic probation—what happens now?
202   What if personal problems are causing me to fail academically?
203   What help is available if I'm failing academically?
209   How can I relax while taking a test?
216   Help! How can I get personal tutoring in a subject?
220   How can I get control of my time?
226   How can I improve my reading speed?

Registration and Records

Registration
101   How do I discontinue all classes after I've registered?
119   Tips on advance registration.
120   Late registration.
112   Add/drop procedures for classes.

Records
109   How do I remove an incomplete or get a grade change on my record?
122   Keeping my academic record current and correct.
123   How to obtain an end-of-semester/term grade report.
124   How to obtain a transcript of credits.
125   Obtaining credits by examination.

Employment—Now and Later

111   How can I get a job on campus?

TABLE 1   (Cont.)

150 How to prepare for the job interview.
151 Preparing an employment résumé.
152 Using the services of the Placement Center.
384 What about questionable employment practices?

Home Sweet Home
180 How do I resolve a dispute with my landlord?
181 How can I avoid problems that might be encountered in off-campus living?
182 I'm having trouble finding housing. Who can help?
354 Considerations in ending a housing contract.
358 What to look for in a housing contract.
388 What steps can I take if my landlord won't return my security deposit?

Traffic, Cars, Bikes, etc.
103 How do I appeal a traffic ticket on campus?
112 How do I obtain a parking permit?
113 How do I register my vehicle?
114 Where can visitors park on campus?
116 How to obtain a bicycle license.
117 How to register my motorcycle on campus.
118 Obtaining a nonresident permit for an out-of-state vehicle.
386 No fault insurance—what is it? Does it apply to me?
387 What are the traffic court procedures in Provo?
389 I am an out-of-state driver. What driving and license requirements apply to me?

Financial Assistance
Financial Aids
275 Types of financial aid available at BYU.
276 Qualifying for (and borrowing limits under) a BYU student loan.
277 Can I get government loans or grants at BYU?
278 Can BYU help me apply for a student loan from my bank?
279 Financial aids available to law students.
280 Financial aids available to graduate students.
281 Does BYU have scholarships or grants based on financial need?

Scholarships
290 How do I qualify for a scholarship?
291 How and when do I apply for a scholarship?
292 Are BYU scholarships renewable?
801 The Air Force ROTC scholarship program—how to apply.
803 The Army ROTC scholarship program—how to apply.

Personal Questions
Strictly Personal
201 Who can I talk to about my personal problems?
202 What if personal problems are causing me to fail academically?
207 I've never had a date since coming to BYU. What can I do?
208 I am lonely. How can I make friends?
209 How can I relax while taking a test?
210 What can I do about my overweight problem?
211 How can I get rid of a bad habit?
212 How can I get rid of my self-defeating behavior?
213 My spouse and I need help in communicating.

(Table 1, cont.)

214 My friend is talking about suicide. What should I do?
215 Need help relaxing now?
221 How can I deal with my fear of failure?
222 How can I feel more comfortable with the opposite sex?
223 What are some tips on resolving interpersonal conflicts?
224 What can I do if I feel depressed?
225 How can I overcome feelings of inferiority?

Helps and Hints
203 What help is available if I'm failing academically?
204 How should I select a major?
205 I am undecided about a major. What should I do?
206 How can I find out about career alternatives?
216 Help! How can I get personal tutoring in a subject?
217 How can I improve my memory?
218 How can I improve my ability to make decisions?
219 How can I determine what is really important to me?
220 How can I get control of my time?
490 Help for personal or family problems at the Timpanogos Mental Health Center.

The Honor Code and You
301 I know of a violation of the Honor Code. What should I do?
302 What happens if I'm referred to University Standards?
303 What if my roommate leaves unpaid bills?
304 Why dress and grooming at BYU?
305 Hair-length standards confuse me. What is the code for men?
306 Are my rights protected if I'm accused of violating the Honor Code?

The Crime Scene
320 I know of a crime. What should I do?
321 If someone commits a crime against me, what should I do?
322 I am a girl and concerned about my self-protection. What should I do?
323 I know of narcotic or drug activity. What is my responsibility?
324 How can I protect my property from theft?
381 What are my rights if I'm arrested?

Tips to the Consumer
102 The ombudsman: the person to see when no one else will help.
350 If I've had difficulty with a local business, what can I do?
351 When University red tape gets me down, to whom can I turn?
352 Exactly what is "buyer's right to cancel?"
353 What to check in an installment contract.
354 Considerations in ending a housing contract.
355 Buying on credit—the pros and cons.
356 What to do when the salesman calls.
357 Insurance policies: the do's and don'ts.
358 What to look for in a housing contract.
390 Consumer tip of the month from your ombudsman.

Legal Stuff
352 Exactly what is a "buyer's right to cancel?"
380 What legal services are available to students?
381 What are my rights if I'm arrested?

TABLE 1   (Cont.)

382   I'm from out-of-state, living in Provo. What are my rights in Provo?
383   Small claims court: the "people's court."
386   No-fault insurance—what is it? Does it apply to me?
387   What are the traffic court procedures in Provo?
388   What steps can I take if my landlord won't return my security deposit?
389   As an out-of-state driver, what driving and license requirements apply to me?

You and Your Health

General Information
402   What services are available at the health center?
404   How do I make an appointment at the health center?
405   Are student medical records considered to be confidential?
406   How do I obtain ambulance service on campus?
407   What are the services at the urgent care area of the health center?
409   Selecting a physician in a new community.
414   What constitutes a "good" physical exam?

Preparing for Emergencies
214   My friend is talking about suicide. What should I do?
406   How do I obtain ambulance service on campus?
469   If someone has stopped breathing, what can I do?
476   When a person is having a seizure or "fit," what can I do for him?

Health Insurance Plans
410   To what benefits am I entitled under the new health center plan?
411   How are private insurance claims handled?
412   What hospital insurance plan is offered by the University?

Getting the Needle (Immunizations)
420   Do I need flu shots? If so, how many? And when may I have them?
421   Why do I need a series of shots rather than one?
422   What is a "booster" shot?
423   What shots do I need when planning to travel to a foreign country?
424   Why is gamma globulin given to people traveling to certain areas?
425   Why do I have to wait fifteen minutes after receiving an injection?
426   Can I give blood while taking allergy shots?
427   What is rubella?
428   Why shouldn't I get pregnant for the three months after a rubella shot?
429   Who should not receive immunizations?

Premarital Concerns
44   Why a blood test and physical examination before marriage?
441   If I need a premarital examination, how do I make the appointment?
442   How might I seek premarital counseling?

Tell Me Doctor (Medical Problems)
460   What is infectious mononucleosis and how contagious is it?
461   I have a sore throat. What can I do about it?
462   What are the benefits of taking vitamin E?
463   I have a vaginal discharge. Should I see a doctor?
464   I have a very irregular menstrual period. What would you recommend?
465   Would thyroid relieve my fatigue and would it be a useful medication in weight control?
466   Is there a cure for acne?

TABLE 1   (Cont.)

468   I'm dizzy all the time. What can I do about it?
469   If someone has stopped breathing, what can I do?
470   I'm a full-time married student. Can I get maternity care through the health center?
472   I feel so tired all the time. What causes this and what can I do about it?
473   What is hypoglycemia? Who suffers from this disease?
474   How can I prevent high blood pressure?
475   What signs and symptoms indicate a need for an eye exam?
481   Health foods and fad diets.

VD, Drugs, and Medications
471   What is VD? How is it treated?
477   Agencies for the diagnosis and treatment of VD.
478   Is it unsafe to take your roommate's drugs or medications without medical supervision?
479   Drug treatment and referral agencies available in the area.
480   Taking tranquilizers.

Mental Health
490   Help for personal or family problems at the Timpanogos Mental Health Center.

For the International Student

500   What should I do when my visa expires?
501   What should I do when my passport expires?
502   What is "alien registration"?
503   How do I obtain a work permit?
504   How do I qualify for and obtain a practical-training visa?
505   What should I do when planning to leave the United States?
506   How do I change my visa status?
507   What is a "host family"?
508   English in class gives me difficulty. How do I improve?
509   How do I file income tax and obtain a social security refund?

Student Government

General
600   What is "student government" at BYU?
601   How can I participate in student government?
602   How can I run for a student office?

Getting Involved
607   Opportunities for women in student government.
608   Setting up a student-community service project.

Military Officer Programs

800   Opportunities in the Air Force ROTC.
801   The Air Force ROTC scholarship program—how to apply.
802   Opportunities in the Army ROTC.
803   The Army ROTC scholarship program—how to apply.

particular behavior you are trying to eliminate. It is kept confidential. You can sign up for a self-defeating behavior workshop at the Personal Development Center, Room C-273, in the Smoot Administration Building or by calling extension 3035. Workshops can be provided to fit *your* schedule.

DOES IT WORK?

At least three criteria can be used to evaluate the effectiveness of the Tele-Tip approach. First of all, is there a demand on the system? That is, do the students use it? Demand, if continued, suggests that the method is meeting some need. Second, what type of answers are being sought? This reveals to some extent the kinds of needs present in the student community. Finally, do individuals do anything differently as a result of having received information and counseling through access to the telephone tapes? Not all of these criteria can be evaluated yet. However, some preliminary data are rather meaningful.

Table 2 summarizes the demand on the Tele-Tip system during the initial months of operation and immediately following the introduction of the expanded question list. For a 25,000-student university a rather high and sustained level of demand for taped responses to stated problems was achieved. The initial demand was very high, partially because of curiosity. The heaviest demand usually occurred in the late afternoon and evenings (Tele-

Tip is in operation from 7:00 A.M. to 10:45 P.M. six days a week). Approximately 6,000 individual tape requests were received in the first sixty-one days of operation. Some 3,380 requests were made during the first twenty-three days of operation of the expanded list shown in Table 1. An increased demand was normal and expected in view of the large increase in topic listings. The most "popular" topics have been those dealing with personal, medical, or academically related questions.[3] Demand does vary with the timeliness of certain problems and other community events.

Do students change their behavior and act on the basis of information and advice provided in these taped answers? That answer is only partially available,

[3] This pattern might have been predicted. Individuals reluctant to ask personal questions in face-to-face situations may not hesitate to do so when their anonymity is maintained.

TABLE 2   Statistics on Requests by Topic Areas and Times

	Sample Periods		
	November–December 1973	January–February 1974	September 1974
Tapes Available (N)	66	95	163
Topic Areas			
Administrative[a]	15 percent	9 percent	23 percent
Academic assistance	—	—	11 percent
Personal	58 percent	47 percent	36 percent
Honor code	11 percent	5 percent	2 percent
Crime	—	2 percent	1 percent
Personal health	14 percent	34 percent	19 percent
International students	2 percent	3 percent	1 percent
Consumer and legal	—	—	6 percent
Total requests	3,661	2,272	3,380
Days in operation	35	26	23
Average requests per day	105	87	147

[a] Includes various subtopic areas like "Registration and Records," "Financial," "Traffic," "Employment," and "Home Sweet Home."

through a random-sampling procedure (see Table 3). Students tell us verbally that they think the idea is great. They also suggest additional topics. Some 29 percent of those calling indicate that they have made additional contacts suggested in the tape requested. Many of the taped answers provide information or suggest actions that need not involve second parties. Realistically, we recognize that the very design of the system for anonymity of the caller may preclude a thorough analysis of the behavior-change criterion.[4]

Regardless of limitations in achieving a complete assessment, we know that the Tele-Tip system is being *used* by students. Logically, the greater the extent to which correct information and expert advice are disseminated to students, the greater the chances of ap-

propriate behavior on the part of students.[5]

We do note with interest (see Table 3) that one of the major remaining problems in making the system more effective is broader distribution of the list of tapes available through Tele-Tip. The second random survey of students indicated that only 35 percent of the group reported having lists of tapes available for reference—this following the distribution of 20,000 brochures at the time of registration. These data also support an initial indication that students who become aware of a system like this and use it tend to use it again. Continued evaluation and development of the Tele-Tip approach will focus on analysis of the list of problems to be offered, continued dissemination of the tape list throughout the student community, and accumulation of data on the third and most critical criterion of effectiveness—does it lead to changed behavior on the part of the students who use it?

[4] *Editors' note:* Possibly. One strategy may be to select a few students who acknowledge using Tele-Tip and carefully to examine their behavior relevant to the problem area for which they requested help. Another strategy would be to see whether the addition or deletion of tapes on selected topics increases or decreases the frequencies of certain problem behaviors associated with those topics.

[5] *Editors' note:* The authors are to be congratulated for not relying on logic alone, however. Results gathered empirically often defy "logic."

TABLE 3   Results of Survey of Student Awareness and Use of Tele-Tip

	April 1974	*October 1974*
N Sampled	100	196
Reported some awareness of the system (purpose, and so on)	63 percent	64 percent
Knew of someone who had used it	25 percent	28 percent
Had used it personally	18 percent	25 percent
Percentage of those using the system who initiated a follow-up contact or actions as a result of information given	—	29 percent
Had a list of tapes available for reference	25 percent	35 percent

references

Gelso, C. J. & McKenzie, J. D. Effect of information on students' perception of counseling and their willingness to seek help. *Journal of Counseling Psychology*, 1973, **20**, 406–411.

McGuire, J. M. & Noble, F. C. Motivational level and response to academic encouragement among low-achieving college males. *Journal of Counseling Psychology*, 1973, **20**, 425–430.

Moses, D. (Ed.) Improving academic performance. Unpublished manuscript, Academic Standards Office, Brigham Young University, 1971.

45.   CAREER GUIDANCE IN THE COMMUNITY COLLEGE

JEFF FERGUSON   Moorpark College

The counseling and guidance faculty at Moorpark College started to work on career education with the results of college research and a needs-assessment survey for guidance. Like students in many community colleges, our students vary markedly in age. The mean age of our population, almost evenly balanced between sexes, is twenty-two years; slightly more than one fourth of our students are over thirty years of age. Even though our average student is several years past high-school graduation, our continuing research has yielded some remarkable findings. Although not conclusive, our tabulations indicate that more than 75 percent of all entering students expressed desire to enroll in a transfer program (to a four-year institution) and that fewer than 20 percent actually transferred. Also approximately 55 percent of our population had undeclared or undecided majors. Our needs-assessment survey, in conjunction with county high-school polls, indicated a clear demand for career education.

STRATEGIES FOR INTERVENTION

As a direct method of intervention we offer group guidance classes for our main target population: the "undecided" student.[1] These classes, modified after field testing, enable students to explore career, educational, and personal alternatives through the use of structured exercises and self-assessment instruments. An integral part of this experience is learning and using decision-making skills. Secondary target populations include those who have made tentative career decisions and seek more information or want to validate or test decisions.[2]

[1] *Editors' note:* "Decided" students should not be overlooked. Some of them may need more help than the "undecided" students because they may have arrived at their "decisions" without learning how to make them wisely. If the goal of a career-guidance program is to teach the decision-making *process,* then candidates for learning *how* to make decisions could come from both "decided" and "undecided" groups.

[2] *Editors' note:* Good.

Supplementing direct service to individuals in groups, we use various media as means of intervention. Our career center, containing a large library of mixed-media career information, has a classroom for guidance groups and offices for counselors and a paraprofessional. Working with a receptionist and student helpers, our center staff actively publicizes many services, like guest speakers and career films.

Consultation and training are yet another method of intervention. Here our target is members of other institutions and communities whom we engage in workshops, conferences, conventions, and visits in order to share our approach to career guidance. An additional part of this training comes from our published career-development workbook, a leader's guide, and a student journal for guidance classes (Ferguson, 1974).[3]

The purpose of using direct service and media as intervention methods is both remedial and preventive, whereas consultation and training serve a developmental purpose. Both the guidance classes and the career center serve those students and community members who have made, or may be making, personally inappropriate career decisions. Also, both methods enable them to acquire the skills needed to plan career decisions.

[3] Readers may order *The Career Guidance Class* from Walter T. Metcalf and Associates, 2034 Ciprian Avenue, Camarillo, California 93010. The cost is $5.50 a copy, which includes postage and handling (California residents add 6 percent sales tax).

GUIDANCE CLASSES

We want our students to become aware of and to explore the many dimensions of career choice and to learn the planning skills necessary to act on their goals. For these reasons, we discarded some of the traditional tools of vocational guidance: we do not use test batteries, nor do we rely exclusively on career libraries, expecting information to "teach"; we also do not attempt to "fit" a person to a job. Instead, we systematically examine the major components of career development. We explore career choice holistically—integrating career, educational, and personal alternatives in consideration of individual values.

We explore the process of career development in eight-week classes. Given a limited counseling staff, the duration of our groups enables us to serve twice as many students as the normal full-semester class. We limit class size to fifteen students, and our total contact time, excluding one-to-one counseling, is twenty-four hours per group. Of course, group size and duration may be altered.

First Week

In the initial period, we cover introductions, expectations, a career-development model, self-awareness of values, and career resources. Because our groups are listed in a schedule with other college classes, the group members are often strangers to one another. Given our setting, we do not conduct systematic pregroup interviews; however, during academic counseling or through the catalogue or other publicity (counseling brochures or newspaper announcements), students may select themselves as appropriate group members. Our first task is to become acquainted. There are a variety of ways to do this. One successful "ice breaker" that we use is the name game. One volunteer states his name and the name of the person next to him; the next person names himself and the two people who preceded him. This process continues, with the number of people named increasing by one each time until all have been named. Then we do an exercise we call "pairing." We ask people to mill about the room and to select partners whom they do not know. Then each pair takes a few moments to become acquainted. Afterward, we share what we have learned about our partners in the large group.

We then move to a discussion of expectations. We ask the students, "Why are you here?" or "What do you expect to accomplish by the end of this group?" This is a critical part of the group process. Lacking pregroup interviews, the counselor can now hear the expectations of each group member. Occasionally, a student wants something magical to occur (for example, "Tell me what job I'm best suited for" or "What jobs can I count on being there when I graduate?"). This is the time verbally to reinforce those behaviors (stated expectations) appropriate to the metagoal of the group and to begin shaping inappropriate behaviors (like unrealistic expectations) toward attainable goals. Also at this time we review some guiding principles for group behavior, like tolerance of individual differences and confidentiality.

As a starting point for career exploration, we begin by reviewing the objectives of the career-development model (Cunha, 1972), reproduced in Ferguson (1974). This serves to clarify some basic facts or truths about the process vital to career choice.

We then introduce group members to the concept of values. There are many ways to learn about values. In planning the class, we decided to avoid simulated experiences when possible and to emphasize exercises with personal applicability. One such exercise is called "occupational status." We present students with an alphabetical list of fifteen occupations (randomly selected to cover a variety of work settings, salaries, education or training required, and so on). We ask them to rank these occupations according to their personal standards of status or prestige. Next, we ask them to reach consensus (subgroups five to seven) on ranking the occupations. We then compare and contrast individual with individual, individual with group, and group with group rankings. Clearly, there are many questions to examine in such a discussion. Such questions might include: "What is a value?" "What values emerge as being important to you?" "How are the differences we find applicable to career choice?" Throughout the classes, through similar exercises, members learn to examine their values and, in the process of making decisions, learn to formulate priorities based on these examinations.

Beside discussions centered on the components of career choice, group members complete a number of paper-and-pencil instruments. Most of these are contained in a journal or student workbook[4] designed to enable the student to proceed systematically through the awareness-accommodation-action levels of the career-development model. One such entry follows.

I Am, I Said
I want _____.
I need _____.
Three words I would like said about me:
_____ _____ _____.
I am proud of _____.
I would like to change _____ about myself.
One thing I can do which I couldn't do a few years ago is _____.
If all goes poorly in the next five years, I will be doing _____.
If things go well in the next five years, I will be doing _____.

We use this exercise to explore the relation of self-concept to career choice. Also, on the first day we administer a questionnaire as a pretest measurement of objectives.

Second Week

We continue to examine values and start to look at the function of decision making (thinking about decisions, taking responsibility for decisions, and limitations on decision making). We may begin by reviewing the previously completed journal entries from the student workbooks. These entries are kept by each student for future personal reference; they may be used in individual counseling, or students may want to share their responses with the group.

[4] The journal or student workbook may be reproduced from *The Career Guidance Class* with the written consent of the publisher.

Some of the entries are designed for group use. For example, one exercise we use to examine personal values and personal decision-making strategies is entitled "What, What, What." We ask students three questions: "What have you always wanted to do in your life?" "What's keeping you from it?" and "What action can you take in the next year to accomplish your goals?" A typical response might be "Travel," "Time and money," "Save more money." The exercise yields data about personal priorities which are frequently stated as very general goals. This provides an opportunity to shape certain behaviors —in particular, the ability to move from a general statement of goals to specific statements of clearly defined objectives. Thus, we reinforce the behaviors (stated goals or objectives) that are appropriately specific.

At this stage, we begin to examine the differences between critical decisions and lesser ones. A valuable source of information in the decision-making process is a consideration of limitations. Some limitations are personal, like ability or willingness to consider a particular goal; others are societal, like racism or sexism. There are a variety of ways to examine these limiting factors on personal decision making. For example, one way we look at sexism is through a list we call "It's a Man's World." Sample statements from this list are:

Hire him; he's got great legs.
Occupation: "Househusband."
Blondes have more brains.
Behind every successful woman, there's a good man.
Charles, have you figured out how you can combine a career and marriage?

Introducing your husband: "Meet the little man."

Our deodorant is mild enough for a man yet strong enough for a woman.

I'd like you to meet Mrs. and Mr. Alice Turner.

You've taken the solemn vows—I now pronounce you woman and husband.

In addition to a group focus on limitations, individual counseling may be an appropriate supplemental tool.

Third Week

In the third week we begin to focus on self-assessment as it is related to work. Consistent with the goals of the group, we instruct the students that self-assessment instruments can be useful in confirming some things for themselves, suggesting career areas to explore, raising questions not previously considered, and providing systematic means of examining personal data. Because group members commonly view such instruments as "tests," which somehow magically help to select "best" or "most suitable" careers, we reiterate the goals of the group consistent with exploring developing career choices. All the instruments we use, whether purchased from a publisher or developed by us, are "self-scored" by each group member. This method helps to remove the mystery and stigma of "testing" and enables a student to see how his responses to each question determine the final summary data of a self-assessment instrument.

Among the instruments we use is the "Work Values Inventory" (Super, 1968). This tool enables the user to organize his values as they are related to career preferences. Another exercise

we use to explore values asks the question, "Why work at all?" For this exercise, we instruct group members to suppose that each of them had a guaranteed tax-free income of $2,000 a month for life. Questions like "How would you use your time?" "Why would you choose such activities?" and "What personal values and/or needs would you be fulfilling?" help group members order their personal priorities.

Fourth Week

Building on previous group work, we introduce a decision-making model in the fourth week. When we first use the model, we call it "A Tentative Career-Related Decision," for several reasons: First, career development is a continuous, life-long process; second, we cannot realistically expect definite career choices from our limited intervention; and, third, we know that other important decisions (for example, on marriage or education) may be related to career decisions. Therefore, even though a decision may be tentative and not career-specific, it is still possible to shape exploratory career behavior. The decision-making model gives the student a specific tool to use in working through the steps leading to some goal-related action. The action is defined by the group member in conjunction with the counselor and is stated as a clear objective.

A Tentative Career-Related Decision
Decision: State a tentative career-related decision.
Alternatives: What are your alternatives? List at least five.

Information: List the information you need for each alternative.
Outcomes: What are the expected outcomes for each alternative? What might you gain? What might you lose?
Plan of Action: What action do you plan to take now?

Action:
Conditions:
Amount:

For most group members, this guide represents the first systematic approach to considered decision making. Because they are acquiring new skills, we plan a variety of associated learning activities. First, we model the use of the decision-making strategy in a simulated case. Then we select an appropriate group member as a live model. And we divide into subgroups, using all group members as teacher-learner models.

Fifth Week

We continue to review the decision-making process in the fifth week, introducing career-planning clusters and educational alternatives. By this time, group members have worked through the decision-making model at least once and have formulated plans of action. Having acquired earlier awareness of career clusters or fields, they now learn to act on this information by means of the "Self-Directed Search" (Holland, 1970). This instrument is designed to direct a career search toward one or more fields. Students add these results to sheets summarizing the major self-assessment instruments used in the group. Combining this information with the other journal entries gives group members a systematic means of

focusing on particular career fields. Much of the remaining group time is spent gathering, analyzing, and using occupational information in the career center.

Sixth Through Eighth Weeks

Group members now have a variety of data and skills to enable them to be more specific about career alternatives. Several guides are useful tools toward this end: For example, "Getting Helpful Information" and "An Occupation and I" (Stewart, 1969) and a mini-interview serve as models for career investigation.

A Mini-Interview
What do you like most about your job and why?
What do you like least about your job and why?
How did you decide to get into this field and what steps did you take to enter the field?
What personal qualities do you feel would be most important in your work and why?
If you had it to do over, would you make the same career choice? Why?

In the final sessions, group members work in the career center and convene in a group room to review their individual career development. During the last meeting students complete the posttest and anonymously evaluate the counselor and course content.

MEASUREMENT OF OBJECTIVES

As a means of evaluating the effectiveness of our intervention, we administer a questionnaire before and after the course in order to measure attainment of our objectives. Basically, the questionnaire asks students to rate themselves on a 6-point scale. The pre- and postcourse means, based on a sample of 296 students, are shown below.[5]

[5] *Editors' note:* Evaluating the attainment of decision-making competences is difficult. Self-ratings are one method. Other methods are described in Article 46. Some innovative thinking and careful evaluation will be needed to develop still better assessments of decision-making skills.

An assessment of self-reported outcomes indicates that we are achieving some of our objectives. All but one of the items revealed a positive change. There was a marked increase in the abilities to identify and rank values; to identify, formulate, and act on decisions (goals); and to state goals as clear, attainable objectives formulated as plans of action. As counselors search for systematic means to improve decision-making skills, some of the methods reported here may be useful.

How would you *rate your ability*?

| 1. Don't know | 2. Poor | 3. Fair |
| 4. Good | 5. Very good | 6. Excellent |

	Before	After	Difference
1. To identify and rank your values?	3.5	4.7	+1.2
2. To identify your interests?	4.8	5.3	+0.5
3. To appraise your abilities or compentencies?	4.2	4.5	+0.3
4. To identify, formulate, and act on decisions that are important to you?	4.2	5.2	+1.0
5. To identify, formulate, and act on your career goals?	3.2	5.0	+1.8
6. To identify, formulate, and act on your personal goals?	2.7	5.2	+2.5
7. To identify, formulate, and act on your educational goals?	3.8	5.5	+1.7
8. To generate and consider alternatives for a decision important to you?	4.3	4.7	+0.4
9. To gather and appraise information for a decision important to you?	4.3	4.3	0.0
10. To weigh the consequences or outcomes of various alternatives you would consider for an important decision?	4.2	5.0	+0.8
11. To state your goals as clear, attainable objectives?	2.8	5.0	+2.2
12. To formulate a plan of action to activate your important decisions?	3.7	5.3	+1.6
13. Every occupation is related to some other occupations by some similarities; this relation is referred to by "career clusters," "job families," or "fields." For whatever occupation(s) you have considered or are considering, how would you rate your ability to recognize and describe various other	3.7	4.3	+0.6

occupations in your considered career
cluster or field?

14. In any field, or group of simliar   3.3   4.2   +0.9
careers, there are various *levels*
of specialization, and there are
several *entry routes* to different
occupations. For whatever occupation(s)
you have considered or are considering,
how would you rate your ability to
identify levels and entry routes for
your considered field?

references

Cunha, J. Career development: A California model for career guidance curriculum K-adult. *California Personnel and Guidance Association Monograph*, 1972, No. 5. (ED 075 672)

Ferguson, J. (Ed.) *The Career Guidance Class.* Camarillo, Calif.: Metcalf, 1974.

Holland, J. *Self-directed search.* Palo Alto: Consulting Psychologists Press, 1970.

Stewart, N. Exploring and processing information about educational and vocational opportunities in groups. In J. D. Krumboltz & C. E. Thoresen (Eds.), *Behavioral counseling: Cases and techniques.* New York: Holt, Rinehart and Winston, 1969. Pp. 56–61.

Super, D. *Work values inventory.* Palo Alto: Houghton Mifflin, 1968.

ASSESSMENT

46. *EVALUATION OF PROBLEM-SOLVING COMPETENCE*

G. BRIAN JONES   American Institute for Research, Palo Alto, California

One of the main goals of the counseling and guidance movement in the United States, and perhaps of the educational system generally, is to develop the personal decision-making or problem-solving abilities of its clients (Rothney, 1958; Gelatt, 1962). Such problems involve decisions that were once relatively simple but are now quite complex (for example, choice of an occupation), as well as new decisions that must be confronted (for example, how to increase leisure time). Lack of ability to perform the behaviors required in problem situations invariably leads to ineffective behavior (D'Zurilla & Goldfried, 1968). As the possible results of inadequate problem-solving competence are examined, it is understandable that assisting individuals in learning how to solve problems wisely is advocated as a priority goal for counseling (Krumboltz, 1967).

The cognitive process and the overt behaviors manifested by individuals in problem-solving situations are learned. In fact, as Skinner (1953) and Brim and his colleagues (1962) have observed, the problem-solving behaviors that now appear to be habitual responses probably have been learned in earlier problem-solving contexts. Training and evaluating overt problem-solving behaviors may be an effective and efficient strategy for improving what individuals actually do in problem situations. Such an approach contrasts with other strategies for direct intervention in cognitive processes based on the questionable assumption that cognitive training and assessment will also result in desirable changes in overt behaviors.[1]

PROBLEM-SOLVING SKILLS

What behaviors are requisite to effective personal problem solving? A multitude of conceptualizations and models of problem-solving phenomena is available (for example, Dewey, 1933; Polya, 1945; Simon, 1957). Such descriptions have been based on the results of research or logic. The problem-solving paradigm in Table 1 represents an attempt to systematize common problem-solving factors reported in the literature. This paradigm serves as a framework upon which our efforts at evaluating problem-solving competence have

---

[1] *Editors' note:* Perhaps the best strategy is to focus on both "cognitive" and overt behaviors. For example, teaching people to talk to themselves differently (as in self-instruction) can be very helpful in reducing problem situations. See articles 9, 37, and 55 for examples of how to change covert behaviors.

been based. Though the behaviors are grouped into skill areas, no inference is made that these areas represent steps in problem solving or an optimal sequence of responses.

Considerable controversy has developed over whether the focal point of problem-solving training and evaluation should be the process or the product of that process. Bross (1953) suggests that the criterion for judging good or bad problem solving is pragmatic (What is the outcome of the decision? Did it work?). Leaning more toward a process orientation, Gelatt (1962) states that a good decision is one for which the decider has considered the alternatives and is willing to accept the consequences. Halpern (1967) makes a cogent case for examining problem solving in terms of its process.

It is unnecessary to pledge allegiance to either side of the controversy. Measures of problem-solving effectiveness can include assessment of both process behaviors and the products of such behaviors.

EVALUATION OF GENERAL PROBLEM-SOLVING SKILLS

A major difficulty in problem-solving research and training is the development of assessment instruments. Outlined here are three instruments that we have developed for one problem-solving skill. Space limitations preclude description of an experimental study in which we employed these instruments, but the interested reader may wish to consult Nelson and Jones (1969).

TABLE 1   Paradigm for Problem Solving

General Process Skills	*Specific Problem-Solving Behaviors Grouped by Behavioral Skill Areas*

A. *Planning Emphasis*—decision-making and performance activities involved are in these problem-solving behaviors but the emphasis is upon using a planned approach to understanding the problem and gathering information on it in order to expedite subsequent problem-solving activities.	1. Perceiving, delineating, and commiting to work on, the problem.
	  a. Perceiving a personal problem when it exists.
	  b. Inhibiting the tendency to respond impulsively, passively, or by avoiding the problem.
	  c. Stating the conditions that would exist if the problem were resolved.
	  d. Specifying discrepancies between current personal status and those levels that would exist if the problem were resolved.
	2. Searching for, evaluating, and utilizing the information.
	  a. Formulating a strategy for searching for information relevant to the problem.
	  b. Knowing and evaluating sources of information.
	  c. Efficiently utilizing the sources of information.
	  d. Evaluating the reliability and accuracy of information received and its relevance to the problem.
	  e. Being willing to consider new information relevant to the problem even when it conflicts with that presently held.

B. *Decision-Making Emphasis*—planning and performance activities are involved in these problem-solving behaviors. Planning skills are ones which are particularly important following the decision-making activities implemented here.	3. Generating and considering multiple alternative problem solutions.
	  a. Generating several viable courses of action or alternative solutions to the problem.
	  b. Knowing possible outcomes associated with each alternative.
	  c. Calculating the subjective and objective probabilities of each outcome's occurrence.
	  d. Using some personal standards or criteria for determining the desirability of possible outcomes.
	  e. Considering each alternative in light of the information gathered on its possible outcomes and in relation to the conditions that would exist if the problem were resolved.
	4. Selecting the most desirable alternative problem solutions and formulating plans for implementing these alternatives.

TABLE 1   (Cont.)

a. Knowing and considering various rules or philosophies for selecting an alternative problem solution.

b. Selecting a preferred alternative problem solution to be implemented and knowing the rationale for the choice of this alternative.

c. Selecting, and knowing the rationale for the selection of, a second alternative problem solution to be used in case certain contingencies arise thwarting implementation of the first choice alternative.

d. Detailing a plan for carrying out the preferred alternative problem solution.

e. Knowing some conditions under which the second alternative problem solution might be implemented.

C. *Implementation Emphasis*—activities here involve what has been referred to as "student managed performance." However, decision making (relative to evaluating one's problem-solving behavior) and planning (relative to revising or changing plans for implementation) are both involved in these activities.

5. Implementing specific plans related to selected alternatives.

a. Until such time as other plans appear more appropriate, exhibiting the behaviors necessary to implement the plan for the chosen alternative.

b. Correctly judging whether the plan of implementation should be modified, or replaced with a plan for implementing the second choice or other alternative.

c. Implementing a plan for the second or other alternative as a result of information collected while acting on the preferred alternative.

6. Analyzing the process and product of problem solving.

a. Ascertaining if the problem has been satisfactorily solved by comparing present conditions with those previously specified for problem solution.

b. In terms of the model presented here, analyzing the positive and negative aspects of the behaviors emitted during the problem-solving process.

c. In terms of the previously specified conditions for problem solution, analyzing the positive and negative aspects of the solution and the results of the problem-solving process.

d. Knowing what has been learned (i.e., principles and techniques) that will be of help in future problem contexts.

e. Applying these principles and techniques to future problems when appropriate.

Evaluating the Ability to Generate and Consider Alternatives

The problem-solving skill that we selected for our first training and evaluation efforts was the generation and consideration of alternative solutions (or courses of action) before selecting one for implementation. Example behaviors are included in Table 1 under category 3.

We developed two simulation instruments for assessing client behaviors in relation to this skill. Simulations have at least two advantages. First, the problem situations to which clients are exposed can be standardized, and, second, the problems are of a real-life type. The second simulation presented here has an additional advantage in that the problem situation is somewhat individualized because each subject selects a hypothetical individual to assist him with one of his own personal problems. Behaviors exhibited in these simulations are objectively quantifiable and thus amenable to statistical analysis.

Hypothetical Problem Situation. Seated in a semidarkened room, clients are given oral and written instructions and a sheet describing briefly thirty-two slides that are available in envelopes on a nearby table.[2] They are informed that, when the projector is switched on, they will be confronted with a description of a problem situation facing a hypothetical student, Jerry, and that they will be allotted ten minutes to decide on a solution to Jerry's problem.

[2] The set of thirty-two slides can be purchased at cost for approximately $16.08 by writing to Director, Youth Development Research Program, American Institutes for Research, P.O. Box 1113, Palo Alto, California 94302.

They are informed that, in order to assist them in arriving at a decision, their "Instruction Sheet and Slide Program" describes a number of slides providing information that might be useful in arriving at a solution to Jerry's problem. The slides are placed in categories, and each presents a statement describing Jerry's interests, abilities, values, and background experiences; available activities in which Jerry could participate; several alternative courses of action that could be taken; and several consequences that could result from each alternative action. Each category of slides is placed in a separate envelope on a nearby table. Clients are allowed to select as many slides, in any order, as they wish and use as much of the ten minutes as they need.

Trained observers record the following for each client. First is the number of slides presenting possible solutions to the problem viewed (this measure is accepted as an indication of the number of alternatives to which they have given some consideration). Second is the emphasis (or degree of attention) given to slides in the "alternative" category (a ratio of the number of seconds spent viewing alternative slides to the total number of seconds spent viewing all available slides, multiplied by the number of alternative slides viewed). Third is the number of slides viewed from the "outcome" category; by reviewing an "alternative" slide found inside each information envelope, a client learns about a specific alternative solution to the problem, but he has to open at least one other package within the same information envelope to learn about the possible outcomes of that alternative. Fourth is the emphasis (or degree of attention) given to the consideration of outcomes (a ratio of the number of seconds spent viewing slides from the outcome category to the total number of seconds for all slides, multiplied by the number of outcome slides). Finally, the problem solution selected is recorded; of the six alternative solutions to the problem, three are deliberately structured to be more appropriate, based on the information available.

Personal Problem Situation. In this second situation clients are given oral and written instructions telling each of them to think of a problem that he currently is facing. The problem should be of real importance; for example, it might be related to something the client wants to achieve, like overcoming an undesirable behavior. The key task in this simulation is the selection from any array of alternative hypothetical people the one the subject feels would most like to assist him in solving this personal problem.

Information on each of six hypothetical individuals is placed in a series of five packets.[3] Inside one of these five packets is a photograph of the individual; the other packets each contain a tape cartridge providing information on the hypothetical individual's interests, values, abilities, and background (previous significant experiences and future plans). A general description of each hypothetical individual is also provided.

Observer records in this simulation yield measures of the number of hypo-

[3] A booklet containing information and the photographs contained in these packets can be purchased at cost for approximately $1.00 from Director, Youth Development Research Program, American Institutes for Research, P.O. Box 1113, Palo Alto, California 94302.

thetical individuals about whom each client samples some information (providing an indication of the number of alternatives considered) and the emphasis (or degree of attention) that each client gives to each alternative. For the latter measure, a score is obtained by assigning 5 points to each client's first information selection from each alternative available, 4 points to a second selection from the same alternative, and so forth. Through this weighting procedure, both the breadth and depth of selections are rewarded. For this instrument, the final choice is not scored, for there are no "correct" responses.

Evaluating the Need for Training in Problem Solving

The "Checklist for Solving Problems in Real Life" is composed of twelve statements describing personal problem-solving behaviors. It is reproduced in Figure 1. It is designed to assess clients' needs and desires for training in effective problem-solving behaviors. They decide whether or not statements 1–10 accurately reflect their usual problem-solving behaviors. If they do, they place check marks in the column labeled "True"; if not, they check the column marked "False." The statements are counterbalanced so that a "true" response sometimes denotes a desirable and at other times an undesirable personal problem-solving behavior. Statements 1–10 on this instrument are designed to reflect whether or not the subject typically exhibits behavior in each of the six skill areas of problem solving (listed in Table 1) when he attempts to solve his own personal problems.

Statements 11 and 12 give each client an opportunity to express in two ways a desire to receive training in effective personal problem solving. In response to statement 11, they can express an interest in general improvement of their problem-solving behavior, whereas in response to statement 12, they can make a specific request for training in the behaviors mentioned in statements 1–10. Each client's responses to these statements before and after exposure to the various training experiences are examined for changes in his self-reports of personal problem-solving behaviors and changes in his requests for assistance (that is, responses to statements 11 and 12). Clients are also asked to circle the number of each statement specifying behavior with which they want help. On the first of these two measures, it is expected that training should increase the number of problem-solving behaviors that clients claim to perform. Training should reduce the assistance requests recorded in the second measure.

Directions: This is not a test. The purposes of this checklist are to find out how high school students solve problems in their personal lives and to discover if students would like help in learning how to solve these problems better. We are talking not about math or science problems, but rather about personal problems that come up from time to time in your life such as:

1. what courses to take next year
2. how to meet new friends
3. what vocation to select
4. how to get along better with your fellow students.

STEP 1   On the reverse side of this page, sign your name in the space provided and circle your present grade level. We need this information so that we can provide help in solving problems to the students who want it.

STEP 2   Read each of the statements on the reverse side of this page. These statements describe how people sometimes go about solving problems. Read each statement carefully. Then do the following:

STEP 3   If you usually do the behavior described when you solve problems in your life or the statement describes how you feel, place a check mark ($\checkmark$) in the column marked "True" to the right of that statement.

If you do not do the behavior described when you solve problems in your life or the statement does not describe how you feel, place a check mark ($\checkmark$) in the column marked "False" to the right of that statement.

For example, read statement one. If you usually do consider many different ways to solve a problem before trying to solve it, you would make a check mark ($\checkmark$) in the column marked "True." However, if you usually do not consider many different ways to solve a problem before trying to solve it, you would check the column marked "False."

FIGURE 1   Checklist for solving problems in real life. (This material was prepared under Contract #OEG-0-8-70109-3530(085), Research Project #7-0109, with the Office of Education, U.S. Department of Health, Education and Welfare, May 1969.)

(Figure 1, cont.)

STEP 4 As you make a check mark for each statement, circle the number of every statement that describes a behavior you'd like to improve. For example, read statement number one again. If you'd like to learn how to consider many possible solutions to a problem, circle number one, after you place the check mark in one of the answer columns.

Remember now that this is not a test.

Be honest and careful in making your answers. Your answers are confidential. They will be used to help students like you. Be sure to sign your name on the line on the reverse side of this page. This way your counselors and teachers will know which students would like help.

Begin now. Be sure to answer all the statements.

YOUR NAME _____ Grade (circle one)   9   10   11   12

Read each statement carefully. Place a check mark in the appropriate column.

	True	False
1. When solving a problem, I usually do consider many different possible solutions to it.		
2. I usually do not not have a good method or strategy that I use to look for possible solutions to the problems that come up in my life.		
3. After solving a problem, I usually do study the method I used to solve it (in order to learn from my experience).		
4. When trying to solve a problem I usually do not know how to tell if a piece of new information I find will help me in solving my problem.		
5. When I've decided on a plan for solving a problem, I do not figure out exactly what needs to be done to carry out the plan.		
6. I usually do know about and consider the possible results, good and bad, of each possible solution to my problem.		
7. I usually do not know how to find information which will help me solve a problem.		
8. I usually do not decide what things I want in a solution to a problem; that is, I do not know how to tell a good solution from a bad one.		
9. I usually do not know how to define a problem; that is, I usually do not know exactly what the problem is.		
10. I usually do pick out a second way to solve a problem to use in case something goes wrong with my first solution.		
11. I do want to learn how to solve my personal problems better.		
12. I do want to learn how to do all the problem-solving behaviors talked about in these statements.		

Do not forget to circle the number of each statement that described a behavior you would like to improve.

EVALUATION STRATEGIES IN TWO SKILL AREAS OF A TRAINING PROGRAM

As we focused on the development of a "Program for Effective Personal Problem Solving" (PEPPS) for high-school students, we had to design strategies for use in the evaluation of preliminary drafts of our training materials and procedures.[4] In their orientation materials for PEPPS, students are told:

The first step in developing this program involved finding out what people who are good problem solvers do. It was found that they seem to have skills in six areas and that these can be applied to most personal problems. Each of the six general skills which are important in personal problem solving is made up of several more specific behaviors. These skill areas are briefly described here. Later in the program you will get a separate booklet for each skill area, which will show you how to get that skill if you have not already learned it, and how to use it in solving a personal problem.

After their introduction to the six skill areas summarized in Table 1 students

are helped to identify the areas on which they should work, and then they are given access to materials and activities in priority areas. Resources for each area include an explanation of the behaviors that the skill area entails, examples of students performing these behaviors, exercises to help students practice these behaviors, a simulated problem that the students are asked to solve using the most effective behaviors they know, and an opportunity to apply such behaviors to personal problems that they select. A placement test helps students to assess themselves in order to identify skills on which they should work.

Program resources for two of the six PEPPS areas have been pilot-tested. Students' subjective reactions to each performance objective, instructional or counseling procedure, and item of the learning materials were collected. In addition, unanticipated side effects were recorded from student comments written on the PEPPS materials and verbalized during individual interviews. These data were examined for constructive suggestions that would improve the program.[5]

---

[4] The "Administrators Manual" and the "Student Orientation Booklet" for this program can be purchased at cost for approximately $5.50 from Director, Youth Development Research Program, American Institutes for Research, P.O. Box 1113, Palo Alto, California 94302.

[5] The brief report of this study is entitled "PEPPS Field Test Summary." It can be purchased at cost for approximately 50 cents from Director, Youth Development Research Program, American Institutes for Research, P.O. Box 1113, Palo Alto, California 94302.

references

Brim, O., Glass, D. E., Lavin, D. E. & Goodman, N. *Personality and decision processes.* Stanford: Stanford University Press, 1962.

Bross, I. D. *Design for decision.* New York: Macmillan, 1953.

Dewey, J. *How we think.* (Rev. ed.) New York: Heath, 1933.

D'Zurilla, T. J. & Goldfried, M. R. *Cognitive processes, problem-solving, and effective behavior.* Paper presented at the meeting of the American Psychological Association, San Francisco, September 1968.

Gelatt, H. B. Decision-making: A conceptual frame of reference for counseling. *Journal of Counseling Psychology,* 1962, 9, 240–245.

Halpern, G. Assessment of decision processes. *Proceedings of the 75th Annual Convention of the American Psychological Association,* 1967, 361–362.

Krumboltz, J. D. Future directions for guidance research. In John M. Whiteley (Ed.), *Proceedings of the invitational conference on research problems in counseling: Reevaluation and refocus.* St. Ann, Mo.: Central Midwestern Regional Educational Laboratory, 1967. Pp. 199–219.

Nelson, D. E. & Jones, G. B. *An experimental evaluation of methods of teaching students to consider alternative problem solutions.* (Technical Progress Report for Project No. 7-0109.) Washington, D.C.: Office of Education, Department of Health, Education and Welfare, 1969.

Polya, G. *How to solve it; A new aspect of mathematical method.* Princeton: Princeton University Press, 1945.

Rothney, J. W. M. *Guidance practices and results.* New York: Harper, 1958.

Simon, H. A. *Administrative behavior.* New York: Macmillan, 1957.

Skinner, B. F. *Science and human behavior.* New York: Macmillan, 1953.

PART 4

METHODS
FOR PREVENTING
PROBLEMS
AND DEVELOPING
RESOURCEFULNESS

Increasingly, counselors are assuming responsibility for interventions to prevent the occurrence of certain problems or to develop the capabilities of individuals for dealing with future problems. The old model of one-to-one counseling will probably always be with us, but the problems of society are so immense that merely treating victims one at a time seems comparable to bailing a leaking boat with a thimble. Or, as Robert E. Taylor put it, "I'm so busy chasing pigs I don't have time to build a fence."

Ways must be found to reach more people faster. The methods used for preventing problems and developing resourcefulness on a broader scale are not all that different from the methods used for treating individuals. But adaptations are necessary to make these methods more efficient in reaching more people. The methods described and illustrated in this section generally meet one or more of the following criteria.

1. *They are designed to benefit people who have not specifically asked for help.* Counselors generally think of themselves as working only with people who have requested their services. But there are large numbers of people who could benefit from counselor services yet will never see a counselor and cannot ask for help. Some caution must be exercised here in order to ensure that counselors are not providing unwanted services and are not in some way violating the best interests of other people. But few people would argue that teaching nutritional principles to parents violates the rights of their children. The children are the beneficiaries, even though they have never asked for help. Similarly, teaching parents and teachers positive methods of child rearing will have long-range benefits for the children, even though the children themselves never ask for help.

2. *They are designed to reach large numbers of people.* Traditional counseling methods are designed to benefit one person at a time. The methods described here are designed to benefit families, classes, school and prison communities, and other groups of individuals, however they may be collectively defined.

3. *They may have indirect effects.* When the speed limit was lowered to 55 miles an hour, traffic fatalities and injuries showed a sharp decline. This effect may have resulted from discouraging people from driving long distances or from the fact that the energy crisis called public attention to the ecological dangers of automobile use, or it may even have been an artifact of some other cause. But the intervention does seem to have been associated with some general improvement in the human condition. Thousands of human beings are now alive and healthy, apparently as a result of the reduction in the speed limit. No one knows exactly which individuals benefited. Maybe you are one who is alive today because of it. Similar indirect effects seem likely to occur from preventive interventions that counselors might initiate. The beneficiaries may be unknown and untraceable. The only way that evidence can be accumulated to document the effects is through longitudinal assessment of the frequency of certain types of incidents or behaviors.

4. *They are self-perpetuating.* Some of these preventive interventions are designed to generate the means for their own continuation. Some organizations live on long after the founders have resigned. Instructional materials have an impact long after the author has forgotten about them. In some training programs each new set of leaders trains the next set of leaders. Arrangements like these permit the intervention to have continued impact.

5. *They may involve changes in ground rules or organizational structures.* The rules by which we live and work can have profound effects on the ways in which people are rewarded or punished for their efforts. Changing the rules can sometimes make the game more fair and enjoyable. Counselors have operated for years under sets of rules that have never been fully explicated or examined against alternatives. Counselors have often been rewarded for stating good intentions without ever having had to show that they have benefited anyone. Efforts are afoot to change the rules so that counselors and others can demonstrate the effectiveness of what they practice. Exactly how these rules should be changed is a controversial issue, but certainly counselors have a big stake in the outcome and should take action to influence the ways in which rules are stated.

TRAINING FAMILY MEMBERS

47. *TEACHING PARENTS HOW TO DO A BETTER JOB*

MARCIA McBEATH   Shoreline Public Schools, Seattle, and University of Washington

"Mommy, buy me some candy. I want some gum. Gimme a dime. Buy that cereal. *Mommy*, buy me some candy!" Does that sound like a familiar grocery-store scene?

"If I've told you once, I've told you a hundred times. Hang up your coat when you come in the door. Don't throw it on the couch."
"Make your bed *before* you go to school."
"Stop hopping up and down from the table."
"Can't you leave your little brother alone?"
"No. You can't stay up any longer. It's already a half hour past your bed time."
Do you hear yourself saying any of these things?

With these examples I generally introduce the idea of a workshop for parents on using a positive approach to changing children's behavior. Explaining what is meant by a positive approach is also done by means of examples.

A first-grade teacher brought a Snoopy doll and doghouse to class. When the children were misbehaving, she would put Snoopy's paws in front of his eyes and tell the children how badly he felt. If they continued to misbehave, she would move him into the doghouse. However, this demonstration did not work very well. So, after learning about the theory of positive reinforcement, she made a slight change. When the children came in the next day, the Snoopy doll was inside the doghouse. When questioned, the teacher said, "Snoopy doesn't feel very well right now, but let's see what happens."

As soon as the children were working nicely, she put his nose out of the door, saying, "Oh, you children are doing so well, Snoopy is starting to come out of his house."

This continued throughout the day until he was all the way out at the end. Later, the teacher had two things to report. One was that this method had continued to work over a period of time. The other was that one of her students had said, "We have to work a lot harder to get Snoopy *out* of the dog house than we used to work to put him in."

SETTING UP THE WORKSHOP

Workshop meetings are held once a week for five weeks. Each is a two-hour session with a fifteen-minute refreshment break. Participants are provided with outlines for taking notes. This outline also helps to keep the workshop leader from digressing too often.

Name tags for participants are helpful. A list of names is circulated each week for attendance. The room in which the workshop is to be held should have tables that can be arranged both for a speaker and for small group discussions. A blackboard is needed. A

16-millimeter projector and screen are used during the second session.

Parents are told that each will be expected to try a behavior-change project. However, they should not begin their projects until after the third session.

Although twenty to twenty-five is a nice group size, it is possible to work with more. However, for larger groups, some help is needed during the small-group discussions.

After the last session, each parent who has attended a majority of the meetings is presented with a "reinforcer"—a certificate that proclaims him a "Behavior Modifier First Class." Parents are also told that after a month evaluation sheets will be sent to them.

The First Meeting

Examples involving parents are the best teachers. Thus, the workshop starts out with examples and includes them in generous quantities in each session. What better way to explain intermittent reinforcement to parents than by means of the following story?

It is five minutes before dinner. Johnny comes into the kitchen. "Mommy, can I have a cookie?"

"No, Johnny, you'll be eating dinner in five minutes."

Thirty seconds elapse.

"Mommy, can't I please have a cookie? I'm starving."

"No cookie. Now, stop bothering me."

"But, Mommy, I'm hungry."

"No cookie. Go play in the other room."

"Mommy, can I have half a cookie?"

"No. No. No. Can't you see I'm busy?"

A minute later: "Mommy, darling, just give me one little cookie, and I won't bother you any more."

The mother, in exasperation shouts, "Take the cookie and get out of here!"

However, as soon as she reflects on what has happened, she says to herself: "That psychologist said we should be consistent, and mean what we say. If he asks for a cookie tomorrow night, he's not going to get it!"

The next night—same time, same scene.

"Mommy, can I have a cookie?"

"No cookie. Last night I told you you couldn't have one, and then I gave you one. Tonight I mean it!"

A few minutes later, "Mommy, can't I have one little cookie?"

You see, for Johnny, the first five requests do not count at all. He does not even start counting until the sixth time. But, for his mother, after about the eighth request, when the soup is boiling over, the baby is crying, and everyone is asking when dinner will be ready, one of two things usually happens. Either she gives him the cookie because it will get rid of him temporarily,[1] or she screams at the top of her voice, completely "losing her cool"— and this is very rewarding to most children. Either way, Johnny is intermittently reinforced, and this is how persistence in asking for cookies before dinner is developed. It also ex-

[1] *Editors' note:* Giving Johnny the cookie at this point is reinforcing to her, for it removes an aversive event (stimulus) from her kitchen life. Technically this is negative reinforcement for her, because the action that removes the aversive experience (giving him the cookie) is encouraged and strengthened. It is positive reinforcement for the child's whining.

plains the grocery-store scene at the beginning of this chapter.

Although various ways in which behavior is learned, unlearned and changed (for example, through modeling, classical conditioning, and verbal interchanges) are explained, the emphasis is on operant conditioning. This training also begins with a story: "You are having a party. Your five-year-old daughter comes into the room and 'shows off.' Everyone laughs, saying, 'Isn't she cute!' Five minutes later, she is right back in, performing again."

Participants are soon contributing their own stories. At a recent workshop, one parent told about a local candy store with two clerks. Customers would wait in line for one of them even when the other was not busy. After watching for a few minutes, she figured out why. The first clerk, when weighing a pound of candy, always estimated less than a pound on the first try. Then she would add a few pieces to bring the weight up to a pound. The unpopular clerk always estimated just over a pound. That meant she had to take candy out of the bag before giving it to the customer.[2]

In general, the topics discussed during the first session are various ways of changing behavior, the effects of punishment, alternatives to punishment, types of reinforcement, weaning away

from reinforcement, and reinforcing the wrong behavior.

Participants are asked to begin thinking about behavior they would like to change.

The Second Meeting

Before the discussion begins, the parents are asked to write down the behaviors they have considered for their projects. They are told that what they have written may not be what they will eventually decide to work on, but that is all right, for this is just an exercise. They are then asked to turn their papers face down until we are ready to discuss them.

The term "behavior modification" bothers many people. So, the second meeting begins with some often-repeated criticisms of this method and responses to the criticisms. One of the common concerns expressed especially by young adults, both parents and teachers, is "But, aren't you manipulating the child?"

My response is "Yes, but what is teaching and what is child rearing if not manipulating?" When you make a reader out of a nonreader, you are manipulating the child. You decide that the child should learn to read. When you stop a child from hitting and teach discussion of differences in its place, you have determined that the child should not hit and in the same sense are manipulating him.[3]

---

[2] *Editors' note:* A similar phenomenon occurs when a teacher finds a faulty test item in a classroom examination. The teacher can say either "This item shouldn't count, so if you got it right subtract one point" or "This item shouldn't count, so if you missed it add one point." The student's relative standing on the test will be identical under either procedure, but the latter statement will be far more popular.

[3] *Editors' note:* The words "manipulation" and "modification" are cold-sounding, impersonal technical terms. Why not avoid the problem by using more positive terms like "social-learning approach," emphasizing ways of teaching children to learn about themselves and others?

It is to be hoped that, although we start out by imposing our values on our young children, we can help them along the way to learn how to make wise decisions on their own. The important issue is not *how* are we changing a child's behavior but what are the expected outcomes? Are they moral, legal, safe, and ethical? By using a positive approach, I could modify the behavior of a group of children so that they would sit with hands folded for an extended period of time. But I do not believe that this is a good outcome. I could reinforce them for stealing and produce a band of young robbers. Or I could reward them for conformity, so that everyone would draw the same kind of tree. Again, I consider that a poor outcome.

On the other hand, a mother once told me that she was concerned about her four-year-old daughter's swearing. She said: "I've tried everything to get her to stop swearing. I have explained, reasoned, punished. I tried washing her mouth out with soap, and that didn't work. I even tried Tabasco sauce and that didn't work."

Here, the *method* was cruel. I would rather hear the child swear than think of her having Tabasco sauce forced into her mouth in order to change her behavior.[4]

After the various criticisms are discussed, we talk about pinpointing the behavior to be changed. Parents are

urged to work on only one behavior at a time. We talk about stating that behavior in objective, measurable terms. This is difficult for some parents, who have written down such ideas as "That he pay attention, be more respectful, or not be so lazy" and "That she have more gumption, be good, not act so immature."

Sometimes it helps for the parent to ask two questions: What does the child do? What does he look like while doing it? A few minutes are spent in groups, rewording the original behavior descriptions that the participants have written.

Next we talk about collecting baseline data. I emphasize that this is not an essential part of changing behavior. We do it as an experimental aspect of the workshop. If parents take data before starting the project, they will have an objective measure of their results.[5] Methods of counting are discussed and parents are asked to bring the base-line data to the next meeting. They are warned that frequently the behavior magically disappears during this counting stage and told that, if it does, they should merely choose other behaviors and start again. They are also told not to change any of their previous ways of handling their children for one more week. They are informed that in the following week we shall try to figure out antecedents and consequences for their individual projects.

Finally, the film P.A.T.C.H. (Pos-

---

[4] *Editors' note:* One should be concerned about both *how* he does something and *what* he ends up accomplishing. Sometimes a powerful means (like severe punishment) is very effective in one respect but should not be used because of the possible side effects. The "means-end" question is always important to consider.

[5] *Editors' note:* Gathering reliable base-line data for a week or so before a change technique is tried is a very essential step. It forces the parent to observe the behavior, count its frequency, and see whether or not subsequent procedures actually work.

itive Approach to Changing Humans)[6] is shown. It is a training film for teachers, but it demonstrates the theory that has been discussed and its application with normal children.

The Third Meeting

After an initial discussion of any problems encountered in collecting baseline data, the rest of the third meeting is spent on setting up projects. During the first hour, there is a lecture on antecedents, reinforcers and sample change projects, with many examples of each. An antecedent for the child who is slow getting ready in the morning is to help him to lay out his clothes the night before, in the order in which he will

[6] *P.A.T.C.H.*, a nineteen-minute film, is available for purchase or rental from Coronet Instructional Media, 65 East South Water Street, Chicago, Illinois 60601. The cost of the film in color is $150 and in black and white $75. The rental fee is $25 a day. A preview is available to authorized personnel for purchase evaluation, with no obligation other than return postage.

put them on. An antecedent for children who squabble over dish-washing chores is a chart breaking the job into units (see Figure 1). On alternate days one child divides, and the other chooses.

Examples of reinforcers are stars on a chart, the opportunity to stay up later, playing a game with dad, going with the whole family to the movies.

A change project involves a behavior analysis. There is usually an antecedent. Following this, the behavior either is or is not elicited (or stopped, depending upon the project). Consequences follow the behavior.

A mother is trying to stop her young child from interrupting her while she is talking on the telephone. For an antecedent, she tells the child in advance that she will not talk longer than five minutes and that he is not to interrupt her during that time. She sets a timer, which he can see. The behavior is either interrupting or not interrupting. If he does interrupt, he is ignored, and he earns no reward. If he does not interrupt, he earns a point

---

One child divides the jobs by putting an A or a B before each number. The other child decides whether he wants to be A or B.

A_____   B_____

_____1.   Empty dishwasher
_____2.   Clear and wash dining room table and chairs
_____3.   Scrape, rinse, and stack dishes
_____4.   Put dishes in washer, add soap, turn on
_____5.   Wash kitchen table and chairs
_____6.   Grind garbage; wash sink, counters, and stove
_____7.   Take out trash and newspapers
_____8.   Wash extra dishes
_____9.   Sweep floor

FIGURE 1   Antecedent for dishwashing.

plus a hug and a kiss.[7] When he has 5 points on his chart, he and his mother bake a cake together.

A child is a poor eater. She picks at her food and eats very little unless coaxed or fed. The antecedent is to put very small servings on her plate—a tiny portion of meat, a spoonful of mashed potatoes, five peas, followed by an equally small portion of cake (previously displayed). She is told the purpose of this plan and warned that, when the others have finished eating, all plates will be removed. After this, the behavior analysis is simple. Either she eats, feeding herself and without coaxing from others, or she does not. If she does not, she is ignored and her plate removed at the end of the meal with no comment. If she eats, she is included in the family conversation (not about eating), and she is especially listened to when she talks, thus receiving social reinforcement. After five days of success, the whole family goes to a restaurant of her choice for dinner. (If she is apt to choose the most expensive restaurant in town, she should be given a limited choice of three possibilities that fit the budget.)

During the second part of this third session, small groups of four or five participants are formed. Each person describes the behavior that he or she would like to change. The rest of the group listens to the antecedents and consequences being considered and gives feedback. If a participant has not been able to analyze the problem, the others can make suggestions. The workshop leader and assistants circulate to help. Participants are to begin their projects and to be prepared to report back in the following week.

The Fourth Meeting

The fourth meeting is the trouble-shooting session. Parents have had a week to try out their new ideas and what they have learned. Before beginning a general discussion of successes and difficulties, the workshop leader describes several common problems to be considered.

Perhaps the parents' expectations have been too high. It may be necessary to reinforce successive approximations. Or perhaps they have used "if" clauses when it would have been better to use "when." "When you have earned 5 points you may go roller-skating," is preferable to "If you earn 5 points by Saturday, you may go roller-skating." With the second statement, the child might as well earn 0 points as 4 points. With the first, however, persistence finally pays off, even if it takes three weeks.[8] By seeing that it is possible to earn the reinforcer, the child is more apt to try harder the next time.[9]

Some parents forget that responses

---

[7] *Editor's note:* We know of no evidence on the side effects of using hugs and kisses as reinforcers, but some of us on principle prefer to reserve such gestures for spontaneous expressions of affection.

[8] *Editors' note:* Some behaviors have to occur on time, however. If mother wants junior to vacuum the living room before Saturday night's party, it would be inappropriate to reward him if he waits until Sunday morning.

[9] *Editors' note:* The basic point here is excellent. When time is not a crucial factor, the "when-then" strategy enables the child to be successful eventually.

must come right after the behaviors occur. The reward must be immediate, even if it is a star or a point that is later turned in for something that cannot be obtained on the spot.

Application of reward principles does not preclude reliance on other mental-health experts and physicians. The child may have a serious problem that requires special treatment in addition to behavior modification.

Sometimes the use of extinction has to be clarified. It is to be applied only to the specific behavior to be stopped. One mother said that she was going to ignore her child until he picked up his toys. He did everything to gain her attention, from pouring water on the floor to pulling out all the pots and pans. She ignored him for two hours because she did not want to "give in" and thus provide intermittent reinforcement. Examples like this show the importance of follow-up sessions after parents have been presented with the principles and have begun applying them on their own.

After several such examples have been given, the participants begin sharing their experiences with their projects. If the workshop consists of fifteen or fewer people, sharing is with the whole group. When someone has run into a problem, the workshop leader tries to elicit solutions from the rest of the group. When there are more than fifteen, it is preferable to use small groups again, the leader and assistants circulating to help when the groups bog down. If this method is used, it is wise to share with the larger group any problems and suggestions for handling them that may be of interest to all.

By far the greatest percentage of

workshop participants have had dramatic success with their projects. They are usually overwhelmed that such simple ideas work so well. They wonder why they had not heard about these methods before and why more people do not use them.

The Fifth Meeting

The fifth meeting starts with information on additional applications of behavior modification, for example, with autistic children, economically deprived children, psychotic patients, and others exhibiting retarded behavior.

Parents, especially those who have tried the new suggestions made the previous week, are again requested to share their experiences.

Sometimes a parent who had instant success with a project runs into problems later. For example, one mother had been very pleased at how quickly her daughter had learned to pick up her clothes. So she decided to add a new project. She said to her daughter, "You will earn a point each day that I don't yell at you." Not only was this scheme not working, but also the child was crying more frequently and seemed upset. It was pointed out to the mother that her *daughter* was to earn points for the *mother's* behavior, over which she had no control.[10]

Sometime during the five weeks, parents begin to realize that, in order to change their children's behavior, they have to change their own. Often

[10] *Editors' note:* How about having the daughter give Mom a point each day that she does not yell! (Five points would earn Mom a complete kitchen cleanup by the daughter.)

this is hard to do. If there are two parents, they can sometimes reinforce each other for the change. I also suggest that they reinforce themselves.

One mother, who had seven children, reported that, when her project involved an extrinsic, continual reinforcer, she remembered to give the points, and it worked well. Even after she had weaned her children from extrinsic to social reinforcement, the changed behavior continued. Now, however, she was using intermittent reinforcement, and she found it hard to remember to praise the children. It was suggested that she set a timer, and when it rang to praise one of them. With seven children, it would not be too hard to catch one of them being good!

EVALUATION

About 80 percent of the participants have reported success, either verbally or in writing. Some of the evaluation sheets suggest that the ideas have spread to other adult members of the family. Weight control seems to be a popular area. One woman reported success in helping her husband to cut down on his beer consumption.

Some parents reported slow change, whereas others told of dramatic immediate results. One of the latter instances involved a five-year-old girl, who previously had been making her bed occasionally or when reminded. The parents wrote:

We started by talking it over with her and let her put an X on the calendar every time she made her bed and straightened

her room on her own. We praised her and when she reached the agreed upon X's, the family all went out to dinner. We then worked for less X's and baked cookies together. We were shocked as our first project worked. Within a week we noticed the change. The bed making became automatic, even picking up her room, and less misbehavior during the day became very noticeable.

Another parent remembered to catch her son while he was being good, rather than to punish him after he had been bad. She reported:

Our son, who is 13 years old, teases the dog until the dog cries or constantly barks in the front room when everyone is watching TV. I praised him before he would start in, by telling him how much I appreciated his "not teasing the dog." Later on I would ask him if he'd like to play a game of cards. The results were very satisfactory.

Some of the reports indicated that changes in approach had been needed part-way through and that they had been able to diagnose and correct.

Our son (five years old) would mess his undershorts when confronted with a stressful situation. For the project, he could receive three stars a day if there were no dirty undershorts. After getting six stars, he and his daddy and I played a game. After two weeks we changed the system to whereby he gained a star whenever he had a bowel movement in the toilet. He got back into the habit of having his bowel movements regularly in the toilet and then didn't mess his undershorts anymore.

Sometimes two projects were carried out simultaneously for different children in a family. Before the workshop

A. Shoes were strewn all over the house, coat was not hung up.
B. Child would wait too long before going to the bathroom and frequently wet the bathroom floor.
A. Gave praise, hug, and star on a chart when child put shoes away and hung up coat as soon as they were taken off.
B. Gave praise, hug, and star on chart every time child went to bathroom without wetting.

Stars were turned in for reward, i.e. making cookies, reading book with parent, going to Herfy's and Colonel Sanders for dinner, etc. Results—Coat continues to be hung promptly, shoes put away, no wetting, a month or more after stars were discontinued. Praise continues intermittently.

Parents also reported changes in their own behavior. One parent reported:

Prior to the course, child went to his room, screaming, slamming doors and throwing objects when he did not get his way.

After the project the behavior stopped almost immediately and has not returned except very infrequently and even then the duration and intensity of anger is much less. Also I have stopped screaming and yelling almost entirely. I enjoyed the course very much and learned a great deal about myself besides learning about child discipline.

THE WORKSHOP IN OTHER SITUATIONS

The workshop that has been described is one that was adapted from a similar in-service workshop for teachers that I have been using (and revising) for several years. It has also been used with mixed groups of parents and teachers, parent volunteers who work in the schools, parents and teachers of handicapped children, parents of preschoolers, and groups less related to public education, including teachers of anesthesiology and secretaries.

The positive approach is easily understood, usually effective, and widely accepted once it is understood. Children who are trained or educated in these techniques begin to use them themselves. They make for better classrooms and happier homes.

48.   SIBLINGS AS BEHAVIOR-CHANGE AGENTS[1]

NANCY BROWN MILLER AND W. H. MILLER   Neuropsychiatric Institute, University of California, Los Angeles

INTRODUCTION

The major focus of behavior therapy with children has been to identify and

[1] This project has been supported by Easter Seal Research Foundation grant N-7314 (1973-1976).

to train the significant people in the child's environment, primarily parents and teachers. Recently, the importance of peer relationships has been recognized and used successfully (Clement, Roberts & Lantz, 1973) but few systematic attempts to analyze sibling interaction and to involve siblings in the planning and carrying out of behavioral programs in the home have been made (Brown & Cantwell, 1975; Weinrott, 1974).

Little is known about the influences that siblings have on one another, even though the concepts of "sibling rivalry" and "middle-child syndrome," among others, are widely known. One can speculate about the importance of sibling relationships because of the amounts of time and space that siblings share and because of the natural hierarchy that exists simply because of birth order. Also, because of the intense, long-term relationships that siblings are required to have with one another, it is assumed that they do influence and control—or attempt to control—one another on a daily basis.

In this article, the emphasis is on the potential benefits of including siblings in treatment when a traditional approach might involve training only the parents. Thus, although the method used in the case to be presented here was based upon the principles described in *Systematic Parent Training: Procedures, Cases and Issues* (Miller, 1975), the actual treatments were expanded and implemented by siblings, as well as by parents.

THE G FAMILY: A CASE EXAMPLE

At the time of referral to the University of California at Los Angeles, Maria, age four years, had a congenital hip dislocation and was mildly retarded. She had two older sisters, Tracy, who was eleven years old, and Tammy, who was nine years old. Presenting problems included lack of speech, temper tantrums,

whining, noncompliance, throwing food on the floor, refusal to eat, and encopresis and enuresis. The parents reported that Tracy was frequently helpful with Maria, liked to play with her, and tended to overprotect her. Tammy, however, begrudged any time that she had to spend with Maria and in general seemed to resent her.

Data Collection

Before and after treatment the parents filled out the "Missouri Children's Behavior Checklist" (Sines et al., 1969), and the siblings were given the "Family Relations Test" (Bene & Anthony). Home visits were made before and immediately after treatment, as well as three months, six months, and one year after treatment, in order to observe possible changes in compliance by Maria and positive and negative interaction among family members.[2]

Treatment Program

The goal of the first session was learning to define and to observe specific behaviors. They were taught through demonstration and practice during the session, for example, the therapist would have each family member count the frequency of a specific behavior of the therapist, like hand movements, and then compare the results. Words that the family used to describe Maria's behavior, like "whining," were used as examples of defining behaviors in specific, observable terms. The book *Living With Children* (Patterson & Gul-

[2] The "home data" system used in this study was developed by W. H. Miller.

lion, 1968) was given to the family at the end of the session, with instructions for the family to read aloud one chapter each evening.

Beginning in the second session, behavioral principles were introduced; no more than one new principle was presented each week. Principles included praising, prompting, shaping, ignoring, and, finally, punishment. Discussion of didactic material in each session was brief (no more than ten minutes), and the rest of the session was spent on behavior rehearsal, demonstration, and role playing. Many concrete examples, taken from the family interaction in the sessions, were used to improve interaction skills. Previously learned material was reviewed each week.

In Maria G's program three sessions were held in the home. During the first session Maria and her sisters played together in the living room, and the therapist "coached" the sisters in how to involve Maria in play by showing them how to ask her questions (getting her attention, looking at her, asking a specific question, and praising any approximation of a correct response) and how to build with blocks.[3] When it was time to put the toys away, the method of shaping was demonstrated (praising Maria for approximation to obeying, like touching a toy), and the sisters were successful in getting Maria to pick up all her toys for the first time. During the second home session, toilet-training procedures (Foxx & Azrin, 1974) were demonstrated, and each family member took turns in practicing

the behaviors involved in teaching Maria.

During the third session the therapist joined the family at dinner. In previous cases, the senior author had found dinner time to be one of the most effective times to meet with families and to provide guidance and feedback about family interaction. In Maria's family this was the most difficult period of the day. Maria often whined while her mother was cooking, and Mrs. G attended to nearly every instance of Maria's whining. The therapist's strategy was to teach Mrs. G to discriminate Maria's appropriate and inappropriate behavior and to provide more effective consequences. Thus, while preparing dinner, Mrs. G was cued when and how to attend to Maria. With prompting and immediate feedback during a critical time of the day, she was able to recognize and improve her own behavior.

During dinner Mrs. G reported that Maria's throwing food on the floor and demanding more had not occurred for three weeks since the family had begun to ignore it. Suddenly Maria threw her food on the floor and yelled "More!" Tracy quickly turned to her and said, "What do you want, Maria?" Mrs. G said, "Tracy, what's the rule?" Tracy said, "I'm just trying to help her." Tammy said, "The rule is we ignore it." Whereupon she turned her back to Maria and continued to eat. Mrs. G said: "Tracy, everything we do with Maria is a link in a chain. You just broke a link, and now we have to start building the chain again." Tracy turned away from Maria and began to pout, which Mrs. G ignored. Within a few minutes everyone was eating again.

---

[3] Editors' note: This is a good example of live modeling by the therapist.

Later the therapist talked with the family about dinner hour, and a plan was devised by which the siblings and parents would increase positive contingent attention to Maria for desired behavior.

Maria used few words, generally pointing to what she wanted, and she whined a great deal. Before these behaviors had been responded to differently by each family member: Mrs. G had periodically encouraged her to talk but had generally been controlled by the pointing. She had responded to the whining by picking Maria up or becoming angry. The eleven-year-old sibling had patterned her behavior very much on that of her mother but with even greater emphasis on doing things for Maria. The nine-year-old sister had alternated between ignoring Maria and telling her to shut up when she whined. She did not encourage Maria to talk and was generally annoyed by her presence. Mr. G had attempted to get Maria to talk by using food rewards but had quickly become frustrated and upset and had often given the reward to Maria without her having spoken correctly.

In the training sessions the family members were taught to encourage Maria's speech, to model and to reinforce attempts to say words, to respond to speech instead of to pointing, and to ignore whining. Specific instructions and demonstrations with Maria were used to teach the family members how to shape words, to praise approximations, and to correct Maria's mistakes. Each day the siblings and Mrs. G held thirty-minute "speech sessions" with Maria, in which they played with toys, reinforced her clear speech, and kept

records of the correctly spoken words. The results are shown in Figure 1.

By the end of the eight weeks all family members were ignoring the whining, and there were no reports of whining during the last two weeks of the program or at a one-month follow-up interview.

Figure 2 shows the amounts of verbal interaction and of positive verbal interaction between each family member and Maria. The total amount of verbal interaction increased slightly for all of the family. Positive verbal interaction had increased by the end of treatment and was maintained at a high rate by Mrs. G and Tammy for one year. Tracy maintained a high rate through the six-month follow-up, with some decrease by the end of one year.

In Maria's family one of the major complaints was her noncompliance. Whenever her sisters asked her to do something and she refused, they

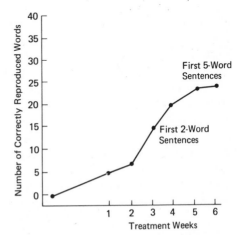

FIGURE 1 Number of correctly reproduced words by Maria during thirty-minute daily training sessions.

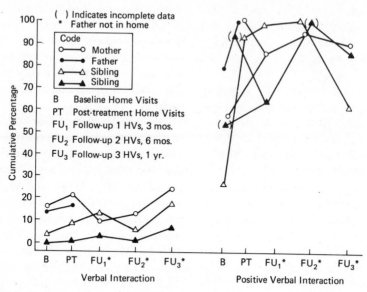

FIGURE 2 Verbal interaction and positive verbal interaction between each family member and Maria.

would usually tell their mother. This resulted in Mrs. G's trying to convince the older sisters to give in or to "forget about it," which upset them. During the program several sessions focused on *how* to give commands (briefly and specifically), *when* to give commands (only when necessary), and *what* to do when Maria complied (praise) or did not comply (repeat the command). In order to emphasize further their important roles, both sisters and Mrs. G were asked to write down at least three commands that they had given Maria each day, and to note whether she had followed or had not followed each command. Figure 3 shows the rate of compliance as reported by the mother and sisters.

Figure 4 shows the results of

Maria's compliance training, based on the observers' data collection. The total number of commands was moderate for UCLA clinic families, and Maria had complied approximately 80 percent of the time during the base-line period. Her rate increased somewhat during treatment, decreased during follow-up, and had increased again one year later. The rate of compliance to the younger sibling shows a steady increase from 55 to 100 percent. Maria's obedience was seldom praised during the base-line period, but praise was increased dramatically by all family members.

Comparing the family's self-reports and the home-visit data, we can see that, during the base-line period, the family had reported little compliance, especially to the siblings, whereas the

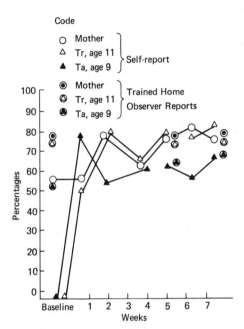

Code

○ Mother
△ Tr, age 11   } Self-report
▲ Ta, age 9

◉ Mother
◍ Tr, age 11   } Trained Home
◕ Ta, age 9   } Observer Reports

FIGURE 3 Percentage of commands obeyed by Maria, as reported by her mother and two sisters.

hyperactivity. He reported no problems with Tracy either before or after treatment. Tammy was reported to have been hyperactive, difficult to manage, and socially immature before treatment and to have shown considerable improvement in all these areas after treatment.

The mother reported many difficulties with Maria before treatment, especially hyperactivity, inhibition, and extreme social immaturity. Following treatment she reported a very significant improvement, especially in confidence and social maturity. For Tracy she reported no problems either before or after treatment. For Tammy she had originally reported aggressive behavior, which she said had decreased considerably after treatment, along with an increase in social interaction.

Family Relations Test

Before treatment, Tracy showed much interaction with Maria, most of it positive; Tammy also showed much interaction, most of it negative, whereas her interactions with other family members were generally positive. Following treatment, Tracy reported even more positive feelings about Maria and reported an increase in the positive behavior that she was receiving from Maria. Tammy showed a great decrease in negative interaction with Maria and also reported receiving a high degree of positive behavior from Maria. Both siblings perceived less total interaction with Maria, but both also reported more positive and less negative interaction with her.

home rater's data indicate a relatively high rate. By the end of treatment the two reports coincided. This may be a result of the family members' (especially the siblings') increasing ability to discriminate compliance in Maria.

Missouri Children's Behavior Checklist

The results on the "Missouri Children's Behavior Checklist," administered before and after treatment, indicate that the parents perceived changes both in Maria and in her siblings. The father reported the greatest improvements in Maria's eating, sleeping, and decreased

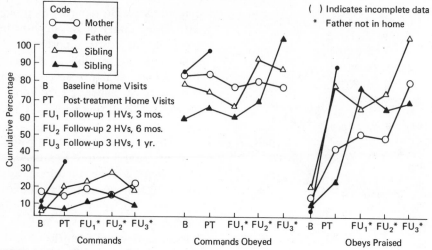

FIGURE 4   Compliance structure for the G family.

PRACTICAL CONSIDERATIONS IN TREATMENT WITH SIBLINGS

Individualizing the Sessions

Session have to be well planned, with a variety of short segments alternating discussion of principles with active role playing and behavioral rehearsal. The structure of the sessions may vary with the age and behavior of the siblings, but generally an hour to an hour and a half per session is adequate. In the G family the siblings maintained their interest for only about ten minutes and then began to grow restless, so didactic presentations were brief, and the emphasis was on active participation.

Sharing Family Secrets

In several sessions it was observed that the siblings did not feel comfortable in talking about one another or their parents. On one occasion in particular, the father had apparently spanked the target child rather severely during the week—contrary to instructions. One of the siblings blurted this out; her father gave her a harsh look and denied it. Sharing secrets is an important problem for both parents and children, and it is necessary at the very beginning of treatment to establish guidelines for the program, including a rule that all behavior in the family that is observed by anyone is subject to discussion in the meetings.

Following Through on Assignments

Siblings occasionally "forget" to write down a required assignment unless they recognize its importance or unless they experience a consequence, like attention from the therapist, for themselves. It may be necessary, especially in the early stages of treatment, for the therapist to call the family between sessions and to talk to each family member about his progress in the program. In Maria's case, the therapist called the family every night for the first two weeks of intervention and talked briefly to each family member.[4]

Presence of the Target Child

Attempting to carry out an organized, efficient session can be very difficult when the referred child is present, particularly when his target behaviors are hyperactivity and a short attention span. The *therapist* decided early that a target behavior for Maria should be the shaping of independent play because she was continually demanding attention from her parents or sisters during the treatment sessions. This approach was partially successful, but Maria's demands were a continual problem.

An ideal plan would be to have the child present for only a *part* of each

session, to allow the family to attend to didactic material and to practice new behaviors in the other parts of the session. The reality is that for many problem children and many families, finding a baby sitter is difficult. Providing a baby sitter in the clinic may be a workable solution.

Participation by Family Members

The dominating parent and the passive child and other familiar combinations present problems that require the therapist's active intervention during the sessions. Siblings often "talk for" one another, and parents often "talk for" children. The therapist has to control who talks when and to ensure equal participation by all family members.[5]

---

[4] *Editors' note:* An excellent plan. The siblings as helpers also need to be reinforced consistently.

[5] *Editors' note:* A helpful technique is to limit talk to the "first person," that is, to statements beginning, "I did this . . ." "I think . . ." "I feel that. . . ."

references

Bandura, A. *Principles of behavior modification.* New York. Holt, Rinehart and Winston, 1966.

Bene, E. & Anthony, J. *The Bene-Anthony family relations test.* London: National Foundation for Educational Research in England and Wales, n.d.

Brown, N. & Cantwell, D. Siblings as therapists: A behavioral approach. Paper presented at the annual meeting of the American Psychiatric Association, Anaheim, Calif., May 1975.

Brown, N. & Guilani, B. The effects of parental modeling in the modification of sibling behavior. Unpublished manuscript, 1973.

Clement, P., Roberts, P. & Lantz, C. Mothers and peers as child behavior therapists. Unpublished manuscript, 1973.

Foxx, D. & Azrin, N. *Toilet training the retarded.* Champaign: Research Press, 1974.

Miller, W. H. *Systematic parent training: Procedures, cases and issues.* Champaign: Research Press, 1975.

Patterson, G. R. & Gullion, M. E. *Living with children: New methods for parents and teachers.* Champaign: Research Press, 1968.

Sines, J. O., Pauker, J. D., Sines, L. K. & Owen, D. R. Identification of clinically relevant dimensions of children's behavior. *Journal of Consulting and Clinical Psychology.* 1969, **33**, 728–734.

Sutton-Smith, B. & Rosenberg, B. *The sibling.* New York: Holt, Rinehart and Winston, 1970.

Tharp, R. & Wetzel, R. *Behavior modifica-tion in the natural environment.* New York: Academic Press, 1970.

Weinrott, M. A training program in be-havior modification for siblings of the retarded. *American Journal of Ortho-psychiatry,* 1974, **44**.

49. MAINTENANCE IN PARENT TRAINING

WILLIAM R. MILLER AND BRIAN G. DANAHER   University of Oregon

Suggestions about child rearing have come from almost every major school of psychology and have been condensed into a variety of books that have been consumed by the public at a voracious rate (for example, Ginott, 1965; Gordon, 1970). For few of these systems, how-ever, has more than anecdotal evidence of efficacy been provided. The behavior-modification approach to child manage-ment has attracted increasing attention during recent years. The application of behaviorally oriented therapy pro-cedures to child management and the evaluation of the effectiveness of such procedures have been extensively re-viewed (for example, Gelfand & Hart-mann, 1968; Patterson, 1971a, 1973). Entire volumes have appeared in pro-fessional circles suggesting further so-cial-learning approaches to clinical aspects of child treatment (Graziano, 1971; Quay, 1968).

One strategy that is frequently ad-vocated involves the parents of "prob-lem children" to understand and to ap-ply behavioral techniques within their home environments. A number of re-ports have described parent-child in-teractions within the clinic playroom (for example, Krapfl, Bry & Nawas, 1969; Russo, 1964; Straughan, 1964; Wahler *et al.,* 1965). In this particular strategy observation and intervention both occur within the clinic setting on the assumption that gains effected in the parent's reaction to the child in the clinic will be generalized to the more "natural" environment.[1]

With the development of reliable observation techniques and increased sophistication, parent training has ex-panded beyond the playroom setting, and trainer-observers have begun work-ing in homes and schools trying ex-plicitly to alter parental behavior (for example, Hawkins *et al.,* 1966; O'Leary, O'Leary & Becker, 1967).

Although the efficacy of shaping appropriate child-rearing behaviors in parents through the help of trainer-observers has been substantially vali-dated in the aforementioned research reports, it does seem apparent that *cost* makes this strategy a less than optimal one for use in applied clinical settings.

---

[1] *Editors' note:* A convenient yet highly questionable assumption made in all counsel-ing. If clients needed help only in their con-sulting-room behavior, then the work of the counselor would be so much easier.

Partly in response to this issue of cost effectiveness, a series of child-management manuals has appeared, emphasizing the behavioral orientation (for example, Krumboltz & Krumboltz, 1972; Patterson, 1971b; Patterson & Gullion, 1968). Unfortunately, reading a manual may not supply the requisite shaping and feedback to ensure a successful outcome (Patterson, 1971a). In order to overcome this problem, these and similar manuals have been used in conjunction with more traditional dyadic and group-therapy settings (for example, Lindsley, 1966; Patterson, 1969, 1971a).

Beyond the issue of treatment economy, concern for the maintenance of change has additional important implications for the *role* of the therapist in the behavior-modification process. Valins and Nisbett (1971) indicate that behavior change perceived as internally controlled is more likely to be maintained than is change attributed to external sources. Treatment approaches that place responsibility for change in the hands of the client might therefore be expected to have greater long-range effectiveness, once contact with the therapist has been terminated, than programs in which the therapist is very salient as the controlling agent.[2]

This case report presents a family that had sought and received successful treatment for one child's behavior problems but had found itself unable to maintain and adapt the program on its own following termination.

[2] *Editors' note:* Herein lies the great advantage of counseling methods that emphasize the client's learning self-control skills.

THE CASE OF MURRAY

The Ks, a lower-middle-class couple in their thirties, made contact with the university psychology clinic in order to seek assistance with the management of their twelve-year-old son Murray, the oldest of three boys. According to the parents' report, Murray was displaying a wide range of disruptive and problematic behaviors. They included aggressive behavior (physical fighting with his brothers and verbal taunting), making noise (banging pots and pans, yelling), destructive acts (kicking the walls and furniture, breaking toys), and "infantile" behavior (crawling around on all fours in public, spontaneous crying). Murray was also of very little help in the household, contributing only token efforts to chores and other family responsibilities. His two younger siblings (aged eleven and nine years) were described by the Ks as much more helpful and certainly much less troublesome.

Murray had been treated previously by a series of physicians, who had prescribed a variety of medications, including Thorazine and Mellaril. When the Ks made contact with the clinic, Murray was being maintained on 125 milligrams of Mellaril daily. The family had also been treated by other therapists who had instituted a behaviorally oriented child-management program for all three boys.[3] The Ks had carried

[3] *Editors' note:* Just because it is labeled a "behaviorally oriented program" does not mean that all the components are present or that the parents are well trained. Counselors who call themselves "behavioral" are like all human beings—capable of distorting principles, omitting steps, and mismanaging treatment.

out the program and had kept records faithfully. The program had been somewhat successful at first, but Murray's behavior had begun to deteriorate again, and the Ks were seeking further assistance.

In addition to their problems with Murray at home, the Ks had serious concerns about his adjustment at school. He had recently entered junior high school with the opportunity to begin "with a clean slate" and to escape the reputation of a "problem child." Early reports from the school indicated that Murray was again running into academic and disciplinary problems, but the Ks still had hopes that he might make a better adjustment in this new setting.

The Ks were seen seven times over a period of five months. During the assessment interviews, when we met with all members of the K family, three major treatment goals were defined: to decrease Murray's disruptive behavior and to increase his constructive behavior within the home setting, to reexamine his need for and use of medication, and to consult with the school and facilitate his adjustment there.

Behavior at Home

Changing Murray's behavior in the home had been the goal of a behaviorally oriented program designed for the Ks by previous therapists. The main features of this previous program, which the Ks were continuing to use when they made contact with clinic, were a list of four house rules, a list of four reinforcers available on a once-daily basis, and a contingency system

which a single infraction resulted in the loss of a reinforcer for the day.

Several serious shortcomings were noted in this program. Perhaps the most obvious of these was the system's "all or none" quality. When a rule had been broken once, the reward was forfeited for the day, and Murray literally had nothing to lose by continuing his rule-breaking behavior. The number of reinforcers lost depended upon the number of *different* rules broken and not upon the *frequency* of rule infractions. For example, one rule forbade name calling. If Murray called someone a single name, he lost a reward for that day. The typical consequence of this system would be a prolonged sequence of name calling for the remainder of the day, sometimes escalating to the loss of other reinforcers.[4]

Another problem with the program was its almost exclusive emphasis upon aversive control. The punishments for rule violation were quite salient, whereas rewards for obedience were much more subtle and delayed.[5] Finally, the program seemed inflexible. No provision had been made for alteration in the system to accommodate the changing needs of the family.

[4] *Editors' note:* A very good point. A whole day is a long time for anyone to be perfect when a high-frequency problem behavior (like offensive language, smoking, or feeling tense) is involved. It is better to use much smaller time blocks, perhaps granting a reward for no swearing in a one-hour or three-hour period.

[5] *Editors' note:* This emphasis on aversive control was perhaps the biggest single mistake: "If you don't stop, I'll . . . [punishment]." Encouraging small steps toward positive behavior is crucial.

Mindful of these shortcomings, we met with the Ks to design a new program that would be sensitive to the *frequency* of target behaviors, incorporate positive reinforcement for desired behavior, and provide for alterations according to changing circumstances. Following the model suggested by Kanfer and Saslow (1969), we asked the Ks to construct three lists: one of behaviors that they would like to decrease, one of behaviors that they would like to increase, and one of potential reinforcers. Point values were then assigned to all elements on the list, so that each desired behavior would earn a set number of points (variable in some instances, like chores, to reflect the extent to which the tasks had been completed), each undesired behavior would result in the loss of a given number of points,[6] and each reward could be purchased for a certain number of points. A child was required to be "in the black" in order to purchase a reward but was free to choose whatever reward he desired (provided that he had sufficient points in his "account").[7]

When the new program had been designed, the entire K family again met with us, and the system was explained to the three boys. They had been anticipating a revised program and seemed enthusiastic about the expanded range of reinforcers and the freedom to choose from among them.

The Ks kept careful data in the weeks that followed. It soon became apparent that even this expanded system would require modification to avoid obsolescence. The Ks, satisfied with the initial effectiveness of the program, were somewhat cautious about suggesting changes at first. We encouraged them to make any changes that seemed appropriate, however, and they were soon confidently modifying the system expediently. Behaviors that no longer seemed troublesome were dropped from the list; new ones were added. The point values for particular behaviors were changed in accordance with the behavioral economics of supply and demand. The Ks seemed pleased that they could adjust the program themselves and took increasing responsibility for doing so. Consultation with the therapists was faded to semi-monthly and finally to monthly meetings. When it became apparent that consultation was no longer required for the program to function, termination was suggested. A new set of program sheets was prepared for the Ks, incorporating the changes that they had made, and arrangements were made for follow-up. Table 1 shows the weekly record sheet used to indicate points earned for performance of household chores. Table 2 shows the record sheet used to indicate points spent through misbehavior and the "purchase" of rewards.

[6] *Editors' note:* One trouble with subtracting points for undesirable behavior is that attention must then be focused on that undesirable behavior, thus rewarding it to some extent. The other difficulty involves achieving "justice." If too many points are subtracted, the child finds all his other efforts discredited and may rebel against the perceived injustice.

[7] *Editors' note:* A point or token system can be very effective in helping to stress positive behaviors and to discourage negative ones. See Reading 17 for an example of this system used with six children in a home setting.

TABLE 1 Points Earned for Various Behaviors[a]

Behaviors	Mon.			Tue.			Wed.			Thu.			Fri.			Sat.			Sun.		
	A	B	M	A	B	M	A	B	M	A	B	M	A	B	M	A	B	M	A	B	M
Get up at first call (3)																					
At breakfast on time (2)																					
Brush teeth after breakfast (5)																					
Brush teeth at bedtime (5)																					
Home from school on time (5)																					
In bed on time (3)																					
Hairbrushing (10)																					
Mow lawn (up to 30)																					
Take garbage out (up to 5)																					
Clean downstairs bathroom (up to 21)																					
Clean upstairs bathroom (up to 21)																					
Pick up back yard (up to 10)																					
Sweep up patio (up to 16)																					
Care for dog (up to 15)																					
Vacuuming (up to 29)																					
Clean your bedroom (up to 38)																					
Wash windows (per window)																					
Vacuum Stairway (up to 15)																					
Wash dishes (up to 30)																					
Dusting (up to 5)																					
Empty wastebasket (up to 10)																					
Daily Totals																					

438

TABLE 2 Points Lost or Spent[a]

Behaviors	Mon. A	B	M	Tue. A	B	M	Wed. A	B	M	Thu. A	B	M	Fri. A	B	M	Sat. A	B	M	Sun. A	B	M
Agitating (3)																					
Teasing dogs (15)																					
Telling lies (10)																					
Physical fighting (15)																					
Arguing and yelling (5)																					
Bothering Mom on phone (15)																					
Lighting matches (25)																					
Stealing (up to 100)																					
Wrestling in house (25)																					
Poor table manners (5)																					
Bothering others' property (5)																					
Name calling (5)																					
Leaving yard (10)																					
Profanity (5)																					
Late to band (M., W., F.) (5)																					
Rewards																					
Bicycling (5 pts./hr.)																					
Swimming (5 pts./hr.)																					
TV privileges for 2 hrs. (10)																					
Visiting a friend (5)																					
Overnight (40)																					
Ice cream at Bob's (10)																					
Having a friend visit (3)																					
Overnight (25)																					
Weekend late bedtime (15)																					
Allowance (2 pts. = 1 cent)																					
Camping trips (100)																					
Daily Totals																					

[a] Murray's points were entered in the columns headed with "M," and the points of his two siblings were entered beneath "A" and "B."

439

Data obtained from the application of the point system just described included frequencies of the major problematic behaviors for all three boys: "agitation," "physical fighting," and "arguing and yelling." Total frequencies of misdemeanors are indicated in Figure 1. As is readily apparent, the frequency with which these problem behaviors were performed consistently decelerated over the course of treatment.

Follow-up data were obtained from the Ks for three full months following the formal date of treatment termination. These data are indicated in Figure 1. The encouraging direction of change suggested by the treatment scores was maintained, and progress even accelerated during this period.

Murray's Medication

The Ks reported that Murray had begun to show less affect and more enuresis, aggressiveness, and infantile behavior when he had been placed on Mellaril. There was also a continual struggle to make Murray take his pills. If Murray failed to take two of his pills through forgetfulness, his parents reported that he would lose control of his temper, destroy things, cry spontaneously, and generally become very difficult to manage. The Ks were thus understandably reluctant to consider the total discontinuation of the drug.

With their permission, however, the family physician was consulted

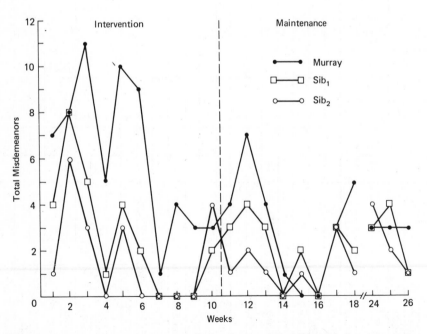

FIGURE 1 Total misdemeanors per week for the three K children during intervention and maintenance.

about Murray's medication. The doctor indicated that Mellaril should certainly not have such marked effects, especially if only a few pills were missed. He supported the idea of reducing the dosage on a gradual and experimental basis, and this plan was suggested to the Ks. They remained reluctant but two weeks later returned to report that Murray was no longer taking his Mellaril. They had decided simply to cease reminding him to take his pills, and he had not asked for them in more than a week. They reported that Murray's enuresis had stopped completely (for the first time in thirteen years), that he seemed less infantile and less prone to crying, and that he seemed somewhat more aggressive. They were pleased with this (although concerned about a possible increase in aggressive behavior) and decided to put the medication away. Five months later Murray was continuing without Mellaril and with marked reduction in enuresis and spontaneous crying.

The School Situation

Three months after the Ks were first interviewed we arranged a conference with Murray's teachers, counselor, and principal. At that time the behavioral program had been in effect in the home for two months, and Murray had been without Mellaril for one month. The conference began with the teachers' reporting their impressions of Murray. We did not specifically request that they report either problems or strengths. To our surprise, five out of six teachers reported very noticeable improvement both in Murray's school work (at least in terms of the amount

of time and effort he gave to it) and in his classroom conduct. They seemed to be having fewer disciplinary problems with him, and he was apparently beginning to relate to his peers in a more positive fashion. The one teacher who did not note improvement reported no change at all. None of the teachers had noticed Murray's abstinence from Mellaril, although all had been aware of the medication. Some had even participated in reminding him to take it. The general evaluation of the school staff was that Murray had improved markedly.

We decided that any intervention in the school setting would be inappropriate. We made contact with the school counselor two months later as a follow-up measure, and he reported that Murray's progress had continued. He also agreed to send a report home to the Ks indicating the school's satisfaction with Murray's improvement.[8]

ISSUES

The case of the K family presents some interesting value considerations inherent in treatment programs involving parent training.

Controlling the Controllers

At times, we were uneasy about the extent and detail of control desired by

---

[8] *Editors' note:* Sometimes improved behavior at home (or school) is not generalized to other settings. An alternative strategy, if needed, would have been to involve Murray's teachers in the point system by having them award points for improved classroom behaviors. See Article 17.

the Ks over their children. As the parents achieved control over Murray's more gross and obnoxious behaviors, they began to add to the list finer and more detailed restrictions. Encouraged by the increasing participation of the boys in household chores, they became more demanding, adding items to the list of desired behaviors as well.

A therapist, in training parents in the technologies of behavior modification and child management, provides considerable control over children but does not necessarily provide limits for the use of this new control. Is the therapist responsible for providing guidelines for the application of these techniques? Should parents be encouraged to apply contingency-management techniques to any and all aspects of their children's behavior or only to a restricted, seriously problematic range? There are no clear answers, yet the questions remain.

Although behaviorally oriented child-management programs frequently appear totalitarian, the control they afford may prove, upon closer inspection, to be less complete. Contract arrangements in families, by which rewards are made contingent upon the occurrence of desired behavior and the absence of undesired behavior, may be viewed as providing countercontrol situations in which both parties are in a real sense "in control" and achieving desired ends. The parents obviously perceive themselves as in control, for the behaviors that have been annoying them decrease and more desirable behaviors increase. As a result, they may find their children more lovable, likable, and easier to live with. The children, on the other hand, are provided with a very tangible means of gaining rewards that they desire. Their world becomes more predictable in this regard, and they also may perceive themselves as in control of the situation. A contingency program, then, can afford countercontrols, providing a system which both parties (parent and child, husband and wife, and so on) can achieve desired changes and are enabled to live together in greater harmony.

The reciprocity of such a system, however, does depend upon its very predictability. If, for example, the parent arbitrarily changes behavior lists, point values, and contingencies, the balance of control tips more heavily to one side, and the child is more likely to see the system as unilateral and oppressive. Such tactics flaunt the parent's control.

Other elements may be incorporated to enhance the feeling of mutual control. A program that depends heavily upon positive control (reinforcement), rather than upon aversive control (punishment), will probably be accepted more readily.[9] Providing choices—for example, allowing the child to choose from a range of reinforcers[10]—also increases perceived degrees of freedom.

---

[9] *Editors' note:* Yes. And positive control permits its recipient to choose whether or not to accept it, whereas aversive control imposes contingencies that are more difficult to avoid.

[10] *Editors' note:* Another way of encouraging reciprocity and interdependence is to involve the child in negotiations about the point system and then gradually to fade the system out on a "trial and success" basis.

Spontaneity and Control

A family may express concern that behavior modification will disrupt "spontaneous" behavior and affection. One means of coping with this concern is to restrict contingency management to a well-circumscribed set of behaviors, namely those that are desired but *do not occur* or those that are undesired but *occur at a high rate*. Indeed, recent research in the area of attribution would suggest that the incautious application of explicit extrinsic reinforcement may "backfire," undermining intrinsic motivation for behaviors that were previously functionally autonomous (Lepper, Greene & Nisbett, 1973; Nisbett & Valins, 1971; Valins & Nisbett, 1971).

Discouragement, Symptom Substitution, and Labeling

A further interesting dilemma was encountered after three months of treatment. The data being submitted by the Ks clearly indicated that Murray's behavior was changing dramatically. The behaviors that had been presented as problematic were well under control, and new behaviors were being modified as well, sometimes by the mere fact that they had been added to the list. Yet, in spite of the obvious progress recorded by the Ks themselves, they were discouraged. The sources of their despair emerged: First, they reported that it seemed that as soon as one behavior was controlled another became problematic; second, they expressed the opinion that, "even though he's behaving, down inside he's still just a deviant kid."

The first of these concerns, which may be thought of as symptom substitution, waned as an increasing number of behaviors came under control. As Bandura (1969) has argued, the emergence of new deviant behavior may be predictable under certain circumstances. If, for example, a target behavior is being maintained as an attention-getting mechanism (A.G.M.), then it may be predicted that other A.G.M. behaviors in a repertoire will be employed when the primary A.G.M. fails.

The second of these concerns may be seen as a labeling problem. It is not surprising that the Ks, having lived with a deviant child for many years, would be reluctant to relabel him as "normal" or "acceptable," even in the face of considerable evidence. We were concerned about the possibility that this "left-over label" might prove a self-fulfilling prophecy. However, the Ks returned the week after they had expressed discouragement quite enthusiastic and reporting that they had begun to rediscover some likable qualities in their son. Had the lag in label change been longer in duration, we might have been obliged to intervene with attitude-change techniques.

references

Bandura, A. *Principles of behavior modification.* New York: Holt, Rinehart and Winston, 1969.

Gelfand, D. M. & Hartmann, D. P. Behavior therapy with children: A review and evaluation of research methodology. *Psychological Bulletin,* 1968, **69**, 204–215.

Ginott, H. G. *Between parent and child.* New York: Macmillan, 1965.

Gordon, T. *Parent effectiveness training.* New York: Wyden, 1970.

Graziano, A. M. (Ed.) *Behavior therapy with children.* New York: Aldine-Atherton, 1971.

Hawkins, R. P., Peterson, R. F., Schweid, E. & Bijou, S. W. Behavior therapy in the home: Amelioration of problem parent-child relations with the parent in a therapeutic role. *Journal of Experimental Child Psychology,* 1966, **4**, 99–107.

Kanfer, F. H. & Saslow, G. Behavioral diagnosis. In C. M. Franks (Ed.), *Behavior therapy: Appraisal and status.* New York: McGraw-Hill, 1969. Pp. 417–444.

Krapfl, J. E., Bry, P. & Nawas, M. M. Uses of the bug-in-the-ear in the modification of parents' behavior. In R. D. Rubin & C. M. Franks (Eds.), *Advances in behavior therapy, 1968.* New York: Academic Press, 1969. Pp. 31–35.

Krumboltz, J. D. & Krumboltz, H. B. *Changing children's behavior.* Englewood Cliffs, N.J.: Prentice-Hall, 1972.

Lepper, M. R., Greene, D. & Nisbett, R. E. Undermining children's intrinsic interest with extrinsic reward: A test of the "over-justification" hypothesis. *Journal of Personality and Social Psychology,* 1973, **28**, 129–137.

Lindsley, O. R. An experiment with parents handling behavior at home. *Johnstone Bulletin,* 1966, **9**, 27–36.

Nisbett, R. E. & Valins, S. *Perceiving the causes of one's own behavior.* New York: General Learning Press, 1971.

O'Leary, L. D., O'Leary, S. & Becker, W. C. Modification of a deviant sibling interaction pattern ·in the home. *Behaviour Research and Ther-*

apy, 1967, **5**, 113–120.

Patterson, G. R. Teaching parents to be behavior modifiers in the classroom. In J. D. Krumboltz & C. E. Thoresen (Eds.), *Behavioral counseling: Cases and techniques.* New York: Holt, Rinehart and Winston, 1969. Pp. 155–161.

Patterson, G. R. Behavioral intervention procedures in the classroom and in the home. In A. E. Bergin & S. L. Garfield (Eds.), *Handbook of psychotherapy and behavior change: An empirical analysis.* New York: Wiley, 1971a. Pp. 751–776.

Patterson, G. R. *Families: Applications of social learning to family life.* Champaign: Research Press, 1971b.

Patterson, G. R. Reprogramming the families of aggressive boys. In C. E. Thoresen (Ed.), *Behavior modification in education: 72nd Yearbook of the National Society for the Study of Education.* Chicago: University of Chicago Press, 1973. Pp. 154–192.

Patterson, G. R. & Gullion, M. E. *Living with children: New methods for parents and teachers.* Champaign: Research Press, 1968.

Quay, H. C. (Ed.) *Children's behavior disorders.* Princeton: Van Nostrand, 1968.

Russo, S. Adaptations in behavioral therapy with children. *Behaviour Research and Therapy,* 1964, **2**, 43–47.

Straughan, J. H. Treatment with child and mother in the playroom. *Behaviour Research and Therapy,* 1964, **2**, 37–41.

Valins, S. & Nisbett, R. E. *Attribution processes in the development and treatment of emotional disorders.* New York: General Learning Press, 1971.

Wahler, R. G., Winkel, G. H., Peterson, R. F. & Morrison, D. C. Mothers as behavior therapists for their own children. *Behaviour Research and Therapy,* 1965, **3**, 113–124.

TEACHING TEACHERS

50. *MEMOS TO A TEACHER*

MARCIA McBEATH Shoreline Public Schools, Seattle, and University of Washington

September 20

To: Robin Gillespie, Syre School
From: Marcia McBeath, School Psychologist
Re: Behavior Modification Consultation

I'll try to summarize some of the things we talked about yesterday.

There are about 6 or 8 students (both boys and girls) who make your teaching really unpleasant. They are not enthusiastic, they talk back, deny wrong-doings, take a long time to settle down when changing from one subject to another, and generally are very negative. You had started some class meetings where each student submitted an idea. Several of them wanted a different seating arrangement, but you feel that presently part of your control is in the seating.

We talked about behavior modification in general, and I told you about my in-service starting October 18. Until then, we discussed four holding measures which you thought you might try, as follows:

1. We will concentrate on trying to change one behavior, which you selected as being at top priority—that of the time involved in changing from one subject to another. A point system will be used, where the amount of the total number of students ready within a set time limit during these changes will be recorded. Those not ready will be ignored. At the end of the day, 5% of the sum will be computed and the students will have that many minutes free time to talk with each other. Much social reinforcement will accompany this project where positive behavior is observed.

2. Deviant behavior will be ignored unless it falls into one of the following four categories:
   a. The child might hurt someone.
   b. The child might hurt himself.
   c. The child might destroy property.
   d. The child is extremely disruptive. (This one is somewhat subjective, but try to determine if he or she is actively preventing others from learning.)

3. Where any of the above behaviors occur, a time-out station will be used where the child will be sent for five minutes. There must be consistency here.

4. You will contact Nancy Post, School Social Worker, to see if she knows of any previous guidance studies on kids you are most concerned about. She may also be able to help you with your group work which I think should continue.

I'll check back with you on 9/26 to see how things are going. Good luck!
cc: Stan Wiklund, Principal
     Nancy Post, School Social Worker

September 27

To: Robin Gillespie, Syre School
From: Marcia McBeath, School Psychologist
Re: Behavior Modification Consultation

Yesterday we discussed the ups and downs of the previous week. After sorting them out, we agreed that a lot of good things had happened, among which were:

1. Time spent in "Time Out" has decreased.
2. The previous day (Tuesday), the students had earned 10 minutes free time which was a good improvement.
3. Several of the children who were borderline behavior problems had caught on immediately to the new system and were now delightful kids.
4. They had been earning points toward an extra P.E. from an earlier project, and because of improved overall behavior, had earned quite a few more points than previously.

The four "downs" were:

1. One boy had an emotional outburst that upset the whole class.
2. You didn't feel well physically one day and knew you would be grouchy but couldn't help it.
3. You changed the seating arrangement and that disrupted things to some extent.
4. Your groups were not too successful because no one talked.

We decided on the following course of action:

1. Continue with last week's project, using heavy social reinforcement when the class behaves appropriately. Be sure to pair points with verbal praise, even if they are quiet because they know you are counting.
2. Make a colorful graph so they will see their improvement. It may not go straight up, but the trend is the important thing.
3. Try to keep a record of the times you use social reinforcement. Reward yourself for increases.

4. Let them know if you do not feel well and tell them to let you know when they don't feel well.
5. Talk to Nancy Post, School Social Worker, about the boy who seems to be having severe emotional outbreaks.
6. If they do not want to talk during your group sessions, tell them that's O.K. and they can use that time as a quiet time.
7. Chris Babin and Sue Jordan, my two School Psychologist Interns, would like to try some group guidance with the 5 or 6 kids who appear to have a really negative attitude. We'll ask Nancy Post to supervise them. Please talk to Nancy about parent permission.

I'll check with you next week. Take care of that cold! Good luck—you're doing a great job.
cc: Stan Wiklund, Principal
      Nancy Post, School Social Worker

October 4

To: Robin Gillespie, Syre School
From: Marcia McBeath, School Psychologist
Re: Behavior Modification Consultation

Last week had its ups and downs again, but in general you said you feel much better about the whole thing.

Ups:

1. The class earned their 100 points on your original project and will have a free P.E. plus the extra bonus of a cake.
2. You had a very good Social Studies discussion on Wednesday so the students showed it was possible.
3. You are able to be firm while still being positive.
4. When students were angry, rather than preach at them, you empathized with them and it worked.

Downs:

1. On the project for time spent between changing subjects, students peaked last Thursday and then declined. However, you felt you have raised your expectations for behavior required to earn the points.
2. You feel students are still not behaving appropriately on their own initiative, but rather because they know you are counting.
3. "Crummy" comments have continued.
4. The student who had an emotional outburst last week, blew up again.
5. Two girls continually try to challenge your authority.

We decided on the following strategies for each of the above "downs."

1. Spell out the criteria for the changing-subjects project, with the help of students. Criteria should be something like this—
   a. Books and materials out.
   b. Sitting in seat.
   c. Not talking to or bothering anyone.
2. In order that this behavior continue into the lesson, let the children know that you will count unobstrusively.
3. Chris Babin and Sue Jordan, School Psychologist Interns, will start their group guidance sessions next Wednesday. Their goal will be to improve the self-image of the five students with whom they will be working. Hopefully, if they feel better about themselves, they will feel better about others. One of the skills they will work on will be communications—how to listen while others talk. Later they plan to use some behavior rehearsal, to help change the overt behavior. They will keep in contact with you for evaluation. Nancy Post will supervise the two interns. You will discuss with Nancy, how to explain this to the group members and then to the rest of the class.

4. We'll ask Nancy to work with the boy with the outbursts, and with his family. From past records recently received, it appears that there are many problems in the home. At school, we'll work on behavior change.
5. Rather than being provoked into a clash of wills with the two girls who challenge you, try to set up some situations where they can have some opportunities for leadership and responsibility (such as being in charge of a bulletin board) and thus be able to feel important in a socially acceptable way. Do not fall into the trap of arguing. Do not respond to a challenge of your instructions.

Robin, I'm glad you feel better about the class. You looked better this week, too, and I suspect that getting over your cold has helped. Keep up the good work (and don't forget to reward yourself for an increase in the positive statements you make). See you next Thursday.
cc: Stan Wiklund, Principal
      Nancy Post, School Social Worker

October 12

To: Robin Gillespie, Syre School
From: Marcia McBeath, School Psychologist
Re: Behavior Modification Consultation

Again both good and bad days. You can express your anger now, without making demeaning comments, and that's good. There's nothing wrong with saying, "It makes me angry when you do such and such." In fact, in expressing anger instead of acting it out, you're a good model for the kids.

You wondered about starting a new project. Let's wait until the in-service starts. The graph is kind of leveling out. We talked about the possibility of a practice session—a kind of behavior rehearsal to make sure the kids understand the specifics for which they earn the points. We decided to try having a student count the points, rather than you, and not until a few minutes after the change (with a signal from you).

Robin, you may not be aware of it, but you have learned a lot in a very short time. I'm really proud of you. I'll bet you'll have student teachers of your own some day (and I'll say, "I told you so!"). I'll see you next week.

cc: Stan Wiklund, Principal

     Nancy Post, School Social Worker

October 18

To: Robin Gillespie, Syre School

From: Marcia McBeath, School Psychologist

Re: Behavior Modification Consultation

Lots of good things happened today. Robin, I think you are beginning to get the feel of using this approach (ignoring inappropriate behavior unless it comes under the four critical categories, and reinforcing the expected behavior). Here are the four things you did today that were great.

1. Child made a "smart" remark. You used to react. Today, although it was hard to do, you ignored it. Child stopped and returned to work.
2. Kids caught you in a mistake. Formerly you would get angry at them for their "disrespect." Today, you agreed you were wrong. Again, it was hard to do, but you did it (bravo) and again the results were encouraging.
3. In lining up for lunch, the rule is that the class leaves only when the line is

ready—a reasonable rule. Before, you would stand in front of them and if it took too long, reprimand them (which is a form of positive reinforcement—attention). Today, you ignored the deviant behavior, returned to your desk and began to work. Peer pressure immediately took over. This is a perfect example of negative reinforcement (the end of the punishment is the reward, and the kids control it themselves rather than you). May I use this example with the in-service?
4. Some of the students who had not formerly worked well independently did so today, and you praised them. We talked about the possibility of even sending a good work slip home if this continues.

We talked about several other things today—some of the possible reasons for your own feelings and behavior, some of the insights you are arriving at, and some ways to attack problems that still exist. One of these was your class group sessions. You said you had put it off for two or three days because of the pressure of academics and you finally called the meeting Wednesday. It went over like a lead balloon. Three suggestions for the group meetings:

1. Have the class decide on a time, and stick to it, even if you have to finish something else at another time.
2. Try it without moving the desks. Maybe the group could sit in a circle on the floor.
3. Ask Nancy to help you with your group sessions. She has had experience in doing this and could be a good asset.

You said that having students count the points is working out well. Two different boys have done it so far. That's good. You were afraid they would not count accurately, but they are. Be sure to let them know they are doing a good job.

You'll continue to have ups and downs, but now you are beginning to recognize what causes the ups and downs. Just because we can recognize something doesn't mean we can always change our own behavior, but you are on the way. Keep up the good work. We talked about my skipping a week, but you felt that at this crucial time you would prefer to continue seeing me weekly. I'll be over next Wednesday.

cc: Stan Wilkund, Principal
      Nancy Post, School Social Worker

October 26

To: Robin Gillespie, Syre School
From: Marcia McBeath, School Psychologist
Re: Behavior Modification Consultation

You reported that things are going better now and you are feeling much more comfortable with your class. Part of it is due to a change in the kids and part to a change in you. Here are some of the things we talked about, followed by our ideas for helping.

1. The kids can work very well for a half-hour without goofing off but then they begin to get restless.
   Suggestion: At the end of about 25 minutes, suggest they get up and stretch for a couple of minutes. Tell them it's a break and let them talk briefly to each other if they want.
2. One boy leans on the back two legs of his chair. Time-out hasn't helped too much.
   Suggestion: Try the "logical consequence" approach. Let him know that whenever he leans on the back two legs, you will remove his chair for ten minutes. He'll have to kneel or stand or sit on the floor. Remember, how-

ever, that it's very important to reinforce him heavily with praise when he sits correctly.
3. Two boys were playing with toy cars during a film. At first you ignored them but when they became so noisy that it was disruptive, you sent them to the office.
   Suggestion: First, take away the object of disruption and tell them you will return it to them when they go home. If they are silent for a few minutes after that, thank them for helping. If taking the objects away does not work, use "time-out." Again, continue to reinforce appropriate behavior after the five-minute "time-out."
4. During classroom discussions, such as social studies, some kids talk out instead of raising their hands.
   Suggestion: They have probably been intermittently reinforced for interrupting, by being responded to when they talk out. Try ignoring them and later praising them for not talking out. Be sure to call on them when they raise their hands. If the interruptions become intolerable, use "time-out."
5. Group meetings still are not too successful.
   Suggestion: Nancy said she'd be glad to come in when you want to have a meeting, and work with you on it.
6. Using the point system to change the behavior of moving more quickly and quietly from one subject to another has worked well enough that you are ready to wean away from counting points.
   Suggestion: When you are ready to wean away, tell the students how much they have improved. They are probably aware of it because of that beautiful graph you have. Tell them you'd like to see if they can continue the behavior without recording points, but you'll still continue to give them free time from time to time. At first, give it to them frequently, letting them know you appreciate how they are trying. Be-

come more and more intermittent, but keep up the praise.

Robin, do you realize that most of the above suggestions were your own, once we analyzed the problems? We discussed the fact that you now can use the theory we've talked so much about, and even though you slip occasionally (after all, who doesn't) that you're well on your way. You asked that I come back in two weeks and I'll be glad to. Keep up the good work.

cc: Stan Wiklund, Principal
       Nancy Post, School Social Worker

November 8

To: Robin Gillespie, Syre School
From: Marcia McBeath, School Psychologist
Re: Behavior Modification Consultation

You said that the new kid you have recording points doesn't always record them and the other students didn't even notice. Now is the time to wean away from keeping points on that project, as we discussed last time. Tell them that you'd like to see if they can continue moving quickly from subject to subject without recording the points, but you will still continue to give them free time from time to time. Be sure to keep up the social reinforcement at first very frequently, and then intermittently.

Your new project, the one you are going to do for the in-service, is to try to get the kids to be quiet during a social studies discussion while someone else is talking. You wanted to try dividing the class into teams. We decided that there might be a problem if all but one in the team try very hard, but because of that one, the team can never earn points. On the other hand, there

may be some peer pressure with teams. We decided on a modified team approach. Each child in the class would get a point if he or she did not talk out or to someone else in the class except when raising a hand and being recognized. In addition, if everyone in a team earns a point, the team will earn a bonus of three points. The discussion will last no longer than 15 minutes. A high school girl who is helping you, will record the points on individual cards which will be on each child's desk. At the end of the discussion, after points are given, she will collect the cards and record the total on a chart. When a total number of points have been earned, the class will have a popcorn party. Again, two things are important. One is to combine this with social reinforcement, and two is to let the kids know that this is to help them learn a good habit that will be useful in Junior High School next year, and that after a while they won't need to depend on points.

You also wondered what to do about the identified Learning Disability (SLD) kids in your class. Since there is apparently no program for them this year, and you do not have training in this area, just do the best you can, and don't worry if they are not achieving at grade level. They *are* learning something. Then, when you are ready to make recommendations next year, be sure that the Junior High School counselor knows they should go into an SLD class in Junior High.

It's fun working with you, Robin— you are so enthusiastic and you learn so fast. You're doing fine on your own, but I'll check back in three weeks.

cc: Stan Wilkund, Principal
       Nancy Post, School Social Worker

November 30

To: Robin Gillespie, Syre School
From: Marcia McBeath, School Psychologist
Re   Behavior Modification Consultation

Congratulations! You have graduated. Or should I say, you have had your commencement exercises, commencement meaning the beginning. Robin, you are more than ready to be on your own in the area of behavior modification because you now can figure out how to use the techniques with your kids better than I can.

Yesterday we talked about the best way of working with individual kids. For example, we decided that with kids like the one who tends to bother others, rather than having him isolated all of the time, that he would have the opportunity to sit near one of the students he chose on the sociogram, with the stipulation that he would move back (either on his own, or at your signal) if he becomes disruptive. After a while, he can try again.

Good things continue to happen. Your problem child was voted vice-president. Your team set-up for social studies discussion groups was going well. (Don't forget to send me a picture of the great chart of the thermometer with the mobile mercury). And there seems to be some improvement in the small group that my interns, Chris and Sue, are working with.

We decided that you would call me if you need any more help. Also, I'll see you at the in-service meetings. I have really enjoyed working with you Robin. Cheers.

cc: Stan Wiklund, Principal
      Nancy Post, School Social Worker

January 7

Marcia,

Behavior modification was a life saver in my room. I couldn't have made it this far without it.

I like its positive approach and reinforcement. It is hard always to reward promptly or praise immediately but overall it is a system that has proved itself.

Most of all I would like to thank you for all the *positive* and *cheerful* assistance you gave me. More than anything this is what spurred me on. I always remember how you encourage me. You are a great *asset* to the district. Thank you.

(signed) Robin Gillespie

51. *SAY, IT'S MY PROBLEM*

HELEN V. TRICKETT   Palo Alto, California, Unified School District

Krumboltz and Thoresen point out in Part One of this book that there are "seven stumbling blocks that counselors face in making the translation" from "amorphous feelings to specific goals." The first stumbling block is presentation of the problem as that of someone else's behavior, rather than that of the referring party. This type of situation was my concern with Kay, a young second-grade teacher. She asked me for consultation to help make

eleven of her parents understand reinforcement theory. The parents, it
seems, had expressed strong disapproval of her use of rewards with her
students.

During our first session, we set two
goals: One was to review Kay's recol-
lections of the "awful" comments made
by the parents about her use of rewards, and the second was to formulate
the problem.

Kay said that she knew the problem exactly: The parents did not know
about nor did they appreciate the value
of the "use of reinforcement" in changing and maintaining children's behavior. She added that she had heard
me talk about reinforcement as important in learning and that she had
read much about the use of M & Ms as
positive reinforcers. I said that I certainly was a proponent of reinforcement theory and that under certain
conditions I thought that M & Ms
could be useful rewards. She nodded
vigorously and said, "What I need is
for you to meet with me and the parents to convince them of the effectiveness of reinforcement." I replied, "That
could be a way to go, if that remained
our conclusion after we reviewed the
parents' 'objections to reinforcement.' "[1]

As Kay recalled the comments, I
wrote them down. Then both of us
looked at those notes. We looked for
possible patterns or similarities in the
comments.

K: *There* is one who objects, really, and
believes *only* in intrinsic reinforcement. She was really emphatic.

C: Yes, now what commonality do the
others have?

K: Let's see, hmm. It looks like they
each talk about candy or material
rewards.

C: Yes, they seem to object to those
specifically and not to reinforcement
generally.

K: Gee, I guess I'll just quit the candy
and go back to my old reward of saying "Good!" Too bad, with the candy,
a couple of kids were beginning to
turn on, too.

C: Tell me more about those turning-on
kids.[2]

K: Well, a couple of them are now completing their work, asking me for
help, and just behaving better! I
shared this with those parents, but
they objected too. I guess they are
hung up on the candy bit. They were
glad their kids did better, though.

C: I'm impressed that you feel you have
brought about some behavior changes
in some children by using a reinforcement technique. We could conclude from this list that all but one
of the parents really object to the
use of candy as a reward and not to
the concept of reinforcement.

K: Say, that's right, but, well, what else
can I do? I get tired of just saying,
"Good!" I mean, it sounds so mechanical, and it doesn't work so well.
I'm sure the kids get tired of it too.
At least all kids love candy! I know I
need a variety of ways to compliment.

C: I couldn't agree more that we need
a variety of reinforcers to keep from
feeling mechanical. We also need to
know some that are unique to a child

[1] *Editors' note:* The consultant did not
deny Kay's request but made it clear that
whatever action was taken would be based
on a joint decision after more facts had been
considered.

[2] *Editors' note:* Note that the emphasis
is on what *does* work.

or meaningful to an individual.[3]

K: How do you get to know more reinforcers and how do you find special ones for a particular child?

C: Perhaps I could help you expand your reinforcement repertoire. . . .

K: How could you do that? That would really be great! Could we start right away? Oh, and how can I handle my complaining parents?

C: Which would you like to choose as your first objective?

K: Handle the complaining parents.

C: What would be the quickest way to do that?

K: Well, of course, quit using candy!

C: That is a fast-action plan! Then what would be your next objective?

K: Could I set up weekly appointments with you and really learn about the

whole notion of reinforcement?

C: I'll get those weekly appointments on my calendar now.

We set two noon-time dates a week apart to review social-learning principles. We set a third date for coming up (between us) with a *list of reinforcers available to Kay for use in the classroom and in the school, as well as a list of reinforcing behaviors that she would feel comfortable using.*

I asked her how she would know whether or not any of these plans had helped her. She declared this list of priorities: The children would change because of her reinforcement plans; the parents would notice the changes; the parents would not object to the method; and Kay would feel better about herself and about how she had encouraged desirable behavior.

We held our sessions on social-learning principles and focused on rein-

---

[3] *Editors' note:* A crucial point: Tailoring consequences to the person is often what makes the difference in using reinforcement successfully. Many of us can not stand M & Ms!

TABLE 1   Resources for Activities in the School Environment Used by the Teacher To Reinforce Second-Grade Children

Resources	Activities[a]
People (peers, teacher, principal, librarian, secretary, custodian)	read or be read to, write for and with, dictate to, study math, share or make music, play P.E. or sedentary game, seek recognition (of accomplishment), tutor, apprentice to
Time (during, before, after school)	rearrange schedule, *gain* for desired or *subtract* from undesired activity, create use of
Space (classroom, outdoors, other school areas— library, offices, multipurpose room)	rearrange own, share, empty, fill up, create use of
Material (books, writing and art materials, furniture, toys, building equipment)	borrow, dispense, ignore, create own

[a] *Choices had to be acceptable to child, teacher, parent, and significant others.*

forcement. We drew up a list of reinforcers all available within the school environment (see Table 1). Kay practiced and learned a variety of individual and particular reinforcers. She also kept records of plans for behavior change, noting the reinforcers to be used (see Figure 1).

After two months, there were no further parental complaints about reinforcement. Kay noted some planned behavior change in each child. At several conferences she shared her techniques with the parents, who might want to use them to modify home behaviors. She then came to me to share a "real discovery": "Say, things are working out just fine, and I remembered that I referred my kids' parents to you, but I really should have referred myself! Say, it's *my* problem I needed to tackle!"

Problem	Margo completes two out of ten paper-pencil tasks weekly.
Objective	Increase by 100 percent papers completed in one week using social reinforcer.
Procedure	1. Use *name* and *comment privately* daily at different stages of paper-pencil task progress.
	a. "Good beginning, Margo!"
	b. "Margo, you are moving along!" At about midpoint in time alloted.
	c. "I'm happy to see you finished one paper (or two) today, Margo."
	2. Make no comment if task-appropriate behavior does not occur at midpoint or end.
Evaluate	1. Review results at end of week with consultant.
	2. Objective reached—continue.
	3. Objective failed—replan social reinforcers, timing, frequency, objective.

FIGURE 1 Teacher's plan for using social reinforcers to modify task-completion behavior of a second-grade girl.

DEVELOPMENT OF ACADEMIC SKILL

52. *TEACHING STUDY SKILLS TO ADULTS*

DAVID M. WARK   University of Minnesota

At the University of Minnesota Evening School course on how to study, the students, whose average age was twenty-seven years, wished to learn or to relearn techniques for college-level studying. The course covered listening, taking notes, concentrating, methods for studying texts, scheduling time and goals, preparing for and taking exams, conquering exam and other anxieties, and individually selected self-improvement projects.

TECHNIQUES

Behavioral methods of teaching study skills have worked well in the course. In general, there are three categories of techniques that can be used by these intact, uninstitutionalized, exuberant, and normal adults.

Self-Observation

The first category contains all of those techniques that encourage the learner to observe himself objectively. Specific examples include charting, counting, measuring, and in some way recording one's own learning behaviors. The actual recording equipment may be a highly sophisticated computer-controlled physiological monitor, or it may be a simple 3 × 5-inch card that a student carries in his pocket and on which he makes a check mark every time he completes a study assignment. Regardless of the equipment, the data have one purpose. They are gathered as a baseline against which to evaluate change in study behaviors. Data collecting was not originally conceived as a modification technique *per se*. Interestingly though, for some students the simple act of charting seems to produce significant behavioral change. About 50 percent of the students tend to increase the number of hours per day that they study after keeping a simple time diary for one week.[1]

[1] *Editors' note:* This is not surprising. Observing one's own behavior systematically over time can do several things. One of them is to provide the basis for self-reinforcement, especially as the person sees some progress being made. See Article 53 for more information on using self-observation to facilitate change.

Stimulus Control

The second category of behavioral skill development techniques includes all those methods that involve changes in the environment. It is axiomatic that study behavior, like all behavior, is under some kind of stimulus control. Changing the stimulus will in most instances change the behavior. Finding or manufacturing a new and nondistracting place to study is one type of environmental modification that can change study time and its effects. Stimulus control also involves more esoteric techniques. Physiological states and internal self-instruction may be considered stimuli for study. Approached in this way, fatigue, self-doubt, and anxiety are not seen as excuses for procrastination; rather, they are treated as merely some of a small set of possible stimuli that should be changed through rest, information, or desensitization, in order to develop study techniques.

Charting and self-observing under a variety of stimulus conditions can assist in the analysis of significant environmental stimuli. Students may find, for example, that they have studied better at certain times of the day, at certain places, or following certain activities. This knowledge of stimulus control over study can be used to plan more effective study strategies.

Consequences

The third category of behavior-control techniques includes self-applied consequences of study. These may be rewards or punishments contracted for by the student and administered according to whether study has been effective or ineffective. The desired effect of these techniques is directly to increase preselected study behaviors, often by reducing undesirable alternatives. In part, the effect may result from direct positive reinforcement of study. It may also be that the processes of self-observation and stimulus change produce effects, regardless of whether or not the consequences are applied. It may also be that, when a free and unrestrained adult volunteers to change his behavior under the guidance of a teacher, reinforcement or punishment is relatively less necessary than in the example of a retarded or institutionalized patient. In any case, contingent consequences are the most obvious and commonly recognized methods of behavior control.

ILLUSTRATIVE APPLICATIONS

Self-Observation: Reading Base Rate

The most common request in the course is for assistance in increasing reading rate. For the students who wish to increase rates, this goal can be chosen as an individual project. However, other students do not wish to devote that much time to rate increase, though they would like some assist-

ance. For them, the technique of charting seems most appropriate and effective.

Each student chooses a book that demands slightly less than his typical reading rate. That is, the sentences should be short enough, the vocabulary familiar enough, and the level of difficulty low enough so that he can read it with good subjective comprehension. The book should be related to an area that is taught in a college course. A book on English Restoration history would be appropriate; a historical novel about the same period would not.

The student counts the number of words in a five-line sample on each of two randomly selected pages. Then he divides the total by ten, in order to obtain the average number of words in a line.

Students are asked to read their selected books for five minutes. They can use a kitchen timer, a wrist watch with a sweep second hand, or a stop watch to time themselves. Reliability of the timer is more important than accuracy. At the end of the five-minute reading period, they count the number of lines read. They convert the number of lines to words per minute in one of two ways. They can use the following formula:

$$\frac{\text{Number of words per line} \times \text{Number of lines read in five minutes}}{5} = \text{words/minute}$$

Or they can go directly to the conversion table provided in the class. The table is particularly helpful to students whose math skills are unreliable.

Students are requested to spend twenty minutes on timed reading on

three different occasions between classes each week. Thus, they bring 12 rate samples to each class. They are encouraged to read at different times and different places, in order to check the effects of those variables on their reading rate. Some students discover that they read faster with more comprehension in the morning hours. They can therefore plan their study time for the early hours, rather than for the more traditional evening hours. Other students find that the places where they study have distinct effects on their reading rates.

Without any particular instruction in class, students who chart their rates generally begin to make increases. These increases may be in steps, with sudden spurts and then plateaus, followed by further spurts. Other students may show steady increases over several weeks. Examples of both patterns are shown in Figure 1. Note that both students stopped charting

their rates after several weeks. However, note also that, when charting was reinstituted in the last week of the course, both students had produced gains in rate. Changes in reading rate earned no consequences of any kind. There was no external or grade payoff for increase rate. The data demonstrate the effects of a type of self-observation on behavior change.[2]

[2] *Editors' note:* The oft-observed increase in reading speed as a function of any type of attention to it is the basis for much quackery. Expensive courses claiming to multiply existing reading rates are unnecessary. The same results can be obtained by the simplest of instructions—or no instructions at all, as documented here.

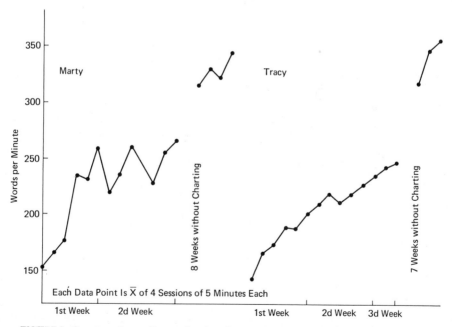

FIGURE 1   Increases in reading-study rates from noncontingent charting.

Stimulus Control: Improving Concentration

One of the most difficult problems for adult students seems to be developing adequate concentration while studying. Students report that their minds wander, particularly when they are studying topics that they do not enjoy. Indeed, when they chart daydreams, some students discover to their amazement that they cannot go more than thirty seconds without thinking about something unrelated to study. Several behavioral techniques to enhance concentration seem to work well, at least with some adults.

As part of the improvement of concentration, students are educated to see that concentration can be a habit.

It is defined as the reduction of competing internal responses while in the presence of books. Students should attempt to associate study with particular locations, times of day, and rituals designed as stimuli just for study and nothing else. Of course, at times they will think of other things. They are taught at those times to stand up and face away from their textbooks. That is, if they are going to daydream, they should do it but while facing away from their books. The book and desk should become stimuli for study, and students can, by means of the simple expedient of standing up, protect that association. Figure 2 shows the data on the decrease in distracting thoughts reported by one student. He was instructed that, whenever he felt like

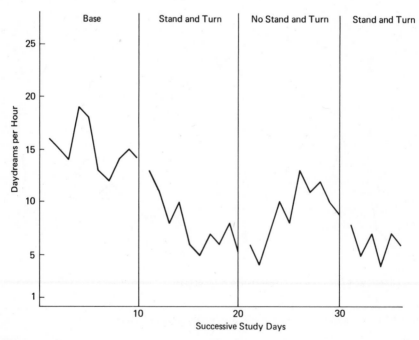

FIGURE 2 Reduction in daydreaming after standing and turning away from reading material.

thinking about something else, he should stand up and turn around.[3]

There are several possible explanations for this reduction in daydreaming. One may have been the gradual transfer of control of study behavior to the desk. Another may be that the student was required to chart daydreaming, a technique of self-awareness. Third, the motor act of standing up and turning around may have changed the internal state of the student sufficiently so that his drop in daydreaming had a physical basis. If so, other types of motor activity, like breathing and stretching, may be helpful in developing concentration.[4]

Consequences: Self-Applied Payoffs for Study

In a unit halfway through the how-to-study course, students are given explicit formal instruction in the techniques of behavioral self-control. They learn a bit about the psychology of reward and punishment, shaping, and contracting. Then they are asked, as part of the course, to apply these techniques to themselves. They choose aspects of their own behavior to observe

[3] *Editors' note:* A similar stimulus-control method has been used successfully with insomniacs, who often experience "racing thoughts" and other cognitive activities that interfere with going to sleep. Each person is instructed to get out of bed and go to another room if he is still awake after fifteen minutes. This is repeated until he falls asleep. See Article 37.

[4] *Editors' note:* Yes, they should be helpful. Various forms of meditation and yoga involve very specific physical (as well as cognitive) activities in order to develop and maintain concentration.

and modify, they select the contingencies, and they apply the payoffs. Of course, not all students are hooked on this technique. Some are satisfied that they have no behavior that they wish to change. Others think that formal programs of self-control are childish games. The instructor has a very important role in getting students committed. A certain amount of modeling and enthusiasm are definitely called for in order to improve the student. Two cases illustrate the effectiveness of the contracting and self-applied payoff approaches (Wark, 1969).

Procrastination Terry was eighteen years old and not working. Although he had the verbal ability of the average university freshman, he had been graduated in the bottom quarter of his high-school class. On the first night of the how-to-study class, he reported that his main problem was starting on his homework. He procrastinated too much. From September 20 until November 18 he did no homework at all. On November 18, following the lecture on behavioral self-modification, he volunteered a contract. He would use fifteen minutes of music as a reward for five minutes of reading his textbook. The contract was signed and witnessed, with great formality, in the class. At the next class meeting, Terry appeared with the chart shown in Figure 3.

Terry was much fussed over by all colleagues because of the chart. Following that presentation, he changed from a silent loner to a rather frequent and lively contributor. He reported at the end of the class that he no longer needed to use the contract but main-

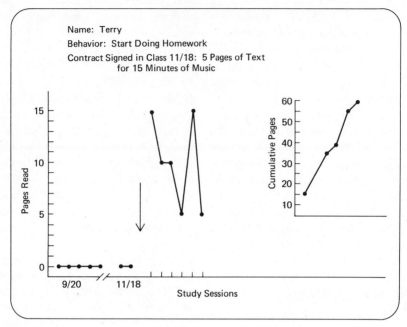

Name: Terry

Behavior: Start Doing Homework

Contract Signed in Class 11/18: 5 Pages of Text
for 15 Minutes of Music

FIGURE 3   Increase in study time rewarded by access to rock music.

tained adequate study output in all of his courses.

Certain variables may account for the effects of the contract. First of all, Terry chose it himself. The procedure probably would not have worked had he been forced. Second, there were a a public commitment and social pressure from the students who had witnessed the signing. Indeed, they were very supportive of Terry when he fulfilled his contract. It is unlikely that he had ever received so much social support for studying in the past. Third, Terry had to pinpoint and record his own behavior in order to make out the chart. Of course, it is impossible to identify the relative effectiveness of these three variables in Terry's case, but, considering his previous study behavior, the increase in output is remarkable.

Persistence   Wayne was a twenty-five-year-old high-school graduate. He had had two years of undistinguished college work. Like Terry, he reported difficulty in starting to study. However, he proposed a mild punishment contract.

Wayne worked as a supervisor over a section of female clerical personnel. He contracted to wear a disreputable and dirty sport coat to work if he had not put in a full hour of study the night before. The results of his contract are reported in Figure 4.

The punishment effect appeared when his clerical staff teased him about the coat. He reported that hanging the

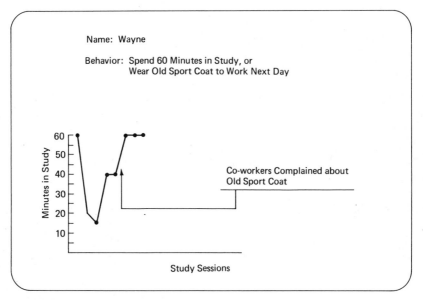

Name: Wayne

Behavior: Spend 60 Minutes in Study, or
Wear Old Sport Coat to Work Next Day

Co-workers Complained about
Old Sport Coat

FIGURE 4   Increase in study time to avoid teasing.

coat over the desk had become sufficient to keep him studying.[5]

[5] *Editors' note:* An interesting finding. Wayne's experience became generalized so that the sight of the old sport coat was sufficient to maintain his studying (an example of negative reinforcement). Perhaps the image or thought of wearing the coat will eventually suffice.

Wayne's case illustrates the effectiveness of social pressure in maintaining a study contract. The primary effect was not owing to self-applied consequences. It was only when his staff began to tease him that he increased his study time. If they had not responded or had not noticed the sport coat, the contingency might not have worked.

references

Emery, J. Systematic desensitization: Reducing test anxiety. In J. D. Krumboltz & C. E. Thoresen (Eds.), *Behavioral counseling: Cases and techniques.* New York: Holt, Rinehart and Winston, 1969. Pp. 267–288.

Wark, D. M. Case studies in behavior modification. In G. B. Schick & M. M. May (Eds.), *The psychology of reading behavior: 18th Yearbook of the National Reading Conference.* Milwaukee: 1969. Pp. 217–228.

Wark, D. M. Test panic, daydreaming and procrastination. In. D. M. Wark (Ed.), *College and adult reading VI: The 6th Yearbook of the North Central Reading Association.* Minneapolis: 1971. Pp. 131–151.

Wolpe, J. *Practice of behavior therapy.* New York: Pergamon, 1969.

Yates, A. *Behavior therapy.* New York: Wiley, 1970.

53. *IMPROVING STUDY BEHAVIORS THROUGH SELF-CONTROL TECHNIQUES*

C. STEVEN RICHARDS   University of Missouri

Developing behavioral self-control entails learning to become one's own therapist and teacher by making specific responses that modify other personal responses. There is already substantial evidence that self-monitoring has therapeutic potential as a self-control technique (Kazdin, 1974b; Thoresen & Mahoney, 1974). This potential can be applied to the clinical problem of college students' underachievement.

THE BIBLIOTHERAPY PACKAGE

Bibliotherapy involves the use of typed handouts that give detailed, self-contained therapeutic instructions. The use of bibliotherapy to teach students self-control techniques requires minimal interaction between students and therapists.[1] Interactions usually involve clarification of handout instructions. We distributed the handouts during several one-hour group sessions spaced over four to six weeks. Students kept the handouts in personal folders. Volunteer college students wishing to improve their study habits formed the subject pool for our controlled treatment studies (see Richards, 1975). The sample handouts presented here are adapted from these treatment studies. Sample handouts are provided for replication purposes, but the samples

here constitute only a subset of some of our bibliotherapy packages.[2]

SAMPLE SELF-MONITORING HANDOUTS

Instructions for Self-Monitoring Study Behavior
HOW TO IMPROVE THE QUANTITY AND QUALITY OF YOUR STUDYING THROUGH SELF-MONITORING:
Self-monitoring entails observing and recording your behavior. Previous research has indicated that self-monitoring study behavior may aid students to improve their study habits and to attain better grades. Self-monitoring (also known as self-recording) is simple and easy to do.[3] Think of self-monitoring as a self-help therapy procedure, rather than a record keeping chore. By self-monitoring your study habits, you provide yourself with structure, information, and a basis for self-evaluation.

HOW TO USE THE SELF-MONITORING SHEETS:
(1) Keep daily records of three types of information: (a) the number of pages read for your Psychology 2 course, (b) the number of hours studied for your Psychology 2 course, and (c) the number of hours studied for all of your courses.

---

[1] *Editors' note:* Written handouts save valuable counselor time and also guarantee that a well-prepared, standardized set of directions is communicated every time.

[2] All of the handouts used in one of the earlier studies are available in appendixes to the author's doctoral dissertation (Richards, 1974). Copies of the dissertation can be purchased from University Microfilms, 300 North Zeeb Road, Ann Arbor, Michigan 48106.

[3] *Editors' note:* A more common term is "self-observation."

(2) Fill in your self-monitoring sheets *every day*.

(3) Keep accurate records—accurate information will be most helpful.

(4) How to fill in the self-monitoring sheets:

    (a) Under # pages read for the Psychology 2 course, include any Psychology 2 related reading (e.g., Munn, Fernald & Fernald; Daniel; Daniel & Chute; reading for labs; etc.).

    (b) Under # hours studied for the Psychology 2 course, include any Psychology 2 related studying (e.g., lectures, seminars, lab reports, readings, etc.).

    (c) Under # hours studied for all courses, include the total time you spend studying each day for all your courses (including Psychology 2: e.g., biology, history, Psychology 2 & English combined).

    (d) Total each column weekly.

    (e) Also estimate how many pages you must read for the next Psychology 2 exam, and set a goal for the total number of hours you want to study that week.[4]

(5) Explanation of the *sample* self-monitoring sheet (see Figure 1):

On Monday, February 18, John Doe read 15 pages of Psychology 2 related material, he studied 1½ hours for Psychology 2, and he studied a total of 4 hours for all his courses. He estimates he must read 250 pages for his next Psychology 2 exam. At the bottom of the sheet, he has summed up his weekly totals. Notice that for the week beginning February 18, he has read a total of 55 pages for Psychology 2, he has studied a total of 9 hours for Psychology 2, and he has studied a total of 30 hours for all his courses. John's total of 30 hours for all courses is 2 hours short of his goal.

If you have any questions, please ask them! Try to follow these techniques precisely.

Further Instructions for Self-Monitoring Study Behavior
HOW TO USE THE SELF-MONITORING GRAPHS:[5]

(1) Keep *daily* records on your graph of the number of pages read for Psychology 102.

(2) Keep an accurate graph—accurate information will be most helpful.

(3) How to mark the plot (line) on your graph:

    (a) Plot only the number of pages you read for Psychology 102 (e.g., Ruch & Zimbardo, Buckhout, seminar reading, etc.).

    (b) Pages read are on the vertical line, dates are on the horizontal line.

    (c) Plot the number of pages you read each day in a *cumulative* manner by adding the number for that day to the previous day's total.

(4) Explanation of the *sample* self-monitoring graph (see Figure 2):

Notice that the plot on the sample graph is cumulative—that is, the line *never* goes down, only horizon-

---

[4] *Editors' note:* Goal setting seems a crucial part of this process. Then self-monitoring will permit the student to determine how close he has come to reaching his goal, thereby setting the stage for self-reinforcement (if the goal has been reached).

[5] The sample self-monitoring sheet and graph have been adapted from different experiments.

Name: JOHN   DOE   Date of Monday: Feb. 18, 1974.
            (FIRST)   (LAST)
Number of pages to be read for the next Psychology 2 exam: 250   (pages).
Goal for weekly total hours (for all courses):   32   (hr).

Self-Monitoring Sheet (sample)			
Date	Number of Pages Read for Psychology 2 (to nearest page)	Number of Hours Studied for Psychology 2 (to nearest ¼ hr.)	Number of Hours Studied for All Courses (to nearest ¼ hr.)
Monday, Feb. 18	15 (pages)	1½ (hr)	4 (hr)
Tuesday	10 (pages)	2 (hr)	5¼ (hr)
Wednesday	13 (pages)	3¼ (hr)	8¼ (hr)
Thursday	0 (pages)	0 (hr)	0 (hr)
Friday	3 (pages)	1¼ (hr)	6½ (hr)
Saturday	0 (pages)	0 (hr)	2 (hr)
Sunday	14 (pages)	1 (hr)	4 (hr)
Weekly Totals	55 (pages)	9 (hr)	30 (hr)

FIGURE 1   A sample self-monitoring sheet.

tally or up. The line should go horizontally if you read 0 pages that day and it should go up if you read 1 or more pages that day. Also notice that on a cumulative graph each day's number of pages is added on to the total for the previous day. For example, in the sample graph, Mr. Doe has read a total of 69 pages by Wednesday, March 21. When the plot reaches the top of the graph (4th of April in the sample graph) you start at the bottom again. The plot on the sample graph is drawn as if Mr. Doe had the same pattern for each week. The steeper the plot, the more you are reading. (The numbers for the sample graph were chosen arbitrarily and are not meant to imply what you should do.)

If you have any questions, please ask them! Follow the instructions carefully.

COMMENTS ON EFFECTIVENESS AND TREATMENT ALTERATIONS

We have found that these self-monitoring techniques are effective in improving students' study behaviors and grades. In one of our controlled treatment studies, involving 108 students (Richards, 1975), self-monitoring proved to be a useful treatment adjunct to advice on study skills (M grade = 2.9), when compared with advice alone (M grade = 2.7), attention-placebo controls (M grade = 2.3), and no-contact controls (M grade = 2.2). Another (unpublished) controlled treatment study with ninety-six students replicated the finding that self-monitoring can change study behavior. Students in the groups that used self-monitoring plus advice on study skills improved their grades

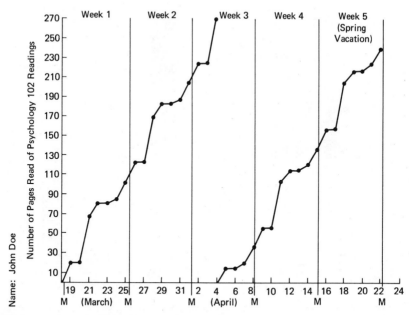

FIGURE 2   A *sample* self-monitoring graph (self-recording graph).

more (M improvement $= .29$) than those in the groups that received advice alone (M decrement $= .04$) or in the attention-placebo and no-contact groups (M decrement $= .28$). Others have also found that self-monitoring can be an effective self-control technique (for example, Johnson & White, 1971; Kazdin, 1974b; Van Zoost & Jackson, 1974).

Our reasearch and clinical experience have suggested three useful alterations in these techniques. First, the self-monitoring procedure should be simplified. For instance, we could delete the graph and have students record only one item on the sheet: the number of hours studied for all courses.[6] Students will not use self-

[6] *Editors' note:* Something valuable

monitoring very long if it is difficult.

Encouraging students to persist in their use of self-monitoring is also facilitated by fading their contacts with the therapist. Hence, the second alteration requires gradually increased intervals between treatment sessions (faded contact), rather than equal intervals between treatment sessions (steady contact). Examination of Figure 3 demonstrates the superiority of faded

might be lost, however. Goals must be set for each course. It seems useful to estimate the number of hours (or pages) one will have to prepare for an examination or to write a paper and then to monitor progress in relation to each goal. Recording *total* study time may only disguise the amount of effort needed for each goal and inhibit the budgeting of time among goals.

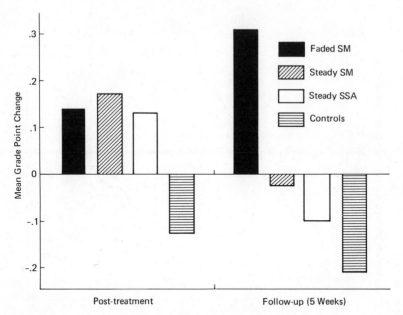

FIGURE 3 Mean exam-grade change from a pretreatment course exam to post-treatment and follow-up course exams (unpublished study). Students ($n = 118$) were in bibliotherapy-style treatment groups involving one of the following conditions: faded therapist contact with self-monitoring emphasis (faded SM), steady therapist contact with self-monitoring emphasis (steady SM), steady therapist contact with advice on study skills (steady SSA), and no treatment and no contact (controls). A grade change of $+1.0$ represents an improvement of one letter grade, for example, improvement from a C to a B.

treatment contact.[7] The results portrayed in Figure 3 are from a controlled treatment study (unpublished) involving 118 students. The fading procedure is one way to cope with the problem of treatment maintenance.

The third suggested alteration entails emphasizing the information-feedback component of self-monitoring (see Kazdin, 1974a) and using self-monitoring mainly with students who are un-

[7] *Editors' note:* The gradual withdrawal, rather than abrupt termination, of contact with the counselor seems a logical procedure for facilitating maintenance of a variety of new behaviors.

aware of their actual study habits. One method of determining who may be classified as "unaware" is to compare students' pretreatment estimates of study behavior (hours per week) with their actual self-monitoring records in the first week of treatment. Very poor matches would be classified as "unaware." We have found that students lacking accurate information about the extent or amount of their study behavior benefit more from self-monitoring (M grade improvement = .54) than those who are already knowledgeable about their study behavior (M grade improvement = .06).

references

Johnson, S. M. & White, G. Self-observation as an agent of behavioral change. *Behavior Therapy*, 1971, **2**, 488–497.

Kazdin, A. E. Reactive self-monitoring: The effects of response desirability, goal setting, and feedback. *Journal of Consulting and Clinical Psychology*, 1974a, **42**, 704–716.

Kazdin, A. E. Self-monitoring and behavior change. In M. J. Mahoney & C. E. Thoresen, *Self-control: Power to the person*. Monterey, Calif.: Brooks/Cole, 1947b. Pp. 218–246.

Richards, C. S. Behavior modification of college students' study behaviors via "self-control" techniques. (Doctoral dissertation, State University of New York at Stony Brook). Ann Arbor: University Microfilms, 1974. No. 74-5511. *Dissertation Abstracts International*, 1974, **34**, 5208B.

Richards, C. S. Behavior modification of studying through study skills advice and self-control procedures. *Journal of Counseling Psychology*, 1975, **22**, 431–436.

Thoresen, C. E. & Mahoney, M. J. *Behavioral self-control*. New York: Holt, Rinehart and Winston, 1974.

Van Zoost, B. L. & Jackson, B. T. Effects of self-monitoring and self-administered reinforcement on study behaviors. *Journal of Educational Research*, 1974, **67**, 216–218.

ASSERTIVENESS TRAINING

54. *ASSERTIVENESS TRAINING FOR WOMEN*[1]

SHARON ANTHONY BOWER   Stanford, California

The "reentry woman" is appearing in increasing numbers at the counseling services of colleges and universities. She is typically a middle-aged housewife who is trying to move out of the home and to reenter the working world of business and professions. Reentry is rarely easy. No Head Start program helps these women, who often feel depressed or anxious because their academic knowledge and skills are rusty. Moreover, they often share the cultural

---

[1] *Editors' note:* The case reported here is that of a "reentry woman." However, the DESC script-writing technique described here has been used successfully in training both men and women to be more assertive.

---

belief that their long years of housewifery have made them passively ineffectual, have rotted their brains, and have rendered them incompetent. To aggravate the problem, many of these women may be reentering against the wishes of their families and friends. The culture typically does not support reentry women as they are forced to change from their traditional roles as homemakers. Counselors see them struggling to define their new roles.

As a reentry woman myself, I was an obvious counselor for such clients who came to Stanford's Institute for Behavioral Counseling. I noticed, however, that their laments about anxiety, depression, and inability to speak up for their rights were not just meno-pausal complaints; I discovered amaz-ingly similar complaints among younger women at a junior college where I was also counseling. Our perspectives must shift, so that we see these women not as needing menopausal painkillers but as needing reorientation in their ways of handling interpersonal problems.

In this paper I describe the evolu-tion of the procedures I am using in assertiveness training for young and old, women and men. In the beginning I could only listen sympathetically to the sad stories of the reentry women, enmeshed as they were in tangles of housework, charity work, overbearing parents or in-laws, rebellious teenagers, and overworked spouses; all were suf-fering exhaustion from continual de-mands on their energies and time, all finding very little comfort in their lives. I soon realized that these women wanted more than a sympathetic ear. One day a client demanded: "Why do you just listen to me ramble on? I'm tired of hearing myself talk!" Some-what stunned, I muttered something about my first duty being to listen sym-pathetically. She replied: "But I don't need any more sympathy. I need some plans for action!"[2]

THE CASE OF JOAN

Joan was a forty-five-year-old woman, separated from her husband and living with her three children and elderly mother. She was returning after twenty-five years of housewifery to the world of full-time work and part-time college. One of her problems was her mother, who was very critical and domineering. Though anxious about her mother's domineering ways, she was in conflict because she needed her mother's help with finances, housekeeping, and baby-sitting. It seemed clear that Joan needed to learn techniques of asserting herself and standing up for her rights against her domineering mother.

First, we had to isolate one or more scenes that were causing her problems. I wanted to know when her mother dominated her, in connection with what subjects, under what circum-stances, and where. To illustrate how questions pinpointed the setting of the problem, here is an edited dialogue taped from the second session:

C: Joan, last time you said you needed plans for action, that you wanted to do more than talk. I agree. To know where we should begin making plans, I need to ask you what is bothering you most today.

J: I'm depressed. I feel like "poor little Joan" all the time.

C: Why do you feel like "poor little Joan"?

J: Oh, my mother—she's always nagging me and the kids.

C: What do you mean "nagging"?

J: She nags. It gets on my nerves.

C: What does she say, for instance?

J: That I shouldn't go to a church I like to go to. She says that it's too far away, that it costs too much gasoline, that it takes too much time to get there.

C: What do you say then?

J: I don't say anything.

C: How does that make you feel?

---

[2] *Editors' note:* Good for her! It would be great if all clients could demand help in implementing action plans. Sympathy and empathy go only so far.

J: She just keeps nagging—she tells me what to do—she won't let me live my life.

C: I get the picture of a demanding mother, but how do you *feel* when she tells you where to go to church?

J: I guess I feel like a little girl again, and she's telling me to come along to Sunday school.

C: How do you feel when she treats you like a little Sunday-school girl?

J: Poor little Joan, that's me.

C: Helpless?

J: Yes—like I'm not old enough to make my own decisions.

C: Have you ever told your mother how her behavior makes you feel?

J: Well, she oughta know.

C: What do you do that should make her know how you feel?

J: Well, when she starts nagging, I throw down my coffee cup, grab my purse, slam the door, and leave as fast as I can get out the driveway.

Many clients who might qualify for assertiveness training will *not* say, "I need to become more assertive." Like Joan, they often begin by saying, "I'm depressed," "I'm exhausted from being torn in a hundred directions," or "Nobody listens to me." Unlike Joan, they rarely proceed to the conclusion that they need action plans for coping with aggravating interpersonal problems. Nonetheless, assertiveness training may be suggested when the client clearly needs it.[3]

[3] *Editors' note:* If the client knew and could perform the actions that would cure her depression, she would not be a client. The counselor has the responsibility for recommending the specific treatment steps that have the greatest likelihood of lifting the client's depression. The client usually does not know what will work and may resist the proposed therapeutic plan.

To begin assertiveness training, we pinpointed a recurrent scene in which Joan was put down. The dialogue given identifies the person who puts her down (nicknamed "the Downer") and what this Downer does that irritates and makes her feel put down (nagging her about church). Typically, Joan felt helpless and would display her anger at her mother in childish ways, hoping that her mother would see the upset that she was causing. But, in fact, her mother appeared totally insensitive to these small storms; it was Joan who would later feel remorse over being angry at her mother's "good-intentioned" advice.

In assertiveness training, a first critical point to be taught is that it is the client who must change her (or his) own behavior. The counselor is not going to change the nagging mother. Through her new assertive behavior, Joan had to become the agent for changing the behavior of her Downer.[4]

I began by concentrating on a specific put-down situation, one that was important to Joan so that she was motivated to change her behavior, as well as one in which her new assertive behavior was likely to succeed. To this end, I asked specific questions, then introduced role playing, as the following excerpt (edited from the second session with Joan) illustrates:

C: Let's analyze what happens to make you feel like a child. Let's pretend that I'm you now, drinking coffee in the kitchen before getting ready to

[4] *Editors' note:* This is a point that counselors and other helpers should really stress: "I can only help you to help yourself. It is you who will be taking action."

go to church. You act out what your mother says and sounds like when she comes into the kitchen. What would you say if you were your mother? You start out as your mother.

J: (as her mother) Joan, don't tell me you're going to that church again? How many times have I told you that church is too far away?

C: That's a very strong voice you have when you talk like your mother. Good! Do you feel like a child when you talk like your mother?

J: No! I feel really strong—like an adult —but that's not really me![5]

C: Well, let's decide whether you *want* to sound stronger. You need to decide what you want to do, or what you *could* do, about this church-going scene.[6] Let's ask: What do you want to do? For instance, you *could* give in—keep the peace—and not go to the church you have been attending.

J: No! I like this church too much to give it up.

C: Well, then, you *could* continue on with the same Sunday morning scene.

J: That is wearing me out. No, not that anymore.

C: You *could* change the scene so it would turn out more to your liking.

J: But how? I've tried. Nothing works.

C: Let's take the scene slowly—like it is in slow motion—so we can see exactly what new lines you can say in a strong voice to your mother. We can even stop the scene if we want to. Let's pretend it is a small scene in a play. In order to know what you should do, let's divide the scene

into four steps or stages. First, you'll need to describe your mother's behavior to her. Next, you'll want to express your feelings about her behavior. Third, you'll ask her to change her behavior in a specific way. Fourth, you'll tell her what you plan to do if she does change and what you'll do if she doesn't change. We'll call this fourth step the consequences or action you'll take. [I came to refer to these four steps at DESC, which means "describe, express, specify, and consequences"].

After this, I elicited from Joan one or two assertive sentences corresponding to each of these points. These sentences provided the outline for the scenario to be role-played and rehearsed, first in the counseling room, later in real life.

C: First, *describe* to me what she is doing when she tells you what church to go to.

J: She just starts hassling me—leading my life.[7]

C: *How* is she hassling you, leading your life? Specifically, what is she saying?

J: She says she doesn't want me to go to the church I'm going to.

C: Does she say something like this: "Joan, you shouldn't go to that church because it is too far away and you're wasting gas"? [Here I am helping Joan to *describe* her mother's behavior by highlighting parts of it.]

J: Yes, that's it.

C: Good! Let's write down the reasons she gives.

C: Let's go on to the second step of

---

[5] *Editors' note:* Should the counselor have reinforced this self-perception of not being strong?

[6] *Editors' note:* The counselor ignored the self-report of weakness and focused instead on getting Joan to assume responsibility for the action she wanted. A smart move!

[7] *Editors' note:* Clients often supply only general complaints. The counselor has to ask more direct questions to pinpoint the specific behaviors of the Downer.

writing a new script for your scene. Here I want you to *express* your feelings about her telling you where to go to church.

J: I don't like her telling me what to do all the time.

C: Let's just talk about how you feel when she brings up the subject of church going. If you were going to tell your mother how helpless and depressed you feel every time she brings up this subject, what would you say to her?

J: It makes me angry—like I'm a little kid who can't make my own decisions when I'm really an adult.

C: Great! I'll write down "little kid," "adult," "own decisions" to remind us of the points you want to make in *expressing* your feelings to your mother. Now let's tackle a third step in writing a script: Tell me what you want your mother to do in this scene to give you what you *need* to be happy. *Specify* exactly what behavior change you need in order to be reasonably happy just about this one scene.

J: I don't want my mother to bring up church going ever again.[8]

C: Do you think your mother will stop telling you where to go to church for all time?

J: No, but I'd like her to stop forever.

C: What is the most reasonable request you could make of her at this time?

J: I think I could reasonably ask her to stop talking about church now, while I'm drinking my coffee. Maybe if I get her to do that, she'll be able to stop tomorrow, too.

[8] *Editors' note:* It is important to help clients ask for reasonable behavior changes. "Ever again" is probably an unrealistic request and should be questioned by the counselor.

C: I'll write these words for step 3: "Stop telling me now where I should go to church." Do those words *specify* the exact behavior you want from your mother?

J: Yes, that's good. What should I do next in this scene?

C: One last step is to stipulate *consequences* for her. Tell her what you'll do if she stops nagging and what you'll do if she continues nagging. But to know what are reasonable rewards or punishments, I need to ask you a couple questions. First, what can you do if your mother does not agree to stop talking—or if she agrees to stop but doesn't live up to the agreement?

J: That's the problem. I can't do anything with her.

C: You do something now. You throw cups and slam doors.

J: But it's impossible to get through to her. What can I do?

C: Just fantasize for a moment. What would you *like* to do?

J: I'd like to walk *calmly* out of the room the first time she mentions church going!

C: Could you tell her you will walk away calmly if she mentions church going again?

J: I should actually tell her what I'll do if she keeps nagging?

C: Yes, that's part of your new assertive behavior.

J: But if I tell her, I have to be able to see myself really doing that, don't I?

C: Yes. Is the consequence realistic in this case? Can you see yourself walking calmly out of the room?

J: Yes.

C: Fine, then your consequence is realistic and not an empty threat. You could—and would—carry it through. But you must also consider whether the consequence fits the crime, so to speak. In other words, is walking calmly out of the room a *reasonable* reaction to your mother's nagging?

J: Yes, I think so.

C: Then, you have to fantasize a bit more: Put yourself in your mother's shoes now and tell me what you think she will do if you walk away.

J: That's easy; she'd keep nagging at me until I get to the car. Then she'd pout when I return home.

C: Are you willing to face the pouting?

J: Yes, but I'd like to avoid it altogether, and just take the kids out of the house for the day.

C: Should I write down these words for our fourth step: "If you continue to comment after I get home, I'll take the kids alone on a picnic for the day."

J: Yes, and I'll do it, too.

C: It is important that you feel you *can* do it; otherwise the sentence would only be an unrealistic threat signifying nothing. Now, how about telling her some positive consequences if she does *not* talk about church going?

J: I though consequences were always negative. What do you mean?

C: What could you tell your mother you would do for her if she *does* keep her end of the agreement not to talk about church going? A positive consequence is a reward for an agreement kept.

J: I should do something nice for her, and tell her ahead of time what I will do if she cooperates? I guess I could tell her that I'd cook Sunday dinner.

C: Are you sure that cooking Sunday dinner would be rewarding to *her*? A positive consequence is something that the other person perceives as rewarding and pleasant.

J: I think so. Anyway I could ask her, and if it isn't, I could suggest that we go on a picnic. I *know* she likes that.

C: It is important that *you* are willing to

cook Sunday dinner or go on a picnic. Are you willing?[9]

J: I don't look forward to coming home from church to cook a Sunday dinner.

C: Then do not offer it as a reward. Instead, choose to do something that you are *willing* to do.

J: The picnic would be rewarding to her, me, and the kids. We like picnicking better than cooking.

C: Fine. It sounds as if you are starting to think about what *you* can do to initiate changes, and that is really assertive thinking! To think of what you can do and say is the way to start on those plans for action you requested in our first session.

I suggested to Joan that the key sentences that we had written down be treated as an actor's script. We agreed what each key sentence must say in order to qualify as assertive language. I pointed out that we could change any clumsy or inaccurate lines now; however, if we did not plan, what she might say later in the heat of an emotional scene would not be so rational or easily erased.

After testing the appropriateness of the language, Joan wrote the final version. For complex scenes, I often have a client take home notes from which to write a more polished script; its availability at the next session saves time. Joan's final assertive script was as follows:

[9] *Editors' note:* Counselors should help clients to choose consequences that are positive for the Downers and for themselves. Cooking Sunday dinner was punishing for Joan, so the counselor helped her to choose a consequence that would be rewarding to herself, as well as to her mother.

Describe	→	"You are telling me not to go to my church and giving your own reasons for why I shouldn't go there."
Express	→	"When you do this, I feel like a child. I believe I am an adult, and adults make their own decisions about where to go to church."
Specify	→	"Stop commenting now on where I should go to church."
Consequences	→	*Positive:* "If you stop commenting now about where to go to church, we can all enjoy a Sunday picnic after church this Sunday." (and) *Negative:* "If you continue to talk about church to me, I'll simply walk out of the room or out of the house. I refuse to listen to you on this subject anymore."

As Joan said this assertive message aloud frequently, it became more natural to her, and she needed her notes less. When she knew her lines, we tape-recorded the scene as we rehearsed it. Then we listened to the playback. After we had practiced each step and had heard the replay, I would ask: "Which words sound strongest to you? Which words could be said more forcefully? Are you varying your voice inflection enough to communicate the emotional force of your message? Would a pause around this important word help emphasize it?"

We underlined the words in the script that she thought should be said more forcibly, made wavy lines under words needing more pitch variation, and inserted a dash (—) for "pause" and a diagonal line (/) for "take a breath." After analyzing her voice, we recorded the scene two more times and played it back. Joan still had difficulty putting the necessary force into her voice; she tended to run out of air and to finish in a soft gasp. So, using the techniques of voice control that actresses use, I taught her to project by breathing correctly, exhaling air gradually as she spoke. I also had her practice her lines as she performed some strenuous activity, like pretending to scour a sink as she said her lines. The harder she scoured, the greater were the strength and force in her voice—a fact that was obvious upon replaying the new tape. Soon she began to discriminate the right voice delivery, commenting, "There I'm good!" or "There I'm too weak."

After rehearsing Joan on expressing her script forcibly, I asked her to say the lines to a mirror in the counseling room. Also, I instructed her to practice her new assertive message in front of her bathroom mirror a couple of times each day. After she felt more confident, I began training her in improvising assertive replies. I used a technique that I call "Downer's Advocate," in which the counselor plays the role of the client's Downer to an increasingly forcible extreme. I took the role of the domineering mother and gradually gave Joan tougher and nastier comebacks than even her mother might be expected to use. Over successive replays of the script, my Downer's Advocate became more vociferous in refuting and denouncing Joan's prepared statements; in other words, Joan was being taught to stand up and say her lines under increasingly heavier fire in successive run-throughs. The surrogate mother would complain, "It seems you can't make a decision about church," "You can't make decisions!" or "You never can make any mature decision. You're just a baby!"

Joan learned how to improvise around her script, how to introduce quick, one-line answers that did not distract her from continuing with her message. As I acted the outraged mother, Joan practiced saying such lines as "Nonsense, I make many careful decisions, and this is one of them!" Improvisation is an important assertive skill that involves thinking up effective answers quickly when unexpected things happen. Its components can be taught once a person has already done the careful planning needed for an assertive message.

Writing and reworking the DESC script provides tangible progress and a sense of starting to gain control over one's destiny. For instance, Joan told me, "I feel stronger and more confident just knowing that I can reach into my pocket for some assertiveness to practice." I concluded assertiveness sessions with Joan four years ago. Recently I wrote her asking for information about her life since then, how assertiveness might have helped her, and which skills had been most useful to her. This is a portion of a longer letter from Joan:

It was so good to hear from you. I have often thought of you and our sessions together and have, on more than one occasion, told friends about those sessions and of their effect on me. As I look back and remember, I'm sure it was the real turning point for me and I am grateful that you came along at that precise time.

The role-playing *with mirror* stands out in my mind, as well as listening to my own voice. I remember the feeling of complete surprise as I listened to myself trying to be assertive and realizing that I was sounding like a child, being whiney instead of an adult being assertive. Also, how the role-playing—using appropriate words—helped me when the time for actual confrontation came!

Vividly, I recall practicing the "script" we worked out. I had misgivings, I confess, especially when I visualized actually saying the words to mother. But when the time came, I remember clearly I used, almost verbatim, the words in the script. I felt a "safety" using the script. Eventually, I became more sure of myself as I saw the effect of my assertiveness and was able to stop using a script and simply be myself (my *new* self). I think now this assertiveness has become much more a part of my personality.

I'm working in a very responsible job and enjoying it tremendously. I use my assertiveness on the job frequently and, I feel, very effectively. I'm the secretary to an executive who is the manager of a department made up of 98% women. I have no trouble with any of these women even though at times I must give orders. I really think the reason is that I have learned to be assertive without being "bossy." I guess what I mean is—I've learned the importance of using appropriate words and tone of voice. I'm sure, Sharon, the root of this lies in our sessions.

The situation with mother is well in hand. Stormy at times but I now feel I am in charge of the problems and can handle them as they arise!

After helping many clients become more assertive and noting the crowds of unassertive people who appear for counseling, I decided to try reaching more people by teaching these techniques to groups. Accordingly, I began classes in assertiveness training at a local community college about three years ago. Each class comprises sixteen to twenty adults (men and women) meeting eighteen hours in one three-hour class a week over a six-week term. (As a rule of thumb, I plan the number of class hours to equal the number of participants.) After developing the training techniques through experience with hundreds of different groups, including personnel in governmental agencies, industries, Stanford University, veterans hospitals, and women's groups, I have written a programmed instruction book that is being prepared for commercial publication.[10]

Assertiveness is not aggressiveness: Assertive behaviors do not hurt other people physically or mentally. Rather, they are aimed at negotiating solutions to problems, at equalizing the balance of social power between the client and a Downer. DESC scripting is one

way to help people speak up and negotiate about their problems. Script writing has two major advantages: first, it provides a specific, easily understood procedure that clients can learn quickly on a one-to-one basis or in classes; second, the DESC techniques can be generalized to help clients solve a variety of other interpersonal problems because they go beyond simple role playing of an isolated scene. The DESC procedure seems to help students analyze their interpersonal problems systematically. Counseling sessions or classes become active "skull sessions," in which problems are pragmatically analyzed and negotiating positions are hewn out and rehearsed.

For clients who feel that the world is often putting them down, who feel stifled and helpless, learning how to assert themselves effectively and how to negotiate for an equal balance of social power can mean the difference between enervating depression and an active, happy, emotional survival. Joan thought that her success in her well-planned scene with her mother was the starting point for her ability to cope with much larger problems requiring assertiveness. Like other students in the assertiveness classes, she believed that with that one assertive script she had taken a giant step into the world of mature communication.

[10] *Editors' note:* Sharon Anthony Bower and Gordon H. Bower, *Assert yourself.* Boston: Addison-Wesley, in press.

55. *DEVELOPING ASSERTIVE BEHAVIOR THROUGH COVERT MODELING*

ALAN E. KAZDIN[1]   The Pennsylvania State University

Modeling has been used increasingly as

[1] Preparation of this paper was facilitated by a grant (MH-23399) from the National Institute of Mental Health.

a behavior-change technique. As it is usually practiced, a client is exposed to live or filmed models, who engage in behaviors that the client wishes to develop (Bandura, 1971; Rachman, 1972). The client learns the behaviors merely by observing others' performances, without overtly rehearsing them. It is assumed that the modeled behaviors are learned because the client symbolically codes the observed performances. The representational processes that code the modeling stimuli subsequently guide the client's behavior. "Modeling" refers primarily to the modification of cognitive processes that guide behavior, rather than to the manner in which modeling stimuli are presented to the client (Bandura, 1970).

Cautela (1971) has suggested that modeling stimuli can be presented in imagination by means of instructions. The client *imagines* a model performing a particular behavior, rather than viewing a live or filmed model's performance. This procedure is called *covert modeling*. It is assumed that the representational processes operative in live modeling are altered through imagination of a model's performance. We have evaluated the effects of covert modeling in assertiveness training for individuals who report themselves as socially inept in expressing their thoughts and feelings and, generally, in sticking up for their rights.[2]

DESCRIPTION OF ASSERTIVE BEHAVIOR

Lack of assertive behavior has received increasing attention as a clinical prob-

lem in recent years. Assertive behavior has been defined differently in various studies, to reflect clients' particular deficits. Yet certain facets of assertiveness are fairly well agreed upon: for example, standing up for one's rights, refusing to comply with seemingly unreasonable demands, making requests and reasonable demands of others, and generally expressing feelings (both positive and negative) overtly to others. Our own work has emphasized improving clients' ability to stand up for their rights, to make appropriate demands upon others, and to refuse unreasonable demands placed upon them. Presumably, clients should be able to express *positive* feelings like approval, love, and affection, as well as negative feelings like anger, dismay, disgust, and irritation. Although this balance may be an ideal, in fact, clients who come to our clinic for treatment rarely cite their inability to express positive feelings as a major source of concern. Of course, this is not to say that expressing positive feelings is not a problem or should not be treated. Yet clients generally wish to exert some counterinfluence on their interpersonal environment when they ordinarily feel helpless. (Of course, a client's judicious use of positive reinforcement, rather than abrasive interactions, may well be the most effective means of controlling the environment in the long run.)[3]

[2] *Editors' note:* Having clients imagine themselves engaged in certain activities is also one of the important procedures in systematic desensitization and other "cognitive" treatments. See Articles 5, 30, and 36.

[3] *Editors' note:* A good point. Many clients can better influence the negative actions of others toward them (their social environment) by treating them in more positive ways, that is, by modeling for others the very actions that they would like others to use toward them. The Golden Rule revisited!

A major consideration in selecting assertive behavior as a problem is that many individuals perceive themselves as having deficits in this area. We recruit sufficient numbers of individuals from the community to fulfill the requirements of research so that various forms of treatment can be compared. Clients are recruited by advertisements in newspapers and announcements on television indicating that free assertive training is available at the psychological clinic at The Pennsylvania State University. Prospective clients are scheduled for individual interviews. During each interview, the client describes the ways in which he feels unassertive and provides examples from his recent behavior. A number of assessment devices are administered during the approximately ninety-minute interview. The assessment battery serves two purposes. First, it allows us to select those individuals whose lack of assertive behavior is consistent on different self-report and behavioral measures. Second, the initial assessment serves as a pretreatment assessment, which is used as a basis for evaluating any change after treatment. (The assessment battery will be briefly described later.)

COVERT-MODELING TREATMENT

Introducing the Procedure

Initially clients receive an explanation or treatment rationale. The rationale, presented by the therapist, provides a social-learning framework for conceptualization of the target behavior. Portions of the rationale are as follows:

We are convinced that being assertive is a skill that one can learn. In fact, assertive behavior probably is learned early in one's family life. Parents have distinct expectancies for certain patterns of assertive behavior. Some parents may expect and support assertive behavior in their children. On the other hand, parents may differ in their expectations for assertiveness for their male and female children. Boys may be encouraged to assert themselves, whereas girls may be discouraged for the same behaviors. Another influence on an individual's assertiveness is how assertive his parents themselves act. Children usually imitate such behaviors in their parents. Similar influences can be made by one's peers. In any case, for our purposes the only important point is that assertiveness or lack of it is *learned*. It can be trained and developed just as any other social behavior. The procedures we will use can help form a foundation for the skills involved in asserting oneself.

In developing behavior such as assertive skills, it is essential to rehearse or practice elements of the skills. Specifically, it is important to rehearse the situations in which assertiveness is the appropriate response. Numerous situations in life require an assertive response of some sort. Learning what these situations are and being able to discriminate appropriate responses are important. People can rehearse situations in their imagination. Imagining certain selected situations can alter one's behavior in those actual situations. For example, to get rid of one's fears, one can imagine carefully selected scenes related to fear and remove the fear. So imagination can strongly influence behavior.

The procedure we are using is based on imagination, practice, and learning. Specifically we are going to have you imagine scenes in the remaining sessions. I will describe a scene to you and have you imagine it. This will continue until we progress through a carefully selected series of scenes. In each session, we will have you practice imagining several scenes so you can learn the behaviors which underlie assertiveness.

The general rationale represents an attempt to overcome preconceptions about supposed psychic determinants of unassertiveness, to which clients often refer. After the rationale, the client is told that he will imagine scenes in which a model (someone other than himself) will engage in various assertive behaviors. Imagining scenes is a novel procedure from the client's point of view. Hence, we give practice scenes in which the client imagines mundane situations unrelated to assertiveness. Practice scenes serve to familiarize the client with the general procedure and, it is hoped, to sensitize him to focus on imagery. Here are two typical practice scenes used:

1. Picture someone eating dinner with you at home. Just picture any other individual sitting at the table and eating dinner with you.
2. Imagine a person in a shoe store being waited on by a shoe salesman.

Clients are instructed to close their eyes and to sit back and relax. The therapist instructs each client to imagine a scene and to raise his index finger when it has been vividly imagined. For the practice scenes, the client is instructed to open his eyes after the scenes are clear. The client describes each scene to the therapist. After the description, the therapist usually asks questions, searching for greater detail. This encourages the client to focus on details of the scene and to include aspects that will add to its clarity.

For example, in the first practice scene, the client is told to imagine the clothes that the imagined individual is wearing, where the scene is taking place, the food and place setting on the table, and various physical attributes of the other person in the scene. Each practice scene is presented twice. After each description, the therapist queries the client about details and makes suggestions for attentiveness to additional details.

During the practice scenes, the client imagines a person engaging in some mundane activity. Typically, we tell a client to imagine someone his own age and sex. (Attributes of the covert model that may enhance treatment will be discussed later.) The person can be anyone other than himself. Once the model has been selected and used as part of the practice scene, the client is told to continue to imagine this person in all of the assertive-training scenes. Presumably, the client selects an individual who can be easily imagined and can be envisioned performing a variety of behaviors.

Treatment Scenes

The treatment consists of four sessions, usually over a two-week period. Across all sessions, a total of thirty-five scenes are presented (five in the first session and ten in each session thereafter). During a given session, each scene is presented twice before proceeding to the next. The scenes are not arranged in any hierarchical fashion but simply provide a variety of different situations in which assertive responses are appropriate.

Each scene consists of *two* basic

ingredients: a description of the situation or context in which the assertive response is appropriate and an assertive response by the person (the covert model) in the scene. As will be discussed later, additional material can be added to the basic scene. However, the minimal ingredients for covert modeling, at least as we have employed the procedure, are the context and assertive behavior by the person in the scene (the model). Five of the scenes employed are presented here.

1. Picture yourself at a concert with a friend. A few people in the row behind you are making a lot of noise and disturbing everyone. It seems they have a comment to make every few minutes which everyone can hear. A person sitting next to you (the model) turns around and says, "Will you people please be quiet."
2. Imagine the person (model) is staying at a hotel. After one night there, he (she) notices that the bed springs must be broken. The bed sags miserably and was very uncomfortable during the night. In the morning, the person goes to the clerk at the desk and says: "The bed in my room is quite uncomfortable. I believe it is broken. I wish you would replace the bed or change my room."
3. Picture yourself in a department store waiting at a counter for a salesperson. In the store the person (model) is returning a gift that he (she) recently received. The salesperson claims that the store cannot give back cash for returned merchandise. The person claims: "I received this for a gift. There is nothing I see that I can use here. Since it is hard for me to get to this store, it is unlikely I will ever shop here again. I think if at all possible you should give a cash refund."
4. Imagine the person (model) in his

(her) apartment around dinner time. The person has an important appointment later in the evening, but friends drop in for a visit. The friends have spent time there. They have finished their coffee but look like they are going to stay for some time. The person is getting somewhat bothered about the appointment and has to leave in a few minutes. While the friends are sitting there and everyone is chatting, the person breaks into the conversation and says: "Say, I'm really glad you dropped in but I have a meeting and have to leave. Perhaps we can get together sometime when we are both free."
5. Imagine the person (model) working in a store. It is lunch time and the person wants to talk to the boss of the business. In fact, the person wants to ask for a raise. He (she) goes over to the boss and says, "I would like to speak to you for a few minutes." The boss says, "Okay, what is it?" The person replies: "Well, I would like to ask for a raise. I have been working here for some time now. I think I do a good job and take my work seriously. I don't have a set figure in mind, but I do think I deserve some salary increase."

During treatment, each scene is described to the client while he is seated with his eyes closed. After a given scene is described, the client is told to signal (as in the practice scenes) when the image is clear. As soon as the client signals, he is told to hold the image as clearly as possible until the therapist says "stop." After fifteen seconds, the therapist says "stop." After five seconds, the scene is presented again. After the first scene has been presented twice, the next scene is presented until all the scenes for that session are completed. Throughout the session, the client's eyes remain closed.

Progression through the scenes is un-interrupted, regardless of whether or not the client has difficulty with a particular scene.

Certain features of our covert-modeling procedure have been decided upon somewhat arbitrarily so that we can provide consistent guidelines for therapists. For example, clients imagine each scene for fifteen seconds after they signal that the image of the scene is clear. We have not determined whether or not this duration is optimal for effecting behavior change. Similarly, we have chosen not to allow a client to imagine a scene more (or less) than twice. In addition, the scenes we use to train for assertiveness are not individualized for specific clients. We employ a standard set of scenes for all clients. The scenes cover a host of situations from everyday experience. There is little doubt that some portions of the treatment are not relevant for all clients. For example, one client may come to us because of an inability to behave assertively in heterosexual interactions. Yet another client may wish to develop assertive behavior in social interactions with colleagues or superiors at work. Because our scenes are not individually tailored, the treatment effects we obtain may be attenuated.[4]

Most of the arbitrary constraints mentioned here are placed upon treatment to permit controlled research. By holding several features of treatment constant, we minimize variability resulting from the administration of treatment. Also, by holding some features constant, we can alter other features and evaluate their effects on outcome.[5] Of course, for the treatment of an individual client not participating in a research project a number of changes might be made. Scenes might be held for varying durations, depending upon their complexity or the degree to which the client has had difficulty in imagining particular situations. Moreover, there might be advantages to allowing the client to practice imagining particular scenes several times. Finally, the scenes probably should be individually suited to the client rather than standardized across all clients. Indeed, the client might select the scenes that he regards as most relevant.

MONITORING CLIENTS' PROGRESS

Covert therapies involve inherent problems, like assessment of the degree to which each client is actually carrying out the procedure. Presumably, the effect of treatment is influenced by the extent to which the client is imagining the material presented by the therapist. Certainly clients should be queried at the end of treatment sessions to determine whether or not they are having difficulty imagining material.

[4] *Editors' note:* An interesting experiment could be devised to test whether or not the standardized scenes described here are as effective as scenes tailored to individual problems.

[5] *Editors' note:* Effective research does not always require this kind of uniformity. Each client can be studied in an intensive experimental fashion, with (in this instance) measures of their unassertive actions used as a "baseline" against which to compare their own progress. Treatments can be tailored to individual problems and still be evaluated.

To assess what the client is imagining, we routinely administer a questionnaire at the end of each treatment session. Information is solicited about the model and aspects of the scenes imagined. Specifically, each client is queried about the sex and approximate age of the model and whether or not the model is someone he knows. Replies to these questions help to determine whether or not the client's imagery diverges from the agreed-upon model or changes across sessions. Other questions at the end of the session are designed to ascertain the degree of difficulty the client has had in imagining the scenes and the extent to which he has become anxious while imagining the scenes. Also he is asked whether or not any consequences have followed the model's behavior in the scenes. Although only the model's assertive responses are described in the basic covert-modeling procedure, it may well be that some clients imagine situations ending favorably (for example, when a model's assertive response is effective), whereas others imagine situations ending unfavorably (when the model is rebuffed or humiliated).[6] An important use of the questionnaire is to determine whether or not self-reported information about the imagined scenes is related to treatment outcome.

Recently we have assessed the client's continuing imagery during the session by having him narrate out loud the events as they are imagined (Kazdin, 1975). To accomplish this, we have extended the amount of time that

he has to imagine and describe a given scene. The client's verbal descriptions are tape-recorded. The tape recordings are subsequently evaluated to determine the extent to which the client has adhered to the scenes as presented, introduced idiosyncratic elements, or extended various features of the scene. Assessment of continuing imagery in this fashion reveals that clients do make some changes in the scenes, although these are relatively infrequent. Changes include elaboration of the basic scene and detailed description of the setting, individuals, or responses of the models in the scene. Overall, the assessment of continuing imagery has not revealed features of the scene introduced by the client that are consistently related to treatment outcome.

EVALUATION OF TREATMENT

To evaluate the efficacy of the covert-modeling assertive-training program, paper-and-pencil inventories and a behavioral role-playing measure are administered before and immediately after treatment. Also paper-and-pencil measures are sent to the clients a few months after training to provide follow-up data. Several paper-and-pencil measures purport to measure assertiveness, particularly refusal behavior and speaking up in social situations. Inventories include the "Conflict Resolution Inventory," the "Action Situation Inventory," the "Wolpe-Lazarus Assertive Training Scale," and the "Rathus Assertiveness Scale."[7]

[6] *Editors' note:* It would probably be a good idea for the client deliberately to include a favorable ending to the imagined scene.

[7] A complete description of the evaluation procedures and outcome data is presented in Kazdin (1974d, 1975).

We also use a behavioral role-playing measure of assertiveness (adapted from Rehm & Marston, 1968; and McFall & Lillesand, 1971). On this test, a client responds orally to prerecorded situations. The client is told to respond to each of ten situations as if he were actually in those situations. A scene is described on tape. At the point in the scene at which the client should respond, a bell sounds on the tape. The client responds spontaneously to the situations. A typical role-playing scene is:

NARRATOR: In this scene, picture yourself standing in a ticket line outside of a theater. You've been in line now for at least ten minutes, and it's getting pretty close to show time. You're still pretty far from the front of the line, and you're starting to wonder whether there will be enough tickets left. There you are, waiting patiently, when two people walk up to someone in front of you, and begin talking. They're obviously all friends, and they're going to the same movie. You look quickly at your watch and notice that the show starts in just two minutes. Just then, one of the newcomers says to his friend, "Hey, the line's a mile long . . . how 'bout if we cut in here with you?"

PERSON IN LINE: "Sure, come on, a couple more won't make any difference."

NARRATOR: And as the two people squeeze in line between you and their friend, one of them looks at you and says: "Excuse me. You don't mind if we cut in, do you?" [Bell cues the subject to respond.]

The client's spontaneous verbal responses are recorded and rated by blind judges on a number of dimensions, including overall assertiveness, duration of the assertive response, latency (time from signal to respond until the client's response), the number of disfluencies in speech, and others.

EFFICACY OF COVERT MODELING

Individuals who receive the covert-modeling scenes described do make substantial improvements in four treatment sessions, as recorded on paper-and-pencil inventories, as well as on the behavioral role-playing measure (Kazdin, 1974d, 1975). Covert-modeling clients show significant gains over control subjects, who go through treatment but imagine all of the scenes *without* the covert model's actually asserting himself. These control subjects imagine only the first portion of each training scene (the context or situation) without the model's behaving assertively. Although control subjects have contact with the therapist and imagine scenes related to assertiveness, at the end of treatment they are not markedly different from clients who have not received any treatment (Kazdin, 1974d). The effects of covert modeling appear to be maintained at least through three or four months of follow-up, at which time subjects are reassessed on paper-and-pencil measures (Kazdin, 1975).

It is one thing to change behavior on assessment devices associated with the clinical setting and quite another to change behavior in "real life" situations. Many clients report successful transfer of training to a variety of situations in their every-day lives. Yet the clients who report this are likely to be a select group, which provides biased results. (An individual for whom assertive training did not work may not have the ability to say that our training program has been useless!) We have attempted to develop unobtrusive measurement procedures to assess behavior outside of our clinic setting. For example, we have explored on a pilot basis requesting individuals to purchase magazines offered at a reasonable price but with unreasonable stipulations, to participate in a lengthy experiment at some personal inconvenience, or to volunteer for a seemingly worthwhile community project. These requests ostensibly are unrelated to the assertive-training clinic and are made in person or by telephone.

There are conceptual, practical, and ethical obstacles that arise in developing "real life" measures of refusal behavior. Although the measures may be designed to assess refusal, in fact, they may assess another construct. For example, asking individuals to complete a seemingly unreasonable task may reflect the extent to which they wish to *help* others, rather than their refusal ability. A practical problem arises in devising measures for use in every-day situations that can be held constant for all clients. A given measure, like selling magazines, often is not applicable to all clients. The ethical considerations also are potentially great because assessment itself may influence how the client perceives himself as a result of having complied or failed to comply with the request. The ethical issues in devising unobtrusive measures are difficult to resolve if such client's rights as informed consent are recognized.

TREATMENT VARIATIONS

The basic covert-modeling procedure outlined here requires that an individual imagine a model asserting himself in a given situation. Yet the basic paradigm leaves a plethora of questions unanswered for the practicing clinician. Should the model that the client imagines be a particular person (like a friend)? What attributes should the model have? Should the model be similar or dissimilar to the client? Should one or many models be used during treatment? What can be added to the covert-modeling scenes to enhance their effects?

Many preliminary answers to these questions can be obtained by extrapolating from the findings about live and filmed modeling (see Bandura, 1971). We have examined some of these questions in analogous investigations with college students who fear harmless snakes and in investigations of developing assertive behavior. Preliminary evidence suggests a number of dimensions that may contribute to the efficacy of covert modeling.

Model-Client Similarity

The basic covert-modeliing paradigm does not specify who the model is or the kind of model to be used. Research on live and filmed modeling suggests that, the greater the similarity between the model and the observer, the greater the effect of modeling on behavior (Bandura, 1971). In covert modeling, we have found that a same-sex model similar to the client in age produces greater avoidance reduction in fearful college students than does a model who is older than the client and of the opposite sex (Kazdin, 1974b). Thus, similarity of the model and client along dimensions (like age and sex) that are seemingly irrelevant to the target behavior appears to contribute to covert-modeling effects.

Similarity of the model to the client may also be important along dimensions directly related to the target behavior (Meichenbaum, 1971). In an analogue study with clients who were "avoidant," models who were similar (that is, showed anxiety) but overcame their anxiety and coped with situations produced greater modeling effects than did models who were not initially anxious (Kazdin, 1973).

The effects of modeling are enhanced when the model is similar to the client in age and of the same sex. Furthermore, it may be advantageous for the model to show behaviors similar to those of the client but overcoming the behavioral problem. At the present time, it is not clear along what other dimensions model-client similarity may be important.

Model Identity

Certainly an interesting question is whether the covert model should be the individual client himself or someone else. When covert modeling was initially posed as a treatment technique (Cautela, 1971), it was defined as a procedure in which an individual imagines someone other than himself. Yet covert modeling bears a resemblance to systematic desensitization. In desensitization, clients imagine *themselves* performing gradations of various behaviors. It might be considered a

version of covert modeling (covert self-modeling). A recent analogue investigation revealed that clients who imagined other people as models did not show greater avoidance reduction after treatment than did clients who imagined themselves (Kazdin, 1974a). Thus, at present there is no reason to favor a covert-modeling procedure in which the client imagines either himself or someone else.[8]

Multiple Models

Covert modeling requires only that a single model be imagined. However, research on filmed modeling suggests that viewing several models is more effective in altering an observer's behavior than viewing only one model (Bandura, 1971). In our covert-modeling studies we have instructed some clients to imagine single models through all treatment sessions and others to imagine multiple models (different models in different sessions). Generally, clients who have imagined several models show greater behavior change (Kazdin, 1974a, 1975b).[9] In view of the evidence from both overt (filmed) and covert modeling, the practicing counselor or therapist should employ different models over the course of therapy.

[8] *Editors' note:* Nobody can be more similar to the client than the client himself. See Article 56, on the self as model.

[9] *Editors' note:* Hmm, we wonder why? These results could reflect a form of conceptual generalization that is aided by the presentation of two or more examples. Or that could reflect a form of succumbing to group pressure, as in the Asch experiments ("Everyone else is doing it, so it must be okay").

Model Reinforcement

Modeling research has shown that consequences following a model's behavior directly influence performance by the individual who observes the model. A client who sees a model rewarded for a particular behavior is more likely to perform that behavior than is a client who views a model who is not rewarded. In covert modeling, it is possible to include material that depicts favorable consequences for the model's behavior in the scenes presented to the client. For example, consider a previously presented scene with the addition of favorable consequences (in italics):

Imagine the person (model) is staying at a hotel. After one night there, he (she) notices that the bed springs must be broken. The bed sags miserably and was very uncomfortable during the night. In the morning, the person goes to the clerk at the desk as says: "The bed in my room is quite uncomfortable. I believe it is broken. I wish you would replace the bed or change my room." *The hotel clerk says, "Certainly, we will have a new mattress and springs put in the room to replace the ones you have now."*

In this scene, there is a consequence that follows the model's behavior. The situation that prompted assertive behavior is resolved favorably. In training for assertiveness, clients who receive scenes with favorable consequences for the model tend to perform more assertively than do those who receive scenes without the consequences. Thus, covert modeling when supplemented with model reinforcement tends to be more effective than covert modeling alone (Kazdin, 1974d, 1976).

Relaxation

The role of clients' relaxation during covert-modeling sessions has not been evaluated. However, research on live and filmed modeling suggests that training clients to be relaxed facilitates modeling. In the investigations showing the effects of relaxation, the target behavior has been anxiety reduction (Bandura, Blanchard & Ritter, 1969; Spiegler *et al.*, 1969). It is not clear whether or not relaxation facilitates modeling when the problem is not clearly related to anxiety. In our own work, we merely instruct the client to sit back and relax while imagining the covert-modeling scenes. Formal relaxation training is not employed. The practicing counselor can proceed by merely asking a client whether or not relaxation facilitates imagery.

CONCLUDING REMARKS

Preliminary work with clients who have response deficits in assertive behavior suggests that covert modeling is indeed effective. Two features of covert modeling make it highly desirable as a counseling and therapeutic technique. First, the procedure is highly flexible. Scenes can be constructed to cover a wide range of problems encountered in treatment. Furthermore, for a given client diverse treatment situations can be readily individualized to cover the areas in which his behavior is deficient. Second, because the procedure relies upon imagery, a client can practice the scenes on his own in the absence of the therapist. Practice by the client should augment the efficacy of treatment. The client may use imagery as a self-control technique to handle problematic situations as they arise in everyday life. Covert modeling has not so far been used extensively in counseling practice. Thus many of its advantages and limitations remain to be enumerated.

references

Bandura, A. Modeling theory. In W. S. Sahakian (Ed.), *Psychology of learning: Systems, models, and theories.* Chicago: Markham, 1970. Pp. 350–367.

Bandura, A. Psychotherapy based upon modeling principles. In A. E. Bergin & S. L. Garfield (Eds.), *Handbook of psychotherapy and behavior change.* New York: Wiley, 1971. Pp. 653–708.

Bandura, A., Blanchard, E. G. & Ritter, B. Relative efficacy of desensitization and modeling approaches for inducing behavioral, affective, and attitudinal changes. *Journal of Personality and Social Psychology,* 1969, **13,** 173–199.

Cautela, J. R. Covert modeling. Paper presented at the fifth annual meeting of the Association for Advancement of Behavior Therapy, Washington, D.C., September 1971.

Kazdin, A. E. Covert modeling and the reduction of avoidance behavior. *Journal of Abnormal Psychology,* 1973, **81,** 87–95.

Kazdin, A. E. Comparative effects of some variations of covert modeling. *Journal of Behavior Therapy and Experimental Psychiatry,* 1974a, **5,** 225–231.

Kazdin, A. E. Covert modeling, model similarity, and reduction of avoidance behavior. *Behavior Therapy,* 1974b, **5,** 325–340.

Kazdin, A. E. The effect of model identity and fear-relevant similarity on covert modeling. *Behavior Therapy,* 1974c, **5,** 624–635.

Kazdin, A. E. Effects of covert modeling and model reinforcement on assertive behavior. *Journal of Abnormal Psychology,* 1974d, **83,** 240–252.

Kazdin, A. E. Covert modeling, imagery assessment, and assertive behavior. *Journal of Consulting and Clinical Psychology,* 1975, **43,** 716–724.

Kazdin, A. E. Effects of covert modeling, multiple models, and model reinforcement on assertive behavior. *Behavior Therapy,* 1976, in press.

McFall, R. M. & Lillesand, D. Behavior rehearsal with modeling and coaching in assertion training. *Journal of Abnormal Psychology,* 1971, **77,** 313–323.

Meichenbaum, D. H. Examination of model characteristics in reducing avoidance behavior. *Journal of Personality and Social Psychology,* 1971, **17,** 298–307.

Rachman, S. Clinical applications of observational learning, imitation, and modeling. *Behavior Therapy,* 1972, **3,** 379–397.

Rehm, L. P. & Marston, A. R. Reduction of social anxiety through modification of self-reinforcement: An instigation therapy technique. *Journal of Consulting and Clinical Psychology,* 1968, **32,** 565–574.

Spiegler, M. D., Liebert, R. M., McMains, M. J. & Fernandez, L. E. Experimental development of a modeling treatment to extinguish persistent avoidance behavior. In R. D. Rubin & C. M. Franks (Eds.), *Advances in behavior therapy, 1968.* New York: Academic Press, 1969. Pp. 45–51.

DEVELOPING LAW-ABIDING BEHAVIOR

56.   *THE SELF-AS-A-MODEL TECHNIQUE: HELPING PRISON INMATES CHANGE*

RAY E. HOSFORD   University of California, Santa Barbara
C. SCOTT MOSS   Federal Correctional Institution, Lompoc, California
GORDON MORRELL   University of California, Santa Barbara

Whether our prisons are to exist as convenient "garbage cans" into which society casts its misfits or whether they are to serve as society's rehabilitative agents is a question that must be answered if we are to find ways of reducing the soaring crime rate in the United States. Since 1870 the *raison d'être* of the American penal system has been to interrupt an individual's destructive patterns of behavior long enough to effect rehabilitation (Commission on Attica, 1972).

If punishment were followed by reduction in subsequent criminal activity, then there would be evidence that incarceration *per se*, our current approach to modifying prison behavior, does indeed serve to rehabilitate the inmate. However, such is not the case. The high rate of recidivism among former inmates suggests that confinement to prisons may, in fact, promote, rather than reduce, subsequent criminal behavior. As Menninger (1968) points out, the crime of punishment is that it does not work. When we imprison an individual, he learns avoidance, escape, and other counteraggressive behaviors, which he uses the rest of his life in getting even with society.[1]

If, as Ramsey Clark points out in his book on crime in the United States (1970), the major chance that the criminal-justice system has to reduce crime lies in rehabilitation of the criminal, then our prisons will have to receive support from society in developing, testing, and evaluating intervention procedures capable of ensuring that, as a result of incarceration, inmates will acquire the specific changes in behavior that they need in order to function successfully in society.

Costello's review (1972) of the research applications of behavior modification in correctional institutions reveals that, in 1972, thirteen programs were in operation in various Federal and state systems. Most of these, however, had been modeled on community-based treatment programs, which have been particularly successful in modifying antisocial behavior among noninstitutionalized delinquent youths. Examples of such programs include those of Montrose Wolf and others at Achievement Place in Lawrence, Kansas;

---

[1] *Editors' note:* The use of punishment as a means of social control just does not seem to work the way it is supposed to. Maybe positive control would work better. These authors describe an encouraging first step, but many more will be necessary to prevent and remediate socially harmful behaviors.

Carl Thoresen's Learning House in Palo Alto, California; Gerald Patterson's Oregon Research Institute Projects, and Roland Tharp and Ralph Wetzel's Behavior Research Project in Tucson, Arizona.

At the Federal Correctional Institution at Lompoc, California, we have been evaluating a variety of behavioral-counseling techniques in order to determine their relevance and effectiveness in correctional counseling. Perhaps better conceptualized as the application of behavioral approaches to counseling, rather than as behavior modification, which all too often is viewed as the standardized application of contingent positive reinforcement (Thoresen & Hosford, 1973), the Lompoc program has involved evaluation of the effectiveness of a variety of behavioral techniques for promoting positive changes, not only among inmates, but among staff as well.

Perhaps most encouraging of the counseling procedures that we have evaluated thus far in our search for effective rehabilitative techniques has been that of social modeling. Basically, social-model counseling consists of determining the specific behaviors that an individual needs to acquire, taking a base rate of related behaviors that he can already perform, and then developing a series of models (often on videotape) that demonstrate sequentially (in terms of difficulty) the specific behaviors to be acquired through imitation systematically reinforced by the counselor. Behavior rehearsal, the counselor's follow-up, and reinforcement as the individual begins to apply these new behaviors outside the counseling sessions are often integral parts

of the total social-model intervention procedure.[2]

THE SELF AS A MODEL

Having the client observe a model who demonstrates a behavior does not necessarily ensure that he will acquire that behavior. As with any counseling technique, a variety of factors serve to enhance or weaken the procedure's effectiveness. For example, the literature contains numerous studies indicating that factors like the model's prestige, competence, status, sex, and ethnic identification influence different clients in different ways (see Bandura, 1969; 1973). And, in some clients, merely observing another person's behavior can arouse any of a variety of negative reactions (McDonald, 1973).

These and other factors influenced us to investigate the effectiveness of having inmates observe their own behavior, that is, serve as their own models, as a means of promoting desired behavioral change. Some research (see Fuller & Manning, 1973) indicates that greater sensory arousal takes place when individuals view their own behavior, rather than that of other people. For example, subjects demonstrate greater activation when listening to themselves (even when not consciously recognizing their own voices) than to others, and individuals observing them-

[2] *Editors' note:* "Structured learning therapy" is another label that has recently been used for counseling that highlights the use of social modeling. See Articles 28 and 33, in which the term "participant modeling" is used to describe a similar approach.

selves performing particular behaviors on videotape demonstrate greater sensory arousal (as measured by GSR ratings) then when giving verbal reports of the same behavior (Carus, 1969). Thus, we hypothesized that consistently viewing himself behaving in ways more appropriate to him and to society should help an inmate not only to learn to perform similarly in subsequent real-life situations but also to develop a more positive self-image.

The Six Steps

Using the self as a model involves six counseling steps.[3] *First*, the inmate is taught how to observe and record his own behavior. This most often involves having him observe himself interacting in a group situation on videotape (we have also used audiotape).

Second, he lists the various behaviors that he has observed and that he might like to change, for example, withdrawing from situations in which he would like to assert himself.

Third, the inmate is asked to select a specific target behavior, usually from among those that he has observed and listed, that he would like most of all to modify. A level of performance (the frequency or quality of performance, or both, that he would like to achieve) is selected as the counseling goal, and base rates are then taken directly from the audio- and videotaped recordings that the client has observed.

[3] For a more detailed discussion of the self-as-a-model procedure, see Hosford & de Visser, 1974.

Fourth, we then construct the social model, or a graduated sequence of models, particularly in cases of anxiety, in which the client is presented performing the goal behavior in the way in which *he desires* to perform it. Only appropriate behavior (behavior that the inmate desires) is presented on the new model tape.[4] Often this positive self-model may consist of excerpts taken directly from the audio- or videotapes that the inmate originally observed. This is possible if he can point out instances in which he has performed in the way he desires. For example, an inmate may be shy in speaking up in a group counseling situation, but from time to time he does enter discussions when he either "forgets to be shy" or finds the topic particularly relevant to him. Instances when he does speak up without any observable anxiety can be edited in to form the positive self-imagery model that serves as the counseling intervention. If the inmate does not, however, observe particular instances in which he is pleased with his behavior, the self-as-a-model tape can be made from a coached, role-played situation in which the client behaves in ways appropriate to his desired counseling goal.

During the *fifth step* of the self-as-a-model technique, the inmate is taught positive self-imagery. He is instructed to observe his modeled behavior carefully and to practice performing

[4] To have the individual observe both his inappropriate and appropriate behaviors may attenuate the acquisition of appropriate behavior and promote greater frequency of the inappropriate behavior (Hosford, 1974).

it covertly in the same way in which he is performing it in the modeled situation. As he progresses, he is encouraged to practice the behavior overtly, first with one of us in the counseling office and then in real-life situations like the group counseling sessions.

The *sixth step* involves the client in monitoring and charting his own performance, keeping data on the frequency and quality with which he is performing his goal behavior in real-life situations. He is asked to share these data with others. In some instances, we have had to construct additional modeled scenes when the behaviors have been particularly complex.

THE CASE OF BOB

The first inmate with whom we used the self-as-a-model technique was a twenty-six-year-old male, who sought counseling for his stuttering problem. Although we explored a variety of problems with him, Bob said that his speech problem was of most concern to him. Because of his anxiety and his feelings of inadequacy related to stuttering, he stated, he had to "buy" his friends. And much of his criminal activity was aimed at obtaining gifts and money, which he used for this purpose.[5]

---

[5] *Editors' note:* This is an instance of how a self-generated rule governs behavior. The rule is "If I am to have friends, I must buy them." One can speculate about a number of questions. What learning experiences led Bob to formulate this rule? When did he actually articulate it—before or after his criminal career started? How could a counselor have discovered his belief in this rule? How could the counselor have successfully in-

We tape-recorded the first counseling interviews, in which Bob discussed a variety of positive and aversive experiences in his life. Frequency counts of stuttering relative to the specific topics about which he was talking were then taken. His stuttering varied considerably as he went from one topic to another. For example, when he was talking about his anxieties associated with stuttering, his stuttering frequency was higher than eight times a minute. However, in describing the most erotic sexual experience that he had ever had, his stuttering dropped to less than once a minute.

Because of these data, we believed that his stuttering was under the control of certain situations. He did not always stutter. Bob viewed himself as a stutterer and often behaved as such. By having him consistently observe himself talking without stuttering, we thought we would be able to help him perceive himself differently and begin to learn through imitation more appropriate speech habits.

We applied the self-as-a-model procedure in the same way as that discussed. Bob was asked to listen to the positive self-model tape, from which all stuttering had been deleted, for at least three hours a week and to practice daily talking in the same way as he did on the model tape. His stuttering rate decreased from 8.7 times a minute to .8 a minute over the twelve-week counseling period.

Whether or not the outcome was

tervened to alter his belief in the rule and the corresponding behaviors? How many other inappropriate patterns of behavior are caused by the adoption of faulty rules?

directly caused by the self-as-a-model procedure, however, cannot be determined. We were not testing a procedure so much as we were trying to help Bob to achieve the goal for which he had sought counseling. Thus, he was also instructed in relaxation techniques, and in some sessions systematic desensitization (Wolpe, 1969) was administered. A follow-up three months later, in which he participated in a tape-recorded group session with other inmates who had experienced some aspects of the behavioral counseling program, indicated that Bob's rate of stuttering had not increased over that of the average for his last three counseling sessions.

THE CASE OF ARNIE

For us the most exciting use of the self-as-a-model procedure within the prison setting *per se*, however, has been with an inmate client, Arnie, who was serving a sentence of life imprisonment.[6] With his admission to the institution there had been an order from the sentencing judge requesting that Arnie receive individual psychotherapy.

Before coming to F.C.I. he had been seen by four court-appointed psychiatrists, who had differed on his mental competence at the moment of the crime. Within three weeks of arriving at the institution, he had begun receiving therapy, which continued for the next two years and totaled 100 hours of individual psychotherapy, an amount far in excess of that given to most other inmates. A variety of counseling techniques, including behavioral techniques (for example, relaxation training and behavior rehearsal), had been used by the four different therapists who had counseled him during this period. To help him recall the reasons why he committed his particular crime, he had also been administered sodium amytal by the prison psychiatrist and the coordinator of mental health. Some clinical evidence, as well as GSR and EEG measurements, indicated that some improvement was taking place but that Arnie was still highly anxious, did not think the therapy beneficial to him, and was withdrawn in his relationships with other inmates.

It appeared to us that Arnie's high anxiety state reduced the effectiveness of much of the counseling, as well as of his interpersonal adjustment to other inmates. Thus, an intensive program of cognitive techniques, systematic desensitization, and the self-as-a-model procedure was begun. Using a programmed text on self-monitoring, we discussed with Arnie different principles and strategies involved in behavioral counseling and how they would apply directly to his problem.[7] This was done to familiarize him with what we were doing and to involve him more directly in the counseling process. Not only did this technique enhance our communication with him, but also we readily noticed that the counseling relationship improved considerably. For

---

[6] For reasons of confidentiality, the reasons for his commitment and any other possibly identifying data have been purposely deleted.

[7] This programmed text on self-monitoring was written by Jules M. Zimmer for use in the Drug Abuse Program, Federal Correctional Institution, Lompoc, California.

example, Arnie entered into the discussions without being asked specific questions, and he was often waiting rather than late for his appointment. As for the original directive, the overall goal still remained: to help him reduce his fear of the unknown and to help him understand and accept the "reasons" why he had committed his particular crime.

Although the self-as-a-model technique was only one of a combination of counseling procedures that we used, it served to reduce Arnie's anxiety about counseling. He became actively involved in setting up some of his own goals, as well as in applying on his own what he was learning during the counseling sessions.

During the initial self-as-a-model session, we familiarized him with the videotaping procedure and the reasons for it. He was also introduced to relaxation training and to building a hierarchy for desensitization. After the interview was completed, we viewed the tape with him and asked that he identify each segment in which he felt relaxed. The segments were then rerecorded on another tape, which was used as the first self-model. This process was continued for the next five weeks. Before each session, Arnie was asked to view the model tape in order to learn to relax more easily during the counseling sessions.

The second self-as-a-model procedure was initiated when he indicated that he wanted to work on some specific behaviors within the institution. Several of these behaviors were identified, and he was asked to role play himself as he would like to behave in each situation. For example, when asked whether or not he had gone to a

particular movie in the prison theater, he would usually indicate that he had not gone because he had been too tense. When asked this same question in the role-playing situation, he responded, "I really like going; I can relax while I see the film." Other situations were role-played—for example, approaching his boss for advice on a work assignment and walking down a corridor in which many people were standing—until most of his specific fears and anxieties about living in the institution had been covered. These role-played instances were then made into a model videotape, which he was to view before each of the following counseling sessions.

The process of watching himself doing on the television screen the things he wanted to be able to do and saying the things he wanted to say proved very reinforcing for Arnie. Within one month, he not only mastered without anxiety his initial desensitization hierarchy, which corresponded closely to role-played modeling situations; he also had begun to report instances in which he had applied his newly learned skills in real-life situations in the prison. These self-reports were also videotaped and served as another self-as-a-model tape, the viewing of which proved very reinforcing for him and an additional incentive to continue counseling.[8]

The self-model tape was particularly helpful in promoting the desensitization process. He reported and we observed that he was able to do many

[8] *Editors' note:* How seldom any of us has the opportunity really to see himself "doing good" on a systematic basis. Maybe we all need such experiences!

things around the institution that he could not do previously, for example, going to movies, walking freely around the prison, watching television with large groups of other men, and entering the dining hall without noticeable anxiety. To help him gain a better idea of his own improvement, we showed him the first videotape that we had made, before any editing had taken place, and had him compare it with the most recent one. He was very pleased with his improvement.

Because of this observable improvement in his behavior and specifically the ease with which he verbalized during the counseling sessions, we asked him whether or not he would like to discuss the details of the crime for which he had been committed. He practiced covertly at first relating experiences without anxiety in a way that he had not been able to do before. Then we explored the details with him while videotaping the session. Again he observed that he was able to talk about the crime, and, as a result, we were able to explore some of his past. We carefully explained how these behaviors might have been learned in the same way as other behaviors and how such learning might have resulted in his criminal behavior. As he was now very familiar with behavioral counseling language and its rationale, he was able to give us the information that we needed in concise language, documented with actual behavioral occurrences that he recalled.

Two weeks later, with Arnie's help, we began to construct a model of his behavior patterns in an attempt to relate his past behavior to that of the present. The main theme was that his

lack of coping skills resulted from the type of reinforcement that he had received from his mother since early childhood. Having been allowed to escape from tense situations, he had never learned to react appropriately when faced with similar anxiety and fear situations later. His mother had made his decisions for him and had solved those problems that had elicited anxiety. Thus, when he found himself in extremely new and fearsome situations (like that in which his crime had been committed), he behaved in familiar ways—escaping from the situation. This theory was presented carefully but deliberately to him while we encouraged him to practice the relaxation exercises whenever he felt any anxiety. At the end of the session, he stated, "This is something I'll have to think about for a while, but right now it seems to fit." A few weeks later he had fully accepted the theoretical explanation, something that previously he had never been able to do; he said that, for the first time, he felt "at peace" with himself.[9]

Several later experiences served to confirm the effectiveness of the self-as-a-model technique. In one of these "tests" Arnie was unexpectedly called in to see the institution's consulting psychiatrist, who periodically visits the prison and who was unaware of the counseling that Arnie had been receiving. Following the interview the psy-

[9] *Editors' note:* An interesting effort at helping the client to gain "insight." Of course, this theoretical model of the reasons for Arnie's past actions may not be "true" (there is no way of knowing for sure), but it may be more helpful and reassuring to him than are other explanations.

chiatrist reported that he had found no mental disorder and stated that "he [Arnie] was a pleasure to talk to . . . he showed no signs of abnormal stress or tension . . . he seemed very relaxed for the circumstances."

Only two days later, Arnie was unexpectedly interviewed by the parole board. Members of this board told us that they had observed many differences in Arnie since they had last spoken to him (one year previously), and they announced that they thought he would be ready for parole, if his present progress continued, in eight months.

The changes in Arnie since we first met him can be described only as exceptional. Although there are many unknown variables that may have affected the outcome, we believe, as does Arnie himself, that using himself as a model to initiate specific kinds of behavior change was a most effective intervention. Videotaping his behavior, editing out the inappropriate responses, and letting him observe only his appropriate behavior served to help him not only to accomplish his main goal but also to acquire some of the knowledge and interpersonal skills that he needed in order to live successfully in society.[10] Indeed, it may be a particular kind of self-feedback, rather than self-feedback *per se*, that best helps a client to achieve a desired change in behavior (Hosford & Brown, 1975). Perhaps the best summary, however, has been supplied by Arnie himself: "With other techniques, it was just talk . . . words wasted. With this, you can really see yourself, and the progress you're making. . . . It makes you work harder. It makes you feel good."

[10] *Editors' note:* As successful as the self-as-a-model technique appears to have been in this case, the adjustment so far is still to a prison society. Whether or not the new-found skills will be transferred to the larger society remains to be seen.

references

Bandura, A. *Principles of behavior modification*. New York: Holt, Rinehart and Winston, 1969.

Bandura, A. *Aggression: A social learning analysis.* Englewood Cliffs, N.J.: Prentice-Hall, 1973.

Carus, F. E. The use of closed circuit television (videotape) and psychogalvanic response to increase the rate of change in student teachers' classroom performance. Unpublished doctoral dissertation, University of California, Berkeley, 1969.

Clark, R. *Crime in America: Observations on its nature, causes, prevention and control.* New York: Simon & Schuster, 1970.

Commission on Attica. *The official report of the New York special commission on Attica.* New York: Bantam, 1972.

Costello, Janis. *Behavior modification and corrections: Current status, future potential.* Washington, D.C.: National Institute for Criminal Justice, 1972.

Fuller, F. F. & Manning, B. A. Self-confrontation reviewed: A conceptualization for video playback in teacher education. *Review of Educational Research*, 1973, **43**, 469–520.

Hosford, R. E. & Brown, S. D. Innovations

in behavioral approaches to counseling. *Focus on Guidance.* 1975, 8, 1–11.

Hosford, R. E. & de Visser, L. A. *Behavioral counseling: An introduction.* Washington, D.C.: American Personnel Guidance Press, 1974.

McDonald, F. J. Behavior modification in teacher education. In *Behavior Modification in Education: 72nd Yearbook of the National Society for the Study of Education*, Part 1. Chicago: University of Chicago Press, 1973. Pp.

41–46.

Menninger, Karl. *The crime of punishment.* New York: Viking, 1968.

Thoresen, C. E. & Hosford, R. E. Behavioral approaches to counseling. In *Behavioral Modification in Education: 72nd Yearbook of the National Society for the Study of Education*, Part 1. University of Chicago Press, 1973. Pp. 107–153.

Wolpe, J. *The practice of behavior therapy.* New York: Pergamon, 1969.

SOCIAL INTERACTION

57. *AN EDUCATIONAL WORKSHOP IN CONVERSATIONAL SKILLS*

THAD A. ECKMAN[1]   Oxnard, California, Community Mental Health Center

The movement toward community-based mental-health services has recently encountered a great deal of criticism, largely because community mental-health centers (C.M.H.C.) have failed to provide alternative methods of

[1] The views expressed here are those of the author and do not necessarily reflect the official policy of the California Department of Mental Hygiene, the Ventura County Mental Health Department, or the Regents of the University of California. The author is deeply grateful to Nancy Austin, Dr. William DeRisi, Jan Levine, and Dr. Larry King for providing the impetus and guidance for constructive change and particularly to Dr. Robert Liberman, who started it all. A special acknowledgment must be made to the clinical staff at the Oxnard Mental Health Center, whose unremitting labor and therapeutic skill have made this program possible. They are Jim Bedwell, Ed Bryan, Aurora de la Selva, Richard Gonzalez, Karen Halter, Gayle McDowell, Monica Myron, Johnie Roberts, and Nancy Sanders.

care for the mentally ill that adequately replace the traditional treatment modes offered by state mental hospitals (Cowen, 1973; Chu & Trotter, 1972; and Schwartz, 1972).

In reference to the Nader task-force report by Chu and Trotter (1972), Farberow (1973, p. 394) makes this statement: "To me, the report issues a clear call for change, not just in form and structure, but in substance and philosophy. It substantiates the feeling that this is a time for innovative ideas in mental health, ideas growing out of creative humanitarian and scientific forces."

The current challenge to provide innovation in treatment requires the development of techniques and programs that will effectively and efficiently reintegrate mental patients into the community. Contemporary C.M.H.C. programs for the most part are clearly not meeting this challenge. One important reason for this failure has been the general reluctance to give up some traditional treatment approaches, even when the effectiveness of these approaches has not been demonstrated.[2]

The growth and popularity of the behavioral movement in community psychology provide an opportunity to promote the types of programs called for by critics of mental-health care. Important strides have been made in behavioral approaches to community mental-health services (Liberman et al., 1974; Liberman, King & DeRisi, 1974; and Spiegler, 1972).[3] Techniques currently being used include a system for developing and specifying individual goals and treatment plans, including the problem-oriented behavioral-progress record; assertion training; systematic desensitization; anxiety-management training; and token economies. The educational-workshop program can be combined effectively with these behavioral techniques and with medical approaches, especially the phenothiazines and other drugs, as well as other comprehensive services in a CMHC, like the mobile emergency team, aftercare and follow-up programs, and outpatient services.

The educational-workship approach was initiated by Spiegler (1972), who began by asking what it is that prevents patients from reentering the community and functioning adequately there. He approached the question from a social-learning point of view and answered by saying that the patients' difficulties arose from their lacking "the necessary self-care, daily living, social, recreational, and vocational skills which enable so-called normal individuals to function in society." With this rationale, Spiegler set about devising a program to teach these behaviors directly to patients in the day-treatment center at a Veterans Administration hospital. At about the same time Liberman and his colleagues initiated a similar approach in the day-treatment program at the Oxnard Community Mental Health Center (OMHC). In this paper we present a description of the program at OMHC.

THE EDUCATIONAL-WORKSHOP MODEL

Before the establishment of the educational-workshop program at OMHC, the mental-health center's day-treatment program operated on a relatively traditional basis. The orientation of the staff and the central focus of the program could be characterized as humanistic and concentrated on *milieu* therapy. A decision was made to change the orientation of OMHC from the traditional model to an educational-behavioral model. After the initial groundwork had been laid, an intensive one-year training program in behavior-modification techniques was conducted for the day-treatment center (DTC) staff. Earlier, a token-economy system had been instituted in the DTC. The transition was made smoothly and successfully. Although both the project

[2] *Editors' note:* Unfortunately, this reluctance to give up familiar methods has not been limited to community mental-health centers.

[3] *Editors' note:* See also Articles 17 and 42.

team and the DTC staff were pleased with the results, they were not entirely satisfied. Despite increases in patient involvement in program activities, participation remained below the desired level and seemed confined to maintenance, clean-up, and cooking efforts. Casual observation indicated that patients still displayed unacceptable amounts of isolate behavior except during structured activities. A study was undertaken to determine the amounts of social participation and nonsocial behaviors exhibited by the patients (Liberman *et al.*, 1974). It was found that fewer than 30 percent of the observed behaviors actually involved social participation, whereas more than 60 percent were nonsocial. In addition, only slightly more than 47 percent of the center's available hours were structured with various types of activity conducive to social participation.[4]

The results of direct observation prompted a restructuring of the day-treatment program. An effort was made to increase the number of structured group activities that would evoke adaptive social behaviors from clients. Many of the clients commented favorably about the evening "school" program, and they lowered the stigma of participation in the DTC program by telling their relatives and friends that they were attending "classes." The project team and the DTC staff decided to extend the workshop model to the day-treatment program and to expand the course offerings to meet the needs of the clientele.

A number of workshops were created to cover a wide variety of subject areas, including conversation skills, personal finance, consumerism, grooming, current events, ethnic exchange, public agencies, vocational preparedness, anxiety and depression management, weight control, and recreation-education-social-transportation. The DTC staff, acting in task forces, gathered course materials. A curriculum was developed and tailored to fit the behavioral objectives specified for each workshop session. A list of terminal behaviors that patients were to be able to perform at the completion of each workshop was created. A lesson plan was written specifying the necessary staff, equipment and materials, schedule of activities, and homework assignments for each workshop session. All of these materials were brought together and placed in a "leader's guide."[5] Leaders and coleaders were assigned to each workshop. The program was arranged so as to permit all day-treatment staff members to rotate through each workshop, first as coleaders, then as leaders, so that every staff member would become proficient at leading each workshop. This system also functioned to alleviate boredom among staff members.[6]

---

[4] *Editors' note:* A good example of how systematic behavior observation can be used in a very direct and relevant fashion to identify necessary change in treatment programs and goals.

[5] Leaders' Guides for the various workshops can be obtained from the author at the Behavior Analysis and Modification Project, Oxnard Community Mental Health Center, 620 South "D" Street, Oxnard, California 93030.

[6] *Editors' note:* Some staff members might develop special interests or competences that could lead to an alternative staffing pattern.

Each workshop was designed to consist of eight weekly sessions. Thus the educational-workshop program operates on an eight-week "semester" basis. Each semester is separated by a two-week semester break, during which a formal workshop evaluation is conducted. At this time the clinical workshop leaders, together with the administrator and the program evaluators, make a thorough review and assessment of all aspects of the program, including objectives, materials, activities, methods and outcomes.

When the decision to institute the educational-workshop model was made, it was also decided to refer to patients as "students" and to therapists as "counselors," in an effort to reduce the social stigma that is frequently associated with a mental-health center.[7]

The contingencies in the token economy were rearranged and integrated into the schedule of workshop activities. Work-related tasks, particularly housekeeping chores, were deemphasized in favor of participation in workshop activities. The greatest number of credits could be earned for active involvement and participation in workshop activities and for completion of classroom and homework assignments.

Two months after the educational-workshop program had begun, direct observations of patient behaviors were made again. The results indicated that social participation had increased by nearly 40 percent since the initial observations. Nonsocial behaviors had decreased by more than 44 percent. The data from the direct observation study reveal an important relationship between the amount of structured activity in the program and the amount of social participation by clients. After the workshop program was begun the amount of structured activity increased from approximately 48 percent to nearly 84 percent, even when social participation was rigorously defined as talking, nonverbal involvement like behavioral rehearsal, and attending with head and body oriented toward the speaker.

WORKSHOP COURSES

The topics covered by the workshop courses range from personal care and daily living skills to community involvement. Although each course has a particular specified set of goals, the central focus of every workshop is to maximize available opportunities for patients to learn the necessary self-help skills that will permit effective reentry into the community and at the same time to provide the necessary skills and information for dealing with problems in daily living.

AN EXAMPLE: THE CONVERSATION-SKILLS WORKSHOP

One of the more popular workshop courses offered at OMHC is "Conversation Skills." The conversation-skills workshop assists students in developing verbal facility in social settings. It is especially suited for people who have

---

[7] *Editors' note:* An excellent idea. Designating people as "patients" or "clients" can encourage them to act in passive, dependent ways.

never learned appropriate verbal skills or who have not used them for a long time. The workshop sessions are designed to provide instruction in the basic skills necessary to initiate conversation with others, to maintain conversations that are pleasant and personally rewarding, and to terminate conversations in a manner that is socially acceptable. The workshop aims to reduce speech disfluencies and other habits that may interfere with effective interpersonal communication.

The conversation-skills workshop is designed to accommodate lower-functioning patients who have difficulties in verbalizing in social situations. One important function of the workshop is to prepared individuals for personal-effectiveness training (PET), a special form of group assertion training that forms the nucleus of the OMHC day-treatment program (King, Liberman & Roberts, 1974). Students must be referred to the conversation-skills workshop by their counselors. Referrals are made on the basis of the counselors' observation of specific behaviors like low rate of verbal interaction, lack of spontaneity in groups, failure to elaborate topical content in the context of conversation, speech dysfunctions that interfere with the rate or frequency of conversation (repetition of content, blocking, pauses longer than four seconds, repetitious sounds), and too frequently changing the topic of discussion.

Workshop-session activities center around a variety of situations in which the demand characteristics require great deals of verbalization by participants, like conducting "man on the street" interviews, show-and-tell exercises, games that necessitate a high rate of verbal responding, and so on. Because the participants are lower-functioning individuals, a great deal of modeling and behavioral rehearsal take place. This allows the workshop leaders and other participants ample opportunity for feedback and social reinforcement. Feedback sessions are considered extremely important in this workshop and are programmed directly into the leader's guide as a structured activity. Audio and video devices are used to instruct students directly in techniques of giving and receiving feedback.

The conversation-skills workshop is evaluated both before and after training by the workshop leaders and independent observers (usually two other day-treatment staff members or volunteer workers). Basic components of conversation skills have been operationally defined, including posture, eye contact, use of hands, voice level and tone, verbal fluency, and content. Behavioral observations are taken at the beginning and end of each semester. When students demonstrate sufficient improvement they are graduated to the personal-effectiveness training program, in which more sophisticated interpersonal skills are learned.

Session 1

In the first session a general assessment of the student's basic conversation skills is conducted. Direct behavioral observations are recorded by two observers. The categories of behavior observed include posture, eye contact, use of hands, voice level and tone, verbal fluency, and verbal content (see Figure 1). A brief training session is conducted

Posture (P)
1. Slouch—head down, shoulders rounded, back curved.
2. Stoop—head up but shoulders rounded, back curved.
3. Rigidly erect—head up, shoulders straight, back straight, all limbs held in tight control.
4. Erect—head up, shoulders and back relaxed but straight.
5. Relaxed and poised—head up, limbs relaxed, poised and coordinated control of shoulders, back, and stomach.

Eye Contact (EC)
1. Closed—eyes closed or not visible.
2. Hooded—eyes partially closed, or open but averted (for example, looking at the floor).
3. Open—sidelong glances at others.
4. Open—looks directly at others for brief intervals.
5. Open—looks directly at others, more or less continuously.

Use of Hands (UH)
1. None.
2. Restrained—hands are interrupted in gesture, hands "imprisoned."
3. Some gestural accompaniment to conversation.
4. Hands used intermittently for emphasis and exclamation.
5. Uninhibited use of hands as basic part of interaction.

Voice Level and Tone (VL)
1. Inaudible.
2. Barely audible, mumbling.
3. Audible, but irregular modulation of volume and intonation.
4. Consistent audible volume and intonation.
5. District appropriate tonal inflection, volume; clearly audible.

Fluency (F)
1. Inarticulate, silent.
2. Disfluencies such as stuttering, lisps, hesitations.
3. Interruptions in discourse (for example, *aah, um, ya know*).
4. Repetition of one idea.
5. Consummate conversationalist—fluent multitopical conversation.

Content (C)
A. Appropriate—responses are congruent with stimuli.
I. Inappropriate—psychotic verbalizations, "word salad."

FIGURE 1   Conversation-skills ratings (component behaviors).

for the observers prior to the assessment so as to ensure an acceptable level of reliability among raters.

The general assessment procedure is carried out with each student individually. The student is called into the conference room and introduced to the workshop leaders and the observers. The basic rationale and procedures for the conversation-skills workshop are explained to him. Next the procedure for the assessment is explained, and instructions are provided as follows:

In this first workshop session we want to make an assessment of the general conversation skills you now have. We are particularly interested in how you initiate, maintain and terminate a conversation. Here is what I want you to do. When I tell you to begin, I want you to walk over to _____ [insert co-leader's name] and introduce yourself. Sit down and begin a conversation. You may talk about anything you care to. Continue talking until you hear this sound [co-leader sounds a timer]. Then end the conversation as you normally do. When you finish, we will repeat this procedure with _____ [insert the name of the workshop leader].

The observers station themselves behind the workshop co-leader and face the student. They are twelve to fifteen feet away from the student and slightly to the side (one observer on each side), so as to be as unobtrusive as possible. The raters begin making observations when the workshop leader signals them with a flashlight. The leader positions himself behind the student (so the student cannot detect the flashlight signal) and faces the observers. The leader cues the student to begin and then signals the raters who begin the observations. The raters watch the student's behavior for five seconds and then record the first behavior on the rating form coded according to the categories in Figure 1. The leader signals the beginning of each five-second observation interval with a brief flash of the flashlight. He signals the end of the five-second observation interval with a quick double flash of the flashlight. The double sig-

nal alerts the raters to begin the recording interval, which is ten seconds in duration. The observation procedure continues (five-second observation, followed by ten-second recording interval, followed by five second observation, and so on) until each of the six behaviors (P, EC, UH, VL, F, C) has been observed four times. These behaviors are observed in turn in the order in which they appear on the rating form. When all observations are complete, the leader signals the student to end the conversation by sounding the timer.

The workshop leader and co-leader now exchange roles, and the entire procedure is repeated. Thus each student is observed in conversation with both the workshop leader and the co-leader.

When the observations have been completed, the workshop leaders provide the student with feedback about his performance and positively reinforce appropriate performance behaviors. The student is thanked for his cooperation and told what to expect in the next workshop session.

Comparison of average performance ratings for each behavior plus the workshop leader's subjective evaluation provides information about each student's relative strengths and weaknesses in basic conversation skills.

Session 2

Students meet as a group in the second session of the conversation-skills workshop. The goal of this session is to provide them with experience in increasing voice volume and decreasing the duration of pauses in conversation. This goal is achieved by creating an artificial situation in which loud talk and temporary loss of social propriety are highly reinforced. This situation is developed in the course of playing the game "PIT" (Parker Brothers), a game that seeks to recreate the loud, rapid-fire bidding of the Chicago commodities market (hence the name "PIT"). The game must be played aggressively to be played well. The object of the game is to "corner" the market in any of the commodities offered for bidding. Participation must be continual if success is to be achieved.

Instructors demonstrate how to play the game by playing with the students in a rigorous and animated manner. Shouting and reaching are encouraged.

During the initial stage of learning the game, one of the workshop leaders moves freely around the table, coaching (prompting) players who are experiencing difficulty with procedures, while the other leader plays the game (modeling) along with the students. The object of the game is to produce a high degree of participation and to have fun in a situation requiring a high degree of social interaction. The game as it is used in this workshop has several advantages. It provides the staff with an opportunity to "break the ice" with a new group of students and to model voice volume and enthusiastic participation for the benefit of the students.

The game is followed by a feedback session and general discussion of activities during the game.

A homework assignment, to be prepared for the next workshop session, is then given. Each student is asked to write on a card (permanent product of assignment) the title and major features of a story that he will relate to the group at the next session. The workshop leader demonstrates the assignment for the students and tells them why it is being made (to practice voice volume with the voice-light feedback indicator).

Session 3

The conversation-skills workshop relies heavily on a social learning model. Feedback and reinforcement are crucial components of nearly every workshop activity. Although feedback and reinforcement from workshop leaders have a great deal of impact on students, interaction among group members is also extremely important in fostering new learning, maintaining enthusiasm, and creating cohesiveness among participants. To this end, the goal of the third workshop session is to provide instruction in techniques for giving feedback and ways to use feedback.

The session begins with a minilecture (five minutes) on appropriate and effective feedback techniques. The discussion centers around the necessity of feedback if learning is to take place and the importance of emphasizing positive feedback.

The minilecture is followed by a brief demonstration, which exemplifies the efficacy of high-quality feedback. A student is given a piece of chalk and is asked to draw a line exactly six inches long on a chalkboard. When he has done so, he is asked to draw a line exactly six inches long. The leader has him repeat this twice more, being careful not to give him any feedback whatever about the accuracy of his performance. This is labeled "condition A." Next the student is asked to repeat the task on an adjacent area of the chalk board. He does this four times again, but this time he is provided with minimal feedback: "Yes, that is right" or "No, that is not right" after each response. This is labeled "condition B." Now he is asked to repeat the task (to draw a line exactly six inches long). He does this four times again, but this time he is provided with slightly higher-quality feedback: "That's a little too long" or "That's a little too short." This is labeled "condition C." Finally, the student is asked to repeat the task again. This time he is given the highest-quality feedback for this task. After each of the four responses, the leader says "That is one inch too long," "That is two inches too short," or the like. This is labeled "condition D." It is pointed out that in each successive condition feedback has become progressively higher in quality. It is emphasized that learning of any sort will proceed more rapidly and will be more efficient when the very highest-quality feedback is provided. The students are asked to discuss other examples that parallel the demonstration.

The voice light is then introduced as a feedback device for voice loudness. The voice light is a small instrument with a voice-activated relay that turns on a light bulb when voice volume reaches a specified intensity. It is explained to the participants that the object of the activity is to light the voice light as many times as possible during the exercise.

Each student in turn is asked to tell the story he has prepared as a homework assignment. While the story is being told, the other students record on wrist counters the number of times that the voice light is caused to light. Having students record the number of voice-light flashes provides an incentive to attend to the desired behavior, as well as to the person telling the story. The group's attention and the clicking sounds of the wrist counters provide a source of immediate reinforcement for the story teller.

Each student's performance is tape-recorded for immediate playback. When the student finishes telling his story, group members are asked to comment on his performance. The feedback is guided so that appropriate behaviors can be reinforced. Those portions of the audiotape that highlight the student's performance are played back as an additional source of feedback.[8]

As a homework assignment for the next workshop session, each student is asked to bring an object that has special meaning for him and that he can describe to the group. It may be a souvenir, a keepsake, or a gift.

Session 4

The fourth workshop session is designed to provide an opportunity for students to practice verbal fluency and voice loudness, as well as basic nonverbal conversation skills like eye contact and gesturing. A second goal for this session is to help participants to desensitize themselves to speaking befor a small group.

[8] *Editors' note:* A client can become his or her own model (see Article 56). Note that the emphasis is on the best parts of the student's performance.

The session begins with a brief review of appropriate feedback procedures. Emphasis is placed on those aspects of conversation skills most relevant to the present task: voice fluency and loudness, eye contact, and use of hands.

Each student has brought with him an object to discuss before the group. The workshop leader models the show-and-tell procedure for the students, and the co-leader points out specific behaviors that are to be imitated by the students.

Students take turns making their presentations. Each performance is tape-recorded for immediate playback. Feedback is also solicited from group members following each performance. An attempt is made to guide the evaluation so that desirable behaviors can be positively reinforced. Students are encouraged to comment on specific ways to improve, rather than to point out mistakes.

Here is a partial transcript from a feedback session:

LEADER: That was a fine discussion Jim. You looked relaxed and the words just seemed to flow.

ALICE: Yes, every word was crystal clear. [Jim's presentation centered around methods of growing crystals. Alice's pun was the first time she had spoken out in the group without prompting from the group leader]. I could hear everything you said all the way over here. That's a real improvement over last time.

GEORGE: I could really be involved this time because Jim was looking right at us. It felt like he was talking to us instead of lecturing us.

MAY: Not only that! He used his hands to show us how big the crystals get to be [gestures].

JANET: The thing I liked best was that Jim really got into it. You know what I mean?

CO-LEADER: Yes, there was a lot of enthusiasm in your tone of voice Jim. What do you think Al?

AL: [after a pause] Well, that was pretty good but he slouched a lot.

LEADER: How could Jim improve on that Al?

AL: He could stand up straighter and hold his head up more. You look more comfortable when you stand up straight Jim.

LEADER: Let's listen to the part of Jim's presentation that I thought was particularly good.

After each member has had an opportunity to give his presentation and to receive feedback, a homework assignment is made for the next session. Each student is asked to bring an article to "sell" to another group member. The item should have some qualities that make it an attractive buy and will provide some selling points. The article will not actually be sold. It serves only as a "prompt" to elicit appropriate verbal behavior by the "seller."

Session 5

In session 5 students practice maintaining appropriate voice volume and verbal fluency for minimum periods of three minutes. After a brief review of feedback procedures, the workshop leader gives instructions for the session's activity. Each student is instructed to give a sales pitch for the item that he wishes to "sell." It is suggested that he point out the features of the item that make it valuable, interesting, useful, and so on. It is indicated that he should strive to create a need for the article, just as an actual salesman might.

The workshop leader then models the procedure for the students and asks the co-leader to provide feedback on the performance. The co-leader serves as a model for appropriate evaluation.

When each student has had an opportunity to participate in the activity and receive feedback, the assignment is made for the next session. Students are asked to write on a card the titles of topics about which they would like to be interviewed. The topics can be anything that the students will feel comfortable discussing: generally hobbies, jobs, meaningful experiences, or unusual things the students have done.

Session 6

In the sixth workshop session students practice techniques for initiating, maintaining, and terminating conversation. They also practice directing the course of conversations.

The workshop leader describes the interview activity for this session, using examples of well known interviewers: television talk-show hosts, news reporters, and entertainers. He models the types of techniques used for initiating, directing, maintaining, and terminating conversations, with special emphasis on the importance of elaborating an answer to a question. The leader discusses questioning techniques that elicit elaborate responses, questions that cannot be answered with simple "yes" or "no." Students are also instructed in the techniques of "active listening," reflection, and so on.

Each group member conducts an interview and is interviewed by another group member. During each interview, the leader and co-leader sit closely behind the participants, so that cues and prompts can be given when necessary. The interviews are tape-recorded for immediate playback and as guides for feedback from the group.

The homework assignment for the next session is for each student to write on a card two "opening lines" that he might use to initiate a conversation with a stranger. The opening lines can be statements or questions, as long as they are appropriate to the contexts and likely to be successful in initiating conversations.

Session 7

The seventh session provides an opportunity for students to learn some rules for conversation that may help them to become more interesting and attractive to others.

After reviewing the homework assignment and discussing the goals for this session, the workshop leader begins the first exercise.

LEADER: When you want to begin a conversation with someone there are some rules you can use to help you be more interesting and attractive to the other person. The first rule is to practice showing interest in the other person by giving a compliment. People will respond more favorably to you after you give them a compliment.

CO-LEADER: Pick three people in the group. Approach each one in turn and pay them each a compliment. Follow up the compliment with a second comment or question. Watch as I do it with Nancy. Hi! That's a very unusual watch you're wearing. May I ask what kind it is?

NANCY: Do you like it? It's a Seiko.

COLEADER: Oh yes, that's that Japanese watch I've seen advertised. Is it easy to get them repaired?

LEADER: Notice how Jack kept the conversation going by his second statement and question.[9]

When everyone has had an opportunity to practice the first exercise, the group leader states the second conversation rule.

LEADER: Practice showing interest in the other people by getting them to talk about themselves.

CO-LEADER: Watch as I do it with May. Hi! Do you come here often?

MAY: No, this is the first time I've done my laundry here.

CO-LEADER: Say, is there any reason to use just cold water in a machine? I mean, does it really help make the clothes last longer—or is all that just commercial talk?

MAY: No, I think it is better—but I don't do it myself, just used to the old way, I guess. Maybe if I had my own machine I'd experiment with cold water.

CO-LEADER: No machines where you live either, huh?[10]

MAY: No way—the landlord says he's going to put them in but you know landlords.

LEADER: Notice how Jack got May to start to talk. He showed an interest in her by asking a direct question,

asking for advice (which he may or may not have needed) and then he asked a question that opened up a topic of conversation—apartment living, landlord, rents, etc.

After everyone has practiced the second exercise, the workshop leader explains the next conversation rule to the group.

LEADER: When you want a conversation to continue, try to use open-ended questions. These are questions that can't be answered with a "yes" or "no." They require some statement of opinion or choice or attitude. There are several areas that are gold mines for conversation topics. One is current events, another is show biz— TV, movies, sports—and the other is books and magazines. Forget the weather for conversation unless right now you're having the worst storm, heat wave, rain, or flood of the century.

CO-LEADER: With two different people (not the same ones you've been talking to this session) start and maintain a conversation for at least two minutes with each person using open-ended questions about current events, show biz, and sports or books and magazines. Watch as I do it with Al. What do you think of the CIA disclosures?[11]

AL: Oh, I think it's pretty much being exaggerated by the newspapers and TV.

CO-LEADER: I don't know—I think that there's a lot of truth in it. Weren't those assassination plots really something?

[9] Editors' note: The leader could also point out that nobody is perfect in avoiding yes-or-no questions, not even the co-leader.

[10] Editors' note: Hmm, this co-leader was probably absent during session 6!

[11] Editors' note: Well done, co-leader.

AL: Yes, it sure seems like bad judgment.

CO-LEADER: What do you think will happen next?

Upon completion of this exercise, the workshop leader gives the homework assignment for the next session. Each student is asked to practice one of the three exercises presented in this session and to report the results of the practice session at the next workshop meeting. Students are asked to note on cards the two behaviors (eye contact, posture, use of hands, verbal fluency, voice volume, and so on) that received the most positive feedback and the two behaviors that need the most improvement.

Session 8

The primary goal for the eighth session is to provide an opportunity for students to learn appropriate techniques for self-disclosure.

The workshop leader begins the session with a minilecture (five minutes) on the importance of self-disclosure in making conversations personal and in prompting feelings of affiliation. A significant part of the discussion is devoted to how and when to use "I statements."

LEADER: An important element of conversation is giving out information about ourselves: where we come from, where we're going, how we feel about things—our personal attitudes and beliefs. When used properly, these kinds of comments add a personal quality to the conversation. When used too much in a conversation, self-disclosure can turn people

off. Too many statements starting with "I" can be a bore.

CO-LEADER: Have a two-minute conversation with each of two people. Use at least four "I statements" in the conversation, but not more than eight. Get feedback from the group.

When all group members have practiced the exercise and received feedback, the workshop leader introduces a second exercise.

LEADER: Finding out about the other person is one way of showing interest in them. The best way to find out about the other person is to ask questions. Try not to ask questions that are too personal and try not to make your efforts too intense. Don't make your conversation sound like an interrogation or an interview.

CO-LEADER: With two people (different from those you spoke to in the first session) find out at least four things about them in two minutes of conversation. Don't ask more than four questions.[12] Some good questions to use are "What do you think of . . ."; "What was your high school like?" "What's going to happen in the Rams' game tomorrow the way they've been playing lately?"

When the self-disclosure exercises have been completed, an evaluation of each student's basic conversation skills is carried out in precisely the same manner as in the initial evaluation delineated in session 1. Students engage

[12]*Editors' note:* A more advanced version of this assignment is to find out four things about another person without asking *any* questions.

in six-minute conversations with the workshop leader and with the co-leader while observers rate behaviors according to the specified criteria for posture, eye contact, use of hands, voice level and tone, verbal fluency, and verbal content.

SOME OBSERVATIONS ABOUT EFFECTIVENESS

Depending upon the initial levels of the students' skills in the various behavioral categories, the workshop has been effective in increasing basic conversation skills in from 75 to 90 percent of the cases, according to the results of the behavioral observations. This does not mean that at the completion of the workshop students possess thorough repertoires of conversation skills and strategies. But, for the most part, students do make significant gains.

Perhaps the most important indication of the workshop's effectiveness is in the reports of day-treatment staff members at the mental-health center and family members of the students. Staff members report that clients are more receptive to other therapeutic interventions and that many clients initiate more frequent social contacts after participating in the workshop. A common observation is that students who have attended the conversation-skills workshop nearly always participate to some extent in class activities in other workshops without prompting.

Family members are enthusiastic about the workshop. They are pleased to see improved communication skills in the home, even if it is only so much as a student's soliciting a family member

as a practice partner for a homework assignment.[13]

FUTURE DIRECTIONS

Despite the relative degree of success attained by the OMHC educational-workshop program in reducing isolate behavior and increasing social participation and acquisition of social skills, there remains a desire to emphasize community involvement even more strongly by programming direct community interventions focused intensively on individual problems and concerns. A move is presently underway to begin shaping the day-treatment program in the direction of a personalized system of instruction (PSI) as delineated by Keller (1968), Wilson and Tosti (1972), and others. This approach will further promote the OMHC goal of meeting the individual needs of its clients. When this method is adopted, each workshop session will become a "learning module." The behavioral objectives will be clearly specified in quantifiable terms and pre- and posttraining assessment devices based on behavioral performance tests will be created for each module. Each student will be tested before enrolling in a particular workshop session and admitted only if he fails to achieve a specified criterion. Once enrolled, students will focus on particular

[13] *Editors' note:* Assessing new behaviors in the natural environment is difficult but crucial in determining the effectiveness of treatments. Most of the evaluations so far have been conducted within treatment sesions. The anecdotal data from outside are useful in formulating feasible systematic external evaluations.

levels of proficiency before moving on to more complex or sophisticated levels.

Students from a neighboring college will become an integral part of the proposed program. They will act as cohorts of the workshop leaders by assisting in the implementation of instructional modules. Students will also work closely with patients and their primary therapists in the development of personalized programs. Under the supervision of the therapist, each student will accompany a patient into the community to assist him in carrying out assignments by prompting, modeling, on-the-spot rehearsal, and reinforcing him as he performs the assigned tasks. Students will also collect data, using a behavioral-observation technique, on the rate and quality of patients' performances.[14] To avoid the motivational problems frequently encountered with volunteer workers, the students will receive course credit for their involvement in the OMHC day-treatment program. Students will also attend weekly seminars at which problems and strategies will be discussed under the direction of a consulting psychologist who is a professor at the college that the students attend.

[14] *Editors' note:* A good, inexpensive way of collecting evidence in the natural environment, providing on-the-spot training, and developing future therapists.

references

Cataldo, M. & Risley, T. R. The development of a general evaluation program for residential institutions. Paper presented at the fifth Banff International Conference on Behavior Modification, Banff, March 1973.

Chu, F. D. & Trotter, S. *Task force report: The mental health complex. Part I: Community mental health centers.* Washington, D.C.: Center for Study of Responsive Law, 1972.

Farberow, N. L. The crisis is chronic. *American Psychologist,* 1973, **28,** 5.

Keller, F. S. Good-bye, Teacher. *Journal of Applied Behavior Analysis,* 1968, **1,** 79–89.

King, L. W., Liberman, R. P. & Roberts, J. An evaluation of personal effectiveness training (assertive training): A behavioral, group therapy. Paper presented at the annual conference of the American Group Psychotherapy Association, New York, 1974.

Liberman, P. R., DeRisi, W. J., King, L. W., Eckman, T. A. & Wood, D. Behavioral measurement in a community mental health center. In P. O. Davidson, F. W. Clark & L. A. Hamerlynck (Eds.), *Evaluation of behavioral programs in community, residential, and school settings.* Champaign: Research Press, 1974. Pp. 103–139.

Liberman, R. P., King, L. W. & DeRisi, W. J. Behavioral analysis and modification in community mental health. In H. Leitenberg (Ed.), *Handbook of behavior modification.* Englewood Cliffs, N.J.: Prentice-Hall, in press.

Spiegler, M. D. School days—creditable treatment. Unpublished manuscript, University of Texas, 1972.

Wilson, S. R. & Tosti, D. T. *Learning is getting easier: A guide-book to individualized education.* Individual Learning Systems, San Rafael, Ca., 1972.

DRUG ABUSE

58.   DRUG-ABUSE PREVENTION: REINFORCEMENT OF ALTERNATIVES

RICHARD W. WARNER, JR.   Auburn University
JOHN D. SWISHER[1]   The Pennsylvania State University

Although some experts still view the drug problem as a fad among youth and frequently parallel it to goldfish swallowing, it is now apparent that the drug problem pervades the very fabric of this society. Alcohol is finally being recognized as a major drug problem. "Over-the-counter drugs" are widely abused, and estimates of aspirin-related deaths range from 500 to 800 annually. In effect, concern about heroin and other serious drugs has been generalized to a broader concern about drug abuse that affects all members of this society.

In the past most programs developed for prevention purposes have focused on information about drugs and drug abuse. As discussed elsewhere (Warner, Swisher & Horan, 1973; Abrams, Garfield & Swisher, 1973), the empirical data suggest that this kind of approach has little effect on attitudes toward the abuse of drugs or the actual use of drugs. The kind of approach that does appear to make some difference in these matters is one that focuses on

the affective (attitudinal), behavioral (alternatives), and cognitive (informational) domains. The behavioral group counseling program described here does focus on these three areas and has evolved from a series of programs conducted by the authors and their colleagues. The same basic program has been used with individuals ranging from ninth grade through college.

The overall objective of the program is to focus on positive ways of experiencing life, rather than on the negative aspects of drug abuse. As counselors in a prevention program, we seek to equip young people with the knowledge, attitudes, and alternatives for experiencing life before a drug decision is made, rather than waiting until they are involved with drugs and then trying to modify their behavior. In one sense, what we are doing is consistently reinforcing current attitudes and attempting to increase the frequency of current behavior.

TARGET POPULATION

The basic program has been designed for students in junior high school through college. In public schools it is most appropriate to develop the program as a companion to a program that focuses on the informational aspects of drugs and drug abuse. If no

[1] The authors are deeply indebted to the many fine and dedicated colleagues who have worked with us on these projects. The excerpts from actual counseling sessions were taken from a tape prepared by the authors and entitled "Drug Abuse Prevention: Counseling for Involvement in Living." This tape is available from the American Personnel and Guidance Association, 1607 New Hampshire N. W., Washington, D.C. 20009.

such program is available, then it is recommended that the basic counseling program described here be extended by at least one session so that additional information can be incorporated. As in most counseling programs, the participants should be there on a voluntary basis. We have handled this requirement by introducing the program to all students in a particular grade. In this way all participants are informed of the values of the counselor and the purpose of the sessions, and they are given the choice of participating or not if they choose to attend the first group session. With junior- and senior-high-school students, permission to participate has also been obtained from parents on signed permission sheets. The participants are told that the counselor is opposed to the abuse of drugs and that the objective of the group sessions is to focus on alternative ways of experiencing life without the use of artificial aids like drugs.

TRAINING OF GROUP LEADERS

Although the group leaders in most of the programs have been trained as counselors, several programs designed on this model have used classroom teachers, community leaders, parents, and young people as group leaders. It is helpful if the group leaders have had some previous training in skills related to counseling, but it is not absolutely necessary. When leaders have had some training in counseling, a forty-hour training program has been used, and it should be extended for those with little prior training.

The forty hours of training for leaders is composed of the following elements.[2]

Didactic (sixteen hours)
1. Overview of drug education
2. Pharmacology of drugs
3. The facilitative dimensions in counseling
4. Reinforcement and extinction procedures
5. Alternatives to drug abuse
6. Use of modeling techniques
7. Evaluation methodology
8. Analysis of tape recordings

Experimental (twenty-four hours)
1. Ten hours of training in the facilitative dimensions of empathy, respect, and genuineness
2. Ten hours of training in the use of reinforcement techniques, modeling, and cuing
3. Four hours of training in group leadership skills

TOPICAL OUTLINES OF SESSIONS

The program is designed to be carried out in six one-hour group counseling sessions. If younger students (in junior high school) are involved, it is recommended that the length of each session be reduced and that the number of sessions be increased to seven or eight.[3] Group size should not exceed ten or be

[2] A more detailed description of the training program is available from J. Swisher, 1001 University Drive, State College, Pa. 16801.

[3] *Editors' note:* Group size should vary according to the skills and experience of the leader. Some leaders may be able to handle larger groups of fifteen or so.

smaller than six. The following is a suggested guide for group leaders.

1. Session 1
   a. Ensure that everyone *at least* knows each other member's name.
   b. Set ground rules
      (1) Focus of the group will be on alternatives to drug abuse
      (2) Discussions will be confidential
      (3) "Volunteer" nature of the group
      (4) Everyone *belongs* just because he chose to come to the sessions
      (5) Everyone has a right to be heard
      (6) Everyone has an obligation to listen to another's point of view
   c. Set *overall* goals for group discussion. In all six sessions the topics covered will be
      (1) Who uses drugs? Distinguish between use and abuse.
      (2) Why do people abuse drugs?
      (3) What happens to people who abuse drugs?
      (4) What are some alternatives to drug abuse?
   d. Perhaps the most important goal for the first session is to *establish a relationship* with the group members. Unless they feel that you can be *trusted*, that you *care* about them (their feelings and opinions), that you are *genuine*, that you are trying to *understand*, and so on, you will have a most difficult time as a *reinforcer* and a *model* of healthy attitudes toward drugs.[4]
2. Session 2
   a. Review session 1 briefly

   b. Discuss "who uses drugs" (parents, kids, doctors, mothers, and so on); distinguish legal and illegal use, use and abuse
   c. Introduce a taped model if you are using one, and discuss
   d. If time permits, begin to discuss "Why people abuse drugs"
   e. Summarize discussion
3. Session 3
   a. Review session 2
   b. Discuss "what happens to people who abuse drugs" (physical and psychological aspects, legal aspects, job and family problems, and so on)
   c. Summarize discussion
4. Sessions 4–6
   a. Briefly summarize the first three sessions
   b. Discuss "the alternatives to drug abuse" (hiking, skiing, going to college, marriage, experiencing reality, and so on); remember that alternatives are *unique* for each individual. Discussion of a particular alternative should touch upon both a *description* of it *and* the *philosophy* or *value* of that alternative for the individual: "Why is this alternative satisfying for you?" Ask participants to describe recent experiences with alternatives.[5]

In all sessions the group leader tries to *reinforce* socially healthy attitudes and reported behaviors that reflect such attitudes and positive alternatives to drugs. It is not necessary (or even desirable) to reinforce *every time*. Constantly interrupting a person to reinforce statements will help to break down communication.

[4] *Editors' note:* Well said! Skills in building good relationships are essential if modeling and reinforcement are to have optimum effects.

[5] *Editors' note:* Note that the basic rationale of teaching alternatives is similar to that of the drug-treatment program described in Article 15.

The many ways to reinforce include

1. Attention: Look at the person with interest
2. Clarification: "What I hear you saying is . . ."
3. Posture: Lean toward the person speaking
4. Voice: Warm, interested, friendly
5. Smiling
6. Nod of head: indicating agreement
7. "Uh-huh"
8. "That's a good idea"
9. "Tell us more about that"
10. *Selective* reflection: Reinforcing positive aspects of a statement that may contain both positive and negative attitudes; for example,

I: I'd like to try drugs, *but I'm afraid of what might happen.*
YOU: "You seem to be saying that drugs might harm you. Could you tell us a little more about that?"

Self-defeating (negative) responses should be *ignored* or *minimally* reinforced.

USE OF SOCIAL MODELS

At first we used former drug abusers as social models within the groups. This procedure did not work satisfactorily because the models made as many pro-drug as anti-drug statements. Since then we have used a taped model. Although not completely necessary, the taped model does add an important stimulus to the early discussions. If a leader uses a modeling procedure in the group, we recommend that the model be a formerly drug-abusing peer of the target population and that he be interviewed on tape by a counselor. In this way the counselor can take the model through the whole sequence of the drug experience with emphasis on the current state of being "beyond the use of drugs." Leaders are cautioned to obtain prior permission from both the model and his parents for use of the tape. This has never been a problem in our programs.

The tape of the model should be introduced in the first or second session. The group leader should cue group members to focus on the reasons why the model is no longer using drugs and on what kinds of things the model is now involved in that are "beyond drugs."

EXAMPLES FROM SESSIONS OF DIFFERENT GROUPS

Session 1

LEADER: The reason I asked you all to come down here really is that most of you have participated in one form or another in a unit in school that has to do with drug abuse. These units have provided you with some information about drugs, but what I would like to do here, if you people are willing, is to spend some time discussing your feelings about drug abuse and on something we might call a natural high. What I'm kind of hoping is that by discussing these topics we might develop some ways of experiencing life and the highs it can provide without a reliance on artificial things such as drugs. I don't have any real ground rules except that we keep what we share with one another within this group; and, while I would like you to try this for one or two sessions, if you don't feel this group will meet your needs please feel free to drop out. O.K.—let's try to start—maybe the first place to start is to try to look at why we think a lot of young people are into drugs— and what do we really mean by drug abuse?

FRANK: I've been trying to do as much reading on it as possible and I've come up with—you have the marijuana, the hashish, which is very close to it, and then you have the pills and different drugs like heroin and things like that. This alcohol thing is the number one drug and, as far as I can see, I haven't come up with any kind of reasoning that says that marijuana is less or worse than alcohol, in fact from people I talk to—they seem to think that marijuana is less harmful than alcohol and of course, if you use it to excess, it could get the best of you.

LEADER: You include alcohol as a drug and you are saying that there is some debate about marijuana and alcohol, but anything to excess is going to be a problem.

HELEN: I think that social standards has a lot to do with it—to be in with your friends and stuff—when your friends do it you have to do it too, as far as going on with drugs.

LOUISE: Well, it just depends on what social surrounding you are in and, if you're in with a party where everyone is drinking beer, the chances are you're not going to start smoking, but if you go to a party where a lot of your friends are at this party, even if you are in college, and everyone is smoking marijuana, I think you'll be more induced to smoke marijuana with them. I don't think that it's just all for high school.

LEADER: How do some of the rest of you feel?

Session 2

JACK: There's one thing that a lot of people say—in society, when there is something the matter, you take a pill for it, you know, indigestion or headache, anything like that—so if someone has some sort of hassle, that could be one reason they take drugs.

KRIS: Usually one thing around here they hear a lot—kids have always heard a lot about drugs and their parents have cut it down to do you smoke grass, etc., it's a role of life, they've tried it and they've liked it, that's what it does—their parents told them and they went against them.

LEADER: I'm not sure I understand you. Are you saying the parents told them not to and that's the reason the kids did—I see some of you shaking your heads—is that one of the main reasons kids begin?

JACK: I think so, yes. I feel that way.

JOE: It seems also the atmosphere around here—you call it drug shopping—you always hear about the local pushers and it doesn't seem that way—you'll see a guy has a joint and it doesn't strike you that he's a pusher, but if your parents call him a pusher and it really puts you out— but really, actually they are.

LEADER: By law, even if they're giving it away, they are a pusher. It's one of those kind of unique things about the law.

Session 3

LEADER: Anyone else gone through that kind of thing or think that they're beyond drugs?

JACK: At times I don't feel that way you know—anybody gets it, if you've gone straight you know it takes a while—it takes a long time—I feel like going and getting so rapped out in my head at times it isn't funny, so what I do is go get drunk—that doesn't help matters either. It's a big hassle.

LEADER: Using drugs is a boring kind of thing after a while?

ROD: It gets really commonplace—yeah, you're not doing it for the first time.

JACK: Say it's Tuesday, it's time for my acid.

LEADER: So once the novelty wears off —once the novelty is gone, what you're saying is there is very little reason for taking drugs. Am I reading you right there?

JIM: Actually, I'm considerably—I haven't gotten really deep into drugs. I sorta like grass and hash and speed once in a while—I can see where if I got into too much I'd get into a rut—I can see that's not too cool—I really don't mind it—you know—now and then.

LEADER: Jim, what do you think has kept you from maybe going in as far as some other people? Has it been things they've said to you or things that you've decided for yourself?

JIM: I'm not really sure. I think I would try asking them if I thought after I used it there would be any problems then I'd stop. I think I might try experimenting with it to see how it was.

LEADER: What do you think, Pat?

Session 4

LEADER: Maybe a way of putting it is what turns you on, using someone's words, naturally, as opposed to what turns you on by what you might think. What are some of those other things you do? Listen to music?

HELEN: I don't know—it's pretty hard to come up with a few alternatives off hand.

LEADER: Let's just throw it out as a general idea rather than trying to make it fit there. What are your peak moments?

DAVE: There are always people around up here, but when you get close friends together, my personal group, the question of drugs never comes up because of—we sit just talking to each other. I think usually there is music in the background, but very seldom something special that we listen to.

LEADER: But the important thing there is, the group is together.

DAVE: Yes. And we get deeply involved in each other—I mean, talk about personal things and feelings and whatever happens to be happening to one of us at the time. Everyone else seems to get excited about it and you have a close relationship like that even if you're studying for an exam or you're talking about your problems—if someone is happy about something, you're sharing it, so I think you're using someone else's happiness to get you high and it seems to work.

LEADER: They'll share your high, or happiness, or difficulties.

SARAH: When you are in with a group—it's really crazy how much you look forward to being a part of that group and go and talk to the people—no matter what's happening —go and talk to the people.

LEADER: Gary, what turns you on?

GARY: Well, I don't know—really not too much here—but, I'm in this one class I have this term—the way it is structured you can't help but get close to everyone and you don't necessarily have to talk about deep things. You can get to know others very well, but just the fact that you're close to the person and you know that you're close with the person, this turns me on.

RESULTS

The initial investigation of the basic approach described here was undertaken with a program involving ninth ($n=108$)- and eleventh ($n=108$)-graders. Four different treatment groups were used in the project: A social-reinforcement group with a former drug-abusing model, a social-reinforcement group with a nondrug-abusing model, a relationship-counseling group, and a standard health-unit group. Pre and post measures were gathered by means of a forty-item knowledge scale, a fourteen-item attitude scale, and a thirty-five-item behavioral scale.[6] The results indicate that all four groups experienced significant gains in knowledge about drugs. All three of the counseling groups experienced nonsignificant improvements in attitudes toward the abuse of drugs, whereas the attitude scores of students in the health unit had moved in the prodrug direction (Swisher, Warner & Herr, 1972). Reported drug use was so small on the behavioral scale as to make measurement impossible.

A second investigation following the same basic model with college students ($n=316$) produced almost exactly the same results. At this point a modification in the program was made: The procedure of including the models in the group was dropped, and the use of an audiotaped model was substituted. A subsequent investigation with ninth-graders ($n=119$) demonstrated that the modified approach produced a significant positive change ($+15.17$ points) in participants' attitudes toward the abuse of drugs. No measures of changes in behavior or gains in knowledge were obtained (Warner, Swisher & Horan, 1973).

Schroeder and Swisher (1973), in another investigation using a random-assignment posttest-only design with junior-high-school students ($n=90$), found that the behavioral approach had been more successful than either a standard health unit or an independent-study program both in changing students' attitudes in a healthy direction and in reducing the degree of illegal drug use. The behavioral group had a mean attitude score 2.6 points better than that of the health-unit group and 2.7 points better than that of the independent-study group. Although reported use was rather small for all groups (experimental-use level), the behavioral group reported a mean use of .34, whereas the health-unit group reported a mean use of 1.07 and the independent-study group reported a mean use of 1.00. Both the attitude and use differences are rather small, but the differences are in the desired direction. This fact, coupled with the results of the study by Warner, Swisher, and Horan (1973) and the general lack of positive results from other programs reported in the literature, indicates that

---

[6] Readers interested in examining the newest form of this scale are referred to L. A. Abrams, E. F. Garfield, and J. D. Swisher, *Accountability in Drug Education* (1973), available from the Drug Abuse Council, Inc., 1828 L Street N.W., Washington, D.C. 20036.

the use of social-reinforcement groups is a viable approach to the extremely difficult problem of drug abuse.

No objective long-term follow-ups of participants in any of the programs have been carried out. However, counselors who operated the three school programs reported here have had continued contact with some of the participants and have reported that they believe that the groups have had continued positive impact on participants.[7]

[7] *Editors' note:* The initial effects seem promising, and some more objective follow-up of long-term effects would seem most worthwhile.

references

Abrams, L. A., Garfield, E. F. & Swisher, J. D. *Accountability in drug education.* Washington, D.C.: Drug Abuse Council, 1973.

Schroeder, J. & Swisher, J. D. Alternatives to drug abuse: A behavioral approach. Unpublished manuscript, Pennsylvania State University, 1973.

Swisher, J. E. & Warner, R. W. A comparison of four approaches to drug abuse prevention. Harrisburg: Governor's Justice Commission of Pennsylvania, 1971.

Swisher, J. D., Warner, R. W. & Herr, E. L. An experimental comparison of four approaches to drug education. *Journal of Counseling Psychology,* 1972, **19**, 328–332.

Warner, R. W., Swisher, J. D. & Horan, J. J. Drug abuse prevention: A behavioral approach. *NASSP Bulletin,* 1973, **57**, 49–54.

PERSONAL APPEARANCE

59. *IMPROVING CLIENTS' GROOMING*

JANICE ARNDT PRAZAK   Walker and Associates, Minneapolis
KATHLEEN SCHMOLKE BIRCH   Catholic Social Services, Racine, Wisconsin

Loretta was forty-two years old when she was referred to the Minneapolis Rehabilitation Center for vocational help. She had spent most of her life in a small rural community and had recently been institutionalized for several months for emotional problems that had occurred after her husband died. Within a short time the center staff had determined that she had sufficient skills for light office work. Good skills, a pleasant personality, and even a special training program in job-interview skills, however, were not going to be sufficient to help Loretta to find a good job.[1] One quick look revealed that her appearance would be a major barrier to employment. She wore an

[1] See J. A. Prazak, "Learning Job-Seeking Interview Skills," in Krumboltz & Thoresen (1969).

ill-fitting cotton dress stiffened with too much starch, her hair was tangled, 1950s-vintage bright-red lipstick was smeared carelessly around her mouth, and white bobby sox were bunched around the ankles of her unshaven legs.

A few years before Loretta would probably have been referred to a staff social worker with the dictum, "Do something about the way she looks." If the social worker had sufficient skills, time, and motivation, a quick, intensive effort might have resulted in Loretta's looking acceptable for a job interview. However, it is likely that she would have lost her job as soon as she reverted to her old grooming habits. Fortunately, the "How to 'LOOK' for a Job" grooming program had been developed.[2] At the same time that Loretta was being evaluated and improving her job skills she spent a few hours a week in this grooming program. When she left the center after five weeks her hair was combed into a smooth style, she wore a simple tailored dress purchased at a thrift shop, pantyhose were seen on her shaven legs, and her makeup was subtle and attractive. Within a short time Loretta was hired to do clerical work and occasional receptionist duties in a small office. As this grooming program had taught Loretta not only how to improve her appearance but also how to maintain it, she was still on the job and looking well groomed when her counselor saw her a few months later.

The Minneapolis Rehabilitation

[2] The "How to 'LOOK' for a Job" grooming program was developed in 1972 by J. A. Prazak, K. S. Birch, and Cynthia Christofferson Lesher.

Center is a private, nonprofit vocational-rehabilitation agency that receives clients with physical, emotional, sociocultural, learning, and other problems. Clients include both men and women aged sixteen to sixty years with intelligence levels (I.Q.s) from approximately 70 to 120 and above. All clients have vocational problems for which the center provides vocational evaluation, counseling, social work, and other services.

The center staff had realized for some time that appearance is a major barrier to their clients' being hired or obtaining jobs commensurate with their skills. One survey indicated that approximately 40 percent of the clients who came to the center had grooming problems of such significance that they would likely have difficulty being accepted by employers.

Many sporadic attempts had been made by the center's staff over the years to change clients' poor grooming habits. Initial efforts had included a grooming-lecture program, which predictably had failed to have any significant impact. One-to-one and small-group grooming programs had been instituted, but they took considerable staff time, and their content and quality were dependent on the grooming knowledge and skills of the staff people involved. One of these earlier efforts had also included an arrangement with a local beauty school to beautify female clients. The immediate results were terrific, for clients returned with lovely professional coiffures, but the long-range impact was zero. Clients had learned nothing more than how to have someone else do their hair. In a few days the new hairdos would deteriorate and clients would look the same as before.[3]

After years of experimenting with various low-key approaches to grooming, it was decided that in order to make substantial and lasting changes in clients' grooming behavior a systematic program would have to be developed. The program was to meet the following criteria: It had to be appropriate for both men and women clients of the type seen by the center, it had to be replicable in other settings serving similar types of clientele, it had to prove effective in changing clients' appearances, and it had to be focused on changing appearances for jobs and job interviews.

[3] *Editors' note:* Some alternative strategy would be necessary to create a really permanent wave.

TABLE 1

Area	Standard
Hygiene and cleanliness	Body must be free from odor (from perspiration, bad breath, and so on)
Shaving for men	Face must be clean-shaven, or beard, moustache, and sideburns must be neatly trimmed
Shaving for women	Underarms and legs must appear clean-shaven
Manicure (women)	Hands and nails must appear smooth and clean, nails shaped
Feminine hygiene	Client must have no obvious feminine-hygiene problems during menstrual periods or at other times
Shampooing	Hair must appear clean (free from dirt, grease, and visible dandruff)
Setting hair	Client can use rollers and pins to set hair in attractive style
Combing hair	Client arranges own hair in neat, attractive style
Skin types (women)	Client must cleanse face properly and care for her skin
Acne and troubled skin	Client's complexion must be clean and clear; blemishes, if present, must be healing
Basic make-up	Female client must wear a minimum of makeup, properly applied (for example, colored makeup base, lipstick, and cheek color)
Advanced makeup	Client must wear basic makeup plus eye makeup attractively applied
Poise and posture	Client sits, stands, and walks straight and tall (unless physically handicapped)
Exercise	Client's body is firm, or he knows and uses daily exercise routines to firm body
Dieting	Client who is over- or underweight knows how to select proper diet for weight problem
Laundering	Client's clothing is clean, and he knows how to launder his own clothing
Caring for clothes	Clothing is in good repair, and client knows how to mend tears and sew on buttons
Ironing and pressing	Client's clothing is free from wrinkles
Dry cleaning	Client's nonwashable clothing (like coats and suits) appears clean
Shopping	Client knows how to select appropriate clothing for himself and where to purchase it economically
Dressing for interviews	Client dresses appropriately for the type of job that he is seeking

GOALS

In order to develop a grooming program the effectiveness of which could be evaluated, measurable criteria, reflecting current community standards for acceptable job-seeking appearance, were defined (Table 1).

The standards given in Table 1 did not completely eliminate subjective judgments. Whenever possible, however, an attempt was made to define standards in terms that permitted reliable ratings by observers. The reason was that the impact of the program was to be measured in two ways: improvement in appearance observed by the grooming instructor and other professional staff and improvement in grooming knowledge as measured by a pre- and postprogram quiz.

PROGRAMS

Each area listed became an independent program module. A client could be involved in any combination of program modules that was suited to his needs. This gave the program greater flexibility than others, which require the client to progress through an entire prearranged sequence. The modular structure was also adopted to make it possible for the client himself to select the modules in which he wished to participate. It was thought that, if the client were given a role in the selection of his own program, he would be more highly motivated to participate. The development staff also wished to assess whether or not clients were indeed capable of selecting grooming modules appropriate to their needs.

Content for the program was developed from professional knowledge, practical experience, and the use of books and pamphlets on personal appearance.[4] Letters were sent to many companies that manufacture grooming products, to solicit free samples and pamphlets for use in the program. The response of these companies was very gratifying. Their generosity supplied the program with samples of shampoo, toothpaste and toothbrushes, hair conditioner, lipstick and eye makeup, hair spray, and other products that could be used in the program and distributed to clients.[5]

The final program consisted of cassette tapes for each module, synchronized with colored slides illustrating each program step. An "Introduction to Grooming" module offered a brief overview of the program and allowed the client to select the other modules in which he wished to participate. A practice laboratory was arranged and equipped with a sink, mirrors, and grooming supplies. Three program manuals were written to provide additional information and facilitate program implementation an instructor's manual, a student workbook, and a reference manual.[6]

Presentation of the modules was

[4] The first author is also trained and licensed in cosmetology and has taught at a nationally established personal-improvement school.

[5] A 40 percent discount on beauty products is given to programs working with the handicapped by the Helena Rubinstein Company, 767 Fifth Avenue, New York, New York 10022.

[6] For information about obtaining these manuals write to Janice Prazak, Walker and Associates, 123 East Grant Street, Minneapolis, Minnesota 55403.

scheduled so that clients could be trained in one or two modules at a time, have a day or so to practice and bring their appearance up to each module standard, and then go on to the next module. The clients could then move by successive approximation to the ultimate grooming goal of demonstrating appropriate appearance for a job interview. This kind of gradual learning gives the clients an opportunity to receive verbal reinforcement for each step that they make in improving their grooming. It also helps to ensure that the knowledge and improvement gains that they make will be maintained. Many new skills must be learned, and many new habits must be acquired if a client is to achieve and maintain an improved personal appearance. Learning to put in a hair roller properly, for example, may require practice over several days for some women—particularly those who are physically or intellectually handicapped. A client who is expected to assimilate these and other new skills in one or two saturation sessions could easily become discouraged. For this reason gradual-learning techniques are used. This program was designed so that each module shown would be attended by two or more clients. The small-group approach enabled the instructor to provide sufficient individual attention to each person and also offered the opportunity of peer-group reinforcement.[7]

_____

[7] *Editors' note:* An excellent point. As the effects of appropriate grooming are social, a small group provides opportunities for modeling, guided practice, positive feedback, and encouragement.

Application to the Case of Deborah

In this section we describe the program as it was experienced by one client. Deborah was a twenty-two-year-old borderline-retarded woman, who had grown up in a rural community. She weighed 210 pounds, had never shaved her legs or underarms, took baths only occasionally (using laundry soap), did not know how to set her hair, and had never used deodorant. During her two-day initial orientation to the center, Deborah viewed the sound-slide "Introduction to Grooming." (This module consists of a series of color slides projected on a screen, accompanied by a cassette tape recording.) The first slide shows a distinguished-looking man behind a desk in a personnel office. He says:

Hello. My name is Mr. Brock, and I am the personnel manager at the ABC company. I understand you are interested in getting a good job. I see many people who come to my office looking for work. Do you know what the first thing is that I notice about them? Their appearance. I have seen a lot of people make or break their chances of getting a good job because of their appearance. Let me show you some of the people in my waiting room, and you will see what I mean.

The slides then show several applicants in varied states of good and poor grooming. Mr. Brock describes what he thinks of the appearance of each of them. When he has finished his talk about the importance of appropriate appearance, a second voice tells the client:

So you want to know how you can look right for a job interview. We have a program here at the center that can help you. This program is divided into twenty-one parts called "modules." We would like you to decide for yourself which of these modules you would like to work on so you can be helped in the areas in which you need help the most. We will show you a preview of each of these modules, and after each one is described you should check "yes" on the list in front of you after the name of the module if you want to see it, and "no" if you think you do not need help in that area.

Deborah heard and saw each module briefly described. A short sales talk has been made for each module. For example, in "Shaving for Women" the tape says: "Ladies, maybe you are wondering whether really modern girls should shave their legs and underarms or whether they should 'go natural.' Perhaps some of you are interested in learning about methods of shaving or removing hair without shaving. This module will give you some of the information and answers you may need."

As the information about each module was presented Deborah checked the areas that she wanted. Her vocational counselor (or social worker) also completed a similar checklist, checking those areas in which he thought that she needed some help. The grooming instructor, who was observing this introductory session, also checked a similar list based on her observation of Deborah's appearance. (These preliminary checklists by staff members also provide base-line data on how the client looks initially and can be compared with lists checked by the professionals after the client completes the program, to assess whether or not change has occurred.)

Deborah's grooming-program schedule was a combination of the areas that she had checked and the additional areas checked by professional staff. This ensured that, for example, if she had failed to check "Shampooing," which she obviously needed, she would still take that module. Deborah participated in all of the modules that were appropriate for women because she needed so much grooming help.[8]

In each module Deborah was presented with technical information about how to perform the grooming necessary for that module. Colored slides illustrated each step. In "Shampooing," for example, she was told specifically how to wash her hair:

First, wet your head and hair with warm water.

Now apply about a capful (about a teaspoonful) of shampoo to your hair.

Massage the shampoo through your hair.

Now, curve your fingers as though you were holding a ball in your hand. Use the tips of your fingers to massage your hair and scalp thoroughly.

The shampooing module continued telling Deborah to suds and rinse again and to listen for her hair to squeak when she had finished. After viewing the module, Deborah and the other clients in the group discussed what they had seen and asked questions of the

---

[8] *Editors' note:* Having the client take some responsibility right in the beginning for what is to be changed often helps to motivate him to make changes. It also permits modeling of a more independent role for clients, rather than the passive-dependent one that is so often encouraged by professional helpers.

instructor. They then had a laboratory practice session in which they either actually shampooed their hair` or at least practiced the shampoo manipulations on dry hair and planned to shampoo that evening at home.[9]

Before viewing each module, Deborah took a ten-question quiz to assess her prior knowledge about that area. Following completion of the module, she took a similar test to see how much she had learned. The scores on these tests were used to determine whether or not she had understood and assimilated the information presented. This helped the program developers to review and improve the content and presentation methods, in order to make them as effective as possible.

As Deborah progressed through each program module, she was rewarded by grooming instructors, peers, and her social worker and counselor for the improvements that she made in her appearance. In order to help her to organize a grooming schedule, she was told to make a chart showing what she must do each day of the week. Baths were to be taken every day; hair had to be washed and set on Mondays, Wednesdays, and Fridays; deodorant was to be used daily; and she was to check weekly to see whether or not her legs and underarms needed shaving.

Four weeks after she had started the grooming program, Deborah was bathing, shaving, using deodorant, and washing and setting her hair. She had difficulty limiting her diet to low-calorie foods but did manage to lose three pounds during the program.[10] Just before she left the program Deborah went out on her own to a local Goodwill store and purchased a "new" outfit to wear to job interviews. Her new grooming habits not only brought her the rewards of praise and favorable attention from staff and peers but resulted in a new job as well. She was hired as a kitchen helper at a local hospital.

Use of Rewards and Reinforcement

It was decided that verbal praise from peers and staff would be the most natural reinforcement method to use for this program, for praise and favorable attention are the rewards that one most typically receives for being well groomed. If clients are attuned to look for this kind of reinforcement from their friends, families, and coworkers, they are more likely to maintain good grooming habits. When working with individuals who are in an environment like the center, sheltered workshops, and state hospitals, it is possible to structure this environment so that an individual is ensured recognition for behavior changes. One of the techniques used successfully in this program to ensure verbal reinforcement was to send a daily note to the staff working with each client who was in the grooming program. The note indicated the particular area of grooming that was being worked on each day. In many instances the changes were so obvious that notes were not needed, but in others (like manicuring) the staff needed reminders to compliment clients' on their progress.

[9] Editors' note: Great! Clients need the opportunity to try out a new skill immediately after it has been presented.

[10] Editors' note: Not bad for a starter. Perhaps even more weight loss will occur after counselors read articles 9, 10, and 60.

In some instances it was necessary to establish more specific reward systems in order to effect change. An example illustrates this. Seventeen-year-old Sue was socially and intellectually immature. Her most significant grooming problem was excess weight. Information on dieting and encouragement to diet had little effect. Because Sue enjoyed conversing with the grooming staff, it was decided to use conversation time as a reward for losing weight. Sue weighed in twice weekly. Each time that she lost a pound she earned conversation time with the grooming-staff member of her choice. Eventually Sue lost thirteen pounds and was continuing to follow her diet when she left the program.

An individualized reward system was also used to help Frank to improve his grooming. He was thirty-three years old and had been in and out of mental hospitals for eleven years. When he was in the hospital the essentials of grooming (baths, deodorant, shaving, clean clothing) were regulated by the institution. On his own, however, Frank was not able to manage a regular grooming routine. He both looked and smelled unclean.

In discussions with his counselor, it was learned that Frank really enjoyed his coffee breaks from the evaluation workshop and looked forward to them. It was decided to use additional coffee-break time as a reward for grooming improvements. Frank was told that for each grooming standard he met each day he could add five minutes to his coffee break. After two weeks of these extended coffee breaks, Frank's appearance had improved so much that he attracted a girlfriend. This new reinforcer was so strong that he no longer needed the extra coffee-break time to maintain his appearance.[11]

Staffing

The "How to 'LOOK' for a Job" grooming program uses nonprofessional staff as instructors. It was developed so that it could be staffed by a technician or other nonprofessional—or perhaps a volunteer. The three program manuals and the sound-slide presentation are so comprehensive that a beautician or other grooming professional is not needed to teach the program. It is essential, however, that an instructor work with the clients during the program, in order to help them learn the techniques and to provide reinforcement.

EVALUATION[12]

After six months of trial operation, the program had involved 220 men and

---

[11] *Editors' note:* Frank is more likely than Sue to maintain the new grooming behaviors. He now has someone in his natural environment to reinforce his new behaviors, whereas Sue is still dependent upon conversations with staff members. To maintain new client behaviors, the counselor must find ways to transfer the reinforcing contingencies to the natural environment.

[12] Evaluation of the program was conducted by K. S. Birch and Judith A. Klein as part of the fulfillment of requirements for the degree of Master of Social Work from the University of Minnesota. The statistics provided are taken from their research report, "Development and Evaluation of a Grooming Program in a Vocational Rehabilitation Center" March 1973.

women, aged sixteen to fifty-eight years, who were clients of the center. They evinced problems (in addition to grooming) of mental retardation, chemical dependence, delinquency, physical handicaps, and emotional maladjustment.

For fifteen of the twenty-one modules clients' changes in knowledge were significant at the .01 level. In two modules changes were significant at the .05 level. It was therefore concluded that seventeen of the twenty-one modules provided significant levels of change in knowledge.

Figure 1 shows the percentage of clients who improved in each module. In seventeen of the twenty-one modules 70 percent of all clients met the module standards after completing the program.

There was only 57 percent agreement between the clients' selection of modules for themselves and the selections of the grooming instructor or other professionals on their behalf. The grooming instructor or counselor made 1,504 separate selections of modules on behalf of clients. The clients made 903 separate selections of modules that agreed with the selections by either the grooming instructor or the counselor. Apparently, in many instances, the staff thought that clients needed more grooming help than the clients thought that they needed. The program developers still believe that providing clients with opportunities to select their own programs is worthwhile. Clients did succeed in making appearance changes, and it is possible that their involvement in program selection helped to ensure

their commitment to the program and to improve their motivation.[13]

Poor grooming is one of the most significant yet the most often ignored barriers to employment and other rehabilitation goals. In this day of individualism some professionals fear that attempts to change clients' appearance will be seen as chauvinistic. Yet undeniable standards of acceptable grooming do exist in the social and employment community. If a client is not acquainted with these standards and if he is not helped to meet them, he is likely to fail to achieve larger goals in the areas of competitive employment and socialization.

Many professionals fail to realize that "common knowledge" about basic hygiene and grooming which has been part of their own upbringing, is not necessarily "common" to all people. Many individuals who are poorly groomed or unclean simply lack basic information about how to care for their bodies and their appearance.

The developers of this program learned that when grooming problems are approached honestly yet sensitively, clients are receptive to change. They enjoy the benefits of improved grooming, and their chances of succeeding in other life areas are greatly increased.

[13] *Editors' note:* It appears that clients were expected to take some modules recommended by the staff, even though the clients themselves did not choose to do so initially. Perhaps the differential success rate on the various modules reflects the extent of client selection. Certainly the data could be analyzed to see whether or not self-selected modules were accomplished more successfully than staff-selected modules.

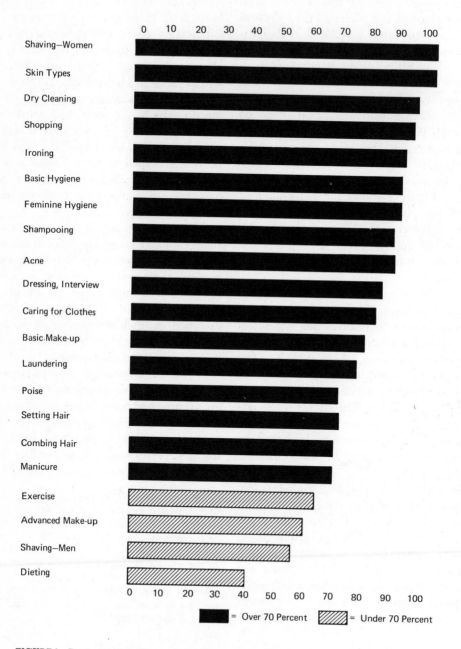

FIGURE 1 Percentage of clients who improved in each module.

reference

Krumboltz, J. D. & Thoresen, C. E. *Behavioral counseling: Cases and techniques.* New York: Holt, Rinehart and Winston, 1969.

PHYSICAL CONDITIONING

60. USING CONTRACTS TO CONTROL WEIGHT AND TO IMPROVE CARDIOVASCULAR PHYSICAL FITNESS

BARBARA VANCE   Brigham Young Unviersity

After much agonizing and soul searching Janet finally made an appointment with a personal-development consultant[1] at the university. She had not had a date since she had arrived at the university seven months previously as a freshman, and her grades were growing worse instead of better. It was obvious to the consultant after talking with Janet for a few minutes that her primary problem—at least socially—was obesity. Janet finally admitted that she thought her other problems would be solved if she could just lose some weight. She had tried every fad diet suggested by her friends or that she had read about in magazines. But she could never manage to stay on any diet very long. The consultant was well aware of the poor prognosis for overweight individuals in counseling. Should he suggest to Janet that she take a fitness course in physical education, see a medical doctor about her prob-

lem, or join a local "obesity anonymous" group? Or should he assist Janet in developing and following through on a weight-control contract?

Todd's roommates in the dorm had become alarmed lately because of his increasing moodiness and sudden outbursts of anger in overreaction to minor incidents in the dorm. They had finally prevailed on him to make an appointment with Dr. Jones in the counseling service, who had a reputation among the students as a "cool guy." During his first conversation with Dr. Jones, Todd revealed the heavy pressures that he was under to maintain a high grade-point average in his physics major, so that he could apply for a graduate scholarship. He felt forced to give up almost all activities other than studying in order to maintain his grades. His grades were improving slightly, but he had noticed some "personality changes" lately. He knew that he was overreacting negatively to too many situations but did not know how to control himself. It was almost more than he could handle just to maintain a tight study schedule, and he was getting very little exercise. He often felt depressed while

---

[1] The term "personal-development consultant" is replacing "counselor" at some high schools and colleges, in order to denote a broader range of activities in the instructional environment of students than those typically ascribed to "counselor."

studying. Dr. Jones knew that his depression and overreaction to minor events probably were at least partially related to his lack of exercise.[2] If he suggested that Todd take a fitness course in physical education right then, he knew that Todd would not take the time in an already overloaded class schedule. Should he suggest that Todd come in once a week to talk over his problems just to tide him over to the next semester? Should he suggest that Todd go to the health center for some tranquillizers? Or should he try a cardiovascular endurance-program contract with Todd?

Janet and Todd each had several presenting problems. Each problem could be stated in behavioral terms and identified as a goal for counseling. The rule here is twofold: First, work on *one* problem at a time; second, let the client select the problem that he wishes to solve first. Janet wanted to work on her overweight problem. Todd, after some discussion wtih Dr. Jones, decided that he wanted to work on his exercise problem, even though he had a very full academic schedule. He thought that exercise could help him to overcome his moodiness and overreaction to minor events.

If Janet and Todd wanted to learn new physical *skills*, they probably would have been wiser to take one or more skills courses in the physical-education department. However, their identified problems were related to

----

[2] *Editors' note:* Dr. Jones' interests and values are showing. Todd sounds as if he is developing into a "Type A"—the term used by some cardiologists for a person who is trying to do too much and who exhibits hostile feelings and actions toward others.

physical behavior that had already been learned but had to be increased in frequency. Therefore these problems could be considered motivational. But where does a counselor begin on such problems?

DEVELOPING A SELF-CONTRACT

Early in 1973 I was asked to assist members of the faculty of physical education at the university to develop an individualized instructional program on physical fitness that would eventually be required of all 8,000 incoming freshmen each year. Two activity programs were considered imperative in this course, one in cardiovascular endurance and one in weight control, including both diet and exercise. The goal of these two activity programs was to develop motivation within each student to continue his cardiovascular-endurance program and, if necessary, his weight-control program throughout his lifetime. Obviously the faculty could not monitor each student's progress beyond his time at the university. However, if a student achieved and maintained good physical fitness throughout his college career, he would be more likely to continue it afterward. Two members of the physical-education faculty and I kept this goal in mind as we prepared the activity programs for the physical-fitness course. A cardiovascular-endurance program and a weight-control program contract were developed. Figures 1 and 2 are examples of the weight- and cardiovascular-program contracts.

The development and formative evaluation of self-contracts with forty-

Semester __Fall__   Year __197_

1. Name _____Janet_____   Age __18__ Sex __F__ .

2. Current Percent Body Fat __35__ . Desired Percent Body Fat __16__ .

3. Present Weight __170__ . Pounds To Be Lost __32__ . Target Weight __138__ .

Week	Exercise	Duration	Weekly Exercise Periods	Exercise Rein- forcer(s)	Weight To Be Lost	Desired Calorie Intake	Diet Rein- forcer(s)
1	Swimming	20 min.	3	5 points each period	2	1800	1 hr. TV, ½ hr. read book
2	”	”	”	”	”	”	”
3	”	”	”	”	”	”	”
4	”	”	”	”	”	”	”
5	”	”	”	”	”	”	”
6	”	”	”	”	”	”	”
7	”	”	”	”	”	”	”
8	”	”	”	”	”	”	”
9	”	”	”	”	”	”	”
				Go to movie for each 30 points			Parents have promised new ward- robe when I achieve target weight

Student's Signature: _____

Contract Approval Date: _____ Approved by: _____

Progress Check Date: _____ Approved by: _____

Contract Completion Date: _____ Approved by: _____

FIGURE 1   Weight-control program contract.

three students are described here. As counseling is an individualized instructional process, counselors may wish to use similar contracts and processes to assist their clients with physical-fitness problems.

Specifying the Behavior

What is the desired behavior? This was our first problem in developing the physical-fitness activity programs. For the overweight individual, is it satis-

Semester __Fall__   Year __197_

1. Name ___Todd___   Age __20__   Sex __M__

2. Beginning Fitness Category: ⓪ (Beginner)   III (Average)
                                 I (Very Poor)   IV   (Good)
                                 II (Poor)   V   (Excellent)

3. Desired cardiovascular exercise(s): _____Jogging_____

Week	Days	Exercise	Distance	Duration	Points/ Day	Points/ Week	Reinforcers
1	5	Jogging	1 mile	13:30	2	10	2 points each exercise period
2	5	"	"	13:00	2	10	"
3	5	"	"	12:45	2	10	"
4	5	"	"	11:45	3	15	"
5	5	"	"	11:00	3	15	"
6	5	"	"	10:30	3	15	"
7	5	"	1.5 miles	18:30	3	15	"
8	5	"	"	17:30	3	15	"
9	4	"	"	16:30	4.5	18	"
10	3	"	1 mile	9:30	—	21	"
	2	"	1.5 miles	15:30			

Student's Signature: _____
Contract Approval Date: _____ Approved by: _____
Progress Check Date: _____ Approved by: _____
Contract Completion Date: _____ Approved by: _____

FIGURE 2 Cardiovascular-endurance program contract.

factory to identify the behavior as "to lose X number of pounds"? Loss of weight is not a behavior. It is a result of several behaviors like physical activity and eating. For the individual who has a low cardiovascular-endurance fitness level, is it satisfactory to identify behavior as "to achieve X level of fitness"? Achieving a given level of cardiovascular-endurance fitness is not a behavior but results from several activities.[3]

A weight-control worksheet and a cardiovascular-endurance worksheet

[3] Editors' note: A good point. Losing so many pounds or achieving a certain level of physical fitness is a behavioral goal or outcome. To accomplish such a goal certain behaviors must be increased, and other behaviors must be decreased.

with accompanying instructions were developed to assist each student to determine his ideal daily caloric intake and his ideal daily cardiovascular-endurance exercise respectively. A unique feature of the weight-control program was the determination of percentage of body fat and the computation of ideal weight on the basis of percentage of body fat, rather than according to a height-weight chart.[4] The weight-control program also included regular exercise. The individual tends to lose lean body mass, as well as fat, in a program of weight loss by diet only.[5] The cardiovascular-endurance program is based on the "aerobics" system developed by Cooper (1970) for males and by Cooper and Cooper (1972) for females. Individualized instructions for completing the weight-control and cardiovascular-endurance program worksheets are available in Allsen, Harrison, and Vance (1976).

Using pertinent information from his worksheets, the student fills out the top of his weight-control program contract, items 1–4 (see Figure 1), and items 1–3 in his cardiovascular-endurance program contract (see Figure 2). He then fills in each of the columns on the contract, with the exception of

those dealing with his reinforcers. Each row in the contract summarizes one week of the program. That is, during the first week of a weight-control program the student indicates his choice of exercise (column 2), how long he plans to exercise during each exercise period (column 3), how many times he will exercise during the week (column 4), how much weight he will lose that week (already filled in for column 6),[6] and how many calories he must eat each day to lose two pounds a week (column 7).

During the first week of the cardiovascular-endurance program the student indicates the days (at least four) of the week that he will exercise (column 2), the name of the desired exercise (column 3), how far or to what degree he will exercise (column 4), how long he will exercise each day (column 5), how many "aerobics" points he will receive for each day of exercise (column 6), and how many "aerobics" points he will achieve for that week (column 7). The information for these columns is obtained from the respective worksheets described in Allsen, Harrison, and Vance (1976).

There are rows for each week of the program on each contract because the student is required in the course to engage in his weight-control or cardiovascular-endurance program for a given number of weeks during the semester. For counseling purposes, it may not be necessary to have the separate rows for

---

[4] Skin calipers were used to determine percentage of body fat. Skin-caliper tests can be given by trained personnel in most college physical-education departments. More readily available techniques are now being studied. For more information on these techniques, write to P. E. Allsen, Physical Education Department, Brigham Young University, Provo, Utah 84602.

[5] Editors' note: A very important point. See Article 9 for another example of weight control through changing many habits, including certain thoughts.

[6] Editors' note: This column could be left blank too, so that each student could set his or her own own target. Two pounds a week is a reasonable maximum, however. Overambitious goals lead to crash programs that fail.

each week of the weight-control program because each week would produce essentially the same information. However, the individual may wish to change his desired exercise or the duration of his exercise later in his program.

The cardiovascular-endurance program will gradually change his program from week to week as that student's cardiovascular endurance increases, unless he is on a cardiovascular-maintenance program. If he is on a maintenance program he probably is not a candidate for counseling related to cardiovascular endurance. Thus, space should be allowed on the cardiovascular-endurance program contract for each week of the program. It may be wise to furnish additional spaces for weeks on the contract for clients at such low cardiovascular-endurance levels that they require the full sixteen-week "aerobics" conditioning program recommended by Cooper (1970) and Cooper and Cooper (1972).

Determining Reinforcers

Before completing his contract the student is asked to determine his reinforcers and then to select from this list of reinforcers those that he will use periodically to reward himself for achieving intermediate goals. As an aid in listing his reinforcers, he is furnished with a copy of the personal-reward list (see Figure 3).

When he completes this list, he selects those reinforcers that he can control and that are most likely to reinforce his daily exercise and daily caloric intake. The token system of rewards is explained to the student in his instructional materials, in the event that he

may wish to give himself so many points for each exercise activity or each day that he eats no more than his desired daily caloric intake. These points can be accumulated for larger, more tangible rewards later on.

Clients who wish counseling assistance for weight-control or cardiovascular-endurance problems usually have problems that are relatively severe compared with those of the average person. Therefore, they should be encouraged to use tangible reinforcers quite frequently, especially at the beginning of their programs to start them and keep them going. Larger rewards can also be added periodically on the basis of a token system.

The target weight for an obese person like Janet looks remote compared to that of a girl who has only ten or fifteen pounds to lose. Thus, intermediate rewards must be frequent and powerful—and may have to be changed occasionally to prevent satiation. The desired reinforcers are selected from the personal-reward list and added to columns 5 and 8 on the weight-control program contract (Figure 1) or to column 8 of the cardiovascular-endurance program contract (Figure 2).

Recording Behavior

Students in the course attend class only when they wish to take mastery checks on written material, receive assistance from the instructor or student proctor, or have their progress on their cardiovascular-endurance and weight-control programs checked. When the weight-control program or the cardiovascular-endurance program contract is completed, it is checked by the student's

Questions	Answers
1. What kinds of things do I like to have?	Nice clothes; words & music to popular songs
2. What are my major interests?	Watching TV; movies; reading novels and magazines; talking to friends
3. What are my hobbies?	Needlepoint, playing guitar, reading historical fiction
4. What kinds of people do I like to be with?	My roommates; my best friend; my family
5. What do I like to do with these people?	Rap; go to movies; go swimming
6. What do I do for fun, for enjoyment and relaxation?	Watch TV; go to movies; read novels and magazines
7. What would be a nice present to receive?	A whole new wardrobe when I'm not fat
8. What kinds of things are important to me?	Dating; getting good grades; pleasing my parents and friends
9. What would I do if I had an extra $5? $10? $50?	Go out for a steak dinner Buy a new blouse Buy a new guitar
10. What are activities I engage in every day? (Don't overlook the obvious and commonplace activities such as brushing teeth, combing hair, dressing, etc.)	Brush teeth; dress in morning; get ready for bed; wash hair; eat; watch TV; talk with roommates; make bed; comb hair; walk to class
11. What would I hate to lose?	My guitar; my guitar music; money
12. What are my favorite foods?	Hot fudge sundaes; chocolate cake; steaks; pie; candy bars

FIGURE 3   Personal-reward list.

instructor or proctor to make sure that computations are correct and that reinforcers are realistic. It is then signed by the student and his instructor or proctor. The student agrees to come in for a progress check on his contract during a specified period at midterm.

Now the student actually begins the terms of his contract. It is extremely important that he record his *daily* behavior. This gives him daily evidence and reminders of his progress. A student may not feel actual physical changes in weight loss or cardiovascular endurance for several days or even weeks, but at least he can have daily evidence of the specific behaviors leading to the desired changes.[7]

Figure 4 is a sample of the weight-control program progress log. Each day the student records which week of his

[7] *Editors' note:* This daily "feedback" on appropriate behaviors is often crucial in the beginning. Too often the obese client, for example, becomes quickly discouraged when no obvious evidence of his "starvation" regime occurs, the scale still reads "heavy," his clothes are still tight, and the mirror still reveals a fat person. Self-reward for changing eating behaviors can bolster morale.

Name **Janet** . Age **18** . Sex **F** .
Current Percent Body Fat **35** . Desired Percent Body Fat **16** .
Current Weight **170** . Pounds To Be Lost **32** . Target Weight **138** .

Week	Day and Date	Exercise	Duration	Exercise Reinforcers	Calorie Intake	Weight	Diet Reinforcer(s)
1	M	Swimming	22 min.	5 points	1800	170	1 hr. TV; ½ hr. read
1	Tu				1800	170.5	”
1	W	Swimming	25 min.	5 points	1800	169.5	”
1	Th				1800	169.5	”
1	F	Swimming	20 min.	5 points	1800	169.0	”
1	S				1800	169.5	”
1	Su					169.0	”
2	M	Swimming	25 min.	5 points	1800	168.0	”
2	Tu				1800	168.0	”
2	W	Swimming	21 min.	5 points	1800	167.5	”
2	Th				1800	167.5	”
2	F	Swimming	25 min.	5 points — movie	1800	167.0	”
2	S				1800	166.0	”
2	Su					166.0	”
3	M	Swimming	23 min.	5 points	1800	165	”
3	Tu				1800	166	”
3	W	Swimming	20 min.	5 points	1800	165	”
3	Th				1800	164.5	”
3	F	Swimming	24 min.	5 points	1800	164	”
3	S				1800	164	”

FIGURE 4 Weight-control program progress log.

program he is on (column 1); the day of the week and the date (column 2); his exercise for the day, if any (column 3); the duration of his exercise (column 4); the reinforcer(s) due for his exercise, if any (column 5); the actual caloric intake for that day (column 6); his weight that day (column 7); and any reinforcers earned for sticking to the desired number of calories that day (column 8).

Figure 5 is a sample of the cardiovascular endurance program progress log. Each day the student records which week of the program he is on (column 1); the date (column 2); the day of the week (column 3); the name of the exercise (column 4); how far or to what extent he has engaged in the exercise (column 5); how long he has exercised that day (column 6); how many exercise or "aerobics" points he has earned for the day (column 6); how many "aerobics" points he has accumulated during the week, if it is the last day of the week (column 7); and the reinforcer that he has earned for his exercise that day, if any (column 8).

Students are instructed to put their progress logs in conspicuous spots, where they can fill in appropriate information immediately.[8] They are urged to exercise at the same time each day, in order to make it easier to establish the habit of exercise. It is easier to talk yourself out of an exercise period when that exercise period is not at a consistent time in the daily schedule. Those on a weight-control program are en-

couraged to weigh themselves at the same time every day (preferably in the morning when body liquids are at their lowest levels) and in the same clothes (like pajamas early in the morning).

Checking Progress

During the progress check at midterm each student brings his progress log, as well as his copy of his contract. The progress check includes a fitness appraisal to check percentage of body fat and cardiovascular-endurance level. This same fitness appraisal is given to the student before he prepares his contract and is also given to him again as a final measure of his achievement on his contract. If desired, the student may wish to take such body measurements as the circumference of his upper arms, chest or bust, waist, thighs, and calves, especially if he has taken these measurements at the first fitness appraisal. Students may find it quite reinforcing to discover that their waist measurements are smaller and their chest and bust measurements are larger, even though they have gained some weight on a cardiovascular-endurance program (because of natural increases in muscle tissue as a result of exercise).

During the progress check the student may wish to change some of the terms of his contract. Perhaps he feels that his exercise goal is too high and that he needs to reduce the amount of time that he engages in exercise. Or perhaps he finds just the opposite, that he wants to increase the time that he spends in exercise. Or he may wish to change from one exercise to another that he thinks he will like better. Perhaps he finds his reinforcers not real-

---

[8] *Editors' note:* And where friends or relatives can provide some intermittent social reinforcement for sticking to the plan.

Name ___Todd___

Age ___20___ Sex ___M___

Beginning cardiovascular endurance level ___0___

Exercise(s): ___Jogging___

Week	Date	Day	Exercise	Distance	Duration	Points/Day	Points/Week	Reinforcer(s)
1	10/20	M	Jogging	1 mile	14:00	2		2 pts.
1	10/21	Tu	"	"	14:00	"		"
1	10/22	W	"	"	13:45	"		"
1	10/23	Th	"	"	13:45	"		"
1	10/25	S	"	"	13:30	"	10	"
2	10/27	M	"	"	13:30	"		"
2	10/28	Tu	"	"	13:15	"		"
2	10/29	W	"	"	13:15	"		"
2	10/30	Th	"	"	13:00	"		"
2	11/1	S	"	"	13:00	"	10	"
3	11/3	M	"	"	13:00	"		"
3	11/4	Tu	"	"	13:15	"		"
3	11/5	W	"	"	13:00	"		"
3	11/6	Th	"	"	13:00	"		"
3	11/8	S	"	"	12:45	"	10	"
4	11/10	M	"	"	12:45	"		"
4	11/11	Tu	"	"	12:30	"		"
4	11/12	W	"	"	12:15	"		"
4	11/13	Th	"	"	12:00	"		"
4	11/15	S	"	"	11:45	"	10	2 stereo cassettes

FIGURE 5   Cardiovascular-endurance program progress log.

istic and would like to change the type or the ratio of reinforcement.[9]

Progress checks are especially important for clients working on physical-fitness programs in counseling. They will need instruction in the selection and use of reinforcers in particular. As the goal of the counselor is to assist the client to the point at which he can carry on without frequent help from the counselor, it is important that the client learn what his reinforcers are and how to control them in the service of desirable goals like physical fitness. And the verbal reinforcers offered to the client when he shows his counselor a "good" progress log should not be underestimated. If the client is struggling to stick to his contract, he will need help from his counselor to determine whether he needs to "slice the behavior thinner" or change his reinforcers. Therefore, each counseling session is a form of progress check once the client has started on his program.

Occasionally the counselor may have to assist his client to determine some effective self-punishers when reinforcers do not seem to work. Punishers usually are not necessary for clients on a cardiovascular-endurance program. However, clients on weight-control programs may have to use self-punishment for a while. Physical punishers usually are "no no"s. However, deprivation or "removal" punishers may be effective. One form of effective punishment for a recent client was giving her best friend a $10 bill whenever she failed to lose the two pounds that she had contracted to lose each week. She only lost one $10 bill! One antifeminist client gave his counselor a signed check for $25 made out to the National Organization of Women with the agreement that the check would be mailed whenever he failed to lose two pounds in a given week. There was never any reason to send the check![10]

The obese person often needs some simple guidelines to assist him in his weight-control program. The following guidelines were prepared to assist the students in our physical-fitness program.

1. Beware of accepting invitations to dinner where you might be tempted to go off your diet or to snack. It will take time to adjust to your new eating patterns. When you learn the basic food plan for your diet from week to week, you can then accept invitations with the understanding that you may not be able to eat everything served.
2. Avoid boring or fatiguing situations that cause you to think of food or to nibble between meals.
3. Learn what tempts you to snack, and avoid the temptation.
4. Eat only the food listed on your daily food plan. Don't cheat, or your blood sugar level will take a big leap and then take an even bigger dive. You will feel worse then if you had avoided the forbidden food in the first place.
5. Don't read or watch TV while eating. This leads to thoughtless overeating.
6. When shopping be sure to use a list,

[9] *Editors' note:* It is an excellent idea to build in a periodic review of the contract. More realistic terms can be specified after some initial experience.

[10] *Editors' note:* Perhaps these contingencies or arrangements constitute negative reinforcement more than punishment. An aversive situation is constructed (agreeing to the contract involving a potential loss), and it can be avoided only by meeting the terms of the contract (losing weight).

to shop for what's on the list only, to take only enough money for what's on the list, to avoid putting high-calorie foods on the list, and never to shop when you are hungry!

7. When eating, try the following: Serve yourself on small dishes, say a dessert plate instead of a dinner plate, so small servings will look large; lay down your eating utensil between bites; chew the food in your mouth and swallow it before you take the next bite; learn to savor the food you eat; measure your servings with measuring cups, spoons, and a small food scale. The eye is not a very good judge of serving size.

8. Cook vegetables in as little water as possible for as short a time as possible. They will look better, taste better, and be more nutritious.

9. Always eat three regular meals a day. If you try to cram all your daily calories into one or two meals your body will not be able to handle all the nutrients at once, and some calories will be stored as fat. In addition, waiting so long between meals affects blood-sugar level and causes undue fatigue and irritability. Be good to yourself. Eat good meals and acceptable snacks in between.

10. Never eat fewer than 1,200 calories a day unless you are under the care of a medical doctor. Even if your weight-control program calls for fewer than 1,200 calories, consume 1,200 calories a day until you have lost the desired amount of weight.

Evaluation of Contracts

During the fall of 1973 and the winter of 1974, forty-three undergraduate students used a pilot form of the instructional materials for the physical-fitness course, including the weight-control and cardiovascular-endurance activity programs and contracts. These students were volunteers for the physical-fitness courses and were not typical of those who might ordinarily seek counseling for physical-fitness problems, for their fitness problems were not extreme. Only three of these students were males. Of this sample, twenty-one engaged in a weight-control program, and twenty-two engaged in a cardiovascular-endurance program.

All twenty-one students on the weight-control program were female. Twenty of them achieved the terms of their contracts in the ten-week contract period. At the beginning of the program the range of percentage of body fat was from a low of 18.7 percent (good) to 35.8 percent (obese). At the end of the contract period all students had lost some body fat, ranging from a loss of 3 percent to a loss of 13 percent. The one girl who had not achieved the terms of her contract said, in answer to the question "How has this weight-control program affected you?":

I have not done as well as I would have liked to. Living in the dorms, the food is almost all fattening and it is difficult to really know just how many calories you are taking in. Also, due to pressure from friends to go get ice cream, pizza, etc., no one seemed to care much that I was on a diet. Instead they, 3 of which [sic] are overweight, tried to discourage me from staying on it.

This response illustrates some of the basic reasons why counseling the overweight has such a poor prognosis in general. It takes time to lose weight. In the meantime, other, more immediate, but counterproductive reinforcers are available in the environment to lure the individual away from the best-laid behavioral plans.

Those twenty individuals who had met the terms of their weight-control contracts suggested that they needed no reinforcers at all other than the reinforcement intrinsic in the weight loss itself.[11] And thirteen of these twenty had had more than twenty-seven percent body fat, in other words, were obese! Several of them found it very

[11] *Editors' note:* Remember that these students were volunteers. Because weight loss is slow and erratic, especially in the beginning, reinforcement for changes in eating habits may be critical for clients with more serious problems.

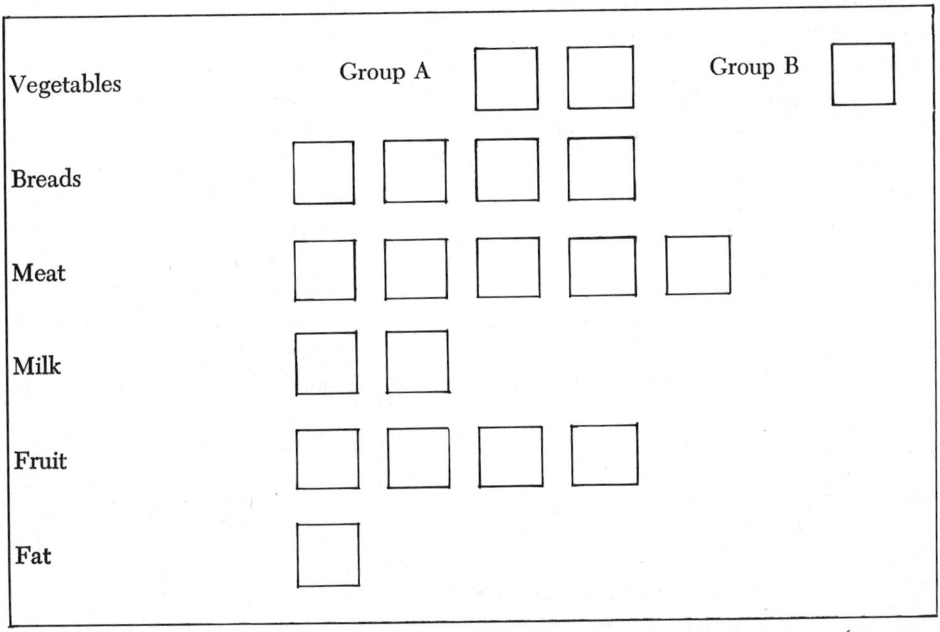

helpful to keep track of the foods they ate daily from the food-exchange lists (Allsen, Harrison & Vance, 1976) on a 3×5-inch card, similar to the one shown in Figure 6, each day. The card indicates the total number of servings daily (admissible for a given number of calories per day) from each of the six food-exchange groups. The students found it very simple to make their own cards and to carry a card each day, marking off each serving of food on it as they ate their meals.

Of the twenty-two students on the cardiovascular-endurance program, three were male. Table 1 presents the number of students in each cardiovascular-endurance level before and after the contract period. Five students

FIGURE 6 Sample of the daily food-plan card used by Janet (for 1,800 calories). Each box represents one serving from the food-exchange list in Allsen, Harrison & Vance (1976). Janet checked a box each time she ate a serving from any of these categories. She used a different card each day to record the food she ate.

TABLE 1   Number of Students in Each Cardiovascular-Endurance Level Be-
fore and After the Contract
Period

Cardiovascular Endurance Level	Before	After
Excellent	0	0
Good	1	10
Fair	9	11
Poor	12	1
Very poor	0	0

had made no change at all in endurance level during their contract period, fourteen had moved one level upward, and three had moved two levels upward. This is considered good to excellent progress. The five students who had not made progress were inconsistent in meeting the terms of their contracts. Inconsistent exercise is considered by some exercise physiologists to be worse than no exercise at all.

Here are some typical comments received when students on the cardiovascular-endurance program were asked, "How has this cardiovascular endurance program affected you?"

I sleep very soundly, and I don't require as much sleep to be alert and efficient as I used to. It certainly is easy to fall asleep now and I don't wake 'til morning.

I am more "awake." I don't just drag through the day.

My appetite is more controlled since I started exercising. And I REALLY notice that I feel like I have more energy. I am able to sleep a lot better, and now I'm to the point where it isn't hard to pull myself out of bed at 6:00 every morning to swim.

This cardiovascular endurance program

has improved my life and my way of living. . . . My appetite has increased, but the foods I want to eat are more nutritious. I can run faster than I have before. I feel better during the day, think better, breathe deeper, and sleep more soundly.

The students on the weight-control program were encouraged to choose cardiovascular-endurance exercises for their weight-control programs; their comments on exercise are similar to those just quoted.

The students using the cardiovascular-endurance program, almost without exception, suggested that external reinforcement was unnecessary. They found the almost immediate increase in physical well-being was enough reinforcement. However, these students were taking a physical-education course and were in a "physical fitness" atmosphere every time they came to class. External reinforcers may be necessary for the counseling client with a physical-fitness problem who is not taking a physical-education course.[12]

I personally made all kinds of excuses not to jog until I found a friend who liked to jog before her team-tennis matches. She took me to the track with her and helped me to learn how gradually to break myself in. Then I bought myself a good-looking jogging outfit, including a pair of shoes that made me feel as if I were walking on a cloud. So I felt good in my new outfit and gained further confidence because I had learned some basic rules of track use and how to warm my body up.

[12] *Editors' note:* Of course, counselors may find that the most effective therapy would be to persuade their clients to sign up for physical-fitness classes.

From then on I could be an independent jogger. I did not particularly like to run, but the feeling afterward was great, and thus intrinsic reinforcement kept me going. Jogging is "the exercise I hate once a day"—but I love the results! It might be necessary for the behavioral counselor to leave his stuffy office and assist a client on a cardiovascular-endurance program break into the "real world" of exercise.

Janet, who wanted to lose weight, and Todd, who needed a cardiovascular-endurance program, are typical of those clients who may come to counselors for assistance. A weight-control contract or a cardiovascular-endurance contract may be just what the client needs to achieve success in such a behavior area.

references

Allsen, P. E., Harrison, J. & Vance, B. *Fitness for life: An individualized approach.* Dubuque, Iowa: William C. Brown Company, 1976.

Cooper, K. H. *The new aerobics.* New York: Bantam, 1970.

Cooper, M. & Cooper, K. H. *Aerobics for women.* New York: Bantam, 1972.

PEER COUNSELING

61. *PEER COUNSELING: A GUIDANCE PROGRAM AND A BEHAVIORAL INTERVENTION*

BARBARA B. VARENHORST Palo Alto, California, Unified School District

The year was 1970. As a psychologist in the Palo Alto, California, schools' guidance department and the coordinator of an ESEA Exemplary Guidance Program grant, I was attempting to assess the needs of consumers of guidance services. In doing so, I interviewed and talked with counselors, teachers, administrators, and even students. Counselors told me: "I don't have enough time to see most of my counselees. The ones with serious problems take most of my time." Teachers frequently answered my questions: "Counselors don't know the average student. They are either working with problem kids or helping those who are going to college." The students said things like: "I don't talk to my counselor about my personal problems. He doesn't know me. He doesn't have time. Besides, it's hard to talk to someone across a desk"; "I talk to my friends about my problems, and they talk to me. I don't always know what to say or do, but I like it better this way. We know one another"; "This is a cold school. It's hard to make friends here, and lots of times

I have to admit to myself that I feel lonely."

There were other comments, in different words but centering on the same themes: Counselors feel burdened with heavy counseling loads and "crisis" cases, finding it hard to reach the middle group of students with normal developmental concerns; there is not enough time to get to know students in sufficient depth for them to feel comfortable discussing personal problems; they turn to other students for help, and many students feel lonely and isolated. How could a guidance program meet these varied needs?

Often in my past counseling work I had longed for a corps of students I could "take off the shelf" and give to other students as friends: to meet a need that I could not fulfill even with professional skill and genuine interest in the students I was counseling. When I did find a student willing to help in this way, he really did not know how to go about it. His behavior seemed forced and phony.

From remembering my own experiences in counseling and thinking of the comments that I had heard, the idea of a secondary-school peer-counseling program began to emerge. At that time a few models of peer counseling had been tried at the college level. Perhaps it would also work with junior- and senior-high-school students. As a result of my musings, the Palo Alto peer-counseling program was developed. Now in its fifth year of operation, it has become established and has been replicated in other districts. Further work is planned to extend and improve the program.

GUIDANCE PROGRAM AND BEHAVIORAL INTERVENTION

Peer counseling was started as a program to meet the specific need to extend the services of adult counselors to students infrequently seen by them, to teach students how to be more effective in helping their friends, and to reduce loneliness and isolation in our six secondary schools. Experience with the training part of the program has proved peer counseling also to be a powerful behavioral intervention for helping trainees with their own problems. The *program* has a rationale, a structure, specific activities and events, specific personnel with designated responsibilities, and organized routines. It becomes a behavoral *intervention* as the training and subsequent working with other students teach students skills that increase their own repertoire of behaviors: the discrimination and use of appropriate behaviors to achieve desired personal outcomes, the discovery of alternative ways of solving problems, and the experience of reinforcement that motivates trainees in their development as mature, responsible young adults.

PEER COUNSELING AS A GUIDANCE PROGRAM

The peer-counseling program is composed of several parts. First, there is an eighteen-hour training course in counseling skills for junior- and senior-high-school students. Second, there is identification of students and situations that call for help from trained peer counselors; they are called "assignments" in the program and in the subsequent matching of peer counselors with assignment requests. Third, there is continuing supervision and training in weekly "practicum" groups, in which experiences with assignments are discussed and further help to counselors can be given. Finally, the program has been expanded to include a training course for adults, to prepare them as supervisor-trainers of future peer-counseling training groups.

The program follows a scheduled sequence of events and activities. Early in the school year students in secondary schools are informed of the program through bulletins, visits to individual classes, and articles in newspapers. They are invited to take the training course to become peer counselors. Following an orientation meeting, those planning to enroll are assigned to the several afternoon and evening training classes. These groups are mixtures of ten to twelve students of different ages and schools. Each group is trained by two adults who have previously taken the supervisor-trainer course. When students have finished training, those wishing to continue as counselors are assigned to practicum groups that meet weekly. Counseling assignments are distributed in these meetings, which are also led by trained adults, and continuing monitoring of counseling work is conducted through these meetings. As students are being trained, the coordinator is in contact with counselors and teachers in schools in order to identify potential assignments. In this way, opportunities for informing the school community about the program and for creating a base of awareness and possible support are provided.

The basic personnel necessary for the program to function include at least a part-time coordinator, adult supervisor-trainers, and some secretarial help. As it has functioned, only the coordinator and the secretary have been paid. The supervisors have continued to volunteer their time in exchange for being involved in meaningful ways with students.

A clear description of the rationale, program development, and specifics of the training curriculum is given in detail elsewhere (Hamburg & Varenhorst, 1972). However, a discussion of the developmental phases may help to illustrate key factors needing attention if the program is to be replicated with success.

The Pilot Year

Identifying the Population To Be Served Soon after the idea of a secondary-school peer-counseling program emerged, I sought the consultation of Dr. Beatrix Hamburg, a child psychiatrist on the faculty of Stanford Medical School. Since that time we have worked together in establishing, developing, and evaluating the program. We had no established models to use and no experience of other programs to guide us. Therefore, at every step of the way care was exercised to control for mistakes that would eliminate the program before it had been tried.

The purpose of peer counselors was stated in terms of possible target populations that they might help. We wanted students to be working with students new to Palo Alto, lonely and isolated students, and those physically and mentally handicapped. We did not want them to be working with severely disturbed peers, those deep in the drug culture, or those who clearly needed the help of adult professionals. It was believed that peer counselors might serve as an effective bridge between troubled students and professionals who could help. We found that, by clearly establishing the purpose and the target population first, we were able to convince school decision makers of its value, to establish a guide for developing the curriculum, and to provide specifics for potential recruits. Other districts might have different purposes or potential "clients," but the purpose should be determined first, so that the training and evaluation can be tailored to it.[1]

Public-Relations Work   Long before students heard of the program, the groundwork had been laid for its support through systematic consultation with critical individuals and groups. The superintendent was consulted; meetings were held with the district's psychological staff, counselors in each building, and P.T.A. councils at all six secondary schools. Carefully worded announcements were put in PTA newsletters and school bulletins. The questions frequently asked included "Are students capable of dealing with problems of another when perhaps they have numerous problems of their own?" "Would students care enough to be trained and be interested enough to give of their time and energy?" What will this involve of my time as a counselor? How will they be related to counselors?" Some of the answers had to be found during the pilot year; others required prior clarification of how the program would function.[2]

It cannot be emphasized enough— public relations is a vital step in starting such a program. I could give numerous examples of how the program benefited from, even was saved by, time spent in preparing people for the initiation of this innovative use of student resources. When the emerging program was discussed, guidance personnel could speak with some knowledge. They were not caught off base, uninformed. This built support even affecting a school-board election, during which candidates were asked about peer counseling.

Developmental Guidelines   Two distinct decisions have influenced the quality and character of this program. First, it was decided that the program would be open to all students in grades seven through twelve, *without* any entry screening. If a student was elim-

---

[1] *Editors' note:* An admirable sequence. So often counseling and clerical services are developed first, and then problems are "fitted" to existing programs—somewhat analogous to Humpty-Dumpty's admonition to Alice: "Here's the answer, Here's the answer. Now, what's the question?"

[2] *Editors' note:* A peer-counseling program may be seen as a threat by many people. Parents worry that their faults will be discussed in public; counselors worry that their jobs will be taken over by students; administrators worry that some catastrophe will result in a lawsuit. The active cooperation and support of key individuals and groups must be sought in advance of starting an innovative program like this one.

inated he or she did it personally, merely by dropping out. Operators of the program have tried never to hurt anyone connected with its function or activities; screening can hurt. Although objections were raised over this issue, even to the point of questioning the training of specific individuals, by accepting all who came we were able to discover the counseling-intervention aspect of peer counseling. Students with problems, those who were less successful in school, the so-called "losers," learned alternative solutions to problems, useful personal skills, and improved self-concepts as results of the training.[3]

Second, the decision to require evidence of commitment resulted in stronger group morale and earned community and school support for the program's continuation. Certain hurdles were established, for example, requiring attendance at all twelve training sessions. If an absence was necessary, a makeup session was required. Training was held in a centrally located school. All students had to come there by means of their own transportation. They came by car or on foot—and every training room was usually filled with bikes. As training was held outside school hours, students were being asked to use their free time. This meant that peer counseling had to hold a high priority in their time and values. Commit-

ment was mentioned so frequently that year that the week before Easter vacation a student asked, "Aren't we going to meet during vacation?" Being tired myself, I was stunned by the question. When I said that we would not be meeting, she replied: "You keep talking about commitment. I'm ready to come next week!"

The Curriculum   Basically the curriculum involves three skill areas: communication skills, that is, how to talk effectively with someone whom you do not know in order to establish a relationship of trust leading to possible help with a problem; alternatives for dealing with such generalized problems as family relations, cliques, school relationships, health problems, and peer relationships (for example, how to make more friends); and the strategies and ethics of counseling as opposed to giving advice. This last topic involves referrals, how to start working with a student, confidentiality, and the limits and description of the peer-counseling role. The curriculum has an established format that is followed by all trainers. Although training is conducted in a group setting, it is *task* and *time* oriented, as opposed to the orientation of other "counseling" groups to encounters or sensitivity training. Copies of the curriculum may be ordered through the Palo Alto Guidance Department.[4]

Qualifications of Trainers   The original trainers were twelve people hand-

[3] *Editors' note:* An "elitist" version of peer counseling was avoided here. The peer counselors can be "coping models," helping others who share their same problems, rather than "mastery models," who have not suffered some of these problems and who may unwittingly communicate that goals are unattainable.

[4] The curriculum may be ordered from the Palo Alto Unified School District, 25 Churchill Avenue, Palo Alto, California 94306. The cost is $2.

picked on the basis of certain requirements. They had to have earned reputations for being successful with adolescents, be skilled in small-group techniques, be flexible enough to modify a curriculum outline to meet the immediate needs of a training group better, and be willing to volunteer their time for approximately two and a half hours a week. Finding extremely able initial trainers certainly helped to launch the program. A total of 152 high-school juniors and seniors completed the twelve-week training. Experience has since shown that the best trainers may or may not be guidance personnel. Teachers, and even administrators, are also effective and also enjoy doing the training.

The Developmental (Second) Year

The pilot year had been used to develop the framework of a program and had demonstrated that students are interested in being involved in helping their peers. Support from parents whose children had taken the training was enthusiastic. The school community was still waiting to see what would happen.

The second year was spent in developing the program into a functioning extension of guidance services and in taking steps to establish it as an integral part of the district's educational program. Several major components were added:

1. The initiation of practicums
2. Implementation of peer-counseling services on assignments
3. Initiation of the adult training course for potential supervisor-trainers

The Practicums   Approximately ninety students from the pilot training courses were ready to continue as counselors at the beginning of the second year. What were they to do? Where were the needy students who could be helped? The practicum groups were quickly formed to prevent loss of eagerness and enthusiasm. Initially these meetings were spent in reviewing the spring training. The practicums were to be used to deal with specific problems that peer counselors might have in carrying out their assignments. Therefore, no formal curriculum was prepared, and much of the usefulness of these early practicum meetings was a function of the adult group leaders. Gradually, as students received and began assignments, typical concerns began to emerge. The topics discussed included:

1. How does one relate to an elementary student? What do I do with a fourth-grade child who loses his temper and gets out of control?
2. How do I know when and what to do to conclude a counseling relationship?
3. How do I handle *my* feelings when my "counselee" doesn't seem to need me anymore?
4. I feel I've "blown" my first contact with my counselee. What can I do now?
5. How do I handle my own discouragement? The person I work with doesn't show any signs that I'm helping him at all. How can I tell if I'm making any progress?
6. How do you start a personal relationship without appearing phony or artificial?[5]

[5] *Editors' note:* These questions, of course, are not unique to young adolescents but are shared by most people learning how to be effective counselors.

Because of the students' attendance and their comments, the practicums proved to be an essential addition to the successful implementation of the program. The practicum concept also has proved to be a vital part of the total operation, serving as a communication link, a continuing training class, a method of supervision, and a unifying force to maintain morale.

Assignments Students *are* screened for appropriate assignments. Not all students are capable of dealing with others even after training, Some students do not feel ready. Many feel more comfortable starting with assignments in elementary schools. Although the final decision on an assignment rests with the coordinator, the students seem to sense accurately what they can do and, in a sense, screen themselves. For example, our experience has shown that no student who did not yet seem ready for an assignment, a judgment based on performance in training classes, ever has asked for one.[6] Some have asked to help with other training groups, which has been interpreted as seeking further training for themselves.

Although many peer counselors requested and started with elementary-school assignments, many of them ultimately requested assignments in their own schools or with peers closer to their own ages. A typical junior- or senior-high-school assignment would be helping a foreign student, working with a new student, or helping with orientation programs. It is believed that

[6] *Editors' note:* Undoubtedly some students who could do good jobs hesitate to volunteer and miss some opportunities for overcoming their self-doubts.

greater use could be made of this counseling resource at the secondary-school level.

Adult Training Course Of the initial twelve trainers, five were from outside the district. In order for the program eventually to become a district program, it was essential to establish a broader base of support and involvement among school personnel. Also, with additional training of students anticipated, a bigger corps of trainers was needed. Consequently, in January of the second year, the first course for adults was offered. It was open to all school personnel, including classified employees and parents in the community. Twenty-five adults completed this course, which followed closely the course given to students. Of those twenty-five, ten were parents. Those wishing to go farther as supervisor-trainers were assigned to work with "veteran" leaders of the pilot training classes, which proved to be their practicum experience.

Since that first adult class, approximately 140 additional adults have taken the training. Some have come from other districts, in order to take the first steps in replicating the program in their schools. Most who enroll are teachers. Not all district counselors or psychologists have enrolled, nor is there pressure for them to do so.

Knowledge of the curriculum, activities to achieve the training goals, and step-by-step procedures are essential for a trainer to be successful. However, another necessary ingredient is skill in group dynamics. Even though a person has taught for ten or fifteen years, he may be ineffective in molding group unity or in skillfully dealing with issues that come up about personal concerns of group members. To meet this training need, several sessions on group processes are being added to the adult training course.

IS THE PROGRAM SUCCESSFUL?

The Experimental (Third) Year

Success means different things to different evaluators. Possible criteria for success of the peer-counseling program could include the numbers of students taking the training and continuing as counselors, the numbers of students helped by peer counselors, the changes in behavior of those receiving peer-counseling assistance, increased support and use of the program by the school and community, and the development of skills by students as a result of the training.

Considerable effort was put into collecting evaluation data during the third year of operation, when the program was first funded for a three-year period by the National Institute of Mental Health. On the basis of the grant proposal, more attention was given to evaluating the outcomes of training in the self-concepts and behaviors of peer counselors than to the "delivery" services of the program.

Program evaluation data are incomplete and limited, for various reasons to be explained. A more thorough and systematic method of collecting such data should be developed and implemented in order accurately to evaluate the program by the criteria mentioned. The data that have been collected have been summarized in the following way.

Numbers of Students Trained and Working as Counselors During four years of training, 520 students have completed the eighteen-hour training course. Of each group trained, approximately 75 percent have continued in the program, many until they have been graduated. Some may work a year and drop out for a year, depending upon their activities and academic responsibilities. Some drop out after training because of graduation or because they move away. Others find that they do not enjoy working with others in this way.

These statistics should be studied in view of the ultimate goal of this program which is to become a nonprogrammed program. This means if training in development of interpersonal skills is provided in a systematic way, students may then use what they have learned in all subsequent personal relationships. They can then reach out in natural ways to help friends who need help, approach new students who appear in class, notice classmates who are depressed, and practice listening and effective problem solving in family and school involvements without being assigned to do so.

Numbers and Types of Assignments It is difficult to tabulate accurately the numbers of students helped by the program for a very good reason: Increasingly, peer counselors are "taking on" assignments that come to them naturally. As the program does not provide offices or badges, peer counselors are not specifically visible. Despite this, they are becoming known and sought by troubled students. These peer-counselor contacts are infrequently reported for the records.

However, *formal* assignments, those requests in writing for peer counselors, are recorded. The numbers vary from year to year, depending upon the need. In the first year of using counselors in formal assignments, the following activities were tabulated.

*Number of Peer Counselors Working on Particular Assignments*___

23 helped students with social problems
 4 worked with physically handicapped students
19 tutored and dealt with associated personal problems
 4 assisted in orienting new students and maintained a relationship
 4 worked with particular counseling groups
 3 received training and then conducted structured interviews for district study
 4 tutored and assisted on social adjustment of foreign students
 4 assisted in peer-counseling training groups
 4 worked with educationally and mentally retarded
 2 assisted elementary-school children with development of physical skills

Effectiveness of Peer Counselors An evaluation of the effectiveness of peer counselors is made in connection with formal assignments. The data are not complete because of less than 100 percent return from adults who have requested peer-counseling services. The evaluations are based on information reported on the form depicted in Figure 1. This form is sent to all who have had peer counselors working with their students or clients. The charts here report the results for the 1972–1973 school year.

Raters were asked to evaluate peer-counselor effectiveness on a 10-point scale with respect to three areas: behaviors of counselees before and after receiving counseling help, perceptions of each counselee's attitude before and after receiving counseling, and the relationship between the peer

Behavior Change	
Change	*Percentage of Counselees*
Behavior remained the same	29
Improved 1–3 points on behaviors measured	25
Improved 3 or more points	24
Did not respond to questions on behavior	22
Perceptions of Counselee's Attitude	
Same attitude (no change)	35
Improved 1–3 points	38
Improved more than 3 points	16
No response	11

Relationship Between Counselor and Counselee	
Feelings of Relationship with Counselee	*Percentage of Perceptions*
Very warm relationship	62
Warm relationship	25
Neutral	13

1. Name of supervisor: _____

2. Name of peer counselor: _____

3. Name of the counselee: _____

4. Description of the assignment:

5. How many hours per week did the peer counselor work with the counselee: _____ Total No. of Weeks _____

6. General change in the counselee with respect to the stated problem (please circle appropriate number):
No improvement   1   2   3   4   5   6   7   Much improvement
Specific comments:

7. Specific changes in the counselee:
Where it applies, mark a B for behaviors noted before the intervention of the peer counselor and mark an A for behaviors observed after the intervention of the peer counselor on a scale of 1–7. One represents poor (highly noticeable negative behavior) and 7 good (total absence of these behaviors).

	Poor	1	2	3	4	5	6	7	Good
(EXAMPLE: disrupts class)			B					A	

Check if applicable, then rate: Poor   1   2   3   4   5   6   7   Good

_____ Lacks study skills _____

_____ Disrupts class _____

_____ Appears to be
rejected by his/her
peer group _____

_____ Demonstrates
unhappiness or
depression _____

_____ Seems apathetic
toward making new
friends _____

_____ Lacks coordination
in physical
activities _____

_____ School attendance _____

_____ Rebellious toward
authority _____

8. Counselee's attitudes—before and after (mark B and A as in No. 7):
Poor   1   2   3   4   5   6   7   Good

FIGURE 1 Evaluation of the peer-counseling intervention.

(Figure 1, cont.)

Check if applicable, then rate:

_____ Apathetic	_____	Caring
_____ Withdrawn	_____	Outgoing
_____ Excitable	_____	Calm
_____ Sad	_____	Happy
_____ Uncooperative	_____	Cooperative
_____ Moody	_____	Even-tempered
_____ Suspicious	_____	Trusting
_____ Aloof	_____	Friendly
_____ Insecure	_____	Confident
_____ Distracted	_____	Attentive

9. Relationship between peer counsleor and counselee:
   Distant _____ Very warm
   $\quad\quad\quad\quad$ 1 $\quad$ 2 $\quad$ 3 $\quad$ 4 $\quad$ 5 $\quad$ 6 $\quad$ 7

10. (a) Do you plan to request a peer counselor again?* Yes_____ No_____
    (b) If no, please explain:

11. Do you have any suggestions or recommendations for the peer-counseling program?

If you would like to request a peer counselor at this time or for the next school year, please call extension 4278 and have your name put on our requestor's list.

---

counselor and the counselee. As noted on the form, specific behaviors and attitudes were identified for evaluation.

Some raters did not think that the form was appropriate for reporting their estimates of the relationship outcomes and sent in evaluation comments. These comments offered subjective evidence of effectiveness, as well as support for the program itself. Examples of comments include:

An enormous amount of behavior change took place as verified by independent observers.

Class reacted favorably to peer counselors. They are extremely responsible, reliable, and perceptive to the needs of the children. The class looked forward to their help and presence. They felt fortunate to have them the whole year.

Did not improve significantly on her subjects, but she did improve her peer problems. Began to take more risks.

We were very pleased with Doug's work with our students and believe him to be exceptionally capable in peer counseling. In fact we sincerely hope that he might be available to work at this school next year. We would hope that our request for this time be given top priority and that we are enabled to begin working with him earlier in the year.

School and Community Support The comments quoted indicate the kind of support coming from school personnel for the program. The fact that requests for services increase each year indicates belief in what peer counselors can do. Secondary-school counselors are finding a variety of ways in which peer counselors can help and are leaning more and more on them for their capabilities including reaching severely turned-off students. The enthusiastic response to these services has almost become a problem. Teenage students cannot do everything, nor should they be so pursued and pressured that they sacrifice their own school responsibilities as students.

BEHAVIORAL INTERVENTION

Because of the absence of screening, a wide variety of students enrolled in the training. Great differences in ability to handle personal problems and in skills for helping other peoples existed. The curriculum is designed to teach particular skills and is so structured that trainees can use their own concerns as material. Essentially, students learn how to help others by helping one another in the training sessions.

Formal evaluations are made, in order to measure the extent to which students do in fact acquire the skills thought necessary to function as peer counselors. Observations and self-reports have revealed the impact of training, as well as of group support, on the personal lives of trainees. The behavioral observations of individual peer counselors in the years after training seem to be the most powerful evidence that peer counseling is an effective behavioral intervention.

Abilities Taught in Training

We attempt to teach certain abilities that continue also to be emphasized in practicum groups:

1. Ability to approach a stranger and engage in constructive conversation
2. Ability to listen to another, including nonverbal communication
3. Ability to observe and evaluate the behaviors of others
4. Ability to talk with others about personal problems and feelings
5. Ability to use decision-making counseling in dealing with personal problems, health problems, school problems, and peer-relations planning
6. Ability to develop alternative actions when faced with a problem
7. Ability to apply interpersonal skills to the initiation of a first meeting with a student needing help
8. Ability to develop observational skills in order to distinguish abnormal from normal behavior and to identify behaviors related to differences among drug problems, feelings of isolation, and extreme nervous habits
9. Ability to use referral resources as sources of help for students
10. Ability to demonstrate awareness of the ethics and strategies of counseling

Training includes such learning activities as role playing, practice followed by feedback, observational tasks, and discussion. A typical exercise is focused on learning to talk to someone the trainee fears or finds difficult to be with. Students are asked to develop verbal descriptions of a teacher who might be hard to approach about a sensitive subject. When this is done, one person takes that teacher's role, and one by one members of the group attempt to talk with him or her about different sensitive issues, like a grade felt to be unfair or obtaining an assignment after having been late to class. Students experience what can happen in such situations and talk about alternatives or more effective ways of approaching such a teacher. One student said, "I'm not going to admit to any guilt in asking for that assignment." Another student replied, "But see what you have to lose by not doing it—and what you could gain if you did." The first student sat in silent reflection.

Evaluation

Evaluation data are obtained by asking supervisor-trainers to complete the assessment form included in this chapter (see Figure 2). Such a form is completed for each student at the beginning of training and immediately following, as well as at the start of practicum groups and the end of the year.

The general results calculated for the 1972–1973 trainees and practicum peer counselors indicate significant learning of skills during both the training and the practicum sessions. The results are reported in Table 1.

Table 1 shows how the ratings of training supervisors changed over the period of peer-counselor training. The lowest mean score is reported for the beginning of the training program pretest (4.631). At that point none of the students had received any training. By the time students had been rated in the training program posttest, the mean score of supervisors' ratings had risen to 5.467. This change is statistically significant at the .01 level.

The mean score for supervisors' ratings for the practicum pretest was 5.1. Students entering the practicum had already completed the training program. As we would expect, they scored higher than students who had received no training whatever. However, it is interesting to note that they actually scored lower on the pretest for the practicum than they did on the posttest for the training program. This decline probably represents the effects of summer vacation. Finally, we note that the highest mean score of all (5.67) is the rating for students at the end of the practicum sessions.[7] This score is also statistically significant (at the .01 level or better) from the mean pretest score for practicum students (5.1).

Behavioral Change

The self-reports and behavioral observations of students reveal the personal dimension of intervention. No systematic efforts have been made to collect such data, although plans are underway to do a longitudinal study of peer counselors.

Among the comments from students that have been reported are these: "It was the most important thing

[7] *Editors' note:* These subjective ratings have some limitations, suffering partly from "hello-goodbye" effect and partly from the fact that the supervisors have some vested interest in their own supervisees' improvement.

TABLE 1

	Mean of All Items Means: TRAINING PROGRAM	Mean of All Items Means: PRACTICUM
Pretest	4.631	5.100
Posttest	5.467	5.670

Name of Trainee: _____ Name of Supervisor: _____

Although we know that you have had only a short time to get to know your trainees in the peer-counseling program, we would like you to make an initial assessment of traits which we will stress in the training program. Later, when the training program has been completed, we will compare this base-line data with your final assessment of the trainee's skills in the same general areas.

First Impression

What is your initial subjective reaction to the trainee (please circle one):
1. Positive: The trainee is the kind of person you would immediately like to get to know better.
2. No strong impression at this point.
3. Negative: The trainee puts you off by some behaviors or habits. (Perhaps is not too responsive to friendly overtures or is openly hostile?).

On a scale of 1 to 4, 1 being *most like* and 4 being *least like*, rank how well you feel the trainee fits the person described in the following statements. If you absolutely cannot judge, mark a 0.

1. *Most like*   2. *Like*   3. *Unlike*   4. *Most unlike*

Group and communication skills

_____ 1. The trainee is able to form an easy and relaxed relationship with the group.

_____ 2. The trainee is able to contribute feelings about himself to the group and at the same time is willing and interested in listening to other group members.

_____ 3. The trainee makes a conscious effort, through eye contact, positive verbal communications, etc. to draw out various group members in an exchange of ideas. (In other words, the trainee appears to make good use of interpersonal skills to facilitate communication.)

_____ 4. The trainee exhibits the ability to converse in a nonjudgmental, nonthreatening manner with others in the training group.

_____ 5. The trainee is open to suggestions directed at him or her by other members of the group.

_____ 6. The trainee exhibits nervous habits and mannerisms that could interfere with successful counseling.

Problem-solving and counseling skills

_____ 7. In a problem-solving situation the trainee exhibits the ability to effectively formulate a plan of action and is able to integrate constructive suggestions.

_____ 8. The trainee offers positive suggestions to other members who present their problems to the group.

FIGURE 2 Supervisor's assessment of trainee's skills (pre- and post-ratings).

(Figure 2, cont.)

_____ 9. In what areas do you think the trainee will need additional work?
(please check the appropriate items)
_____ Dominates the group
_____ Overly passive
_____ Lacks self-confidence
_____ Lacks responsibility
_____ Overly opinionated and inflexible
_____ Overly identifies with the problems that are brought up

I did in four years of high school"; "After training I could start a conversation with a stranger. I don't always do it, but I now know how"; "I came into peer counseling because I didn't have any friends. The training caused me to look at some things in myself I had been avoiding and to learn how to deal with them"; "I learned not to interrogate a person in conversation"; "I learned I could do things I didn't know I could and to feel good about myself because of it."

One girl reported that she had had problems with her parents since she had been in elementary school. She had tried everything from drugs to running away. After the session on family problems, she decided that she had nothing to lose by trying some of the alternatives suggested. She found that they worked, and for the first time in years she was getting along with her parents and enjoying it.

One girl had been heavily into the drug culture since the ninth grade. The program directors were criticized for accepting her as a peer counselor. But she was effective in working with certain types of students and was one of the most faithful attenders at the practicum sessions. Her fellow peer counselors repeatedly gave her support and help in working with her own problems, never seeming to tire of coming to her aid when she needed it. Gradual changes developed, and she was finally graduated with a high-school scholarship to go on to college.

Many such examples could be mentioned to illustrate significant changes in peer counselors' lives. Perhaps these students could and would have been reached by other counseling services offered in the school—or perhaps they would have gone unnoticed, never finding the right moment to seek the help that they needed. They did receive some counseling in the activities and training of peer counseling, at the same time providing services to others —feeling good about themselves, rather than shame or guilt about their problems. These incidents alone seem sufficient reason for implementing a peer-counseling program.

references

Hamburg, B. & Varenhorst, B. Peer counseling in the secondary schools: A community mental health project for youth. *American Journal of Orthopsychiatry*, 1972, **42**, 566–581.

Varenhorst, Barbara B. Hello me—Hello you! Peer counseling intervention. In A. M. Mitchell & C. D. Johnson (Eds.), *Therapeutic techniques: Working models for the helping professional*. Fullerton: California Personnel and Guidance Association, 1973. Pp. 185–203.

COUNSELOR ACCOUNTABILITY SYSTEMS

62. ACCOUNTABILITY FOR COUNSELING PROGRAMS

GARY PRAZAK   Walker and Associates, Minneapolis

Accountability has become a popular concept in the human-service professions in the 1970s. There are few who would not agree that accountability in the abstract is a good idea. However, there is no clear agreement as to what accountability means, who is to be held accountable, for what, and to whom.

Until recently it was assumed that professionals had to be held accountable only for faithfulness to the teachings of their particular disciplines. So long as an individual was considered professionally competent and reliable, no one questioned his performance with clients.

Some organizations hold their staffs accountable for "process": being at work on time, conducting themselves in a professional manner, working hard, spending required numbers of hours with clients, keeping good records of activities.

More recently the term "accountability" has taken on a more focused meaning as service personnel have had their efforts called into question by providers of funds, legislative bodies, the general public, and recipients of services. More concern is being shown about the *results* of services than about the services themselves.

Many believe that holding a professional provider of human services accountable for what he does is somehow a reflection on his credibility. Yet, unless professionals are held accountable, a program cannot establish that it is indeed accomplishing what it purports to accomplish, and indeed it may not be accomplishing the best possible outcomes.

In this paper we shall describe an accountability, or performance, evaluation system based on results that were developed in two manpower programs and shall discuss the impact of accountability and its implications for counselors. The programs in which these accountability systems were installed were two federally funded manpower programs serving disadvantaged clients and welfare recipients in a metro-politan area: the Work Incentive Program and the Concentrated Employment Program. The general goal of both programs was employment for clients, and both were staffed primarily with counselors. Together the two programs employed a total of sixteen counselors. Because of their similarities, they will be described here as a single program, and the evaluation system will be presented as a composite of two.[1]

WHAT IS ACCOUNTABILITY?

The major reason that accountability causes providers of human services, including counselors, anxiety is that few people understand what it means and how it will affect them personally. Simply stated, a system of accountability involves evaluating the performance of an organization and its staff in the accomplishment of clearly specified *objectives* and then applying appropriate *consequences* to that performance.[2]

[1] *Editors' note:* The particular accountability system described here would be relevant only to counseling agencies that share the same goal—maximizing employment for their clients. However, because accountability systems for counselors are so new, it seems valuable to present a concrete example that other counseling agencies may use as a starting point. A more general model may be found in Krumboltz (1974).

[2] *Editors' note:* Some of us prefer to define "accountability" as a system for providing feedback about the accomplishment of results *without* specifying consequences.

Author's comment: That is an information system, not an accountability system. Accountability implies some sort of consequences, it is to be hoped positive ones.

Editors' reply: Only if it is defined that way.

Counselors who anticipate "being held accountable" are primarily concerned about the two major elements of *objectives* ("How am I going to be measured?") and *consequences* ("How will these measures be used against me?").[3] Robert Walker describes "accountability performance evaluation" as requiring three major elements: goal setting, feedback on performance results to the providers of services, and consequences (see Walker, 1972). The system described here was among the first in the country to include all these major elements.

HOW IS AN ACCOUNTABILITY SYSTEM DEVELOPED?

In order to develop an accountability system based on performance evaluation, it was necessary to develop objectives related to both effectiveness and efficiency, measures of performance, performance expectations, definitions of who was to be served, and provisions for consequences based on actual performance.

Goals and Objectives

The most critical and most difficult part of the development of an accountability system for any organization is clarifying the goals and specifying the objectives to be achieved. At first, it might appear that a counseling program aimed at achieving employment for its clients would by its nature have

[3] *Editors' note:* Counselors should be encouraged to ask, "How will these measures benefit me?"

easily defined objectives. Not so at all. The program described here had been operating for several years, yet the administrators, staff, and board could not readily agree on just what they were in business to accomplish. The issue of setting specific objectives is not usually confronted until it is decided that performance evaluation should be based on the accomplishment of those objectives! Because of the differing views on what the program should accomplish, the objectives were set after considerable negotiation.

The negotiation process resulted in selection of objectives that covered both the quantity and quality of results achieved. The objective for quantity was to optimize the percentage of clients obtaining stable full-time jobs and earning at least the Federal minimum wage. The Federal reporting system for the program had not yet defined what constituted a "job," which allowed the program to take credit for people with seasonal, part-time, and low-paying jobs. The objective for the quality of jobs obtained was to optimize the average hourly salary.

The staff, particularly the counselors, also wanted the objectives to reflect accomplishments of those clients who had not found employment. In recognition of the fact that the program could not find good jobs for everyone, the objective of having people referred to and accepted for services by other community agencies and programs that might meet these clients' needs or hired for temporary or part-time jobs was also adopted.

Additional objectives were set, in order to encourage efficiency in the program. One objective was to minimize the length of time that people were receiving services in the program. If the program could help people in less time, it could serve more people, and the cost per person would be reduced. The efficiency of the program was separately measured for those clients who were "successful" (obtained jobs) and "unsuccessful" (did not obtain jobs).[4] (See Table 1.)

[4] *Editors' note:* A counselor who was trying to "beat the system" might detect a weak point here. It appears that one could receive some credit for speedily processing unsuccessful clients. Counseling a thousand unsuccessful clients in one day should not bring any credit; on the other hand, taking one day is better than taking two days.

Author's comment: The weighting of various objectives does not allow a counselor to beat the system and come out looking like a good performer when in fact he is not. It does encourage counselors to limit program length for those who cannot be helped by that program.

TABLE 1   Performance Measures, Expected Performance Levels, and Weights of Measure

Measures	Goals Expected	Relative Weight (in percentages)
Percentage of clients employed at least 90 days	50	60
Average hourly salary	$2.50 an hour	10
Average program length (successful clients)	120 days	15
Average program length (unsuccessful clients)	60 days	10
Percentage of "unsuccessful" clients finding lesser jobs or receiving services through other community agencies	30	5

Measures

Measures were then developed for each of the objectives. This involved defining terms, deciding when measures would be taken, who would be measured, and who would do the measuring. The measures proved to be the easiest part of the system to develop. The most difficult part was identifying the objectives and expressing them in a specific manner, using clearly defined terms. In this program it was also decided to apply the measures to individual counselors, as well as to the overall program. The counselors all had equivalent case loads and received the same numbers of randomly assigned new clients. This made it possible to apply the same measures to all counselors, to compare their results, and to hold them accountable for results.

Expectations

In order to establish a general perspective for viewing information on performance, expectations were set for each measure. Expectations reflect the degree to which the organization believes an objective can reasonably be achieved in view of the nature of the population and other factors. For example, the expected goal set for the first measure, percentage of terminated clients employed at least ninety days, was 50 percent. Without some standard or bench mark against which to compare actual performance, the data have no real meaning or are subject to interpretation and value judgments by each reader. A program must indicate not only what it is trying to accomplish, for example, finding people jobs, but also the *degree* of accomplishment aimed at. In this program the expectations were set after data on actual program performance were available for several months. Expectations must be set at levels that are both reasonable and achievable but not so low as to do a disservice to the clients and the community.[5]

[5] *Editors' note:* Setting expectations may not be necessary and may in fact be harmful if they become used as standards. As expectations are established rather arbitrarily on the basis of past experience changing conditions may make them obsolete. An improved economic climate, for example, may make it easy for 60 percent of the clients to find jobs, and then some counselors may not even try to help the other 40 percent because they are already so far ahead of what has been expected. An alternative would be for each counselor to use his own previous month's results (or those of the same month a year before) as a basis for comparison with this month's results.

Author's comment: Expectations can be changed to reflect changes in the economic climate or changes in the program's services. Experience has shown that counselors do not stop at the goal but work to exceed it. Not to make such goals explicit leaves each counselor and supervisor to apply his own personal and arbitrary standards to performance. Simple comparison with previous performance might lead a very successful counselor whose results have slipped a bit to conclude that he has been unsuccessful. On the other hand, a counselor whose performance is very low might conclude that his performance has been great because it has increased from 5 percent to 10 percent success. You cannot have accountability without specifying the level of performance that is desired. You are missing the whole point, editors.

Editors' reply: The argument hinges on the premises. If you want the accountability system to compare counselors with one another and to specify a minimum acceptable success level, you are quite right. If you want every counselor to be constantly working to improve his previous record, we are right.

Weights

The objectives were not considered to be equal in value, so relative weights were set for each measure. The measure for the percentage of clients employed at least ninety days was considered to be most important and was assigned a weight of 60 percent out of a possible 100 percent. This meant that this measure would make up 60 percent of the overall program's performance "score." The weighting makes it impossible for a counselor to "look good" in the system without achieving on those measures given the most weight.

WHO IS SERVED?

The characteristics of the clients served were monitored along with information on results. New clients coming in for services and those being terminated were described in terms of such characteristics as age, sex, education level, length of unemployment, minority status, number of dependents, previous involvement in other employment programs, presence of disability or drug problems, and history of legal involvement. Such information is important for interpretation of the data on results. Obviously, a program serving older alcoholics with limited education and long periods of unemployment will place a smaller proportion of individuals in good, permanent jobs than will a program serving mostly young high-school graduates without problems. The characteristics of the clients therefore affect the performance expectations. One of the easiest ways to improve performance reports is to be more selective about who is served. Without a mechanism for monitoring the characteristics of clients, a program or counselor can appear to be achieving better results while the improvements may be primarily owing to careful selection of clients.[6]

FEEDBACK

The accountability system provided the program staff with its first objective feedback on performance. The staff members were given monthly reports on their performance and the performance of the total program. Information was anonymously provided on the performance of all counselors so that each could compare his performance with those of the others.[7] Counselors, as well as their supervisors, often underrate or overrate their own performance when they have no information on actual performance and no objective basis for comparison either with the performances of others or with some clearly stated organizational objectives and expectations.

The good performers, as well as those whose performance had clearly been inadequate, were now readily identified, and administrators and supervisors were often surprised by the performances of certain counselors. Without objective results supervisors

[6] *Editors' note:* A good point. And the data might also be useful in pinpointing the techniques that seem to work best with different kinds of clients.

[7] *Editors' note:* Anonymity is good, but we bet the word gets around.

Author's comment: It does, but that is each counselor's own choice.

often judge counselors on the basis of their "style," rather than their accomplishments.

Performance reports were also regularly provided to the board and the agencies providing the funds for the program, in order that the director could, in effect, be held accountable for the results of the overall program. Board members indicated that they found the performance reports, with rather simple data on results, much more useful than the extensive reports on activities that they had been receiving. A sample report is provided in Table 2.

CONSEQUENCES

A performance evaluation system introduces accountability only when there are consequences for both good and poor performance. Good performance must be rewarded in order to be maintained, and action must be taken to correct poor performance.[9] Sometimes a program can provide financial incentives to outstanding performers. Although the program illustrated here

[9] *Editors' note:* For some people, feedback on their performance constitutes a sufficient consequence in itself.

TABLE 2   Sample Performance Summary Report

Total Program index score: 93		Month: November
Measures	*Index Score*[a]	*Data*
Percentage of clients employed at least 90 days	110	This month 27 out of 50 clients terminated had been employed at least 90 days; this is 54 percent.
Average hourly wage	145	The average hourly wage of these employed clients is $2.95 an hour.
Average program length (successful clients)	70	The average number of program days for the successful terminees was 132.
Average program length (unsuccessful clients)	55	The average number of program days for the unsuccessful terminees was 78.
Percentage of "unsuccessful" clients receiving lesser jobs or accepted for services by community agencies	100	This month 4 out of a possible 13 "unsuccessful" terminees received other benefits; this is 31 percent.

[a] *The "index score" is a weighted standard score, with 100 defined as goal-level performance, that which the program is striving to achieve; 50 as minimal performance; and 150 as optimal performance. Specific values are set for each of these levels for each measure. For example, for the measure "percentage of clients employed at least ninety days" the goal was set at 50 percent. Achievement of 50 percent would be shown as an index score of 100. Minimal performance on this measure was set at 30 percent and optimal performance at 70 percent. The use of the index score permits comparison of performance on various measures and, through the relative weights, permits a single score of overall program performance, combining the performances on all measures, to be calculated.[8]*

[8] *Editors' note:* Index scores also have a disadvantage in that they disguise the direct measures on which they are based. A more direct alternative procedure would be to graph by month the percentage of clients employed at least 90 days, the average hourly wage, etc.

Author's comment: We always present both the data and the index scores.

could not provide financial incentives, we did find that simple recognition was rewarding and reinforcing to staff. Unfortunately, providing even simple verbal recognition of good performance is a behavior foreign to many administrators. However, recognition from peers and informed self-satisfaction appeared to be significant reinforcers. The data on poor performance were used to determine where the entire program needed technical assistance and where individual counselors needed special supervisory help.[10]

WHAT HAPPENS WITHOUT ACCOUNTABILITY?

Without clearly defined program objectives, performance expectations, and all the other elements of accountability, counselors tend to "do their own thing." Each pursues his own goals, and the focus tends to be on process, style, and activities, rather than on results achieved by clients. For example, in this program two counselors were randomly assigned the same kinds of clients. One strongly encouraged extensive training and education for her clients. Her personal goal was to help a few people each year to find really good jobs, no matter what the time or cost involved. The other counselor pushed people into hastily chosen jobs in order to achieve the goal of putting as many people as possible back to work each year.

Without an accountability system and its clear definition of goals and

performance feedback there was no way of determining which of these was the better performer in the system. Before the accountability system was installed these counselors were given no directions for balancing the quantity and quality of results to be achieved. The client's chance assignment to one counselor, rather than to another, might have dramatically affected the probability of his obtaining some useful benefit. This chance element is reduced when all the counselors are working toward the same clearly established objectives and are held accountable for achieving them.

IMPACT OF ACCOUNTABILITY ON COUNSELORS

There is a wide range of staff reactions to accountability. Some welcome the opportunity to demonstrate their accomplishments. Others are fearful that expectations will be unrealistic or that they will no longer be able to pursue their own goals with clients and will be required to work toward goals set by the administration with which they may not agree. Adequate involvement of all levels of staff in the development of an accountability system, particularly in selecting the objectives and setting expectations, soon dissipates this anxiety.[11] However, a few counselors actually will choose to leave, rather than to be held accountable for achievement of results. Some apparently believe that measurement of results will

---

[10] *Editors' note:* A constructive use of an accountability system!

[11] *Editors' note:* Staff participation in establishing the system is essential.

cramp their style or that it is somehow unprofessional.[12]

Staff reactions to accountability are very dependent upon the manner in which the system is developed and upon how the data are used by supervisors and administrators. One supervisor refused to accept some of the performance objectives selected and the expectations agreed upon by the rest of the staff and administration. He neglected to review performance results with his counselors and instead continued to spend long hours reviewing case records. His counselors soon "got the message" that results were less important to their supervisor than was the process of counseling, and they shifted at least some of their efforts to maintaining the kind of case records that this supervisor wanted to see. As a result, the outcomes of this segment of the staff suffered.

The accountability system did change counselors' behavior in several ways. The more effective counselors were sought out by those who were not doing as well and were asked to share their ideas and techniques. The use of the program's support services, like basic education, testing, and various skill-training resources also changed. Counselors began to use less often those support services that they thought were not really contributing to achieving program goals and increased their use of those that they found effective. Eventually support staff became much

more responsive to counselors and changed their services to make them more relevant to the overall program goals. Basic education, for example, changed its emphasis from teaching basic skills for their own sake to helping clients to acquire those specific skills needed for particular training courses or for specific jobs.

Figure 1 shows the change during the first year following the installation of the accountability system. The dramatic increase in results is owing in large part to the clarification of program goals. Everyone knew what he was expected to achieve and began to receive feedback that his performance was improving. The reinforcers for the staff were primarily recognition provided by some of the supervisors and individual counselors' finding out for themselves just how well they were doing, compared with others and with the program's goals. The importance of feedback and verbal reinforcement became obvious when the administrators of one program failed to provide any recognition of improved performance and instead criticized the program for failing to meet their expectations for certain other activities unrelated to results.[13] Consequently, the performance

---

[12] *Editors' note:* Perhaps they want to counsel toward objectives other than those reinforced here, or perhaps they judge that they could not be successful in accomplishing these outcomes.

Author's comment: Exactly!

[13] *Editors' note:* Possibly there remain some unstated objectives desired by certain administrators or staff members. For example, an additional objective might be that each client later report that he had been treated humanely. If humane treatment were made an explicit objective, then a counselor's promptness in keeping appointments might affect the client's report. If humane treatment is not an explicit objective, then promptness may be irrelevant. Certain counselor activities (like promptness and filling out forms for administrative information) make life easier

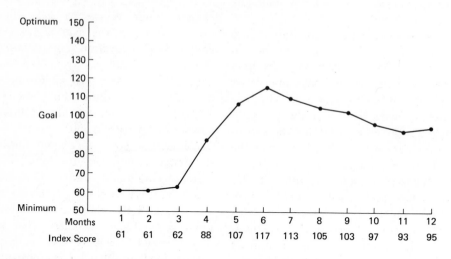

FIGURE 1 Overall performance of all counselors combined.

curve began to drop off after several months. In addition to providing continual reinforcement for results, an accountability system also should be reviewed periodically to determine that the objectives, measures, and performance expectations are still relevant.[14]

---

for administrators, even though they are related only tangentially to the accomplishment of major client outcomes. The answer may be to make these secondary, implicit objectives explicit.

Author's comment: These are process objectives and should not be confused or mixed with "results objectives."

Editors' reply: The distinction is important, but for clients to consider that they received humane treatment *can* be specified as a "results objective," even though in your system it has not yet been done. Look at it this way: If too many clients were to complain of inhumane treatment, the financial support for your whole program might be eliminated.

[14] *Editors' note:* A crucial point! The system cannot possibly be perfect at the beginning, if ever. But, by deliberately build-

The clients served by a program using an accountability system clearly benefit. More of them achieve better results when a program and its staff are held accountable for accomplishments.

Accountability is still in its infancy. There is much to be learned about how to achieve it—and still more about how to convince professionals and organizations that it should be achieved. Everyone seems to agree that program evaluation is good, but too few are ready to invest the time and effort necessary to achieve it. Yet, until organizations elect or are required to hold themselves accountable for results, professionals have no proof that they are doing a good job, and clients will continue to have no assurance of achieving significant benefits.

ing in a process for evaluating and revising, a staff can improve the process, add or revise goals, and develop more precise and economical means of assessing progress.

references

Krumboltz, J. D. An accountability model for counselors. *Personnel and Guidance Journal,* 1974, **52,** 639–646.

Walker, Robert A. The ninth panacea: Program evaluation. *Evaluation,* Fall 1972.

INDEX

Abel, G. G., 227, 240, 344–349
Abramovitz, A., 316
Abrams, L. A., 510
Abramson, E. E., 106
Academic skills. *See* Study skills
Accountability, effect on counselors, 562–564; defined, 557; evaluation system, 556–565; feedback, 560–561; goals, 557–558; measures for, 558–559
"Action Situation Inventory," 481
Activity schedules, use in treatment of depression, 67–74
Adolescents, drug-abuse prevention for, 510–517
Aerobics System (Cooper), 531, 532
Aggression, reduction of, behavior contracts and, 170, 181–186; group approach to, 174–180; point system and, 164, 175, 177; preschooler-parent, effects on, 199–201; turtle technique and, 157–162. *See also* Classroom behavior
Agoraphobia, 257–258
Agras, W. S., 234, 250
Alberti, R. E., 342
Alcohol Behavior Research Laboratory, 144, 145
Alcoholics Anonymous, 144
Alcoholism, 144–150
Allsen, P. E., 531, 539
Alvoro, R. W., 389–405

American Cancer Society, The, 125, 126, 129, 130
American Institute for Research, 405
American Psychiatric Association, 235
Anant, S. S., 234
Anthony, J. L., 427
Anton, J. L., 6, 67–74
Anxiety, reduction of, classroom behavior and, 265–268; generalized, 321–325; hierarchies test for, 272–277; kung fu, use in, 312–316; sexual, 37
Anxiety index, 250
Anxiety management training, 320–325
Arieff, A. J., 226
Arkowitz, H., 36, 38, 42
Assertive behavior, defined, 476–477; measurements of, 481
Assertiveness training, 499; covert modeling techniques and, 475–486; enuresis, effects on, 217–219; job-linked, 299–300; participant modeling in, 262–263; role-playing in, 30–34, 469–474, 482; shyness, effects on, 29–36; for women, 467–475
Athletic skill. *See* Physical fitness
Attention-getting mechanism (A.G.M.), 444
Audiotapes, on conversation skills, 503, 504; on decision making, 389–405; on grooming skills, 520, 521; Tele-tip, 389–397